Panama

Matthew D Firestone

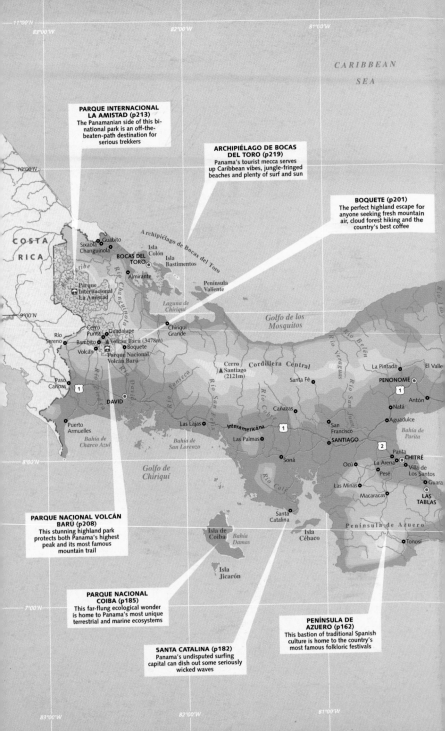

PARQUE INTERNACIONAL LA AMISTAD (p213)
The Panamanian side of this bi-national park is an off-the-beaten-path destination for serious trekkers

ARCHIPIÉLAGO DE BOCAS DEL TORO (p219)
Panama's tourist mecca serves up Caribbean vibes, jungle-fringed beaches and plenty of surf and sun

BOQUETE (p201)
The perfect highland escape for anyone seeking fresh mountain air, cloud forest hiking and the country's best coffee

PARQUE NACIONAL VOLCÁN BARÚ (p208)
This stunning highland park protects both Panama's highest peak and its most famous mountain trail

PARQUE NACIONAL COIBA (p185)
This far-flung ecological wonder is home to Panama's most unique terrestrial and marine ecosystems

SANTA CATALINA (p182)
Panama's undisputed surfing capital can dish out some seriously wicked waves

PENÍNSULA DE AZUERO (p162)
This bastion of traditional Spanish culture is home to the country's most famous folkloric festivals

CARIBBEAN SEA

COSTA RICA

Sixaola
Guabito
Changuinola
Isla Colón
BOCAS DEL TORO
Isla Bastimentos
Almirante
Península Valiente
Archipiélago de Bocas del Toro
Laguna de Chiriquí
Golfo de los Mosquitos
Parque Internacional La Amistad
Río Sereno
Cerro Punta
Guadalupe
Bambito
Volcán Barú (3478m)
Volcán
Boquete
Parque Nacional Volcán Barú
Chiriquí Grande
Cerro Santiago (2121m)
Cordillera Central
La Pintada
El Valle
Paso Canoas
DAVID
Santa Fé
PENONOMÉ
Natá
Antón
Puerto Armuelles
Las Lajas
Interamericana
San Francisco
Cañazas
SANTIAGO
Aguadulce
Bahía de Charco Azul
Bahía de San Lorenzo
Las Palmas
Soná
Ocú
Panta
CHITRÉ
Bahía de Parita
Golfo de Chiriquí
La Arena
Pesé
Villa de Los Santos
Guara
Santa Catalina
Isla Cébaco
Las Minas
Macaracas
LAS TABLAS
Isla de Coiba
Bahía Damas
Península de Azuero
Isla Jicarón
Tonosí

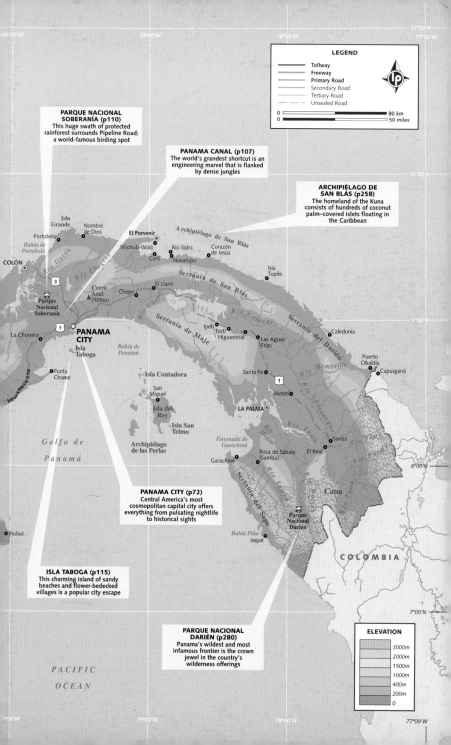

LEGEND

▬▬▬	Tollway
▬▬▬	Freeway
▬▬▬	Primary Road
▬▬▬	Secondary Road
▬▬▬	Tertiary Road
▬ ▬ ▬	Unsealed Road

0 _____ 80 km
0 _____ 50 miles

PARQUE NACIONAL SOBERANÍA (p110)
This huge swath of protected rainforest surrounds Pipeline Road; a world-famous birding spot

PANAMA CANAL (p107)
The world's grandest shortcut is an engineering marvel that is flanked by dense jungles

ARCHIPIÉLAGO DE SAN BLÁS (p258)
The homeland of the Kuna consists of hundreds of coconut palm–covered islets floating in the Caribbean

PANAMA CITY (p72)
Central America's most cosmopolitan capital city offers everything from pulsating nightlife to historical sights

ISLA TABOGA (p115)
This charming island of sandy beaches and flower-bedecked villages is a popular city escape

PARQUE NACIONAL DARIÉN (p280)
Panama's wildest and most infamous frontier is the crown jewel in the country's wilderness offerings

ELEVATION

	3000m
	2000m
	1500m
	1000m
	400m
	200m
	0

Isla Grande
Nombre de Dios
Portobelo
Bahía de Portobelo
El Porvenir
Wichub-Walá
Río Sidra
Corazón de Jesús
Archipiélago de San Blás
COLÓN
Río Gatún
Río Chagres
Cartí
Nusatupo
Isla Tupile
Cerro Azul (950m)
Chepo
El Llano
Serranía de San Blás
Parque Nacional Soberanía
Río Chepo
Serranía del Darién
La Chorrera
PANAMA CITY
Isla Taboga
Ipetí
Torti
Higueronal
Río Cañazas
Las Aguas Frías
Caledonia
Bahía de Panamá
Serranía de Majé
Punta Chame
Isla Contadora
Santa Fe
Río Membrillo
Puerto Obaldía
Capurganá
San Miguel
Meteti
Isla del Rey
Río Chucunaque
Isla San Telmo
Archipiélago de las Perlas
Ensenada de Garachiné
Río Tuíra
Yaviza
Río Tupisa
Garachiné
Boca de Sábalo (Sambú)
El Real
Río Tuíra
Río Balsas
Cana
Interamericana
Pedasí
Serranía del Sapo
Río Sambú
Parque Nacional Darién
COLOMBIA
Bahía Piña
Jaqué
Golfo de Panamá
PACIFIC OCEAN
LA PALMA

60°00'W   79°00'W   78°00'W   77°00'W
11°00'N   10°00'N   9°00'N   8°00'N   7°00'N

On the Road

MATTHEW D FIRESTONE Coordinating Author

This shot was taken at the Boca de Cupe checkpoint at the start of the infamous Darién Gap. Here, my guide and I registered with police before heading on foot to the ANCON field station in Cana. The blue dye on my skin is *jagua*, a traditional dye used by the Emberá to decorate their bodies during celebrations.

DON'T MISS

Panama City (p72) is arguably the most cosmopolitan Latin American capital. With its eclectic mix of international restaurants and all-night clubs, it's hard to have a bad time here. Of course, you shouldn't let the good life distract for you too

long – the Caribbean stylings of Archipiélago de Bocas del Toro (p219) are just a quick plane ride away. Although it's hard to pull yourself away from these laid-back islands, don't miss Panama's 'other Caribbean,' namely the Archipiélago de San Blás (p258). Home to the fiercely independent Kuna, these culturally rich islands are the perfect place to slow down (or possibly get stuck) for a while.

You should set aside some time for the far-flung Isla de Coiba (p188), a genuine 'Lost World' of ecological wonders. Hikers should head to Parque Nacional Volcán Barú (p208), home to Panama's highest volcano and its most famous highland trail. Serious explorers should head to the Darién (p273), though a little preparation is in order before you tackle this frontier region. And if you've got your board in tow, don't miss the surf paradise of Santa Catalina (p182), home to the country's largest swells.

See full author bios page 330

THE SECRETS OF PANAMA

Unfettered by tourist crowds, Panama's natural gifts shine. Although most travelers to Central America set their sights on tourist-soaked Costa Rica, in Panama it's hard to shake the feeling that you're in on a secret the rest of the traveling world has yet to discover. Most of Panama's highlights are still very much off-the-beaten-path destinations, but this is likely to change in the years to come. With highland cloud forests, vast tracts of wildlife-rich jungle, a cosmopolitan capital city and two coastlines teeming with sparkling beaches and vibrant coral reefs, Panama is so much more than just a canal.

Natural Wonders

From cloud forests to Caribbean beaches, Panama overflows with natural wonders. In the span of a few hours, you can explore dense jungles and lounge on sunkissed beaches. However, Panama's greatest natural wonder is the incredible abundance and variety of wildlife. With the full complement of neotropical fauna including 900 species of birds, Panama is a naturalist's dream.

Author Tip

Before arriving in Panama, be sure to pick up a copy of *A Guide to the Birds of Panama*, by Robert Ridgley and John Gwynne. Owning a copy of the foremost field guide to Panama's birds will greatly enhance your wildlife-watching experience.

❶ Archipiélago de Bocas del Toro

Panama's top tourist destination (p219) is a postcard-perfect stretch of tropical islands dotted with white-sand beaches, mangrove forests and enough positive Caribbean vibes to soothe your travel-worn soul.

❷ Archipiélago de San Blás

Consisting of over 300 coconut palm–fringed islands and islets floating in a sea of turquoise, the Archipiélago de San Blás (p258) is as close as you can get to paradise in this lifetime, blending idyllic relaxation with cultural discovery.

❸ Darién Province

Few destinations in the Americas can conjure up images of impenetrable jungles, impassable mountains and remote frontiers quite like the infamous Darién (p273), home to everything from indigenous Emberá and Wounaan villages to rare neotropical fauna.

❹ Isla de Coiba

With its remote location and difficult access keeping the crowds away, the far-flung ecological wonder of Isla de Coiba (p188) is simply unforgettable.

❺ Monkeys & Cats

A variety of primates swing from the rainforest canopy in Monumento Nacional Isla Barro Colorado (p113), including white-faced capuchins, howler monkeys and the only population of Geoffroy's tamarins in Central America. On the forest floor, big cats prowl at night, leaving their tracks behind for hikers to discover.

❻ Birds

Regarded as one of the top birding destinations in the world, Cana (p286) abounds with rare tropical species including macaws, toucans, quetzals, motmots and trogons.

Outdoor Adventures

There's no secret as to why Panama is regarded as one of Central America's top outdoor destinations. On land, you can explore tropical cloud forests, climb extinct volcanoes or trek through virgin jungle. In the water, you can surf across barreling waves and dive among hammerheads.

Author Tip
Several of Panama's top destinations, including Isla de Coiba and the Darién, are difficult to access without a tour operator. Even if you're a staunch independent traveler, you might want to consider joining one of the tours in Ancon Expeditions' portfolio of offerings; see p89.

❶ Hiking

Hikers will be overwhelmed by the sheer number of easily accessible trails available in Panama including those in the famous Parque Internacional La Amistad (p213).

❷ Climbing

Serious climbers should head straight for Volcán Barú (p209), an extinct volcano that serves as Panama's highest point and the centerpiece for Parque Nacional Volcán Barú (p208).

❸ Trekking

While there's no shortage of locales boasting multiday treks to test your mental and physical stamina, few can compare to Panama's famous Sendero Los Quetzales (Quetzals Trail; p209).

❹ Surfing

While neighboring Costa Rica fills up with surfers, the secret about Bocas del Toro (p219) is slowly getting around. Travelers in the know can choose from a variety of gnarly breaks stretching along the coast.

❺ Diving & Snorkeling

Wedged between the dark blue Pacific and the turquoise Caribbean, Panama brims with world-class diving and snorkeling spots, such as Portobelo (p250). Underwater explorers can snorkel and dive everything from sunken airplanes and cargo ships to vibrant coral reefs and enormous rock gardens.

❻ Rafting & Kayaking

Panama offers two raging white-water runs, namely the Ríos Chiriquí and Chiriquí Viejo (p204). Would-be rafters should head to the highland town of Boquete (p201), the unofficial river-running capital of Panama.

Cultural Tapestries

The variety of Panama's natural beauty is rivaled only by the incredible multiculturalism of Panamanians. From the soaring steel and glass towers of the modern capital city to the modest palm and thatch riverside houses of the Darién, Panama is a richly woven tapestry of cultural diversity.

2

Author Tip

When visiting indigenous communities in Panama, please be aware of your surroundings, and be sensitive to the plight of your hosts. Revenue from tourism can play a vital role in the development of a region, but a living community should never be treated as a human zoo.

❶ The Kuna

Interacting with the Kuna in a sustainable manner is one of the highlights of any visit to Panama, especially since the group resides in the Archipiélago de San Blás (p258), one of the country's top natural wonders.

❷ The Emberá

Environmental degradation of the Darién (p273) is threatening the future of the Emberá, but a visit to these communities provides insight into the lifestyle of one of the most fascinating indigenous groups in the Americas.

❸ Ngöbe-Buglé

Panama's largest indigenous population, the Ngöbe-Buglé, retain their own autonomous region that is largely confined to the Chirquí highlands (p201). Like their pre-Columbian ancestors, they predominantly survive on subsistence agriculture, and continue to retain their rich artisan tradition.

❹ Península de Azuero

The site of Panama's first cry for independence, the Península de Azuero (p161) is fondly referred to by most Panamanians as the heart and soul of the country.

❺ Creoles

In the historic town of Old Bank on Isla Bastimentos (p229), you'll hear Gali-Gali, the distinct Creole language of Bocas del Toro Province, which combines Afro-Antillean English, Spanish and Ngöbe-Buglé.

❻ Urbanites

Upholding its claim to be the most cosmopolitan capital in Central America, Panama City (p72) is an urban playground of eclectic restaurants, swish bars and all-night dance clubs.

Contents

Regional Map Contents

Destination Panama

After centuries of occuuption by the Spanish and later the Americans, Panama has recently cast off the last throes of colonialism. On December 31, 1999 the US relinquished control of the Panama Canal and closed its military bases. Over 4000 Panamanians employed by the US military lost their jobs immediately and the US took with them an economic impact of up to US$350 million. Polls taken prior to the withdrawal showed that a majority of Panamanians did not want the US to pull out completely because of the economic consequences.

Although there was both international and national skepticism regarding Panama's ability to run the canal, Panama has defied expectations, racking up impressive safety records and decreasing transit time for ships passing through the canal by more than 10%. Today, the canal remains the lifeline of the country's economy and there are hopes that it will bring greater wealth in the future.

In October 2006, under the leadership of President Martín Torrijos, Panamanian voters overwhelmingly endorsed an ambitious project to expand the canal. At an estimated cost of US$5 billion, the expansion will widen and deepen existing navigation channels in addition to creating a third set of locks. By enabling increased canal traffic and the passage of larger vessels, the Panamanian government is betting that higher revenues from canal tolls will inject a much needed boost into the country's economy.

The campaign for the canal expansion was endorsed by the country's rich, elite and powerful, who stand to make quite a bit of money from increased shipping traffic. Of course, this is ultimately contingent on whether or not the government can actually pull it off and critics argue that the project's final price tag may be too high to recoup.

Meanwhile real growth is happening in the economy, and President Torrijos' probusiness attitude has thus far pleased many investors. With the increase of trade and the continued flow of foreign investment, Panama's future is looking brighter than ever.

The future for Panama's natural wonders is less certain. With tourism and foreign investment making convenient bedfellows, developers are increasingly viewing Panama with dollar signs in their eyes. Real-estate moguls and wealthy investors are envisioning cruise-ship ports, giant beach resorts and gated retirement communities.

Fortunately there is hope. Several conservation organizations, most notably Asociación Nacional para la Conservación de la Naturaleza (ANCON; National Association for the Conservation of Nature), envision Panama's tourism developing slowly and sustainably. However, the road ahead is paved with potential misfortune, especially on the battlegrounds of Parque Nacional Coiba and Isla Bastimentos.

In the end, the future of Panama will be dependent on the speed at which the country's tourism sector develops. Unlike neighboring Costa Rica, which has exploded as an international tourist destination in recent years, Panama has been slow to capitalize on its potential. However, this has allowed players on both sides of the investment/conservation line to step back and assess the situation. Hopefully, Panama will adopt a low-volume, high-profit model of tourism in the near future.

FAST FACTS

Population: 3.2 million

Annual growth rate: 1.56%

Life expectancy at birth: 75.19 years (US 78)

Infant mortality rate per 1000: 15.96 (US 6.37)

Adult literacy: 92.6%

GDP: 25.3 billion

Unemployment rate: 8.8%

Population below poverty line: 37%

Number of bird species: 940

Number of endangered species: 105

Getting Started

Traveling is all about spontaneity, and plenty of people jump on the plane to Panama without making a single plan. However, although Panama is a fine country for spontaneous adventuring, you'll get more out of your trip if you do a bit of planning before you go.

For starters, there are a few destinations in Panama where advance reservations are a good idea. This is especially true for the Comarca de Kuna Yala (p258), where the demand for flights far exceeds the supply. Fortunately, you can book your outbound and inbound flights in advance (see p264). Advance reservations for Isla Barro Colorado (p113), an outpost for the Smithsonian's Tropical Research Institute (STRI), are also necessary.

If you're planning a trip with the country's leading tour operator, Ancon Expeditions (see the boxed text, p89), advance reservations are usually necessary. This is especially true for their more popular destinations, such as the far-flung corners of the Darién (p273) and the remote island of Coiba (p185).

Panama is a country for any budget. There is a plethora of budget accommodations around the country as well as many decent, inexpensive restaurants. At the other end of the scale, there are five-star lodges overlooking the sea and charming B&Bs tucked away in the mountains. So, whether you're shoestringing or spending Benjamins like they were going out of style, the only thing limiting your trip to Panama is your imagination.

WHEN TO GO

Panama's high tourist season corresponds with its Pacific-side dry season, from mid-December to mid-April. During these months, there is relatively little rain in Panama City and elsewhere south of the Continental Divide. North of the mountains, on the Caribbean side of Panama, it rains all year round. However, it tends to rain less in February, March, September and October than it does the rest of the year.

The best time to visit Panama really depends on what you plan to do. If you intend to spend most of your time on the Pacific side, you might want to visit in December or January, when there's generally little rain and the weather is pleasant. Bear in mind, however, that hotel prices and airfares are generally higher from mid-December to mid-April.

See Climate Charts (p294) for more information.

If you'll be doing any serious hiking, the dry season is the most comfortable time to do it. For planning purposes, be aware that Panama's mountains can get very cold at night; if you're considering camping at altitude (in Boquete, El Valle or Cerro Punta, for example), be sure to bring warm clothing.

If you'll be spending most of your holiday surfing, bear in mind that swells are fairly constant in the Pacific year-round, though offshore winds from December to mid-April can add a few meters to curl. However, Caribbean swells are a bit more fickle, and are usually dependent on weather patterns in the region.

Other outdoor pursuits are also weather dependent. Rafting is at its best is Chiriquí Province from May to December when the rivers are running high, while diving is best from December to mid-April when the dry season lends better visibility.

Some of Panama's colorful festivals draw enormous crowds, and are well worth attending if you're in the area. The Península de Azuero is very popular for its Carnaval (Mardi Gras; p151) – the celebrations are held on the four

---

DON'T LEAVE HOME WITHOUT...

- Learning at least a few basic phrases in Spanish (see Language, p320)
- A poncho for rainy days and wet boat trips
- A mosquito net for trips into the jungle – or a night's rest in well-ventilated quarters
- Decent insect repellent (30% to 50% DEET)
- A flashlight (torch)
- Binoculars, if you're planning to do any bird-watching
- Sun protection – sunscreen, sunglasses, a hat
- Warm clothes for chilly nights in the mountains
- An ATM card or a Visa/MasterCard with (known) pin number
- An alarm clock for catching early-morning flights (to/from Comarca de Kuna Yala, for instance)
- An appetite for fresh seafood
- A thirst for cold lager

---

days leading up to Ash Wednesday. Panama City's Carnaval is also popular (and one of the world's largest; p89). Hotel reservations during Carnaval are a must and should be made well in advance. Panama has a number of other festivals worth catching, especially on the Península de Azuero; see the boxed texts, p151 and p163.

COSTS & MONEY

Prices in Panama tend to be slightly higher than in other parts of Central America, such as Guatemala and Nicaragua, though they are about on par with Costa Rica.

Throughout the country, you can get a budget hotel room for about US$15 to US$20 a night, while die-hard shoestring travelers can probably find some questionable digs for about US$10. In recent years a number of backpacker-friendly hostels have popped up around the country, particularly in Panama City, Bocas del Toro and Boquete – a dorm bed at any of these places will set you back less than US$10 a night.

Good, inexpensive food isn't hard to come by. You can eat *comida corriente* (set meals) at Panamanian restaurants for about US$2 to US$4 no matter where you are in the country. Buses and taxis are also reasonable – a two-hour bus ride costs a few dollars, while a cab ride in the capital costs the same. All in all, if you're traveling frugally, it's possible to get by on US$20 to US$30 a day in Panama.

Midrange accommodations are reasonably priced in Panama, and compared to other parts of Latin America, you tend to get a lot more for your money. You can eat at better restaurants for US$5 to US$10 a person and stay in decent quarters for US$20 to US$40 a night. Add in a flight or two (Kuna Yala, Bocas), a few activities (national-park fees, snorkeling and/or boat trips), a nightly cocktail or two and you can easily get by on US$55 to US$65 a day.

With that said, you'll get more value for your money if you can split the costs with someone. At midrange hotels, single rooms aren't much cheaper than doubles, and you'll save money on excursions if there are more of you to share the cost.

If you're looking to have a blow-out vacation, there are numerous ways to experience Panama's natural and cultural riches at the top end. There

TOP 10

PANAMA

• Panama City

Costa Rica

FAVORITE FESTIVALS

The legacy of colonial Spain lives on in the many colorful celebrations that take place throughout Panama.

1 Feria de las Flores y del Café, 10 days in January, Boquete (p205)

2 Carnaval, four days prior to Ash Wednesday (February or March), Las Tablas (p168) and Panama City (p89)

3 Feria de Azuero, late April or early May, Villa de Los Santos (p164)

4 Corpus Christi, 40 days after Easter (May or June), Villa de Los Santos (p164)

5 Nuestra Señora del Carmen, July 16, Isla Taboga (p116)

6 Fiesta de Santa Librada and Festival de La Pollera, July 21, Las Tablas (p168)

7 Festival del Manito Ocueño, third week of August, Ocú (p159)

8 Feria de la Mejorana, September 23 to 27, Guararé (p166)

9 Festival of Nogagope, October 10 to 12, followed by the Kuna Feria, October 13 to 16, Isla Tigre (p263)

10 Festival de Cristo Negro, October 21, Portobelo (p253)

HISTORICAL READS

For such a small country, Panama has a voluminous history, as evidenced by the many books about the pirates, the visionaries and the demagogues who've all left their mark on the narrow isthmus.

1 *Old Panama and Castilla Del Oro*, CLG Anderson

2 *The Sack of Panama: Sir Henry Morgan's Adventures on the Spanish Main*, Peter Earle

3 *Panama: Four Hundred Years of Dreams and Cruelty*, David Howarth

4 *The Path Between the Seas: The Creation of the Panama Canal*, David McCullough

5 *How Wall Street Created a Nation: JP Morgan, Teddy Roosevelt and the Panama Canal*, Ovidio Diaz Espino

6 *Emperors in the Jungle: The Hidden History of the US in Panama*, John Lindsay-Poland

7 *Panama: The Whole Story*, Kevin Buckley

8 *The Noriega Mess: The Drugs, the Canal, and Why America Invaded*, Luis Murillo

9 *America's Prisoner: The Memoirs of Manuel Noriega*, cowritten with Peter Eisner

10 *A People Who Would Not Kneel: Panama, the United States, and the San Blás Kuna*, James Howe

THE FAMOUS & THE INFAMOUS

The lure of this lush country has been felt by some of history's most fascinating – and notorious – characters. Panama's most famous sojourners and residents include the following.

1 Christopher Columbus, whose only attempt at founding a colony in the New World failed miserably in present-day Veraguas

2 Francis Drake, who, between raids on Spain's gold-filled warehouses in Nombre de Dios, managed to find time to sail around the world

3 Vasco Núñez de Balboa, who was the first European to lay eyes on the Pacific

4 Ferdinand-Marie de Lesseps, who followed his success at Suez with the tragic failure of the Panama Canal endeavor

5 Paul Gauguin, day laborer on the Panama Canal, and struggling artist

6 Graham Greene, whose love affair with the country led to his invitation to attend the signing of the 1977 Torrijos-Carter treaty

7 Frank Gehry, the highly acclaimed architect whose love of Panama will soon be manifest in the Biodiversity Museum

8 Valentín Santana, who is king of the Teribe – the only group in all of the Americas still governed by a monarch

9 Colonel Manuel Antonio Noriega; one of Florida's most infamous prisoners, he's set for release when this book goes to print

10 Rubén Blades, a Grammy Award–winning, Harvard-educated lawyer and one-time presidential candidate (placing third)

are several excellent all-inclusive lodges throughout the country, which are designed for everything from wildlife-watching to sportfishing. Travelers looking to part with a little cash can also take advantage of the decadent restaurants in Panama City, secluded B&Bs in the highlands and luxury ocean-side resorts along the coasts.

TRAVEL LITERATURE

Anyone who doubts that Panama is still an overlooked country has only to take a look at its selection of travel literature. Unlike Guatemala, Peru or even Nicaragua, there are very few accounts of travel within the country. This is good news for would-be travel writers but bad news for anyone wanting to get something other than a historical look at the country. *Travelers' Tales Central America,* published in 2002, has only three stories about Panama, but they are interesting tales (one touches on life in Isla de Coiba's penal colony, while another provides an interesting account of shamanism and the Kuna). It's a decent book for those interested in learning about other Central American countries. Among the most notable contributions is Guatemalan Nobel-laureate Rigoberto Menchú's piece on indigenous village life in the Guatemalan highlands.

For a fictional look at one of Panama's spiciest cultures, read the work of short story–writer José María Sanchez. His work was first published in the 1940s but was rereleased in an anthology titled *Cuentos de Bocas del Toro* (Tales of Bocas del Toro). Set in that beautiful province, where the author was born and raised, these fun stories – whose protagonists are driven by the sensuous, baroque excesses of the tropical jungle and sea – possess a language charged with powerful imagery.

Although *Panama*, by Carlos Ledson Miller, is a work of fiction, the story takes readers on a journey through the political turmoil of the country during the Noriega years. The author, who lived in Panama as a boy, also takes readers further back in history, giving snapshots of Balboa's arrival in 1514, Sir Henry Morgan's sacking of Panama City in the 17th century and more recently the 1964 student riots that later led to the Torrijos–Carter treaty that returned the canal to Panamanian hands.

Getting to Know the General, by Graham Greene, is a biased but still fascinating portrait of General Omar Torrijos and the Panamanian political climate of the 1960s and '70s, by one of England's finest 20th-century writers.

INTERNET RESOURCES

IPAT (www.ipat.gob.pa in Spanish) The official website of Panama's national tourism department.
Lanic (http://lanic.utexas.edu/la/ca/panama) Outstanding collection of links from the University of Texas Latin American Information Center.
Lonely Planet (www.lonelyplanet.com) The popular Thorn Tree forum, travel news and links to other useful sites.
Panama Info (www.panamainfo.com) Panama's best web-based travel resource, with lots of practical information as well as info on provinces and historical background.
Visit Panama (www.visitpanama.com) IPAT's English version of its website, with a small selection of practical and historical info, a few articles and links to other sites.

HOW MUCH?

Dorm bed in Bocas del Toro US$7

Surfboard rental in Santa Catalina per day US$10

Cozy mountain cabin for two in Boquete US$50

Flight from Panama City to San Blás US$35-65

Two-tank dive off the coast of Portobelo US$80

Itineraries
CLASSIC ROUTES

THE BEST OF PANAMA
Two Weeks

For a taste of all that Panama has to offer, this classic travelers' route will take you to colonial cities, the locks of the canal and two far-flung Caribbean getaways.

In **Panama City** (p72), the country's vibrant capital, start your journey at **Panamá Viejo** (p82), the ruins of Spain's first Pacific settlement. After its sacking by pirates, the settlement was moved to present-day **Casco Viejo** (p78), where you'll find colonial buildings, 18th-century churches and scenic plazas amid the old quarters. And of course, you shouldn't leave the capital without a daytrip to the nearby **Miraflores Locks** (p107) of the Panama Canal.

From Panama City, take a quick flight to **Bocas del Toro** (p217), where you can snorkel coral reefs, surf great breaks and soak up the Caribbean vibes. Fly back to the capital and then grab another quick flight to the **Comarca de Kuna Yala** (p258), a string of hundreds of pristine islands that are lorded over by the Kuna. At the end of your trip, return to Panama City for a bit of urban decadence in open-air **restaurants** (p94) and salsa-infused **nightclubs** (p100).

CARIBBEAN SEA

Bocas del Toro

Comarca de Kuna Yala

Miraflores Locks

PANAMA CITY

Golfo de Panamá

PACIFIC OCEAN

DRIVING THE INTERAMERICANA   Two Weeks

From Panama City, head west along the Interamericana to the string of **beaches** (p125) along the Pacific coast. Whether you settle on a quiet strip of sand or live it up in the lap of luxury, chances are you'll find what you're looking for. When you're ready for a detour, take the turnoff for **El Valle** (p130), a mountain retreat surrounded by lush cloud forests and green peaks. Head back to and continue along the Interamericana, taking a quick stop to shop for some Panama hats at **Penonomé** (p139), then take the turnoff for **Santa Fé** (p179), a tiny highland town amid sparkling rivers and gorgeous waterfalls.

If you're starting to miss the beach, backtrack to the Interamericana and take a detour to **Santa Catalina** (p182), a serious surfer's destination worthy of taking down your boards from the roof rack. Get your fill of sun here before heading via **David** (p194) to the popular town of **Boquete** (p201) in Chiriquí. Once in Boquete, you can hike into nearby forests, lounge in hot springs, take a canopy tour and fill up on mountain-grown coffee.

If you've got your own wheels, hit the Interamericana for a route that passes through the interior and alternates between scenic beaches and highland cloud forests.

ROADS LESS TRAVELED

CARIBBEAN COASTAL EXPLORER   Three Weeks

Starting in Panama City, ride the luxury train along the historic **Panama Railroad** (p246) through the Canal Zone to **Colón**. Although there's little reason to linger in this infamous city, you shouldn't miss the historic Spanish forts that guard the bay in **Portobelo** (p250). Divers will want to explore the underwater world along this stretch of coast while history buffs should head to the Unesco World Heritage site of **Fuerte San Lorenzo** (p249).

Anyone looking to slow things down a bit should check out the windswept beaches of **Isla Grande** (p254), which are perfect for surfing, sunning or simply lazing about. When you're ready, head back to the capital and then grab another quick flight to **El Porvenir** (p265) in Kuna Yala. From here, you can head as far south along the archipelago as your time and money will carry you. Of course, serious adventurers should consider taking a sailboat to Colombia – see p263 for details.

If you're looking to get off the beaten path, this seafarer route will bring you from the well-trodden Canal Zone to the farthest reaches of Kuna Yala (and possibly even Colombia).

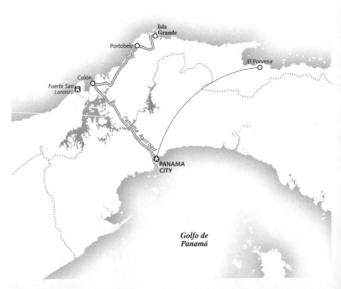

ADVENTURES ACROSS THE ISTHMUS
Three Weeks

From Panama City, travel by bus to the tourist town of **Boquete** (p201) in the Chirirquí Highlands. From here, your first destination should be an ascent up **Volcán Barú** (p209), an extinct volcano that is also Panama's tallest point. After checking out the panoramic views of both the Pacific and the Caribbean, head back to Boquete and grab a bus via **David** (p194) to **Cerro Punta** (p212). From here, you can hike the along the **Sendero Los Quetzales** (p209), a stunning mountain pass that winds through wildlife-rich cloud forest. Now that you've acclimatized yourself to Panama's outdoors, your next stop should be the **Parque Internacional La Amistad** (p213). The Panamanian side of this binational park is virtually undeveloped and largely unexplored. Your final stop will require the services of Ancon Expeditions (p89), but no self-respecting adventurer can leave Panama without trekking through the jungles of the **Parque Nacional Darién** (p280).

If you're the kind of traveler who gets their kicks hiking through dense jungles and scaling towering peaks, then check out this seriously rugged route through Panama's wilderness.

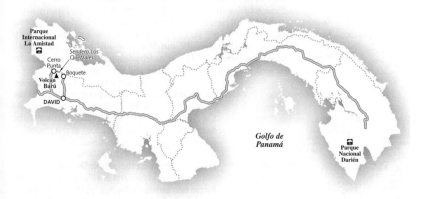

TAILORED TRIPS

WORLD HERITAGE SITES

Panama's five Unesco World Heritage sites provide visitors with a chance to discover the remainders of its storied past, a plethora of neotropical wildlife and the indigenous cultures that lie inside its borders.

The 576,000-hectare **Parque Nacional Darién** (p280) is Panama's crown jewel, with lush primary rainforest, an astounding range of animal life and Emberá and Wounaan villages scattered through remote jungle. Inside the park, **Cana** (p286), with its hundreds of tropical avian species, is regarded as one of the top birding destinations in the world.

Panama City is home to the ruins of **Panamá Viejo** (p82), the first European settlement on the Pacific coast of the Americas. On the other side of town lies the colonial district of **Casco Viejo** (p78).

Travel north of Panama City to reach several Spanish forts along the Caribbean coast. The well-preserved ruins of **Fuerte San Lorenzo** (p249) stand guard over the mouth of the Río Chagres. Further east near the historic town of Portobelo stands the impressive **Fuerte San Jerónimo** (p252).

In the western part of the country, it's back into the rainforest at **Parque Internacional La Amistad** (p213), a binational park shared with Costa Rica. Panama's newest Unesco World Heritage site is **Isla de Coiba** (p188), a far-flung yet pristine island that is the center of a vast marine park.

WILDLIFE-WATCHING

Close to downtown Panama City, the **Parque Natural Metropolitano** (p82) is an excellent (and convenient) place to get a taste of the country's wildlife. Of course, serious birders should head to the **Parque Nacional Soberanía** (p110) in the Canal Zone, which is home to the famous Pipeline Road. Nearby is the Smithsonian Tropical Research Institute on fauna-rich island of **Monumento Nacional Isla Barro Colorado** (p113), and you can spot lounging crocodiles on the banks of the canal during the jungle cruise out there. Little-visited **Parque Nacional Omar Torrijos** (p142) in nearby Coclé Province also boasts rich wildlife, well-maintained hiking trails and few tourists.

Turtle lovers shouldn't miss nesting season on **Isla de Cañas** (p173), **Isla Iguana** (p170) or in the marine park near **Isla Bastimentos** (p229). On the Caribbean coast, four species of turtle come to the **Humedal de San-San Pond Sak** (p236). If you're looking for marine life such as whales and dolphins, the best spots are **Parque Nacional Coiba** (p185) and the reefs and islands in the **Golfo de Chiriquí** (p198).

In the mountains and highland cloud forests, **Parque Internacional La Amistad** (p213) and **Parque Nacional Volcán Barú** (p208) have trails for seeking rare birds, such as the resplendent quetzals, and several species of primates including howlers and capuchins. For unparalleled wildlife viewing, there's no better place than **Parque Nacional Darién** (p280).

ISLAND & BEACH HOPPING

A short flight from Panama City, **Isla Contadora** (p119) has a dozen fine beaches –
and the country's only nude one. The charming island of **Isla Taboga** (p115)
is closer in, with beaches, hiking trails and fine views. The windswept **Isla
Grande** (p254) is a favorite of weekending urbanites, while the hundreds of
islands of the **Comarca de Kuna Yala** (p258), with their white sands, coconut
palms and countless coral reefs, are among Panama's loveliest. Just west of
the capital along the Interamericana lie a string of
beaches (p125), which range from low-key fishing
settlements to resort getaways.

Head to the Península de Azuero for fine, untouched beaches on **Isla Iguana** (p170) and serious
surf on **Playa Venao** (p171). Even better surf – and
fantastic diving – is found at **Playa Santa Catalina**
(p182). For a pure island getaway, head to Boca
Brava in **Golfo de Chiriquí** (p198) where local fishers
can show you all the secret snorkeling spots, or
join an expedition out to **Isla de Coiba** (p188). And
of course, don't miss out the islands and beaches
of Panama's ultimate tourist destination, namely
the **Archipiélago de Bocas del Toro** (p219).

FLOATING ON A CLOUD

Panama's highlands are teeming with wildlife-rich cloud forests. The quickest
escape from the hustle and bustle of the capital is **El Valle** (p130), a tiny town
in the crater of an extinct volcano that is sur-
rounded by forest-covered mountains. Further
west in Veraguas Province is the town of **Santa
Fé** (p179), which abounds with towering waterfalls and hiking trails. Panama's highland tourist
capital is **Boquete** (p201), which provides access
to the Chiriquí Highlands and is the traditional
starting point for hikes up **Volcán Barú** (p209).
Nearby, the mountain town of **Cerro Punta** (p212)
is the traditional starting point for the **Sendero Los
Quetzales** (p209), the country's finest cloud forest
trail. For a taste of the cloud forest without all the
tourist crowds, there's no better place than **Parque
Internacional La Amistad** (p213).

History

LOST PANAMA

The coastlines and rainforests of Panama have been inhabited by humans for at least 10,000 years, and it's estimated that several dozen indigenous groups including the Kuna, the Ngöbe-Buglé, the Emberá, the Wounaan and the Naso were living on the isthmus prior to the Spanish arrival. However, the historical tragedy of Panama is that despite its rich cultural history, there are virtually no physical remains of these great civilizations.

Unlike the massive pyramid complexes found throughout Latin America, the ancient towns and cities of Panama vanished in the jungles, never to be seen by the eyes of the modern world. However, tales of lost cities still survive in the oral histories of Panama's indigenous communities, and there is hope amongst Panamanian archaeologists that a great discovery lies in waiting. Considering that much of Panama consists of inaccessible mountains and rainforests, perhaps these dreams aren't so fanciful.

Old Panama and Castilla Del Oro, by CLG Anderson, is a narrative history of the Spanish discovery, conquest and settlement of Panama as well as the early efforts to build a canal.

What is known about pre-Columbian Panama is that early inhabitants were part of an extensive trading zone that extended as far south as Peru and as far north as Mexico. Archaeologists have uncovered exquisite gold ornaments and unusual life-size stone statues of human figures as well as distinctive types of pottery and *metates* (stone platforms that were used for grinding corn).

Panama's first peoples also lived beside both oceans, and fished in mangrove swamps, estuaries and coral reefs. Given the tremendous impact that fishing has had on the lives of Isthmians, it seems only fitting that the country's name is derived from an indigenous word meaning 'abundance of fish.'

NEW WORLD ORDER

Panama: Four Hundred Years of Dreams and Cruelty, by David A Howarth, is a readable history of the isthmus from Balboa's 1513 exploration through 1964. The best sections are those dealing with the conquistadores and buccaneers.

In 1501 the discovery of Panama by Spanish explorer Rodrigo de Bastidas marked the beginning of the age of conquest and colonization in the isthmus. However, it was his first mate, Vasco Núñez de Balboa, who was to be immortalized in the history books, following his discovery of the Pacific Ocean 12 years later.

On his fourth and final voyage to the New World in 1502, Christopher Columbus went ashore in present-day Costa Rica and returned from the encounter claiming to have seen 'more gold in two days than in four years in Spain.' Although his attempts to establish a colony at the mouth of the Río Belén failed due to fierce local resistance, Columbus petitioned the Spanish Crown to have himself appointed as governor of Veraguas, the stretch of shoreline from Honduras to Panama.

TIMELINE

11,000 BC	2,500 BC	100 BC
The first humans occupy Panama, and populations quickly flourish due to the rich resources found along both coastlines.	Panama is home to some of the first pottery-making villages in the Americas, such as the Monagrillo culture dating from 2500 to 1700 BC.	Panama becomes part of an extensive trade network of gold and other goods that extends from Mesoamerica to the Andes.

Following Columbus' death in 1506, King Ferdinand appointed Diego de Nicuesa to settle the newly claimed land. In 1510 Nicuesa followed Columbus's lead, and once again tried to establish a Spanish colony at Río Belén. However, local resistance was once again enough to beat back Spanish occupation, and Nicuesa was forced to flee the area. Leading a small fleet with 280 starving men aboard, the weary explorer looked upon a protected bay 23km east of present-day Portobelo and exclaimed: *'¡Paremos aquí, en nombre de Dios!'* ('Let us stop here, in the name of God!'). Thus was named the town of Nombre de Dios, one of the first Spanish settlements in the continental New World.

Much to the disappointment of Columbus' conquistador heirs, Panama was not abundant with gold. Add tropical diseases, inhospitable terrain and less than welcoming natives to the mix, and it's easy to see why Nombre de Dios failed several times during its early years as a Spanish colony. However, a bright moment in Spanish exploration came in 1513 when Balboa heard rumors about a large sea and a wealthy, gold-producing civilization across the mountains of the isthmus – almost certainly referring to the Inca empire of Peru. Driven by equal parts ambition and greed, Balboa scaled the Continental Divide, and on September 26, 1513, he became the first European to set eyes upon the Pacific Ocean. Keeping up with the European fashion of the day, Balboa immediately proceeded to claim the ocean and all the lands it touched for the king of Spain.

THE EMPIRE EXPANDS

In 1519 a cruel and vindictive Spaniard named Pedro Arias de Ávila (or Pedrarias, as many of his contemporaries called him) founded the city of Panamá on the Pacific side, near where Panama City stands today. The governor is best remembered for such benevolent acts as ordering the beheading of Balboa in 1517 on a trumped-up charge of treason as well as ordering murderous attacks against the indigenous population, whom he roasted alive or fed to dogs when the opportunity permitted.

Despite his less than admirable humanitarian record, Pedrarias established Panamá as an important Spanish settlement, a commercial center and a base for further explorations, including the conquest of Peru. From Panamá, vast riches including Peruvian gold and Oriental spices were transported across the isthmus by foot to the town of Venta de Cruces, and then by boat to Nombre de Dios via the Río Chagres. Vestiges of this famous trade route, which was known as the Sendero Las Cruces (Las Cruces Trail), can still be found today throughout Panama.

As the Spaniards grew fat and content on the wealth of plundered civilizations, the world began to notice the prospering colony, especially the English privateers lurking in coastal waters. In 1572 Sir Francis Drake destroyed Nombre de Dios, and set sail for England with a galleon laden with Spanish

Among those who made the famous crossing of the isthmus were 1000 indigenous slaves and 190 Spaniards, including Francisco Pizarro, who later conquered Peru.

1513	1519	1671
Balboa endures a tortuous trek from the Atlantic to the Pacific, and becomes the first European to lay eyes on what he dubbed the 'South Sea.'	Pedrarias founds the city of Panamá, which becomes a major transit point for gold plundered from Peru and brought by galleon to Spain.	Henry Morgan overpowers Fuerte San Lorenzo, and then sails up the Río Chagres to sack the city of Panamá. After suffering a crushing defeat, a new walled city is built a few kilometers away in present-day Casco Viejo.

gold. It was also during this expedition that Drake climbed a high tree in the mountains, thus becoming the first Englishman to ever set eyes on the Pacific Ocean.

The Sack of Panamá: Sir Henry Morgan's Adventures on the Spanish Main, by Peter Earle, is a good read for those wanting an account of the Welsh pirate's looting of Panamá in 1671.

Hoping to stave off further ransacking and pillaging, the Spanish built large stone fortresses at Portobelo and Fuerte San Lorenzo. However, these fortifications weren't enough to stop the Welsh buccaneer Sir Henry Morgan from overpowering Fuerte San Lorenzo and sailing up the Río Chagres in 1671. After crossing the length of the isthmus, Captain Morgan destroyed the city of Panamá, made off with its entire treasure and arrived back on the Caribbean coast with 200 mules loaded with loot.

After Panamá burnt to the ground, the Spanish rebuilt the city a few years later on a cape several kilometers west of its original site. The ruins of the old settlement, now known as Panamá Viejo (p82), as well as the colonial city of Casco Viejo (p78), are both located within the city limits of present-day Panama City.

Of course, British privateering didn't cease with the destruction of Panamá. In 1739 the final nail in the coffin was hammered in when Admiral Edward Vernon destroyed the fortress of Portobelo. Humiliated by their defeat and robbed of one of their greatest defenses, the Spanish abandoned the Panamanian crossing in favor of sailing the long way around Cape Horn to the western coast of South America.

THE EMPIRE ENDS

On October 27, 1807, the Treaty of Fontainebleau, which defined the occupation of Portugal, was signed between Spain and France. Under the guise of reinforcing the Franco-Spanish army occupying Portugal, Napoleon moved tens of thousands of troops into Spain. In an act of military genius, Napoleon ordered his troops to abandon the ruse and seize key Spanish fortifications.

SALVAGING SUNKEN GALLEONS

During the period of colonization between the 16th and 18th centuries, Spanish galleons left home carrying goods to the colonies and returned loaded with gold and silver mined in Colombia, Peru and Mexico. Many of these ships sank in the Caribbean Sea, overcome by pirates or hurricanes. During these years, literally thousands of ships – not only Spanish but also English, French, Dutch, pirate and African slave ships – foundered in the green-blue waters of the Caribbean.

The frequency of shipwrecks spurred the Spaniards to organize operations to recover sunken cargo. By the 17th century, Spain maintained salvage flotillas in the ports of Portobelo, Havana and Veracruz. These fleets awaited news of shipwrecks and then proceeded immediately to the wreck sites, where the Spaniards used Caribbean and Bahamian divers, and later African slaves, to scour sunken vessels and the seafloor around them. On many occasions great storms wiped out entire fleets, resulting in a tremendous loss of lives and cargo.

1698	1739	1821
The ill-fated Darien scheme establishes a Scottish trading colony in the region, though it fails soon after, and plunges Scotland into economic depression. The resulting financial losses heavily influence the union of Scotland with England in 1707.	Following numerous pirate attacks, Spain abandons the transisthmian trade route in favor of sailing around Cape Horn in South America.	Simón Bolívar leads the northern swath of South America to independence from Spain, and Panama joins the newly formed union of Gran Colombia.

Without firing a single shot, Napoleon's troops seized Barcelona after convincing the city to open its gates for a convoy of wounded soldiers.

Although Napoleon's invasion by stealth was successful, the resulting Peninsular War was a horrific campaign of guerrilla warfare that crippled both countries. As a result of the conflict, its subsequent power vacuum and decades of internal turmoil, Spain lost nearly all of its colonial possessions in the first third of the century.

Panama gained independence from Spanish rule in 1821, and immediately joined Gran Colombia, a confederation of Colombia, Bolivia, Ecuador, Peru and Venezuela, a united Latin American nation that had long been the dream of Simón Bolívar. However, internal disputes lead to the formal abolishment of Gran Colombia in 1831, though fledgling Panama retained its status as a province of Colombia.

BIRTH OF A NATION

Panama's future forever changed from the moment that the world's major powers learned that the isthmus of Panama was the narrowest point between the Atlantic and Pacific Oceans. In 1846 Colombia signed a treaty permitting the US to construct a railway across the isthmus, though it also granted them free transit and the right to protect the railway with military force. At the height of the California gold rush in 1849, tens of thousands of people traveled from the east coast of the US to the west coast via Panama in order to avoid hostile Native Americans living in the central states. Colombia and Panama grew wealthy from the railway, and the first talks of an interoceanic canal across Central America began to surface.

The idea of a canal across the isthmus was first raised in 1524 when King Charles V of Spain ordered that a survey be undertaken to determine the feasibility of constructing such a waterway. In 1878, however, it was the French who received a contract from Colombia to build a canal. Still basking in the warm glory of the recently constructed Suez Canal, French builder Ferdinand-Marie de Lesseps brought his crew to Panama in 1881. Much like Napoleon before him, Lesseps severely underestimated the task at hand, and over 22,000 workers died from yellow fever and malaria in less than a decade. By 1889, insurmountable construction problems and financial mismanagement had driven the company bankrupt.

The US, always keen to look after its investments, saw the French failure as a lucrative business opportunity that was ripe for the taking. Although they had previously been scouting locations for a canal in Nicaragua, the US pressured the French to sell them their concessions. In 1903, Lesseps' chief engineer, Philippe Bunau-Varilla, agreed to the sale, though the Colombian government promptly refused.

In what would be the first of a series of American interventions in Panama, Bunau-Varilla approached the US government to back Panama if it declared

At one time the Panama Railroad was the highest priced stock on the New York Stock Exchange at US$295 a share.

The Panama Railroad website www.trainweb .org/panama contains photographs, historical information and fascinating travelogues – one dated from 1868, written by Mark Twain.

1855	**1856**	**1878**
An estimated 12,000 laborers die during the construction of the Panama Railroad, particularly from malaria and yellow fever. Despite being only 76km long, the Panama Railroad requires 304 bridges and culverts.	The US intervenes in Panama for the first time in a conflict that becomes known as the Watermelon War of 1856. The war starts when white US soldiers mistreat locals, which causes large-scale race riots that the Marines eventually put down.	The French are granted the rights to build a canal though Panama. After malaria and yellow fever claim over 22,000 lives, the French declare bankruptcy and abandon the project altogether.

its independence from Colombia. On November 3, 1903, a revolutionary junta declared Panama independent, and the US government immediately recognized the sovereignty of the country. Although Colombia sent troops by sea to try to regain control of the province, US battleships prevented them from reaching land. Colombia did not recognize Panama as a legitimately separate nation until 1921, when the US paid Colombia US$25 million in 'compensation.'

GROWING PAINS

Following independence, Bunau-Varilla was appointed Panamanian ambassador to the US, though his first act of office paved the way for future American interventions in the region. Hoping to profit from the sale of the canal concessions to the US, Bunau-Varilla arrived in Washington, DC before Panama could assemble a delegation. On November 18, Bunau-Varilla and US Secretary of State, John Hay, signed the Hay-Bunau-Varilla Treaty, which gave the US far more than had been offered in the original treaty. In addition to owning concessions to the canal, the US was also granted 'sovereign rights in perpetuity over the Canal Zone,' an area extending 8km on either side of the canal, and a broad right of intervention in Panamanian affairs.

Despite opposition from the tardy Panamanian delegation as well as lingering questions about its legality, the treaty was ratified, ushering in an era of friction between the US and Panama. Construction began again on the canal in 1904, and despite disease, landslides and harsh weather, the world's greatest engineering marvel was completed in only a decade. The first ship sailed through the canal on August 15, 1914.

In the years following the completion of the canal, the US military repeatedly intervened in the country's political affairs. In response to growing Panamanian disenchantment with frequent US interventions, the Hay-Bunau-Varilla Treaty was replaced in 1936 by the Hull-Alfaro Treaty. The US relinquished its rights to use its troops outside the Canal Zone and to seize land for canal purposes, and the annual sum paid to Panama for use of the Canal Zone was raised. However, increased sovereignty was not enough to stem the growing wave of Panamanian opposition to US occupation. Anti-US sentiments reached a boiling point in 1964 during a student protest that left 27 Panamanians dead and 500 injured. Today, the event is commemorated as Día de Los Mártires (National Martyrs Day).

As US influence waned, the Panamanian army grew more powerful. In 1968, the Guardia Nacional deposed the elected president and took control of the government. Soon after, the constitution was suspended, the national assembly was dissolved and the press were censored, while the Guardia's General Omar Torrijos emerged as the new leader. Despite plunging the country into debt as a result of a massive public works program, Torrijos was successful in pressuring US President Jimmy Carter

For all things canal-related visit www .pancanal.com, with historical information, photographs and even webcams of the canal in action.

1902	**1909**	**1914**
US President Theodore Roosevelt convinces the US Congress to take control of the abandoned French project. At the time, Colombia was in the midst of the Thousand Days War.	Colombian President Rafael Reyes presents a treaty that will recognize Panamanian independence, but the matter is dropped due to popular and legislative opposition - it is not raised again until 1921.	The canal is finally completed, owing to the efforts of 75,000 laborers, many thousands of whom perish during the construction.

into ceding control of the canal to Panama. The Torrijos-Carter Treaty guaranteed full Panamanian control of the canal as of December 31, 1999, as well as a complete withdrawal of US military forces.

THE RISE & FALL OF NORIEGA

Still feeling truimphant from the recently signed treaty, Panama was unprepared for the sudden death of Torrijos in a plane crash in 1981. Two years later, Colonel Manuel Antonio Noriega seized the Guardia Nacional, promoted himself to general and made himself the de facto ruler of Panama. Noriega, a former head of Panama's secret police, a former CIA operative and a graduate of the School of the Americas, quickly began to consolidate his power. He enlarged the Guardia Nacional, significantly expanded its authority and renamed it the Panama Defense Forces. He also created a paramilitary 'Dignity Battalion' in every city, town and village, its members armed and ready to inform on any of their neighbors showed less than complete loyalty to the Noriega regime.

Things went from bad to worse in early 1987 when Noriega became the center of an international scandal. He was publicly accused of involvement in drug trafficking with Colombian drug cartels, murdering his opponents and rigging elections. Many Panamanians demanded Noriega's dismissal, protesting with general strikes and street demonstrations that resulted in violent clashes with the Panama Defense Forces. In February 1988 Panamanian President Eric Arturo Delvalle attempted to dismiss Noriega, though the stalwart general held on to the reins of power, deposing Delvalle and forcing him to flee Panama. Noriega subsequently appointed a substitute president that was more sympathetic to his cause.

Noriega's regime became an international embarrassment. In March 1988 the US imposed economic sanctions against Panama, ending a preferential trade agreement, freezing Panamanian assets in US banks and refusing to pay canal fees. A few days after the sanctions were imposed, an unsuccessful military coup prompted Noriega to step up violent repression of his critics. After Noriega's candidate failed to win the presidential election in May 1989, the general declared the election null and void. Meanwhile, Guillermo Endara, the winning candidate, and his two vice-presidential running mates were badly beaten by some of Noriega's thugs, and the entire bloody scene was captured by a TV crew and broadcast internationally. A second failed coup in October 1989 was followed by even more repressive measures.

On December 15, 1989, Noriega's legislature declared him president and his first official act of office was to declare war on the US. The following day, an unarmed US marine dressed in civilian clothes was killed by Panamanian soldiers while exiting a restaurant in Panama City.

The US Army's School of the Americas, previously based in Panama, trained some of the worst human rights abusers in Latin America – including Manuel Noriega. For information on the school's history visit www.soaw.org.

1964	**1968**	**1977**
The riots of January 9 (now known as Martyrs' Day) escalate tensions between Panama and the US regarding occupation rights of the Canal Zone. Twenty Panamanian rioters are killed and over 500 are wounded.	The Panamanian army overthrows president-elect Arnulfo Arias after just 11 days in office. Seizing the power gap, General Omar Torrijos becomes Panama's leader.	The Torrijos-Carter Treaty is signed, allowing for the complete transfer of the canal and the 14 US army bases from the US to Panama by 1999.

US reaction was swift and unrelenting. In the first hour of December 20, 1989, Panama City was attacked by aircraft, tanks and 26,000 US troops in 'Operation Just Cause,' though the US media preferred to label it 'Operation Just 'cuz.' Although the intention of the invasion was to bring Noriega to justice and create a democracy better suited to US interests, it left more than 2000 civilians dead, tens of thousands homeless and destroyed entire tracts of Panama City.

On Christmas Day, the fifth day of the invasion, Noriega claimed asylum in the Vatican embassy. US forces surrounded the embassy and pressured the Vatican to release him, as entering the embassy would be considered an act of war against the tiny country. However, the US memorably used that psychological tactic beloved of disgruntled teenagers, namely bombarding the embassy with blaring rock music (Van Halen and Metallica were among the selections). The embassy was also surrounded by mobs of angry Panamanians calling for the ousting of Noriega.

'On Christmas Day, the fifth day of the invasion, Noriega claimed asylum in the Vatican embassy'

After 10 days of psychological warfare, the chief of the Vatican embassy persuaded Noriega to give himself up by threatening to cancel his asylum. Noriega surrendered to US forces on January 3, and was flown immediately to Miami where he was convicted of conspiracy to manufacture and distribute cocaine. Although he was sentenced in 1992 to 40 years in a Florida prison, he is scheduled to be released on good behavior at the end of 2007.

MODERN WOES

After Noriega's forced removal, Guillermo Endara, the legitimate winner of the 1989 election, was sworn in as president, and Panama attempted to put itself back together. The country's image and economy were in shambles, and its capital had suffered damage not only from the invasion itself, but from widespread looting that followed. Unfortunately, Endara proved to be an ineffective leader whose policies cut jobs and cost his administration the popularity it initially enjoyed. By the time he was voted out of office in 1994, he was suffering from single-digit approval ratings.

In the 1994 elections, the fairest in recent Panamanian history, Ernesto Pérez Balladares came into office. Under his direction, the Panamanian government implemented a program of privatization that focused on infrastructure improvements, health care and education. Although Pérez Balladares allocated unprecedented levels of funding, he was viewed as corrupt. In the spring of 1999, voters rejected his attempt to change constitutional limits barring a president from serving two consecutive terms.

In 1999 Mireya Moscoso, the widow of popular former president Arnulfo Arias, Panama's first female leader and head of the conservative Arnulfista Party (PA), took office. Moscoso had ambitious plans for the country, and promised to improve education, health care and housing

1983	1988	1989
Following Torrijos' death in a plane crash in 1981, former CIA operative Manuel Noriega rises to power and ushers in an era of repression.	US President Ronald Reagan invokes the International Emergency Economic Powers Act, freezing Panamanian government assets in US banks and prohibiting payments by American businesses to the Noriega regime.	The US invades Panama, and extradites Noriega to Miami where he is later convicted on charges of conspiracy and drug trafficking.

for the two-thirds of Panamanians who were below the poverty line. She also promised to generate much-needed jobs and to reduce the staggering unemployment rate.

As Panama celebrated its centenary in 2003, unemployment rose to 18% while underemployment reached 30%. In addition, Moscoso angered many over her wasteful spending – as parts of the country went without food, she paid US$10 million to bring the Miss Universe pageant to Panama. She was also accused of looking the other way during Colombian military incursions into the Darién, implying indifference to the terrorism occurring inside the country's borders. When she left office in 2004, Moscoso left behind a legacy of gross incompetence, failing to fulfill even a single campaign promise.

Panama is currently under the leadership of Martín Torrijos, a member of the Revolutionary Democratic Party (PRD) and the son of former leader Omar Torrijos. Although there is still much debate regarding the successes and failures of his administration, he has already implemented a number of much-needed fiscal reforms including an overhaul of the nation's social security. Furthermore, his proposal to expand the Panama Canal was overwhelmingly approved in a national referendum on October 22, 2006.

1994	1999	2006
Ernesto Pérez Balladares is sworn in as president after an internationally monitored election campaign. Balladares emphasizes his party's populist Torrijos roots rather than its former association with Noriega.	Mireya Moscoso becomes Panama's first female president after a free and fair election. The US ends nearly a century of occupation of Panama by closing all of its military bases and turning over control of the canal.	Seventy-eight per cent of voters cast a 'yes' ballot in support of an expanded canal – voter turnout is only 44%.

The Culture

THE NATIONAL PSYCHE

At the crossroads of the Americas, the narrow isthmus of Panama bridges not only two continents, but two vastly different paradigms of Panamanian culture and society. While one sphere of Panama clings to the traditions of the past, the other looks to the modernizing influences of a growing economy. These forces often tug in opposition to one another, which raises the question: what exactly is the Panamanian national character?

In some ways this disorientation is only natural given the many years that Panama has been the object of another country's meddling. From the US-backed independence of 1903 to the strong-armed removal of Noriega in 1989 – with half-a-dozen other interventions in between – the USA left behind a strong legacy in the country. Nearly every Panamanian has a relative or at least an acquaintance living in the USA, and parts of the country seem swept up in mall-fever, with architectural inspiration straight out of North America. Panamanians (or at least the ones that can afford to) deck themselves out in US clothes, buy US-made cars and take their fashion tips straight from Madison Avenue.

Others are not so ready to embrace the culture from the north. Indigenous groups like the Emberá and Kuna struggle to keep their traditions alive as more and more of their youth are lured into the Western lifestyles of the city. On the Península de Azuero, which maintains its rich Spanish cultural heritage through traditional festivals, dress and customs, local villagers raise the same concerns about the future of their youth.

A People Who Would Not Kneel: Panama, the United States and the San Blás Kuna, by James Howe, describes the struggles the Kuna underwent in order to gain the independence they enjoy today.

Given the clash between old and new, it's surprising the country isn't suffering from a serious case of cognitive dissonance. However, the exceptionally tolerant Panamanian character weathers many contradictions – the old and the new, the grave disparity between rich and poor, and the stunning natural environment and its rapid destruction. In fact, much of this tolerance begins in the family, which is the cornerstone of Panamanian society, and plays a role in nearly every aspect of a person's life. Whether among Kuna sisters or Panama City's elite, everyone looks after each other – favors are graciously accepted, promptly returned and never forgotten.

This mutual concern extends from the family into the community, and at times the whole country can seem like one giant extended community. In the political arena, the same names appear time and again as nepotism is the norm rather than the exception. Unfortunately, this goes hand-in-hand with Panama's most persistent problem: corruption. Panamanians view their leaders' fiscal and moral transgressions with disgust, and are far from being in the dark about issues. Yet they accept things with patience and an almost fatalistic attitude. Outsiders sometimes view this as a kind of passivity, but it's all just another aspect of the complicated Panamanian psyche.

LIFESTYLE

In spite of the skyscrapers and gleaming restaurants lining the wealthier districts of Panama City, nearly a third of the country's population lives in poverty. Furthermore, almost three-quarters of a million Panamanians live in extreme conditions, struggling just to satisfy their basic dietary needs and living on less than a dollar a day. Those hardest hit by poverty tend to be in the least populated provinces: Darién, Bocas del Toro, Veraguas, Los Santos and Colón. There are also a substantial number of poor people living in the slums of Panama City, where an estimated 20% of the urban population lives. Countrywide, 9% of the population lives in *barriados* (squatter) settlements.

In the Emberá and Wounaan villages of Darién, traditional living patterns persist much as they have for hundreds of years. The communities are typically made up of 30 to 40 *bohíos* (thatched-roof, open-sided dwellings), and survive on subsistence agriculture, hunting, fishing and pastoralism. However, life can be extremely difficult in these frontier villages – the life expectancy is about 10 years below the national average and the majority of the Emberá and Wounaan communities lack access to clean water and basic sanitation.

For the *campesinos* (farmers), life is also hard. A subsistence farmer in the interior might earn as little as US$100 a year, far below the national average of US$7400 per capita. The dwelling might consist of a simple cinderblock building, with a roof and four walls and perhaps a porch. Families have few possessions and every member assists with working the land or contributing to the household.

The middle and upper class largely reside in Panama City environs, enjoying a level of comfort similar to their economic brethren in Europe and the USA. They live in large homes or apartments, have a maid, a car or two, and for the lucky few a second home on the beach or in the mountains. Cell phones are de rigueur. Vacations are often enjoyed outside of the country in Europe or the USA. Most middle-class adults can speak some English and their children usually attend English-speaking schools.

Celebrations, weddings and family gatherings are a social outlet for rich and poor alike, and those with relatives in positions of power – nominal or otherwise – don't hesitate to turn to them for support.

POPULATION

The majority of Panamanians (65%) are mestizo, which is generally a mix of indigenous and Spanish descent. In truth, many non-black immigrants are also thrown into this category, including a sizable Chinese population – some people estimate that as much as 10% of the population is of Chinese ancestry. There are also a number of other sizable groups: about 14% of Panamanians are of African descent, 10% of Spanish descent, 5% of mixed African and Spanish descent, and 6% are indigenous. Generally, black Panamanians are mostly descendants of English-speaking West Indians, such as Jamaicans and Trinidadians, who were originally brought to Panama as laborers.

Indigenous Groups

Of the several dozen native tribes that inhabited Panama when the Spanish arrived, only seven now remain. Perhaps the most well-known group in the West, due to their distinctive dress, are the Kuna (p259), who inhabit the Archipiélago de San Blás and run their native lands as a *comarca* (autonomous region). Regarded as having one of the largest degrees of sovereignty in Latin America, the Kuna are fiercely protective of their independence and routinely introduce new legislation to protect their lands from foreign cultural invasion. In recent years, this has resulted in barring foreigners from owning property in the *comarca*, imposing restrictions on tourism in San Blás and introducing standard fees for photography and video throughout the region. However, this tenacity has proved successful as one of the highlights of visiting San Blás is witnessing first-hand the vibrancy of the Kuna's unique culture.

The Emberá and Wounaan (p275) inhabit the jungle of the eastern Panamá Province and the Darién, and although both groups distinguish themselves from one another, the difference is more linguistic than cultural. Historically, both groups have eked out a living on the edges of the jungles through

Formal marriage is rare outside of the middle and upper classes. Some estimate that 60% of children are born to short-term unions.

hunting, fishing, subsistence farming and rearing livestock, though rapidly increasing deforestation has reduced the extent of their traditional lands. Today, the majority of Emberá and Wounaan inhabit the fringes of the Darién and live beyond the range of destruction brought forth by loggers, farmers and ranchers. However, an increasing number of communities are turning to tourism for survival, particularly in the Canal Zone where traditional lifestyles are no longer feasible. Sadly, Panama's most recent immigrants are Emberá refugees from Colombia, who fled heavy fighting in the Chaco region by the thousands in early 2004.

The website www.dule nega.nativeweb.org has stories and poems of the Kuna people, as well as a complete list of publications about their culture.

Panama's largest indigenous group is the Ngöbe-Buglé (p193), who number close to 200,000 and occupy a *comarca* that spans the Chiriquí, Veraguas and Bocas del Toro Provinces. Similar to the Kuna, the Ngöbe-Buglé enjoy a high degree of political autonomy and have been extremely successful in managing their lands and protecting their cultural identity. Unlike the Emberá and the Wounaan, the Ngöbe-Buglé have largely resisted outside cultural interventions, primarily since their communities are scattered amongst huge tracts of undeveloped land. In recent years, the youth have been increasingly heading to the cities for work, and missionaries have made numerous inroads in their attempt to convert the indigenous population to Christianity. Religion aside, the Ngöbe-Buglé continue to live much as they have throughout history by relying almost exclusively on subsistence agriculture.

The Naso (Teribe; p237) inhabit mainland Bocas del Toro and are largely confined to the Panamanian side of the binational Parque Internacional La Amistad. Unlike other indigenous population groups, the Naso do not have an independent *comarca* of their own, which has resulted in the rapid destruction of their cultural sovereignty in recent years. Another strike against them is the tremendous tourism potential of the international park, which has prevented the Panamanian government from coming to their aid. Today, traditional villages are rapidly disappearing throughout the region and only a few thousand Naso remain. However, in an effort to ensure their cultural survival, a few villages have banded together to create an ecological center near the Wekso entrance to the park, which aims to draw more visitors to the region and employ more Naso as tourist guides.

The country's other two indigenous groups are the Bokotá, who inhabit Bocas del Toro Province, and the Bribri, who are found both in Costa Rica and in Panama along the Talamanca reserve. Both of these groups maintain their own language and culture, but their numbers and political influence are less than the groups previously mentioned.

SPORTS

Owing to the legacy of US occupation, baseball is the preferred pastime in Panama. This is indeed a rarity in Latin America where football (soccer) is normally the national craze.

Although there are no professional teams in Panama, the amateur leagues host games in stadiums throughout the country. Panamanians have their favorite teams, but are usually more interested in their favorite players in the US major leagues. Mariano Rivera, the record-setting Panamanian pitcher for the New York Yankees, is a national hero, and New Yorkers and Yankees fans alike can easily strike up a conversation with most Panamanians. Batting champ Rod Carew, another Panamanian star, was inducted into the Hall of Fame in 1991. Roberto Kelly, who played for the Yankees for many years, is also fondly remembered.

Boxing is another popular spectator sport and it has been a source of pride to Panamanians (and to Latin Americans in general) ever since Roberto Durán, a Panama City native and boxing legend, won the world championship lightweight title in 1972. He went on to become the world champion in the welterweight (1980), light middleweight (1983) and super middleweight (1989) categories.

MULTICULTURALISM

Panama is a rich melting pot of cultures with immigrants from around the globe as well as a diverse indigenous population. Shortly after the Spanish arrived, slaves were brought from Africa to work in Panama's mines and perform grunt labor in the colony. Slaves that escaped set up communities in the Darién jungle, where their descendents (cimarrones) still live today. Subsequent waves of immigration coincided with the construction of both the Panama Railroad in 1850 and the Panama Canal – both the French effort in the late 1800s and the American completion in the early 1900s. During these times, thousands of workers were brought to Panama from the West Indies, particularly Jamaica and Trinidad.

Workers also came from the East Indies and from China to labor – and many to die – on these massive projects. The majority of the Chinese settled in Panama City, and today you can see two Chinatowns (one is near Casco Viejo, the other in El Dorado). In fact, there are two daily Chinese newspapers and even a private school for the Chinese. The term for Chinese Panamanians is 'Once' (pronounced 'awn-say').

Mixed offspring – and mixed marriages – are increasingly common today. Among the East Indian community, Hindus complain that their culture is disappearing: where once it was common for young men to return to India to find a bride, this is no longer the case. This intermixing of races happens across the nation, although indigenous groups and whites – representing each end of the economic scale – are least likely to marry outside of their group.

Although Panama is a much more racially tolerant society than many other Latin American countries, there is distrust among groups, particularly between indigenous groups and mestizos. This stems largely from mestizo land grabs – by loggers, ranchers and settlers – that have pushed indigenous communities off their lands. Indigenous communities also view the government as corrupt and largely indifferent to their plight – to some extent, they are in fact correct.

Class distinctions also persist. While politicians from the president on down take pride in mingling with the public and maintaining some semblance of a classless society, the whites (rabiblancos) control the majority of the wealth and nearly all of the power. Within that group are several dozen wealthy families who are above the law – people able to escape arrest by mentioning the names of others who could complicate life for a lowly police officer.

In Panama, members of a certain class marry only members of that same class. And at the almighty Union Club (the social club of Panama City), memberships are rarely given to people with dark skin.

Racism is abhorrent no matter where it's found, but racism in Panama is mild compared to the brand found in many other countries. Panama has no counterpart to the Ku Klux Klan and there are no skinheads committing hate crimes. For all its inequities, Panama is closer to the ideal in this respect than most developed nations.

Torrijos helped end the historical monopoly of power by white Panamanians.

MEDIA

Panama has a number of daily newspapers – ranging from sensationalist rags to astute independents. However, in Panama City, the most popular form of mass media is television and some 75% of all homes own a TV set. Mainstream broadcast views tend to represent business and the oligarchy, which is for the most part what urban viewers want to hear. Outside the capital however, radio is the most important medium. There are approximately 90 radio stations on the dial, though most Panamanians have two or three favorites – morning talk shows are particularly popular and represent a wide range of viewpoints.

Unfortunately, Panama still has some horrendous laws that make freedom of the press nothing more than a myth. Government officials who take offense from criticism directed against them can have the journalist imprisoned, for 'not showing them respect.' This is a legacy of Noriega, who used such laws to suppress the voices of critics. Furthermore, many international human-rights and press-advocacy organizations have decried Panama as supporting one of the most repressive regimes in the Americas because of the various 'gag laws' that bureaucrats can use to stifle opposition.

> 'Religion in Panama can best be observed by walking the streets of the capital'

In recent years, nearly 100 journalists and writers nationwide were facing potential prison sentences for publishing material that 'offended the honor' of one or another public figure. A typical incident occurred in August 2003 when two journalists from *El Panamá America* were sentenced to prison for one year (later commuted to a US$600 fine) for 'harming the dignity and honor' of supreme court justice Winston Spadafora. They were punished for an article which described Spadafora's use of public funds to build a road to Iturralde, which led almost exclusively to Spadafora's private estate.

In 2002 Victor Ramos of La Prensa was brought to justice for a political cartoon involving Pérez Balladares, the former president. After Balladares boasted publicly about all of the 'little toys' at his disposal – a private oceanfront residence, a plane and a helicopter among other things – Ramos' cartoon placed the former president's list next to another that itemized the scandals that had dogged his political career. Among the well-documented scandals was a US$51,000 campaign check that Balladares received in 1994 from a Colombian drug trafficker, as well as the mysterious disappearance of millions of dollars allocated for the construction of a bridge over the Panama Canal. Although prosecutors targeted Pérez Balladares in corruption investigations, they claimed there was insufficient evidence to prosecute him.

In spite of President Moscoso's pronouncement to repeal these laws during her term, she and her cronies used these 'gag laws' to suppress dissent. At the time of writing, it was still unclear whether the current administration under Torrijos will employ the same tactics.

RELIGION

Religion in Panama can best be observed by walking the streets of the capital. Among the scores of Catholic churches, you'll find breezy Anglican churches filled with worshippers from the West Indies, synagogues, mosques, a shiny Greek Orthodox church, an impressive Hindu temple and a surreal Baha'i house of worship (the headquarters for Latin America).

Freedom of religion is constitutionally guaranteed in Panama, although the preeminence of Roman Catholicism is also officially recognized, with 77% of the country filling its ranks. In fact, children in school have the option to study theology, though it is not compulsory. Protestant denominations account for 12%, Muslims 4.4% and Baha'i 1.2%. Additionally, the country has approximately 3000 Jews (many of them recent immigrants from Israel), 24,000 Buddhists and 9000 Hindus.

In addition to the mainstream world religions, the various indigenous tribes of Panama have their own belief systems, although these are fading quickly due to the influence of Christian missionaries. As in other parts of Latin America, the evangelical movement is spreading like wildfire.

Although Catholics are the majority, only about 20% of them attend church regularly. The religious orders aren't particularly strong in Panama either – only about 25% of Catholic clergy are Panamanian while the rest are foreign missionaries.

WOMEN IN PANAMA

Women enjoy more opportunities in Panama than they do in most other Latin American countries. At the forefront of the country's political arena is the PNF (Feminist National Party), which was founded in 1923 and is one of the oldest feminist parties in Latin America. Historically, the PNF has been strongly critical of the male-dominated government and has secured numerous social reforms for women and children. In 1941, the PNF helped women secure the right to vote, while in 1981 they helped ratify the law that eliminated all forms of discrimination against women.

'Women enjoy more opportunities in Panama then they do in most other countries'

In spite of these advances, women still face many obstacles in Panamanian society. Machismo and gross stereotypes are more prevalent in rural areas than in urban ones, but even in the cities women have to face lower wages and sexual harassment, and are nearly twice as likely to be unemployed. Although women make up nearly half of the workforce, they make up only 10% of the country's legislature.

Overall, women are having fewer children and are having them later in life. Many postpone motherhood to enter the workplace – a pattern that exists in Europe and the USA. Panama also has a growing number of single mothers, particularly at the bottom income bracket. This problem is compounded by the facts that women have no right to an abortion (it's illegal in Panama) and that the teenage pregnancy rate is high.

In indigenous communities, women face many hardships, including poor access to health care and a low level of prenatal care. Prevailing stereotypes also means that girls are less likely to attend school – among indigenous populations, over half of women are illiterate compared to one-third of men. Women also enter motherhood at much younger ages and bear more children than their mestizo counterparts. At the same time, they are expected to work and help support the household.

One of the most positive signs that things are improving for indigenous women is the 2004 election of a female governor over the Comarca de Emberá–Wounaan. She was chosen by the general congress, made up of both Emberá and Wounaan in the Darién Province.

Of course, the single greatest accomplishment for women in the political area was the presidential election of Mireya Moscoso. When Moscoso left office in 2004, she was one of only 12 female heads of state in the world. This historic achievement places Panama ahead of many other countries in both the developed and the developing world.

ARTS

Panama's art scene reflects its ethnic mix. A slow spin on the radio dial or a close-up look at Panamanian nightclubs will reveal everything from salsa and jazz to reggae and rock 'n' roll.

The country has a few impressive painters and writers, some of whom are internationally recognized. There is also fair representation in dance, theater and other performance arts, which are managed by the Instituto Nacional de Cultura (INAC).

Traditional Panamanian products include woodcarvings, textiles, ceramics, masks and other handicrafts.

Inauguración de La Fe
(Inauguration of La Fe),
by Consuelo Tomás, is a
collection of tales depicting the idiosyncrasies of
the popular neighborhoods of Panama City.

Literature

Several of Panama's best novelists wrote around the midcentury. *El Ahogado* (The Drowned Man), a 1937 novel by Tristán Solarte (pen name for Guillermo Sánchez Borbón, a well-known poet, novelist and journalist), ingeniously blends elements of the detective, gothic and psychological genres, along with a famous local myth. *El Desván* (In the Garret), a 1954 novel by Ramón H Jurado, explores the emotional limits of the human condition. *Gamboa Road Gang,* by Joaquín Beleño, is the best work of fiction about the political and social events surrounding the Panama Canal.

Music

Salsa is the most popular music in Panama, and live salsa is easy to find, particularly in Panama City. Jazz, which was brought to Panama from the US, and calypso music from the West Indies can also be heard in clubs in Panama. Rock 'n' roll, in both English and Spanish, is played on most Panamanian FM radio stations, and some decent bands play it in Panama City clubs.

The country's most renowned salsa singer, Rubén Blades, is something of a national hero. Raised in Panama City, Blades has had several international hits, appeared in a few motion pictures and once even ran for president – he finished third. For more on Blades, see the boxed text on opposite.

For the lowdown on the
Panamanian music scene
as well as a guide to its
most famous and greatest, take a look at www
.panama1.com/Music
_of_Panama.php

The jazz composer and pianist Danilo Pérez is widely acclaimed by American and European jazz critics. He has recorded with jazz greats from around the world and is currently serving on the faculty of the Berklee College of Music and the New England Conservatory of Music in Boston, USA.

Los Rabanes is the most popular rock 'n' roll group in the country. Panamanian folkloric music *(típico)*, in which the accordion is dominant, is well represented by Dorindo Cárdenas, the late Victorio Vergara (whose band lives on as Nenito Vargas y los Plumas Negras) and the popular brother–sister pair of Sammy and Sandra Sandoval.

Handicrafts

Panama's handicrafts are varied and often of excellent quality. The Wounaan and Emberá in the Darién create some beautiful woven baskets. These indigenous groups also sell carvings of jungle wildlife from *cocobolo*, a handsome tropical hardwood, and tiny figurines from the ivory-colored *tagua* nut.

The Kuna of the Comarca de Kuna Yala are known worldwide for their *molas* – the blouse panels used by women in their traditional dress and sold

BUYING A MOLA

A *mola*, a traditional Kuna handicraft, is made of brightly colored squares of cotton fabric laid atop one another. Cuts are made through the layers, forming basic designs. The layers are then sewn together with tiny, evenly spaced stitches to hold the design in place. *Mola* means 'blouse' in Kuna, and Kuna women make *molas* in thematically matching but never identical pairs. A pair will comprise the front and back of a blouse.

Regardless of the design, Kuna believe the very best *molas* should always have the following characteristics:

- Stitches closely match the color of the cloth they are set against.
- Stitches are very fine and neatly spaced.
- Stitches are pulled evenly and with enough tension to be barely visible.
- Curves are cut smoothly and the sewing follows the curves of the cut.
- Outline strips are uniform in width, with no frayed edges.

GREAT PANAMANIANS: RUBÉN BLADES

Rubén Blades Bellido de Luna was born on July 16, 1948, and is a famous salsa singer, songwriter, lawyer, actor, politician and all-around Renaissance man. As a songwriter, Blades is often referred to as the 'Latin Bruce Springsteen' and is revered for bringing lyrical sophistication to salsa and creating intelligent dance music. Today, his music remains incredibly popular in Panama and is admired throughout Latin America and in the West. Despite his failed attempt at winning the Panamanian presidency in 1994, Blades is now serving as the Minister of Tourism under President Martín Torrijos.

Raised in a middle-class neighborhood in Panama City, Blades inherited his musical talents from his mother, a Cuban immigrant who played the piano and sang on the radio, and his father, a police detective who played the bongos. Inspired by the doo-wop singing of Frankie Lymon & the Teenagers, Blades began singing North American music in his early teens. However, influenced by the political upheaval in Panama during the mid-60s, Blades became increasingly patriotic and for a brief period refused to sing in any language other than Spanish.

While studying at the prestigious University of Panama, Blades continued to pursue his musical pursuits. He regularly performed with popular Panamanian groups such as Conjunto Latino and Los Salvajes del Ritmo, and recorded a best-selling album with Bush and the Magnificos in 1968. Shortly after, his reputation had spread to New York, and Blades was asked to join the legendary band of Joe Cuba, but he rejected the offer in order to complete his studies.

After graduating with degrees in political science and law, Blades worked as a lawyer at the Bank of Panama. In 1974, Blades abandoned his law career and moved to the US to pursue his music, staying temporarily with his exiled parents in Miami before relocating to New York City. Blades started out by taking a position in the mailroom at the Latin-orientated Fania Records and spent most of his spare time composing songs. One year later, he had replaced Tito Allen as featured vocalist in Ray Barretto's salsa band following a successful audition in the Fania Records mailroom.

Eventually, Barretto left the salsa band to start a Latin fusion project and Blades took control of the group, which he named Guarare. For their first project, Blades composed and sang lead on Barretto's recording 'Canto Abacua', which went on to become an international chart-topper. As a result, Blades was named Composer of the Year by *Latin New York* magazine. At the same time, Blades was also playing regularly with Willie Colón's band, and their collaboration reached its apex with the three-million-copy-selling album *Siembra*. This record-smashing LP included the song 'Pedro Navaja', which remains the biggest-selling single in salsa history.

Unfortunately, Blades' propensity to write politically charged lyrics was not universally accepted. In 1980 Blades became embroiled in a controversy over his song 'Tiburon', which railed against American political and military intervention in the Caribbean and was eventually banned from the radio in Miami. Shortly after, Blades tried to terminate his contract with Fania Records, though he was unable to break his contractual obligation. As a result, he recorded a number of self-proclaimed throw-away albums before going on to form his own band, Los Seis de Solar, in 1982. Over the next few years, Blades experimented with a fusion of Latin, rock, reggae and Caribbean music while simultaneously completing a master's degree in international law at Harvard University and breaking into Hollywood.

The same year he formed Los Seis de Solar, Blades got his first acting role in the film *The Last Fight*. Portraying a singer-turned-boxer, Blades' character seeks to win the championship against a fighter who was portrayed by the real life world champion boxer Salvador Sánchez. In the years to follow, Blades appeared in a string of movies including *The Milagro Beanfield War* (1988), *The Two Jakes* (1990), *Mo' Better Blues* (1990), *Devil's Own* (1997) and *Cradle Will Rock* (1999). However, his most memorable performances were in Paul Simon's Broadway musical *The Capeman* (1997) and in the cult movie *Once Upon a Time in Mexico* (2003).

In 2004, Blades ran an unsuccessful campaign for the presidency of Panama, though he did manage to finish in third place, with 20% of the vote. Since 2004 Blades has been serving as Panama's Minister of Tourism, though his tendency to favor foreign investment over environmental conservation has thus far garnered him mixed support.

as crafts. Molas symbolize the identity of the Kuna people to outsiders, and their colorful and elaborate designs often depict sea turtles, birds and fish. For more information on *molas*, see the boxed text on p40.

Ocú and Penonomé produce superior Panama hats. For more information on Panama's most famous fashion accessory, see the boxed text on p141.

Polleras (elaborate traditional outfits of Spanish origin) are handmade in Guararé and in other villages in Las Tablas Province. Also available on the Azuero Peninsula are handcrafted festival masks from Villa de Los Santos and Parita.

To learn about the Kuna as well as the culture, history and sewing of their world-famous *molas*, visit www .quiltethnic.com/kuna .html.

Painting

Trained in France, Roberto Lewis (1874–1949) became the first prominent figure on Panama's art scene. He painted portraits of the nation's leaders and allegorical images to decorate public buildings. Among his most notable works are those in the Palacio de las Garzas (p81) in Panama City. In 1913 Lewis became the director of Panama's first art academy, where he and his successor, Humberto Ivaldi (1909–47), educated a generation of artists. Among the school's students were Juan Manuel Cedeño and Isaac Benítez, as well as the painters who would come to the fore in the 1950s and 1960s. This group includes Alfredo Sinclair, Guillermo Trujillo, Eudoro Silvera and others. Most of these artists are still active today and their works are occasionally shown in local galleries.

Michel Perrin's *Magnificent Molas: The Art of the Kuna Indian* contains photographs of 300 fabric works of art. Perrin describes the vivid relationship between Kuna art and culture.

The largest Panamanian art exposition – the Bienal de Arte – is held every two years at the Museo de Arte Contemporáneo (p87) in Panama City.

Photography

Panama has several gifted photographers, including Iraida Icaza, Stuart Warner and Sandra Eleta. Icaza, who lived for many years in Tokyo and now resides in New York, makes abstract art using photographic equipment. Her work is bold and innovative.

Warner, who has spent much of his life in Asia, the Middle East, Europe and the USA, captures the human spirit in beautiful landscapes and portraits.

Sandra Eleta's portraits of the black inhabitants of Panama's Caribbean coast (particularly of Portobelo, where she resides part of the year) have made her one of the most important photographers in Latin America.

Food & Drink

Panama's resplendent coastline and verdant interior produce a culinary bounty, from tropical fruits to *frutas del mar* (fruits of the sea). Throughout the country, bustling outdoor markets brim with such exotic specialities as mangoes, guavas and passion fruit, while fishers ply their catch of day, be it red snapper, spiny lobster, king crab or octopus. However, Panama remains fiercely true to its Latin roots by featuring rice and beans prominently at most meals. And of course, Panamanians love a good beef fillet, which isn't too hard to find given the abundance of cattle ranches throughout the country.

Despite its small size, Panama's culinary landscape varies considerably from region to region. Along the Caribbean coast, West Indian flavors are evident in Bocas del Toro, while traditional cooking methods of the Kuna people feature prominently in the Comarca. In the interior, hearty country-inspired cooking that's heavy on the beef and corn is usually on the menu, while indigenous groups in the Darién continue to subsist on rice, beans, yucca and plantains. The crown jewel in Panama's plate of gastronomic offerings, though, is its cosmopolitan capital, which is home to some of the finest restaurants in Latin America.

Owing to its rapidly growing international community, Panama City offers everything from French and Italian to Japanese and Chinese with a dash of Lebanese and African in the middle. While there's no shortage of cheap and cheerful neighborhood eateries, Panama City is the perfect place to lighten up the wallet, pack on a few extra kilos and wine and dine to your heart's (and stomach's) content.

STAPLES & SPECIALITIES

In most Latin American countries, the core of the Panamanian diet is rice and beans, a healthy and hearty staple that can be served a dozen different ways. In fact, a meal is not considered to be a meal unless there's rice, and it's not surprising that this versatile grain is seemingly served alongside everything. As for the beans, they're usually served lightly spiced with herbs, and also seem to be served with everything.

Panamanians have much love for the venerated plate of rice and beans, though most will secretly tell you that they'd prefer to eat meat three times a day. Urban dwellers can satisfy this carnivorous fix with *bistec* (steak) and *carne asado* (roast meat), though the working class are loyal to *ropa vieja* (literally 'old clothes'), a spicy shredded beef combination served over rice. Of course, Panamanians from all walks of life can agree that the national dish of *sancocho*, a fairly spicy chicken-and-vegetable stew, is simply delicious.

In restaurants, snack bars and just about anywhere food is sold, you'll undoubtedly come across empanadas, which are fried corn turnovers filled with ground meat. If you get them fresh, they're a fine treat. Another favorite is the *tamale*, which is cornmeal with a few spices and chicken or pork that's wrapped in banana leaves and boiled. Also keep an eye out for the Panamanian speciality known as *carimañola*, which is a roll made from ground and boiled yucca that is filled with chopped meat and then deep fried.

As in Costa Rica, *gallo pinto* (literally 'spotted rooster') is traditionally served at breakfast, and consists of a soupy mixture of rice and black beans. Although Westerners may be initially be put off by the idea of eating rice and beans for breakfast, a heaping plate of *gallo pinto* will start your day off right, and the stuff goes down well with *natilla* (a cross between sour cream and custard) and *huevos fritos/revueltos* (fried/scrambled eggs).

New World Kitchen: Latin American and Caribbean Cuisine, by Norman Aken, contains only one purely Panamanian recipe, but you'll find dozens of other 'Pan-Latin' and 'Pan-Caribbean' dishes that show culinary influences from the isthmus.

Another item you might see at breakfast is a side of *tortillas de maíz,* which is usually served alongside eggs or roast meat. Unlike those found in Mexico and Guatemala, Panamanian tortillas are much thicker, and are essentially deep-fried cornmeal cakes. If you have a sweet tooth, don't miss out on the *hojaldras*, which are deep-fried masses of dough that are served hot and covered with sugar – think of them as a Panamanian doughnut.

At lunch, many Panamanians opt for a simple *comida corriente* (set meal), which is also known as a *casado* (literally 'married'). Known as the meal of the working class, this inexpensive set meal 'marries' either beef, chicken or fish to *arroz* (rice), *frijoles* (black beans), *plátano* (fried plantain), chopped *repollo* (cabbage) and possibly an egg or an avocado.

Dozens of Panamanian recipes (in Spanish) are listed on www.critica.com.pa/archivo/recetas.

Since vegetables don't grow well in the tropics, yucca and plantains take the place of leafy greens at most Panamanian eateries. Yucca is most often served in fried cubes that are heavily salted and perfect for curing a hangover or preventing one in the morning. Plantains are usually served as either *patacones* (fried green plantains cut crossways) or *plátanos maduros* (ripe plantains baked or broiled with butter, brown sugar and cinnamon). Unlike vegetables, fruits are plentiful in Panama, and the climate is just right for nourishing a range of exotic tropical specialities including papayas, mangoes, *piñas* (pineapples), melons, *maracuyá* (passion fruit) and *guanábanas* (soursops, or custard apples).

You'll find excellent *ceviche* throughout the isthmus. To get a handle on preparing this delicious seafood dish, take a look at *The Great Ceviche Book,* by Douglas Rodriguez.

True to its moniker – Panamá means 'abundance of fish' in several indigenous languages – seafood is abundant along both coastlines. In the Caribbean, common everyday foods include shrimp, king crab, octopus, grouper and red snapper. Unfortunately lobster and grouper are heavily overfished, so you might want to skip these if they're out of season. In Bocas del Toro, you'll find a West Indian influence to the dishes – seafood is often mixed with coconut milk, and coconut rice and coconut bread are common staples. Further south in the Comarca de Kuna Yala, traditional cooking styles involve grating coconut over fresh fish that is cooked over hot coals.

Along the Pacific coast, *corvina* (sea bass) is the most sought-after catch of the day, and it's usually served either *a la parilla* (grilled) or as *ceviche* (raw fish marinated in lemon juice). In fact, *ceviche* is one of the most popular foods in the country – classic Panamanian *ceviche* includes sea bass or *conchas* (shellfish), chopped onion and *ají chombo* (one of the hottest chili peppers in the world). However, due to rapidly decreasing sea-bass stocks, *ceviche* is increasingly offered with *langostinos* (jumbo shrimp) or *pulpo* (octopus).

DRINKS
Alcoholic Drinks

The national alcoholic drink is *seco,* which is distilled, like rum, from sugarcane, and is popular in the rural areas. Order a *seco con leche* (*seco* with milk) in a martini lounge in Panama City and you'll likely receive some odd looks, but you'll make some new friends if you order one in the provinces.

The output of Panama's largest *seco* factory, Seco Herrerano, is 36,000 1L bottles every day.

By far the most popular alcoholic beverage in Panama is *cerveza* (beer), and the most popular local brands are Soberana and Panamá, as well as the higher-alcohol Balboa and Atlas. All of these beers fall somewhere between pilsner and lager, and although they're not overly flavorful, they do the trick when served ice cold on a hot day. A large Atlas at a typical cantina can cost as little as US$0.50; the same beer can cost you US$2.50 at a decent restaurant.

Interestingly enough, one beer company distributes Balboa and Panamá, while another distributes Soberana and Atlas – Panamanians often jest that

---

TRAVEL YOUR TASTE BUDS

Think you've got a strong palate, an iron gut and the will to travel your taste buds? Here's our top-five list of Panama's less than popular culinary oddities.

Mondongo (tripe soup) Unless you grew up eating the stuff, it's difficult for most people to dig into a hot, steamy bowl of boiled intestines. Assuming you can forget about what you're eating, where they came from and what used to pass through them, consistencies such as chewy, stringy and spongy don't exactly get the mouth watering and the stomach grumbling.

Ceviche de pulpo (octopus *ceviche*) Sushi aficionados the world over may disagree with us, but it takes a bit of mental preparation to put a piece of raw octopus in your mouth. Although the citric acid in the lemon juice arguably cooks the octopus, it's still rubbery and hard to chew, and it's difficult to describe the feeling of the suckers sliding down your throat.

Vino de Palma (Palm Wine) The preferred firewater of rural *campesinos* (country folk) throughout Panama, palm wine is the fermented sap of the *palma de corozo* tree. After burning your innards, inducing temporary blindness and killing a few million brain cells, you will be treated to one of the worst hangovers of your life, the likes of which has been known to last for up to two days.

Chicharrones (Fried Pig Skin) Although hot, salty and oily are usually good adjectives for describing a snack food, it's hard to eat pig skin if you've ever seen one rolling around in its own filth. Of course, 'pork rinds' are a popular snack food in the US, though the real thing is less like a pork-flavored potato chip and more like a greasy slab of pork-flavored fat.

Seco con leche (Rum-type liquor and milk) The preferred cocktail of rural *campesinos* across Panama, *seco con leche* is a cool and frothy mix of fresh milk and hard liquor. Sure, it goes down smooth enough, but don't even think about chasing it with beer lest you want to discover how quickly it can come up.

---

they're loyal to their favorite brands. We have our favorites too, though we'll let you decide which one quenches your thirst best!

Wines on offer in Panama generally come from Chile, Argentina, Spain and the USA, though the quality is poor and as a result wine isn't particularly popular. However, Panama City has a growing number of restaurants and bars where you can find good-quality wines.

Nonalcoholic Drinks

Panama sits firmly in the tropics, which means that there is no shortage of exotic juices on offer. Fresh fruit juices, sweetened with heaped tablespoons of sugar and mixed with water or milk, are known as *chichas* and are common throughout the country. Popular offerings include *piña* (pineapple), *sandía* (watermelon), *tamarindo* (tamarind), *guanábana* (soursop), *mango* (mango), *melón* (cantaloupe), *fresa* (strawberry), *zarzamora* (blackberry), *zanahoria* (carrot) and *cebada* (barley).

A nonalcoholic drink found in Panama and nowhere else is the *chicheme*. This delicious concoction consists of milk, sweet corn, cinnamon and vanilla, and is rumored to have health-giving properties.

Coffee is traditionally served very strong and offered with cream or condensed milk. Café Durán is the most popular of the local brands, and this being Central America, it's quite good. Cappuccinos are increasingly available in Panama City, David, Boquete and Bocas del Toro.

Tea (including herbal tea) is available in the cities, but is incredibly difficult to find in towns. Note that the milk in Panama is pasteurized and safe to drink.

WHERE TO EAT & DRINK

Panama has eating establishments to suit every budget. At the low end are *cafeterías* (simple eateries), where food is served either buffet-style or as

Eating & Drinking in Latin America: A Menu Reader and Restaurant Guide, by Andy Herbach and Michael Dillon, is a sensible choice if you plan to travel in other parts of Latin America. The guide features local specialities and unusual dishes.

comida corriente. In either case, meals rarely cost over US$3, the atmosphere is informal and the service is courteous but to the point.

Panaderías are bakeries, and are a good choice for a quick bite. Most have a few tables and a countertop where you can peer at the goods. Coffee and other drinks are available at most bakeries.

Restaurante is a term that, like its English counterpart, covers a wide spectrum of dining options. Most restaurants open for lunch from noon to 3pm and dinner from 6pm to 10pm. On weekends, restaurants in Panama City stay open until midnight or even 2am, depending on their location. Not all places open for breakfast – those that do open at 7am or 8am. Even at the best places in Panama City, you rarely need reservations. If there's a wait, by the time you finish a cocktail at the restaurant-bar (or one nearby), your table will be ready.

> The pain caused by the capsaicin in chili peppers causes the brain to produce natural endorphins to create a sense of wellbeing.

VEGETARIANS & VEGANS

As with the rest of Latin American, vegetarians and vegans traveling in Panama should have few problems subsisting on rice and beans – it may be dull, but this hearty staple packs in your daily protein requirements. Vegetarians will be happy to learn that eggs and local cheeses feature prominently on most menus, while vegans will be more than satisfied with the variety of fresh tropical fruits on offer.

The best places for vegetarians to eat are in Panama City, which has a handful of places where you can put together a meatless meal. Lebanese, Thai and Chinese places are good options. Also keep an eye out for supermarkets and vegetable stands, where you can get the ingredients to put your own meal together.

Be aware that Panamanian dishes often contain 'hidden' meat products – vegetable soups usually are made from meat stock, and *patacones* are often fried in lard.

EATING WITH KIDS

If you're traveling with the little ones, be advised that only a handful of Panamanian restaurants have high chairs or special kids' menus. All the same, most Panamanians are quite accommodating to diners with children.

Cities with the widest varieties of restaurants are Panama City, Bocas del Toro, Boquete and to a lesser extent David. In any of these towns, it's easy

---

PANAMA'S TOP FIVE EATS

- **René Cafe** (Casco Viejo, Panama City; p95) René Cafe is an alfresco charmer where you can dine on electic tapas while watching pedestrians pass through the Plaza de la Independencia.

- **Limoncillo** (Bella Vista, Panama City; p97) Limoncillo is one of the city's most stylish restaurants – the daily specials are almost as artistic as the original paintings that adorn the walls.

- **Palo Alto** (Boquete, Chiriquí Province; p208) A rustic restaurant where you can soak up the charm of the highlands while dining on the catch of the day (usually river trout) and listen to the sounds of the rushing Río Palo Alto.

- **La Casbah** (Isla Colón, Bocas del Toro Province; p228) This much-loved Bocas restaurant offers a wide variety of European-inspired dishes that are accented by fresh produce and exotic spices.

- **Roots** (Isla Bastimentos, Bocas del Toro Province; p234) This Isla Bastimentos institution is perched over the water, but the views shouldn't distract you too much from the seriously fresh seafood.

DOS AND DON'TS

- When you enter a restaurant, and when you sit down at a table, it's polite to say *'buenos dias,'* *'buenas tardes'* or *'buenas noches'* (depending on the time of day) to those near you.

- When you leave a restaurant, it's polite to say *'buen provecho'* (bon appetit) to those near you.

- It's customary to leave a 10% *propina* (tip), which is usually included in the bill. Always look to see if the tip has been added.

- Don't eat animals that are endangered or at risk of being endangered. These include *tortuga* (sea turtle), *huevos de tortuga* (turtle eggs), *cazón* (shark), *conejo pintado* (paca), *ñeque* (agouti), *venado* (deer) or iguana. *Langosta* (lobster) is heavily overfished, particularly in the Comarca de Kuna Yala. By eating lobster, you may be contributing to its extinction in these waters – this is especially important during the mating season from March to July.

---

to find something for even the most finicky child. And, of course, nearly every town has at least one pizzeria, which is where you're most likely to see Panamanian parents with little children or teenagers.

Supermarkets in Panama boast a wide range of products, and are great spots for loading up on snack items before a bus trip.

Very few visitors to Panama have a problem with sickness from food preparation, and that includes kids as well as adults. Cleanliness and hygiene are particularly high in Panama, and the tap water is safe to drink in most provinces (Bocas del Toro being a notable exception).

For more information on traveling with kids, see p293.

> For loads of Panamanian recipes in English head to www.czbrats.com /Menus/recmenu.htm.

HABITS & CUSTOMS

Urbanites in Panama tend to have a small repast at breakfast time – usually just coffee and a roll. In the countryside, however, it's not uncommon to start the day off with something bigger, such as eggs, *carne asado* and tortillas. Generally, lunch is the big meal of the day, often followed by a short siesta to beat the heat of the day. Dinner usually consists of soup or salad and bread.

Panamanians are open and informal, and treat their guests quite well. If you have the good fortune to be invited into a Panamanian's home, you can expect to be served first, receive the biggest portion and perhaps even receive a parting gift. On your part, flowers or wine are a fine gift to bring, though the best gift you can offer is extending a future dinner invitation to your hosts.

> Get some Latin culinary inspiration at www .boyds.org/recipes.htm.

EAT YOUR WORDS

Don't know your *pipas* from your *patacones*? A *batido* from a *bolita*? Get beneath the surface of Panama's plentiful cuisine by learning the lingo. For pronunciation guidelines, see p320.

Useful Phrases
Another (beer) please.
    Mas una (cerveza), por favor   mas *oo*·na ser·*ve*·sa por fa·*vor*
Do you have an English menu?
    ¿Hay una carta en inglés?   ai *oo*·na *kar*·ta en een·*gles*
I'd like ...
    Quisiera ...   kee·*sye*·ra ...
I'm a vegetarian.
    Soy vegetariano/a. (m/f)   soy ve·khe·te·*rya*·no/a
The bill, please.
    La cuenta, por favor.   la *kwen*·ta por fa·*vor*

Menu Decoder

almojabanos (al·mo·kha·*ba*·nos) – similar to *tortilla de maíz*, except hand-rolled into small sausage-sized pieces

batido (ba·*tee*·do) – milkshake made with fresh fruit, sugar and milk

bocas (*bo*·kas) – savory side dishes or appetizers

bolitas de carne (bo·*lee*·tas de *kar*·ne) – snack of mildly spicy meatballs

carimañola (ka·ree·ma·*nyo*·la) – a deep-fried roll made from chopped meat and boiled yucca

carne ahumada (*kar*·ne a·oo·*ma*·da) – smoked, dried (jerked) meat

ceviche (se·*vee*·che) – marinated raw fish or shellfish

chichas (*chee*·chas) – heavily sweetened, fresh fruit drinks

chicheme (chee·*che*·me) – nonalcoholic drink consisting of milk, sweet corn, cinnamon and vanilla

comida corriente; casado (ko·*mee*·da ko·*ryen*·te; ka·*sa*·do) – set meal of rice, beans, plantains and a piece of meat or fish

corvina (kor·*vee*·na) – a flavorful white fish; Panama's most popular fish dish

empanada (em·pa·*na*·da) – corn turnover filled with ground meat, chicken, cheese or sweet fruit

gallo pinto (*ga*·lyo *peen*·to) – literally 'spotted rooster'; a soupy mixture of rice and black beans

hojaldres (o·*khal*·dres) – fried dough, similar to a doughnut; popular with breakfast

huevos fritos/revueltos (*we*·vos *free*·tos/re·*vwel*·tos) – fried/scrambled eggs

licuado (lee·*kwa*·do) – shake made with fresh fruit, sugar and water

mondongo (mon·*don*·go) – tripe

patacones (pa·ta·*ko*·nes) – fried green plantains cut in thin pieces, salted, pressed and then fried

pipa (*pee*·pa) – coconut water, served straight from the husk

plátano maduro (*pla*·ta·no ma·*doo*·ro) – ripe plantains baked or broiled with butter, brown sugar and cinnamon; served hot

raspados (ras·*pa*·dos) – shaved ice flavored with fruit juice

ropa vieja (*ro*·pa *vye*·kha) – literally 'old clothes'; a spicy shredded beef combination served over rice

sancocho (san·*ko*·cho) – a somewhat spicy chicken-and-vegetable stew; Panama's national dish

seco (*se*·ko) – alcoholic drink made from sugarcane

tajadas (ta·*kha*·das) – ripe plantains sliced lengthwise and fried

tamales (ta·*ma*·les) – spiced ground corn with chicken or pork, boiled in banana leaves

tasajo (ta·*sa*·kho) – dried meat cooked with vegetables

tortilla de maíz (tor·*tee*·lya de ma·*ees*) – a thick, fried cornmeal tortilla

Food Glossary

BASICS

a la parilla	a la pa·*ree*·lya	grilled
azúcar	a·soo·*kar*	sugar
cuchara	koo·*cha*·ra	spoon
cuchillo	koo·*chee*·lyo	knife
frito	*free*·to	fried
hielo	*ye*·lo	ice
mantequilla	man·te·*kee*·lya	butter
pan	pan	bread
plato	*pla*·to	plate
sal	sal	salt
servilleta	ser·vee·*lye*·ta	napkin
sopa	*so*·pa	soup
taza	*ta*·sa	cup
tenedor	te·ne·*dor*	fork
vaso	*va*·so	glass

MEAL TIMES

desayuno	de·sa·*yoo*·no	breakfast
almuerzo	al·*mwer*·so	lunch
cena	*se*·na	dinner

FRUITS & VEGETABLES

aguacate	a·gwa·*ka*·te	avocado
ensalada	en·sa·*la*·da	salad
fresa	*fre*·sa	strawberry
guanábana	gwa·*na*·ba·na	soursop
manzana	man·*za*·na	apple
maracuyá	ma·ra·koo·*ya*	passion fruit
naranja	na·*ran*·kha	orange
piña	*pee*·nya	pineapple
zanahoria	sa·na·o·rya	carrot
zarzamora	zar·za·*mo*·ra	blackberry

SEAFOOD

camarón	ka·ma·*ron*	shrimp
filete de pescado	fee·*le*·te de pes·*ka*·do	fish fillet
langosta	lan·*gos*·ta	lobster
langostino	lan·gos·*tee*·no	jumbo shrimp
pescado	pes·*ka*·do	fish
pulpo	*pool*·po	octopus

MEATS

bistec	*bis*·tek	steak
carne	*kar*·ne	beef
chuleta	choo·*le*·ta	pork chop
hamburguesa	am·boor·*gwe*·sa	hamburger
salchicha	sal·*chee*·cha	sausage

DRINKS

agua	*a*·gwa	water
bebida	be·*bee*·da	drink
café	ka·*fe*	coffee
cerveza	ser·*ve*·sa	beer
leche	*le*·che	milk
ron	ron	rum
vino	*vee*·no	wine

Environment

Although still largely undiscovered, Panama is slowly gaining fame for its vast tropical forests, hundreds of pristine islands and the astounding biodiversity stretching its full length. Although the country itself is only slightly bigger than Ireland or Austria, Panama is home to an incredible variety of landscapes. In the span of a few days, you can easily climb mountains and trek across valleys, hike through highland cloud forests and verdant jungles and take a dip in both the Caribbean Sea and the Pacific Ocean.

As the secret about Panama's remarkable environment spreads, more and more visitors arrive on the isthmus with one thing in mind: experiencing the wildlife which the country has in spades. On land, Panama's rainforests support countless creatures from the tiny agoutis that scurry across the canopy floor to the mighty jaguars that prowl the forests by night. In the sea, shallow coral reef beds support countless varieties of tropical fish, while pelagic animals including hammerheads and manta rays search for food in deeper waters. In the air, over 900 avian species dart across the sky, making Panama one of the top birding destinations in the world.

Unfortunately, Panama also has grave environmental threats, coming from the hands of loggers, developers and indifferent or corrupt government agencies, who don't understand that the country's finest gem – its natural beauty – is rapidly disappearing. The principal threat to Panama's ecology is deforestation, which is picking up momentum throughout the country, most notably in the Darién. In addition, the balance between environmental conservation and infrastructure development is threatening to tip in favor of the latter, particularly in tourist hot spots such as Isla de Coiba and Bocas del Toro. Fortunately, the unexpected delay in the tourism boom may buy enough time for both sides to reach an agreement that is both sustainable and profitable.

In April 2004 Panama, Costa Rica, Colombia and Ecuador signed an agreement creating a Pacific marine corridor to preserve the area's ecosystems.

THE LAND

Panama is both the narrowest and the southernmost country in Central America. The long S-shaped isthmus borders Costa Rica in the west and Colombia in the east. Its northern Caribbean coastline measures 1160km, compared to a 1690km Pacific coastline in the south, and its total land area is 78,056km. By comparison, Panama is roughly the same size as South Carolina.

Panama is just 50km wide at its leanest point, an impressive statistic given that it separates two great oceans. The Panama Canal, which is about 80km long, effectively divides the country into eastern and western regions. Panama is also home to two great mountain ranges, which run along Panama's spine in both the east and the west. The highest point in the country, Volcán Barú, is located in Chiriquí Province, and is also the country's only volcano.

Like all of the Central American countries, Panama has large, flat coastal lowlands, covered in places by huge banana plantations. There are about 480 rivers in Panama and 1518 islands near its shores. The two main island groups are the San Blás and Bocas del Toro archipelagos on the Caribbean side, but most of the islands are on the Pacific side. Even the Panama Canal has islands, including Isla Barro Colorado, which has a world-famous tropical rainforest research station.

WILDLIFE

The country's rich biodiversity owes a great deal to its geological history. Around 65 million years ago, North and South America were joined by a land bridge not unlike what exists today. Around 50 million years ago however, the continents split apart and remained separate from one another for millions of years.

During this time, unique evolutionary landscapes were created on both continents. In South America, there was an astonishing diversification of many species. The land soon gave rise to many bird families (toucans and hummingbirds included), unique neotropical rodents (agoutis and capybaras) and groups like iguanas, poison dart frogs and basilisks. In North America, which collided repeatedly with Eurasia, animal species that had no relatives in South America (horses, deer, raccoons, squirrels and mice) flourished.

The momentous event that would change natural history for both continents occurred around three million years ago when the land bridge of Panama arose. Species from both continents mingled as northern animals went south and southern animals went north. Many found their homes in the lush forests and wetlands along the isthmus, where the great variety of plant species created ideal conditions for nourishing wildlife.

Today, the interchange of species between North and South America is limited to winged migrations, though this annual event can be breathtaking to behold.

A Neotropical Companion, by John Kricher, is an excellent book for learning about ecology, evolutionary theory and biodiversity in the New World tropics.

Animals

Panama's biodiversity is staggering – the country is home to 218 mammal species, 226 species of reptile, 164 amphibian species and 125 animal species found nowhere else in the world. Panama also boasts 940 avian species, which is the largest number in Central America.

Bird-watchers consider Panama to be one of the world's best birding sights. Quetzals, macaws, amazons, parrots and toucans all have sizable populations here, as do many species of tanager and raptor. The best bird-watching site in the country is Cana (p286) in Parque Nacional Darién, where you can see four species of macaw, golden-headed quetzals and black-tipped cotingas. Another fantastic birding spot is Parque Nacional Soberanía (p110), where hundreds of species have been spotted along the famous 17km-long Pipeline Rd.

One of the most sought-after birds is the harpy eagle, the national bird of Panama. With a 2m wingspan and weights of up to 20lb, this raptor is the world's most powerful bird of prey and a truly awesome sight. The bird is recognized by its huge size, its broad, black chest band with white underneath, its piercing yellow eyes and its prominent, regal crests. The harpy's powerful claws can carry off howler monkeys and capuchins, and it also hunts sloths, coatis, anteaters and just about anything that moves. It's best spotted in the Parque Nacional Darién around Punta Patiño (p281).

More famous than the harpy eagle is the elusive, emerald-green quetzal, which lives in habitats throughout Central America, but some of the best places to see it are in Panama. The male has an elongated wing covert (train) and a scarlet breast and belly, while females have duller plumage. Parque Nacional Volcán Barú (p208) is a top spot for sighting them, as is Parque Internacional La Amistad (p213). They are best spotted in the breeding season from March to June when males grow their spectacular trains and start calling for mates.

Panama's geographical position also makes it a crossroads for migratory birds. Out of the country's 940 bird species, 122 occur only as long-distance migrants (ie they don't breed in Panama). From August to December, North American raptors migrate south into Central America by the millions – at times, there are so many birds that they make a black streak across the sky. The canopy tower in Panama's Parque Nacional Soberanía (p110) is a particularly good vantage point for watching this migration.

In Bocas del Toro, keep an eye out for kettling hawk migrations – October is the best month to see them in large numbers. The migration of turkey vultures over the islands in early March and again in October is another striking sight. These big, black-bodied, red-necked birds can streak the sky and are able to soar for long periods without a single flap as they migrate between southern Canada and Tierra del Fuego.

Primate lovers are also drawn to Panama. Among the country's many species – including white-faced capuchins, squirrel monkeys, spider monkeys and howler monkeys – are some fascinating varieties. The Geoffroy's tamarin, for instance, is found nowhere else in Central America. These tiny, gregarious monkeys can live in groups of up to 40 in lowland forest, and many weigh less than a pound. They're identified by their whistles and chirps, mottled black-and-brown fur, white chests, and of course, their diminutive stature. They can be spotted in Parque Natural Metropolitano (p82), Monumento Nacional Isla Barro Colorado (p113) and in the Darién (p273).

Big cats prowl the jungles of Panama and although you'd be extremely fortunate to catch even a glimpse of one, their prints are easy to come across. Jaguars, pumas, ocelots, jaguarundis and margays are all found on the isthmus. The jaguar is the biggest of the bunch and is the largest cat in the Americas. Jaguars (and pumas) both need large tracts of land in order to survive. Without them the big cats gradually exhaust their food supply (which numbers 85 hunted species) and perish. They are excellent swimmers and climbers and are commonly spotted resting on sunny riverbanks.

Panama's offshore waters host a fascinating assortment of creatures. Reefs found off both coasts support a plethora of tropical fish, and visitors to the national marine parks might spot humpback whales, reef sharks, bottlenose dolphins, and killer or sperm whales. Underwater, whale sharks, black- and white-tip sharks and occasionally tiger sharks also visit.

One of Panama's biggest coastal draws is the sea turtle. Of the world's seven different species, five can be seen in Panama at various times throughout the year (see the boxed text, opposite). All sea turtles originally evolved from terrestrial species and the most important stage of their survival happens on land when they come to nest. Although you'll need a bit of luck and a lot of patience, the experience of seeing hatchlings emerge is unparalleled.

Arribadas (arrivals) are rare events that occur when thousands of female sea turtles flood the beach to lay their eggs. This happens occasionally on Isla de Cañas (p173) when 40,000 to 50,000 olive ridleys come to nest at a single time. This chance event most likely occurs in the wet season (usually September to October) during the first and last quarter of the moon. Although scientists are not entirely sure why these mass arrivals occur, a common theory is that *arribadas* are a defense mechanism to overwhelm would-be predators.

Monkey's Bridge: Mysteries of Evolution in Central America, by David Rains Wallace, tells of the colorful evolutionary unfolding of fauna and flora on the isthmus, beginning three million years ago and ending in the present.

Endangered Species

According to the World Conservation Monitoring Centre, there are over 100 species threatened with extinction within Panama. Among the animals appearing on its 'red list' for Panama are the jaguar, the spectacled bear, the Central American tapir, the American crocodile, all five species of sea turtle that nest on Panamanian beaches and dozens of birds, including several eagle species and the military and scarlet macaws.

The Panamanian legislature has implemented laws to curb illegal hunting and logging, but the laws are widely ignored due to an absence of enforce-

SEA-TURTLE NESTING

Turtle	Nesting season	Peak	Hot spots
leatherback	Mar-Jul (Caribbean) Oct-Mar (Pacific)	April-May (Caribbean) Nov-Jan (Pacific)	Isla Bastimentos Humedal de San-San Pond Sak
loggerhead	May-Sep (Caribbean)	no peak	Isla Bastimentos Humedal de San-San Pond Sak
green	May-Oct (Caribbean) Jun-Dec (Pacific)	Aug-Oct (Caribbean) no peak	Isla Bastimentos Humedal de San-San Pond Sak
hawksbill	Apr-Oct (Caribbean) Apr-Nov (Pacific)	Jun-Jul (Caribbean) Jun-Jul (Pacific)	Isla Bastimentos Humedal de San-San Pond Sak
olive ridley	year-round (Pacific)	Jun-Nov (Pacific)	Isla de Cañas

ment. For example, keeping a parrot, toucan or macaw in a cage is a fineable offense in Panama. However, not only can you see them in cages outside many residences, but many hotel managers apparently believe that tourists enjoy seeing large tropical birds in itty-bitty cages.

You can help reduce the threat to Panama's endangered species. If you see caged animals at a hotel, complain to the manager, take your business elsewhere and report the crime to **ANCON** (National Association for the Conservation of Nature; ☎ 314 0060), the country's largest private conservation organization. Although it should go without saying, please refrain from eating *tortuga* (sea turtle), *huevos de tortuga* (turtle eggs), *cazón* (shark), *conejo pintado* (paca), *ñeque* (agouti), *venado* (deer) or iguana.

Please remember that buying items such as jaguar teeth, ocelot skins or turtle shell products, directly contributes to these animals' extinction.

Plants

Humid, tropical rainforest is the dominant vegetation in the canal area, along the Caribbean coast and in most of the eastern half of the country – Parque Nacional Darién (p280) protects much of Panama's largest tropical rainforest region. Other vegetation zones include dry tropical rainforest and grassland on the Pacific coast, cloud forest in the highlands, alpine vegetation on the highest peaks and mangrove forest on both coasts and around many islands. Among the flora, Panama has over 10,000 species of plant including approximately 1200 orchid species, 675 fern species and 1500 species of tree.

NATIONAL PARKS

Today, Panama has around 40 national parks and officially protected areas, and about 25% of the country's total land is set aside for conservation. In many of the national parks and protected areas, you'll find mestizo and indigenous villages scattered throughout. In the most successful scenarios, the communities help protect and maintain the park and its wildlife.

To enter a national park, travelers must pay US$3 (US$10 if it's a national marine park) at ANAM (Autoridad Nacional de Ambiente; Panama's national environmental authority) headquarters in Panama City (p75), at a regional ANAM office or at an ANAM ranger station inside the park being visited. Permits to camp or stay at an ANAM ranger station (US$5 to US$10) can be obtained in the same places as well.

In Panama City, the 265-hectare Parque Natural Metropolitano (p82) protects vast expanses of tropical semideciduous forest within the city limits.

A Field Guide to the Orchids of Costa Rica and Panama, by Robert Dressler, has 240 photos, and almost as many drawings, of orchids within its 274 pages.

NATIONAL PARKS & OTHER PROTECTED AREAS

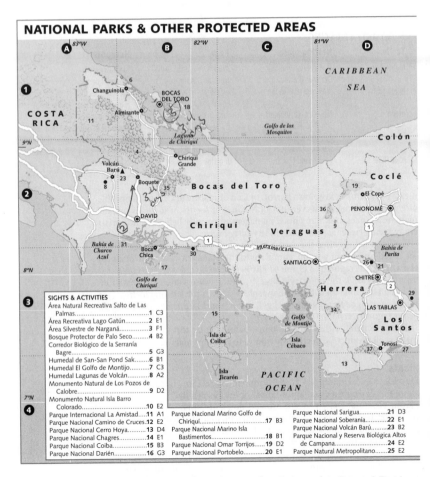

SIGHTS & ACTIVITIES

A short distance from the capital and situated in Panamá Province, Parque Nacional Soberanía (p110) is a birder's paradise – in a single day, you can see hundreds of different avian species. Lush rainforest abounds here, as it does on the nearby biological reserve of Monumento Nacional Isla Barro Colorado (p113), where scientists study the area's incredibly rich biodiversity.

In Coclé Province, Parque Nacional Omar Torrijos (p142) is a lovely national park that remains largely overlooked owing to its difficult access – you'll need a good 4WD, or plan on walking a bit (at least one hour) to reach the entrance. Once there you'll be rewarded with some prime bird watching through lovely forest, and the possibility of viewing both the Atlantic and Pacific Oceans.

In contrast to many of Panama's other national parks, the small Parque Nacional Sarigua (p156), just outside of Chitré in Herrera Province, is not the place to encounter lush forests or abundant wildlife – which is precisely the point. The desertlike wasteland exists as a sad and potent reminder of the future of Panama if greed wins out over environmental responsibility.

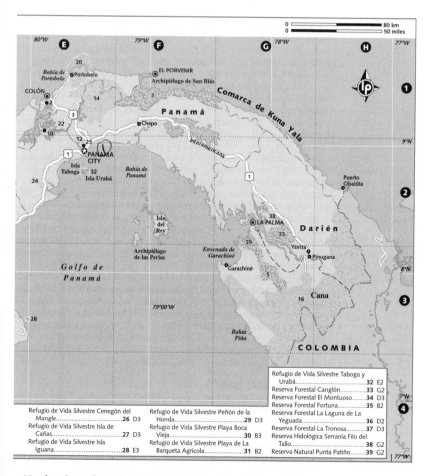

Nearby, the Refugio de Vida Silvestre Cenegón del Mangle (p158) is a mangrove forest and wildlife refuge that's a prime nesting ground for herons and other bird life. It also contains a series of pools said to have therapeutic properties.

Although the province of Los Santos has no national parks, there is an attractive wildlife refuge and a protected area frequented by nesting sea turtles. The Refugio de Vida Silvestre Isla Iguana (p170) near Pedasí offers some pristine snorkeling and if you're lucky you might spot some humpback whales in the area. Nearby, Isla de Cañas (p173) is a major nesting site for olive ridley sea turtles.

In Veraguas, Parque Nacional Coiba (p185) is one of the largest marine parks in the world. It contains Panama's largest island, the 493-sq-km Isla de Coiba, which is regarded by scientists as a biodiversity hotspot. Also in Veraguas is the 32,577-hectare Parque Nacional Cerro Hoya (p190), which protects some of the last remaining patches of dry tropical forest on the Península de Azuero. Unfortunately, the park has little infrastructure and getting there is a challenge.

The San Lorenzo Project protects the forests, wetlands and coastal regions surrounding former US military base Fuerte Sherman in Colón Province - visit www.sanlorenzo.org.pa.

In Chiriquí Province, along the coastline south of David, the impressive Parque Nacional Marino Golfo de Chriquí (p198) is a 14,740-hectare national marine park that protects 25 islands and numerous coral reefs – the aquatic life here is astounding. In the highlands, the 14,300-hectare Parque Nacional Volcán Barú (p208) surrounds Panama's only volcano – its fertile soil nourishes a wide variety of plant and animal life, making it a fine destination for hikers and bird watchers. At 3478m, Volcán Barú's summit is Panama's highest peak. Also in Chiriquí is the majority of the Panamanian side of the binational Parque Internacional La Amistad (p213). Although largely unexplored, La Amistad offers several excellent day hikes and you can easily hire local indigenous guides to lead you on overnight excursions.

In the Archipiélago de Bocas del Toro, Parque Nacional Marino Isla Batimentos (p231) protects various areas of the archipelago and is an important nature reserve for many species of Caribbean wildlife. Turtles nest on its beaches and its abundant marine life makes for great snorkeling and diving. On the mainland is the other sector of Panama's share of the binational Parque Internacional La Amistad (p237). Wekso, as this sector of the park is called, is home to several different indigenous groups, pristine rainforest and abundant wildlife. Near the border with Chiriquí Province, the Bosque Protector Palo Seco (p239) contains several hiking trails through lush cloud forest high in the Talamanca range.

Panama's crown jewel is the Parque Nacional Darién (p280), which boasts 576,000 hectares of wildlife-rich rainforest. The heart of this Unesco World Heritage site is Cana, a former mining valley that is now regarded as one of the best birding spots in the world. The Darién is also home to the Reserva Natural Punta Patiño (p281), a 26,315-hectare wildlife reserve on the southern shore of the Golfo de San Miguel. This private reserve is one of the best places in the country to see the harpy eagle, Panama's national bird.

ENVIRONMENTAL ISSUES

According to 2003 figures published by the EIU Country Report, 44.4% of Panama is covered by forest and just over 25% of its land is set aside for conservation – this is more than any other Central American country. Panama's forests also contain the greatest number of species of all the New World countries north of Colombia.

Tropical rainforests cover just 7% of the earth's surface but account for 50% of the world's biodiversity.

Unfortunately, it is uncertain as to whether Panamanians will be able to live in harmony with their wilderness areas in the years to come. A little over 50 years ago, 70% of Panama's total land mass was covered by forest, which gives a quick indication of one of the country's gravest environmental problems: deforestation. Despite the presence of a growing environmental movement, the majority of Panamanians – especially the urban poor and rural farmers – are unconcerned with the rainforest's destruction. This is especially true in the Darién, which is currently serving as ground zero for the ongoing deforestation.

Additionally, Panama's national parks are staffed by few park rangers. Although their areas of coverage are colossal, many rangers aren't given patrol vehicles or radios. In Parque Nacional Darién for instance, there are usually no more than 20 rangers assigned to protect 576,000 hectares – an area larger than some countries. These rangers are generally unarmed and poorly paid, and spend most of their day trying to figure out what they are going to eat for dinner. Meanwhile illegal hunting, settling and logging take place in their park. Unless the Panamanian government gets serious, it may not be long before the country's protected areas are nothing more than national parks on paper.

In recent years, increased foreign investment coupled with the desire to improve tourist infrastructure have started to threaten several of Panama's most pristine ecosystems. For instance, on Isla de Coiba, environmentalists and developers are debating to what extent (if any) hoteliers should be allowed to develop the island as a commercial tourist destination. In addition, on Isla Bastimentos in Bocas del Toro, a massive luxury residential project aimed at foreign retirees will likely change the face of this once remote island. Unfortunately, money talks in Panama and the sad reality is that virgin rainforest is not nearly as profitable as all-inclusive resorts and oceanside condos.

Deforestation

To get an idea of Panama's ecological future, one need only glimpse at what happened (and what's continuing to happen) in the Darién. The region north of Yaviza – the town where the Interamericana presently ends – was covered with virgin forest just over three decades ago. Unfortunately, everything changed when the highway was extended from Chepo to Yaviza.

The loggers initially sought big trees within easy reach, felling all the giants near the highway and trampling young trees with their machinery. Once the giant trees were gone, the loggers cut roads perpendicular to the highway, which led into tall stands of hardwoods. After those stands were chopped down and removed, more roads were cut and yet more stands were leveled.

Right behind the loggers were thousands of settlers looking to eke out a living by turning the trampled vegetation left by the loggers into cropland. With the mature trees gone, all that was required to create cropland was an ax and a match. After some crackling, sizzling and a lot of smoke, the would-be subsistence farmers had fields for planting. Of course, all of this is not only legal, but actively encouraged by Panamanian law.

However, the story doesn't end here. In a healthy rainforest ecosystem, huge, exposed tree roots prevent heavy rains from washing away the thin layer of nutrient-rich topsoil found in tropical forests. But, if you take out the trees, a big storm over a denuded area will quickly carry the topsoil into rivers and out to sea, leaving only the nutrient-deficient lower soil where the vibrant jungle once stood. In the span of only two to three years, the soil in the Darién couldn't support a decent harvest and little more than grass grew on it. Since grass is what cattle eat, the ranchers stepped in and bought fields that frustrated farmers could no longer use.

Today the succession of loggers, farmers and ranchers continues in northern Darién Province, although now the loggers must drive far up the side roads they've made to find trees. The farmers are still a step behind the loggers, unintentional nomads employing the slash-and-burn method so widespread in the developing world. And everywhere the settler-farmers go, ranchers move in behind them. Worse yet, as if bent on speeding the Darién's destruction, the Panamanian government is currently paving the Interamericana all the way to Yaviza.

Isla de Coiba

Currently, one of the hottest environmental topics in Panama is the fate of Isla de Coiba (p188). This rainforest-covered island and Unesco World Heritage site is set in one of the largest marine parks in the world – scientists often compare Coiba to the Galapagos Islands.

Owing to the presence of a penal colony, this island and its surrounding waters remained untouched, but now that the prison is being phased out, developers and members of the government see glorious tourism possibilities for this ecological gem. What they have in mind is building a few hotels, perhaps a megaresort or two on the island and in nearby Santa

A good website to help you learn about the astounding natural riches of Isla de Coiba is www .coibapanama.com, which contains photographs as well as links to conservation organizations in Panama.

SAVE THE RAINFOREST

Why should we as humans start getting more serious about saving the rainforest? Even though most of us don't encounter one in our daily lives, rainforests and their future survival affect each and every one of us in more ways than we realize. Here's why.

Carbon Sink Effect

Some of the most common media buzzwords these days are 'climate change' and 'global warming,' and particularly to what extent we are negatively impacting the health and sustainability of the planet. As developing nations around the world continue to modernize, global carbon emissions are on the rise, and evidence of the greenhouse effect can already be felt across the planet.

One of the best defenses humans have against rising carbon dioxide levels is the tropical rainforest. Specifically, tropical rainforests limit the greenhouse effect of global warming by storing carbon and hence reducing the amount of carbon dioxide in the atmosphere. But our best defense against climate change is rapidly being destroyed the world over. In a frightening example of the interconnectedness of human societies, the deforestation of Latin America rainforests is impacting global ecosystems, such as the increasing desertification of the Sahel in Africa.

Unfortunately, the total picture is even bleaker. In 2004, scientists announced that the world's tropical forests may become less able to absorb carbon dioxide. In areas of the forest where there was no human activity such as logging or burning, scientists discovered that bigger, quicker-growing species were flourishing at the expense of the smaller ones living below the forest canopy. Since plant growth is dependent on carbon dioxide, the team hypothesized that tropical rainforests are getting an extra boost from rising levels of global emissions.

As a result of changing rainforest dynamics, specifically the decline of densely wooded sub-canopy trees, the ability of tropical rainforests to act as a carbon sink is in jeopardy. This reality, however frightening it may be, affects each and every one of us.

Bioprospecting

In October 2003 the scientific journal of the Ecological Society of America published an article on one of the most fascinating scientific research projects ever undertaken in Panama – one that could have long-lasting implications for rainforest conservation around the globe.

Several US scientists developed a program in Panama of 'bioprospecting' or scouring the rainforest for compounds that may one day become new drugs. They set up six labs and hired Panamanian cell biologists and chemists to develop and run experiments. Although the labs have funding far below those in the USA and Europe, researchers have already starting producing remarkable results and have published their findings in a number of academic journals.

The results of all this places a great deal of importance on the rainforest's biodiversity, especially since further research – and by necessity conservation – potentially equals cures for widespread diseases. It is also slowly attracting the attention of large pharmaceutical companies, and could lead to a huge investment in helping to both unlock the mysteries of the rainforest and consequently preserve them. Ultimately this would make conservation both the end and the means.

Intrinsic Value

Climate change and bioprospecting aside, a simple argument for saving the rainforest is simply that its intrinsic value is enough to warrant increased conservation efforts. Panama's natural vegetation was originally almost all forest, though much of this has been cleared during the past few generations to create pastures and agriculture land. As a result, the destruction of rainforest has already wiped out countless flora and fauna species that will never be known again. Even beyond the plants and animals that actually inhabit the forests, deforestation negatively impacts migratory animals that pass through the forests annually, such as bats, butterflies and birds.

Deforestation and habitat destruction have also threatened the traditional cultures of the Emberá and Wounaan, who have lived in the rainforest for generations. While humans the world over lament the destruction of this crucial ecosystem, it is the original denizens of the rainforests that have already lost the most.

Catalina, plus a cruise-ship dock and so on. Former President Mireya Moscoso signed a law in 2002 allowing developers to exploit the island, though progress has been delayed due to the opposition imposed by ANCON, the country's largest private conservation organization.

Red Frog Beach Club

Foreigners have been buying up real estate on the islands of Bocas del Toro for decades, but nothing has alarmed Panamanians quite like the planned community of the Red Frog Beach Club (RFBC) on Isla Bastimentos. This massive luxury residential complex will be comprised of oceanside condos and villas, an all-inclusive resort hotel, three marinas and an 18-hole golf course. More importantly, it will completely transform the face of the island that was formerly home to working-class West Indians and nesting sea turtles.

Despite protests from concerned residents, local expats, environmentalists and marine biologists, nothing seems to be slowing down the progress of construction. Unfortunately, there is little evidence to suggest that the RFBC will be anything other than a total environmental disaster.

For more information on the precarious future of Isla Bastimentos, see the boxed text on p232.

ENVIRONMENTAL ORGANIZATIONS

In spite of the majority of Panamanians being indifferent to the environmental devastation occurring within the country, there are a few organizations striving to protect the country and its biodiversity, which cannot always be said for ANAM, the largely useless national environment authority. The following resources are good places to learn about Panama's natural (and threatened) riches:

ANCON (☎ 314 0060; www.ancon.org in Spanish) Founded in 1985 by academic and business leaders, ANCON has played a major role in the creation of national parks and on many occasions has spurred ANAM into action. Ancon Expeditions, although no longer part of the nonprofit organization, still leases land from the conservation organization and employs some of the top naturalist guides in the country; see also p89.

Associación Napguana (☎ 227 5886; napguana@pty.com) An NGO founded and run by the Kuna working on preserving the ecology of the islands and other development issues.

Conservación del Parque Nacional Volcán Barú (☎ 263 4963; www.volcanbaru.cjb.net, http://usuarios.lycos.es/quetzales, in Spanish) A conservation organization dedicated to safeguarding the future of Parque Nacional Volcán Barú.

Corredor Biológico Mesoamericano del Atlántico Panameño (☎ 232 6601; www.cbmap.org) This Panamanian-focused conservation organization is allied with the Central American Environment and Development Commission.

Dobbo Yala (☎ 261 7229; www.dobboyala.org.pa) This NGO is run by indigenous professionals, who work in conservation and development projects in indigenous communities.

Institute for Tropical Ecology and Conservation (ITEC; ☎ 352-367-9128 in USA; www.itec-edu.org) In addition to offering courses and research grants on tropical ecology, ITEC works with marine turtles and promotes local environmental education and antipollution awareness in the Bocas del Toro area.

PEMASKY (Project for the Study & Management of Wild Areas of the Kuna Yala; ☎ 316 1236; geodisio@yahoo.com) This grassroots movement, led by the Kuna, has helped keep settlers and loggers out of the mainland rainforests of Kuna Yala.

The Smithsonian Tropical Research Institute's website, www.stri.org, contains information about current research in the rainforest labs and upcoming seminars, and recent publications about tropical ecology and biodiversity topics.

Panama Outdoors

There's no shortage of reasons why Panama is one of the top outdoors destinations in the Americas. For starters, the abundance and variety of Panama's neotropical wildlife is simply astounding – primates swing from trees, whales breach offshore and butterflies dart across the forest floor. Of course, Panama's rich birdlife is a shining example of its biodiversity, with everything from parrots and macaws to toucans and trogons. With over 900 avian species found within its borders, Panama is arguably one of the greatest birding destinations in the world.

Of course, to fully appreciate Panama's wildlife, you're going to have to get out of Panama City and head straight for the country's forests, rivers and seas. Whether you opt for a mountain ascent or a cross-jungle trek, Panama's rainforests are ripe for independent or guided exploration. If you're looking to make a splash, you can navigate raging rapids in either a kayak or a white-water raft, or simply take a relaxing jungle cruise and spot wildlife along wooded banks. If you fancy a face-to-face encounter with an enormous hammerhead shark (or merely a school of rainbow-colored reef fish), both the Pacific and Caribbean are brimming with diving and snorkeling destinations.

If we still haven't piqued your interest, fear not as Panama's outdoor pursuits don't stop here. Whether you're an aspiring angler or a seasoned fisherman, Panama rivers and oceans teem with tropical fish. Or, if you prefer to use a little self-propelled power to explore the countryside, Panama's small size and modern infrastructure are the perfect combination for cyclists. And of course, let's not forget about Panama's legendary surf breaks, which span both the Pacific and the Caribbean coastlines, and offer everything from barreling beach breaks to 4m-high walls.

'Panama is arguably one of the greatest birding destinations in the world'

BOAT TRIPS
River Trips
Nearly 500 rivers carve the rugged landscape of Panama, the majority of which are lush, jungle-shrouded waterways. Whether you're looking to unwind on a relaxing jungle cruise or take a motorized dugout upriver to a remote indigenous village, there are several recommended tour operators that can help fulfill your wildest *Heart of Darkness* fantasies.

Ancon Expeditions of Panama (☎ 269 9414; www.anconexpeditions.com), located in Panama City (p89), offers an excellent day trip, the 'jungle boat adventure,' which consists of a cruise up the Panama Canal and a trip around some of the pristine islands of Lago Gatún. This journey passes close to the shoreline to allow for maximum wildlife viewing and is a great choice for kids. Ancon Expeditions is also the exclusive tour operator in the Darién (p273).

Canal & Bay Tours (☎ 314 1339; www.canalandbaytours.com in Spanish) offers partial canal transits every Saturday morning. Boats depart from Panama City, travel through the Miraflores Locks to Lago Miraflores and back, and then cruise out into the bay for scenic views of the city. This is by far the best way to appreciate the canal, and one of the highlights of any trip to Panama.

Panama Jet Boat Explorer (☎ 720 4054; www.panamajetboatexplorer.com) operates a variety of day trips in Chiriquí and Bocas del Toro Provinces, which involve cruising up jungle rivers and stopping in Ngöbe Buglé villages. It's owned by a safety-conscious American expat, and comes well recommended by readers.

For those looking for more off-the-beaten-path adventure, there are loads of opportunities in the Darién (p273). With the help of guides from Ancon

Expeditions, you can cruise up the Río Mogué to visit the indigenous village of Mogué, where you can interact with the Emberá people and, with a little luck, spot a rare harpy eagle. More independently minded travelers can also arrange transit up the Río Sambú, though this ambitious expedition is best reserved for truly intrepid spirits.

Finally, in the Wekso sector of the Parque Internacional La Amistad (p237), wanderlust-ridden travelers can penetrate the rugged mainland of Bocas del Toro. By traveling upriver on motorized dugouts, you'll pass by several indigenous villages perched on the edge of the jungle.

Ocean Trips

Bordering the Pacific and the Caribbean, Panama is a seafarer's dream of tropical seas, deserted islands and far-flung remote destinations. Whether you relax on a palm-fringed Caribbean isle of white sands and cool breezes, or wind down the day with a cold beer and a Pacific sunset, chances are you'll find peace of mind and an open ocean in Panama.

Barcos Calypso (☎ 314 1730; US$10 roundtrip) has daily departures from the Causeway in Panama City to the nearby Pacific island of Isla Taboga. This flower-ringed tropical island is a popular weekend escape for beach-starved urban dwellers, though the ocean trip itself is one of the highlights, especially if you get lucky and spot a pod of whales.

In Bocas del Toro, the *taxis marinos* (water taxis) ply the waters of the archipelago, and can whisk you away to remote beaches and snorkeling sites for a few dollars. This is one of the best ways to travel, particularly if you're in search of a secret surf break or fishing spot.

MV Coral Star (in USA ☎ 800-215-5169; www.coralstar.com) is a 115ft live-aboard ship that offers first-class passage to the Unesco World Heritage Site of Parque Nacional Coiba. Centered on the former penal colony of Isla de Coiba, this national park is a veritable lost world of unique flora and fauna. Ancon Expeditions (p89) also runs ocean trips to the island, which emphasize naturalism and ecology. Note that although it is possible to hire local fishermen and boat captains to take you out to Coiba, this is not recommended as the seas can get extremely rough in these parts.

Stretching from the Golfo de San Blás to the edge of the Colombian border, the 226km-long Archipiélago de San Blás (p258) is arguably the best destination in Panama for ocean explorers. Run as an independent *comarca* (autonomous region) by the Kuna, the archipelago consists of hundreds of coconut-fringed islands and islets surrounded by turquoise waters. Independent travelers can travel by small boat between the islands, though anyone with more time on their hands shouldn't pass up the opportunity to travel by yacht to Colombia (see p263).

HIKING

Hiking opportunities abound in Panama, and it's simply impossible to list everything that awaits you in one place. However, whether you're looking for a walk in the park or a multiday trek, Panama will certainly deliver, especially since the country offers everything from dry tropical rainforests and highland cloud forests to humid jungles and blistery mountain peaks.

Starting near the capital on the shores of the canal, the Parque Nacional Soberanía (p110) contains a section of the old Sendero Las Cruces (Las Cruces Trail), which was used by the Spaniards to cross between the coasts. Closer to Panama City, the Parque Nacional Metropolitano (p82) boasts a number of short but rewarding hikes in plush rainforest that literally skirts the edge of the capital.

The Panama Guide, by Nancy Schwalbe Zydler and Tom Zydler, is the best cruising guide to the isthmus of Panama. It offers piloting directions, charts, anchorages, history, and even instructions for transiting the Panama Canal.

HOW TO HIKE SAFELY & RESPONSIBLY

Before embarking on a hiking trip, consider the following points to ensure a safe and enjoyable experience:

- Pay any fees and possess any permits required by local authorities.
- Be sure you are healthy and feel comfortable walking for a sustained period.
- Obtain reliable information about physical and environmental conditions along your intended route.
- Be aware of local laws, regulations and etiquette about wildlife and the environment.
- Walk only in regions, and on trails, within your realm of experience.
- Be aware that weather conditions and terrain vary significantly from one region to another, or even from one trail to another. Seasonal changes can significantly alter any trail. These differences influence the way walkers dress and the equipment they carry.
- Before you set out, ask about the environmental characteristics that can affect your walk and how local, experienced walkers deal with these considerations.

To help preserve the ecology and beauty of Panama, consider the following tips when hiking:

Rubbish

- Carry out all your rubbish. Don't overlook easily forgotten items, such as silver paper, orange peel, cigarette butts and plastic wrappers. Make an effort to carry out rubbish left by others.
- Never bury your rubbish: digging disturbs soil and ground cover and encourages erosion. Buried rubbish will likely be dug up by animals, who may be injured or poisoned by it. It may also take years to decompose.
- Minimize waste by taking minimal packaging and no more food than you will need. Take reusable containers or stuff sacks.
- Sanitary napkins, tampons, condoms and toilet paper should be carried out despite the inconvenience. They burn and decompose poorly.

Human Waste Disposal

- Contamination of water sources by human feces can lead to the transmission of all sorts of nasties. Where there is a toilet, please use it. Otherwise, bury your waste – dig a small hole 15cm (6in) deep and at least 100m (320ft) from any watercourse and cover the waste with soil and a rock.

Washing

- Don't use detergents or toothpaste in or near watercourses, even if they are biodegradable.

If the urban grind of Panama City is a little too much to handle, do what most of the capital dwellers do and head for the hills. Within a few hours' drive of Panama are two popular highland retreats, namely El Valle (p130), which is nestled into the extinct volcano now known as Valle de Antón; and Santa Fé (p179), which is surrounded by rivers, waterfalls and cloud forests. Both towns serve as rural retreats for stressed-out Panamanians, and offer abundant walking and hiking in a pristine mountain setting.

Chirquí Province is home to two of Panama's most famous hikes, namely Volcán Barú and the Sendero Los Quetzales (Quetzals Trail), both of which are located in Parque Nacional Volcán Barú (p208). Ascents up Barú, which is Panama's highest peak, provide successful trekkers with views of both oceans on a clear day. The trek typically begins in the highland town of Boquete (p201), which also offers numerous walks and hikes up and down slopes

- For personal washing, use biodegradable soap and a water container (or even a lightweight, portable basin) at least 50m (160ft) away from the watercourse. Disperse the waste water widely to allow the soil to filter it fully.

- Wash cooking utensils 50m (160ft) from watercourses using a scourer, sand or snow instead of detergent.

Erosion

- Hillsides and mountain slopes, especially at high altitudes, are prone to erosion. Stick to existing trails and avoid short cuts.

- If a well-used trail passes through a mud patch, walk through the mud so as not to increase the size of the patch.

- Avoid removing the plant life that keeps topsoils in place.

Fires & Low-Impact Cooking

- Don't depend on open fires for cooking. Cook on a lightweight kerosene, alcohol or Shellite (white gas) stove and avoid those powered by disposable butane gas canisters.

- If you are trekking with a guide and porters, supply stoves for the whole team.

- If you patronize local accommodation, select those places that do not use wood fires to heat water or cook food.

- Fires may be acceptable below the tree line in areas that get very few visitors. If you light a fire, use an existing fireplace. Don't surround fires with rocks. Use only dead, fallen wood. Remember the adage 'the bigger the fool, the bigger the fire.' Use minimal wood, just what you need for cooking. In huts, leave wood for the next person.

- Ensure that you fully extinguish a fire after use. Spread the embers and flood them with water.

Wildlife Conservation

- Do not engage in or encourage hunting. It is illegal in all parks and reserves.

- Don't buy items made from endangered species.

- Avoid attracting wildlife by not leaving food scraps behind you. Place gear out of reach and tie packs to rafters or trees.

- Do not feed the wildlife as this can lead to animals becoming dependent on hand-outs, to unbalanced populations and to diseases.

Camping & Walking on Private Property

- Always seek permission to camp from landowners.

that are dotted with coffee plantations. The cross-mountain trek known as the Sendero Los Quetzales typically starts in the town of Guadalupe, and winds through virgin cloud forest that is riddled with resplendent quetzals, the Mayan bird of paradise.

For a truly off-the-beaten-path adventure, hikers should head to the Las Nubes sector of the Parque Internacional La Amistad (p213), the Panamanian side of this binational park and biological corridor. The hiking trails in La Amistad are scarcely developed and only accessible with a guide, and there are few places in Panama as rugged and uncharted as this enormous national park.

The crown jewel of Panama's wilderness offerings is undoubtedly the Darién, which is centered on the Unesco World Heritage Site of Parque Nacional Darién (p280). Often regarded as one of the last great wildernesses in the Americas, this sprawling expanse of primary and secondary forests forms a virtually impenetrable frontier with Colombia. Despite concentrated security problems along the border, the national park is not only accessible but highly recommended for anyone with young hearts and intrepid spirits. To truly experience the wonders of the Darién, arrange a tour through Ancon Expeditions (p89), which is the exclusive operator in the province.

CYCLING

Owing to its compact size and modern infrastructure, Panama is the perfect country to unleash a little pedal power. As with all long-distance cycling, you need to prepare yourself both physically and mentally for the rigors of the road, though these helpful tips will have you on the road in no time.

Generally speaking, the roads in Panama are the best in Central America, though this doesn't mean much once you leave the Interamericana. Fortunately, the highway is in good condition from the Costa Rican border to Panama City. Although it does get narrow in spots, you can cycle between most major destinations with relative ease. When it comes to the intersecting roads, however, they range from recently paved and paved with potholes to dirt roads and full-on mud bogs – bring plenty of spare parts and always be prepared for the worst.

The Darkest Jungle: The True Story of the Darién Expedition and America's Ill-Fated Race to Connect the Seas, by Todd Balf, tells the harrowing tale of the 1854 expedition that ended in tragedy in the untamed jungle.

The major factor when considering a lengthy bike ride is the weather. No matter what bike you're on, it's not entirely safe to ride in the rain. Throughout much of the country, the rains are confined to mid-April to mid-December, though on the Caribbean side you can expect rain virtually year-round. If the rains do start to fall however, in Panama you're never more than a few hours' away from the nearest accommodations.

There is one decent biking store in the country, namely **Bicicletas Rali** (Map pp74-5; ☎ 263 4136; www.rali-carretero.com in Spanish; Via España) in Panama City where you can buy bikes and accessories and have repairs done. Beyond the capital, you're essentially on your own, but never underestimate the prowess of the village mechanic.

DIVING & SNORKELING

Panama's underwater world spans two great oceans, and abounds with colorful coral gardens, towering rock shelves, sunken wrecks and a rich diversity of marine life. Fans of multicolored reef fish and bathtub-warm water should head for the Caribbean, while more advanced divers in search of enormous pelagic animals and remote dive sites should head to the Pacific.

Listing all of Panama's diving and snorkeling spots is an exercise in futility – there are literally thousands of spots along both coastlines that are ripe for underwater exploration. In fact, if you have snorkeling gear and you're near the ocean, chances are you'll come across something of interest. With that said, there are three major spots in Panama that have a deserved reputation for fine scuba diving: the archipelago of Bocas del Toro (p219), the Caribbean town of Portobelo (p250) and the Pacific island of Isla de Coiba (p188).

Owing to its status as Panama's top tourist destination, the Caribbean islands of Bocas del Toro are home to a thriving dive community. Unfortunately, Bocas diving leaves something to be desired, and it's a far cry from other Caribbean diving destinations such as the Bay Islands or Belize. The main problem is that the underwater visibility is extremely poor – nearly 40 rivers deposit silt into the seas around the islands, which turn the water a murky green. However, things tend to clear up a bit during the dry season, and it's worth remembering that a bad day of diving is still better than a good day of work. Local dive shops include **Starfleet Eco-Adventures** (☎ 757 9630; www.explorepanama.com/starfleet.htm) and **Bocas Water Sports** (☎ /fax 757 9541;

HOW TO DIVE SAFELY & RESPONSIBLY

Before embarking on a scuba diving, skin diving or snorkeling trip, carefully consider the following points to ensure a safe and enjoyable experience:

- Possess a current diving certification card from a recognized scuba diving instructional agency (if scuba diving).
- Be sure you are healthy and feel comfortable diving.
- Obtain reliable information about physical and environmental conditions at the dive site (eg from a reputable local dive operation).
- Be aware of local laws, regulations and etiquette about marine life and the environment.
- Dive only at sites within your realm of experience; if available, engage the services of a competent, professionally trained dive instructor or dive master.
- Be aware that underwater conditions vary significantly from one region, or even site, to another. Seasonal changes can significantly alter any site and dive conditions. These differences influence the way divers dress for a dive and what diving techniques they use.
- Ask about the environmental characteristics that can affect your diving and how local trained divers deal with these considerations.

Please consider the following tips when diving and help preserve the ecology and beauty of reefs:

- Never use anchors on the reef, and take care not to ground boats on coral.
- Avoid touching or standing on living marine organisms or dragging equipment across the reef. Polyps can be damaged by even the gentlest contact. If you must hold on to the reef, only touch exposed rock or dead coral.
- Be conscious of your fins. Even without contact, the surge from fin strokes near the reef can damage delicate organisms. Take care not to kick up clouds of sand, which can smother organisms.
- Practice and maintain proper buoyancy control. Major damage can be done by divers descending too fast and colliding with the reef.
- Take great care in underwater caves. Spend as little time within them as possible as your air bubbles may be caught within the roof and thereby leave organisms high and dry. Take turns to inspect the interior of a small cave.
- Resist the temptation to collect or buy corals or shells or to loot marine archaeological sites (mainly shipwrecks).
- Ensure that you take home all your rubbish and any litter you may find as well. Plastics in particular are a serious threat to marine life.
- Do not feed fish.
- Minimize your disturbance of marine animals. Never ride on the backs of turtles.

Warning: as there are only four decompression chambers in the entire country – one in Colón, one at Lago Gatún and two in Panama City – divers should avoid taking unnecessary risks. If you stay down too long or come up too fast, you'll be in serious trouble.

www.bocaswatersports.com) on Isla Colón and the **Dutch Pirate** (☎ 6567 1812; www .thedutchpirate.com) on Isla Bastimentos.

Another popular dive center is the historic town of Portobelo – here, you'll find 16 major dive sites in the adjacent Caribbean waters. Although the visibility here is also poor, there is an excellent variety of underwater attractions including a 110ft cargo ship, a C-45 twin-engine plane, soft coral-laden walls, off-shore reefs and rock gardens. Local dive shops include **Scubaportobelo** (☎ 448 2147; www.scubapanama.com) and **Twin Oceans Dive Center** (☎ 448 2067) as well as **Jimmy's Caribbean Dive Resort** (☎ 682 9322; www .caribbeanjimmysdiveresort.com) in the nearby town of Nombre de Dios.

The best diving in Panama, hands down, is around Isla de Coiba, which is the centerpiece of a national marine park. Here, divers are on the look-out for enormous sharks including schools of hammerheads, black-tips and white-tips as well as the occasional tiger or whale shark. **Scuba Coiba** (☎ 263 4366; www.scubacoiba.com), on the coast in the town of Santa Catalina, can arrange equipment rental and transport.

It's also worth mentioning that the Comarca de Kuna Yala (p258) is studded with fine coral reefs, though the Kuna prohibit dive operators from working in the archipelago. As a result, visitors will have to be con-tent with snorkeling, though it's some of the best on offer in Panama.

And, in case you've been wondering, the answer is yes – it is in fact possible to dive the Pacific and Atlantic Oceans in one day. **Scubapan-ama** (☎ 261 3841; www.scubapanama.com; cnr Av 6a C Norte & Calle 62 C Oeste, El Carmen, Panama City) offers bicoastal dives, as well as personalized tours around the country.

When you're making travel plans, bear in mind that the Caribbean Sea is calm during the dry season (mid-December to mid-April), though it can be fairly treacherous due to high winds and strong currents during the rainy season (mid-April to mid-December). On the Pacific side, ocean temperatures are warmest during the dry season, though strong winds are common during February and March.

In the margin:
In the Darién's Bahía Piña, more International Game Fish Association world records have been broken than anywhere else on the planet.

FISHING

Panamá means 'abundance of fish' in several indigenous languages – with 1518 islands, 2988km of coastline and 480 major rivers, there's no problem finding a fishing spot. Freshwater anglers usually set their sights on trout and bass, while serious sport-fishers ply the seas for trophy fish including tarpon, sailfish and marlin.

The majority of freshwater angling in Panama can be pursued inde-pendently, especially in the highlands of Chiriquí and Veraguas, which are home to several fish-filled rivers and streams. However, one recommended operator is **Panama Canal Fishing** (☎ 6678 2653; www.panamacanalfishing.com), which runs organized tours in the Canal Zone. Its signature tour involves fishing for peacock bass in Lake Gatún and the Chagres River.

For deep-sea fishing, Panama offers three world-class areas – Bahía Piña, the Pearl Islands and Isla de Coiba – all of which are served by ex-tremely professional fishing outfits. Bahía Piña, which has produced more International Game Fish Association (IGFA) world records than any other body of water in the world, is served exclusively by the Topic Star Lodge (p289). Although you have to pay to play at this millionaire's retreat, Piña is sportfishing at its best, and the chance to break a world record is clearly worth the price of admission.

On the private island of San José in the Archipiélago de las Perlas, the all-inclusive Hacienda del Mar (p121) resort offers chartered fishing trips along this stunning stretch of the Pacific. This exclusive luxury lodge is one of the most remote destinations in Panama, though it offers unparalleled professionalism and the opportunity to catch some enormous trophies.

The seas around Isla de Coiba are home to several species of sport-fish including yellow-fin tuna, wahoo, dolphin, Spanish mackerel, jacks and rooster fish. Although it's difficult (and expensive) to access, the chance to fish the waters around this far-flung ecological jewel should not be missed. **Coiba Adventure** (☎ 999 8108; www.coibadventure.com) is one of Panama's top sport-fishing operations, and offers a variety of tours that combine deep-sea fishing with island exploration.

SURFING

While everyone (and their mothers) seems to have discovered Costa Rica, Panama is still garnering popularity among the international surfing community. Of course, Panamanian surfers and a few knowledgeable foreigners have always known about the great breaks that lie off both coasts of this relatively undiscovered surfers' paradise.

Although the joy of Panama is riding some of the lesser known surf breaks – or even discovering your own – the country is home to two world-class spots, namely Santa Catalina (p183) and the archipelago of Bocas del Toro (p224). Of course, even these are significantly less crowded than similar spots in neighboring Costa Rica.

The best months for Santa Catalina are February and March, but the surf breaks here year-round. The face of a typical wave at Santa Catalina is 2m, though during February and March, waves with 4m faces are fairly common.

Isla Bastimentos and Santa Catalina boast the best surfing in the country. On good days you can find waves with 4m faces. If there's a strong swell, you can expect 5m.

TOP 10 SPOTS TO GET YOUR SURF ON

Think you've got what it takes to paddle into Panama's sickest waves? The following is a list of the country's 'Top 10' legendary surf spots:

1 **Punta Teta (Panamá Province)** Point break over rocks to the south of the Río Teta mouth. Lefts and rights with good tubes, especially at medium tide going up.

2 **Playa Venao (Los Santos Province)** South Venado. Sand-bottom beach break popular with local surfers. This spot catches just about any swell. Best surfed at medium to high tide.

3 **Playa Santa Catalina (Veraguas Province)** Sharp rock bottom right and left break. Main wave is the right. Incredible tubes, long rides with lots of power. Surfed mostly medium to high tide.

4 **Punta Brava (Veraguas Province)** Just west of Estero. Point breaks at low tide over sharp rock bottom. Has lefts and rights, but the lefts are the best. Very powerful. Has a great tube section.

5 **Morro Negrito (Chiriquí Province)** Near Morro Negrito town. About five breaks, variety of lefts and rights with occasional tubes.

6 **Dumpers (Bocas del Toro Province)** Isla Colón. Reef-bottom left break with a very steep drop, big tube and short ride. Reef is sharp and tricky.

7 **Playa Bluff (Bocas del Toro Province)** Isla Colón, road's end. Long beach renowned for board-breaking powerful surf. The tubes here are incredible.

8 **Carenero (Bocas del Toro Province)** Isla Carenero, five-minute boat ride from Bocas town. Reef break with 200m peeling lefts, with great tubes. Boat drop-off, pickup at reef. Booties recommended.

9 **Silverbacks (Bocas del Toro Province)** Isla Bastimentos. Reef bottom with waves up to 5m on good swells. Large right with big drop, big tube, but relatively short ride. Not for beginners.

10 **Playa Grande (Colón Province)** Mainland, east of Isla Grande. Beach break with some reef. Waves break left and right.

If you're ready to hit the surf, see the Panama Surfer's Map on pp68–9.

SURFER'S MAP

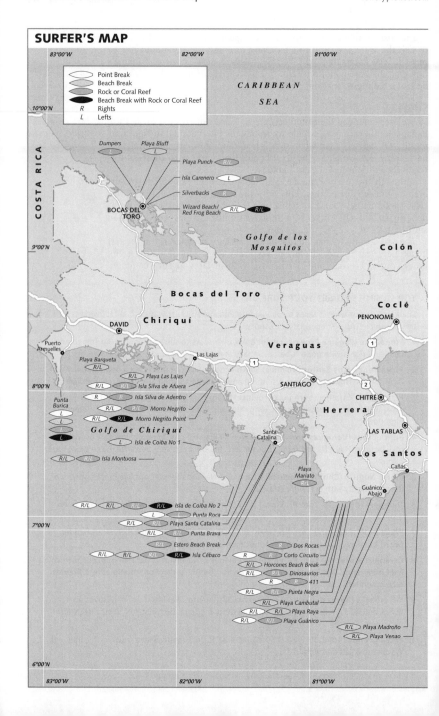

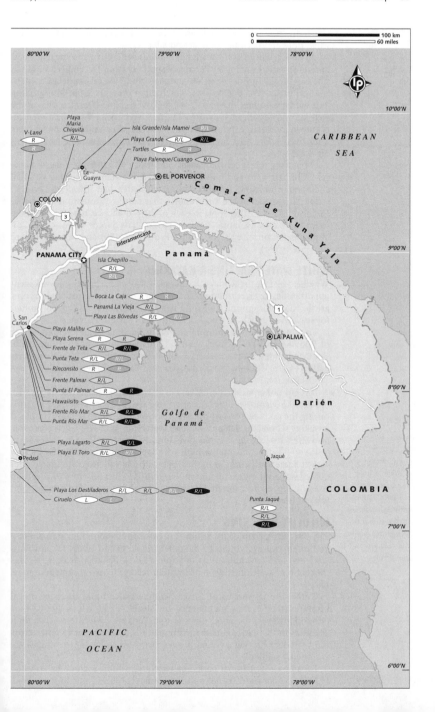

Generally speaking, waves here are at their best during medium to high tide when rides approaching 150m are possible.

On the Caribbean side, the islands of Bocas del Toro offer some of the best and most varied surfing in Panama, especially from December to March. The top breaks in Bocas are Isla Carenero and Silverbacks. Isla Carenero is a reef break near Bocas town, which often presents 200m-long peeling lefts with great tubes. It breaks over shallow reef and is comparable to the well-known Restaurants break in Tahiti. Silverbacks, off Isla Bastimentos, is known for its large, powerful right with a big drop and big tube; it offers a relatively short ride, breaking over reef and is comparable to Hawaii's big-wave spots.

For surfing tours, contact **Panama Surf Tours** (☎ 672 0089; www.panamasurftours .com). This company is run by Panama native Jon Hanna, a former national champion who knows Panama's surf scene better than anyone else.

Jon also prepared the surf reports that appear throughout this book. Detailed lists of surfing spots in each of the provinces can be found on the following pages: Panamá Province (p126), Los Santos Province (p172), Veraguas Province (p183), Chiriquí Province (p199) and Bocas del Toro Province (p224).

WHITE-WATER RAFTING & KAYAKING

Whether you take to the water by raft or kayak, Panama boasts some excellent opportunities for river running. The country's most famous white-water runs are the Ríos Chiriquí and Chiriquí Viejo, though there are also opportunities for sea kayaking in both Bocas del Toro and Chiriquí Provinces.

The unofficial river-running capital of Panama is the highland town of Boquete (p201). Located near the Ríos Chiriquí and Chiriquí Viejo, Boquete is home to the country's top rafting outfits, namely **Chiriquí River Rafting** (☎ 720 1505; www.panama-rafting.com) and **Panama Rafters** (☎ 720 2712; www .panamarafters.com).

If you'd rather tackle these rivers by kayak, **Kayak Panama** (☎ /fax 993 3620), based at XS Memories hotel and sports bar (p137) in Santa Clara, runs trips during the rainy season (April to November). The world famous US-based kayaking school, the **Nantahala Outdoor Center** (in US ☎ 800-232-7238; www.noc.com), also offers several highly rated kayaking adventures in Panama every year.

If you'd rather take to the high seas, **Exploration Panama** (☎ 720 2470; www .explorationpanama.net) works in conjunction with Chiriquí River Rafting to offer guided sea kayaking excursions in the Golfo de Chiriquí. On the Caribbean coast, independently minded travelers can rent kayaks at **Cap 'n Dons** (☎ 757 9248) on Isla Colón.

The Tapir's Morning Bath: Mysteries of the Tropical Rainforests and the Scientists who are Trying to Solve Them, by Elizabeth Royte, is a fascinating introduction to tropical ecology and a travelogue documenting Royte's 'education' on Isla Barro Colorado.

WILDLIFE WATCHING

The bio-rich terrain of the isthmus boasts some astounding animal life – you might see everything from spider monkeys and sloths to capybaras (rodents) and crocodiles (just to name a few!). Panama also offers magnificent bird-watching due to its location relative to two continents and its narrow girth.

Unlike the savannahs of Africa, wildlife-watching in the neotropical rainforest is an exercise in patience and stealth – a little luck doesn't hurt either. However, the good news is that Panama's wildlife reaches high densities in the national parks. Although it's unlikely you'll come across top predators like jaguars and pumas, primates and lesser mammals are commonly sighted.

Panama's top national parks for watching wildlife include La Amistad (p237), Volcán Barú (p208) and the Darién (p280). Closer to the capital,

Parque Natural Metropolitano (p82) and Parque Nacional Soberanía (p110) are easily accessible.

Bird-watching

With more than 900 species of birds in Panama, all you need to do to spot feathered-friends is to get a good pair of binoculars and hit the trails. Two popular spots include Pipeline Road (p110) in Parque Nacional Soberanía and the Sierra Llorona Panama Lodge (p247) in Colón Province.

Panama's avian species are at their best in the legendary Cana Valley, which is regarded as one of the top birding destinations in the world. This phenomenal wildlife preserve can only be accessed via organized tour with the highly recommended Ancon Expeditions (p89).

The **Panama Audubon Society** (☎ 224 9371; www.panamaaudubon.org), located in Panama City, organizes the annual Christmas bird count on Pipeline Road, and runs birding expeditions throughout the country.

Panama City

Undoubtedly the most cosmopolitan capital in Central America, Panama City is both a gateway to the country's natural riches and a vibrant destination in its own right. As a thriving center for international banking and trade, Panama City sports a sultry skyline of shimmering glass and steel towers that is reminiscent of Miami. Not surprisingly, the city residents often joke that Panama City is the 'Miami of the south,' except that more English is spoken.

Although there's no shortage of fine dining and chic dance clubs, visitors are often drawn to Casco Viejo, a dilapidated neighborhood of historic buildings and cobbled streets reminiscent of old Havana. Abandoned in favor of more stylish neighborhoods, Casco Viejo lay crumbling on the edge of the sea for decades. However, following an ambitious reclamation of this colonial district in recent years, it is priming itself to charm and enchant visitors once more.

The city's architectural diversity is rivaled only by its cultural diversity. Urbanites here hail from all over Latin America, the Caribbean, Asia and, increasingly, North America and Europe. Given the ethnic diversity, it's no surprise that the capital boasts a wide array of restaurants, with everything from Panamanian-style ceviche and bluefin tuna sushi to tikka masala and chicken kebabs. Not far from the city, you'll also find some impressive adventure opportunities, from hiking through tropical rainforests to skirting along the jungle on a train ride to Colón.

Whether you measure the pulse of the city by the beat of the salsa clubs on Calle Uruguay or by the staccato of the street vendors' voices in Casco Viejo, chances are you'll slip into the rhythm of this Latin playground

---

HIGHLIGHTS

- Exploring historic **Casco Viejo** (p78), a rapidly gentrifying neighborhood of colonial buildings, soaring churches and grand plazas

- Reconnecting with the past at the ruins of **Panamá Viejo** (p82), the original Panama City c1519

- Hiking through **Parque Natural Metropolitano** (p82), 265 hectares of rainforest just 10 minutes from downtown

- Dining on Spanish tapas, Italian pastas and Panamanian specialities at any of the capital's fine assortment of **restaurants** (p94)

- Partying like a rock star on **Calle Uruguay** (p100), home to the city's most sophisticated nightlife

---

| ■ POPULATION: 450,000 | ■ AREA: 2561 SQ KM | ■ ELEVATION: SEA LEVEL |

HISTORY

Panama City was founded in 1519 by the Spanish governor Pedro Arias de Ávila (Pedrarias) not long after Balboa first saw the Pacific. Although the Spanish settlement quickly became an important center of government and church authority, the city was ransacked and destroyed in 1671 by the English pirate Sir Henry Morgan, leaving only the stone ruins of Panamá Viejo.

Three years later, the city was reestablished about 8km to the southwest in the area now known as Casco Viejo. Although the city's peninsular location meant that it was well defended, the destruction of the Caribbean port at Portobelo in 1746 dealt a heavy blow to the Spanish overland trade route. Panama City subsequently declined in importance, though it returned to prominence in the 1850s when the Panama Railroad was completed, and gold seekers on their way to California flooded across the isthmus by train.

After Panama declared its independence from Colombia on November 3, 1903 in the Parque de la Independencia, Panama City was firmly established as the capital of the new nation. Since the Panama Canal was completed in 1914, the city has emerged as a center for international business and trade.

The city's only major setback in recent times occurred in 1989, when it was invaded by the USA to oust dictator Manuel Noriega from power. The capital suffered damage both from the invasion itself and from the subsequent looting, and several residential blocks of the El Chorrillo district were destroyed by combat-ignited fire.

Today, Panama City is by far the wealthiest city in Central America, and residents are wholly optimistic about the future – and with good reason. Following the handover of the Canal in 1999, and the subsequent closure of American military bases in the country, Panama City is finally in charge of its own destiny. Furthermore, a spate of foreign investment and the recent referendum to expand the Panama Canal means that the capital is likely to continue its remarkable boom.

ORIENTATION

Panama City stretches about 20km along the Pacific coast, from the Panama Canal at its western end to the ruins of Panamá Viejo to the east.

Near the canal are Albrook airport, the Fort Amador Causeway and the wealthy Balboa and Ancón suburbs built for the US canal and military workers. The Puente de las Américas (Bridge of the Americas) arches gracefully over the canal.

The colonial part of the city, Casco Viejo (also called San Felipe and Casco Antiguo), juts into the sea on the southwestern side of town. From here, two major roads head east through the city.

The main drag is Av Central, which runs past the cathedral in Casco Viejo to Parque Santa Ana and Plaza Cinco de Mayo; between these two plazas, the avenue is a pedestrian-only shopping street. At a fork further east, the avenue becomes Av Central España; the section that traverses the El Cangrejo business and financial district is called Vía España. The other part of the fork becomes Av 1 Norte (José D Espinar), Av Simón Bolívar and finally Vía Transístmica as it heads out of town and across the isthmus toward Colón.

Av 6 Sur branches off Av Central not far out of Casco Viejo and undergoes several name changes. It is called Av Balboa as it curves around the edge of the bay to Punta Paitilla, on the bay's eastern point; it then continues under various names past the Centro Atlapa to the ruins of Panamá Viejo.

Generally, *avenidas* (avenues) run east–west, while *calles* (streets) run north–south. Av Central and Vía España form the boundary – *avenidas* south of Vía España are labeled *sur* (south) while *calles* east of Vía España are labeled *este*.

INFORMATION

Bookshops

El Hombre de la Mancha (Map p79; ☎ 263 6218; Calle 52; ⌚ 10am-9pm Mon-Sat) A Spanish-language bookstore favored by Panamanians.

Exedra Books (Map p79; ☎ 264 4252; Vía España at Vía Brasil; ⌚ 9:30am-9:30pm Mon-Sat, 11am-8:30pm Sun) Easily one of Central America's best bookstores.

Librería Argosy (Map p79; ☎ 223 5344; Vía Argentina near Vía España) A bookstore and cultural institution owned by a cheerful Greek immigrant.

Emergency

Ambulance ☎ 228 2187, 229 1133
Fire ☎ 103
Police ☎ 104

PANAMA CITY

PANAMA CITY

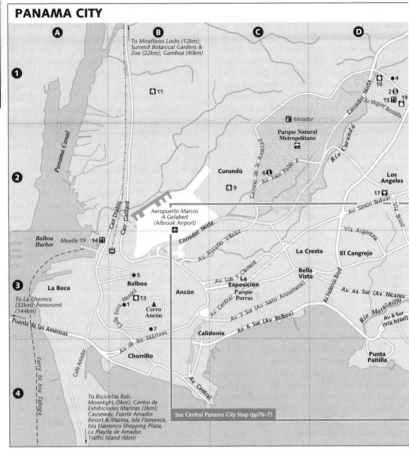

Internet Access

Internet cafés are plentiful in Panama City, especially in the El Cangrejo banking district.

Evolution Planet (Map p79; Av 1a A Norte; per hr US$1; ☿ 9am-4am)

La Red (Map pp76-7; per hr US$1; ☿ 10am-midnight) In Casco Viejo, facing Parque Santa Ana.

Libraries

Earl S Tupper Tropical Sciences Library (Map pp76-7; ☎ 212 8113) A world-class resource for information on tropical biology and conservation.

Maps

Instituto Geográfico Nacional (Tommy Guardia; Map pp76-7; ☎ 236 2444; ☿ 8am-4pm Mon-Fri) Just off Av

Simón Bolívar opposite the Universidad de Panamá. Has an excellent collection of maps for sale.

Medical Services

Medicine in Panama, especially in Panama City, is of a high standard.

Centro Médico Paitilla (Map pp76-7; ☎ 265 8800, 265 8883; cnr Calle 53 & Av Balboa) Has well-trained physicians who speak both Spanish and English.

Money

ATMs are abundant throughout the city. The Banco Nacional de Panamá counter at Tocumen International Airport is one of the few places in Panama City that exchanges foreign currency.

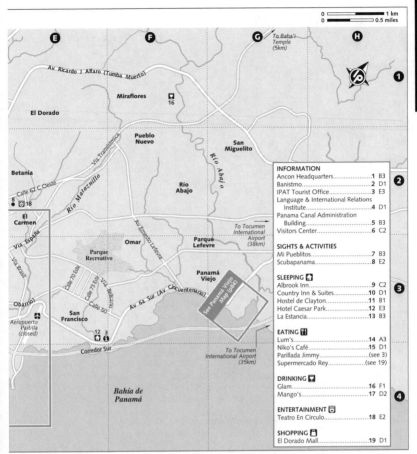

Banistmo (Map p79; Vía España) Changes Amex traveler's checks with no fee; US$5 transaction for other types.
Panacambios (Map p79; ☎ 223 1800; Ground fl, Plaza Regency Bldg, Vía España; 8am-5pm Mon-Fri) Buys and sells international currencies.

Post
Many hotels sell stamps and some will mail guests' letters.
Main Post Office (Map pp76-7; Ave Balboa btwn Calles 23 & 24; 7am-5:45pm Mon-Fri, 7am-4:45pm Sat) Holds poste restante items for 30 days.

Telephone
Tarjetas (phonecards) valued at US$3, US$5 and US$10 can be purchased at pharmacies for local and regional calls at any card phone.

Tourist Information
All the IPAT offices give out free maps. The usefulness of a given office depends on the individual employees. Note that few IPAT employees speak English.
Autoridad Nacional del Ambiente (ANAM; Map pp76-7; ☎ 315 0855; 8am-4pm) ANAM can occasionally provide maps and information on national parks. However, they are not organized to provide much assistance to tourists. Located inside Building 804 of the Albrook district.
IPAT (Map pp74-5; ☎ 226 7000; www.panamainfo .com; Vía Israel, San Francisco; 8:30am-4:30pm Mon-Fri) Panama's tourism bureau is headquartered at the Centro Atlapa in the San Francisco neighborhood. Enter at the rear of the large building. IPAT gives out free maps and information on things to see and do.

PANAMA CITY

CENTRAL PANAMA CITY

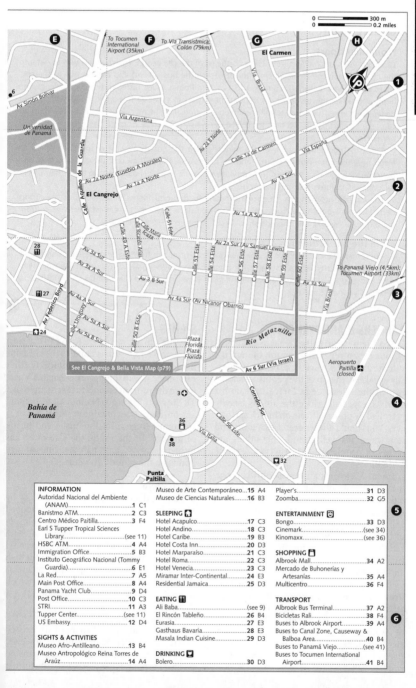

GETTING INTO TOWN

From the Airports
Tocumen International Airport is 35km northeast of the city center. The cheapest way to get into the city is to exit the terminal, cross the street (to the bus shelter) and catch a bus to the city. Buses are marked 'España-Tocumen' (US$0.25, two hours). Much faster and costlier, taxis can be hired at the Transportes Turísticos desk at the airport exit. Beside it is a taxi stand, with posted prices. Unlicensed taxi drivers will assail you, offering rides at ridiculously high prices, but you can take a *colectivo* (shared taxi) for US$10 per person (for three or more passengers) or US$12 per person (for two passengers).

Buses to Tocumen depart every 15 minutes from the bus stop north of the Plaza Cinco de Mayo near the corner of Av Central and Av Justo Arosemena. They cost US$0.75 and take one hour to reach the airport. A taxi from downtown to the airport should cost no more than US$12 for one, US$15 for two or more people.

The Albrook airport north of Cerro Ancón handles domestic flights. Buses ($0.25) to the airport depart from the bus stop in front of the Legislative Palace. However, the easiest way to get to/from the airport is by taxi, and the ride should cost between US$2 and US$4.

From the Bus Terminal
All long-distance buses arrive at the Albrook bus terminal; from here there are connections throughout the city. Routes (such as Vía España, Panamá Viejo) are displayed in the front window and cost US$0.25. If you arrive after dark, it is recommended that you take a taxi (US$2 to US$4) to your destination.

DANGERS & ANNOYANCES

Casco Viejo is currently the focus of an ambitious urban renewal program, though it's still very much a work in progress. Generally speaking, the tip of the peninsula southeast of the Iglesia de la Merced is safe for tourists, especially since the area is heavily patrolled by police officers on bicycles. However, you should always exercise caution, and stay where it's well lit and where there are plenty of people around. Always take taxis at night.

Casco Viejo gets an undeserved bad rep, though you should not underestimate how quickly the neighborhood can change. As you move away from the tip of the peninsula, you will be entering high-density slums and plenty of tourists have been the target of criminal activity. Other high-crime areas include Curundú, El Chorrillo, Santa Ana, San Miguelito and Río Abajo.

There are occasional reports of robbery near the ruins of Panamá Viejo – don't go after sunset, and always keep an eye out.

When walking the streets of Panama City, be aware that drivers do not yield to pedestrians. Sometimes it's best to approach intersections like Panamanians – look both ways then run like hell.

SIGHTS

Panama's major sights are found to the west in Casco Viejo, which is home to the last remnants of the city's colonial heritage. Further east on the way to the airport is Panamá Viejo, where the ruins of Spain's first settlement lie. To the north is Parque Natural Metropolitan, an enormous tract of rainforest that serves as welcome refuge from the hustle and bustle of the city. In the south, the Causeway has numerous restaurants, bars and fine vantage points on the edge of the ocean.

Casco Viejo

Following the destruction of the old city by Henry Morgan in 1671, the Spanish moved their city 8km southwest to a rocky peninsula on the foot of Cerro Ancón. The new location was easier to defend as the reefs prevented ships from approaching the city except at high tide. The new city was also easy to defend as it was surrounded by a massive wall, which is how Casco Viejo (Old Compound) got its name.

In 1904, when construction began on the Panama Canal, all of Panama City existed where Casco Viejo stands today. However, as population growth and urban expansion pushed the boundaries of Panama City further

EL CANGREJO & BELLA VISTA

0 _____ 200 m
0 _____ 0.1 miles

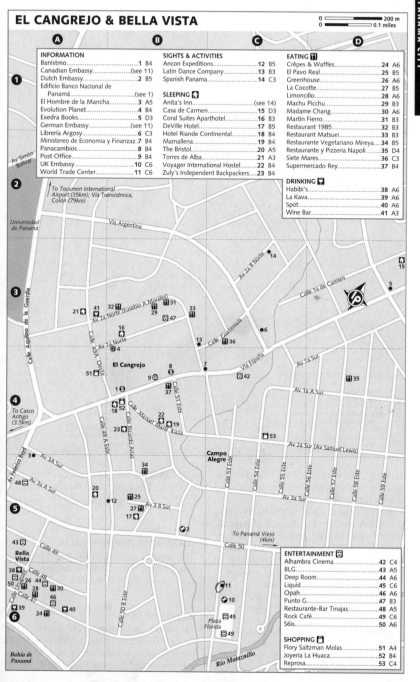

INFORMATION
Banistmo.....................................**1** B4
Canadian Embassy.................(see 11)
Dutch Embassy..........................**2** B5
Edificio Banco Nacional de
  Panamá................................(see 1)
El Hombre de la Mancha............**3** A5
Evolution Planet........................**4** B4
Exedra Books.............................**5** D3
German Embassy....................(see 11)
Librería Argosy.........................**6** C3
Ministereo de Economia y Finanza..**7** B4
Panacambios..............................**8** B4
Post Office..................................**9** B4
UK Embassy..............................**10** C6
World Trade Center..................**11** C6

SIGHTS & ACTIVITIES
Ancon Expeditions...................**12** B5
Latin Dance Company...............**13** B3
Spanish Panama.......................**14** C3

SLEEPING
Anita's Inn...............................(see 14)
Casa de Carmen.......................**15** D3
Coral Suites Aparthotel............**16** B3
DeVille Hotel...........................**17** B5
Hotel Riande Continental.........**18** B4
Mamallena...............................**19** B4
The Bristol...............................**20** A5
Torres de Alba.........................**21** A3
Voyager International Hostel.....**22** B4
Zuly's Independent Backpackers....**23** B4

EATING
Crêpes & Waffles......................**24** A6
El Pavo Real.............................**25** B5
Greenhouse...............................**26** A6
La Cocotte................................**27** B5
Limoncillo................................**28** A6
Machu Picchu...........................**29** B3
Madame Chang.........................**30** A6
Martín Fierro............................**31** B3
Restaurant 1985.......................**32** B3
Restaurant Matsuei...................**33** B3
Restaurante Vegetariano Mireya...**34** B5
Restaurante y Pizzeria Napoli.....**35** D4
Siete Mares...............................**36** C3
Supermercado Rey....................**37** B4

DRINKING
Habibi's...................................**38** A6
La Kava....................................**39** A6
Spot...**40** A6
Wine Bar..................................**41** A3

To Tocumen International
Airport (35km); Vía Transístmica,
Colón (79km)

Universidad
de Panamá

Av Simón
Bolívar

Calle Aquilino de la Guarda

Via Argentina

Av 2a B Norte

Calle 1a de Carmen

Av 2a Norte (Eusebio A Morales)

Calle Guatemala

Calle 49A Oeste

Av 1a Norte

El Cangrejo

Via España

Av 1a Sur

Calle 51 Este

Calle Manuel María Icaza

Calle Ricardo Arias

Av 1a A Sur

Av 2a Sur (Av Samuel Lewis)

Campo
Alegre

Calle 52 Este
Calle 53 Este
Calle 54 Este
Calle 55 Este
Calle 56 Este
Calle 57 Este
Calle 58 Este
Calle 59 Este

Av 3a Sur

To Casco
Antigo
(3.5km)

Av Federico Boyd

Av 3A Sur

Av 3a A Sur

Av 3 B Sur

To Panamá Viejo
(4km)

Calle 50

Bella
Vista

Calle 49

Calle 48

Calle 50 Este

Calle 47

ENTERTAINMENT
Alhambra Cinema.....................**42** C4
BLG..**43** A5
Deep Room................................**44** A6
Liquid.......................................**45** C6
Opah..**46** A6
Punto G....................................**47** B3
Restaurante-Bar Tinajas.............**48** A5
Rock Café.................................**49** C6
S6is..**50** A6

SHOPPING
Flory Saltzman Molas................**51** A4
Joyería La Huaca.....................**52** B4
Reprosa....................................**53** C4

Plaza
Florida

Bahía de
Panamá

Río Mataznillo

CASCO VIEJO

0 _____ 200 m
0 _____ 0.1 miles

To Parque Santa
Ana (50m); Plaza
Cinco de Mayo (800m)

Muelle Fiscal

Bahía de
Panamá

To the Causeway
(7.5km)

Parque
Herrera

Plaza de la
Independencia

Parque
Bolívar

Bahía de
Panamá

Plaza
de
Francia

east, the city's elite abandoned Casco Viejo, and the neighborhood rapidly deteriorated into an urban slum.

Today, Casco Viejo is gradually being gentrified, and the buildings that have already been restored give a sense of how magnificent the area must have looked in past years. International recognition of these efforts by the community resulted in the area being declared a Unesco World Heritage Site in 2003. However, part of the allure of strolling along Casco Viejo's cobbled streets is the dilapidated charm of the crumbling buildings, abandoned houses and boarded-up ruins.

The restoration of Casco Viejo is still a work in progress, so please be aware of your surroundings and exercise caution while exploring this fascinating neighborhood.

The following places are located on map p80.

PLAZA DE LA INDEPENDENCIA

This **plaza** is the heart of Casco Viejo, and was the site where Panama declared its independence from Colombia on November 3, 1903.

IGLESIA DE SAN JOSÉ

This **church** (Av A) protects the famous *Altar de Oro* (Golden Altar), which was about the only thing of value salvaged after Henry Morgan sacked Panamá Viejo. According to local legend, when word came of the pirate's impending attack, a priest attempted to disguise the altar by painting it black. The priest told Morgan that the famous altar had been stolen by another pirate, and even convinced Morgan to donate handsomely for its replacement. Morgan is said to have told the priest, 'I don't know why, but I think you are more of a pirate than I am.' Whatever the truth, the baroque altar was later moved from the old city to the present site.

TEATRO NACIONAL

Built in 1907, the interior of this ornate **theater** (☎ 262 3525; Av B) has been completely restored, and boasts red and gold decorations, a once-magnificent ceiling mural by Roberto Lewis (one of Panama's finest painters) and an impressive crystal chandelier. Performances are still held here – to find out about them, or just to have a look at the theater, go around to the office door at the side of the building.

PLAZA DE FRANCIA

At the tip of the southern point is this **plaza**, which displays large stone tablets and statues dictating the story (in Spanish) of the French role in the construction of the canal. The plaza is dedicated to the memory of the 22,000 workers, most of them from France, Guadeloupe and Martinique, who died trying to create the canal. Most were killed by yellow fever and malaria, and among the busts is a monument to the Cuban doctor Carlos J Finlay, who discovered how mosquitoes transmit yellow fever. His work led to the eradication of the disease in Panama.

On one side of the plaza are nine restored **dungeons** that were used by the Spaniards and later by the Colombians. Although they're now home to some rather upscale art galleries and restaurants, you can still see the dungeons' original stonework. Also on the plaza are the **Teatro Anita Villalaz** and the **Instituto Nacional de Cultura** (INAC; ☎ 211 4034; ☻ 8:30am-4pm Mon-Fri). INAC is responsible for maintaining the country's museums and other cultural institutions. There is a small gallery on the 1st floor that displays works by Panamanian artists.

PASEO LAS BÓVEDAS

This **esplanade** runs along the top of the sea wall built by the Spanish to protect the city. From here, you can see the Puente de las Américas arching over the waterway and the ships lining up to enter the canal.

PALACIO DE LAS GARZAS

The **presidential palace** (Av Alfaro) is named after the great white herons that reside here. The president of Panama lives on the upper floor.

CLUB DE CLASES Y TROPAS

This abandoned **ruin** (Calle 1a Oeste) was once the favorite hangout of General Noriega, though it was virtually destroyed during the 1989 invasion. Some fresh paint was selectively applied in early 2000, when scenes from the movie *The Tailor of Panama* were filmed here.

PARQUE BOLÍVAR

In 1826, in a schoolroom opposite this park, Simón Bolívar held a meeting urging the union of the Latin American countries. After many struggles against Spanish domination, Bolívar succeeded in liberating Bolivia, Colombia, Ecuador, Peru and Venezuela, and he created Gran Colombia, which encompassed all these states. Although Bolívar was unable to keep Gran Colombia together, he is nonetheless venerated as a hero throughout Latin America.

MUSEO DE ARTE RELIGIOSO COLONIAL

Housed beside the ruins of the Iglesia y Convento de Santo Domingo, this **art museum** (☎ 228 2897; cnr Av A & Calle 3; admission US$1; ☻ 8am-4pm Tue-Sat) has a collection of colonial-era religious artifacts, some dating from the 16th century.

Just inside the doorway of the ruins is the **Arco Chato**, a long arch that had stood here, unsupported, for centuries. It reportedly played a part in the selection of Panama over Nicaragua as the site for the canal since its survival was taken as proof that the area was not subject to earthquakes. Sadly, it collapsed in 2003.

MUSEO DEL CANAL INTEROCEÁNICO

This impressive **museum** (☎ 211 1995; Calle 6a Oeste; admission US$2; ☻ 9:30am-5:30pm Tue-Sun) is housed in a beautifully restored building that once served as the headquarters for the original French canal company. The Panama Canal Museum (as it's more commonly known) presents excellent exhibits on the famous waterway, framed in their historical and political context. Signs are in Spanish, but English-speaking guides and audio tours (US$5) are available.

MUSEO DE HISTORIA DE PANAMÁ

This modest **museum** (☎ 228 6231; Calle 6a Oeste; admission free; ⏲ 8:30am-3:30pm Mon-Fri) has a small selection of exhibits covering Panamanian history from the colonial period to the modern era.

Parque Natural Metropolitano

Up on a hill to the north of downtown, this 265-hectare national park protects vast expanses of tropical semideciduous forest within the city limits, and serves as an incredible wilderness escape from the trappings of the capital. It has two main walking trails, the **Nature Trail** and the **Tití Monkey Trail**, which join to form one long loop. The loop is also home to a 150m-high *mirador* (lookout) that offers panoramic views of Panama City, the bay and the canal all the way to the Miraflores Locks.

Mammals in the park include *tití* monkeys, anteaters, sloths and white-tailed deer, while reptiles include iguanas, turtles and tortoises. More than 250 known bird species have been spotted here, and there are fish and shrimp living in the Río Curundú, which runs along the eastern side of the park.

The park was the site of an important battle during the US invasion to oust Noriega. Also of historical significance are the concrete structures just past the park entrance, which were used during WWII as a testing and assembly plant for aircraft engines.

The park is bordered on the west and north sides by Camino de la Amistad and to the south and east by Corredor Norte; Av Juan Pablo II runs right through the park. Pick up a pamphlet for a self-guided tour in Spanish and English at the **visitors center** (Map pp74-5; ☎ 232 5516; admission US$1; ⏲ 8am-5pm Mon-Fri, to 1pm Sat), 40m north of the park entrance. Rangers offer one-hour tours to groups of five or more (US$6 per person), but you need to call in advance.

Additionally, the **Panama Audubon Society** (☎ 224 9371; www.panamaaudubon.org) holds its monthly meeting at the visitors center from 7:30pm to 9:30pm on the second Thursday of every month. The meetings are open to the public and often feature interesting speakers. Both English and Spanish are spoken here. These meetings provide an excellent opportunity to get to know some Panamanian birders and to learn more about tropical bird species.

An international team of scientists from the Smithsonian Tropical Research Institute (STRI) have set up a **crane** in the park to study the forest canopy, which is home to a complete ecosystem 30m to 50m up from the ground. Although the crane was previously off-limits to the public, **Ancon Expeditions** (see the boxed text on p89) was recently awarded permission to take tourists up to the treetops. This is a highly recommended experience that will provide you with an entirely different view of the rainforest, though you will need to book in advance as the number of tourists allowed up on the crane per day is limited.

Panamá Viejo

Founded on August 15, 1519, by Spanish conquistador Pedro Arias de Ávila, the city of Panamá was the first European settlement along the Pacific. For the next 150 years it profited mainly from Spain's famed bullion pipeline, which ran from Peru's gold and silver mines to Europe via Panamá. Because of the amount of wealth that passed through the city, the Spaniards kept many soldiers here, and their presence kept the buccaneers away.

In 1671, 1200 pirates led by Henry Morgan ascended the Río Chagres as far as Venta de Cruces and then proceeded overland to Panamá. Although the city was not fortified, it was protected on three sides by the sea and marshes, and on the land side was a causeway with a bridge in its middle to allow tidal water to pass underneath. But to the bewilderment of historians, when Morgan and his men neared the city, the Spanish soldiers left this natural stronghold and confronted the buccaneers in a hilly area outside town.

It was the first of their many mistakes. When the two forces met in battle, the Spanish infantry left their ranks after mistaking a repositioning of some of Morgan's men for a retreat. The Spanish soldiers ran after the pirates, leaving a high position for a gully. French sharpshooters within Morgan's band were delighted by the development and opened fire on the Spaniards from nearby knolls. The first volley of musket fire dropped about 100 soldiers, and the Spanish force fell to pieces. Soon after, nearly everything of value was either plundered and divvied up or destroyed by fire.

LOCAL VOICES: MAYOR NAVARRO & THE FUTURE OF TOURISM IN PANAMA

Juan Carlos Navarro is the founding director of ANCON, the country's most prominent private conservation organization. Harvard-educated, and renowned for his sharp wit and piercing intellect, he is currently serving his second term as the mayor of Panama City.

■ **What makes Panama a unique tourist destination?** For a long time, Panama has been one of the world's best kept secrets. You know, all of us who live here, especially those folks who appreciate and respect our natural and cultural heritage, have always known that Panama was fantastic. And then suddenly, just a few years ago, word started getting around that Panama has a lot to offer and people started getting interested in the country for the first time. So now, I think we're currently undergoing a phase of intense interest and scrutiny from the international tourism industry.

■ **What is your vision for the future of tourism in Panama?** Currently, a lot of Americans, Canadians and Europeans are coming to Panama to buy second homes. And, because of the canal expansion and the climate of general well-being and safety in Panama, our country is attracting a lot of international and local investment. So, when you put all that together in a pot and stir it, you have a lot of interest and pressure for us to develop tourism in Panama. This of course has a very good side and a very bad side. The good side is that tourism is one of the few opportunities we have in hand to generate foreign revenue, income and jobs in a relatively short period of time. The difficult part of the equation is that in order for tourism to be sustainable, it has to take into account the culture, the environment and other intangibles. As an example, you can build massive hotels to promote beach tourism almost anywhere in the world. But, if you want to build long-term value, there must be more than that.

■ **What model of tourism would work well in Panama?** The model I like is one of heritage tourism. It is important to develop Panama as a destination for people who seek extraordinary landscapes, be it coastlines, mountains or tropical rainforests. But, I am also interested in developing Panama as a destination for people who want to learn about our history, our indigenous cultures and our natural heritage. I think that if we manage to achieve this in an intelligent way, then we can build sustainable tourism in Panama. In my opinion, quality tourism in Panama would be low volume and preferably high income so that we can receive the greatest possible economic impact and the least possible environmental and cultural shock. For me, that would be my ideal and my vision for where we should go. However, how do you achieve this model within a high pressured environment of tremendous capital investment by both local and international investors? That's our challenge!

■ **What makes Panama City unique in Latin America?** What I like about my city is that it is fast paced and cosmopolitan, and that we were born open to the world. We were founded in 1519, and we are the oldest city on the Pacific in the Americas. Although Panama City has evolved since its founding, it has always been an extremely dynamic and diverse place. Today there are very few places on Earth where you can have an authentic Chinese dim sum in the morning, fried fish with cold beer at noon, and world-class Italian pasta in the evening. You see, the one thing that Panamanians have is our joie de vivre. We are a joyful, smart and creative people, and we just love to share our country with the world.

For the next three centuries, what remained of the abandoned city – mostly beams and stone blocks – served as a convenient source of building materials. Yet most of the remnants of the one-time metropolis were still intact as recently as 1950, when the limits of modern Panama City reached the ruins in the form of a squatter settlement.

Unfortunately, by the time the government declared the ruins a protected site in 1976 (Unesco followed suit in 1997), most of the old city had already been dismantled and overrun.

Today much of Panamá Viejo lies buried under a poor residential neighborhood, though the ruins are a must-see, even if only

PANAMÁ VIEJO

INFORMATION	Catedral de Nuestra Señora de la Asunción	Iglesia y Convento de San Francisco.**13** B3
IPAT tourism office...........................**1** A3	(Our Lady of the Assumption	Iglesia y Convento de Santo Domingo
	Cathedral)......................................**7** C2	(Church and Convent of St Dominic)
SIGHTS & ACTIVITIES	Hospital de San Juan de Dios (Hospital of St	....**14** C2
Cabildo de la Ciudad	John of God)....................................**8** B3	Museo de Sitio Panamá Viejo...........**15** C3
(City Hall)......................................**2** C3	Iglesia de San José (Church of St	Puente del Matadero (Bridge of the
Casa Alarcón...................................**3** C2	Joseph)..**9** C1	Slaughterhouse)..........................**16** A3
Casa de los Genoveses (Slave	Iglesia y Convento de la Compañía de	Puente del Rey (Bridge of the King).**17** C1
Market)...**4** D2	Jesús..**10** C3	
Casas de Terrín...............................**5** C2	Iglesia y Convento de la Concepción.**11** C3	**SHOPPING** 🛍
Casas Reales (Royal Houses)...........**6** D3	Iglesia y Convento de La Merced......**12** A3	Mercado Nacional de Artesanías......**18** C3

to stand on the hallowed grounds of one of Central America's greatest cities.

ORIENTATION & INFORMATION

The ruins of Panamá Viejo are not fenced in, so you can visit them anytime, though for safety reasons it's probably best to explore the area during the daylight hours. So little of the original city remains that its size, layout and appearance are the subjects of much conjecture.

The city was founded on a coastal bar alongside a shallow cove. The primary government buildings were at the mouth of the cove, which was rather spacious and could be used as a port. Panamá was also home to all of the major Catholic religious

orders – the Franciscans, Dominicans, Jesuits and Augustines – all of which had churches and convents in town. The best houses and most of the convents were built on the narrow strip of land along the beachfront.

The colonial city seems to have followed a grid plan, with blocks of various sizes and a main square (the visible remains of Panamá Viejo are certainly laid out that way). The lots tended to be narrow, and the houses often consisted of two or three stories. The suburbs that developed to the north and northwest lacked planning, and there are foundations of common houses and hovels scattered along crooked lanes.

It requires a fertile imagination to visualize the city before the arrival of Captain Morgan and his men. The churches, some of which faced the sea, were the most outstanding buildings. All were rectangular, with stone outer walls, timber roofs, internal wooden supports and a lack of towers. The adjoining convents had inner courts surrounded by wooden galleries, and the larger ones had enclosed gardens and orchards.

Most of the better houses were built of timber and placed wall to wall, with small inner courts, open-air kitchens and separate wings for the servants. Some had ground-floor galleries and balconies, and most had plain exterior walls. A few of the fancier homes were built of stone and their ruins remain. The poor had far simpler dwellings, usually thatched huts built with inexpensive materials such as reeds.

The following sites are featured on Map p84.

RUINS

The center of power resided at the **Casas Reales** (Royal House), a complex ringed by timber ramparts and separated from the city proper by a moat. Within the complex were the customs house, the royal treasury, a prison and the governor's house. Despite the obvious historical importance of the site, past governments have allowed sections of the property to be used as a landfill and for horse stables. Only scattered walls remain of the once impressive structures.

The **Catedral de Nuestra Señora de la Asunción** (Cathedral of Our Lady of Asunción), built between 1619 and 1626, is the best-preserved building of the ruins. In traditional fashion, it was designed so that its two side chapels gave the cathedral a crosslike shape when viewed from the heavens. The bell tower was at the back of the church and may have served double duty as a watchtower for the Casas Reales. The main facade, which faced the Plaza Mayor (Grand Plaza), is gone – only the walls remain.

Also facing the Plaza Mayor were the **Cabildo de la Ciudad** (City Hall) and the **Casas de Terrín**, houses built by one of the city's wealthiest citizens, Francisco Terrín.

Immediately north of the cathedral are the massive ruins of **Casa Alarcón**, the town's best-preserved and largest known private residence, which dates from the 1640s. Just north of the former residence is the **Iglesia y Convento de Santo Domingo** (Church & Convent

of St Dominic), the best-preserved church of the ruins. The convent dates from the 1570s, though the church was built 20 or more years later.

Arriving a decade or so after the Dominican friars were the Jesuits, who built the **Iglesia y Convento de la Compañía de Jesús** (Church & Covent of the Company of Jesus), whose stone ruins are likewise visible today. Just west of the Jesuits' facilities are the spacious ruins of a church and convent, the **Iglesia y Convento de la Concepción**, which were erected by the nuns of Nuestra Señora de la Concepción (Our Lady of the Conception). Most of the ruins, which cover the better part of two blocks, were part of the church – little remains of the convent.

Between the nuns' church and the sea was the city's sole hospital, the **Hospital de San Juan de Dios**. Unfortunately, much of the hospital's remains were scattered when Av Cincuentenario and a side road were put in not long ago. Also bordering the avenue, two blocks west of the hospital's ruins, are the remains of the **Iglesia y Convento de San Francisco**, the facilities erected by the Franciscans. The church faced the sea and stood on a massive base.

Continuing two blocks west along Av Cincuentenario, you'll arrive at the ruins of the **Iglesia y Convento de La Merced**. Erected by the Mercedarian friars in the early 17th century, the buildings actually survived the fire that swept the city following Morgan's assault. However, the church's facade is missing because the friars dismantled it and moved it to Casco Viejo, where it can be seen today.

Further west and paralleling the modern bridge is the **Puente del Matadero** (Bridge of the Slaughterhouse), a horribly over restored stone bridge that took its name from a nearby slaughterhouse, and which marked the beginning of the Camino Real to Portobelo. A much more significant bridge is the **Puente del Rey** (Bridge of the King), which is visible from Av Cincuentenario near the northern edge of town. Built in 1617, it may be the oldest standing bridge in the Americas.

About halfway between Puente del Rey and the Iglesia y Convento de Santo Domingo lies the **Iglesia de San José** (Church of St Joseph), which belonged to the Augustine order. Marking this building as special were its vaulted side chapels, an architectural feature seldom seen in Panama.

MERCADO NACIONAL DE ARTESANÍAS

Panamá Viejo buses ($0.25) coming from Plaza Cinco de Mayo will drop you off at this **artisans market** (☉ 9am-6pm), which lies beside the bulk of the ruins.

MUSEO DE SITIO PANAMÁ VIEJO

Adjacent to the artisans market is this **museum** (admission US$2; ☉ 9am-5pm), which contains a rather impressive scale model of Panamá Viejo prior to 1671 as well as a few surviving colonial artifacts. All signs are in Spanish, though a brochure and tape recording recount the site's history in English.

The Causeway

At the Pacific entrance to the Panama Canal, a 2km palm tree-lined *Calzada* (Causeway) connects the four small islands of Naos, Culebra, Perico and Flamenco to the mainland. The Causeway is the popular place to be in the early morning and late afternoon when residents head here to walk, jog, skate and cycle, or simply escape the noise and pollution of the city. The Causeway also offers sweeping views of the skyline and the old city, and you can see flocks of brown pelicans diving into the sea here most times of the year. Others arrive here simply to savor the pleasant breeze at one of the Causeway's many restaurants and bars.

At the Causeway entrance, **Bicicletas Rali** (☉ 8am-6pm Sat & Sun) operates a booth where you can rent a bicycle for US$3 per hour or rollerblades for US$1 per hour.

If you don't have your own vehicle, it's most convenient to take a taxi to the Causeway (US$4 to US$6) and to hail another when you're ready to return to town – any of the restaurants or bars can call one for you.

FLAMENCO SHOPPING CENTER & FUERTE AMADOR RESORT & MARINA

At the end of Isla Flamenco, you'll find one of the city's newest attractions, the **Fuerte Amador Resort & Marina** (☎ 314 0932; www.fuerteamador .com). This complex contains a two-story shopping center, a marina, a cruise ship terminal and a number of restaurants and bars. At night, these open-air spots are a big draw, providing a fine setting for cocktails or a decent meal.

At the marina, daily boats leave for the nearby resort island of **Isla Taboga** (p115).

CENTRO DE EXHIBICIONES MARINAS

The **Marine Exhibitions Center** (☎ 212 8000, ext 2366; admission US$1; ☉ 1-5pm Tue-Fri, 10am-5pm Sat & Sun), operated by the Smithsonian Tropical Research Institute (STRI), includes an informative marine museum with signs in English and Spanish, two small aquariums and a nature trail through a patch of dry forest containing sloths and iguanas.

There are many exhibits at the center, including a small six-sided building with sweeping views of the Bahía de Panamá, which was built by Noriega for intimate gatherings. Today it houses a museum containing exhibits on the history of Panama's indigenous cultures.

At the museum you can also learn about the role that Panama's marine resources play in the country's economy, and the destructive and wasteful effects of harvesting fish and shrimp by net. All of the text is illustrated with high-quality photos.

Outside the museum is something to thrill ship enthusiasts: large, intelligent illustrations of vessels that allow visitors to glance out at the ocean and identify the types of ships waiting to transit the canal. There's a telescope that you can use free of charge to peer onto the boats and get an idea of what it's like to be a crew member on these tankers.

Two large aquariums, also part of the marine center, are 50m from the museum. One contains fish from the Pacific, the other fish from the Caribbean, allowing you to compare the two sets. You'll be struck by the difference – fish from the Caribbean are much more colorful, and much larger than fish from the Pacific. Staff on hand can explain to you the reasons for the differences.

Dry forests once lined Central America's Pacific coast. Relatively easy to clear and burn for agriculture, these forests have now all but disappeared. However, the forest that you can see from the center, which lines the shore just south of the Puente de las Américas, is a surviving patch of dry forest. There's even some dry forest near the aquariums – keep your eyes open for three-toed sloths as well as other wildlife.

Museums

Sadly, the establishment and preservation of museums is not a governmental priority in Panama City. Those that do exist are mostly

THE SECRET LIFE OF THE CAUSEWAY

All four of the Causeway islands once comprised Fort Grant, which was established in 1913 to guard the southern entrance to the canal. Between 1913 and WWII, the USA made Fort Grant into the most powerful defense complex in the world.

In 1928, two 14-inch guns with ranges up to 44km were brought to Panama. Mounted on railway carriages, they could be moved across the isthmus via the Panama Railroad to defend either entrance to the canal (the Pacific-side emplacement for the railroad guns was on Culebra). You can still see the tracks today on the driveway leading up to the Centro de Exhibiciones Marinas. The concrete rooms nearby, now used by marine-center staff, once housed the guns' ammunition.

In 1941 the Japanese assault on Pearl Harbor showed that carrier-based aircraft could attack successfully far beyond the range of artillery. Suddenly obsolete, many of the big guns were retired from service even before the end of WWII. However, in 1942 the US military was still determined to bulk up their defenses, and paid the enormous cost of US$400,000 to build a command post on Isla Flamenco.

The Causeway, its four islands and a chunk of the peninsula leading to the Causeway, were turned over to Panama in October 1979 in compliance with the Torrijos-Carter Treaty of 1977. Today, part of the Fuerte Amador shopping center is built on a massively protected bombproof structure that was needed 'for use in case of emergency and vital to the security of important data,' according to the US general who ordered its construction. Even today, the US military will not disclose what data was so important that it needed to be stored at the center of a rock island.

the products of extraordinary efforts by individuals who took it upon themselves to move a bureaucratic mountain and create institutions in which Panama's human and natural histories could be preserved.

Foremost among this select group of individuals was the late Reina Torres de Araúz, the country's most distinguished anthropologist. Before she passed away in 1982 at age 49, she successfully battled for the creation of seven museums – including the anthropology museum that bears her name.

The strength of Panama City's museums lies not in a single institution or two but in their variety. In the capital city there are museums devoted to religious colonial art, natural science, Panamanian history, contemporary art, the Panama Railroad and the canal. Unfortunately, signs at all the museums are in Spanish only, and literature in other languages generally is not available.

In addition to those listed in the Casco Viejo section (p81), Panama City is home to several other interesting museums.

The **Museo Antropológico Reina Torres de Araúz** (Map pp76-7; ☎ 262 8338; Av Central near Plaza Cinco de Mayo; admission US$2; ☒ 9am-4pm Mon-Fri) shows the rich cultural heritage of Panama with a collection of pre-Columbian artifacts and exhibits.

The small **Museo Afro-Antilleano** (Map pp76-7; ☎ 262 5348; cnr Av Justo Arosemena & Calle 24 Este; admis-

sion US$1; ☒ 8:30am-3:30pm Tue-Sat) has exhibits on the history of Panama's West Indian community, particularly their work building the railroad and later the canal.

Museo de Arte Contemporáneo (Map pp76-7; ☎ 262 8012; near Av Los Mártires, Ancón district; admission free; ☒ 9am-4pm Mon-Fri, to noon Sat, to 3pm Sun) is a privately owned museum with an excellent collection of works on paper by Latin American artists, and the occasional temporary exhibition by a foreign or national artist.

Museo de Ciencias Naturales (Map pp76-7; ☎ 225 0645; Av Cuba, btwn Calles 29 Este & 30 Este; admission US$1; ☒ 9am-3:45pm Tue-Sat) has sections on geology, paleontology, entomology and marine biology, as well as an impressive display of taxidermy.

At the time of publication, construction on the **Museo de la Biodiversidad** (Museum of Biodiversity; www.biomuseopanama.org), designed by world-renowned architect Frank Gehry, was well underway. This much-anticipated museum will be located at the tip of the Causeway.

Panama Canal Murals

The story of the monumental effort to build the Panama Canal is powerfully depicted in murals mounted in the rotunda of the **Panama Canal Administration Building** (Map pp74-5; Balboa Heights; admission free; ☒ 7:30am-4:15pm Mon-Fri).

The murals tell the story of the canal's construction through four main scenes: the digging of Gaillard Cut at Gold Hill, where the canal passes through the Continental Divide; the building of the spillway of the Gatún Dam, which dammed the Río Chagres and created Lago Gatún; the construction of one of the giant lock gates (the canal uses some 80 of these gates); and the construction of the Miraflores Locks near the Pacific entrance to the canal. A frieze located immediately below the murals presents a panorama of the excavation of Gaillard Cut.

The murals were created by William B Van Ingen of New York, an outstanding artist who had achieved considerable fame for his murals in the Library of Congress in Washington, DC, and those in the US Mint in Philadelphia. Van Ingen agreed to produce the murals for US$25 per sq ft; the finished murals cover about 1000 sq ft.

According to a leaflet at the administration building, Van Ingen and two assistants first made charcoal sketches of canal construction activities during two visits to Panama in 1914. Van Ingen then painted the murals on separate panels in his New York studio. The panels were shipped to Panama and installed during a three-day period in January 1915 under the artist's personal supervision. The paintings have the distinction of being the largest group of murals by an American artist on display outside the USA.

The building is closed on weekends, but guards will usually let you in between 10am and 2:30pm if you ask them politely.

Mi Pueblito

At the foot of Cerro Ancón, on the western side of town, **Mi Pueblito** (My Little Village; Map pp74-5; Av de Los Mártires; admission US$1; 9am-9pm Tue-Sun) features life-size replicas of rural villages found on the Península de Azuero, in Bocas del Toro and in the Darién. It also features extensive shops selling handicrafts from throughout the country and a handful of decent restaurants. Folk dances accompanied by live music are staged on Friday and Saturday at around 6pm – they're touristy but still worth a look.

Baha'i House of Worship

On the outskirts of Panama City, 11km from the city center on the Transisthmian Hwy, the

---

> **DAY TRIPS FROM PANAMA CITY**
>
> Looking to get out of the city for the day? Here are some author-tested suggestions.
>
> ■ Laying eyes on the awe-inspiring **Panama Canal** (p107)
>
> ■ Spotting feathered friends along Pipeline Rd in **Parque Nacional Soberanía** (p110)
>
> ■ Visiting the world-famous tropical biology center on **Isla Barro Colorado** (p113)
>
> ■ Escaping to the flower-dotted island of **Isla Taboga** (p115)
>
> ■ Surfing gnarly breaks along the **Pacific Coast** (p122)

---

white-domed **Baha'i temple** (☎ 231 1137; 10am-6pm) looms like a giant egg atop the crest of a hill. The inside is surprisingly beautiful, with a fresh breeze always present. The Baha'i House of Worship serves all of Latin America.

Information about the faith is available at the temple in English and Spanish; readings from the Baha'i writings (also in English and Spanish) are held Sunday mornings at 10am. Any bus to Colón can let you off on the highway, but it's a long walk up the hill. A taxi from Panama City costs around US$10.

COURSES
Dance

Located one block from Vía España near the Hotel Riande Continental, the **Latin Dance Company** (Map p79; ☎ 265 7964) offers classes in salsa, merengue and hip-hop for students aged five to 65. Three classes are held in the evenings starting at 5:30pm, and there are several Saturday classes as well. Classes cost US$5 plus the US$5 enrolment fee. Or if you plan on sticking around for a while, sign up for 10 days (US$50) or one month (US$80) of unlimited classes.

Language

Located in the suburban El Dorado neighborhood, the **Language & International Relations Institute** (ILERI; Map pp74-5; ☎ 260 4424; isls.com/panama/schools/ileri.html; Camino de la Amistad) offers four hours of one-on-one instruction per day, five days a week. Costs start at US$300 for the first week (with lodging, meals, trips and activities), and then decreases with each subsequent week. The weekly rate without lodging starts at US$200.

The immensely popular language school, **Spanish Panama** (Map p79; ☎ 213 3121; www.span ishpanama.com; Av 2a B Norte), gets rave reviews from travelers. It has a similar structure to ILERI's: four hours of one-on-one classes daily and homestays with meals for US$375 per week (long-term discounts are available). They also offer a 'backpacker special,' which includes classes with dorm stay for US$275 per week.

PANAMA CITY FOR CHILDREN

Panama City has a variety of attractions that are suitable for kids. With excellent rainforest nearby, consider a day tour with Ancon Expeditions (see below). Some of the best options for kids include visiting an **Emberá village** (p112), touring the old cannon-lined forts in **Portobelo** (p250), cruising along **Lago Gatún** (p123) on a jungle boat or taking a moderate hike through **Parque National Soberanía** (p110).

The **Panama Canal Railway** (p246) that links the two oceans provides a lovely journey along the canal and through rainforest. Kids might also enjoy a visit to the **Miraflores Locks** (**p107**), especially since the new museum there has lots of eye-catching multimedia exhibitions and is touch-friendly in parts. And of course, if you need a respite from the heat (or the rain), head to **Multicentro** (p102) – this mall has dozens of shops and restaurants, a movie theater and an internet café.

FESTIVALS & EVENTS

Although not as famous as the celebrations in Rio de Janeiro or New Orleans, Carnaval in Panama City is celebrated with the same level of unrestrained merriment and wild abandon during the four days preceding Ash Wednesday. From Saturday until the following Tuesday, work is abandoned and masks, costumes and confetti are brought to the fore. For 96 hours, almost anything goes.

The festivities formally begin with a coronation ceremony on Friday, during which a Carnaval queen and her attendants are chosen from candidates representing a variety of social clubs, volunteer organizations, neighborhoods and private groups. Throughout her reign, the queen presides over all official receptions and is the center of attention in the daily parades scheduled each afternoon.

Officially, the craziness starts slowly, with a small parade on Saturday that consists of little more than the queen and her court. Unofficially, the cork is way out of the bottle by then. Vía España fills with people, and everyone is in high spirits and partying in an atmosphere that is sexually charged and free of class distinctions. Music pours from all directions and spontaneous dancing breaks out everywhere. Masquerade characters cavort among the crowd. Colorful street vendors

---

ANCON EXPEDITIONS OF PANAMA

Ancon Expeditions of Panama (Map pp74–5; ☎ 269 9415; www.anconexpeditions.com; El Dorado Bldg, Calle Elvira Mendez) is the for-profit arm of ANCON (Asociación Nacional para la Conservación de la Naturaleza; National Association for the Conservation of Nature). It enables a portion of all proceeds from ecotours to be used in the ongoing fight to protect Panama's natural heritage.

Because of its conservationist aims, Ancon Expeditions has been able to recruit the country's foremost nature guides, all of whom are avid birders, speak flawless English and are extremely enthusiastic about the environment. They are excited about their occupations and offer a level of service that is simply superb. In Panama, the standard for nature guides and tours is set by Ancon Expeditions.

Ancon Expeditions' tour offerings are extensive, and they have regularly scheduled departures to every corner of the country, from the Chiriquí Highlands (p201), Bocas del Toro (p217) and Isla de Coiba (p188) to the Canal Zone (p107) and Kuna Yala (p258). The company is also the exclusive tour operator for the Darién (p278), and manages the world-famous Cana field station popular with bird-watchers, and the Punta Patiño lodge.

If you're interested in arranging a daytour around the city or to the Canal Zone, it is sometimes possible to stop by the office and book everything on-site. However, due to the popularity of Ancon Expedition's tour offerings, it's recommended that you book prior to your arrival in Panama, especially if you're planning on joining a multiday tour.

wander through the throngs of people, and improvised entertainment abounds. The party moves indoors at night – into cantinas, private clubs and hotels – where combos play Afro-Cuban and typical Panamanian music, and the dancing and drinking continue till dawn.

The celebration, the origins of which have been obscured with the passage of time, kicks into a higher gear on Sunday, when folk dance groups decked out in Panama's national costumes join the queen and her attendants in the afternoon parade down Vía España, traveling from near Vía Brasil to near Av Federico Boyd (the exact beginning and ending points vary from year to year). To cool the sunbaked masses, fire and garden hoses are turned on the crowd at every opportunity. The amount of water sprayed on party-goers during Carnaval in Panama City during these four festive days equals the amount the city uses during the previous four *months*.

The madness peaks on Shrove Tuesday with the biggest parade of all. Floats of all sizes rule the avenue, separated by bands of gaily dressed people walking slowly in themed formations – not the least conspicuous of which is the traditional entourage of transvestites. Most of them carry a razor in each hand as a warning to macho types that a punch thrown at them will not go unanswered.

Carnaval officially closes with the first rays of sunlight on Wednesday morning, when the hardiest celebrants appear on the beach of the Bahía de Panamá to bury a sardine in the sand – a symbolic gesture intended to convey the end of worldly pleasures for the Lenten season.

SLEEPING

There are dozens of hotels in Panama City with guest rooms ranging from dimly lit concrete cells to luxurious high-rise suites.

In the past, accommodations in Casco Viejo were best avoided – that is of course unless you were looking to rent a place by the hour. Today however, this rapidly changing neighborhood is home to a handful of recommended accommodations, and bedding down in Casco Viejo is a great away to soak up its Old World charm.

The neighborhoods of La Exposición and Bella Vista are home to a number of fairly standard budget and midrange hotels. Although the districts are newer than Casco Viejo, they're not quite as new and shiny as the banking district.

The fast-paced vibe of modern Panama City is best experienced in El Cangrejo, the modern banking district that's chock-full of soaring steel and glass. Most of the hotels in this neighborhood are pricey affairs, though you can't beat the views from high up.

The final option is the former US-occupied neighborhoods of Clayton, Albrook, Cerro Ancón and Amador, which are located in the Canal Zone adjacent to the Miraflores Locks. Although you're a taxi cab away from the downtown, staying out here is a welcome respite from the noise and congestion of Panama City.

Casco Viejo

The following accomodations are featured on Map p80.

Hospedaje Casco Viejo (☎ 211 2027; www.hospedaje cascoviejo.com; Calles 8a Oeste; dm US$7, s without/with bathroom US$10/12; Ⓟ Ⓠ) A welcome addition to the Casco Viejo scene, this warm and inviting colonial-mansion-turned-hospedaje is arguably the best deal in town. Whether you bed down in the dormitory or splurge on a private bathroom, it's hard to beat these prices, especially since guests can take advantage of the communal kitchen, free wi-fi and the open-air courtyard. The *hospedaje* is located down a quiet side street next to the Iglesia de San José and is just a few blocks away from the quarter's trendiest bars and restaurants.

Pensión Colón (☎ 228 8506; cnr Calles 12 Oeste & B; s/d US$9/10, s/d with private bathroom US$10/11; Ⓟ) Originally built to house Panama Canal workers, this handsome hotel has an impressive lobby complete with the original ornate Spanish tile work. On the exterior, the Pensión Colón evokes the Casco Viejo of old. Unfortunately, the place has seen many years of neglect, though a sagging mattress and a leaky sink are offset by the incredible views from the balcony.

our pick Luna's Castle (☎ 262 1540; www.lunascastle .com; Calle 9; dm/d incl breakfast US$9/22) From the same twisted minds that brought you Mondo Taitu and Hostel Heike in Bocas del Toro (p226), Luna's Castle is, bar none, the best backpacker spot in Panama City. Housed in a creaky, colonial mansion near the water's edge, Luna's Castle masterfully blends historic Spanish colonial architecture with funky, laid-back backpacker vibes. Although it's the newest accomodation in the capital, the owners' winning formula of professional service, international atmosphere and shoestring prices are sure to make this a legendary stop on the Gringo Trail. In the evenings, the attached 9th Avenue Bar is the best pick-up joint in the city for anyone smitten with an incurable case of wanderlust.

Casa Mar Alta (☎ 211 3427; www.casamaralta.com; Calle 2a, Casco Viejo; master bedroom/2nd bedroom US$95/125; P ▣ ✖) Located at the core of Panama City's most atmospheric neighborhood, Casa Mar Alta is a beautifully restored 19th-century mansion with two lavish guest rooms. The finest feature of this penthouse apartment – and the reason it's often favored for magazine photo shoots – is the exquisite tile work throughout. Guests also have access to the dining room where breakfast is served each morning, as well as the stunning rooftop terrace, which has unspoiled views out to the sea. There really is no substitute for the exquisite penthouse, but you will need to book in advance as it's extremely popular.

La Exposición

The following accomodations are featured on Map pp76–7.

BUDGET

Residencial Jamaica (☎ 225 9870; cnr Av Cuba & Calle 38 Este; d with private bathroom US$20; P ✖) This coral-pink palace offers secure, clean rooms in a mellow corner location. The light-filled rooms are a good deal at this price, especially since they come with air-con and private hot-water bathrooms. What makes this place worth considering is how well it's maintained – the management cares and it shows.

Hotel Acapulco (☎ 225 3832; Calle 30; s/d with private bathroom US$20/22; P ✖) A discernible step up from the standard hotel fare that runs chockablock in this part of town, the Acapulco combines professionalism with a certain no-nonsense style. This is reflected in the spotless rooms complete with air-con, private hot-water bathroom and French-door laden balconies. There is a simple recipe for success here: low prices, decent standards and a friendly staff.

Hotel Andino (☎ 225 1162; Calle 35; s/d with private bathroom US$22/25; P ✖) Rooms at the Hotel Andino lack charm, but they're big, clean and equipped like a start-up apartment. Request a king-size for extra play space, and you can also

get a two-burner stove for some self-catering adventures. If you don't feel like leaving the hotel at all, there's a bar and restaurant here, making it a convenient choice if you just have to crash overnight between bus departures.

Hotel Marparaíso (☎ 227 6767; Calle 34 Este; s/d US$22/28; P ▣ ✖) Travelers in the know choose Hotel Marparaíso, simply because they'll pick you up at the airport for free, which will save you some serious cash. The rooms themselves are fairly unremarkable, though at least you can take a hot shower, watch some satellite TV and blast the air-con while recuperating from a long flight. Growing in popularity, the downstairs bar and restaurant is a great place to chat up other travelers.

MIDRANGE & TOP END

Hotel Venecia (☎ 227 7881; Av Perú near Calle 35 Este; s/d/f/executive rooms US$25/30/35/40; P ✖ ▣) The Venecia is one of the newer hotels in this rapidly aging neighborhood, and its cheerily painted exterior is subtle compared to the over-the-top Venetian theme inside. If you can look past all the Roman tapestries, replica urns, fake artwork and stock tourist photos, the Venecia is actually good value for the money. Brightly lit rooms are adorned with modern furnishings, and the downstairs restaurant serves up some good spaghetti.

Hotel Caribe (☎ 225 0404; cnr Calle 28 & Av Perú; s/d with private bathroom US$28/34; P ✖ ▣) Psychedelic and slightly retro – by default rather than design – this 250-room hotel has an intrigue that grows on you. Lurid orange and brown dominate the color scheme and the lighting is terrible, but there's something surreal about the rooftop pool overlooking the city. Summer days in the capital are stifling and sticky, so there's something to be said for the cheapest room in town with a pool.

Hotel Costa Inn (☎ 227 1522; www.hotelcosta inn.com; Av Perú near Calle 39 Este; s/d US$40/45; P ✖ ▣ ▣) A discernible step up in quality and service, the Hotel Costa Inn offers no-nonsense rooms in a part of town famous for surprises. However, the real perk of the Costa Inn is paying a midrange price for upscale amenities, including a gym and pool. Airport shuttle and city tours are available, and there's a reputable travel agency on the premises.

Hotel Roma (☎ 227 3844; www.hotelromaplaza.com; Av Justo Arosemena at Calle 33; d from US$60; ste US$100;

P ⊠ ⬛ ⬛) Another top pick for high quality and service, the Roma offers sparkling rooms with modern accents that are a world beyond the drab interiors of its neighboring hotels. If you're travelling with the little ones, the family-style suites are great value and the rooftop pool will keep everyone's temperatures down. A pleasant restaurant and bar on the 1st floor serves up a good mix of Panamanian favorites and Western standards.

Miramar Inter-Continental (☎ 214 1000; www.mi ramarpanama.com; Av Balboa near Av Federico Boyd; d from US$165; P ⊠ ⬛) This Panama City landmark hotel has hosted the likes of Hillary Clinton, Mick Jagger, Jimmy Carter, Alberto Fujimori, Sting, Ernesto Zedillo, Andres Pastrana and Def Leppard – not at the same time of course. Gorgeous guest rooms brimming with all the creature comforts face either the gleaming expanse of the Bahía de Panamá or the shimmering towers of the financial district. The Miramar is also home to an impressive list of amenities including an informal marina-side restaurant, a fine-dining restaurant, a piano lounge, an upscale dance club, spa and workout center, beauty salon, tennis courts and an enormous pool complete with its own island.

El Cangrejo & Bella Vista

All of the following accomodations are featured on Map p79, unless otherwise noted.

BUDGET

Zuly's Independent Backpackers (☎ 6605 4742; www .geocities.com/zulys_independent_backpacker; Calle Ricardo Arias 8; s/d within dm US$7/11; ⬛ ⊠) The cheapest dorm bed in the city can be yours at this low-key spot, which occupies the original premises of Voyager International Hostel. Zuly's is brand new and still working out the kinks, so it has a long way to go yet. But the warm, friendly atmosphere is likely to make it a popular choice amongst backpackers.

Voyager International Hostel (☎ 260 5913; www .geocities.com/voyagerih/english.html; Calle Maria Icaza; dm/d US$8/17; ⬛ ⊠) Panama City's original hostel boasts incredible wraparound views of the city in its new location, and it's worth mentioning that Voyager essentially invented the idea of a hostel in Panama. Unfortunately, its reputation amongst backpackers has dropped in recent years and the management doesn't seem intent on reinvesting any money into the property.

Mamallena (☎ 6538 9745; www.mamallena.com; Calle Maria Icaza; dm US$10; ⬛ ⊠) Literally next door to Voyager, Mamallena is one of the newest hostels in Panama City, and offers clean and comfortable air-conditioned dorm rooms and basic shared facilities. This is a good deal for your money and unfussy travelers looking to save a buck or two will leave here feeling satisfied. Unfortunately, the atmosphere is as sterile as a hospital waiting room, which means that the quality of your time at Mamallena depends on the company.

Casa de Carmen (☎ 263 4366; www.lacasadecarmen .com; Calle 1a de Carmen 32, El Carmen; dm/tr per person US$10/13.50, d US$20-30, apt US$45; P ⊠ ⬛) Located in a beautiful converted colonial home near Vía Brasil in the district of El Carmen, this festive hostel is undoubtedly Panama City's loveliest budget accommodation – lovely to the point of being hard to get into, so book ahead. All of the rooms here are painted a different shade, but share the same detailed forethought of high ceilings, slung-up hammocks, warm incandescent light and tiled bathrooms with scalloped sinks. Guests of all ages congregate in the cosy communal kitchen, lounge area or on the lush patio. The friendly owners, who have a wealth of knowledge of the city and countryside, add to the familial atmosphere.

Anita's Inn (☎ 213 3121; www.hostelspanama.com; Av 2a B Norte; dm US$10, s from US$15; ⬛ ⊠) Affiliated with Spanish Panama (p89), this cozy guesthouse is conveniently located in the same building as the language school. If you're brushing up on your Spanish, you couldn't ask for a better place to call home. Even if you're just passing through and happy to speak English, the communal atmosphere, comfortable rooms and relaxing location make Anita's an excellent choice.

MIDRANGE & TOP END

Coral Suites Aparthotel (☎ 269 3898; www.coral suites.net; Calle D; ste from US$80; P ⊠ ⬛ ⬛) This handsome all-suites hotel is a good choice for traveling executives who require their amenities, or long-term visitors to the capital in need of more than a hotel room. Simple and functional suites feature spacious bathrooms, luxury mattresses and a fully equipped kitchen for all your culinary needs. Coral Suites really stands out at this price range when you consider the full gym, rooftop pool and business center.

Torres de Alba (☎ 269 7770; www.torresdealba.com .pa; Av Eusebio A Morales; ste from US$90; [P] [X] [R]) One of the newest hotels in El Cangrejo, the suites at Torres de Alba are expertly designed and outfitted with spacious living and dining areas, marble bathrooms with fine American-made fixtures and hot-water showers boasting hydrotherapy-style pressure. If you're looking to stay in shape, you can also do a few laps in the rooftop pool or pump some iron in the well-stocked workout center. Despite all of this, suites at Torres de Alba are under US$100 a night, and there are discounts for long-term stays.

Hotel Riande Continental (☎ 265 5114; www.hotel esriande.com; Calle Ricardo Arias & Vía España; d from US$110; [P] [X] [R]) This well-located upscale hotel has that swinging, tropical style more common to Havana than Panama, thanks to the open architecture, cool breezes and abundance of fresh-cut flowers. The rooms themselves have four-poster federalist-style beds and enough space to do somersaults, though you'll be disappointed if you get a room in the old tower. If you can afford it, upgrade to a suite and you'll be treated to eye-popping skyline views from the sitting area, the bed and even the walk-in closet. Of course, the real action at the Riande happens at the poolside – grab a cocktail and watch it all swirl by.

Hotel Caesar Park (Map pp74–5; ☎ 270 0477; www .caesarpark.com; Calle 77 Este near Vía Israel, San Francisco; ste from US$125; [P] [X] [R]) This gigantic hotel is like a slice of Vegas transplanted to Panama City: flashy, rococo, bodacious and stacked with facilities, amenities and services – it even has the casino, but is short an Elvis impersonator. Part of the Westin Hotels and Resorts chain, this is where heads of state usually stay when they visit Panama, so you never know who you may bump into in the athletic club and spa, swimming pool, business center, dance club or mall. There are 361 suites on offer here, each of varying shape and size, though all of them boast great views of the soaring skyline.

DeVille Hotel (☎ 206 3100; www.devillehotel.com.pa; Av Beatriz Cabal near Calle 50; ste from US$175; [P] [X] [□]) The boutique concept is executed impeccably at this sweetheart of a hotel that has won a devoted clientele for its classy, tasteful digs and sterling service. While it's comfortable and functional enough for the most distinguished executive travelers, it's also undeniably romantic – a hard balance to strike. All

of the 33 rooms are suites and offer luxury par excellence. Among the features in your beautifully appointed room, expect to find an antique dresser from Thailand, glistening with inlaid mother of pearl; a marble-topped antique table set with Louis XV chairs; and the finest-quality US-made mattresses with custom bed linen made of Egyptian cotton and goose-feather pillows.

The Bristol (☎ 265 7844; www.thebristol.com; Calle Aquilino de la Guardia; d US$295, ste from US$335; [P] [X] [□]) An impossibly intimate, elegant hotel with marble at every turn, you'll sense the difference at the Bristol the moment the door is swept open for you. Oriental carpets, flamboyant orchids and lots of precious woods abound, and that's just the lobby. There are only 56 rooms at this 'Leading Small Hotel of the World', which, coupled with the 24-hour butler service, means you'll be scrupulously looked after.

Canal Zone

All of the following accomodations are featured on Map pp74–5.

Hostel de Clayton (☎ 317 1634; www.hosteldeclayton .com; Calle Guanabana edificio 605B; dm US$11.50, tw without/ with private bathroom US$13.50/15; [P] [□] [X]) Reminiscent of an army barracks (well, it was!), this unique hostel is located on the site of the former US army base of Clayton, though today it's one of the city's up and coming residential areas. The rooms and amenities here are perfectly suited to the budget traveler, and it's definitely cool to close your eyes for the night in the former belly of the beast. But the real reason you're staying here is to explore the area's quiet, suburban setting and attractive gardens.

La Estancia (☎ 314 1417; www.bedandbreakfastpan ama.com; Casa 35, Quarry Heights, Ancón Hill; d/ste US$55/85; [P] [X]) Perched atop Cerro Ancón and surrounded by tropical flora and fauna, La Estancia is a small apartment building converted into a tranquil B&B that boasts some great views from its lofty locale. Pastels and clean lines abound, and the quaint rooms exemplify functional simplicity with no knickknacks to clutter things up. Breakfasts (included in the room cost) are excellent here, and best enjoyed on the patio while gazing upon the Puente de las Américas.

Albrook Inn (☎ 315 1789; www.albrookinnpanama .com.pa; Calle Hazelhurst 14, Albrook; d/ste US$60/80; [P] [X]) Set amid lush greenery in a tranquil area removed from the chaos of downtown, the new Albrook Inn near Albrook airport is a fine choice if you're trying to make an early morning domestic flight. Bright rooms with picture windows make the most of the ample sunlight and surrounding gardens, and are far removed from the congestion and pollution of the downtown area. The 2nd-floor suites are well priced, especially considering they come with three beds, a fully equipped kitchen and a cozy lounge area.

Country Inn & Suites, Panama Canal (☎ 211 4500; www.countryinns.com/panamacanalpan; Amador Av & Pelicano Av; d/ste US$110/125; P ⚙ ♨) In a peaceful setting on the water overlooking the canal, this Panamanian installment of the American-owned Country Inn is reminiscent of a retirement community in Panama City, Florida. Cookie-cutter architecture aside, all of the rooms here are outfitted with all the trimmings and the private balconies overlooking the Puente de las Américas are a nice touch. There's also an enormous swimming pool complete with hot tub, which casts a resort-like ambience on the whole property.

EATING

Panama City has literally hundreds of places to eat, from the gritty working-class hole in the wall to the garden bistro, with everything in between. Reflecting its large immigrant population, Panama City also offers an enticing palette of cuisines from every corner of the globe.

In the past, the district of Casco Viejo was the best place in the city for budget travelers to find a cheap plate of rice and beans and whatever meat was cooking out back. Today however, the urban renewal of the district has attracted a number of boutique eateries and European-inspired cafés.

The neighborhood of La Exposición reflects its working-class roots, though there are a number of good spots hidden along its back streets. On the other hand, Bella Vista, the self-proclaimed restaurant district, is the best spot in the city for lightening the wallet and satisfying the tastebuds.

With so many salaried earners on their lunch break, the banking district of El Cangrejo is home to a number of pricey eateries. They also tend to be slighty more conservative and less trendy than the Bella Vista offerings.

Owing to the wealth of city denizens and the popularity of dining out, Panama City is the only place in the country where reservations are a good idea. Although you can probably get a table most days of the week, don't even think about just showing up on Friday or Saturday night without phoning ahead.

For groceries and self-catering, stop by the 24-hour Supermercado Rey, which has several locations throughout the city. Panama City is also home to a number of street vendors selling everything from shaved ices to empanadas.

Casco Viejo ~ Monday

All of the following eateries are featured on Map p80.

EL DONALDO

With nightlife to rival Miami and an old city with European airs, Panama City unabashedly has it all, not to mention the fact that it's less than one hour away from mountains, beaches and rainforests. Not surprisingly, some seriously swish high-rise apartments are going up by the dozen, and it's not just Panamanians that are getting in on the real estate action.

In 2005 the American Association of Retired Persons (AARP) ranked Panama as the No 4 place in the world to retire, dubbing Panama City the 'Dubai of the Western Hemisphere.' This is in part due to the government's generous pension program, which enables foreigners who can prove a guaranteed income of $500 per month to cash in on everything from discounted medical expenses to home-closing costs.

In fact, the real-estate boom is so lucrative that even 'The Donald' himself is getting in on the action. Invigorated by the success of his absurd reality TV show, Donald Trump has already begun construction of the Trump Ocean Club, a US$220 million project that will boast a 65-story condominium tower, an international casino and a private beach club.

Although it will still be years before the flock of American retirees transform Panama into another West Palm Beach, how The Donald can be stopped is anyone's guess.

Café Coca Cola (Av Central; plates US$1-3; ⏱ 7:30-11pm) A neighborhood institution near Plaza Santa Ana, Café Coca Cola is an old-school diner, complete with chess-playing senoras and no-nonsense waitresses. It's also air-conditioned and chock-full of TVs playing the latest Latin American football matches, which makes Coca Cola something of a hang-out spot for Casco Viejo's working class. Of course, all of this shouldn't distract you from the real reason you're here, namely to fill the stomach without breaking the bank on hearty platefuls of rice, beans and the featured meat of the day.

Granclement (Av Central; gelato US$2.50-3.50; ⏱ noon-8pm) Nothing beats the tropical heat like a cool scoop of mango gelato and there's no better gourmet spot in the city than this European-style ice cream shop. With French owners who refuse to skimp on quality or authenticity, Granclement serves up the perfect accompaniment to a leisurely stroll through the old streets of Casco Viejo or along the waterfront. If you want to speed things up a bit however, there's also a real Italian espresso machine on the premises that will get you exactly where you need to go.

Brooklyn Cafe (Calle 1a Oeste; coffee & pastry US$2-3, meal US$5-6; ⏱ 7:30am-7pm daily) Owned by a warm Panamanian woman who fondly recalls her time in the States, this NYC-style café is the perfect spot to linger over a frothy cappuccino and a buttery muffin. Of course, those with bigger appetites should stop by for the daily *plato ejecutivo* (US$5), a slightly upscale version of the traditional Panamanian lunch that is served in restaurants throughout the country. Although it's only been around for a short while, the Brooklyn Cafe is fixing to become the neighborhood coffee shop and it's already won a mountain of praise from scores of devotees.

Café de Asís (☎ 262 9304; Calle 3a Este; mains US$7-12; ⏱ from 6pm) Located on the ground floor of a beautifully restored 19th-century building, Café de Asís is perhaps the most charming spot in Panama City. With outdoor tables spilling out into the Parque Bolívar and over-looking the soaring spires of the Iglesia de San Francisco, the Old World atmosphere here is Casco Viejo at its best. The food at Asís can easily hold its own, and the fresh Peruvian-style ceviche and the house sangría pretty much complements everything on the menu perfectly.

closed sunday

Manolo Caracol (☎ 228 4640; cnr Av Central & Calle 3 Oeste; mains US$10-17; ⏱ noon-3pm & 7-10:30pm Mon-Fri, 7-11pm Sat) Arguably the most famous restaurant in Panama City, Manolo Caracol offers fixed-price five-course lunches (US$10) and seven-course dinners (US$17) that change daily. The menu emphasizes seasonal produce, locally raised meats and freshly caught fish, but it's the imaginative recipes and flawless presentation that have helped vault the restaurant's reputation. Manolo is also located in a historic colonial mansion complete with the original tiling, historic tapestries and hewn-wood furniture, which completes the restaurant's warm and intimate atmosphere.

René Cafe (☎ 262 3487; Calle 7a Este; mains US$12-16; ⏱ noon-3pm & 7-10:30pm Mon-Fri, 7-11pm Sat) With an unbeatable location underneath the shadows of the Iglesia Catedral and overlooking the Plaza de la Independencia, this relative new-comer is primed to become one of the most popular restaurants in the city. Drawing on the successes of Manolo Caracol, René Cafe also offers fixed-price five-course lunches (US$12) and seven-course dinners (US$16) that change daily. However, the difference is that René emphasizes the international nature of the capital by infusing traditional Panamanian favorites with influences as broad as Pan-Asian and Continental cuisine to create some truly unique tapas.

Restaurante Las Bóvedas (☎ 228 8058; Plaza de Francia; mains US$16-22; ⏱ from 6pm, closed Sun) This utterly unique French restaurant is set in the vaults of a 300-year-old fort that housed political prisoners for most of the 19th century – fortunately for the crowds who converge here on the weekends, the ghosts of the past haven't had a deleterious effect on the cooking. Specializing in local seafood with a French twist, the menu varies daily, subject to the catch of the day, but always includes a fish fillet, mixed seafood and a cut of steak just to round things out a bit. A guitarist performs in the last vault nightly except Friday and Saturday, when there's jazz; the music usually starts around 9pm.

La Exposición & Bella Vista
BUDGET & MIDRANGE
Restaurante Vegetariano Mireya (Map p79; cnr Calle Ricardo Arias & Av 3a Sur; items US$2-3; ⏱ 6am-10pm Mon-Sat) Mireya is a budget traveler's delight, especially if you're a vegetarian on a desperate search for

nutrition in this meat-lover's paradise. Tasty cruelty-free offerings include eggplant parmesan, soy burgers and freshly squeezed tropical juices, and there's no shortage of healthy snacks available for purchase. Even if you're not a vegetarian, skip on the cow for a day and mix things up a bit – your body will thank you.

El Rincón Tableño (Map pp76-7; cnr Calle 27 Este & Av Balboa, La Exposición; meals US$2-4; 7:30-11pm) The menu changes daily at this open-air cafeteria-style eatery, but the type of food never does: it's always 100% working-class Panamanian. Typical items include *sopa de carne* (meat soup), *camarones guisados* (shrimp in tomato sauce), and *ropa vieja* (literally, 'old clothes'; marinated shredded beef served as a stew), and there's a choice of a half-dozen or so natural fruit juices, each priced under US$1. Panama City has no shortage of upscale international eateries, but sometimes it's refreshing to simply stick to your roots.

Crêpes & Waffles (Map p79; 269 1574; Calle 47 Este, Bella Vista; mains US$4-7; noon-11pm) Crepe and waffle lovers rejoice at this popular spot in nightlife-rich Bella Vista, which is an ideal place to grab a quick bite before hitting the bars and clubs. Spinach, ricotta and tomato are good standbys, though the truly hungry should opt for the more filling *lomito á la pimienta* (strips of roast beef with pepper sauce). Owing to its increasing popularity, Crêpes & Waffles franchises are popping up all over the city, which is a good thing – there's nothing quite like wrapping your dinner up in a thin and savory pancake package.

Masala Indian Cuisine (Map pp76-7; 225 0105; Calle 42 Este, Bella Vista; mains US$5-9; noon-11pm) Nothing complements hot and humid tropical climes quite like a fiery plate of Indian curry and an ice-cold Kingfisher lager. Housed in a historic Bella Vista mansion that's been redecorated with colorful textiles and Indian art, Masala offers a full complement of traditional dishes from the subcontinent. Although nonadventurous eaters can stick to more Westernized dishes like tikka masala and tandoori chicken, iron-stomach masochistic types should pile on the heat with dishes like lamb vindaloo.

El Pavo Real (Map p79; Av 3 B Sur near Calle Ricardo Arias, Bella Vista; plates US$5-9; noon-midnight Mon-Sat) A mix of Panamanians and expats gather over games of darts or pool at this British pub-restaurant made famous by John le Carré's

thriller *The Tailor of Panama*. (The British Foreign Service employee/best-selling novelist spent a lot of time here while conducting research for his book. The pub-restaurant's owner, Sarah Simpson, is also an ex-BFS employee. Coincidence?) The pub grub here is tasty and filling, and offerings include burgers, chicken-breast sandwiches and fish 'n' chips. There is also occasional live music and there's never a cover charge.

Lum's (Map pp74-5; 317 6303; Corozal Oeste off Carretera Diablo, Bldg 340, Ancón; mains US$6-10; from 11am Mon-Sat) Occupying an old cavernous hangar that once housed machinery for the Panama Canal, Lum's has a long history of serving up ribs, steaks and other hot-off-the-grill mains. Today it's the expat's restaurant of choice, especially since its satellite TV, pool table, foosball and healthy offering of tap beers packs in the crowds on weekends. Located just west of La Exposición in Ancón on the edge of the canal, Lum's is one of the most of the popular restaurants in the Canal Zone.

Gasthaus Bavaria (Map pp76-7; 265 6772; Calle 50, Bella Vista; mains US$7-12; noon-11pm Mon-Sat) Hands down the best German restaurant in the capital, Gasthaus Bavaria serves up all of your favorite dishes from the motherland, as well as enough traditional beers to inspire your own mini-Oktoberfest any time of the year. Although you're welcome to try anything on the menu, the favorite is the Jaeger Schnitzel, a breaded sausage with a mushroom cream sauce – definitely not for the weak of heart. Of course, even if you were foolish enough to leave your appetite behind, don't pass up the complimentary cheesy puffs served alongside pints of rich, fragrant Warsteiner beer.

Ali Baba (Map pp76-7; 225 0159; Panama Yacht Club, Av Balboa near Calle 40 Este, La Exposición; mains US$10-15; lunch & dinner) This landmark restaurant capitalizes on its stunning location on the 2nd floor of the Panama Yacht Club. The views of the bay here are stunning and it's easy to pass away the hours just staring at the boats bobbing up and down on the sea. Popular with the business crowd during lunch hours and with romantic couples at night, Ali Baba features an eclectic menu including Spanish paellas, thin-crust pizzas and, befitting the name, an ample selection of Middle Eastern dishes. There's live music on the weekends.

Restaurante Matsuei (Map p79; 264 9562; Calle Eusebio A Morales, Bella Vista; mains US$11-15; noon-

11:30pm Mon-Sat, 6-11:30pm Sun) Although Japanese restaurants come and go in Panama City with the same frequency as transiting ships, Matsuei has a long and proud history stretching back over a quarter of a century. True to its Japanese roots, the sushi bar stretches across the entire restaurant and is easily one of Panama's finest raw fish experiences – much of the fish is imported from Miami, so you can expect to see everything from *unagi* (eel) to *maguro* (tuna) on offer. Even if you're not tempted by fresh sushi, Matsuei is known for its piping hot sukiyaki and lightly fried tempura, as well as countless other Japanese standards.

TOP END

Martín Fierro (Map p79; ☎ 264 1927; Calle Eusebio A Morales; steaks US$12-20; ☯ noon-3pm & 6-11pm Mon-Sat, noon-9:30pm Sun) For top quality sirloins, porterhouse cuts and filet mignon, there is only one name in Panama City, and it's Martín Fierro. The quality of meat served here is unparalleled – top selections include the best in US-imported New York rib steaks, grass-fed Argentinean fillets and locally raised Panamanian cuts. And of course, nothing washes down braised beef quite like a deep and bold glass of red wine, and Martín Fierro has no shortage of Chilean standards to round out your meal.

Madame Chang (Map p79; ☎ 269 1313; Calle 48, Bella Vista; mains US$14-18; ☯ noon-3pm & 6-11pm Mon-Sat, noon-11pm Sun) The top Chinese restaurant in town offers Oriental opulence in the center of a historic Bella Vista home. Although Western palates fearful of Asian cuisine will find familiar favorites, serious aficionados should choose any of the traditional offerings including *pato al estilo Pekin* (Peking duck), *filete 'tit pang'* (sizzling sliced beef with oyster sauce) and *pichón en pétalos de lechuga* (a combination of duck, chicken and pigeon, served on a bed of crispy rice noodles). In a country where Chinese food is often a sorry excuse to serve up day-old fried rice, Madame Chang is a breath of fresh lotus-scented air.

Eurasia (Map pp76-7; ☎ 264 7859; Calle 48, Bella Vista; mains US$15-20; ☯ noon-3pm Mon-Fri, 7-10:30pm Mon-Sat) Dining at Eurasia is a rich, sensory experience, starting with the lavishly adorned restaurant complete with marble floors and hanging original artwork. The experience continues with impeccable service and daring fusion cuisine including Vietnamese shrimp rolls with orange sauce, and onion soup with tofu and duck breast. Entrées similarly range across the continents with dishes such as jumbo shrimp in tamarind sauce and coconut milk with rice pilaf or tuna breaded with *ajonjolí* (sesame) seeds and caramelized in honey.

Limoncillo (Map p79; ☎ 263 5350; Calle 47 near Calle Uruguay, Bella Vista; mains US$15-20; ☯ noon-3pm & 7-10:30pm Mon-Fri, 7-11pm Sat) Panamanian chef Clara Icaza Angelini cooked at some of the best restaurants in New York before returning to her roots and opening one of Panama City's top restaurants. The menu changes every few months, but you can always count on a fresh and creative assortment of plates with delicate spices, such as pan-roasted grouper with grilled asparagus or sautéed sea scallops with Thai red curry sauce. Incredibly stylish and decorated with an eye for detail, Limoncillo benefits from Angelini's family of artists – many of the paintings, photographs and sculptures in the restaurant were made by her relatives (some are for sale). *Closed Su.*

La Cocotte (Map p79; ☎ 213 8250; Av 3 B Sur, Bella Vista; mains US$15-25; ☯ lunch Mon-Fri, dinner Mon-Sat) Fine Parisian cuisine reigns supreme under the stewardship of Chef Fabien Migny, who studied at the Ecole Hotelliére Belliard while simultaneously training at the renowned Restaurant Jamin de Joel Robouchon in Paris. Appetizers like *pâté de canard* (duck pâté) meld nicely with mains of *confit de canard* (roasted duck) or fresh salmon in a red wine sauce, and everything is expertly topped off with *crêpes soufflées au chocolat* (chocolate soufflé crepes). The fixed-price lunch (US$13) is a good way to sample Migny's cuisine without breaking the bank, though there are certainly less enjoyable ways to spend your hard-earned money.

Restaurante 1985 (Map p79; ☎ 263 8541; Chalet Suizo, Calle Eusebio A Morales; plates from US$20; ☯ 11:30am-midnight Mon-Fri, 5:30pm-midnight Sat & Sun) Restaurant goers with very large expense accounts should consider a meal of unparalleled decadence at Restaurante 1985, one of the city's most highly regarded culinary institutions. Located inside the Chalet Suizo (Swiss Chalet), this French restaurant provides impeccable service, elegant decor and an extensive wine list. *Steak morilles* (steak with morel mushrooms), lobster Provençal, shrimp cognac and the many changing daily specials highlight the talents of Chef Willy Diggelmann.

El Cangrejo & Bella Vista

Niko's Cafe (Map pp74-5; Calle 51 Este near Vía España; mains US$2-4; ☺ 24hr) Spawned from the dreams of a Greek immigrant who once sold food from a cart, Niko's has become one of Panama City's most successful restaurant chains, with several locations throughout the city. The secret is simple: serve fresh, hearty portions of inexpensive food in a laid-back cafeteria-style ambience and the crowds will file in. Open 24 hours to serve all of your late-night snack attacks, Niko's serves up everything from made-to-order breakfasts, Panamanian staples, Greek gyros, Italian pastas and every kind of meat from grilled chicken and fried cutlets to greasy burgers to T-bone fillets.

Restaurante y Pizzeria Napoli (Map p79; ☎ 262 2446; Calle Estudiante at Calle 16; pizzas US$4-8; ☺ 11am-11pm Wed-Mon) Panama's oldest pizzeria serves up delicious, wood-fired pizzas at a no-nonsense speed. Although they're piping hot and extra cheesy, the pizzas aren't the only thing on the menu, and you can't go wrong with any of the past offerings such as ravioli or a hearty dish of fettuccine alfredo. Of course, no matter what you choose, you'll enjoy the classic atmosphere of open-air tables with red-checked tablecloths and rapidly moving waiters shuffling between the tables.

Machu Picchu (Map p79; ☎ 264 9308; Calle Eusebio A Morales 16, El Cangrejo; mains US$7-10; ☺ 11am-3pm & 6-11pm) Machu Picchu is a low-key but traditional restaurant where blue-vested waiters make the rounds among a mix of Peruvian expats and in-the-know Panamanians. True to its roots, the authentic menu has a long list of Peruvian specialities including pan-fried sea bass served with cream sauce, topped with shrimp or a half-a-dozen other ways. And of course, nothing quenches your thirst and cleans your palate quite like a pisco sour, Peru's sometimes sweet and sometimes tart national drink.

Parillada Jimmy (Map pp74-5; ☎ 226 1096; Av Cincuentenario; mains US$7-12; ☺ 11:30am-11:30pm) The long open porch with high ceilings and wrought-iron chandeliers lend a farmhouse feel to this Panama City institution. The grill flares in the corner giving an indication of the specialities served here, namely some serious cuts of beef, meaty chicken breasts and fresh country-style sausage. Although it's located in the San Francisco district just east of the old Aeropuerto Paitilla, Parillada Jimmy still packs in lunchtime diners from the business district and it's always hopping with the after-work crowd.

Greenhouse (Map p79; ☎ 269 6846; Calle Uruguay; mains US$8-12) This stylish restaurant and lounge draws its name from its enclosed patio, which puts you in touch with tropical greenery – inside, stained-glass windows, an artfully displayed fish tank and a nice, relaxed vibe completes the setting. Pleasant but sedate waiters bring warm towels as refreshment, before you dine on a variety salads and tasty bites from the grill, such as *corvina* (flavorful white fish) and steak burgers, as well as wraps and quesadillas. At night, the restaurant puts the electronic music up a notch as a young good-looking crowd holds court over round upon round of expertly mixed martinis.

Siete Mares (Map p79; ☎ 264 0144; Calle Guatemala; mains US$12-18; ☺ 11am-3pm & 6-11pm) Artful lighting and a few impressionistic paintings scattered along the exposed brick walls sets the mood for some serious seafood dining, which attracts suits from all corners of Panama City's financial district. The speciality here is lobster, though if the sea hasn't been bountiful, you can choose from a wide variety of options including sea bass, jumbo shrimp and red snapper. Despite the fact that the street is lined with countless other eateries, the crowds flocking in front of Siete Mares are testament to the fact that seafood here is about as fresh as it gets.

DRINKING

Bars and clubs open and close with alarming frequency in Panama City, though generally speaking, nightlife is stylish, sophisticated and fairly pricey. With that said, the well-to-do denizens of Panama City love a good scene, so it's worth scrubbing up, donning some nice threads and parting with a bit dough. You might regret blowing your budget in the morning, but that's the price you pay to party with the beautiful people.

Big areas for nightlife are localized in four parts of town: Casco Viejo, La Exposición, Bella Vista and the Causeway. Bars in Casco Viejo are generally subdued and cater to an older crowd, though there's nothing quite like sipping a perfectly crafted cocktail in a crumbling colonial mansion.

As one of the older parts of the modern downtown, La Exposición isn't nearly as hip and trendy as some of the more fashionable

---

LOCAL LORE: CAPTAIN MORGAN

After sacking Panamá in 1671, Captain Henry Morgan burnt the city to the ground, massacred its inhabitants and made off with the richest booty in the Americas, though his infamous exploits didn't end there. Because his actions violated a peace treaty between England and Spain, Morgan was arrested and conducted to England the following year, but he was acquitted on the questionable account that he had no prior knowledge of the treaty. In 1674 Morgan was knighted before departing for Jamaica to take up the post of Lieutenant Governor.

Although Captain Morgan is best remembered for his nefarious exploits at sea, the last several years of his life in Port Royal (the 'Sodom of the New World') is the stuff of legends. At the time, the pirate capital of the Caribbean was known as the richest, nastiest city in the world, and was famous for its gaudy displays of wealth and loose morals. Here, Morgan spent the last years of his life spending the riches of Panamá, though the actual events surrounding his death remain a mystery.

In 1688, at the age of 53, Captain Morgan suddenly died, leaving behind an immense personal fortune. Although his death has been attributed to tuberculosis and dropsy (edema), the local lore has it that world's most infamous pirate simply drank himself to death – it's fitting that Captain Morgan's legacy should live on in the form of syrupy-sweet spiced rum.

---

districts. However, there are still a few hidden gems out there, so keep your ears to the ground and don't be afraid to explore.

The district of Bella Vista is home to the always fashionable Calle Uruguay, a strip of trendy bars and clubs that's reminiscent of Miami's South Beach. Although you have to pay to play here, though there's nothing quite like a night in Panama City's playground of the rich and sexy.

At the Isla Flamenco shopping center on the Causeway, you'll find a number of nightlife spots, ranging from packed dance clubs to more low-key watering holes. However, the vibe here is not unlike what you might find in Las Vegas, so shop around and pick the theme that you like, be it a pirate bar or an Egyptian club.

For the latest on what's happening in the city, be sure to pick up a copy of *La Prensa* (www.prensa.com in Spanish). Weekend listings are available in the Thursday and Friday editions or on its website; look for the 'De Noche' section.

Half the fun of drinking in Panama City is finding a hidden gem, though here's a few of our favorite spots to get you started.

Platea (Map p80; Calle 1a Oeste) With exposed brick walls and a small, intimate stage, this jazz club wouldn't feel out of place in Greenwich Village, minus the Spanish of course. As the night wears on, a more mixed crowd is attracted to this swinging spot, making for some excellent people-watching over expertly crafted *mojitos*.

Bolero (Map pp76-7; Calle 42) This elegant, understated Cuban bar and restaurant hosts live salsa and merengue bands on Friday and Saturday, and a live DJ most other nights. Although there's no dance floor here, the young and fiesty crowd occasionally dance among the tables when the music starts to peak.

Player's (Map pp76-7; Calle 42) This British-style pub is outfitted with dark-wood furniture and gleaming fixtures, which lends a proper Anglo feel to this watering hole. The pool table here is hopping most weeknights, and the Friday night rock performances draw in a good mix of Panamanians and expats from around the globe.

Mango's (Map pp74-5; Plaza Edison, Vía Brasil) Despite being a little far away from the action, this hidden bar-restaurant becomes a fairly popular gathering spot on weekends. Local DJs play a wide mix of sounds ranging from hip-hop and drum 'n' bass to electronica and reggaeton, sometimes packing the dance floor, sometimes clearing it.

Spot (Map p79; Calle 47) One of Panama City's best karaoke bars, this place attracts would-be divas and maestros who belt out Latin favorites to the often packed bar room. The Spot has a festive vibe and it's a good place to meet some new friends, especially if you don't mind embarrassing the hell out of yourself.

Wine Bar (Map p79; Av Eusebio A Moralel) This stylish Italian bistro showcases the fruit of the vine, with over 200 selections on offer from around the globe. Accompanying the wine list are appetizers like smoked salmon with toasted almonds and carpaccio with capers. Live jazz starts at 9pm most nights of the week.

La Kava (Map p79; Calle Uruguay) The handsome La Kava attracts a young indie-rocker crowd and an eclectic mix of other laid-back types. Local rock bands perform on Thursday nights, and if old Nirvana covers don't cut it, you can always retreat to the mellow lounge space in the next room.

Habibi's (Map p79; Calle Ricardo Arias) The open patio is a scenic spot for Lebanese cuisine, while the upstairs is a colorful lounge resembling a sheik's tent where you can imbibe *cuba libres* (rum and cokes) after taking a few hits off the hookah. A belly dancer often appears on Friday and Saturday nights to add a splash of color to the scenery.

Traffic Island (Map pp74–5; Isla Flamenco Shopping Plaza) Located on Isla Amador, Traffic Island has a stunning open-air location and boasts sweeping views across the water to the Panama City's soaring skyline. Salsa and merengue set the tone for a variety of tropical drinks, and if the music puts you in the mood, there's plenty of nearby places to dance in the complex.

ENTERTAINMENT

It's hard not to have a good night out in Panama City, especially since the capital is home to the most sophisticated clubs in Central America.

If you're not looking to get blotto, there are numerous ways to spend a moonlit (or rainy) evening in the city. A good place to start is the arts section in the Sunday edition of *La Prensa* or the back pages of the *Panama News*.

Panamanians have a love affair with Hollywood and there are many air-conditioned cinemas in and around the city. Panamanians also love to gamble, and there are a few flashy casinos where you can get in on the action. There are also opportunities in the capital to see traditional folk dancing and live performances of music and theatre.

Nightclubs

Panama City has a wide selection of nightclubs – gay, straight, cruisy and sedate. DJs usually pull from a broad repertoire, from salsa and merengue to UK and US '80s classics, with electronic music (house, drum 'n' bass) liberally added to the mix. Most clubs don't open their doors before 11pm, so plan

your evening accordingly. As in most other Latin American cities, people dress to the nines when they go out – women typically don a skirt, blouse and heels for a night out dancing, while men tend to stick to slacks or designer jeans and a collared shirt. You can be sure that you'll constantly be surrounded by the latest fashions, so go all out and dress to impress. Note that at most clubs, you'll be denied entry if you're wearing sneakers or shorts.

Due to a severe parking shortage, it's best to take a taxi if you go out in the Calle Uruguay area, even if you're renting a vehicle in Panama. Also, remember to bring identification with you, as you might be asked for it. Most clubs have a cover charge of US$5 to US$15, though this varies greatly depending on the place, the date and the time.

Much like the city's bar scene, clubs come and go, and what's hot one minute is on the out the next. However, don't be afraid to follow the crowds and use your intuition – there's no shortage of great spots to party it up.

Here are a few of our favorite clubs to get you started.

S6is (Map p79; Calle Uruguay) Pronounced '*seis*' (as in the number 'six'), this intimate club plays a fine selection of electronic music to a laid-back mix of people. This is a good choice if you want to bypass the mega-club scene and just kick back with a good cocktail and soak up the loungey vibe.

Liquid (Map p79; Calle 53 Este) This sleek and ultramodern electronic club is heavy on the polished metal and the tubular lighting. Rotating DJs spin even heavier beats from around the globe to a fairly well-dressed crowd that's not afraid to let their hair down and sweat it out.

Deep Room (Map p79; Calle 48) Panama City's favored after-hours spot, Deep Room doesn't get going until sometime after 2am. However, the multilevel space attracts top DJs and there's no better place to be when the sun is about to rise above the horizon.

Opah (Map p79; Calle 47) The latest incarnation of this storied Bella Vista Club, Opah is a favored spot for the beautiful people and their hangers-on. The polished club is a good spot for dancing. Electronic music, '80s and salsa are the DJs' repertoire of choice, though you really never know what's in store for you here.

Rock Café (Map p79; Calle 53 Este) One of three large clubs in the Plaza Florida, Rock Café packs in the crowds with its steady stream of everything from classic rock to modern riffs. Its all-you-can-drink nights for one low price is a great way to live it up and cancel whatever it is you have planned for tomorrow.

Bongo (Map pp76-7; Calle 42) This combination live-music hall and dance club is one of the best spots in the city to hear (and dance to) live salsa bands. DJs fill the space the rest of the time, though the atmosphere is always festive and the music is always danceable.

Zoomba (Map pp76-7; Plaza Pacifica, Punta Pacifica) Located in the upscale district of Punta Pacifica, this stylish club attracts a mixed-crowd, but everyone is certainly well-to-do. This club has a much warmer feel than other dance clubs, and features an eclectic mix of music including salsa, ambient and world beats.

Bucaneros (Map pp74-5; Isla Flamenco, Amador) Sure, the cowboy theme is a bit overdone at this popular dance spot at the end of the Causeway, but a good time is certainly had by all here. Plus, you can't beat the open-air location, the tropical cocktails and the stunning views of Panama City's illuminated skyline.

Karnak (Map pp74-5; Isla Flamenco, Amador) Around the corner from Bucaneros, this Egyptian-themed club is even more over-the-top than its cowboy brethren. Although arguably better suited to Las Vegas, there's a fun time to be had here and the energetic crowds certainly enjoy themselves.

GAY & LESBIAN VENUES

Although Panama City is far from being a liberal or even tolerant society when it comes to the topic of gay rights, the city does have several excellent gay clubs. Be sure to check out the nightlife-rich websites www.farraurbana.com, www.rumbanight .com and www.chemibel.com, which list new gay clubs in town as well as upcoming parties (in Spanish).

BLG (Map p79; Calle 49) Located in the heart of Panama City's nightlife scene, this out-and-proud club serves an incredibly diverse clientele. Owing to its trendy location and increasing popularity, BLG sees its share of top-notch DJs, and it's hard not to have a good time when there's a free open bar included in the cover charge (from US$25).

Punto G (Map p79; Calle D) Sexed-up bare-chested bartenders in spandex and cowboy hats serve the crowd at this raucous establishment, and the occasional tranny show makes for a fine interlude between the serious dancing. This unmarked club is next to the restaurant Ginza Teppanyaki, though the interior is certainly more lavish than its nondescript exterior.

Glam (Map pp74-5; Av Ricardo J Alfaro, Tumba Muerto) In an industrial area north of downtown, Glam proudly stands as the biggest gay dance club in the country. Saturday is generally the best night to go, when a wild and celebratory crowd fills the dance floor until late in the morning, though talented DJs spin house, drum 'n' bass, soul and Latin classics here every night. This place is best reached by taxi – it's located in front of the Club de Montana.

Cinemas

Panama City's modern movie houses show mostly Hollywood films (with Spanish subtitles) for US$2 to US$4. For listings and show times, pick up a copy of *La Prensa* or go to www.prensa.com and click on 'cine.'

Alhambra (Map p79; Vía España, El Cangrejo) Occasionally screens independent films.

Cinemark (Map pp76-7; Albrook mall) Next to the Albrook bus terminal.

Kinomaxx (Map pp76-7; Multicentro shopping center) Near Punta Paitilla.

Casinos

None of the casinos in Panama City are on the verge of stealing business away from the megacasinos of Las Vegas, but there are three attractive and popular houses of chance in the capital city. All are located inside top hotels: the Hotel Caesar Park (p93), the Miramar Inter-Continental (p92) and the Hotel Riande Continental (p93).

Traditional Dance

A good place to see traditional Panamanian folk dancing is the **Restaurante-Bar Tinajas** (Map p79; ☎ 263 7890; Av 3a A Sur near Av Frederico Boyd; ⊗ closed Sun) Sure, it's touristy, but nicely done just the same. Shows are staged here on Tuesday, Thursday, Friday and Saturday nights at 9pm; there's a US$5 entertainment fee, as well as a US$5.50 minimum per person for drinks and food. It is highly recommended to make a reservation before dining.

Theater

Teatro Anita Villalaz (Map p80; ☎ 211 4017; Plaza de Francia) A historic spot in Casco Viejo to see live performances.

Teatro En Círculo (Map pp74-5; ☎ 261 5375; Av 6 C Norte near Vía Transístmica) Plays and musicals are scheduled regularly.

Teatro Nacional (Map p80; ☎ 262 3525; Av B at Calle 2) Casco Viejo's lovely 19th-century playhouse stages ballets and concerts in addition to plays.

SHOPPING

The city has a number of markets where you can purchase handicrafts native to regions throughout the country. Here you'll find a range of handmade goods from baskets made in Emberá villages to *molas* (traditional textiles) from Kuna Yala.

Mi Pueblito (Map pp74-5; Cerro Ancón; admission US$1; ☺ 10am-10pm Tue-Sun) Scattered throughout this life-size replica of rural villages you'll encounter a huge selection of high-quality crafts – perfect for one-stop shopping. For more information on this complex, see p88.

Mercado Nacional de Artesanías (Map p84; Panamá Vieja; ☺ 9am-4pm Mon-Sat, to 1pm Sun) With a picturesque location next to the historic ruins of Panama Viejó, this large artisan's market is a great place to shop for memorable souvenirs. For more information, see p82.

Mercado de Buhonerías y Artesanías (Map pp76-7; ☺ 9am-5pm Mon-Sat) This bustling outdoor spot, located behind the Museo Antropológico Reina Torres de Araúzis, is a great place to shop, especially if you've just finished perusing the anthropology museum and have a new-found appreciation for Panama's crafts.

Baskets

The Emberá and Wounaan people in Darién Province (p275) produce some beautiful woven baskets of incredibly high quality. There are two types: the utilitarian and the decorative. The utilitarian baskets are made primarily from the *chunga* palm, but can contain bits of other plants, vines, bark and leaves. They are usually woven, using various plaiting techniques, from single plant strips of coarse texture and great strength, and are rarely dyed. These baskets are often used for carrying seeds or harvesting crops.

The decorative baskets are much more refined, usually featuring many different colors and are created from palm materials of the *nahuala* bush and the *chunga* palm. The dyes

are 100% natural, and are extracted from fruits, leaves, roots and bark. Typical motifs are of butterflies, frogs, toucans, trees and parrots. The baskets are similar in quality to the renowned early 20th-century Chemehuevi Indian baskets of California.

You can often buy baskets at any of the markets.

Huacas

It's possible to purchase high-quality replicas of *huacas* – golden objects made on the isthmus centuries before the Spanish conquest and placed with indigenous leaders at the time of burial. The indigenous population believed in an afterlife, and the *huacas* were intended to accompany and protect their souls on the voyage to the other world.

The *huacas* were mainly items of adornment, the most fascinating items being the three-dimensional figure pendants. Most took the form of a warrior, crocodile, jaguar, frog or condor. Little else is known about the exact purpose of these golden figures, but each probably held mystical, spiritual or religious meaning.

You can purchase exact (solid gold) and near-exact (gold-plated) reproductions of these palm-size objects. They are available at reasonable cost at **Reprosa** (Map p79; ☎ 269 0457; cnr Av 2 Sur & Calle 54 Este; ☺ 9am-7pm Mon-Sat). Also available here are well-priced necklaces made of black onyx and other gemstones. If you're looking for something special to bring back for a loved one, this is the place to come.

Jewelry

Because of their proximity to mineral-rich Colombia and Brazil, the jewelry stores here often have high-quality gems at excellent prices. Beware: there are many fake gems on the world market, as well as many flawed gems that have been altered to appear more valuable than they really are. One of the city's most reputable jewelry stores is **Joyería La Huaca** (Map p79; cnr Calle Ricardo Arias & Vía España) in front of the Hotel Riande Continental. A high-quality sapphire ring there costs about one-third less than you would pay in Europe or the USA.

Malls

The capital has a growing number of shopping malls, all of which highlight the increasing love of Americana in Panama. Consumerism aside, these air-conditioned spots can be a good place to escape the heat, especially if you're travelling with the kids.

Albrook mall (Map pp76-7; 10am-9pm Mon-Sat, 11am-8pm Sun) Next to the bus terminal, this mall has a cinema, supermarket and dozens of stores.

El Dorado mall (Map pp74-5; Vía Ricardo J Alfaro; 10am-9pm Mon-Sat, 11am-8pm Sun) Near one of Panama City's newer Chinatowns, El Dorado also has restaurants, shops and a cinema.

Isla Flamenco Shopping Plaza (Map pp74-5; 10am-10pm) Small, but nearby you'll find the best selection of open-air restaurants in the city.

Multicentro (Map pp76-7; 10am-9pm) Also has a cinema and shops, along with many outdoor restaurants.

Molas

A popular handicraft souvenir from Panama is the *mola* – a colorful, intricate, multilayered appliqué textile sewn by Kuna women – for more information, see p263. Small, simple souvenir *molas* are widely available in Panama City, and can be bought for as little as US$5, but the best ones can fetch several hundred dollars.

Most upscale hotels have authentic *molas* for sale in their gift shops, though **Flory Saltzman Molas** (Map p79; 223 6963; Calle 49 B Oeste) has the best selection.

GETTING THERE & AWAY
Air

International flights arrive at and depart from **Tocumen International Airport** (238 4160), 35km northeast of the city center. For information on getting to and from the airport see p78.

International airlines serving Panama City include:

American Airlines 269 6022
Continental Airlines 263 9177
COPA 227 2672
Delta 214 8118
Grupo TACA 360 2093
LAB 264 1330
Lufthansa 223 9208
Mexicana 264 9855
United Airlines 225 6519

Panama's domestic airlines are **Air Panama** (316 9000; www.flyairpanama.com/tickets) and **Aero perlas** (315 7500; www.aeroperlas.com).

Domestic flights depart from **Albrook airport** (315 0403), aka Aeropuerto Marcos A Gelabert, in the former Albrook Air Force Station near the canal. For information on getting to and from the airport, see p78.

All flights within Panama last under one hour. Prices vary according to season and availability. Flights within Panama are inexpensive and will save you lots of time getting around. Flights listed below are approximate one-way fares:

Bocas del Toro (US$60; Air Panama 2 per day Tue, Thu, Sat & Sun, 1 per day Mon, Tue, Fri Aeroperlas 2 per day Mon-Fri, 1 Sat-Sun)
Chitré (US$25; Air Panama 2 per week)
David (US$60; Air Panama 2 per day Mon-Sat, 1 per day Sun Aeroperlas 2 per day Mon-Sun)
El Porvenir (San Blás) (US$35; Air Panama 1 per day Aeroperlas 3 per week)
Isla Contadora (US$30; Air Panama 4 per day Sat & Sun, 2 per day Mon-Fri Aeroperlas 4 per day Sat & Sun, 2 per day Mon-Fri)
La Palma (Darién) (US$40; Air Panama 1 per week Aeroperlas 3 per week)
Playón Chico (US$40; Aeroperlas per day)
Puerto Obaldía (Darién) (US$40; Aeroperlas 1 per week)
Río Sidra (San Blás) (US$35; Air Panama 1 per day Aeroperlas 4 flights per week)

Boat

Barcos Calypso (314 1730; roundtrip US$10) has departures to Isla Taboga from Panama City at 8:30am and 3:00pm Monday, Wednesday and Friday, 8:30am on Tuesday and Thursday and 8:30am, 10:30am and 4:00pm on Saturday and Sunday. Ferries depart Isla Taboga at 9:30am and 4:00pm Monday, Wednesday and Friday, 4:30pm on Tuesday and Thursday and 9:00am, 3:00pm and 5:00pm on Saturday and Sunday.

Ferries depart from La Playita de Amador, which is located behind the Centro de Exhibiciones Marinas on the Causeway (p86). The easiest way to reach the dock is by taxi (US$4 to US$6).

For more information on Isla Taboga, see p115.

For information on sailing to Colombia, see p263.

Bus

The shiny and new Albrook terminal, near the Albrook airport, is a convenient one-stop location for most buses leaving Panama City. The terminal includes a food court, banks, shops, a sports bar, storage room, bathrooms and showers. A mall lies next door, complete with a supermarket and cinema.

Local buses from the city's major routes stop at the terminal, and behind the station there are direct buses to and from Tocumen International Airport. To get to the station from the city, take any of the frequent buses that pass in front of the Legislative Palace or along Vía España (look for the 'via Albrook' sign in the front window).

Major bus routes are:

Aguadulce (US$5; 3hr; 33 daily, 6am-8pm)

Antón (US$3.50; 2hr; every 20min, 6am-6pm)

Cañita (US$3.75; 2½hr; 11 daily, 6:40am-5pm)

Chame (US$2.50; 1¼hr; 37 daily, 5:10am-10pm)

Changuinola (US$24; 10hr; 1 per day at 8pm)

Chitré (US$6; 4hr; hourly, 6am-11pm)

Colón (US$2.50; 2hr; every 20min; 5am-11pm)

David (US$12.50; 7-8hr; 13 per day; expresos US$15; 5-6 hr; 2 per day at 10:45pm & midnight)

El Copé (US$6; 4hr; 9 daily, 6am-6pm)

El Valle (US$4; 2½hr; many buses, 7am-7pm)

Las Tablas (US$6.50; 4½hr; hourly, 6am-7pm)

Macaracas (US$7; 5hr; 5 daily, 7am-3:30pm)

Ocú (US$6; 4hr; 8 daily, 7am-5pm)

Penonomé (US$4; 2½hr; 48 daily, 4:45am-11pm)

Pesé (US$6.50; 4½hr; 6 daily, 8:15am-3:45pm)

San Carlos (US$3.50; 1½hr; 25 daily, 5:10am-10pm)

San José, Costa Rica (Panaline US$25; 1 daily; noon; Tica Bus US$25; 11am)

Santiago (US$6; 4hr; 20 daily)

Soná (US$7; 6hr; 6 daily, 8:30am-6pm)

Villa de Los Santos (US$6; 4hr; 18 daily; 6am-11pm)

Yaviza (US$15; 7-10hr; 8 per day; 5am-3:45pm)

Buses to Balboa, Ancón and the Canal Zone (Miraflores and Pedro Miguel Locks, Paraíso and Gamboa) depart from the bus stop on Av Roosevelt across from the Legislative Palace. All fares are less than US$1.

Car

Many car rental agencies lie clustered around Calle 49 B Oeste in El Cangrejo. Daily rates run from US$30 to US$55 per day for the most economical cars, including insurance and unlimited kilometers.

Rental car companies in Panama City include:

Avis Albrook airport (☎ 264 0722, 315 0434); Tocumen airport (☎ 238 4056)

Barriga Tocumen airport (☎ 269 0221, 238 4495)

Budget Albrook airport (☎ 263 8777, 315 0201); Tocumen airport (☎ 238 4069)

Dollar Tocumen airport (☎ 270 0355, 238 4032)

Hertz Albrook airport (☎ 264 1111, 315 0418); Tocumen airport (☎ 238 4081)

National Albrook airport (☎ 265 2222, 315 0416); Tocumen airport (☎ 238 4144)

Thrifty Albrook airport (☎ 264 1402, 315 0144); Tocumen airport (☎ 238 4955)

Train

The **Panama Railway Company** (PCRC; Map pp74-5; ☎ 317 6070; www.panarail.com; Carr Gaillard) operates a glass-domed luxury passenger train from Panama City to Colón (US$22 one-way, US$35 for a round-trip), leaving at 7:15am and returning at 5:15pm every day. It's a lovely ride that follows the canal, and at times the train is surrounded by nothing but thick vine-strewn jungle. If you want to relive the hey-day of luxury train travel for an hour or two, this is definitely the way to do it. For more information on the history of this storied railway, see the boxed text on p246.

GETTING AROUND
Bicycle

The best spot to rent bicycles in Panama City is at **Bicicletas Rali** (☎ 220 3844; ☷ 8am-6pm Sat & Sun), which operates a booth at the Causeway entrance. You can rent a bicycle for US$2.50 per hour or rollerblades for US$1 per hour.

Bus

Panama City has a good network of local buses (nicknamed *diablos rojos* or 'red devils'), which run every day from around 5am to 11pm. A ride costs US$0.25, and we promise you've never seen anything quite like these tricked-out street rockets. Buses run along the three major west-to-east routes: Av Central–Vía España, Av Balboa– Vía Israel, and Av Simón Bolívar–Vía Transístmica. The Av Central–Vía España streets are one-way going west for much of the route; eastbound buses use Av Perú and Av 4 Sur; these buses will take you into the banking district of El Cangrejo. Buses also run along Av Ricardo J Alfaro (known as Tumba Muerto). There are plenty of bus stops along the street, but you can usually hail one from anywhere. Many of these buses stop at the Albrook bus terminal, the bus station near the Albrook airport.

The Plaza Cinco de Mayo area has three major bus stops. On the corner of Av Central and Av Justo Arosemena, buses depart for Panamá Viejo and the Tocumen International Airport. Buses for the Albrook domestic airport depart in front of the Legislative Palace. Buses depart from the station on Av Roosevelt, opposite the Legislative Palace, for the Balboa and Ancón area (including the Causeway) and other destinations. A ride usually costs no more than US$1.

Taxi

Taxis are plentiful. They are not metered, but there is a list of standard fares that drivers are supposed to charge, measured by zones.

The fare for one zone is a minimum of US$1; the maximum fare within the city is US$4. An average ride, crossing a couple of zones, would cost US$1.25 to US$2, plus US$0.25 for each additional passenger. Always agree on a fare before you get into the cab. Taxis can also be rented for US$8 an hour.

Watch out for unmarked large-model US cars serving hotels as cabs. Their prices are up to four times that of regular street taxis. You can phone for a taxi:

America ☎ 223 7694
America Libre ☎ 223 7342
Latino ☎ 224 0677
Metro ☎ 264 6788
Taxi Unico Cooperativa ☎ 221 3191

Panamá Province

Panamá Province has a rich history of pirates, plunder, pearls and the world's most daring engineering marvel. Even before Henry Morgan's raid of Panamá, pirates such as Sir Francis Drake used Isla Taboga as a hideout and springboard for attacks on the mainland. Further off the coast, an even better hideout was the remote Archipiélago de las Perlas (Pearl Islands), which was named by Vasco Núñez de Balboa upon learning of the abundance of pearls in this area.

Today Panamá Province is more famed for the canal than for anything else. Cutting through the province, the canal can be explored by visiting its locks, riding a boat through its watery recesses or hiking along its jungle-clad shore. The entirety of the Panama Canal watershed is federally protected land, which makes the area one of the most accessible and best-studied tropical rainforests on the planet.

The province's attractions serve as popular day trips or minibreaks for Panama City's weekend warriors. The charming island village of Taboga is undergoing something of a revival, but its unhurried pace hasn't changed much since the days when visitors such as Gauguin sojourned here. Along the coastline, a string of beaches attracts everyone from sun-worshippers to wave-seeking surf junkies. Farther flung are the Archipiélago de las Perlas, which draw everyone from the moneyed elite to the occasional *Survivor* television series.

Although it's the most populated province in the country, Panamá can be as big or as small as you want it to be. Tranquil rainforests and sizzling beach scenes are yours to explore and the comforts of the capital are never more than an hour away.

HIGHLIGHTS

- Laying eyes on the awe-inspiring **Panama Canal** (opposite), an engineering marvel in the midst of an expansion

- Spotting feathered friends along Pipeline Road in **Parque Nacional Soberanía** (p110), one of the world's premier bird-watching sites

- Visiting the world-famous tropical biology center on **Monumento Natural Isla Barro Colorado** (p113), the most studied patch of rainforest in the world

- Escaping the urban grind of the capital on a day trip to the flower-dotted island of **Isla Taboga** (p115)

- Soaking up the sun, surfing gnarly breaks and making the most of romantic hideaways along the Pacific Coast **beaches** (p122)

| POPULATION: 1,460,000 | AREA: 11,887 SQ KM | ELEVATION: SEA LEVEL TO 1000M |

HISTORY

Throughout the 16th and 17th centuries, the Spanish used the isthmus as a transit point for shipping plundered gold between Peru and Spain. The main route was the famous cobblestoned Camino Real (King's Hwy), which linked Panamá to Portobelo, and served as the only road across the isthmus for hundreds of years. In the 1700s, however, the route was abandoned in favor of shipping gold around Cape Horn owing to repeated pirate attacks, the most famous of which was Sir Henry Morgan's sacking of Panamá Viejo in 1671.

As early as 1524, King Charles V of Spain had ordered a survey to be undertaken to determine the feasibility of constructing a transisthmian water route. But it wasn't until the 1880s that any country dared to undertake the momentous project of carving a trench through dense jungles and mountains. The first canal attempt came from a French team led by Ferdinand-Marie de Lesseps, who was riding high on his prior success building the Suez Canal.

Sadly, he and his colleagues grossly underestimated the difficulties and some 22,000 workers died during the construction attempt. The majority of deaths were due to yellow fever and malaria, which lead to the establishment of an enormous quarantine on Isla Taboga – at the time, it was not yet known that mosquitoes were the disease vector.

Several decades later, the Americans learned from the mistakes of the French and succeeded in completing the canal in 1914. Today the waterway rests firmly in the hands of the Panamanian government and the face of the canal is rapidly changing as ambitious expansion plans slowly unfold.

AROUND PANAMA CITY

No visit to Panama City would be complete without taking a day trip to its famous waterway – just remember that the Canal Zone is much, much more than just the canal.

PANAMA CANAL

The canal is truly one of the world's greatest engineering marvels. Stretching for 80km from Panama City on the Pacific side to Colón on the Atlantic side, the canal cuts right through the Continental Divide. Nearly 14,000 vessels pass through the canal each year and ships worldwide are built with the dimensions of the Panama Canal's locks (305m long and 33.5m wide) in mind.

Ships pay according to their weight, with the average fee around US$30,000. The highest amount paid was around US$200,000, paid in 2001 by the 90,000-ton French cruise ship Infinity; the lowest amount was US$0.36, paid in 1928 by Richard Halliburton, who swam through.

The canal has three sets of double locks: Miraflores and Pedro Miguel Locks on the Pacific side and Gatún Locks on the Atlantic side. Between the locks, ships pass through a huge artificial lake, Lago Gatún, created by the Gatún Dam across the Río Chagres, and the Gaillard Cut, a 14km cut through the rock and shale of the isthmian mountains. With the passage of each ship, a staggering 52 million gallons of fresh water is released into the ocean.

In a referendum that took place in 2006, Panamanian voters overwhelmingly endorsed an ambitious project to expand the Panama Canal. The US$5.25 billion plan, which calls for the largest expansion of the canal since it opened in 1914, will widen and deepen existing navigation channels as well as enable the construction of a third set of locks.

At present, the canal can only handle ships carrying up to 4000 containers, though the new locks and larger channels will allow the passage of ships carrying up to 10,000 containers. Although supporters say that the cost of the upgrades will be met from increased tolls (supplemented by a $2.3 billion loan), opponents claim that when the work is finished in 2014, the canal will still be unable to meet world shipping needs.

For more information on the expansion, see the boxed text on p111. For more information on the history of the canal, see p30.

Sights

MIRAFLORES LOCKS

The easiest and best way to visit the canal is to go to the **Miraflores Visitors' Center** (☎ 276 8325; www.pancanal.com; admission to viewing deck/full-access US$5/8; ☹ 9am-5pm), located just outside Panama City. The recently inaugurated visitors center features a large, four-floor

lonelyplanet.com

PANAMÁ PROVINCE

PANAMÁ PROVINCE

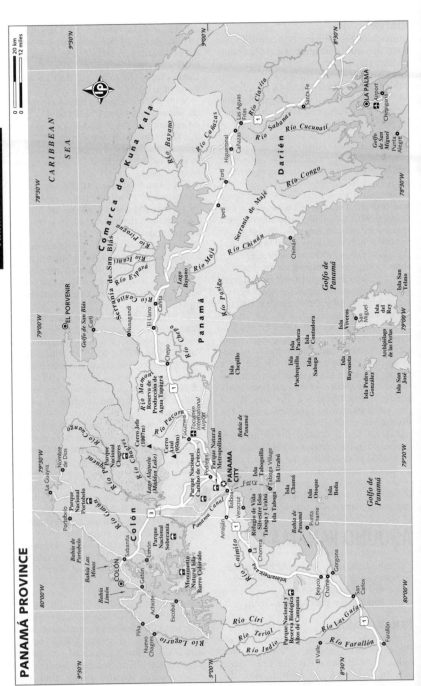

museum, several viewing platforms and an excellent restaurant overlooking the locks. Tip: the best time to view big liners passing through is from 9am to 11am and from 3pm to 5pm, when they are more frequent.

To get there, take any Paraíso or Gamboa bus from the bus stop on Av Roosevelt across from Legislative Palace in Panama City. These buses, passing along the canal-side highway to Gamboa, will let you off at the 'Miraflores Locks' sign on the highway, 12km from the city center. It's about a 15-minute walk to the locks from the sign. Otherwise, you can take a taxi; there's a 30-minute wait at the locks and from there you get driven back to the capital. Expect to pay no more than US$15 for the round-trip – agree on the price beforehand.

OTHER LOCKS

Further north, past the Miraflores Locks, are the **Pedro Miguel Locks**, which can be seen from the highway to Gamboa. One hundred meters beyond the locks there's a parking strip where onlookers can watch ships transit the canal.

On the Caribbean side, the **Gatún Locks** have a viewing stand for visitors and a small replica of the entire canal that lets you place the locks in context. For more information, see p245.

Activities

CANAL TRANSITS

Canal Bay & Tours (☎ 314 1339; www.canalandbay tours.com) offers partial canal transits every Saturday morning. Boats depart from Muelle (Pier) 19 in Balboa, a western suburb of Panama City. They travel through the Miraflores Locks to Lago Miraflores and back, and then cruise out into the bay for scenic views of the city. These tours last 4½ hours and cost US$99 per person – it's a good idea to make reservations in advance. One Saturday every month, the company also offers full transits, from Balboa to Cristóbal on the Caribbean coast, passing all three sets of locks. The transit takes all day (from 7:30am to 5:30pm) and costs US$149. Check the company's website for dates of upcoming transits.

The highly recommended **Ancon Expeditions** (p89) also offers regularly scheduled canal transits, though it's a good idea to book in advance as this is one of the company's most popular offerings.

FISHING

If you're looking to reel in the big one, get in touch with **Panama Canal Fishing** (☎ 6699 0507; www.panamacanalfishing.com), which runs organized tours in the Canal Zone. Their signature tour involves fishing for peacock bass in Lago Gatún and the Chagres river.

CANAL ZONE

The Canal Zone is home to a number of impressive attractions, especially if you're into wildlife-watching, hiking and birding. On a day trip from Panama City, you could first visit the Miraflores Locks, then the Summit Botanical Gardens & Zoo, and finish at the Parque Nacional Soberanía and the Fundación Avifauna Eugene Eisenmann. With prior arrangements, you could also take an organized tour of Isla Barro Colorado, one of the world's most famous tropical research stations, or an Emberá or Wounaan village on the shores of the Río Chagres. If you want to spend the night in the area, it's worth parting with a little cash for the experience of staying at either the Canopy Tower or the Gamboa Rainforest Resort.

All of the attractions in the Canal Zone are located along the highway that runs from Panama City to Gamboa, the small town where the Río Chagres enters Lago Gatún. They can be reached by taking the Gamboa bus, which departs every half-hour from Av Roosevelt across from the Legislative Palace in Panama City.

Summit Botanical Gardens & Zoo

Ten kilometers past the Miraflores Locks are the **Summit Botanical Gardens & Zoo** (☎ 232 4854; admission US$1; ☽ 8am-4pm), which were established in 1923 to introduce, propagate and disseminate tropical plants from around the world into Panama. The gardens are home to over 15,000 plant species, the majority of which are laid out along well-marked trails and paths. Summit is also home to a small zoo, which was originally setup to help GIs identify animals while they were out serving in the jungles.

Today, Summit is expertly managed by a young conservationist who has idealistic plans for the park's future. The star attractions at the zoo include an enormous harpy eagle compound, a tapir area and a rapidly expanding jaguar enclosure. Since the aim of the park is to promote environmental education, strong

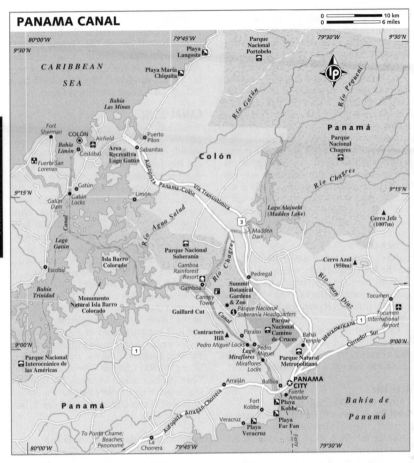

attempts have been made to highlight the native flora and fauna of Panama through a series of natural enclosures that mimic rainforest habitats.

Parque Nacional Soberanía

A few kilometers past Summit, across the border into Colón Province, the 22,104-hectare **Parque Nacional Soberanía** (admission US$3) is one of the most accessible tropical rainforest areas in Panama. It extends much of the way across the isthmus, from Limón on Lago Gatún to just north of Paraíso, and boasts hiking trails that brim with a remarkable variety of wildlife.

Hiking trails in the park include a section of the old **Sendero Las Cruces** (Las Cruces Trail), used by the Spanish to transport gold by mule

train between Panama City and Nombre de Dios, and the 17km **Pipeline Road**, providing access to Río Agua Salud, where you can walk upriver for a swim under a waterfall. A shorter, very easy trail is the **Sendero El Charco** (The Puddle Trail), signposted from the highway, 3km past the Summit Botanical Gardens & Zoo.

Pipeline Road is considered to be one of the world's premier birding sites – not surprisingly, it is intensely popular with birders, especially in the early morning hours. Over 500 different species of birds have been spotted on the trail and it's fairly likely you will spot everything from toucans to trogons.

A healthy cluster of golden-collared manakins is usually found at the end of the

THE FUTURE OF THE CANAL

On October 22, 2006, 78% of voters cast a 'yes' ballot to show their support for an expanded canal. Although only 44% of registered voters turned out for the election, this single event was the only measure of approval that the government needed to usher in a US$5.25 billion mega-project, which will stretch over seven years and finish in conjunction with the canal's centennial in 2014.

Not surprisingly, the country's rich, elite and powerful formed the backbone of the campaign, especially since the increase in traffic and volume through the canal will inject a huge boost into the Panamanian economy. The country will maintain its current role as the maritime logistics center in the Americas and everything from the Free Trade Zone of Colón to the international financial hub of Panama City is likely to boom.

Of course, all of this is ultimately contingent on whether or not the government can actually pull it off, though skeptics should note that this plan has been in the making for over five years. In fact, the organizing minds behind the expansion do not belong to any specific political or financial group, and transcend both the Panama Canal Authority and the central government.

The rational for the expansion is that the demands of the international maritime shipping community have changed. Although as much as 4% of the world's total sea commerce traverses the Panama Canal, the Suez Canal, which is capable of handling larger vessels, serves over 6%. Furthermore, the Panama Canal is already operating at over 90% of its maximum capacity and will reach its saturation point in less than five years.

Supporters also argue that the threat of competition in regards to alternatives to the canal underscores the importance of this project. Nicaragua has already announced plans to construct a US$20 billion interoceanic route and Mexico is currently working to improve its Pacific and Atlantic ports as well as its internal transportation networks.

However, the biggest challenge the Panama Canal faces is to lure in the enormous post-Panamax vessels, which currently depend on either the US Trans-continental Railway or the Suez Canal. But proponents of the canal expansion are hoping that this lucrative market will adopt the Panama route, especially as trade volumes between Asia and the continental east coast increase.

Businesspeople throughout Panama are also forecasting an increase in tourism, especially since the new locks will be able to accommodate large cruise ships. This ultimately will lead to an increase in tourist infrastructure throughout the country, especially in the rapidly developing Canal Zone.

Of course, the biggest question on everyone's mind is how the project is going to be financed, especially considering that there is no guarantee that the expansion will generate higher revenues and offset the construction costs. Furthermore, critics from all sectors of society are pessimistic that the government can actually pull off the project at its stated price tag.

The current plan is to borrow US$2.3 billion, with the remainder of the money to come from both the Panamanian government and the Panama Canal Authority. Since it's estimated that the value of tolls will increase significantly over the next 20 years, the hope is that the expected flow of post-Panamax vessels through the canal will eventually pick up the tab. In the meantime, however, the project will need to acquire an incredible volume of financial resources.

In the end, the success of the project will ultimately be determined by whether or not Panama receives the international backing it's hoping for. Fortunately, Panama has thus far done an exemplary job running the canal since the US pullout, though it remains to be seen whether or not this ambitious project will ruin the country's economy. Commentators from all sides of the political spectrum are chiming in with their views, but the truth of the matter is that, at this point, it's anybody's guess.

first 100m of the road, on the left-hand side. Other typical sounds on the first 2km of the road come from white-bellied antbirds, black-bellied wrens, collared aracaris, keel-billed toucans and buff-throated woodcreepers. Also keep an eye out for rarities such as the tiny hawk, the hook-billed kite, the great jacamar and the black-tailed trogon.

In order to fully appreciate the wildlife on Pipeline, it's wise to hire a guide – it's one of the world's premier birding sites, and it would be a shame to give it short shrift. A recommended

---

BRINGING BACK THE HARPY

Panama's national bird, the harpy eagle, was once found in lowland rainforests throughout Central America. But, these large, bold eagles are often the targets of hunters, which lead to their extirpation from the Canal Zone during the 20th century. The **Peregrine Fund** (www.peregrinefund.org), an international organization dedicated to the conservation of the world's raptors, has created a small captive, breeding nucleus of harpy eagles unable to return to the wild (usually due to injury) at the Neotropical Raptor Center near Panama City.

Ultimately, the Peregrine Fund aims to reinstate these birds throughout their former range, but it's a long road: a female released in 1998 was retrapped and brought back into human care after she repeatedly strayed outside protected areas in the Canal Zone. A male harpy eagle hatched in 1997 and released in Parque Nacional Soberanía in 1998 was not so fortunate – he was shot by a hunter in 2000.

Recognizing that the cooperation of local people is essential in preserving this species, the Peregrine Fund is now also devoting resources to wildlife education in villages surrounding officially protected areas. For more information on the project, and to learn how you can get involved, visit the Peregrine Fund's website.

---

operator is **Ancon Expeditions** (see p89), which runs regular trips to the park. Another option is to stop by the **Fundación Avifauna Eugene Eisenmann** (see right), which is located near the entrance to Pipeline.

The **Río Chagres**, which flows through the park and supplies most of the water for the Panama Canal, is home to several **Emberá** and **Wounaan** communities (see p275). Although the Darién is the ancestral home of these two indigenous groups, a wave of migration to the shores of the Río Chagres commenced in the 1950s. However, following the establishment of the national park in the 1980s, the government culled the practice of slash-and-burn agriculture, which has severely affected their livelihood. Today, several villages are turning to tourism for survival.

Before visiting these communities, it's important to realize that over the past 50 years, both the Emberá and the Wounaan have had a turbulent history of land grabs, legal battles and political misrepresentation. As a result, both groups have been forced to modernize, though the Emberá and the Wounaan still maintain their incredibly rich cultural heritage. If you arrive expecting to see villagers living traditional lifestyles in harmony with the land, then you will be disappointed. However, the Emberá and the Wounaan still have a lot to show to visitors, especially their traditional dances, music, handicrafts and the surrounding national park that has become their de facto home.

The neighboring Emberá community of **Ella Puru** (☎ 6537 7223) and Wounaan community of **San Antonio** (☎ 6637 9503) regularly receive tourists and with prior notice you can arrange a pick up from the docks in Gamboa. Tour prices vary from US$20 to $US30 per person depending on the activities you arrange and there is no shortage of possible excursions, ranging from guided rainforest walks to watching traditional dances.

For more information on the plight of the Emberá in Panamá Province, see the boxed text, opposite.

FISHING

Fishing is permitted on the Río Chagres and Lago Gatún. Leaflets and information about the park, including a brochure for self-guided walks along the nature trail, are available from **park headquarters** (☎ 276 6370) in Gamboa.

If you're interested in arranging a private tour, contact Panama Canal Fishing (above).

Fundación Avifauna Eugene Eisenmann

At the time of writing, the finishing touches were being applied to the **Fundación Avifauna Eugene Eisenmann** (☎ 264 6266; www.avifauna.org .pa), an ambitious project with the mission to protect Panama's bird fauna and rainforest habitat. The first wave of this project is the construction of a visitors center, hiking trails and a canopy tower near the entrance to Pipeline Road (1.6km from the gate). Successive phases will aim to promote sustainable tourism in the area by using revenues to protect the surrounding environment. As there are currently no facilities for birders accessing Pipeline Road, this project is likely to receive a lot of publicity following its opening launch.

Monumento Nacional Isla Barro Colorado

This lush island in the middle of Lago Gatún was formed by the damming of the Río Chagres and the creation of the lake. In 1923 Isla Barro Colorado (BCI) became one of the first biological reserves in the New World. Since that time, the island has become the most intensively studied area in the neotropics. Home to 1316 recorded plant species, 381 bird species and 102 mammal species, the island also contains a 59km network of marked and protected trails. It is managed by the Smithsonian Tropical Research Institute (STRI), which administers a world-renowned research facility here.

Although the 1500-hectare island was once restricted only to scientists, a limited number of tourists are now allowed to enter as part of a guided tour. The trip includes an STRI boat ride down an attractive part of the canal, from Gamboa across the lake to the island. Tour reservations are essential – book as far in advance as possible. Reservations can be made through the Panama City visitor services office of **STRI** (Map pp76-7; ☎ 212 8026; www.stri.org; Tupper Bldg, Av Roosevelt, Ancón district; adult/student foreign student US$70/40, adult/Panamanian student US$25/12; ☺ 8:30am-4:30pm Mon-Fri).

The boat to BCI leaves the Gamboa pier at 7:15am on Tuesday, Wednesday and Friday, and at 8am on Saturday and Sunday. There are no public visits on Monday, Thursday and on certain holidays. The entire trip lasts four to six hours, depending on the size of the group and on the weather. A buffet lunch (with vegetarian options) is included.

Canopy Tower Ecolodge & Nature Observatory

Located in Parque Nacional Soberanía, this former US Air Force radar station now serves a very different function, namely ecotourism. The **Canopy Tower** (☎ 264 5720; www.canopytower .com; d per person US$130-200, day visit US$85; **P**) is an ecologically-minded three-story, cylindrical lodge and observatory that offers guests the chance to immerse themselves in the sights and sounds of the rainforest. From the third and rooftop levels, you have a 360-degree view over the national park and you can even see ships passing through the canal a mere 2km away. The bird-watching in the surrounding area is top-notch and there's no shortage of other tropical wildlife, including howler monkeys, sloths and a slew of frogs and lizards.

In addition to the viewing platforms, there is also a small ground-floor museum, a tropical biology library, a cozy sitting area and a handful of attractive guest rooms ranging from quaint singles to luxurious four-person suites. Each room is awash in tropical hues,

---

LOCAL VOICES: MELIO & THE PLIGHT OF THE EMBERÁ

Melio is an Emberá who lives along the shores of Río Chagres, which is located within the Panama Canal Watershed and Parque Nacional Soberanía.

- **What is the history of your community?** The father of our community is Antonio Sarco, who is 96 years old. In 1950 he left Río Chico in the Darién and travelled down the Chagres river until he settled here. Antonio was an important man because he knew a lot about survival. Back then, the canal was controlled by America. So, when he contacted the US military, they gave him a job training astronauts and soldiers.

- **What has happened in Río Chagres since then?** Until the national park was created in 1984, we were a free people. We used to hunt, fish, cut down trees and grow crops. Then, once the national park was created, we were told that we had to change. We worried about our survival because everything would be different. We knew that saving the forest was important, but we were nervous about how to survive.

- **How did you survive?** Times were difficult until 1998. Then we were told by the government that we could promote tourism. We were told that we could show our dances, sell our handicrafts and that we wouldn't have to pay taxes. So, that's how we survive now.

- **Do you want to go back to how it was before?** How could we go back? We've lost our skills. And it's too much for us to go back. There is more income with tourism. In the Darién, the Emberá still live like before. But here, it's different.

THE CANAL ZONE: THE GRASS WAS GREENER ON THE OTHER SIDE *Ivan Hoyos*

Before coming to Panama, most travelers have a mental image of the Panama Canal as an industrial area where ships are raised and lowered through a system of locks. However, the Panama Canal and the surrounding Canal Zone are in fact an oasis of public green space, national parks and wildlife reserves.

The Panama Canal relies on the rainforest that embraces the channel to guarantee a continuous volume of water and to reduce the impact of erosion. As a result, Panama created a series of national parks, including Parque Nacional Soberanía, in order to safeguard this watershed. These very same forests also provide a sanctuary for the high diversity of flora and fauna that live on the banks of the canal, including jaguars, monkeys, sloths and hundreds of species of tropical birds. Unfortunately, while other countries are rushing to safeguard what little natural habitats they harbor, Panama seems to be thinking otherwise. The current development boom is placing an ever-increasing pressure on our natural landmarks, and residents of the Canal Zone are up in arms.

When Panama received the lands and properties once controlled by the US, Panama inherited a 'Garden City.' Former military bases such as Clayton and Albrook, and civilian communities such as Cardenas and Los Rios, provided families with playgrounds, soccer fields, swimming pools and public areas for recreation. As a result, the cities of Panama and Colón inherited the much-needed green space and recreational areas otherwise not found in these high-density urban environments. Furthermore, the masterfully planned communities yielded architecture unique to Panama – perfectly lined, red-tiled roofs and wooden houses on stilts are a sight that is not matched anywhere else in Central America.

However, with the ever-increasing demand for luxury apartments and gated communities, the 'Law 12' legislation was approved by the Panamanian Government in 2007. This ill-conceived law allows a developer to change the current zoning regulations without any regard for the natural surroundings. Green areas could soon become the site of multiple high-rise constructions, such as the ones found in the high-density districts of Paitilla and Punta Pacifica in Panama City. Mature rainforest areas and old historical homes could vanish, only to be converted into ostentatious gated communities. As a result of this law, Panama's historical, natural and architectural patrimony is in grave danger.

As a mockery to concerned Panamanians such as myself, billboards at the main entrances of Albrook and Clayton display high-rise buildings with catchy slogans like 'in harmony with nature.' Although these billboards are promising tranquility and peace in a natural surrounding, they are setting a precedent for what could turn the Canal Zone into a cornucopia of cement and glass.

Fortunately, there are organizations such as the Confederación de Comunidades de las Áreas Revertidas (Confederation of Communities in the Canal Zone) and the Comite Pro Defensa Camino de Cruces (Path of the Crossings Pro-Defense Committee) that are striving to put an end to harmful legislation like Law 12. Though these organizations are comprised primarily of residents from the Canal Zone, they have also reached the interest of Panamanians from as far as away as Chiriquí Province and the Azuero peninsula.

Beyond zoning laws, the Canal Zone is facing other devastating issues, such as the destruction of the mangrove ecosystems of Colón to make room for container yards, ship holding pens and shopping malls. There are even talks of building a massive port on the west bank of the Pacific entrance of the canal, which would eliminate one of the healthiest tracts of dry deciduous forest in Panama. Unfortunately, the future of the Canal Zone is very bleak for anyone concerned with protecting the environment.

As a concerned Panamanian, I hope that property developers and local authorities realize that travelers visit Panama for its premier natural heritage, and not to see an ever-increasing urban jungle.

Ivan Hoyos is a life-long resident of the Canal Zone and is an active promoter of environmental issues throughout Panama.

natural hardwoods, firm beds and a few hammocks to help you pass the time easier. Rates include three meals and guided nature walks in Parque Nacional Soberanía. Even if you're not spending the night, a day visit will allow you to visit the viewing platforms and partake in a few guided walks through the park.

To reach the Canopy Tower, pass the entrance to Summit on your way to Gamboa, and take the second road to the right – the turnoff is marked with a Canopy Tower sign. Follow the road for exactly one mile until you reach the top of Semaphore Hill and the entrance to the hotel.

Gamboa Rainforest Resort

Near the junction of the Panama Canal and the Río Chagres, 9km past the turnoff for Canopy Tower on the road to Colón, is the US$30-million **Gamboa Rainforest Resort** (☎ 314 9000; www.gamboaresort.com; villas from $150, d from US$225; P 🖳 🕱 🕱). Although it's just a resort located in a rainforest as opposed to an environmentally friendly ecolodge, it's hard to deny the grandeur of this place. The main building has sweeping vistas of the jungle-flanked Río Chagres, an awesome panorama of river and rainforest seen through windows three stories high – all 110 luxurious guest rooms offer slices of the same view. Flanking the driveway to the main building, there are also 65 colonial villas that once housed the administrators who managed canal dredging operations a century ago.

Holding true to its resort moniker, it's hard to get bored here. Guests can take advantage of the on-site golf course, spa, gym, marina, swimming pool and bar-restaurant. There's even an aerial tram that brings you up into the canopy, as well as healthy offering of guided nature walks and birding trips. If you're planning on spending a few days here, check the website for special package deals, which often include activities, meals and transfers.

One note of caution: we have received complaints from readers about Gamboa's 'Monkey Island' tours, where the highlight is feeding a colony of monkeys on a small island in Lake Gatún. Although we probably don't have to say it, let's be perfectly clear about this – feeding wildlife is an environmentally detrimental practice that should not be encouraged. Please do not frequent tours of this nature and don't be afraid to inform the management of Gamboa about the ill-effects of this practice.

PACIFIC ISLANDS

Wedged between two oceans, Panamá is an island-hoppers dream – spend some time on the Pacific side of things, especially if you're a fan of fiery sunsets and scenic coastlines.

ISLA TABOGA
pop 1000

A tropical island with only one road and no traffic, Isla Taboga is a pleasant place to escape from the hustle and bustle of Panama City. Although it is only 20km offshore, the 'Island of Flowers' is covered with sweet-smelling blossoms at certain times of the year. First settled by the Spanish in 1515, the quaint village of Taboga is also home to the second-oldest church in the western hemisphere. However, the main appeal of the island is its string of sandy beaches lapped by warm waters, which can quickly rejuvenate even the most hardened urbanite.

Isla Taboga is currently in the midst of an image makeover. Ferries for the island now depart from the most exclusive of berths, namely the Causeway (p86. Also, rumors abound that the now-defunct Hotel Taboga will be knocked down to make way for a sophisticated resort. In the meantime however, Taboga still serves as a laid-back day trip from Panama City for anyone looking for a little fun in the sun.

History

Taboga is part of a chain of islands that were inhabited by indigenous peoples who resided in thatch huts and lived off the bounty of the sea. In 1515 Spanish soldiers announced their arrival on Taboga by killing or enslaving the islanders and establishing a small colony. Naturally, peace was not established, especially since Taboga became the favorite spot of English pirates.

On August 22, 1686, the ship of Captain Townley was lying in front of Taboga when it was attacked by three Spanish ships armed with cannons. During the ensuing battle, Townley destroyed one of the ships and took the other two vessels captive as well as a fourth ship that had arrived as reinforcement. Afterwards, Townley sent a messenger to the president of Panama demanding supplies, the release of five pirates being held prisoner and ransom for the Spanish captives.

When the president refused to send anything other than medicine, Townley replied that heads would roll if his demands weren't met. When the president ignored the threat, Townley kept his word by sending him a canoe that contained the heads of twenty Spaniards. Townley's message got the president's attention and all of pirate's demands were immediately met.

For years afterward, peace continued to elude the little island. As late as 1819, Taboga was still sought after for its strategic location, a fact made abundantly clear when the pirate Captain Illingsworth and his party of Chileans sacked the island and killed most of its inhabitants.

During the 1880s, when the French took a stab at digging a canal across the isthmus, Taboga became the site of an enormous sanatorium for workers who had contracted malaria or yellow fever. The Island of Flowers might well have earned its name from all the flowers placed on graves here. Sadly, Taboga's centuries-old cemetery has been looted so many times that it looks like it was hit by artillery fire.

Real artillery fire also took a toll on Taboga. The US Navy used the broad hill facing the town for artillery practice during WWII and even installed a number of anti-aircraft guns and machine-gun bunkers atop the island. Although they were abandoned in 1960, these ruins can still be visited today.

In recent decades, peace has finally come to Taboga, though the island is continually assailed by weekend vacationers from Panama City and groups of foreign tourists.

Orientation & Information

Ferries from the Causeway in Panama City tie up at a pier near the north end of the island. As you exit the pier, you'll see the entrance to the abandoned Hotel Taboga to your right. To your left, you'll see a narrow street that is the island's main road. From this point, the street meanders 5.2km before ending at the old US military installation atop the island's highest hill, Cerro El Vigia.

For more information on the island, seek out the excellent English-language site, www.taboga.panamanow.com.

Sights

There are fine **beaches** in Taboga in either direction from the ferry dock. Many visitors head straight for the Hotel Taboga, to your right as you walk off the ferry dock; the hotel faces onto the island's most popular beach, arcing between Taboga and tiny Isla El Morro.

Walk left from the pier along the island's only road for about 75m until you reach the fork. If you take the high road, you will come to a modest **church**, in front of which is a simple square. This unassuming church was founded in 1550 and is the second-oldest church in the western hemisphere; inside is a handsome altar and lovely artwork.

Further down the road is a beautiful public garden, which bears the statue of the island's patroness, **Nuestra Señora del Carmen**, who is honored with a procession every July 16. The statue is carried upon the shoulders of followers to the oceanside, placed on a boat and ferried around the island. Upon her return she is carried around the island, while crowds follow and everyone else watches at their windows. The Virgin is returned to her garden shrine and the rest of the day is one of rejoicing. Seemingly everyone partakes in games, fire-breathing or dancing.

For a fine view, you can walk up the **Cerro de la Cruz** hill on the east side of the island to the cross on the top. At the top, look for abandoned bunkers that were used by US troops during WWII. If you look below and to the right of the old cross, you'll also see a white-and-brown pile of rubble amid thickening vegetation. This is the ruins of a Spanish cannon emplacement put here 300 years ago to protect the island from pirates.

Activities
SNORKELING

On weekends, when people are most likely to visit Taboga, fishermen at the pier can take you around the island, allowing you to see it from all sides and reach some good snorkeling spots. Caves on the island's western side are rumored to hold treasure left by pirates. During the week, when the small boats aren't taking people around, you can still snorkel around Isla El Morro, which doesn't have coral, but attracts some large fish.

DIVING

Taboga offers typical Pacific-style diving, with rocky formations and a wide variety of marine life. The beauty of the Pacific is enhanced by the schools of fish that roam about: on a good dive you can expect to see jack, snapper, jewfish, eels, rays, lobsters and octopuses. With a little luck, you may also come across old bottles, spent WWII-era shells and artifacts from pirate days. **Scubapanama** (Map pp74-5; ☎ 261 3841; www.scubapanama.com; cnr Av 6a C Norte & Calle 62 C Oeste, El Carmen, Panama City) offers periodic dive trips to the island.

BIRD-WATCHING
The islands of Taboga and nearby Urabá are home to one of the largest breeding colonies of brown pelicans in the world. The colony has contained up to 100,000 individual birds, or about half of the world population of this species. A wildlife refuge, the **Refugio de Vida Silvestre Islas Taboga y Urabá**, was established to protect their habitat, and covers about a third of Taboga as well as the entire island of Urabá, just off Taboga's southeast coast. May is the height of nesting season, but pelicans can be seen from January to June.

WHALE-WATCHING
On your way to and from the island, keep an eye on the ocean. On rare occasions during August, September and October, migrating humpback and sei whales can be seen leaping from the water near Taboga in spectacular displays.

Sleeping & Eating
Most people choose to visit Isla Taboga as a day trip from Panama City, though there are a handful of places to stay on the island.

Kool Hostel (☎ 690 2545; luisveron@hotmail.com; dm/ house US$10/25) Perched on a hill overlooking the bay, this clean and comfortable family-run hostel is a good place to bed down if you want to extend your time on the island. Rooms are fairly standard and lacking in personality, but there are shared hot-water bathrooms and a communal kitchen. Guests can rent bikes, snorkel gear or fishing tackle. To reach the hostel, turn left as you exit the dock and walk for a few minutes until you see a sign leading you up the hill.

Vereda Tropical Hotel (☎ 250 2154; veredatropical hotel@hotmail.com; d from US$45; ✷) Atop a hill with commanding views, this beautiful hotel is one of the most charming places to stay on the island. Colorful rooms, some with balconies, are stylishly decorated and have high ceilings, comfortable beds and shutters that open onto the village or the sea. The open-air restaurant, with sunny adjoining patio, serves tasty meals

prepared by the talented Portuguese chef. Vereda Tropical is located about 100m past the path leading up to Kool Hostel.

Aquario (mains US$4-7; ✷ 7am-10pm) This simple eatery along the main road in the center of town is a good spot for traditional Panamanian food. Peel a few more bucks out of your wallet and sample the catch of the day, which was most likely caught just a few hundred meters from where you're sitting.

Getting There & Away
The scenic boat trip out to Isla Taboga is part of the island's attraction. **Barcos Calypso** (☎ 314 1730; roundtrip US$10) has departures from Panama City at 8:30am and 3:00pm Monday, Wednesday and Friday, 8:30am on Tuesday and Thursday, and 8:30am, 10:30am and 4:00pm on Saturday and Sunday. Ferries depart Isla Taboga at 9:30am and 4:00pm Monday, Wednesday and Friday, 4:30pm on Tuesday and Thursday, and 9:00am, 3:00pm and 5:00pm on Saturday and Sunday.

Ferries depart from La Playita de Amador, which is located behind the Centro de Exhibiciones Marinas on the Causeway (p86). The easiest way to reach the dock is by taxi (US$4 to US$6).

ARCHIPIÉLAGO DE LAS PERLAS
In January 1979, after the followers of the Ayatollah Ruholla Khomeini had forced Shah Mohammed Reza Pahlavi to pack up his hundreds of millions of dollars and flee Iran, the shah looked the world over and moved to Isla Contadora. It's one of 90 named islands in the Archipiélago de las Perlas, or Pearl Islands, any one of which is fit for a king – or a shah.

Named for the large pearls that are found in its waters, the Pearl Islands are comprised of 90 named islands and over 100 unnamed islets, each surrounded by travel magazine–worthy, white-sand beaches and turquoise waters. Isla Contadora is the best-known island of the group, especially since the island is home to the palatial mansions of the rich and powerful. The Pearl Islands were also the site of the popular US TV show *Survivor,* which filmed the 2003 season of their sensationalist series on an unnamed island in the chain.

History
True to its name, it was pearls that initially brought the archipelago to the Old World's

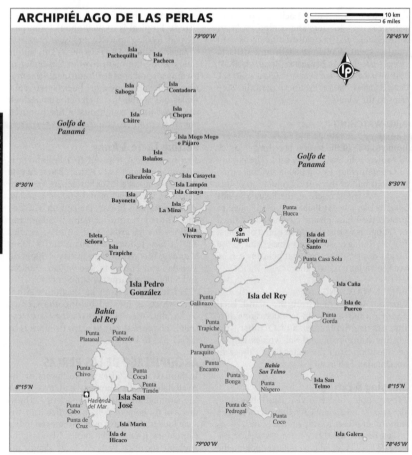

ARCHIPIÉLAGO DE LAS PERLAS

attention. Vasco Núñez de Balboa, within days of his discovery of the Pacific Ocean, learned of nearby islands rich with pearls from a local guide. Balboa was anxious to visit the islands, but he was told that a hostile chief ruled them, and cautiously decided to postpone the visit. Nonetheless, Balboa named the archipelago 'Islas de las Perlas,' and declared it and all its undiscovered riches Spanish property. The year was 1513, and Balboa vowed to return one day to kill the chief and claim his pearls for the king of Spain.

However, before he could fulfill his vow, Spanish governor Pedro Arias de Ávila, who loathed the great explorer for his popularity with the king, dispatched his cousin Gaspar de Morales to the islands in order to secure the pearls spoken of by Balboa. Once on the islands, Morales captured 20 chieftains and gave them to his dogs to tear to pieces. The purportedly hostile chief, a man named Dites, saw the futility of warring with the Spaniards, and instead presented Morales with a basket of large and lustrous pearls. Unfortunately, this only enhanced the Spaniards' desires to control the archipelago and it took just two years to exterminate the islands' indigenous population.

In 1517, the same year that Morales raided Las Perlas, Pedrarias (as the governor was often called) falsely charged Balboa with treason, and had him and four of his closest friends beheaded in the Caribbean coastal town of Aclá.

LOCAL LORE: LA PEREGRINA

The oysters that abound in the water of archipelago have produced some of the world's finest pearls. However, none are as celebrated or well documented as the La Peregrina (The Pilgrim Pearl). This enormous, pear-shaped white pearl weighs 203.84 grains or 31 carats. When it was discovered 400 years ago, it was considered so magnificent that the slave who discovered it was given his freedom.

In the mid-16th century, the pearl was given to King Phillip II of Spain, who later presented it as a wedding gift to his wife, Queen Mary of Scots. Later it belonged to the Bonaparte family, though it was eventually acquired by the British Marquis of Abercorn from the son of French emperor Napoleon III.

In 1969 it was purchased for US$37,000 by actor Richard Burton for his wife, Elizabeth Taylor. Today, the pearl is still owned by Ms Taylor, who has one of the largest private jewelry collections in the world. Of course, it's worth noting that La Peregrina was briefly lost for a period of time when her pet dog scampered away with the pearl in its mouth!

In the years that followed Morales' arrival in the archipelago, the Spaniards harvested the islands' oyster beds. However, since they had slain the entire population of the islands, they had to import slaves from Africa to collect the oysters. Today the descendants of the first slaves who came to the Archipiélago de las Perlas live on the islands.

Orientation & Information

With few exceptions, tourists visit only four of Las Perlas: Isla Contadora, which is the most accessible, developed and visited island; Isla San José, which is the site of an exclusive resort; and neighboring Islas Casaya and Casayeta, which are frequented by pearl shoppers. However, since less than a dozen of the Pearl Islands are inhabited, there are ample opportunities here for independent exploration, especially if you have a sense of adventure and the help of a local guide.

Isla Contadora

pop 350

Isla Contadora (Counting House Island) was the historic accounting center for pearls before they were shipped off to Spain. Today however, there's not much accounting being done on the island, especially since the island's residents are multimillionaires, the majority of which probably haven't filed their tax returns in quite some time.

Owing to its close proximity and frequent air connections to Panama City, Isla Contadora is the only island in the archipelago with a developed tourist infrastructure. For the most part, Contadora is a prestigous destination that caters to its wealthy residents and moneyed tourists from the mainland. However, the beaches on the island are spectacular, the snorkeling is worldclass, and the island is a great jumping off point for independent exploration of the archipelago.

ORIENTATION & INFORMATION

Isla Contadora is only 1.2 sq km in size and nearly all of its tourist facilities are on the northern side of the island, within walking distance of the airstrip. The other side consists primarily of forest, palatial homes and secluded beaches.

There's a **ULAPS Health Clinic** (☎ 250 4209; ⏱ 24hr) a short walk from the airstrip. If no one answers the door, walk around to the back of the facility to the house there – it's the doctor's home and he doesn't mind being disturbed if someone's in need.

SIGHTS & ACTIVITIES

Beaches

Isla Contadora is home to no less than 12 beaches, all of which are covered with tan sand and are virtually abandoned except during major holidays. Five beaches are particularly lovely: Playa Larga, Playa de las Suecas, Playa Cacique, Playa Ejecutiva and Playa Galeón. Although spread around three sides of the island, all can be visited in as little as 20 minutes in a rented four-wheeler.

Playa Larga (Long Beach), which is located in front of the Hotel Contadora Resort, is always crowded, but it's the best place for spotting marine life. Around the corner to the south is **Playa de las Suecas** (Swedish Women's Beach), where you can sunbathe in the buff legally – the Swedish women are

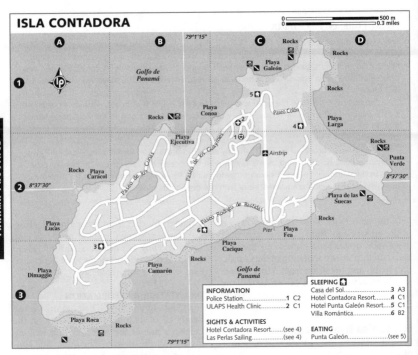

ISLA CONTADORA

INFORMATION	
Police Station	1 C2
ULAPS Health Clinic	2 C1

SIGHTS & ACTIVITIES	
Hotel Contadora Resort	(see 4)
Las Perlas Sailing	(see 4)

SLEEPING	
Casa del Sol	3 A3
Hotel Contadora Resort	4 C1
Hotel Punta Galeón Resort	5 C1
Villa Romántica	6 B2

EATING	
Punta Galeón	(see 5)

the ones with blond hair, blue eyes and sunburnt skin. Continuing west 400m, you'll find **Playa Cacique**, a fairly large and unvisited beach that's a good choice if you want a little peace and quiet. On the northern side of the island, **Playa Ejecutiva** (Executive Beach) is another intimate escape – the large house on the bluff to the east is where the shah of Iran once lived. **Playa Galeón** (Galleon Beach), to the northeast, is another good spot for snorkeling, though the surf can really pick up here at times.

Snorkeling & Diving

The snorkeling and diving around Contadora is fantastic. There are five coral fields near the island and within them you can expect to see schools of angelfish, damselfish, moray eels, parrot fish, puffer fish, butterfly fish, white-tip reef sharks and a whole lot more. Even in the waters off Playa Larga, the most popular of Isla Contadora's beaches, you can often spot sea turtles and manta rays.

The coral fields are found offshore from the following places: the eastern end of Playa de las Suecas, Punta Verde, near the southern end of Playa Larga, both ends of Playa Galeón and the western end of Playa Ejecutiva. In addition, although there is little coral at the southwestern end of the island, there is a lot of marine life among the rocks in front and east of Playa Roca.

Snorkeling and diving trips can be arranged at the Hotel Punta Galeón Resort or the Hotel Contadora Resort (see opposite).

Sailing

One of the best ways to appreciate the beauty and isolation of the Archipiélago de las Perlas is to explore them on a chartered sailboat. **Las Perlas Sailing** (☎ 250 4214), located just before the Hotel Contadora Resort, offers a number of trips ranging from one-hour circumnavigations of the island (US$15 per person) to four-hour excursions (US$40 per person) to nearby islets. If you have had previous experience with boats, Las Perlas will also rent one- and two-person sailboats as well as a whole range of motorboats. You can also arrange sportfishing excursions here, but an outing will set you back a few hundred dollars.

Four-Wheeling

Contadora lends itself to getting around in a four-wheeler – in fact, it's the only way to get around the island aside from walking. You can rent them at the Hotel Punta Galeón Resort or the Hotel Contadora Resort (see below) for US$20 per hour.

SLEEPING

All of the accommodations listed below will meet you at the airport and provide transportation (via golf cart) to the resort or hotel.

Casa del Sol (☎ 250 4212; www.panama-isla-contadora.com; r from US$55; ❄ ▣) Located in a pleasant residential neighborhood, this adorable inn is surrounded by a native tropical wooded area of towering palms and tropical flowers. Each of the five rooms on offer are individually decorated and have just the right amount of personal touch. The friendly owners have a wealth of knowledge about Contadora and will go out of their way to make sure you enjoy your time here.

Villa Romántica (☎ 250 4067; www.contadora-villa-romantica.com; d from US$80) Overlooking the lovely beach of Playa Cacique, this small inn caters to anyone looking for a romantic getaway, though the vibe here is more 'Vegas Weekend' than 'Hawaiian Honeymoon.' Rooms decked out in odd murals come complete with waterbeds and are centered on a large open-air restaurant and hot tub. This is definitely one of the island's more unusual spots and it can be a lot of fun if you're in the right mindset.

Hotel Contadora Resort (☎ 264 1498; www.hotelcontadora.com; d from US$160; ❄ ▣ ▣) This hulking monstrosity of French Colonial design has deteriorated over the years, but it still manages to fill up with unsuspecting guests. The landscaped grounds are beautiful – and the golf course, swimming pool and tennis courts are an attractive lure – but the rooms are poorly maintained.

Hotel Punta Galeón Resort (☎ 214 3719; www.puntagaleon.com; d from US$165; ❄ ▣ ▣) The best hotel on the island has a dramatic location, perched on a cliff up above Playa Galeón. Several white-washed thatch buildings with modern interiors are connected by an attractive boardwalk that's perfect for slow struts and long gazes out to the sea. There's also no shortage of amenities on offer, including a swimming pool, a spa and a handful of bars and restaurants.

EATING

Unfortunately, Isla Contadora has something of a reputation for terrible and overpriced food. The main problem is that everything needs to be shipped from the mainland, which leaves something to be desired in terms of price and freshness.

Even if you're not staying at the resort, **Punta Galeón** (mains US$9-15) is probably your best bet for a decent meal. There is usually a fair selection of fresh seafood on offer and the attached bar has the best liquor selection on the island.

GETTING THERE & AWAY

Air Panama (☎ 316 9000; www.flyairpanama.com/tickets) and **Aeroperlas** (☎ 315 7500; www.aeroperlas.com) fly direct from Panama City to Isla Contadora (round-trip US$60, 20 minutes). Each airline has two daily departures on weekdays and four daily departures on weekends.

GETTING AROUND

Because the island is only about a square kilometer in size, there are no taxis. Hotels shuttle guests to and from the airport via golf cart, and there is no shortage of four-wheelers for rent.

Isla San José

Home to the most exclusive resort in the Pearl Islands, Isla San José has a dark and overlooked history as a US chemical weapons testing ground. During a 2001 inspection, the entire island was placed under temporary quarantine following the recovery of unexploded ordinance, which lead to a tiff between Panama and the US over who should pick up the cleaning bill.

History aside, most of the 45.3 sq km island is covered in a bank of rainforest that's networked by all-weather roads installed by the US military decades ago. With the exception of the roads, the only development on the island is a gorgeous resort at the cliff's edge.

our pick **Hacienda del Mar** (☎ 269 6634, 269 6613 in Panama City; www.haciendadelmar.net; cabin from US$360) presently has the island's 37 tan-sand beaches, nine year-round rivers and seven accessible waterfalls all to itself. The resort is the creation of Aeroperlas President George Novey, who spared no expense in the construction of his resort. Each of the 12 stand-alone luxury cabins is overflowing with amenities and overlooks a picture-perfect sweep of beach and a lonely sea. Although most guests are

PANAMÁ PROVINCE

PIRATES IN THE BAY

From the late 17th century, the Bahía de Panamá, home to the Pearl and Taboga island groups, was the scene of pirate exploits unsurpassed anywhere in the New World. After Henry Morgan's successful 1671 sacking of the city of Panama, other buccaneers were enticed to enter the area and to try their hands at plundering and pillaging Spanish territory and ships along the Pacific coast. Many are the stories of pirates using the Archipiélago de las Perlas as a hideout and springboard for attacks.

One of the era's most significant escapades occurred in May 1685 near Las Perlas when the largest number of trained seamen and fighters ever assembled under a buccaneer flag in the Pacific played cat-and-mouse with a Spanish armada of 18 ships. The pirate fleet consisted of 10 French and English vessels united under the English captain Edward Blake. Because his fleet was deficient in cannons but sufficient in muskets, it was Blake's policy to avoid long-range fighting. Despite his fleet's inferior numbers, he itched for a close encounter with the Spaniards.

When the two great forces crossed paths on May 28, Blake ordered two of his principal ships (one led by a Frenchman, the second by an Englishman) to initiate an attack on the Spanish fleet. Fearing the Spaniards' cannons, both men refused to obey. Blake's crew exchanged shots with the Spanish vice admiral, but Blake, seeing the imprudence of continuing battle with the odds stacked against him, ordered his slower ships to flee while his and another fast vessel delayed the conquistadores.

The Spaniards opened fire with their big guns, but the pirates managed some risky evasive maneuvers between rocky islets at the northern end of the archipelago, and their pursuers gave up the chase. Blake's ships anchored off the archipelago's Isla Pacheca that night, fully expecting the Spanish armada to engage them the next day. Instead, for reasons that mystify historians, the Spanish admiral ordered his fleet to return to Panamá. In the days that followed, dissent arose among the buccaneers, and the short-lived French–English pirate confederacy dissolved.

Today, little evidence of the pirates and Spaniards remains in the Archipiélago de las Perlas, with the exception of the distant descendants of the Spaniards and their slaves. Forests once felled to make ships have grown back. Storms, termites and wood worms have destroyed the old Spanish structures – only a church and a stone dam on Isla Saboga and wells on Islas Pacheca and Chapera testify to the Spaniards' presence.

Exploiting this buccaneer reputation, the popular US show *Survivor* brought attention to the islands in fall 2003 by setting their reality TV series here.

content simply soaking up their exclusive slice of paradise, there is an incredible list of tours on offer here and the incredibly professional staff can make all of the necessary arrangements in a blink of an eye.

Air transportation between Panama City and Isla San José is by private charter flight, and must be arranged through Hacienda del Mar in advance.

Islas Casaya And Casayeta

Oysters are still harvested throughout the archipelago, and their pearls are just as legendary as they were when Balboa first arrived. Although pearls are sometimes offered for sale on other islands, the best places to shop for them are Isla Casaya and neighboring Isla Casayeta, about 12km to the south of Contadora.

When you're looking at pearls, you should know that pearl sellers tend to keep their goods in oil, so that they'll have a lovely shine when presented – always dry the pearl that intrigues you before you buy. Prices are generally very reasonable, and there's always room for bargaining.

Accommodations on either Isla Contadora or San José can arrange transportation to the pearl shops on Islas Casaya and Casayeta.

PACIFIC COAST

Every weekend, thousands of stressed-out Panama City residents hop into their cars or board buses and head west on the Interamericana – their destination: the beach.

LA CHORRERA
pop 60,000

One of the first major towns you hit along the Interamerican is La Chorrera, which is famous throughout Panama for its *chich-*

eme, a nonalcoholic drink made from milk, mashed sweet corn, cinnamon and vanilla. Although this heat-quenching beverage isn't likely to make you cancel your beach-going plans, there are some attractive waterfalls near the town that are worth exploring if you can bear to be away from the coast for a little longer.

Orientation

The Interamericana runs from east to west through La Chorrera, slowing to one sluggish lane in each direction as vehicles enter and exit the highway from side streets. However, most people bypass the city on the 28km-long tollway (US$0.50).

Information

There is no tourist office in La Chorrera, but you can obtain reliable information from the **Instituto Nacional de Cultura** (INAC; ☎ /fax 253 2306; Calle Maria Leticia; ☺ 8am-5pm Mon-Fri, 10am-2pm Sat), 75m north of the Interamericana, at the east end of town (the turnoff is 100m before the Super 99 supermarket). The office, located in an art school, can tell you (in Spanish only) about the town's culture and festivals.

There's a small, unnamed internet café just beyond the Super 99. Most banks in La Chorrera are conveniently located on the Interamericana halfway through town. The **post office** (Calle San Francisco) is two blocks south of the Interamericana.

Festivals & Events

La Chorrera is known for its beautiful folkloric dances, which can best be seen during its popular fair. **La Feria de La Chorrera** lasts for 10 days, and is held in late January or early February – dates vary from year to year. The festivities also include parades, a rodeo, the odd cockfight or two and drum dances, which have their origin in African music brought by slaves.

Sights

La Chorrera has only one true tourist attraction, and sadly, it isn't what it once was. **El Chorro** is a series of cascades on the Río Caimito, the last of which takes a 30m plunge into a broad swimming hole. Years ago the Caimito was a raging river and its banks were swathed in pristine jungle. Today much of the river has been siphoned off upstream.

Still, if you're in need of a cool dip, a visit to El Chorro makes for a nice stop, especially if the air-conditioner isn't working in the car. Plus, it's likely that you will have the entire place to yourself, aside from a few local children.

To get here from the Interamericana, turn north onto Calle Larga at the Banistmo and drive 1km until you reach an intersection with a Super La Fortuna market on one side and a Mini Super Pacifico market on the other. Turn right just before the minimarket and then stay to the left of the road. The falls are at the end of this road, 1km from the intersection. You can also hire a taxi (US$1.50 each way) or hail a bus (US$0.35) with 'Calle Larga' scrawled on its windshield.

Sleeping & Eating

Hospedaje Lamas (☎ 253 7887; Av de las Américas; d with fan/air-con US$15/20; P ⚡) Near the west end of town, this old standby features a number of concrete box-style rooms, though the beds are somewhat firm and the showers are somewhat warm. However, it's one of the better places to stay in town and it has less 'hourly guests' than other nearby spots. The building itself is clearly marked, though anyone in town can point out its location to you.

El Chichemito (cnr Calles L Oeste & 26 Norte; snack US$1-3) This is an excellent spot to try *chicheme*, the favored drink in La Chorrera, which goes down nicely with a *boyo chorrenano* (tamale filled with marinated chicken and spice). As you're driving west on the Interamericana, turn right onto Calle 26 Norte (just beyond the 'bbb' shoe store sign) and look for the restaurant, 30m further on the left.

Getting There & Away

East- and west-bound buses stop at the Delta station, opposite the Pribanco bank and Matrox pharmacy on the Interamericana. Buses for Panama City (US$1.25, one hour) leave every fifteen minutes – ask for the express bus or you'll be making frequent stops.

LAGO GATÚN

Adventurous souls might want to venture to Lago Gatún (Gatún Lake), which is easily reached from La Chorrera. With rainforested shores and thousands of tiny islets, Lake Gatún is a gorgeous spot that sees few tourists aside from those on canal transits. However, there's usually a local or two at the lake's edge with a spare boat, and it shouldn't cost you more than a US$25 to go fishing for a few hours.

To get to the lake by car, turn off the Interamericana onto the unmarked road beside the Caja de Ahorros, which is 100m west of the Banco del Istmo and turnoff for El Chorro. Proceed north 800m to the Plaza de 28 de Noviembre, on the right side of the road. Just beyond the plaza, on a corner on the left side of the street, you'll see a butcher shop called Carnicería Victor Loo. Turn left onto the street in front of Victor Loo. (The street is unmarked and no one seems to know the name, hence all these landmarks used as pointers instead of street names. However, most people know this as the road to Mendoza, or 'calle a Mendoza.')

To reach Lago Gatún from here, make your way to Mendoza, then continue on the road for another 5km until you reach the lake's edge. There's a pier there, which is your best option for hiring a boatman. When you've returned with your catch, walk from the pier up the road a little way to the Club Campetre Arco Iris, where there are some bohíos (thatched-roof huts). There, for a few dollars, someone will gladly cook your fish for you.

If you're relying on public transportation, back at the Caja de Ahorres store, catch a bus with 'Mendoza' or 'Mendoza/Represa' on the windshield and tell the driver that you want to go to Lago Gatún (US$1.50).

CAPIRA

Fifty-seven kilometers from Panama City is the nondescript town of Capira, which is home to the famous cheese shop **Quesos Chela** (Interamericana; ◷ 10am-5pm Mon-Sat), an institution that few Panamanian drivers can pass without stopping. It's a plain shop that usually has piping hot fresh cheese (string, mozzarella, farmers, ricotta) and homemade meat empanadas for sale. The cheese shop is right next door to a Texaco and a Mr. Precio supermarket on the right-hand side of the road if you're heading west.

PARQUE NACIONAL Y RESERVA BIOLÓGICA ALTOS DE CAMPANA

This obscure and relatively unknown national park is a favorite of both local and international bird-watchers. Common sightings include the scale-crested pygmy-tyrant,

orange-bellied trogon and chestnut-capped brush-finch, though rare avians including the slaty antwren, the white-tipped sicklebill and the purplish-backed quail-dove are occasionally spotted here.

This park requires at least several hours to be appreciated because it's best viewed on foot. Starting at the road's end, beyond the microwave tower, trails will take you into some lovely forest, which is on the much greener Atlantic slope. The difference between the deforested Pacific and the lush Atlantic slopes is nowhere more evident.

The easy-to-miss turnoff for this national park is 25km southwest of La Chorrera, on the western side of the Interamericana. More specifically, it's at the top of a steep and windy section of the Interamericana known locally as the Loma Capana. From the turnoff, a rocky road winds 4.6km to an **ANAM ranger station** (park fee US$1, per night camping US$5) at the entrance to the park, which is located on Cerro Campana; pay fees here. Camping is allowed but there are no facilities.

No buses go up the road leading to the park. You pretty much need to have your own vehicle, rely on the services of a guide company or do some rather serious hiking to get in. However, getting to the turnoff for the park is easy. Virtually any bus using that section of the Interamericana will drop you there – there's a bus stop beside the turnoff. Getting picked up isn't a problem either as there are many buses that pass by the turnoff during daylight hours.

PUNTA CHAME
pop 390

Just before the Interamericana reaches the coastline, there is a turnoff immediately east of Bejuco, which leads to the tiny sliver of a peninsula known as Punta Chame. The road out to the sea winds past rolling hills before opening up to flat land that consists mainly of shrimp farms and mangroves. Few people live along this 25km road because the brackish water makes farming near impossible, though the environment here is unique to this region, and well worth the diversion.

Punta Chame is a one-road town on a long, 300m-wide peninsula, with residences and vacant lots lining both sides. Although the beaches at Playa Chame on the east coast of the peninsula have lovely tan sand and a wilderness backdrop, they are virtually abandoned due to difficult access. The area also has a notorious reputation for stingrays, so it's best to swim with caution and shuffle your feet while walking out.

To the north of the peninsula is a muddy bay, which is a popular spot for windsurfers. Since equipment rental is not available here, you will need to bring all your own gear. However, the location couldn't be more scenic, and the lack of crowds means that you can pretty much have the bay to yourself.

As you enter Punta Chame, on the right side of the street you'll see a sign for **Fundación Amigos de las Tortugas Marinas** (☎ 227 5091 in Panama City; cabin per person US$30; Ⓟ). The Friends of Sea Turtles Foundation was founded by brother and sister Ramón and Vilma Morales in 1998 to reverse the declining numbers of sea turtles returning to nest on Punta Chame–area beaches every year. Here, there are several hatcheries, where a turtle hunter turned savior hatches sea turtles and releases them when they are of a good size. To help finance their project, the Moraleses built several basic cabins alongside the hatcheries, which are available if you want to bed down for a night. Each cabin has a private cold-water shower and a decent bed alongside a smattering of rustic furniture. Also, if you speak a little Spanish, you'll almost certainly enjoy the company of the Moraleses and their friendly staff.

To get to Punta Chame from the Interamericana, catch a bus at the stop at the Punta Chame turnoff at Bejuco – a bus to the point (US$1) leaves hourly from 6:30am to 5:30pm daily.

BEACHES

Starting just south of the town of Chame and continuing along the Pacific coast for the next 40km are dozens of beautiful beaches that are popular weekend retreats for Panama City residents. About half of these beaches are in Panamá Province, while the remainder are in Coclé Province (p129).

All of the beaches listed in this section can be reached by local bus or taxi at the turnoffs from the Interamericana.

Gorgona

Six kilometers southwest of the turnoff for Punta Chame is the turnoff for Gorgona, a small oceanside community that fronts a curving beach of mostly black sand. Bring your sandals – it gets very hot.

Located near the beach is the **Cabañas de Playa Gorgona** (☎ 269 2433; cabin weekdays/weekends from US$25/35; Ⓟ 🐾 🛏), which is popular with vacationing Panamanian families. It's a fairly large complex of over 40 concrete cabins, each of which has a kitchenette and a private hot-water bathroom. However, the best part of staying here is lounging on the beach property, which is open to all guests and has two pools and a clutch of thatched-roof *palapas*.

Playa Coronado

Four kilometers southwest of the turnoff for Gorgona is the turnoff for Playa Coronado, an affluent beachside community that is a haven for water-sports lovers. The salt-and-pepper beach here is also one of the most

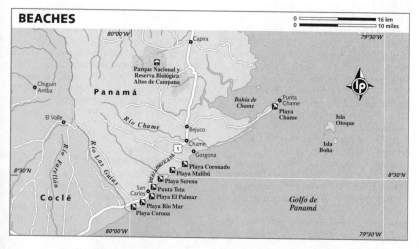

BEACHES

0   16 km
0   10 miles

80°00'W   Capira   79°30'W

Parque Nacional y Reserva Biológica Altos de Campana

Chiguirí Arriba

Panamá

El Valle

Río Chame

Bejuco

Chame

Bahía de Chame

Punta Chame

Playa Chame

Isla Otoque

Isla Boná

Río Las Guías

Gorgona

Playa Coronado

Playa Malibú

Playa Serena

San Carlos

Punta Teta

Playa El Palmar

Playa Río Mar

Playa Corona

Río Perellón

8°30'N

Coclé

Golfo de Panamá

8°30'N

80°00'W   79°30'W

SURFING IN PANAMÁ PROVINCE

The beaches to the southwest of the capital are a popular destination for Panamanian surfers, especially since they're easy to access and offer relatively consistent surf year-round. The following list will help you get started, though don't be afraid to ask local surfers to let you in on their hidden spots. The following beaches and other top spots for surfing are mapped on pp68–9.

- **Playa Malibu** Near Gorgona. Sand-bottom right and left break. Best during medium to low tide. Consistent, good tubes and long rides when there is a strong swell.
- **Playa Serena** In Coronado, past the security gate. Right point break with good tubes. Long rides when the there is a strong swell.
- **Frente de Teta** Rock/sand bottom break at the mouth of the Río Teta. Long lefts at low tide, and rights and lefts at medium to high tide.
- **Punta Teta** Point break over rocks to the south of the Río Teta mouth. Lefts and rights with good tubes, especially at medium tide going up.
- **Rinconsito** Rock-bottom point south of Punta Teta with a long, right break on a good swell. Named after California's famous Rincón break.
- **Frente Palmar** South of San Carlos. Beach break, partial rock bottom that is popular with beginners.
- **Punta El Palmar** South of San Carlos. Rock-bottom point break. Right peeling waves at medium to high tide when there is a good swell.
- **Hawaiisito** South of San Carlos. Rock-bottom point break. Lefts at full high tide. Closes out if there is a strong swell.
- **Frente Río Mar** Somewhat rocky beach break in front of Río Mar. Rights and lefts at medium to high tide.
- **Punta Río Mar** South of the Río Mar, near jutting rocks. Walk and paddle at low tide. Rights best. Breaks only at low tide.

developed strips of sand along the coast and is extremely popular with affluent Panama City denizens.

If you're travelling on a tight budget, a popular destination for shoestringers is the **Sea-SolBeach Coronado Guest House** (☎ 6689 1262; www .seasolbeach.com; dm US$10-12, s/d US$25/30; P ✗ 🖳), which is located on a grassy lot in the center of town. The staff at the SeaSolBeach also work as surfing, kite surfing and windsurfing instructors, so it's fairly easy to arrange lessons or outings and the price is more affordable than you'd imagine. The building itself is well-maintained and has a laid-back atmosphere. It makes for a good place to wind down after a long day of having fun in the sun.

If you're looking to live it up in unchecked luxury, then look no further than the **Coronado Hotel & Resort** (☎ 240 4444; www.coronadoresort.com; d from US$180; P ✗ 🏊 🖳), the granddaddy of Pacific Coast resorts. With more than 100 amenity-laden rooms, a top-notch beachside golf course, swimming pools, tennis courts,

an equestrian center, a casino, a dayspa, a gym, a marina and a whole slew of bars and restaurants, you may not be able to find the time to actually visit the beach. Even if you're not staying here, the town's nightlife revolves around the hotel, so dress smart and stop by the attached nightclub.

Beside the turnoff for Playa Coronado is **Restaurante Los Che's** (Interamericana; mains US$6-12), a long-standing local favorite that is famous for its rotisserie-cooked meats. This is also a great place to sample the local seafood, especially if you stop by the coast during lobster season.

Playa El Palmar

Ten kilometers west of the Playa Coronado is the turnoff for this lovely white-sand beach, which is located in the village of San Carlos. Although much less developed than Coronado, El Palmar is still popular with weekending families from the capital, but the atmosphere is much more low-key.

Hotel Palmar Surf Beach & School (☎ 240 8004; camping per person US$5, r from US$20; P ✕) is an excellent choice for shoestringers who want to surf or learn the ropes. Rooms are extremely basic and minimally furnished, but all you really need after a long day out on the surf is a place to crash. Surf lessons here are US$25 per hour and the friendly owner can also arrange surf trips throughout Panama. And don't worry about not having a board – they're available here for rental.

THE ROAD TO THE DARIÉN

East of the capital, the Interamericana passes through several small towns before arriving at Yaviza, the end of the road – literally.

CHEPO
pop 14,000

Beyond the urban sprawl east of Panama City, the landscape becomes increasingly barren on both sides of the Interamericana. Gas stations and accommodations become somewhat scarce, and the views are monotonous to say the least.

As little as 40 years ago, the highway ended at Chepo and a sign announced the start of the Darién Gap – from Chepo to the Colombian border there was only roadless jungle. Today Chepo is one of several ranching towns along the Interamericana and is notable only for its abundance of gas stations and supermarkets.

Buses leave the Terminal Nacional de Transporte, in the Albrook district of Panama City, for Chepo (US$1.50, 1¼ hours) almost hourly from 6:30am to 5pm.

NUSAGANDI

Just before you reach the town of El Llano, you'll see the turnoff for Nusagandi, a small town inside the **Área Silvestre de Narganá** wildlife reserve. This reserve was created by the Kuna, primarily to try to keep squatters from settling on their land. However, it consists mostly of species-rich primary forest and was a perfect choice for conservation.

The road into the reserve is pretty rough, and you'll need a 4WD vehicle with a strong engine and plenty of clearance. However, it's worth the trip in, especially if you're a birder –

this is the best place in Panama to spot the speckled antshrike, the black-headed ant thrush and the black-crowned antpitta.

At the 17km mark, there's the remote **Burbayar Lodge** (☎ 264 1679; www.burbayar.com; 1st/additional night per person with 3 meals & tours US$115/75 ; P), an ecologically minded, low-impact lodge accommodating up to 14 guests in six simple cabins. A tiny generator provides some electricity, but at night most of the light comes from gas lanterns or candles, lending an old-time feel to the setting. There's primary forest surrounding the lodge, complete with waterfalls, caverns and a trail all the way to the coast in Kuna Yala (27km, six to eight hours). Booking in advance is essential. If you don't have your own car, note that the price includes round trip transportation from Panama City.

IPETÍ
pop 600

Forty-five kilometers east of Lago Bayano, is the town (or towns) of Ipetí-Emberá, Ipetí Kuna and Ipetí Colono – each is occupied by a different cultural group (Kuna, Emberá and Latino). With the help of a local Peace Corps worker, Ipetí has started a community-based tourism project that presents a unique opportunity to learn more about rural Panamanian life.

From the Interamerican, be on the lookout for a faded green sign that says 'bienvenidos' (welcome) – this signals that you have entered the town of Ipetí. From here, turn right at the sign and follow the dirt road for 2km until you reach your first stop, the village of Ipetí-Emberá.

Overlooking the Río Ipetí, this small Emberá village consists of several dozen wood-sided, thatched-roof houses including a Casa Cultural (an open-sided building used as a meeting space), a Casa Medicinal (where healing herbs are grown) and a network of trails leading into the surrounding rainforest. From the village, it's a mere 45-minute walk upstream along the Río Ipetí to a series of natural swimming pools that are fed by small waterfalls. You can also hire one of the villagers to take you up here by dugout canoe, which presents a unique opportunity to wildlife-watch at an unhurried pace. If you want to stay the night, you can either pitch a tent for a few dollars, or arrange a homestay for US$9 per night. If you don't have your own food, you can purchase a simple meal in town for around US$2. There's also a small handicrafts

---

THE END OF THE ROAD

Since the first Interamericana Congress met in Buenos Aires in 1925, the nations of the Americas have devoted considerable money and engineering skills to the completion of a great hemispheric road system. Today, only 150km of unfinished business prevents that system from being realized – the Darién Gap. This defiant stretch of wilderness, which separates the continents of North and South America, is the sole barrier in the way of an otherwise unbroken 30,600km highway winding from Circle, Alaska, to Puerto Montt, Chile.

Until recently, the governments of Panama and Colombia stood poised to construct this missing bit of pavement. However, with the civil war raging in Colombia, and the threat of foot-and-mouth disease spreading to North America, it appears that the hemispheric highway won't be finished any time soon. Until it's completion, the highway on the Panamanian side of the divide will continue to end at the sweaty, ramshackle town of Yaviza in Darién Province. Yaviza and Panama City are separated by 266km of bad road and endless cattle country. Efforts to pave the road all the way to Yaviza began in 2001, though it will take several more years to complete the project.

The drive from the capital to Yaviza currently takes about six hours during the dry season, but will take longer during the rainy season. For information on Yaziva and the Darién Gap see p280.

---

store selling Emberá woven baskets and there is usually someone around that can give you a traditional *jagua* body painting for a few dollars. This hennalike plant extract leaves a temporary tattoo for about a week.

Directly across the highway from the turnoff to Ipetí Emberá is Ipetí Kuna. This is a very traditional Kuna village – many of the residents don't speak Spanish, let alone English – and it's not set up for tourism in the same manner as Ipetí Emberá. However, **Igua** (☎ 595 9500), one of the Kuna chiefs here, leads boat tours to nearby Lago Bayano and can take hikes into the rainforest, though it helps to have a decent command of Spanish.

If you continue up the road 1km you'll reach Ipetí Colono, which is just a few buildings scattered off the highway. Some fine horsemen hail from this village and anyone looking for some impromptu adventure should stop in and inquire about hiring horses – you can reach virgin forest on horseback in under two hours.

TORTÍ
pop 8500

Twelve kilometers past Ipetí is the village of Tortí, which is a useful place to stop for the night if you don't think you can make it as far as Yaviza. The **Hospedaje Tortí** (s/d with fan US$6/8, s/d with air-con US$10/12; P 🐾) isn't the Ritz, but it has a number of relatively clean cinderblock rooms, each with a decent mattress and clean towels. The shared facilities are also passable and although there isn't any hot water, you're not likely to miss it in these parts.

Also in town are three public phones, a health clinic, police and gas stations and several restaurants – these so-called 'conveniences' tend to trail off south of here, so it's best to enjoy them now. If you're looking for a hot meal, **Avicar** (dishes US$2-4) serves traditional country-style Panamanian dishes and you're likely to share a table with some pretty interesting characters in these parts. A grocery store of the same name adjoins the restaurant and it's good place to stock up on supplies before pressing on.

Up the road, you'll reach a leather-goods store named **Echao Palante** (Going Forward; 🕙 10am-8pm). Inside, hard at work, you'll find Pedro Guerra, who has handmade more than 5000 saddles (it takes him a day to make one) and countless belts and sandals over the years.

HIGUERONAL
pop 200

Ten kilometers past Tortí is the village of Higueronal, which is likely the first military checkpoint you'll pass on your way to the Darién. If you're a foreigner, you must enter the building and show your passport to the soldiers, who will note your name and nationality in their ledger before returning your passport. This is done so that if something happens to you, the checkpoint will be able to inform the search party that you passed by here.

If you don't like military checkpoints, either turn around or get used to it – they increase in frequency south of Yaviza.

Coclé Province

Coclé – land of sugar, salt and presidents. More sugar has been refined in this province, more salt has been produced here, and more Panamanian presidents have been born in Coclé than in any other province. These are facts in which the people of Coclé take great pride, but the province isn't just about political legacies and table condiments.

Coclé boasts a medley of landscapes from abandoned coastlines to towering cloud forests, with vast agricultural and pastoral land in between. Edging along the Pacific Ocean, the province is home to a couple of attractive beaches that see their fair share of weekend warriors from Panama City. Edging along the highlands is the mountain town of El Valle, a popular rural retreat. Away from the coast but not quite into the foothills is Penonomé, Coclé's bustling provincial capital and the best place in the country to shop for authentic Panama hats.

Often overlooked by travelers, Coclé lacks the stellar beaches of Bocas del Toro, the pristine national parks of Chiriquí and the cultural heritage of the Península de Azuero. Furthermore, since it's criss-crossed by the Interamericana, Coclé is unfortunately often thought of as drive-through country on the way to more far-flung locales. However, although you certainly shouldn't miss out on Panama's top-attractions, a visit to Coclé will provide you with an authentic off-the-beaten-path trip that is experienced by few travelers.

As not to disappoint those of you whose breath quickened at the earlier mention of salt and sugar, it *is* possible to tour a huge sugar refinery here, and you *can* look out upon salt flats all day. And of course, both can be enjoyed at mealtime, either as sweetener for a cup of Panama's finest or to bring out the flavors of a plate of hearty rice and beans.

COCLÉ PROVINCE

HIGHLIGHTS

- Stopping to breathe in the mountain air in the highland retreat of **El Valle** (p130)
- Taking long walks along empty stretches of beach around **Santa Clara** (p136)
- Shopping for an authentic Panama hat in the regional capital of **Penonomé** (p139)
- Hiking through dense rainforest in the under-touristed **Parque Nacional Omar Torrijos** (p142)

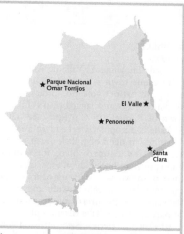

★ Parque Nacional Omar Torrijos

El Valle ★

★ Penonomé

★ Santa Clara

- POPULATION: 214,000
- AREA: 6075 SQ KM
- ELEVATION: 1626M

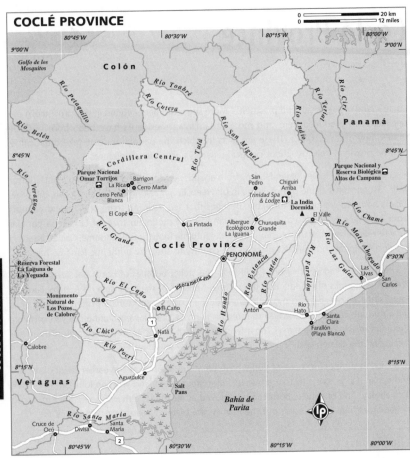

COCLÉ PROVINCE

EL VALLE

pop 6900

Officially known as El Valle de Antón, this picturesque town is nestled in the crater of a giant extinct volcano, and ringed by verdant forests and jagged peaks. Like the town of Boquete in Chiriquí (see p201), El Valle is a popular weekend getaway for urbanites in need of a little fresh air and scenery. It's a superb place for walking, hiking or horseback riding, especially since there is an extensive network of trails leading from the town into the hills and around the valley. Nature lovers, and bird-watchers in particular, won't be disappointed – the nearby forests offer excellent bird-watching, and the valleys of El Valle are home to an impressive set of waterfalls as well as some rare golden frogs.

History

Three million years ago, this volcano erupted with such force that it blew off its top, creating a crater 5km across – one of the largest in the Americas. In the eons that followed, the crater gradually filled with rainwater to create a large lake. However, through erosion or collapse, a breach opened at the present site of Chorro de Las Mozas and the entire lake drained. The resulting flood created an extensive network of waterways, which attracted indigenous populations to the valley. Today, their early petroglyphs can still be seen throughout the valley.

Orientation

The road that heads north to El Valle from the Interamericana becomes Av Central once it hits the eastern edge of the valley. Av Central is El Valle's main street, along which are numerous hotels and restaurants and most of the town's businesses. Many of the roads branching off Av Central lead to yet more hotels and restaurants.

Av Central ends west of the center of town. Here you can turn right and proceed 100m or so until the road forks. The branch to the left – Calle La Reforma – reaches the Cabañas Potosí after about 800m. The branch to the right – Calle del Macho – leads to the canopy tour, a waterfall and to some petroglyphs.

Information

INTERNET ACCESS

An **internet café** (Av Central; per hr US$1; ☯ 8am-6:30pm Mon-Sat, 10:30am-2pm Sun) is on the main road near Motel-Restaurante Niña Delia.

MEDICAL SERVICES

For your health needs, turn to the **Centro de Salud de El Valle** (☎ 983 6112; ☯ 24hr) near the western end of Av Central.

MONEY

Just east of Restaurante Santa Librada is a Banco Nacional de Panama **ATM** (Av Central).

POST

There's a **post office** (Calle del Mercado; ☯ 8am-4pm) behind the handicrafts market.

TOURIST INFORMATION

Instituto Panameño de Turismo (IPAT) operates a small **information booth** (☎ 983 6474) at the center of town next to the handicrafts market, though it is rarely staffed.

Sights

WATERFALLS

Some of the biggest attractions of El Valle are the handful of waterfalls that cascade down the surrounding hillsides into the valley floor. The most accessible of these is the **Chorro de las Mozas** (Young Women's Falls), which is located about 1km outside the southwest corner of town. This is the original site where the prehistoric lake breached, forming the scenic cascades you see today. This is a popular local spot for taking a dip

and lounging about, especially since there's near perfect spring weather in El Valle virtually year round.

The most famous waterfall in the El Valle area is the 85m-high **Chorro El Macho** (Manly Falls; admission US$2; ☯ dawn-dusk), which is located a few kilometers north of town near the entrance to the canopy tour. As its somewhat humorous name implies, this towering waterfall is more dramatic than its dainty counterpart, and makes for some excellent photographs. If the summer sun is beating down more than usual, you can take a refreshing bath at the base of the falls. Here below the falls, you'll find a large swimming pool made of rocks, surrounded by rainforest and fed by river water. There are also a series of short hiking trails here that wind into the surrounding forest.

For an unforgettable aerial view of El Macho, El Valle's famed canopy tour is a truly hair-raising experience – for more information, see p134.

ROCK PAINTINGS

Located in the northwestern corner of the valley, **La Piedra Pintada** (Colored Stone) is a huge boulder adorned with pre-Columbian carvings. Locals often fill in the grooves of the petroglyphs with chalk to facilitate their viewing, but their meaning isn't clearer. That doesn't prevent children from giving their interpretation of the petroglyphs for US$2 (in Spanish only).

One of these interpreters, Seneida Milena Rivera, says she learned the 'story of the rock' at school. Amid a 10-minute explanation of the graffiti-like carvings, she takes her bamboo pointing stick and identifies an x carved into the rock. It represents the burial site of a powerful chief who died many centuries ago, she says. 'The site moos like a cow every time it rains,' she adds.

Due to one report of theft from a vehicle near the entrance of the trail leading to the petroglyphs, it's best to come by bus even if you've got your own wheels. The site can be reached by a yellow school bus with 'Pintada' above the windshield. It passes along Av Central every 30 minutes, from 6am to 7pm (US$0.25 one way).

HANDICRAFTS MARKET

El Valle is home to one of Panama's largest **handicrafts market** (Av Central; ☯ 8am-6pm).

COCLÉ PROVINCE

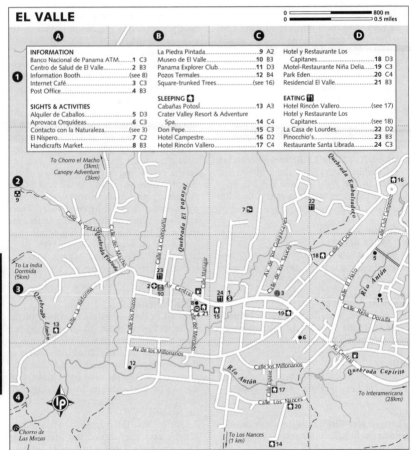

EL VALLE

INFORMATION	
Banco Nacional de Panama ATM......**1** C3	
Centro de Salud de El Valle.............**2** B3	
Information Booth.........................(see 8)	
Internet Café................................**3** C3	
Post Office...................................**4** B3	

SIGHTS & ACTIVITIES	
Alquiler de Caballos.......................**5** D3	
Aprovaca Orquídeas.......................**6** C3	
Contacto con la Naturaleza...........(see 3)	
El Níspero....................................**7** C2	
Handicrafts Market.......................**8** B3	

La Piedra Pintada...........................**9** A2	
Museo de El Valle.........................**10** B3	
Panama Explorer Club...................**11** D3	
Pozos Termales............................**12** B4	
Square-trunked Trees.................(see 16)	

SLEEPING 🏠	
Cabañas Potosí.............................**13** A3	
Crater Valley Resort & Adventure	
Spa...**14** C4	
Don Pepe....................................**15** C3	
Hotel Campestre...........................**16** D2	
Hotel Rincón Vallero.....................**17** C4	

Hotel y Restaurante Los	
Capitanes...................................**18** D3	
Motel-Restaurante Niña Delia......**19** C3	
Park Eden...................................**20** C4	
Residencial El Valle.....................**21** B3	

EATING 🍴	
Hotel Rincón Vallero..................(see 17)	
Hotel y Restaurante Los	
Capitanes.................................(see 18)	
La Casa de Lourdes......................**22** D2	
Pinocchio's..................................**23** B3	
Restaurante Santa Librada..........**24** C3	

Mostly Ngöbe Buglé, but also some Emberá and Wounaan, bring a variety of handicrafts to sell to tourists (most of whom are Panamanians from the capital). If you're self-catering, the market also stocks a good selection of fresh produce from around the country. Although the market runs every day, stop by on Sunday for the full-on affair.

One of the most popular items up for sale in the markets are *bateas,* which are large trays carved from a local hardwood and used by the Ngöbe Buglé for tossing rice and corn. You can also find figurines, colorful baskets made from palms, gourds painted in brilliant colors, clay flowerpots, Panama hats, and birdcages made of sticks.

ZOO

About 1km north of Av Central is a zoo named **El Níspero** (☎ 983 6142; adult/child US$2/1; ⏰ 7am-5pm). Most Latin American zoos are sad, cruel places, and unfortunately this is such a place. Here, for example, there are numerous eagles and hawks in a cage smaller than a walk-in closet, and the margays and ocelots on display look listless and depressed.

If you're sensitive to cage animals, you should probably skip this one. With that said, El Níspero is one of the best places for seeing Panama's golden frogs *(ranas doradas).* These endangered amphibians are unbelievably striking in color, and extremely photogenic. They are also one of Panama's most important cultural symbols, and have

LOCAL LORE: LA INDIA DORMIDA

The locals of El Valle are fond of pointing out features in the peaks surrounding their valley. However, no image is as popular or as storied as that of La India Dormida or the 'Sleeping Indian.' According to local lore, there was once a beautiful native princess that lived in the valley. When the Spanish arrived, the princess fell deeply in love with one of the conquistadores. After a brief but intense romance, she petitioned her father to marry the Spaniard. However, since she was destined to marry someone of royal blood, and the conquistador was busy claiming their native lands for the Spanish crown, her father promptly refused.

Upon having her heart broken, the princess immediately took her own life. After being buried in the hills, earth and dust gradually covered her body, giving shape to the mountain that rises over the valley. However, the legend insists that the princess is merely sleeping, and awaiting the day when her forbidden love can be pursued. Today, locals have popularized the story to serve as a parable for never denying someone's love.

long been revered by the indigenous peoples of the country. Unfortunately, they are extremely sensitive to human intrusion and climate change, so as their numbers continue to deplete, it's increasingly unlikely that you'll see them in the wild.

HOT SPRINGS

Located on the west side of town (follow the signs), **Pozos Termales** (Thermal Baths; Calle los Pozos; admission US$1; 8am-5pm) is the perfect place to soak the afternoon away. The forested complex is remote and rustic, and home to a series of pools with varying temperatures and supposed curative properties. After your bath, there is an area (a bucket, to be more precise) for applying healing mud to your skin. The next step is to take the requisite photo or two, and then head to the showers to rinse off. If you're looking to detox or simply scrub down, this is the perfect place to head.

MUSEO DE EL VALLE

On the eastern side of El Valle's conspicuous church is the very modest **Museo de El Valle** (Av Central; admission US$0.25; 10am-2pm Sun), which contains exhibits of petroglyphs and ceramics left by the indigenous peoples who lived in the area hundreds of years ago. There is also some religious art (the museum is owned by the church next door), mostly statues of Christ and the Virgin, as well as some historical and geological information on El Valle's volcano.

SQUARE-TRUNKED TREES

People who stand to gain from increased tourism to the area like to mention El Valle's *arboles cuadrados* (square-trunked trees), which can be found directly behind the Hotel Camp-

estre. After a short 10-minute hike through the forest, you'll come across a thicket of trees that aren't exactly round, but they're not exactly square, either. You might want to see them for yourself and then ponder, 'What's the big deal even if they are square?'

GARDENS

For the best selection of *orquídeas* (orchids) in the area, visit the pleasant **Aprovaca Orquídeas** (admission free; 9am-4pm). Some 32 volunteers work to maintain the lovely flowers inside the greenhouse and the grounds, and they welcome visitors to show off the 96 varieties of orchids cultivated – it's well worth a visit. Look for the 'Orquídeas' sign on the way into town.

Activities
HIKING

Ringed by 1000m-tall mountains, and surrounded by humid cloud forest, El Valle is a hiker's paradise. From the town center, an extensive network of trails radiates out into the valley and up into the hills, and there are possibilities for anything from short day hikes to overnight excursions.

Serious trekkers should consider excursions to the tops of Cerro Cara Coral, Gerro Gaital and Cerro Pajita to the north, Cerro Gaital and Cerro Guacamayo to the south, and Cerro Tagua to the east. It also possible to make an ascent to the top of La India Dormida (see above). For the most part, the valley floor has been cleared for agricultural and pastoral land, though the peaks remain covered in dense forest.

Although it is possible to hike independently, trails are not always clearly marked,

PANAMA'S NATIONAL FLOWER

While hiking though the forests around El Valle, be sure to look for Panama's national flower, a terrestrial orchid known as the *flor del espiritu santo* or the 'holy ghost orchid.' This stunning flower, which was given its unforgettable name by Spanish missionaries during the colonial era, is perfectly shaped like a red-spotted dove emerging from ivory petals.

The flower is most commonly found along the forest floor beside a trail, but it can also be found growing on the branches of large trees. The orchid blooms from July to October, and has an unforgettable aroma. Please do not pick the flowers or dig up the bulbs as the holy ghost orchid is threatened by overharvesting throughout its range due to its aesthetic and cultural value.

and it is recommended that you seek out local advice before hitting the trails. If you're interested in hiring a guide, **Contacto con la Naturaleza** (Contact with Nature; ☎ 623 4122, 629 3722; elvalledeanton@hotmail.com; Av Central), next door to the internet café, provides bilingual guides for US$5 per hour.

CANOPY TOURS

Although canopy tours are about as prevalent as rice and beans in Costa Rica, they're still quite new to the Panama tourist scene. For the uninitiated, a canopy tour consists of a series of platforms anchored into the forest canopy that are connected by zip lines. Although they were originally used by biologists to study the rainforest canopy, today they function primarily as a way for gringos to get their eco-kicks.

The **Canopy Adventure** (El Valle ☎ 983 6547; Panama City ☎ 612 9176; canopy ride US$40, swim US$2, admission to falls US$2; 8am-4pm) is a suspended ride that uses cables, pulleys and a harness to allow you to view a rainforest from dozens of meters above the jungle floor. You'll be in a harness dangling among jungle trees as you ride from one platform to another (there are six in all), at times gliding over Chorro El Macho.

Although its ecological merit is somewhat questionable, there's no denying the rush you'll get as you soar through the air with your legs flailing to and fro. Of course, unless you like to expose your private parts to strangers, don't do this in a dress or short shorts.

BIRD-WATCHING

The forests around El Valle offer numerous opportunities for bird-watching, especially if you're looking for hummingbirds – commonly spotted species include the green hermit, the violet-headed hummingbird and the white-tailed emerald.

Those planning a bird-watching trip should contact **Mario Bernal Greco** (☎ 693 8213), who is a member of a prominent local conservation group, and is one of the country's top nature guides. If he can't be reached on his cell phone, you can stop by Cabañas Potosí – his mother runs the joint.

HORSEBACK RIDING

Near the Hotel Campestre you'll see a sign for **Alquiler de Caballos** (☎ 646 5813; horse rental per hr US$5, with guide per hr US$10), with a horse mural painted on the side of a building. The stable here has over 30 horses, which make for some fine transportation to explore the nearby mountains. Guides speak Spanish only.

Tours

Based at Crater Valley Hotel, the **Panama Explorer Club** (☎ 983 6939; www.pexclub.com) is an adventure tourism outfit that offers a wide range of activities. Available tours include hiking La India Dormida (US$20 per person, three to four hours), climbing and rappelling (US$20 per person, three to four hours), river kayaking (US$45 per person) and mountain-biking tours (US$10 to US$15 per person).

Sleeping

Although reservations are generally not necessary, be advised that El Valle can get busy on weekends and on national holidays as urban dwellers flee the capital and head for the hills.

Due to the chilly climate, all of the rooms in El Valle have hot water showers.

BUDGET

Motel-Restaurante Niña Delia (☎ 983 6110; Av Central; s/d/tr/q US$12/15/20/25; P) The town's cheapest accommodation has benefited from a recent renovation, though it's still a bare-bones motel beneath the fresh coat of paint. With that said, the six spartan rooms at the Niña Delia are perfectly acceptable if you don't need much more than a bed and bathroom. If you're on a budget, stop by the attached restaurant for all of your favorite Panamanian staples.

Residencial El Valle (☎ 983 6536; residencialelvalle@ hotmail.com; Av Central; s/d US$25/30; **P**) This long-standing budget hotel has earned its deserved popularity through a simple formula. Over the years, the Residencial El Valle has continued to offer clean no-fuss rooms with private hot showers and a personalized level of service. Throw in a few extras like bike rentals, a guide service, an attached handicraft shop and a popular restaurant and you've got yourself a successful hotel.

Don Pepe (☎ 983 6425; hoteldonpepe@hotmail.com; Av Central; s/d US$25/30; **P**) Located next door to Residencial El Valle, Don Pepe follows the same formula as its somewhat more popular neighbor. Fairly basic rooms are sparsely furnished, though they're well cared for by the proficient staff. On a clear night, be sure to check out the starry skies and panoramic view from the roof.

Cabañas Potosí (☎ 983 6181; Calle La Reforma; campsites US$10, d cabin US$40; **P**) Situated about 1.5km west of the town center on peaceful, park-like grounds with lovely views of the craggy ridges ringing the valley. The four stand-alone wooden cabins have two beds apiece with en-suites, and there's level ground here for setting up camp (two-person tent provided). This is a great option if you want a peaceful night's sleep amidst a tranquil forest setting.

MIDRANGE & TOP END

Hotel y Restaurante Los Capitanes (☎ 983 6080; Calle El Ciclo; d/ste US$45/85; **P**) Owned and managed by a former captain in the German merchant marine, this spic-and-span hotel and restaurant runs like a well-oiled ship. On offer are a number of handsome rooms with fine details, firm beds and spacious hot-water bathrooms, as well as a few palatial suites for anyone looking for a little more stretching room. Amenities include an excellent European-inspired restaurant, an open-air café and even a kiddy pool for the little ones.

Los Nances (☎ 983 6126; Calle El Nance; d with breakfast US$50; **P**) This secluded private residence sits high above the valley floor and offers lovely views of the surrounding hillsides. The friendly English-speaking retired couple rents four of their bedrooms, each of which has an intimate personal touch that is evident from the moment you walk in. Since the house is lived in year-round, it's best to phone ahead to let them know you're coming, and it's not a bad idea to ask for directions since the house can be a bit tricky to find.

Park Eden (☎ 938 6167; www.parkeden.com; Calle El Nance; d US$60-120, house from US$195; **P**) Park Eden, overflowing with country charm, is a beautiful retreat – the owner is an American-trained designer, and it shows (his wife is from Ecuador). This gorgeous home offers three very tastefully appointed rooms, plus a separate two-story house, a cottage and a little room behind the cottage. Regardless of which room you choose, staying with the friendly couple is simply a delight, and the house itself is bound to sooth your travel-worn spirits.

Hotel Rincón Vallero (☎ 983 6175; www.rinconvallero .com; Calle Espave; cabin d US$75, ste US$95-125; **P**) Located in a peaceful residential neighborhood, the Rincón Vallero is a contemporary hotel consisting of several cabins scattered around a flower-ringed pond. Although the tranquil ambience of the rustic setting is the main appeal for choosing this spot, guests looking to mingle with one another can congregate in the main building. Here, you'll find a relaxed restaurant (see p136) serving an eclectic mix of food as well as several sitting areas overlooking the gardens.

Crater Valley Resort & Adventure Spa (☎ 215 2330; www.crater-valley.com; per person from US$80; **P**) As its lengthy moniker implies, this resort and spa various offers pursuits ranging from climbing on the rock wall and guided rainforest hikes to soaking in the pool and pampering yourself in the spa. The entire complex sits on beautifully tended grounds that are covered with water features, and the rooms themselves are expertly decorated with tall ceilings, colorfully painted walls and patios with hammocks. Prices vary significantly depending on the time of year, the day of the week and the size of the room, so it's best to book ahead and try to save a bit of cash.

Hotel Campestre (☎ 983 6146; www.hotelcampestre .com; Calle Club Campestre; d US$92; **P**) The oldest hotel in town is a rustic affair with soaring wood beams, vaulted ceilings and a large fireplace, and is located on manicured grounds near the square-trunked tree grove. Unfortunately, the Campestre has seen better days since its opening in the 1920s, and most of the rooms here are starting to show their age. All in all, it's not a bad option if you're looking for a relaxed setting and a certain historic grace, though don't be surprised if the rooms don't meet your expectations.

COCLÉ PROVINCE

Eating

Restaurante Santa Librada (Av Central; mains US$2-4.50)
This cheap and cheerful restaurant serves
hearty portions of Panamanian staples such
as *lomo de arroz* (roast beef with rice) and
bistec picado (spicy shredded beef). If you're
in search of lighter fare, most sandwiches and
breakfasts are under US$2, and the restau-
rant's *sancocho de gallina* (a stew-like chicken
soup) is locally famous.

Pinocchio's (☎ 983 6975; Av Central; pizzas US$3-8;
⊙ 11am-9pm Thu-Sun) This much-loved pizzeria
is your best (and only) spot in El Valle for
tasty and cheap pizzas with a range of top-
pings. Also available here is rotisserie-cooked
chicken, meaty burgers and tacos, though locals and tourists alike swear that the pizzas
here are to die for.

Hotel Rincón Vallero (mains US$6-10) Located be-
side a koi pond, this cozy restaurant serves up
plates of fresh seafood including jump shrimp,
sea bass ceviche and grilled corvina. It also
has an extensive wine and cocktail list, which
makes this a great choice if you're wining and
dining your better half.

Hotel y Restaurante Los Capitanes (Calle El Ciclo;
mains US$8-12) The menu at this fine restaurant
features European cuisine – specials change
daily but always include tasty German staples
like *jager schnitzel* (breaded and fried meat).
Don't miss the freshly baked cakes and pies
or the *batidos* (fruit shakes), as well as the
long list of imported beers including dark and
dreamy *Warsteiner*.

La Casa de Lourdes (mains US$11-15) El Valle's
most beautiful restaurant has the look and
feel of a Tuscan villa. Situated on the back
terrace with stunning views, Lourdes offers
an eclectic menu of dishes like lobster and
sweet corn risotto, pork chop with a port
wine and guava sauce, and blackened corvina
with tamarind.

Getting There & Away

To leave El Valle you can hop aboard a bus
traveling along Av Central; on average, they
depart every 30 minutes. The final destinations are painted on windshields of the bus.
If your next destination isn't posted, catch a
bus going in the same direction and transfer
when appropriate. To reach El Valle from the
Interamericana, disembark any bus at Las
Uvas (marked by both a sign for El Valle and
a pedestrian overpass), about 5km west of San
Carlos. Minibuses pick up passengers at this

turnoff and travel to El Valle (US$1, one hour,
every 30 minutes).

Getting Around

Despite El Valle's small size, taxis ply Av Central all day long. You can go anywhere in town
for US$2.

SANTA CLARA

Although the beach at Santa Clara consists of
sparkling white sand and towering coconut
palms, somehow the tourist crowds seemed
to have passed on by. Needless to say, this is a
great destination if you want to lounge about
for days on end without having to worry about
someone stealing your stretch of sand.

Santa Clara itself is little more than a
sparsely populated fishing village that edges
between patches of dry tropical rainforest and
the vast blue expanse of the Pacific. However,
there's plenty of local flavor here to soak up
in between your beach-lying sessions, and
the high proportion of locals to tourists is a
nice change from some of the country's more
popular destinations.

Orientation

The tiny community of Santa Clara is located
11km southwest of the Interamericana turnoff
for El Valle. There are two Santa Clara turnoffs
from the Interamericana; one is posted for the
town and the other is posted for the beach (Playa
Santa Clara). The first turnoff you'll see as you
come from the east is the turnoff for town.

Activities

A few years ago, the owners of XS Memories
(see opposite) launched **Kayak Panama** (☎ 993
3096; tours per person from US$60) with canoeing guide
Sven Schiffer (☎ /fax 993 3620; vsschiffer@cwp.net.pa).
Now the foremost kayaking agency in the
country, it offers a wide range of excursions,
including trips on the Río Chame and the Río
Santa Maria, salt marsh paddling tours and
kayak trips from the top of the Continental Divide to the Caribbean. Tours have a three-per-
son minimum. Kayak Panama operates only
during the rainy season (April to November).
English, German and Spanish are spoken.

Sleeping & Eating

If you go down the first turnoff for Santa Clara
from the Interamericana for about 1km, you'll
see signs for Balneario Santa Clara, Las Ver-
aneras and Las Sirenas.

GHOSTS OF AN INVASION

About 1km past the Playa Santa Clara turnoff, you'll notice an open area where a wide, paved path stretches straight out from both sides of the Interamericana. This was once a key runway used by Noriega's forces, and it has some interesting history.

(Please note that although there are weeds growing from small cracks in the runway, the runway is occasionally used for private charter flights. As one unsuspecting reader found out, it's not advisable to actually walk down it.)

During the days of the Panama Defense Forces (PDF) there was a major army base here, known as Río Hato, to which the runway belonged. There were many barracks, an armory, a clinic and near the end of a 3km road that runs from the Interamericana to the coast, paralleling the runway, was Noriega's vacation home, near the hamlet of Farallón.

At 1am on December 20, 1989, the 'H-hour' of the US invasion of Panama, two F-117A stealth fighters swooped undetected out of the night sky and dropped two 2000lb bombs near the Río Hato PDF barracks. The bombing marked the first time that the USA's most sophisticated fighter plane was used in combat.

The US Secretary of Defense said at the time that the planes performed their missions flawlessly, precisely hitting their intended targets after flying all night from their base in Nevada. Later, the Pentagon admitted that the pilots had confused their targets, hitting one out of sequence and badly missing the second.

Río Hato was also where the US Army suffered its highest concentration of casualties during the invasion, but most were not the result of combat. Moments after the bombs exploded, an 850-man contingent of army rangers parachuted onto the runway. However, because they jumped from an altitude of only 150m and landed on pavement, many of them sustained serious injuries. More than two dozen members of the elite force were incapacitated by broken legs, torn knee ligaments and other injuries.

One of the most interesting things about all this is not the army's errors in planning the jump, but that the US military acted with great humanity in its bombing. Strange as that may sound, the targets the stealths were ordered to hit were empty fields near barracks filled with young Panamanian soldiers, not the barracks themselves. By dropping bombs near the barracks, the US military hoped to scare the soldiers into surrendering and thus avoid unnecessary bloodshed. In fact, hundreds of Panamanian soldiers at Río Hato did surrender immediately. For all the criticism leveled at the USA during and after the invasion, there were many such instances of restraint that went unmentioned.

Although the building itself is no longer standing, there is an interesting story attached to the former residence of Noriega. One of the main reasons former US President George Bush ordered the invasion was to arrest Noriega and bring him to trial on drug-trafficking charges. A big story on the third day of the invasion was US General Maxwell Thurman's announcement that US soldiers had found more than 50kg of cocaine in Noriega's vacation house. It wasn't until a month later, after persistent questioning from reporters, that the Pentagon admitted that the suspicious substance was actually corn flour used to make tamales.

Restaurante y Balneario Santa Clara (☎ 993 2123; campsites per person US$2; meals US$4-8; P) This popular campsite is a steal – for only a few bucks per night, you can get a private rancho on the beach as well as access to clean toilet and shower facilities. Even if you're not camping here, this is one of the few restaurants in the area, and the catch of the day – whatever it is – tastes fantastic when served in front a Pacific sunset. You can also arrange horseback riding and snorkeling trips here for a few dollars an hour.

XS Memories (☎ 993 3096; www.xsmemories.com; campsite per person US$3, motor home hookup without/with air-con US$8/12, d from US$55; P ⊠ ⊠) Just north of the turnoff for Playa Santa Clara, 100m from the Interamericana, is this American-owned and -run outfit. The property contains three spacious guestrooms with air-con, private hot-water bathrooms and tiled floors, more than 20 water, sewer and electrical hookups for motor homes, an area to pitch tents, an inviting swimming pool and a sports bar with DirecTV that has offers all the latest sporting matches. There's also an excellent restaurant that serves American staples such as juicy cheeseburgers, grilled steaks and pork chops – breakfasts are equally good and filling.

Restaurante y Cabañas Las Veranera (☎ 993 3313; cabins from US$60; P ☒ ☒) These beachside cabañas offer a variety of different sized cabins with en-suite hot-water bathrooms to meet the needs of you and your traveling companions. The loveliest accommodations here are the split-level thatch-cabins, which are built on stilts and overlook the crashing waves. There is also a small restaurant and bar on the beach here, which is perfect for some fresh ceviche, topped off with a sundowner.

Las Sirenas (☎ 993 3235; traducsa@cwpanama.net; d US$90; P ☒) A veritable gem hidden amidst a scenic stretch of coastline, Las Sirenas is a peaceful and secluded spot consisting of several cottages with modern accents and vaulted ceilings. Each cottage is brimming with amenities including air-con, palatial hot-water bathrooms, kitchenettes and dining areas – there is no restaurant on the premises, so you should be prepared to self-cater. The entire complex is set on a lush hillside just 150m from the crashing surf.

Getting There & Away

To get to Santa Clara, just take any bus that would pass through Santa Clara and tell the bus driver to drop you in town. When it's time to leave Santa Clara, just stand at any of the bus stops in town and hail a bus going in the direction you want to go. From Santa Clara, you can catch onward buses west to Antón (US$1, 30 minutes, every 30 minutes) or Penonomé (US$1.75, one hour, every 30 minutes). It's also easy to catch a ride on buses heading as far as David (US$10, 5½ hours, every hour) and points along the way. Heading east, you can find buses to San Carlos (US$1, 30 minutes, every 20 minutes), Chame (US$1.25, 45 minutes, every 20 minutes) and Panama City (US$2.50, 1¾ hours, every 20 minutes).

Getting Around

Except late at night, there are always taxis parked beside the turnoff on the Interamericana for Santa Clara (the town, not the beach). You can take one for US$2 to get to any of the places mentioned previously. The beach is 1.8km from the Interamericana.

FARRALLÓN (PLAYA BLANCA)

About 3km west of the Santa Clara turn-off is the former village of Farallón, which nowadays is starting to slowly adopt its alternative name, Playa Blanca. Prior to 2000, Farallón was just like any other fishing village along the Pacific coast, except of course for the ruins of the Panamanian military base here that was destroyed during the US invasion to oust Noriega. However, when the Colombian-owned Decameron hotel chain opened a resort here at the turn of the millennium, suddenly 'Playa Blanca' was cast as the hottest beach destination in all of Panama.

In 2003, the Spanish-owned Barceló hotel chain opened up a second resort here, which has injected a healthy amount of competition into the local economy. Of course, these days it seems like everyone in Farallón is cashing in, especially since apartments, condos, gated communities and shopping malls are popping up all around town. Needless to say, locals are divided about whether or not this sudden spate of development is exactly what the town needs, though it's unlikely that the boom is going to stop anytime soon. And, it's no small wonder that Farallón survived as long as it did, especially considering that Playa Blanca is one of the most beautiful beaches along the Pacific coast.

The more pretentious the name, the more pretentious the resort, which is why the **Royal Decameron Beach Resort & Casino** (☎ 993 2255; www.decameron.com; all-inclusive per person from US$150; P ☒ ☒ ☒) refers to itself as the Panama's top beach resort. And with more than 600 luxury rooms set on a picture-perfect stretch of powder white sand, and enough pools, bars and restaurants to count on both hands, it may have a point. If you're planning on staying at the 'Decameron' (its proper name is too much of a mouthful for us), it's worth going online as discounted all-inclusive packages are sometimes available if you book in advance.

Of course, the Decameron isn't the only player on the block now, at least not since the **Barceló Playa Blanca** (☎ 264 6444; www.barcelo.com; all-inclusive per person from US$150; P ☒ ☒ ☒) rolled into town. Although it's not nearly as grand in scope as the Decameron, the 200-room Mediterranean-inspired Barceló is worthy competition, especially since it brings to the table a world-class spa, a putting green, an outdoor theater and a marina chock-full of water craft. As with the Decameron, go online to save yourself a few dollars before arriving.

If you're just visiting for the day, and you don't have the cash to blow on a night of hedonistic luxury, both hotels offer day-passes that give you full access to their facilities. Of course, beaches are public land in Panama, so as long as you don't get into trouble, no one is going to stop you from laying out in front of either hotel and working on your tan.

ANTÓN
pop 9000

Antón, 15km west of Farallón, is in the center of a lush valley that's sprinkled with rice fields and cattle ranches. Although it has little to offer the tourist, except of course its natural beauty, its annual **patron saint festival** (January 13 to 16) and its folkloric festival **Toro Guapo** (October 13 to 15) are the best in the province. The people of Antón seemingly live for these events, and it's worth stopping by to partake in the festivities if you find yourself in the area.

As you drive into Antón along the Interamericana, you'll notice several hotels and restaurants as well as a bank and a couple of gas stations. Also along this stretch is the **Hotel Rivera** (☎ 987 2245; d with fan/air-con US$20/30; P ✗ ☎), which is a decent place to rest for the night. Cinderblock rooms with sparse furnishings are anything but special, though the air-con works and the hot water is occasionally turned on. Of course, it's hard to complain at this price, and the inviting pool is a nice amenity, especially when the summer sun is beating down.

Westbound buses including those heading to Penonomé can stop in Antón if you ask the driver in advance.

PENONOMÉ
pop 17,000

The provincial capital of Coclé Province is a bustling cross-roads city with a rich history. Founded in 1581, Penonomé blossomed so quickly that it served as the temporary capital of the isthmus in 1671 after the destruction of the first Panama City (now known as Panamá Viejo) and until Nueva Panamá (now known as Casco Viejo) was founded a few years later.

Today, the lifeline of the city is the Interamericana, which bisects Penonomé and ensures a steady stream of goods flowing in and out. If you're heading west, it's likely that you will pass through here at some point, though it's worth hopping off the bus for the city's two principal attractions, namely its annual festivals and its traditional Panama hats. Penonomé also serves as good jumping off point for the nearby artisan town of La Pintada (p141).

Orientation

Penonomé straddles the Interamericana 144km west of Panama City and 16km northwest of Antón. On the eastern side of town, the highway forks around an Esso gas station. One branch, Av Juan Demostenes Arosemena, goes to the right, and the other, the Interamericana, goes to the left.

Av Juan Demostenes Arosemena is the city's main street. Along it are two banks, a post office and the town church. The avenue actually ends at the church, which faces the central plaza. During Carnaval, the plaza and every street for three blocks around it are packed with people.

Information

For banking, try BBVA (Interamericana) or Banco Nacional de Panamá and Banistmo, both along Av Juan Demostenes Arosemena. All have ATMs.

The **post office** (Av Juan Demostenes Arosemena) is in the Palacio Municipal behind the church. There's a **mercado público** (public market; ☯ 4:30am-3:30pm) that's fun to browse near the central plaza. There is no tourist office in town.

The city's principal **hospital** (Interamericana) is at the eastern end of town.

Festivals & Events

Carnaval, held during the four days preceding Ash Wednesday, is a huge happening in Penonomé. In addition to the traditional festivities (the dancing, the masks, the costumes, the queen's coronation), floats here are literally *floated* down a tributary of the Río Zaratí.

Less popular but still a big crowd pleaser is Penonomé's **patron saint festival**. This festival is generally held on December 8 and 9 (or the following Saturday if both these dates fall on weekdays). Following a special Mass, Penonomé's Catholics carry a statue of the saint through the city's streets. The Mass and procession seem incidental to the celebration that takes place outside the church for two days.

COCLÉ PROVINCE

Sleeping & Eating

Hotel Dos Continentes (☎ 997 9326; fax 997 9390; Interamericana; d from US$20; P) Near the point where the Interamericana forks, Hotel Dos Continentes is the largest hotel in town, and arguably one of the best deals. There are definitely cheaper places to lay your head, though you'll sleep well at night in this secure location with well-lit and spacious rooms, complete with modern hot-water bathrooms and comfortable beds. Ask for a room in the newly renovated section, which will set you back a few extra dollars, but is much, much friendlier on the eyes.

Hotel Guacamaya (☎ 991 0117; hguacamaya@ cwpanama.com.pa; Interamericana; d from US$30; P ✗) A few doors down from the Hotel Dos Continentes, rooms at the Guacamaya are slightly more expensive, though they're significantly more spacious. Regular rooms with modern furniture are nice enough, though it's worth paying a few extra dollars and snagging one of the larger rooms that overlooks the mountains. There is a good restaurant on the premises that serves up all your standard Panamanian offerings.

Parrillada El Gigante (Interamericana; mains US$3-5) A short walk to the west of the Esso station, this pleasant, open-sided restaurant serves traditional country-style food and hot, cheesey pizzas. Courtesy of the Lebanese owner, there are also several Middle Eastern dishes on the menu including falafel and hot pita bread.

Getting There & Away

Buses traveling to and from Penonomé via the Interamericana use a small parking lot opposite the Hotel Dos Continentes as a passenger pick-up and drop-off point. Buses pass through in either direction every 10 to 15 minutes. Area buses, such as those to Churuquita Grande (US$1, 45 minutes, every 30 minutes), Aguadulce (US$1, 30 minutes, every 20 minutes), La Pintada (US$1, every 30 minutes), San Pedro, Chiguiri Arriba (US$1.50, 80 minutes, seven per day) and El Copé (US$1.50, one hour), use a station two blocks southeast of the central plaza. From Penonomé there are frequent buses to Panama City (US$4, 2½ hours, every 20 minutes) and David (US$7, 4½ hours, every 35 minutes).

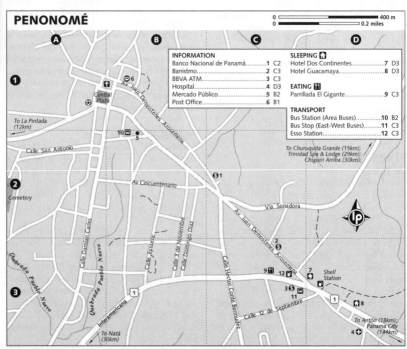

PENONOMÉ

INFORMATION		SLEEPING 🏠	
Banco Nacional de Panamá...........1 C2		Hotel Dos Continentes...................7 D3	
Banistmo...............................2 C3		Hotel Guacamaya......................8 D3	
BBVA ATM..............................3 C3			
Hospital................................4 D3		EATING 🍴	
Mercado Público.......................5 B2		Parrillada El Gigante....................9 C3	
Post Office.............................6 B1			
		TRANSPORT	
		Bus Station (Area Buses)..............10 B2	
		Bus Stop (East-West Buses).........11 C3	
		Esso Station..............................12 C3	

PANAMA HATS

A Panama hat or simply a Panama is a traditional brimmed hat made from a Panama-hat palm (*Carludovica palmata*). Although originally from Ecuador, the hat became popular in Panama during the construction of the canal when thousands of Panamas were imported for use by the workers. After American President Theodore Roosevelt donned a Panama during his historic visit to the canal, the hats became the height of fashion.

Unlike the better-known Panamas from Ecuador, which are woven from crown to brim in one piece, this kind is made by a braiding process, using a half-inch braid of palm fiber, usually of alternating or mixed white and black. The finished braid is wound around a wooden form and sewn together at the edges, producing a round-crowned, black-striped hat. It's a common sight in the rural parts of Panama, and it's not uncommon for political contenders to don hats periodically to appear as 'one of the people.'

Penonomé is known throughout Panama as the place to buy the hats that bear the country's name. The highest-quality Penonomé hats are so tightly put together that they can hold water – prices range from US$10 up to US$150. Surprisingly, there's no one place to buy these hats in Penonomé as they are made in outlying towns and brought to the city for sale. However, many are sold by hat vendors standing outside stores and restaurants near the Esso gas station by the entrance to town. You can also try the **Mercado de Artesanías Coclé** (🕑 8am-4pm) at the eastern end of town and the Mercado de Artesanías La Pintada in the nearby town of La Pintada (see below).

Getting Around

Due to its size and importance, Penonomé has no shortage of taxis. The best place to hail one is by the Esso gas station, near the entrance to town. You can also find one near the central plaza. The fare for any destination in town is not usually more than US$3, and often it's half that.

LA PINTADA

This small foothill town, just 12km northwest of downtown Penonomé, boasts an artisans' market and a cigar factory. If you're staying in Penonomé for the night or simply passing through the area, it's worth stopping at La Pintada to pick up some attractive handicrafts and a few fresh-rolled cigars direct from the source.

La Pintada's famous **Mercado de Artesanías La Pintada** (Pintado Artisans' Market; ☎ 983 0313; 🕑 9am-4pm) specializes in Penonomé-style Panama hats. The material used in Panamas occasionally varies from one town to the next, though here the headgear is made of *bellota* (palm fiber) and also of *pita*, which is related to cactus. There are several *bellota* and *pita* plants growing in front of the market, so you can see what they look like. Other items of particular interest are dolls wearing handmade folkloric costumes, *seco* (the local firewater) bottle covers made from hat palm, and handmade brooms.

The market is easy to find. As you drive through La Pintada on the main road from Penonomé, you'll come to a very large soccer field on the left side of the road. The market is on the far side of this field.

The second obligatory stop in La Pintada is the **Cigars Joyas de Panama** (🕑 /fax 983 0304; joyapan@yahoo.com). The factory's owner, Miriam Padilla, began growing tobacco in La Pintada with three Cubans in 1982, though they went their separate ways in 1987 when the Cubans emigrated to Honduras to open a cigar factory. Left to her own devices, Miriam sent choice samples of her tobacco to tourists and other people she'd met in Panama over the years, seeking investors for a factory. Today Miriam and her son, Braulio Zurita, are La Pintada's largest employers, employing 80 workers who make a total of 22,000 cigars a day. The employees work at rows of desks in a long, concrete-sided, aluminum-roofed, one-story building the size of a large home, which is the pride of the neighborhood.

The cigars are made in an assembly process that begins at one end of the building with leaf separation from stem, and ends at the other end of the building with the packaging of the final product. From here, the cigars are shipped primarily to the USA, France and Spain. A box of 25 of the highest-quality cigars costs US$50 in Panama and twice that outside the country. Joyas de Panama cigars also come flavored – with a hint of vanilla, rum or amaretto. Miriam and Braulio speak English, and cigars are clearly much more than a business to them.

GETTING THERE & AWAY
To get to the factory from the artisans' market, just drive southeast from the market, straight toward Penonomé (ignore the Pana American Cigar Co, which is en route to Joyas de Panama). You'll come to Cafe Coclé, on your right; take the well-maintained dirt road just beyond it (the road that initially parallels the paved road, not the next right). Follow this road about 1km until you see a simple thatched-roof restaurant on the right side of the road immediately followed by the open-sided cigar factory with a corrugated metal roof.

TRINIDAD SPA & LODGE

our pick Trinidad Spa & Lodge (☎ 983 8900; www .posadaecologica.com in Spanish; d US$79-99; P ♠) is an incredible find that's well worth the time it takes to get there – it's reachable by paved road and located in Chiguiri Arriba, 29km to the northeast of Penonomé. The lodge sits atop a summit with sweeping views of green valleys and imposing peaks intermittently shrouded by clouds, looking not so much like a slice of Central America but rather the famous karst formations outside Guilin, China.

The main structure, set amid gardens that attract many species of bird, is home to an outstanding restaurant and bar. Vegetarian items are available, nearly all of the food is grown organically and a selection of Chilean wines accompanies the meals. The building also houses a holistic spa that offers everything from manicures and facials to mud baths and herbal oil massages.

A short walk from the main building are several secondary buildings, which are home to a variety of tranquil rooms outfitted with private terraces, steamy hot-water bathrooms and colonial-inspired furnishings. The premier room here costs a little more (US$99) because word has slipped that it is one of former President Moscoso's favorite rooms – many Panamanian guests now request it.

Guests at the Trinidad are treated to guided hiking tours, ranging from easy nature walks to arduous treks, taking in river, waterfall and forest scenes. Area wildlife

includes three-toed sloths, night monkeys, deer and armadillos. Four species of toucan and many species of hummingbird also live here, and can occasionally be seen from the comfort of the inn's creek-fed swimming pool.

Getting There & Away
To get to the inn from central Penonomé, take the well-marked turnoff for Churuquita Grande, several hundred meters northwest of the Hotel Dos Continentes. Proceed past Churuquita Grande and follow the signs to Chiguiri Arriba and the inn.

Alternately, go to Penonomé's area bus station and take a 'Chiguiri Arriba' bus (US$1.50, 80 minutes). Buses depart at 6am, 10am and 11am and 12:30pm, 2pm, 4:30pm and 6pm.

PARQUE NACIONAL OMAR TORRIJOS & LA RICA
Simply put, Parque Nacional Omar Torrijos (or simply El Copé) is one of Panama's hidden gems, though difficult access and relative obscurity have kept the tourist crowds away. The park encompasses some of the most beautiful forests in Panama, with montane forest on the Pacific side of the Continental Divide and humid tropical forest on the Caribbean side.

El Copé is also home to the full complement of Panama's wildlife, including such rare bird species as the golden-olive woodpecker, red-fronted parrotlet, immaculate antbird and white-throated shrike-tanager, as well as all four species of felines, Baird's tapirs and peccaries.

One of the wonderful surprises to greet visitors to El Copé is the excellent condition of the park's trail system, which was recently given a major makeover by US Peace Corps volunteers, Autoridad Nacional del Ambiente (ANAM) rangers and members of Panama Verde (a Panamanian student ecological group). Another surprise: this park offers the easiest and surest point from which to see both the Pacific and Atlantic Oceans (from the lookout above the cabin).

Orientation & Information
There is a **ranger station** (☼ 6am-8pm; admission per day US$3) just inside the entrance of the park where visitors can pay accomodations and

admission fees. Permits to camp in the park are payable at the ranger station.

Hiking

Next to the ranger station you'll find two side-by-side trails – the leftmost trail follows the ridgeline and summits a nearby mountain in about an hour. Here, you'll be rewarded with panoramic views of both oceans and the surrounding canopy.

If you take the rightmost trail, you'll be following the Caribbean slope of the Continental Divide, though be advised that this trail does not end, and should under no circumstances be attempted without a guide. However, if you can arrange a guide through the ranger station, this is a fantastic trail that passes several rivers, winds up and down several mountain peaks and penetrates deep into the heart of the forest.

Behind the ranger station, you'll find the entrance to a short interpretative trail that points out local species of trees and plants. This trail is only about 500m in length, but it's a great introduction to the flora of the region.

Another hiking option is to spend a night with the Navas family – see below.

Be advised that there are poisonous snakes in the park including the infamous fer-de-lance – as a precaution, inform others of your intentions, always hike in boots and stick to the trails.

Sleeping & Eating

About 200m up the road from the ranger station is a small **cabin** (campsites US$5, r per person US$5) with four beds and a kitchen with simple cooking facilities and basic toilet and cold-water shower. It also has a loft and living room, allowing a total of 10 to sleep comfortably if you have your own gear. Either way, you'll need a sleeping bag – it cools off at night in the mountains so bring some warm clothing as well. If you've brought your own tent, there is a groomed spot alongside the cabin where you can pitch for the night.

Another excellent way of visiting the park is taking advantage of the services of the friendly Navas family. They rent rooms in their **house** (☎ 983 9130; r with meals per person US$15-20) in Barrigon, and they also have a cabaña, **Albergue Navas** (☎ 983 9130; r with meals per person US$15-20), in La Rica, a beautiful community inside the park. Accommodations at both places are rus-

tic, but very well maintained and inexpensive, with all meals included. The family – Santo and Anna Navas and their sons – work as guides, as they have done in the past for scientists and birders. They help to maintain the park and its trails and their knowledge and love of the area is quite apparent.

Barrigon can be reached by car or public transportation from El Copé. From Barrington it's a two- to three-hour hike or a horseback ride to La Rica, where you'll find a cool and pleasant community with a beautiful river and swimming holes, with access to secluded, orchid-covered waterfalls, virgin rain and cloud forest, and excellent bird-watching. ✈

From La Rica, you can take day hikes to the summits of cerros Marta and Peña Blanca, visit the impressive waterfalls of Chorros de Tife and even hike to the ruins of Torrijos' plane; see p137.

La Rica is remote (no phone, electricity or road), and the hiking is strenuous, but it is a nature lover's dream and comes highly recommended. All the arrangements can be made through Santo and Anna Navas (Spanish only). Call ahead, or ask around for the Navas family when you reach Barrigon.

Getting There & Away

The turnoff for this national park is on the Interamericana, 18km west of Penonomé. From the turnoff, it's another 32.8km to the park's entrance. The road, paved for the first 26km, winds through rolling countryside dotted with farms and small cattle ranches. The paved road ends at the small town of El Copé. The remaining 6.8km of the drive to the park is on a dirt road that's so bad that a 4WD vehicle with a very strong motor and excellent tires is needed. There is no public transportation to the park. If you don't have a car, catch a bus from Penonomé to El Copé (US$1.50, one hour) and transfer there in a minibus to Barrigon (US$0.50), the closest village to the park. From there it's a one-hour hike into the park.

If you're driving, take the turnoff as marked from the Interamericana and proceed 26km. You will then see a sign directing you to the park (to the right) and another to the park's Sede Administrativa (administrative office). There's no reason to go to the administrative office, so stay to the right and continue until you reach the park's entrance.

NATÁ

pop 6300

Despite that fact that Natá – founded on May 20, 1522 – is the oldest surviving town in Panama, little remains of this rich history aside from a well-preserved church and a handful of colonial houses. Today, Natá is little more than a sleepy country town, and most of its inhabitants work at the area's sugar refineries or in the fields around town.

Although there's little reason to linger, it's worth stopping in Natá just to take a gander at its historic centerpiece, namely one of the oldest churches in the Americas. The town is also a good base for exploring the ruins at El Caño, one of only two archaeological parks in the country open to the public.

History

In 1515 a chief named Tataracherubi, whose territory covered much of what would later become northern Coclé Province, informed the Spanish conquistadors Alonso Perez de la Rua and Gonzalo de Badajoz of the wealth of his neighbor to the southwest, a chief named Natá. 'Natá has much gold, but he has few fighting men,' was the gist of that conversation.

Naturally, the conquistadors went after Natá's gold. Perez and his 30 men arrived first; Badajoz and his 130 men were not far behind. Perhaps a bit overanxious, Perez and his party soon found themselves amid a large indigenous settlement. Retreat was impossible, but Perez grabbed the native chief and threatened to kill him, and thus forced Natá to tell his warriors to back off.

Then Badajoz and his well-armed soldiers showed up, and Natá was forced to surrender a large quantity of gold. The Christians remained for two months in the village named after the chief before they headed south and plundered more villages. Two years later, the Spaniards, led by Gaspar de Espinosa, returned to Natá and established one of the earliest European settlements on the isthmus.

The Indians, meanwhile, were enslaved. As an incentive to settle in Natá, the ruthless Spanish governor Pedro Arias de Ávila divided the village and its inhabitants among 60 soldiers who agreed to start a pueblo there.

Sights

IGLESIA DE NATÁ

This historic church, which has remained close to its original state after all these years, is reason enough to visit Natá. Following an extensive renovation in the late 1990s, the church's fine colonial facade and a remarkable interior have been restored to their former grandeur.

If you look closely at the altar of the Virgin, you'll notice sculpted fruit, leaves and feathered serpents on its two columns – clearly the influence of its indigenous artisans. The position of the carved angels at its base signifies the power the artisans felt the angels possessed.

Notice also the Holy Trinity painting to the right of the altar. The painting was created in 1758 by the Ecuadorian artist José Samaniego, though for many years it was kept from public view. The reason behind this unscrupulous censorship is that the painting represents the Trinity as three people who all look like Christ, which is not in conformity with Church canon.

Under the floor beneath the painting are three skeletons that were discovered by restorers in 1995 while working on the floor. Surprisingly, no one knows who they are or how many other skeletons may be lying beneath the church's floor.

Father Victor Raul Martinez leads Natá's congregation, and he can usually be found inside the church. He speaks English, and if you ask him politely, he'll unlock a door and lead you up a narrow flight of stairs to the belfry. Once in the belfry, you'll discover four bells, all dating from the 20th century – the original bells were made of solid gold and were stolen years ago.

The choir platform above the entryway was built in 1996 to the specifications of the original. The original columns (the rough ones) that support the church's roof are made of níspero, a hardwood found in Bocas del Toro Province. The smooth columns are new and also made of níspero. The entire ceiling was replaced in 1995 and is made of pine and cedar.

PARQUE ARQUEOLÓGICO DEL CAÑO

This **archaeological park** (adult/child US$1/0.25; 9am-noon & 12:30-4pm Tue-Sat, 9am-1pm Sun) is one of only two sites in the country that are open to the public (the other is Barriles, in Chiriquí Province, p211). Although the site is extremely modest in comparison to large-scale excavations in other countries in Central America, this is perhaps the best place in Panama to get a sense of the country's indigenous traditions.

The site was excavated during the 1920s by an American who allegedly left with most of the objects he came across. The objects that weren't pilfered are now kept in a small museum, which contains dozens of pieces of pottery, arrowheads and carved stones. The objects are believed to date from a culture that lived in El Caño about 1500 years ago. The few signs at the museum are in Spanish only, and the site's caretaker unfortunately can offer little reliable information about El Caño's history.

In addition to the museum, there is a small excavation pit in the park, which contains a burial site in which five skeletons were found in the exact same position as visitors see them today. Nearby there's also a field containing dozens of stone columns that were lined up and stood on end in recent years, though their significance to the lost culture is unknown.

The turnoff for the town of El Caño is on the Interamericana, about 8km north of Natá. The park is another 3km from the turnoff, down an occasionally mud-slicked road. El Caño is not served by bus, but you can take a taxi here from Natá.

Sleeping & Eating

Hotel Rey David (☎ 993 5149; s/d US$18/24; **P** 🔀) If you find yourself stuck in Natá for the night, there's only one place to stay in town, and it's the Rey David. This modest hotel is located on the main road that leads into town from the Interamericana, and consists of 20 simple concrete box-style rooms with private hot water bathrooms and decent beds. This spot is good value and will definitely do in a pinch, though it's unlikely you'd want to spend any more time here than you need to.

Restaurante Vega (mains US$2-4) Two doors up from Hotel Rey David, Restaurante Vega serves traditional Panamanian staples as well as a few Chinese staples. Greasy but filling chow mein and fried lo mein with shrimp are a nice change from all the rice and beans.

Getting There & Away

Natá can be reached by all the buses that use this stretch of the Interamericana, except for the few nonstop buses that cruise between Panama City and Paso Canoas. Buses pass by in either direction every 15 minutes or so. Tell the driver to drop you at Natá, and they'll let you off beside the Restaurante Vega. Often there's a taxi parked in front of the café. You can catch buses eastward to Penonomé (US$1, 30 minutes, every 20 minutes), Panama City (US$4, 2½ hours, every 30 minutes) and points in between. Westward, there are regular connections to Aguadulce (US$0.50, 15 minutes, every 20 minutes), Divisa (US$1, 30 minutes, every 20 minutes), David (US$7.50, 4½ hours, every hour) and points all along the Interamericana.

AGUADULCE
pop 8300

Aguadulce's name is a contraction of *agua* and *dulce* (meaning 'sweet water'), and it is said that this bustling city was named by Spaniards who were pleased to come across a freshwater well amid the arid landscape. Today, the town is known more for its *dulce* as the town is surrounded by fields and fields of sugar cane. From mid-January to mid-March of each year, the cane is cut and then refined at several large refineries in the area. One of these mills, the Ingenio de Azúcar Santa Rosa offers tours – a must-do if you're in the area during the grinding season.

There are salt flats south of downtown, and until recently there was also a sizeable salt works here. Unable to compete with the lower prices of Colombian salt however, the salt works here closed its doors in 1999. Today, the flats now serve as a crucial habitat for marsh and shore birds, and the area is rapidly becoming popular with roseate spoonbills and wood storks, as well as various varieties of local and international birders.

Orientation

Aguadulce is located smack in the center of hot, dry country, 10km south of Natá. Like so many cities and towns in Panama, Aguadulce sits beside the Interamericana, though its downtown is 1km from the highway.

The main road into town from the highway is Av Rafael Estevez. The Hotel Interamericana marks the turnoff. There are always taxis here, and the parking lot next to the hotel is also the town's main bus stop.

To get to Aguadulce's central plaza, drive south on Av Rafael Estevez several blocks until it ends at its intersection with Calle Alejandro T Escobar. Turn left here, onto Calle Alejandro T Escobar, drive 3½ blocks to Av

COCLÉ PROVINCE

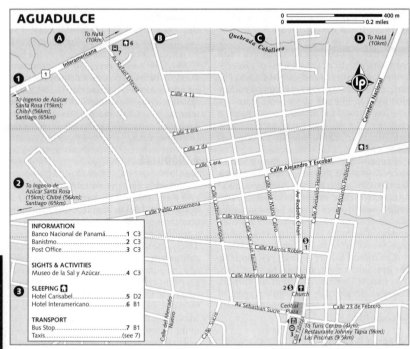

AGUADULCE

Rodolfo Chiari and then turn right. The central plaza and church will appear on your left, four blocks later.

Information

Banco Nacional de Panamá (Av Rodolfo Chiari) Has an ATM

Banistmo (Av Rodolfo Chiari) Has an ATM

Post office (Av Rodolfo Chiari) Near the central plaza, just around the corner from the Museo de la Sal y Azúcar.

Sights & Activities
INGENIO DE AZÚCAR SANTA ROSA

The **Santa Rosa Sugar Refinery** (☎ 987 8101/8102; 🕑 7am-4pm Mon-Fri, 7-11:30am Sat), located 15km west of Aguadulce, is a must-see if you're in the area from mid-January to mid-March. During grinding season, the refinery processes over 6500 tons of raw sugar cane per day.

Because the land here is hilly and rocky, the cane must be harvested by hand. Four thousand people are hired to help with harvesting and production, and they bring the cane in as fast as they can, 24 hours a day, six days a week (on Sunday everyone goes to church). Most of the cane is harvested on company land,

but the mill still buys about 3% of its cane from *campesinos* (farmers), who bring it in on carts pulled by tractors and oxen. Around 135kg of cane enters the mill each second via a huge conveyer belt that's continually fed from trucks coming in from the fields. By day's end, the yield of refined sugar is around 675,000kg (1.5 million pounds). All this cane is sent through grinders that resemble a stack of studded roller pins – except that each one weighs 20 tons and is about the size of a Buick. They spin quickly, and the cane that passes through them is crushed flat.

Occasionally the machine chokes. A 10-second choke results in a pileup of 1350kg of cane, and jackhammers are required to remove the clog. To give you an idea of the grinders' power: when a choke starts to occur, railroad ties are pushed into the grinders. In the fraction of a second it takes for the ties to pass through, they are chewed up as if they were breadsticks, but even as they're pulverized, they act as battering rams, punching bunched-up cane through the machines.

Also on the property is a replica of the original house of the mill's first owner, built in 1911. This museum is nicely done, and contains many exhibits on the history of sugar production in the New World. All its furniture and articles on display are originals.

To book tours, ask for Gonzalo Peréz (he speaks English and Spanish). The refinery would like at least 24 hours' notice to receive visitors.

If you're driving from Aguadulce, the turnoff for the mill will be on the right-hand side of the Interamericana and marked by a sign (there's an Esso station opposite). Take the road 500m, and you'll come to a white guard station with a tiny chapel in front of it. Give your name to the guard and follow instructions.

You can also take a taxi from Aguadulce (which could cost US$25 if the driver waits for you and takes you back to town), or you can catch any bus headed in the direction of the refinery and tell the driver to drop you at the Ingenio de Azúcar Santa Rosa (US$0.50, 20 minutes, every 15 minutes). Be forewarned that the walk from the guard station to the mill is more than 1km down a paved road lined with mature teak trees.

LAS PISCINAS

These popular **swimming pools** are located 9.5km from downtown Aguadulce, just beyond the salt flats and 250m past Restaurante Johnny Tapia. They consist of four 1.5m-high pools constructed in tideland about 150m from the high-water mark. If the tide is out, you can walk over the muddy sand that separates the pools from the shore and take a dip. The water's murky (it's saltwater, after all), but it's not polluted, as the pools are nearly 10km from town. The view from the pools is mostly one of a big, beautiful sky, with distant foothills on one side and the ocean spreading out before you on the other.

The tideland beyond the pools is quite expansive. When the tide is out, you can walk nearly 2km before reaching the ocean. But be careful; once the tide turns, it rises rather quickly, and it's frighteningly easy to be swept out to sea if you're caught in the rush. If you've walked 1km or so beyond the pools and notice the tide rising, head inland immediately.

Once the site of a salt works, today the tidelands serve as an important habitat for various species of birds. When the tide is out,

---

SUGAR IN THE RAW

The origins of the sugar industry are in the European colonization of the Americas, particularly on the islands of the Caribbean. Although it was possible for Europeans to import sugar from the colonies in Asia, the advent of slavery in the New World meant that sugarcane could be grown for a fraction of the cost. This in turn lead to lower prices for the European consumer, which took precedence over the lives of the slaves forced to work in the fields.

During the 18th century, European diets started to change dramatically as sugar increased in popularity. Coffee, tea and cocoa were consumed in greater frequency, and processed foods such as candies and jams became commonplace items. The demand for increased production fueled the slave trade, though the actual process of refining sugar became increasingly mechanized.

In industrial countries, sugar is one of the most heavily subsidized agricultural products. Sugar prices in the US, EU and Japan are on average three times the international market cost as governments maintain elevated price floors by subsidizing domestic production and imposing high tariffs on imports. As a result, sugar exporting countries are excluded from these markets, and thus receive lower prices than they would under a system of free trade.

Brazil, which exports more than a quarter of the world's supply of refined sugar and heads a coalition of sugar exporting nations, has repeatedly lobbied the World Trade Organization to reform the market. For countries like Panama however, sugar production is mainly a domestic industry as it's not profitable to export sugar to countries that levy a high tariff on imports.

Harvesting sugarcane manually is exhausting work as the stalks can grow to a height of 4m, and their thick stalks are fibrous and difficult to cut down. However, it's becoming increasingly common in Panama for sugar cane to be harvested using self-propelled harvesting machines, which has made it difficult for rural farmers to find employment.

The next time you're driving through cane country, look for signs advertising *jugo de caña* as there's nothing quite like a glass of fresh sugar cane juice.

the birding here is fantastic – several species of marsh and shore birds descend on the area in search of food. In fact, the flats are also famous for their jumbo shrimp, which are harvested in great abundance and served in restaurants throughout the country. When the tide is in, keep an eye out for sea lions, which are occasionally spotted swimming near the pools.

The best way to get to the pools is by taxi. Tell the driver to take you to Restaurante Johnny Tapia. From Johnny Tapia, walk south (away from town). On the left side of the road are mangroves, beginning a little way from the restaurant. After you've walked about 100m, you'll see a clearing in the mangroves, and through the clearing you'll be able to spot the pools (if the tide is out).

MUSEO DE LA SAL Y AZÚCAR

This rather unusual **museum** (☎ 997 4280; Plaza 19 de Octubre; adult/child US$0.75/0.25; ☉ 9am-5pm Tue-Sat, 2-5pm Sun) faces the central plaza. As its name suggests, the Museum of Salt and Sugar documents the history of Aguadulce's salt and sugar industries. A good portion of the exhibits also detail the role Aguadulce's salt and sugar have played in Panamanian life.

The museum also contains artifacts including guns, uniforms and swords from the Colombian civil war (1899–1903). It also displays a number of pre-Columbian artifacts, mostly ceramics and tools found in the cane fields nearby. Signage is in Spanish only.

TURIS CENTRO

This modest **recreation area** (☎ 997 3720; free admission, bike/skate rental per hr US$1/1.50, boat rental per 15min US$1.50; ☉ 11am-8pm) is 4km from downtown Aguadulce, on the road to Restaurante Johnny Tapia. Here, in the middle of salt flats and scrub brush, you can rent bikes, skates, or hire paddleboats for the small pond. There's also a children's playground and an inexpensive open-sided restaurant. A taxi here costs about US$2.

Festivals & Events

Aguadulce's biggest celebration is **Carnaval**, which is held the four days before Ash Wednesday, and features parades, floats, Miss Aguadulce ceremonies, and lots of music, dancing and drinking. Other big events include the **patron saint festival** on July 25 and the city's **founding day** on October 18, 19 and 20.

Sleeping & Eating

Hotel Interamericano (☎ 997 4363; fax 997 4975; Interamericana; d US$20; P ☒ ☒) Near Av Rafael Estevez, this popular budget hotel is the best value in town. Cookie-cutter rooms are dimly lit and not much to look at, but you can't beat the price, especially since they come with air-con and private hot-water bathrooms. However, the best perk of staying here is the well-cared-for swimming pool, and the poolside bar-restaurant is a nice touch.

Hotel Carisabel (☎ 997 3800; cnr Calle Alejandro T Escobar & Carretera Nacional; s/d US$25/35; P ☒ ☒) Near the downtown area, the recently renovated Carisabel is easily Aguadulce's best accommodations. Although the building itself isn't particularly attractive, the service here is friendly and professional, and the airy rooms have fresh coats of paint, and the tiled bathrooms are spacious and have steamy showers. There's also an inviting pool here as well as popular bar-restaurant serving country-inspired favorites.

Restaurante Johnny Tapia (seafood US$2.50-3.50; ☉ from 8am) One of the best places to enjoy Aguadulce's nationally famous jumbo shrimp is this very casual beachside diner just past the salt flats, 9km from downtown Aguadulce. Named for its ebullient owner-waiter, this relaxed spot offers everything from shrimp ceviche and shrimp salad to shrimp soup and pan-fried shrimp.

Getting There & Away

Buses arrive and depart from the small parking lot beside Hotel Interamericana on the highway. Destinations west include Divisa (US$1, 30 minutes, every 30 minutes), where you can change for buses to Chitré, Santiago (US$1.75, one hour, every 30 minutes) and David (US$7, four hours, every 45 minutes). Destinations east include Natá (US$0.50, 15 minutes, every 20 minutes), Penonomé (US$1, 30 minutes, every 20 minutes) and Panama City (US$5, three hours, every 20 minutes). A taxi from the parking lot into town costs US$1.

Getting Around

Taxis are the best way to get from one part of Aguadulce to another if you don't feel like walking. Fares rarely exceed US$2, although you can expect to pay a little more at night. Always agree on a price before entering a taxi.

Herrera Province

Herrera Province is centered on the Península de Azuero, a semi-arid landmass that more closely resembles rural USA than the American tropics. Looked upon by Panamanians as their country's heart and soul, the Península de Azuero is one of the country's major farming and ranching centers. It is also the strongest bastion of Spanish culture left in Panama, especially considering that many residents of Azuero can trace lineage directly back to Spain.

However, history and culture didn't arrive in Herrera with the Spaniards. Long before the Spanish conquistadores began carving up the region, Herrera (and even Azuero) was home to the Ngöbe-Buglé, who left behind a rich archaeological record. In fact, much of what we know about the pre-Columbian practices of this indigenous group was obtained from an excavation site near present-day Parita (for more information, see the boxed text, p157). Sadly, the Ngöbe-Buglé were forced out of the province by early colonists, though many were able to later find refuge in the Chiriquí highlands.

Today, Herrera (particularly Azuero) proudly upholds its Spanish legacy, which is best evidenced by the province's famous festivals. In the town of Ocú, the patron saint festival is marked by the joyous parading of newlywed couples through the streets. In the town of Parita, the feast of Corpus Christi is celebrated with great merriment (and a large appetite) 40 days after Easter. In the town of Pesé, lively public re-enactments of the Last Supper, Judas' betrayal and Jesus' imprisonment are performed during the week preceding Easter. All of these festivals, which ultimately revolve around copious amounts of eating, drinking and dancing, provide a window into the rich Spanish heritage of this province. Although Herrera is lacking in terms of traditional tourist sights, partying in the streets with fiercely proud locals is a wonderful cultural experience that complements time spent exploring Panama's more scenic attractions.

HIGHLIGHTS

- Kicking off your shoes, letting your hair down and living it up at any of Herrera's lively **festivals** (p151)
- Strolling through historic **Parita** (p156)
- Birding at **Playa El Aguillito** (p155), a tidal mudflat that attracts rare migratory seabirds
- Beholding the apocalyptic **Parque Nacional Sarigua** (p156), a sad monument to environmental devastation

| ■ POPULATION: 107,830 | ■ AREA: 2341 SQ KM | ■ ELEVATION: SEA LEVEL TO 3478M |

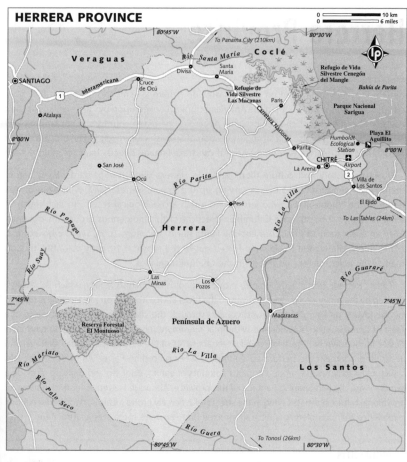

HERRERA PROVINCE

HERRERA PROVINCE

CHITRÉ
pop 46,000

Chitré, the capital of Herrera Province, is the largest city on the Península de Azuero, and the cultural and historic capital of the region. Although the city was founded in 1848, colonial records indicate that there was a village here as early as 1558, which indicates that Chitré is one of the oldest settlements in the country. Today, the city is home to several streets of ornate red-tiled row homes, which hark back to the early days of Spanish settlement.

For most travelers, Chitré serves as a springboard for exploring the peninsula. Highlights include the ceramic shops in La Arena, the Humboldt Ecological Station at Playa El Aguillito, Parque Nacional Sariagua, the historic town of Parita, the *seco* (a distilled liquor akin to rum) factory at Pesé and the wildlife refuge at Cenegón del Mangle, as well as other spots in neighboring Los Santos Province (p161). The sites of some of the peninsula's best festivals are just a quick bus ride away, but Chitré does host a few wild parties of its own (see opposite).

Orientation

The Interamericana connects with the Carretera Nacional (the National Hwy) at the town of Divisa, atop the Península de Azuero. From there, the Carretera Nacional runs southeast 37km to Chitré. From Chitré, it runs 31km further to Las Tablas, in Los Santos Province, then further south toward the southern edge of the peninsula.

LOS FIESTAS DE AZUERO (PART I)

Festivals in the Península de Azuero are famous throughout Panama for their traditional celebrations, many of which revolve around aspects of life in the time of the early Spanish settlers. If your trip to Panama coincides with any of the festivals listed below, it's worth making an effort to visit. You may lose a day or two to a vicious hangover, but partying in the streets with locals until the wee hours of the morning is something you'll never forget.

The following are some of the peninsula's best known festivals:

- Festival of San Sebastián – January 20 in Ocú.
- Carnaval – the four days before Ash Wednesday (February/March) in Chitré and Parita.
- Semana Santa – March/April in Pesé.
- Fiesta de San Juan Bautista – June 24 in Chitré.
- Patronales de San Pablo & San Pedro – June 29 in Pedasí and La Arena.
- Festival del Manito Ocueño, Fiesta Popular, Matrimonio Campesino, El Duelo del Tamarindo & El Penitente de la Otra Vida – August (dates vary) in Ocú.
- Founding of the District of Chitré 1848 – October 19 in Chitré.

For more information on the festivals listed above, see the various town and city listings in this chapter.

For listings of festivals in Los Santos Province, see p163.

Chitré is the first major town the Carretera Nacional encounters as it winds southeast from Divisa. When the highway reaches Chitré, it becomes Paseo Enrique Geenzier, changing name again a dozen blocks further east, to Calle Manuel Maria Correa. The Carretera Nacional re-emerges at the southern end of town.

The town's cathedral and the adjacent central square, Parque Union, are one block south of Calle Manuel Maria Correa between Av Obaldía and Av Herrera. There are numerous hotels and restaurants within a short walk of the square.

Information

For money matters, try **Banco Nacional de Panamá** (Paseo Enrique Geenzier; 🕑 9am-1pm Mon-Thu & Sat, to 3pm Fri) or **HSBC** (Av Herrera; 🕑 9am-1pm Mon-Fri), which lies just north of the cathedral; both have ATMs. **Sanchi Internet** (Calle Aminta Burgos de Amado; per hr US$0.75; 🕑 8:30am-11:30pm), one block west of the park, has reliable connections and keeps regular hours.

Tourist information is available at the new IPAT office in La Arena.

Sights

For information on popular day-trips from Chitré, see p154.

MUSEO DE HERRERA

This anthropology and natural history **museum** (☎ 996 0077; Paseo Enrique Geenzier; adult/child US$1/0.25; 🕑 8am-noon & 1-4pm Tue-Sat, 8-11am Sun) contains many well-preserved pieces of pottery dating from 5000 BC until the time of the Spanish conquest. Some of the pieces that were found at the excavation sites outside Parita are here, although most of those artifacts are on display at the anthropology museum in Panama City (p87).

Also on display are replicas of *huacas* (golden objects placed with indigenous peoples at the time of burial), found on the peninsula, as well as numerous photos of archaeologists at work and maps showing where the pottery and *huacas* were found. Be sure to visit the museum's 2nd floor, where you'll find photos of Azuero residents, authentic folkloric costumes and religious artifacts (including the original bell of Chitré's cathedral, which was cast in 1767). Signs are in Spanish only.

CATHEDRAL

The city's soaring cathedral dates from the 18th century, but was substantially re-modeled in 1988. Today, the entire ceiling is made of polished mahogany, the walls are adorned with near-life-size figures of saints and large, vivid stained-glass windows depicting momentous events in the life of Jesus, and the stations

lonelyplanet.com

HERRERA PROVINCE

CHITRÉ & LA ARENA

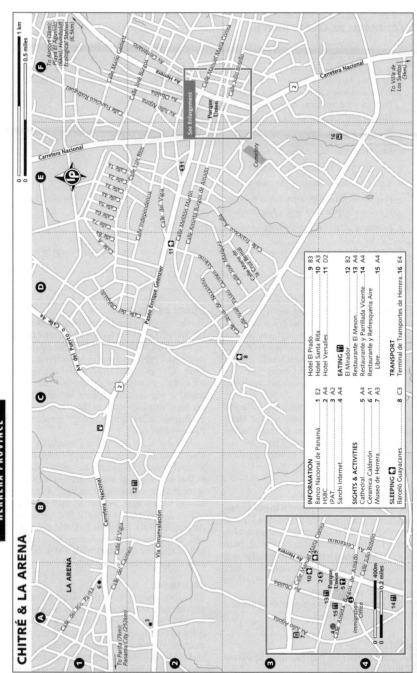

INFORMATION
Banco Nacional de Panamá........**1** E2
HSBC....................................**2** A4
IPAT....................................**3** A2
Sanchi Internet.....................**4** A4

SIGHTS & ACTIVITIES
Cathedral.............................**5** A4
Cerámica Calderón.................**6** A1
Museo de Herrera..................**7** A3

SLEEPING
Barceló Guayacanes...............**8** C3

Hotel El Prado......................**9** B3
Hotel Santa Rita...................**10** A3
Hotel Versalles.....................**11** D2

EATING
El Mirador...........................**12** B2
Restaurante El Meson.............**13** A4
Restaurante y Parrillada Vicente..**14** A4
Restaurante y Refresquería Aire
Libre................................**15** A4

TRANSPORT
Terminal de Transportes de Herrera.**16** E4

of the cross are marked by 4m teak crosses and intricately carved figurines. Unlike many cathedrals that impress through ostentation, this one is striking for its elegant simplicity and fine balance of gold and wood.

Festivals & Events

Chitré's **Carnaval** festivities, held each year on the four days before Ash Wednesday (in February or March), feature parades, folkloric dancing, water fights and lots of drinking. On June 24 Chitré's patron saint festival, the **Fiesta de San Juan Bautista**, starts with a religious service followed by bullfights (the animals are merely teased), cockfights and other popular activities. And on October 19 festivities that celebrate the **Founding of the District of Chitré** (1848) include parades, historical costumes and much merriment.

Sleeping

If you plan to attend any of the festivals in Chitré, you'll have difficulty finding a place to stay if you arrive without a reservation. For Carnaval, rooms often book up months in advance, though you can always visit on a day-trip or plan on sleeping in a hotel outside the city.

Hotel El Prado (☎ 996 4620; Av Herrera; d without/with air-con US$15/20; **P** **⊠**) Although it's certainly not going to win a beauty pageant, this cheap and functional budget hotel offers up cookie cutter rooms that'll do in a pinch. The El Prado is definitely starting to show its age, though the rooms are set back from the street and are fairly quiet, and air-con and occasional hot water are nice perks at this price range. The 2nd-floor restaurant has nice views of the street below, and the hearty plates of traditional Panamanian fare on offer are a good way to absorb all the excess alcohol in your gut if you've been partying too hard.

Hotel Santa Rita (☎ 996 4610; cnr Calle Manuel Maria Correa & Av Herrera; d without/with air-con US$15/20; **P** **⊠**) Santa Rita was one of the city's first hotels, though frequent coats of paint and a little tender loving care have kept it looking younger than its age. The well-maintained rooms have air-con and private hot-water bathrooms, and the private balconies make a nice way to soak up the street scene. As far as budget hotels go, this is great value, and if you squint your eyes just right (and give in a bit to your imagination), you can almost

imagine how elegant the Santa Rita must have been in its heyday.

Hotel Versalles (☎ 996 4422; Paseo Enrique Geenzier near Paseo Carmen Salerno; d/ste US$25/45; **P** **⊠** **⊠**) It certainly would look out of place in Paris, though this French-inspired hotel is easily one of Chitré's best. Spacious guestrooms are a notch above the competition, and feature comfortable beds, air-con and private hot-water bathrooms, though anyone in need of some serious stretching room should consider splurging on the suites. The on-site restaurant and bar is a good place for an evening meal and a nightcap, though the best part of staying at the Versalles is taking a lap or two in the pool – perfect for cooling off after a particularly hot Azuero day.

ourpick Barceló Guayacanes (☎ 996 8969; www .barcelo.com; Vía Circunvalación; s/d/ste US$40/55/80; **P** **⊠** **⊠** **⊠**) Although Chitré isn't exactly Panama's top resort destination, this relatively new addition to the Barceló chain is built around an artificial lake just outside town, and features such four-star amenities as a swimming pool, disco, gourmet restaurant, spa and gym. Although it's not as grand as the Pacific resorts further up the coast toward Panama City, it's easily the most luxurious hotel in Azuero, and a good place to post up for a few days if you want a sophisticated level of comfort. The rooms are excellent value considering they come equipped with modern amenities including air-con, satellite TV and tiled bathrooms with attractive metal accents.

Eating

Chitré's fishermen cast from 2am to 6am and sell their haul soon after their return from the sea, so most of the seafood served in Chitré has been caught the same day. For this reason, Chitré is known throughout the peninsula as having fresh seafood – and it's surprisingly cheap.

Restaurante y Refresquería Aire Libre (Av Obaldia; mains US$3-5; ⏰ 6:30am-10pm) This pleasant open-air café faces the western end of the plaza, and is a good place to soak up the tropical climes and indulge in a bit of people-watching. Good inexpensive Panamanian dishes are on offer including *camarones al ajillo* (shrimp with garlic), though a cup of coffee and some chocolate ice cream is an equally divine choice.

Restaurante y Parrillada Vicente (Av Herrera; mains US$3-6) If you're looking to take a break from all the rice and beans, this greasy-spoon Chinese restaurant serves up all your Latin American–Asian favorites. Brightly painted walls hung with Van Gogh prints form the backdrop to excellent chow mein, chicken with sweet-and-sour sauce and roast pork.

Getting There & Away
AIR
Chitré's airport is northeast of town; follow Av Herrera north from the town square to reach it. A taxi ride there costs US$2.50.

Air Panama (☎ 996 4021; at airport) flies from Chitré to Panama City at least twice a week (US$40).

BUS
Chitré is a center for regional bus transportation. Buses arrive and depart from the **Terminal de Transportes de Herrera** (☎ 996 6426), 1km south of downtown, near Vía Circunvalación. To get to the station, take a taxi (US$1 to US$2) or catch a 'Terminal' bus (US$0.25) at the intersection of Calle Aminta Burgos de Amado and Av Herrera. The terminal has a restaurant that's open 24 hours a day.

Tuasa (☎ 996 2661) and **Transportes Inazun** (☎ 996 4177) buses depart from Chitré for Panama City (one way US$6, four hours, every 45 to 60 minutes from 1:30am to 6pm).

Other buses departing from Chitré operate from sunrise to sunset, and include the following destinations:

Divisa (US$1; 30min; every 15min)
La Arena (US$0.25; 15min; every 15min)
Las Minas (US$2; 1hr; every 30min)
Las Tablas (US$1; 40min; every 20min)
Macaracas (US$2; 1hr; hourly)
Ocú (US$2; 1hr; hourly)
Parita (US$0.50; 15min; every 45min)
Pedasí (US$2; 1hr; hourly)
Pesé (US$1; 20min; every 30min)
Playa El Aguillito (US$0.50; 12min; every 20min)
Playas Monagre & El Rompío (US$1; 30min; every 20min)
Santiago (US$2; 1½hr; every 30min)
Villa de Los Santos (US$0.25; 10min; every 10min)

To get to David or Panama City from Chitré, take a bus to Divisa and then catch a *directo* (direct bus) to either city. Buses leave from the Delta station at the intersection of the Interamericana and the Carretera Nacional. You likely won't have to wait more than 30 minutes. The bus fare will set you back US$7

or US$8. If you're trying to get to Chitré from the Interamericana, ask the bus driver to stop in Divisa. He'll know to stop near the Delta station. At the station, catch any bus heading toward Chitré.

Getting Around
If you need to travel by vehicle, a taxi is the best way to go. They're cheap – most fares in town are between US$1 and US$2.

AROUND CHITRÉ
Some of the most interesting sights in the Azuero Peninsula are just a short bus-ride away from downtown Chitré.

La Arena
Several kilometers west of downtown Chitré, and bisected by the Carretera Nacional, is the famous ceramics center of La Arena. The pottery made in this tiny village mimics the pre-Columbian designs of the Ngöbe-Buglé who once lived nearby. Today, La Arena produces some of the highest quality pottery in the country, and is one of the best places to watch sculptors working their trade. Also, if you're shopping for souvenirs, the prices here for pottery will be lower than anywhere else, and you'll be supporting the artisans directly.

The best of the town's several pottery factories is **Ceramica Calderón** (near Calle del Río Parita & Carretera Nacional), where you can buy traditional painted ceramics at wholesale prices. These pieces are made on the premises in a workshop directly behind the roadside showroom. All the pottery is made by hand with the help of a foot-powered potter's wheel. The artisan who makes most of the ceramics sold here is Angel Calderón, who's been making ceramics professionally for almost 50 years. If you visit Angel's shop, be sure to take a look at the ovens out back – they're quite impressive.

Although there are no places to stay in La Arena, downtown Chitré is just 5km away. A taxi ride from Parque Union to La Arena shouldn't cost you more than US$2, and there are several buses an hour that won't cost you more than a quarter.

Atop a hill in La Arena, **El Mirador** (The Lookout; mains US$3-7; ☒ 4pm-midnight) is a popular spot where tourists from around Panama congregate to take in the views of the city and the surrounding plains. The food is standard at best, though the twinkling lights of Chitré makes for an atmospheric night out. To find the

BIRDING AT PLAYA EL AGUILLITO

Seven kilometers away from Chitré's Parque Union is Playa El Aguillito, which is not so much a sandy beach as it is a mudflat created by silt deposited by two nearby rivers, the Río Parita and the Río La Villa. At low tide, the mudflat stretches more than 2km from the high-water mark across to the surf, and thousands of birds descend upon the mud in search of plankton and small shrimp. Interestingly enough, the actual 'playa' part of the mudflats is artificial and was the result of a failed attempt to create a sunbathing beach by cutting down a mangrove forest back in the 1960s.

Most of the birds that descend on El Aguillito are migratory, flying between Alaska and the tip of South America. For reasons that escape scientists, these birds return during the winter year after year to exactly the same beach – and to no others in the area. This is rather amazing when you consider how many thousands of kilometers the birds fly during a single season, and how many feeding grounds they must pass over.

Playa El Aguillito regulars include roseate spoonbills, sandpipers, warblers, black-necked stilts, white-winged doves, black-bellied plovers, yellow-crowned amazons, yellowlegs and ospreys. The beach is also home to common ground-doves, which are only found in Panama in this one spot. When the tide is high, these birds congregate around salt ponds to the immediate east of Playa El Aguillito.

Of particular interest to birders is the western sandpiper, whose far-flung summer breeding grounds are the Alaskan islands and Siberia. From the fall to the spring, these amazing birds migrate south along the Pacific coast of the Americas, and return to the same feeding grounds each year. For the past several decades, Playa El Aguillito has been visited by thousands of western sandpipers annually, and the birds typically arrive in enormous flocks numbering in the hundreds.

Unfortunately, various factors ranging from environmental pollution to El Niño warming have begun to take their toll on species population, and it isn't helping that feeding grounds such as Playa El Aguillito are endangered. Unfortunately, habitat destruction is on the rise throughout Panama, especially as investors start to eye wetlands and waterfronts as potential fisheries or even beachfront property. In nature, animals don't respect international border lines, and a simple construction project in coastal Panama can have disastrous results for an entire population of birds on a remote Alaskan island.

The good news is that Chitré-born 'friend of the birds' Francisco Delgado is heading the **Humboldt Ecological Station**, which is located toward the northwest end of the beach – look for an 'Estacion Ecologica Alejandro von Humboldt' sign. Since 1983, Francisco and a group of fellow local environmentalists have banded more than 15,000 birds and have monitored them with the assistance of scientists based in other countries.

The work conducted at the station has helped support the conclusion that annually frequenting the same feeding grounds is an important survival mechanism for long-distance migratory birds. Since transcontinental voyages require an enormous amount of energy, reliable feeding grounds are crucial for the birds' survival. This is particularly true for species such as the western sandpiper, which can typically fly for days on end without stopping to eat.

At the station, there are several items on display including a map showing the migratory routes of all the bird species that pass through the area, as well as plans for a much more comprehensive research and conservation center that is awaiting funding. In the meantime, the modest building serves as an ongoing biological research station, and is usually bustling with activity, especially during the busy migratory season when the bulk of the tagging takes place. Francisco himself is usually around to answer questions in English and Spanish, and his legion of assistants and volunteers are an interesting lot to talk to. If Francisco is not around, you can reach him at his **home** (☎ 996 1725).

Playa El Aguillito is reached from Chitré via Av Herrera; it's just past the airport. A bus leaves the Chitré station for the beach every 20 minutes or so from sunrise to sunset. The one-way fare is US$0.50. A taxi ride from town costs US$3 one way.

Mirador from downtown Chitré, head west on the Paseo Enrique Geenzier for about 2.5km and turn left onto the road that begins just past the large 'Chino Bar' sign. At the fork, turn right and continue for another 400m until you reach the top of the hill.

Parque Nacional Sarigua

Ten kilometers north of downtown Chitré, this **national park** (entrance US$3; ⏱ 8am-4pm) is arguably the most important pre-Columbian site in Panama. The Sarigua site has been dated back 11,000 years based on shell mounds and pottery fragments, although much of it has yet to be excavated. Unfortunately, the main hurdle preventing wide-scale excavation is the fact that the entire national park is a 'tropical desert' – or rather, that is what Panama's national environmental authority, ANAM (Autoridad Nacional de Ambiente) would have you believe.

On the contrary, this national park was created in 1984, and consists of 8000 hectares of wasteland that was once dry tropical rainforest and coastal mangrove patches. Simply put, Sarigua is the end product of slash-and-burn agriculture. People moved into the area, cut down all the trees, set fire to the debris, planted crops for a few harvests and then left. Because the forest that had held the thin topsoil in place was removed, the heavy rain that falls here every year carried the topsoil into creeks and then into rivers and out into the sea.

What you see in Parque Nacional Sarigua today is the nutrient-deficient rock that had been underneath the topsoil. Despite the example of Sarigua, the Panamanian government still encourages deforestation throughout the country (most notably in the Darién) to promote the same variety of wasteful and unsustainable agriculture.

What makes matters even worse is that part of the park actually serves as the waste-disposal site for Chitré, Parita and other cities in Azuero. In fact, directly behind the ANAM ranger station (where you pay the entrance fee), you can see garbage poking up out of the ground. Although major dumping has been curtailed in recent years, it's still occurring within the park.

A visit to Sarigua is not for everyone, though it's a sober reminder of the Earth's fragility, and the rapid speed in which we as humans can alter the environment. From the *mirador* (lookout) behind the ranger station,

you can gaze out at the dry, cracked earth and swirling dust storms that used to be a living, breathing ecosystem. If you have your own transportation, you can also drive a few kilometers into the park, though much of Sarigua is off-limits to the public. Not surprisingly, there are a lot of questionable activities taking place (illegal dumping being the first and foremost). The coastal edges of the park are also home to privately owned commercial shrimp farms, which stand as a testament to the rapid destruction of Panama's wetland habitats.

To get here from the Carretera Nacional, take the Puerto Limón turnoff, a couple of kilometers northwest of Parita. After 1km you'll notice the foul smell of a nearby pig farm. After another 1km you'll come to the park turnoff. Follow the signs for 2km, until you come to a structure on the left – this is the ANAM station.

Buses do not go to the park. A round-trip taxi ride to the ANAM station from Chitré costs about US$20.

Parita
pop 4000

Just 6km northwest of downtown Chitré, Parita is one of those hidden gems that travelers love to stumble across. Founded in 1558 and named after the departed Ngöbe-Buglé chief (see the boxed text, opposite), Parita is chock full of colonial structures, the majority of which date from the 18th century. The buildings near the center of town have thick walls and beams as solid as railroad ties, as well as roofs made of red convex tiles – the fancier structures even have sweeping arcades facing out to the street. However, despite its historic core, Parita is known to few people outside the Península de Azuero, so it's unlikely that you will see any tourists here, Panamanian or otherwise.

Parita follows a grid pattern. As you come to intersections near the town's center (which is about 500m from the Carretera Nacional) and glance both ways, you'll see buildings that look much the same as they have for centuries.

The **church** in Parita is the only one in Panama that has its steeple located directly over its entrance rather than over a corner of the structure. This is very unusual as bell towers are always extremely heavy, and therefore are generally built on pillars that rest upon a massive foundation. In fact, it is a major

RECONSTRUCTING THE PAST

During the 1940s, a series of major excavations of indigenous tombs took place just 10km outside Parita. Although there was little structural evidence above ground, the tombs themselves yielded some of the finest pre-Columbian artifacts that have ever been discovered by archaeologists in Panama.

The bulk of the artifacts uncovered were ceremonial pottery, a good portion of which were vessels mounted on tall pedestal bases of two types: painted globular bowls and other bowls in the form of king vulture effigies. The painted globular bowls were brightly colored and adorned with fanciful bird and reptile designs. The more elaborate bowls were shaped to resemble king vultures, with finger-long wings flaring from their sides and bulbous heads and stubby tails at their ends.

In each of the mounds, archaeologists were amazed to discover one incredible artifact cache after the next. For example, in one mound, more than 100 nearly identical red-painted, globular jars with short necks were found. In another, archaeologists found long-necked bottles, 40 painted pots in the form of bird effigies and exquisitely carved batons shaped like stylized alligators, made from manatee ribs. Yet in another mound, were the remains of a young girl with a necklace of hollow gold beads.

However, perhaps the most amazing find was an urn that contained the remains of a single man and a necklace made of more than 800 human teeth. Nearly all the teeth were front incisors, which means that the teeth of at least 200 people were required to make the jewelry. The circumstances under which the necklace was created remain a mystery, though it's not hard to speculate about their origins. Clearly, the indigenous peoples of Azuero were living in violent times.

Of course, ultimately the greatest danger to the survival of these early communities was the arrival of the Spanish settlers, who wasted no time in exterminating the indigenous peoples in Azuero. Unfortunately, their efforts were so effective that what little we do know about these early communities comes from the reports of ruthless conquistadors.

Tantalizing but far from adequate descriptions of the people who created these objects have been left to us by Gaspar de Espinosa and Gonzalo de Badajoz, who led looting expeditions on the peninsula between 1515 and 1525. Since the Spaniards for the most part viewed the natives of Panama as disposable objects, these reports are more a glorification of their conquests than anthropological ethnography. However, they represent one of the few windows we have into the early lives of these communities.

Although today the Azuero Peninsula is best thought of as a dry, semi-arid landscape of cattle ranching farms and massive agricultural plots, in the colonial era the land was completely covered by dry tropical rainforest and thick mangrove patches. As a result, early communities were able to subsist on hunting and fishing, but they did rely on small-scale agriculture, which included rice, beans and manioc. At the time, there were several different indigenous tribes living in the peninsula, though the region was controlled by a powerful Ngöbe-Buglé chief named Parita.

For decades, Parita and his fierce warriors were able to prevent the Spaniards from settling on the peninsula. However, when Espinosa led a later raid on the peninsula, he found to his pleasant surprise that Parita had recently died. Instead of confronting the chief in combat, the raiders found him lying dead in a room containing an astounding 161kg of gold ornaments. Also found near the dead leader were 20 native captives who were lashed to house posts by cords around their necks – these poor souls had been destined to be buried alive with the great chieftain. Also expected to be buried with Parita were his wives and household attendants, who were slaughtered beside the dead chief.

Following the death of Parita, the Spanish rapidly colonized the Península de Azuero and exterminated all of its residents, though a few Ngöbe-Buglé communities were able to safely flee to the jungled mountains in what is now Chiriquí Province. In fact, so fearful were these communities of white people that until only a few decades ago, they continued to place deadly traps along trails to kill or maim outsiders.

HERRERA PROVINCE

curiosity to the residents of Parita that the steeple hasn't collapsed upon the entryway. Although the church was completed in 1723, you'll never see a Parita resident loitering near the entrance.

Beside the church is a grassy square in which cattle-roping demonstrations are held from August 3–7, during the town's patron-saint festivities.

Two doors down from the southeastern corner of Parita's church is a **workshop** (☎ 974 2242/2036) which specializes in the restoration of altars – it is the only such workshop in the country. The artisans working here, Macario José Rodriguez and the twin brothers José Sergio Lopez and Sergio José Lopez, have been restoring the altars of Panama's colonial churches since the 1970s. All three men speak some English and they are very friendly – chances are they'll let you take a look around.

To find the home of one of the country's top **mask makers**, Darido Lopez, return to the Carretera Nacional and find the Shell station near the turnoff. Darido's house is about 100m northwest of the gas station, on the opposite side. Visitors can identify his home by the masks hanging beside his front door. Darido has been making colorful masks for folkloric dancers since the 1960s. While he continues to make masks and satin costumes worn by dirty-devil dancers, these days most of his masks are exported to the USA and to Europe – most cost between US$20 and US$80. (For more information on another of Panama's top mask makers, see p163.)

Although there are no places to stay in Parita, downtown Chitré is just 10km away. A taxi ride from Parque Union to Parita shouldn't cost you more than US$4, and there are several buses an hour that won't cost you more than 50c.

Refugio de Vida Silvestre Cenegón del Mangle

This 775-hectare **refuge** near Parita protects a mangrove forest at the mouth of the Río Santa María, an important wildlife area and nesting ground for wading birds. The most commonly sighted species here are great egrets, cattle egrets and tri-colored herons – in fact, many of the herons that now inhabit the *Palacio de las Garzas* (Palace of the Herons), the official residence of the Panamanian president, came from this reserve.

The refuge is accessed by a 500m-loop trail that follows a boardwalk through the mangrove forest. Along the way, keep your eyes fixed on the eerie waters below as the abundance of wading birds also attracts hungry caimans and crocodiles. The herons are here year round, though opportunistic reptiles tend to congregate during the June to September mating season. Watch your step during this time of year – you really don't want to fall in here!

The primary attraction of the refuge is the birds, though locals claim that the small pools here or **Los Pozos** (the Wells) have health-giving properties. In our opinion, these unattractive muddy puddles seem to be great places for various biting insects to roost, though who are we to argue with lore!

The refuge is not reachable by bus; instead, it's a 45-minute drive north of Chitré via the Carretera Nacional and easily accessible as a day-trip. Take the turnoff to Los Pozos, which is signposted. After 1km the road forks at a church in the village of Paris; take the right branch and it becomes a dirt road. Proceed 4km on this road, after which you'll come to a sign with an arrow showing you where to go and indicating you're 2km from the wells and the entrance to the refuge.

Pesé

pop 2700

The town of Pesé, 19km southwest of Chitré, is famous for its annual Good Friday representation of the Golgotha drama – a re-enactment of Christ's crucifixion. Of course, the real reason why you're probably here has to do with the endless sea of sugarcane plantations that ring the town.

Pesé is home to the country's largest *seco* factory, **Seco Herrerano** (☎ 974 9621; fax 974 9593; admission free; ☺ 9am-5pm Mon-Sat), established in 1936. It's a rather small factory, with only 45 workers, but its output is incredible: 36,000 1L bottles every business day (Monday to Saturday). If you stop by during this time, you can tour the distillery and the mill, and taste some free samples – just have someone else drive you back to Chitré when you're ready to go.

The mill operates only during the harvest season, which lasts from mid-January to mid-March. During this time, you can see tons of sugarcane being fed into huge presses to extract the sweet juice. The juice is then pumped into huge containers, where it ferments. The most impressive aspect about the whole operation is the speed of the pressing and the power of the machinery.

If you wish to take a tour, fax your request at least a week in advance. Send it to Carlos Cedeño. Carlos speaks basic English, so keep your request simple. Don't expect a reply – it's fine to just show up. If you speak Spanish, you can also try calling ahead, though the phone is not always picked up.

Pesé can be reached by frequent buses from the Terminal de Transportes de Herrera in Chitré (US$1, 20 minutes).

OCÚ
pop 9000

About 20km by road west of Pesé, sleepy Ocú would be indistinguishable from neighboring towns were it not for its reputation as one of Panama's top hat-making centers. Not long ago, Ocú, which straddles a loop road that links it and the major towns of Chitré, Pesé, Los Pozos and Las Minas, used to be where Panamanians went to buy the finest panama-style hats made in their country.

Until the 1990s, Ocú's many hat makers could take their intricately braided merchandise to the town square every morning, and expect to have it all sold by noon. Truckers, who were major hat buyers, used to make special trips to Ocú for their headgear. But, once high-quality hats became available in Penonomé (p139), which is conveniently located on the Interamericana, the truckers stopped making special trips to Ocú. Today, local hat makers sell their wares to wholesale vendors who later resell them in Penonomé, though Ocú still retains its proud artisan tradition.

Sights
HAT MAKERS

Today, there are still a fair number of hat makers in Ocú, and if you wish, you can visit some of them and see how a genuine panama hat is made. The finest are so tightly braided that you can turn them over and fill them with water and they won't leak. The time needed to make a hat varies from one week to one month, and prices range from US$25 to US$150 depending on the quality.

If you decide to visit a hat maker, go see Elena Montilla and/or Ezequela Maure – they live only two houses apart at the northern end of town on the main street, Av Central. To find their houses, drive or walk about 1km on Av Central from the town plaza until you reach a fork in the road. A dirt road splits to the left, while the main paved road sweeps right; if you pass the Jorón El Tijera restaurant, in the fork of the road, you've gone too far. Ezequela's house is on the left side of the street, about four houses south of the fork. Elena's house is two doors down. None of Ocú's hat makers speak English.

Festivals & Events

The **Festival del Manito Ocueño**, one of the country's best folklore events, is held in Ocú during the third week in August. The three-day festival was established to maintain the region's traditional culture, and folklore groups from throughout Herrera Province present their dances in traditional dress. The fiesta's climax is a Sunday morning church wedding, after which the couple is paraded through the streets on horseback by friends and family.

Ocú is also famous for its **patron saint festival**, usually held January 20–23. During this festival, an effigy of St Sebastian is paraded through the streets at night, and devotees walk behind the statue carrying lighted candles. This festival includes folklore programs and an agricultural fair.

Sleeping

There are several small hotels in Ocú, but the best place to stay is at the **Habitaciones de Juan Pablo** (☎ 974 1312; d US$10; **P**), a friendly, family-run affair. Just on the edge of town off the road connecting Ocú with the Interamericana (on the left if arriving from the Interamericana), you'll see a sign that reads '*se alquilan habitaciones*' (rooms for rent), marked with a flag. Here, you'll find eight basic rooms, each with two double beds and clean private cold-water bathrooms.

Getting There & Away

Ocú can be reached by frequent buses from the Terminal de Transportes de Herrera in Chitré (US$2, one hour).

SAN JOSÉ

Just outside Ocú, in the small village of San José, lies one of Panama's most organized artisan groups. **Artesanía Ocueña** (www.artesaniasocu .bizland.com) was founded in 1994 by a group of 20 members – all women – who carry on the intricate work of making *montunos* (traditional folklore outfits), *polleras* (traditional dresses from the Península de Azuero) and a range of other handmade items such as tablecloths and place mats. Today, the group numbers about 50 and is receiving international attention (not least from the German government, who helped fund the construction of their workshop/studio in San José). The embroideries here are simply exquisite.

To visit the workshop, take the turnoff (the sign says 'Los Llanos') on the left side of the road as you head north of Ocú in the direction of the Interamericana. The turnoff is about 1km from the central plaza. From there it's a 15-minute drive along a dirt road until you reach the community. You can also catch an 'Ocú–Los Llanos' *chiva* (rural bus; US$0.50) in front of the main plaza in Ocú. If no one's around when you stop in, ask around for **Ana Marín** (☎ 601 7430) or **Guillermina Montilla** (☎ 694 2251). The co-op also sells over the internet.

Los Santos Province

Much like neighboring Herrera Province, Los Santos is centered on the Península de Azuero and is often thought of as the heart and soul of the country. Generations ago, it was here that Panama's cry for independence was first uttered, yet the residents of 'The Saints' Province take great pride in their Spanish history and showcase it in folkloric festivals that date back to the first settlers.

The Fiesta de Corpus Christi in Villa de Los Santos and the Feria de la Mejorana Librada in Guararé are marked by exuberant displays of traditional clothing and dances born in Spain during the Middle Ages. The most intricate *polleras* (the national costume based on dresses worn by Spanish peasants during the 17th and 18th centuries) are made in the village of La Enea. In the provincial capital of Las Tablas, the annual Carnaval is a rowdy affair of unrestrained excess that cannot be rivaled by any other celebration in Panama. The festivities in Los Santos are hedonistic affairs revolving around food, drink and copious amounts of dancing and celebrating. They are some of the most publicized events of the year throughout the entire country, yet few foreign tourists venture into Panama's interior to experience them.

Aside from its festivals, Los Santos is also home to some of the country's best surf spots, though international jet-setters have been slow to catch on. While Bocas del Toro and Santa Catalina continue to attract baby-faced surfers from around the globe, Los Santos is essentially off the map. Whether you partake in centuries-old festivals or catch a ride on an empty break, chances are you'll find what you're looking for in this undertouristed province.

HIGHLIGHTS

- Kicking off your shoes, letting your hair down and living it up at the Carnaval in **Las Tablas** (p167)

- Catching a ride on an uncrowded wave at **Playa Venao** (p171)

- Spotting sea turtles by thousands during their annual nesting at **Isla de Cañas** (p173)

- Shopping for *polleras* (the national dress) in the traditional village of **La Enea** (p166)

- Crying out for independence at 'La Grita', a festival commemorating the birth of Panama, in **Villa de Los Santos** (p162)

★ Villa de Los Santos
La Enea ★
Las Tablas ★
Isla de Cañas ★   ★ Playa Venao

- POPULATION: 86,700   - AREA: 3806 SQ KM   - ELEVATION: SEA LEVEL TO 950M

LOS SANTOS PROVINCE

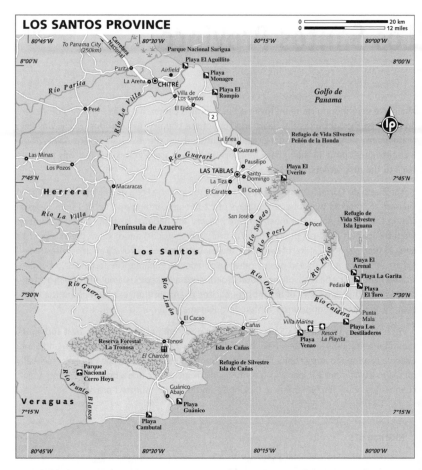

LOS SANTOS PROVINCE

VILLA DE LOS SANTOS

pop 7800

This quintessential Azuero town is where Panama's first move toward independence from Spain began on November 10, 1821. Since then, residents of Los Santos have continued to honor the freedom pangs of their ancestors by throwing one of Panama's wildest parties. Of course, the fun isn't just reserved for one day – on the contrary, the calendar in Los Santos is dotted with enough local and national holidays to keep everyone liquored up and sufficiently entertained.

Aside from its festivals, Los Santos is replete with colonial structures dating back to the early days of the Spanish settlers. It is also home to a noteworthy museum dedicated to

Panamanian independence as well as one of the country's most magnificent churches.

Orientation

The Río La Villa, 4km south of downtown Chitré (p150), marks the boundary between Herrera and Los Santos Provinces. South of the river you'll come to Villa de Los Santos (or simply 'Los Santos') on the Carretera Nacional.

Information

Banco Nacional de Panamá (cnr Av 10 de Noviembre & Calle Tomas Herrera)

IPAT (☎ 966 8013; fax 996 8040; Calle José Vallarino; ⏰ 9am-4pm Mon-Fri) Provides information on any upcoming celebrations in the area.

Police station (Av 10 de Noviembre)

LOS FIESTAS DE AZUERO (PART II)

Festivals in the Península de Azuero are famous throughout Panama for their traditional celebrations, many of which revolve around aspects of life in the time of the early Spanish settlers. If your visit to Panama coincides with any of the festivals listed below, it's worth making an effort to visit. You may lose a day or two to a vicious hangover, but partying in the streets with locals until the wee hours of the morning is something you'll never forget.

Some of the peninsula's best-known festivals include:

- Carnaval – The four days before Ash Wednesday in Las Tablas and Villa de Los Santos.
- Semana Santa – March/April in Villa de Los Santos.
- Feria de Azuero – late April/early May in Villa de los Santos.
- Fiesta de Corpus Christi – forty days after Easter in Villa de Los Santos.
- Fiestas Patronales de Santa Librada – July 20 in Las Tablas.
- Fiesta de la Pollera – July 22 in Las Tablas.
- Feria de la Mejorana, Festival de la Virgen de las Mercedes – September 23 to 27 in Guraré.
- La Grita de la Villa – November 10 in Villa de Los Santos.

For more information on the festivals listed above, see the various town and city listings in this chapter. For listings of festivals in Herrera Province, see p151.

Sights

MUSEO DE LA NACIONALIDAD

This modest **museum** (Calle José Vallarino; adult/child US$1/0.25; �9am-4:30pm Tue-Sat, to 1pm Sun), opposite Plaza Simón Bolívar, occupies the former house where Panama's Declaration of Independence was signed in 1821. In the years that followed, the handsome brick-and-tile residence served as a jail, a school and a legislature. It predates the town's church, but no one knows exactly when it was built.

Inaugurated as a museum in 1974, it contains artifacts related to Panama's independence, which was declared in Los Santos 18 days before it was declared by the government. The museum also contains objects from the era of the Spanish conquest. Pre-Columbian ceramics and colonial-era religious art comprise most of the exhibits, and there's also a lovely garden courtyard.

IGLESIA DE SAN ATANACIO

Villa de Los Santos' church, also alongside Plaza Simón Bolívar, opened its doors to the public in 1782 after nearly nine years of construction. It's a fine example of the baroque style, with lots of intricately carved wood depicting cherubs, saints, Jesus and the Virgin. Almost everything in the church is original, and some of the objects even predate the structure itself. The 12m arch in front of the altar, for example, bears its date of manufacture (1733) and the names of its two creators.

The altar is made of mahogany and rosewood and covered nearly from base to top in gold leaf. In a glass sepulchre in front of the altar is a life-size wooden statue of Christ that is carried through the streets of Villa de Los Santos on Good Friday, behind a candlelit procession.

This church was granted national monument status by the government in 1938 and is truly a national treasure.

MASKS

Carlos Ivan de Leon (☎ 966 9149; Calle Tomas Herrera; �noon-1pm & 6-10pm) makes the most elaborate and frightening masks in Panama at his house near Calle Segundo Villareal. He specializes in one kind of mask; that of the devil for the famous *baile de los diablos sucios* (dance of the dirty devils; see the boxed text on p165). Most of Carlos' masks are sold to professional dancers, but increasingly are being bought by European and American collectors. Several are on display at the IPAT office in Los Santos.

VILLA DE LOS SANTOS

0 — 400 m
0 — 0.2 miles

INFORMATION		
Banco Nacional de Panamá	1	C1
IPAT Tourist Office	2	C1
Police Station	3	C1

SIGHTS & ACTIVITIES		
Home of Maskmaker Carlos		
Ivan de Leon	4	B2
Iglesia de San Atanacio	5	C1
Museo de la Nacionalidad	6	C1

SLEEPING		
Hotel La Villa	7	A3
Kevin's Hotel	8	B2

TRANSPORT		
Buses to Chitré	9	B2
Buses to Las Tablas & Chitré	..(see 13)	
Buses to Panama City	10	C1
Buses to Panama City	11	C1
Taxis	12	C1
Taxis	13	B2

Look out for the house with a black front door and a sign featuring his family name (De Leon) nearby. Carlos speaks Spanish only.

Festivals & Events

For information on Los Santos' biggest festival, the **Fiesta de Corpus Christi**, see the boxed text on opposite.

The anniversary of the historic *grito* (cry), also known as **La Grita de la Villa** (cry of the Village), is celebrated in Los Santos on November 10. This patriotic occasion is usually overseen by the President of Panama and is highlighted by a parade, musical and dance performances and a healthy amount of drinking in the streets.

The **Feria de Azuero** (Azuero Fair, late April/early May) features folkloric dancing, agricultural attractions and various competitions among local singers performing regional songs.

Other notable festivals include **Carnaval**, celebrated four days before Ash Wednesday (February/March) and April's **Semana Santa** (Holy Week).

Sleeping & Eating

With the city of Chitré (p150) just 4km away, there are a range of other sleeping options that may come in handy when Los Santos is packed to the brim during festivals.

Kevin's Hotel (☎ 966 8276; d from US$15-25; P) Set back from the Carretera Nacional, this low-key hotel features a wide range of nearly identical-looking concrete box-style rooms. Of course, the price is right, especially since you can have your choice of amenities including air-con, private hot-water bathrooms and satellite TV for just a few extra dollars. The hotel's restaurant is a popular truck stop and serves hearty dishes including grilled meats and seafood casseroles.

Hotel La Villa (☎ 966 9321; d from US$20-35; P) The best hotel in Los Santos is also a low-key affair, though the swimming pool is a nice touch, especially in the dry and dusty Azuero summer. Rooms of varying sizes and shapes have steamy showers and chilly air-con, and the attached bar-restaurant serves up all of your Panamanian favorites. The best part of La Villa is its colorful design scheme, which incorporates

LOS SANTOS PROVINCE

all of the artisan crafts you'll find at any of Los Santos' festivals.

Getting There & Around

Chitré–Las Tablas buses stop on the Carretera Nacional, and Chitré–Villa de Los Santos buses stop on Calle José Vallarino half a block from the Carretera Nacional. Fares to these destinations or anywhere in the province are usually between US$0.50 and US$2.

Buses to Panama City depart from Calle José Vallarino at Av 10 de Noviembre, and also from Calle Segundo Villarreal a block-and-a-half northeast of Plaza Simón Bolívar.

Taxis are a quick way to get around Villa de Los Santos and between Villa de Los Santos and Chitré. The fare won't exceed US$3 if you stay within these cities. Taxis can usually be found near the bus stop on the Carretera Nacional and northwest of Plaza Simón Bolívar.

PLAYAS MONAGRE & EL ROMPÍO

Ten kilometers northeast of Villa de Los Santos are Playas Monagre and El Rompío, which serve as popular beach day-trips for local families. El Rompío is less frequented than Monagre and thus has less litter, but both have a lot of driftwood on them and the sand is dark and hot on sunny days. Unfortunately, the presence of strong rip currents means that swimming is not a great idea, though there's still plenty of fun in the sun to be had.

A bus leaves the Chitré station for Playas Monagre and El Rompío (US$1, around 20km, hourly) from sunrise to sunset. This bus passes through Villa de Los Santos on the way to the beaches and can be hailed from

the Carretera Nacional in town. Look for a bus with 'Monagre' on its windshield. The fare from Villa de Los Santos to either beach is US$0.50. A taxi ride from Chitré to either beach costs about US$5; a taxi from Villa de Los Santos costs half that.

ROAD TO LAS TABLAS

The Carretera Nacional from Villa de Los Santos to Las Tablas runs mostly past small farms and cattle ranches, with almost no remaining forest in sight – indeed, the province is the most heavily deforested in the country. However, the drive is still scenic in its own right, especially since it passes a few much-loved Azuero institutions.

About 3km southeast of Los Santos along the Carretera Nacional is **Kiosco El Ciruelo** (✪ 6am-10pm Fri-Sun), a rustic trucker stop where everything is cooked on a wood-fire grill. Among the offerings is a traditional speciality of Los Santos Province: tamales made with corn, pork and various spices, and wrapped in plantain leaves.

From Kiosco El Ciruelo, travel another 6km until you see a bright blue public phone on the eastern side of the road. Just beyond the phone is a small hut beside a large pile of coconut husks. Located here is **La Casa de la Pipa** (The House of Coconut Juice), which sells fresh, ice-cold coconut water for US$0.25.

As you travel the two-lane Carretera Nacional toward Las Tablas, you'll occasionally see stands with sausages dangling in front of them. The pork sausages made on the Península de Azuero are nationally famous for their high quality, and a few links of this

---

LOCAL LORE: FIESTA DE CORPUS CHRISTI

The **Fiesta de Corpus Christi** (The Body of Christ Festival), which is held from Thursday to Sunday, 40 days after Easter, is one of the most riotous events in the country. Although the festival has been celebrated throughout the Catholic world ever since Pope Urban IV sanctioned the event in 1264, the local version incorporates the animistic traditions of the Azuero peninsula.

As a means of converting the indigenous peoples of the region, Spanish missionaries used the festival to highlight the concept of good versus evil. At the core of the festival is a series of dances including the famous *baile de los diablos sucios* (dance of the dirty devils), which emphasizes the Christian belief in the Apocalypse. Needless to say, God, heaven and the angels win out in the end, though it doesn't prevent local artisans from creating some truly mind-blowing masks and costumes.

The entire festival attracts hundreds of performers ranging from singers and dancers to theatre troops and magicians. Although it is very much a Catholic festival, the animistic tradition of Azuero lives on in the unique lore that has been passed down from generation to generation.

delicious meat shouldn't cost you more than a dollar or so.

If you're traveling the highway around Carnaval time, you'll also see dozens of smashed-up cars on the roadside. These once belonged to the motorists killed by drunk drivers during Carnaval. Indeed, the police realize that most of the people on the road during Carnaval are intoxicated. However, instead of trying to arrest all the drunk motorists, the police display the old wrecks, hoping the sight will encourage drunks to drive slowly.

With that said, try to avoid any unnecessary highway travel during Carnaval.

GUARARÉ

pop 4200

The tiny town of Guararé, located on the Carretera Nacional between Villa de Los Santos and Las Tablas, is just another sleepy Azuero town that's easily ignored by passing motorists. That is, of course, if you arrive on any day other the days between September 23 and 27, when the town really comes to life for Panama's largest folkloric festival, the **Feria de la Mejorana**.

Begun by Manuel Zárate in 1950 to stimulate interest and participation in traditional practices, the Feria de la Mejorana has become the best place to see Panama's folklore in all its manifestations. Dance groups from all over the country – and even some from other Latin American countries – attend this annual event, which includes a colorful parade in which participants are hauled through the streets in oxcarts.

Folkloric dances that were once part of other celebrations in other places are today sometimes seen only at this event. For example, this is the only festival in which a dance known as La Pajarita (Paper Bird) is performed. In contrast to the various exuberant devil dances, a calm, religious quality pervades La Pajarita.

A good warm-up for the festivities is a visit to the **Museo Manuel F Zárate** (adult/child US$0.75/0.25; 8am-noon & 1-4pm Tue-Sat, to noon Sun). Zárate was a folklorist devoted to conserving the traditions and folklore of the Azuero region. The museum, in Zárate's former home, contains *polleras*, masks, *diablito* (little devil) costumes and other exhibits. It's two blocks behind the church and about six short blocks from the main road (turn off at the gas station).

Just off the Chitré–Las Tablas highway, the **Residencial La Mejorana** (☎ 994 5794; d US$15-30;

(P) (X)) is a fairly large, fairly clean and fairly nondescript hotel, but it's a decent enough place to crash for the night. And of course, if there's a festival in town, you could only be so lucky as to get a room here. Prices vary according to the size of the room, though all are equipped with air-con and private hot-water bathrooms, and have that certain air of sterility to them.

Guararé is beside the Carretera Nacional, 20km south of Villa de Los Santos. You can hop on any bus that travels the highway in the direction of Guararé; you'll be dropped off at the town.

LA ENEA

This small village northeast of Guararé produces the finest *polleras* in Panama. Once the daily attire of Spain's lower classes in the 17th and 18th centuries, the *pollera* is today the national costume and is distinguished by its stirring beauty and elegance. Almost every part of the costume is made by hand, from the attractive embroidery on the blouse and skirt to the delicate filigree ornaments tucked around the gold combs in the hair. The traditional assortment of jewelry worn with a *pollera* can cost upwards of US$20,000.

By convention, the *pollera* consists of two basic pieces: a blouse that rests upon the tops of the shoulders and a long skirt divided into two fully gathered tiers. Each dress requires no less than 10m of fine white linen or cotton cloth. Elaborate needlework in a single color enriches the white background.

One of the best-known makers of the national costume, Ildaura Saavedra de Espina (☎ 994 5527), lives beside Parque de La Enea, in the green-tiled house next door to the small market with 'Roxana' painted over its door. She made her first *pollera* in 1946 at the age of 16 and has been making them ever since, averaging one *pollera* every six months. Ildama sold her first dress for US$300 – today, she charges over US$2000 per dress.

Anyone with a keen interest in needlecraft (and a decent understanding of Spanish) is welcome to visit Ildama. She is accustomed to strangers stopping by her home to marvel at her handiwork and if you're lucky, Ildama will show you her scrapbook, containing photos of many of the dresses she's made.

If you're interested in purchasing a *pollera*, be advised that every dress is made to order – she does not have a rack of them on hand, just sections of the one she's working on.

To reach La Enea, take a taxi (US$2) from Guararé.

LAS TABLAS
pop 9000

Las Tablas is ground zero for the street dancing, booze-soaked celebrations and all-out mayhem associated with the festivals of the Península de Azuero. Home to the country's most famous Carnaval, Las Tablas is the best place in Panama to let go of your inhibitions, get your drink on and seriously cut loose.

As the capital city of Los Santos Province, Las Tablas has a fine church and a small museum devoted to former Las Tablas statesman and three-time president Belisario Porras. The city is also famous for its combined patron saint/*pollera* festival, a colorful mix of religious ceremony and beauty contest.

Orientation

Las Tablas is 31km southeast of Chitré via the Carretera Nacional, which becomes Av Laureano Lopez at the northern edge of town and reemerges as the road to Santo Domingo on the southeastern side of town. Av Laureano Lopez runs for nine blocks before ending at the Museo Belisario Porras, beside the central plaza.

Almost everything of interest to travelers is within five blocks of the plaza. This includes remnants of one of the finest colonial churches on the peninsula, banks, a post office, hotels and restaurants. Further out is a bus station and taxi stands.

Information

Banco Nacional de Panamá (Av Laureano Lopez, near Calle 2)
Banistmo (Calle Belisario Porras)
BBVA (Av Belisario Porras) Bank with ATM.
Post office (Calle 2)
Zona Internet (Calle 8 de Noviembre; per hr US$1; ⏰ 8am-10pm Mon-Sat) Near the plaza.

Sights
MUSEO BELISARIO PORRAS

Opposite the Central Plaza, this **museum** (Av Belisario Porras; adult/child US$0.50/0.25; ⏰ 9am-12:30pm & 1:30-4pm Tue-Sat, to noon Sun) is in the mud-walled former home of three-time president Belisario Porras, during whose administration the

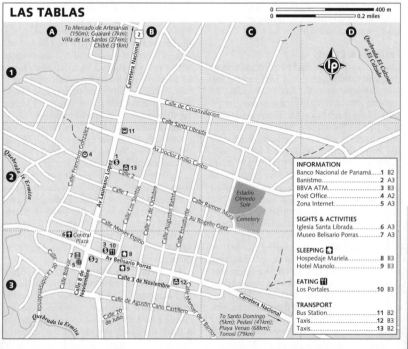

LAS TABLAS

0 _____ 400 m
0 _____ 0.2 miles

To Mercado de Artesanías (150m); Guararé (7km); Villa de Los Santos (27km); Chitré (31km)

Quebrada El Cabezno o El Estudio

Carretera Nacional

Calle de Circunvalacion

Calle Santa Librada

Quebrada la Ermita

Calle Francisco Gonzalez

Av Doctor Emilio Castro

Av Laureano Lopez

Calle 2

Calle 1

Calle Los Santos

Calle 12 de Octubre

Calle Augusto Batista

Calle Ramon Mora

Av Rogelio Gaez

Calle Estudiante

Estadio Olmedo Sole Cemetery

Calle Moises Espino

Central Plaza

Calle 8 de Noviembre

Av Belisario Porras

Calle 3 de Noviembre

Calle Manuel de J Barros

Carretera Nacional

Calle Bolivar

Calle La Independencia

Calle de Agustin Cano Castillero

Calle 20 de Julio

Quebrada la Ermita

To Santo Domingo (5km); Pedasi (41km); Playa Venao (68km); Tonosí (79km)

INFORMATION		
Banco Nacional de Panamá	1	B2
Banistmo	2	A3
BBVA ATM	3	B3
Post Office	4	A2
Zona Internet	5	A3

SIGHTS & ACTIVITIES		
Iglesia Santa Librada	6	A3
Museo Belisario Porras	7	A3

SLEEPING		
Hospedaje Mariela	8	B3
Hotel Manolo	9	B3

EATING		
Los Portales	10	B3

TRANSPORT		
Bus Station	11	B2
Taxis	12	B3
Taxis	13	B2

Panama Canal opened. Porras was president for all but two years from 1912 to 1924. He is credited with establishing Panama's network of public hospitals, creating a national registry for land titles and constructing scores of bridges and aqueducts.

The museum contains many artifacts from Porras' life and serves as a monument to the achievements of this widely revered man. Incidentally, the huge tomb inside the museum, which bears Porras' name, is empty; plans to move his remains here from a cemetery in Panama City were never carried out.

As an interesting aside, all of Porras' male descendants wear their whiskers in his unusual style – a thick, prideful mustache resembling the horns of a Texas longhorn steer.

IGLESIA SANTA LIBRADA

This Baroque-style **church** (Av Belisario Porras) near the central plaza opened its doors on March 9, 1789, but sustained major damage in 1950 during a fire. Although the church was later restored, the walls and the base of the pulpit are original. The painted faces on the ornate 23-karat gold-leaf altar are also original, but the figurines of Christ, the Virgin and the saints were added after the blaze. Cedar wood was used in the construction of the altar, which was renovated in 2001.

Festivals & Events

Las Tablas is perhaps the best place in Panama to spend **Carnaval**, which is held during the four days that precede Ash Wednesday. By tradition, the town is divided into two groups, *calle arriba* (high street) and *calle abajo* (low street), which compete intensely with each other in every aspect of the fiesta. Each *calle* has its own queen, floats and songs. Each day begins with members parading in street clothes and singing songs that poke fun at the rival group. During the parade, jokesters from both sides toss tinted water, blue dye and shaving cream at the other side. No one, onlookers included, is spared – dress expecting to get creamed.

Both sides take a rest during the heat of the day and don costumes or put finishing touches on their floats in the late afternoon. At dusk, the groups' parades begin on parallel streets, led by floats that are followed by musicians seated in the back of flatbed trucks, who are followed in turn by *calle* members. Every night, each *calle* has a different float and dif-

ferent costumes. Crowds pack the sidewalks and fireworks light up the night. The queens make their appearances on Saturday night, dressed at first in gaudily decorated costumes and later in exquisite evening gowns. Their coronation is held on Sunday. Monday is masquerade day and on Tuesday all the women in town who have *polleras* don them and fill the streets.

Another excellent time to be in Las Tablas is July 21, when the provincial capital hosts two big events: the patron saint festival and the *pollera* festival. The **Fiesta de Santa Librada** is a sacred event, and services inside the church are accompanied by street celebrations that recall a medieval fair, with gambling, dancing, singing, bullfights, and excessive eating and drinking – it's a strange juxtaposition of the sacred and the profane. The **Fiesta de La Pollera** is highlighted by a parade of beautiful young women who model the national costume as they pass through the streets, all the while being judged on their grace as well as on the artisanship, design and authenticity of their costumes.

Sleeping & Eating

Hospedaje Mariela (☎ 994 6366; fax 994 7422; Av Belisario Porras; d without/with bathroom US$10/20; P) Occupying the space above an old-school barbershop, the Hospedaje Mariela is the best budget option in town. If you're not too fussy about where you lay your head, a box with a bed and a fan can be yours for next to nothing. If you're feeling a little less than frugal, spring for the private bathroom, but don't expect anything more than lukewarm at best.

Hotel Manolo (☎ 994 6372; Av Belisario Porras; d US$20-30; P ❀) If you're looking for slightly more comfortable lodgings, the Hotel Manolo was rebuilt a few years back and now features a small number of simple but functional rooms with air-con and private hot-water bathrooms. The downstairs restaurant and bar is a popular spot for locals as well as guests, so there are always people around to share a drink with. When you're checking in, be sure to ask for a room with a window – not all of them have one.

Los Portales (Av Belisario Porras; mains US$3-5) Housed in a handsome colonial building, this atmospheric yet low-key spot serves grilled meats and tasty seafood including *corvina ceviche* (sea bass *ceviche*). Before hitting the road, stop by in the morning for a tasty farm-style breakfast to start your day the right way.

Getting There & Away

From Las Tablas' **bus station** (cnr Avs Laureano Lopez & Doctor Emilio Castro) buses run hourly to Santo Domingo (US$0.50, 10 minutes, 5km), Chitré (US$1, 30 minutes), Tonosí (US$3, 1½ hours) and Pedasí (US$2, one hour).

There are 10 daily departures to Panama City (US$6.50, 4½ hours), with additonal buses during festivals.

PEDASÍ

pop 2400

At first glance, Pedasí appears much like any other tranquil town in Azuero – the town center is dotted with historic colonial buildings and many of the town's residents appear to have nothing but time on their hands. Behind the scenes, however, Pedasí is the focus of an intensive push to develop tourism along the southwestern coastline. In case you're wondering why it is that there is so much interest in this rather nondescript place, consider the fact that Pedasí is the hometown of former president Mireya Moscoso. And of course, the nearby wilderness beaches are impossibly picturesque yet virtually abandoned.

For the time being, tourist development seems to be happening slowly in Pedasí, though there are a few major condo projects popping up outside the town limits. In the meantime, Pedasí serves as the gateway to the Azuero coastline (p171), and it's a convenient base for exploring the Refugios de Vida Silvestre Isla Iguana (p170) and Isla de Cañas (p173).

Orientation & Information

The Carretera Nacional passes down the western part of Pedasí, while the beaches start just a few kilometers to the east. A **Banco Nacional de Panama**, with an ATM, is at the northern entrance to town. A new **IPAT office** (☼ 8am-8pm) lies behind the Residencial Pedasí hotel in the north of town. Next door is an **internet café** (per hr US$1; ☼ 9:30am-5:30pm Mon-Fri, to 4pm Sat). The **ANAM** office in the south of town can provide information about Isla Iguana and Isla de Cañas.

Activities

You can arrange to go scuba diving through the **Pedasí Scuba Center** (☎ 995 2405; www.diven fishpanama .com), which is located next door to IPAT. The

center offers diving and boating excursions to Isla Iguana or Isla Frailes (boat hire US$80, two-tank dive US$35), which are both surrounded by large coral reefs. Snorkeling gear (US$10 per day) is also available for rent.

Festivals & Events

Pedasí holds **patron saint festivals** on June 29 and November 25, or the nearest Saturday to them. Although these events are nowhere near as chaotic as some of the more famous festivals in Azuero, they are nevertheless fun affairs, with long parades and lots of merriment. On July 16, a small celebration for fishermen is held at Playa Arenal, a beach 3km northwest of town.

Sleeping & Eating

Residencial Moscoso (☎ 995 2203; s/d US$8/10, s/d with air-con & private bathroom US$15/18; P 🏊) Near the center of town, this pensión is surprisingly low-key considering that the owner is related to Panama's former president, Mireya Moscoso. Although it's a friendly place with personal service, it's probably not a good idea to talk politics while you're staying here. The rooms at Moscoso are fairly basic but well cared for, and you probably won't mind the cold showers one bit.

Dim's Hostal (☎ 995 2303; s/d US$18/25; P) On the main road near the center of town, Dim's has a family atmosphere with a fine backyard, complete with hammocks and a shady mango tree. The delightful owners are also committed to all of their guests, so you can enjoy a fine level of service here despite the budget-friendly prices. A handful of simple rooms have good beds and tiled bathrooms with cold-water showers, though most guests spend their time congregating in the garden.

Dulcería Yely (cakes US$0.25-2) This lovely cake shop on a side street near the Pensión Moscoso serves a variety of delectable sweets including *manjar* cake, which resembles caramel in taste and appearance and is a speciality of the region. If you're in need of something more filling, there are also tasty sandwiches available for takeout for just a few dollars.

Getting There & Away

Buses from Las Tablas leave every 45 minutes between 6am and 4:30pm (US$2, one hour). Buses to the nearby beaches are sporadic, though generally there's one a day at around 8pm that passes the beach en route to Cañas, returning the next morning at around 8am. However, the coastline is easily accessed by private vehicle and a taxi should cost between US$12 and US$16.

AROUND PEDASÍ
Refugio de Vida Silvestre Isla Iguana

This 55-hectare **wildlife refuge** is centered on a deserted island that is ringed by coral fields, though unfortunately many of the reeds died in the 1982–83 El Niño (a change in weather patterns that shifts ocean currents and starves marine life along the eastern Pacific coast).

However, the surviving coral is pretty spectacular and the water is shallow enough to be snorkeled. As with most reefs in the Pacific, the fish here are enormous.

Humpback whales also inhabit the waters around Isla Iguana from June to November. These large sea mammals, 15m to 20m long, mate and bear their young here and then teach them to dive. The humpbacks are the famous 'singing whales' – occasionally you can hear their underwater sounds when diving here.

Unfortunately, although the island is supposed to be maintained by ANAM,

---

RESCUING THE TUNA

In November of 2006, a study published in the journal *Science* suggested that nearly one-third of all global fishing stocks have already collapsed and, based on current trends, it's likely that all global fish stocks will collapse within 50 years. These findings present a sobering reality – in just a few decades, nearly all of the fish present on current menus around the world will be on the verge of extinction.

Although it's easy to dismiss these claims as alarmist, there are countless examples of collapsed fisheries the world over. In the 1970s the Peruvian anchovy fishery collapsed following an El Niño year. In 1992 the virtual extinction of cod in Newfoundland waters forced the Canadian government to impose a moratorium on fishing in the Grand Banks. Today, the sole populations in the Irish Sea and the English channel are highly threatened due to rampant overfishing.

The reason behind overfishing is simply that global seafood production cannot keep up with population growth. Unfortunately, world demand is on the rise, especially as high-quality sashimi-grade fish is increasingly sought after everywhere from North America and Europe to Asia and Australia. Although aquaculture farms act as buffers for certain species like salmon and tilapia, pelagic fish like yellowfin tuna are increasingly threatened.

Yellowfin (ahi) tuna is perhaps the most sought-after fish in the world and its commercial industry is estimated at several billion dollars. Found in subtropical and tropical waters around the world, tuna reach lengths of over 2m and can weigh upwards of 200kg. Although they are typically processed and canned, tuna is increasingly flash frozen and sold in fillets for use as sushi. If left raw, tuna is blood red in color, and has a smooth texture and a rich buttery taste.

In Panama, the Azuero coastline along the Golfo de Panamá is often referred to as the 'tuna coast.' Home to a large population of yellowfin tuna, the tuna coast serves as a benchmark indicator for the health of global stocks.

Thirty kilometers southwest of Pedasí, **Laboratorio Achotines** (Tuna Laboratory; ☎ 995 8166; www.iattc.org) is affiliated with the Inter-American Tropical Tuna Commission, a global regulatory consortium on tuna fishing, and routinely sets quotas for the catches along the Pacific coast of the Americas. In 2002 the laboratory prevented commercial tuna fishing for an entire month along the Pacific coast of both North and South America, and they spent millions of dollars enforcing the ban.

The main purposes of the laboratory are to ensure the future health of yellowfin tuna populations and to promote sustainable commercial fishing. The center studies the spawning patterns of fish held in captivity as well as migratory patterns of tuna in the ocean through the use of radio transmitters. The center has also been successful in establishing an international regulatory commission on the use of certain types of fishing nets, which has played a direct role in reducing the number of dolphins that are killed by tuna fishing in the eastern Pacific, from 500,000 annually to 3000.

Laboratorio Achotines is open to the general public, though you must contact them in advance to arrange a tour of their facilities.

Panama's environmental agency, the main beach is often strewn with litter. Also, the US Navy used the island for target practice during WWII and unexploded ordnance is occasionally discovered here. Needless to say, it's unwise to stray off the island's beaten paths.

Isla Iguana is reachable by boat from Playa El Arenal, a beach 3km northwest of the Accel station in Pedasí. At the beach, boaters can take parties of up to eight people to the island for US$20 each way. Be sure to tell your driver when to return for you.

Azuero Coastline

For information on surfing along the Azuero coastline, see the boxed text on p172.

PLAYAS EL TORO & LA GARITA

The two closest beaches to Pedasí serve as a popular day trip for residents of Pedasí, especially since the ocean here is usually safe for swimming. However, the waves can pick up if there's a strong surge coming in.

At Playa El Toro you can actually drive onto the beach if you have a vehicle, but Playa La Garita is flanked by a rocky slope, and a hike of about 100m through light scrub and dirt (which turns to mud if there's been any recent rain) is required to reach the beach. Despite their close proximity to Pedasí, both beaches are quite isolated and private. Neither offers much snorkeling – the water is simply too murky.

You can hire a taxi in Pedasí to reach these beaches; if you're driving from central Pedasí, turn east off the Carretera Nacional onto the paved street beside the Residential Moscoso and drive about 250m to the Cantina Hermanos Cedeño bar. Then take the dirt road just past the bar for 1km until the road forks. Follow the signs for 2km to the beaches.

PLAYA LOS DESTILADEROS

ourpick The **cabins** (☎ 675 9715, 211 2277; d cabin incl 3 meals US$130; **P**) at this isolated beach are some of Panama's most charming accommodations. The painstaking work that went into these tall, thatched-roof cabins is apparent, from the lovely hand-carved washbasins to the front decks with sea views. Each cabin is fan-cooled and allows plenty of privacy, and waking up to the sights and sounds of the ocean is an experience not to be missed. The owner and designer, Philippe Atanasiades, is one of the

best chefs in Panama, which means that you will eat extremely well while you're staying here. To get here, drive through Pedasí and take the turnoff to the left in El Limon.

RESORT LA PLAYITA

This relaxed **resort** (☎ 996 2225; d cabin US$60; **P**), about 31km southwest of Pedasí, is more of a rustic retreat than an overbearing all-inclusive resort. The grounds are home to three lovely cabins, each beautifully designed with firm beds and private hot-water bathroom; ask for the cabin with ocean views. One thing you should know about La Playita is that the owner has a soft spot for the avian species and there are lots of birds here – particularly ostriches, spotted pigeons and several turkeys – but watch out, as the birds have the run of the grounds.

There's also a pleasant restaurant overlooking the water, and you can rent snorkeling gear (US$6) or arrange boat trips with the owner (US$30). Be advised that if you stay here during the weekend, you'll be sharing the beach with dozens (sometimes hundreds) of revelers who come from Los Santos to party beside the beach. During the week, however, the beach is virtually abandoned aside from the odd fisherman or two.

VILLA MARINA

The next driveway past La Playita leads to **Villa Marina** (☎ 211 2277; www.playavenado.com; d/master bedroom incl 3 meals US$140/150; **P** 🗷), a stunner of an ocean-side B&B that is set amidst tranquil gardens. The standard guestrooms are bright and airy, particularly when the morning light and ocean breezes fill up the room, while the larger master bedroom has French doors that open toward the beach. All of the rooms have luxurious private facilities, and guests can spend their days lounging around on hammocks, horseback riding on the beach, snorkeling and surfing in the sea or on boating and fishing excursions.

PLAYA VENAO

Playa Venao is a long, curving protected beach that's very popular with surfers – there are almost always waves to surf and they break in both directions.

The Playa Venao turnoff is 33km by road southwest of Pedasí, or 2km past the Resort La Playita turnoff. Facilities here are limited to an open-sided restaurant-bar and a nameless

SURFING IN LOS SANTOS PROVINCE

Although few among the international surfing community know about Los Santos, the province is home to some serious surf. The most popular destination for Panamanians is the coastline near Pedasí, though there is no shortage of wicked surf spots to choose from – you may have to work hard to get out here, but it'll be worth it when you see the lack of crowds. The beaches listed below are featured on Map pp68–9.

- **Playa Lagarto** At Pedasí. Beach bottom. Breaks at all tides. Good rights, lefts. Closes out when surf too big.
- **Playa El Toro** Near Pedasí. Rock-bottom point break with lefts, rights. Gets big with a strong swell. Best surfed at medium tide.
- **Playa Los Destiladeros** Near Pedasí. Right point over rock bottom, left point over rock bottom, beack break with pebble bottom. Best at medium tide.
- **Ciruelo** Before Venado. Rock-bottom point break, rarely surfed. Can get really good left tubes when there is a strong swell and no wind.
- **Playa Venao** South of Venado. Sand-bottom beach break popular with local surfers. This spot catches just about any swell. Best surfed at medium to high tide.
- **Playa Madroño** A 30-minute walk from Venado. Surf can get really good, with hollow tubes at low tide. Need to arrive early in the day before the wind picks up.
- **Playa Guánico** A 45-minute walk south of Venado. Two rock-bottom point breaks with rights and lefts. One beach break with rights and lefts.
- **Playa Raya** One hour past Venado. Waves 4m to 5m on big swells with serious tubes. Many big sharks here as well.
- **Playa Cambutal** Beyond Tonosí. Beach breaks with rights and lefts. Catches just about every swell. Best at medium to high tide.
- **Playa Negra** West of Playa Cambutal, around the first point. Point break over rocks, best during medium to high tide.
- **411** West of Punta Negra. Locally famous point break with a long right over a rock ledge. Best during medium to high tide.
- **Dinosaurios** Next to 411. Rock-bottom break with rights, lefts at medium to high tide. Can get very big with strong swells.
- **Horcones Beach Break** West of Dinosaurios. Sand-bottom beach break with rights, lefts. Good most tides.
- **Dos Rocas** Near Horcones. Rock-bottom point break beside two jutting boulders. Can get good rights at medium tide.
- **Corto Circuito** At road's end toward Cerro Hoya. Rock-bottom point break with powerful peak. Breaks over a rock ledge and throws a huge tube, then peels for about 100m with a great wall.

cabaña (per night US$16) that has definitely fallen on hard times – if you stay here, bring a mosquito net. A better option is to bring a tent and camp beside the beach for free, though hardcore Panamanian surfers prefer to sleep in their cars.

Getting here by bus is challenging. One bus from Cañas passes in the morning (between 8am and 9am) en route to Pedasí (US$2). The bus makes the return journey in the evening (Pedasí to Cañas) though it's much easier to take a taxi from Pedasí (US$12 to US$14).

PLAYAS CAMBUTAL & GUÁNICO

Playas Cambutal and Guánico, 16km and 22km away from Tonosí respectively, are two excellent surfing beaches along the southern coast of the Península de Azuero. Both are reachable by dirt road from Tonosí, but access is difficult as neither is served by bus.

If you have your own transportation, give some thought to camping on the beaches between late August and early September as you'll likely see some nesting sea turtles. Since there aren't any stores near the beaches, be sure to take some food with you.

Isla de Cañas

From the end of August through November, thousands of olive ridley sea turtles come ashore at night to lay eggs in the sand on the broad beach of Isla de Cañas (Cane Island). This is one of five places that these endangered turtles nest in such numbers – the others are two beaches on the Pacific side of Costa Rica, and two beaches in Orissa, India, on the Bay of Bengal.

The turtles arrive late at night, so there's no point in hiring the guide during daylight hours. Instead, agree on a meeting place and an hour when the guide can take you. When that time arrives, the guide will walk you across the island to the beach, and if you're lucky, you'll arrive at the same time as the expectant mothers. Please keep in mind that sea turtles are easily frightened, particularly by bright lights such as flashlights and cameras. Instead of hoping to resist the temptation to use these items, just leave them behind – your eyes will adjust to the moonlight and you can take plenty of mental pictures.

You can arrange tours to the island through the Pedasí branch of IPAT (p169) – expect to pay about US$30 for a small group.

There's a small restaurant on the beach as well as some nameless **cabañas** (per person US$10) if you wish to stay on the island. Bring a mosquito net and lots of insect repellent, long pants, a windbreaker or bug jacket and mosquito coils if you have them.

The turnoff for Isla de Cañas is easy to miss. It's beside a bus stop on the south side of the Carretera Nacional, 6.5km west of the turnoff for the town of Cañas; next to the bus stop, there's a brown-and-yellow sign that reads 'Bienvenidos Isla de Cañas via Puerto 2.5km.' The bus stop is served by Toyota Coaster buses that travel between Las Tablas and Tonosí hourly from 7am to 4pm.

From the turnoff, a 5km drive or hike on a dirt road takes you to the edge of a mangrove forest. There's usually a boater there who will shuttle you to and from the island for US$5 per party. If there's no boater to greet you, find the truck wheel hanging from a tree at the mangrove's edge and hit it hard five times with the rusty wrench atop it. If the sun's out and the tide's up – if there's water in the mangrove – a boater will fetch you.

Once you reach the island, you will be approached by a guide. As a rule every foreign visitor must be accompanied by an island guide, who will likely charge US$10 an hour per group when working. If they couldn't make money from the turtles in this way, these people would sell all the turtle eggs they could find on the black market. As it is, about half of the eggs that are laid on the beach are dug up and sold illegally in Panama City – the other half are placed in hatcheries to ensure survival.

MACARACAS
pop 3000

Forty kilometers southwest of Chitré, the tiny town of Macaracas is the site of an annual **folkloric festival** (from January 5 to 10), which is highlighted by several dramatic theatre performances including the popular story of *The Three Wise Men*.

Aside from the festival, the main attraction in Macaracas is the nearby **Rió La Villa**, a secluded river just outside of town that is a great place for taking a swim. It's pretty empty during the week, aside from a few kids ditching school, but it's the place to be on weekends. To get there, take a right off the main road at the San Juan gas station. Continue for 750m until you pass over a metal bridge, then turn right into the gravel lot.

The town's sole lodging is the **Pensión Lorena** (☎ 995 4181; s/d with fan US$8/12, with air-con US$12/15; P ✗), which is located above the pharmacy on the main road through Macaracas. Spartan rooms feature bare beds and cold-water showers, though it'll do in a pinch if you just need a place to lie down for the night. The attached restaurant also serves up hot meals, but don't expect anything more than Panamanian staples.

Buses run between Macaracas and Chitré (US$2, one hour, hourly), and Macaracas and Tonosí (US$2, one hour, hourly) from 7am to 4pm.

Veraguas Province

Nearly 500 years ago, the first attempt by the Spanish to obtain a footing in the continental world was in modern-day Veraguas Province. Lured to the region by the natural beauty of its robust rivers and stunning peaks (as well as the promises of vast gold reserves), Christopher Columbus tried but failed to establish a Spanish colony here. Although the Spanish were successful in founding the town of Concepción, the gold was not to last. Today, the Mosquito Coast of Veraguas remains one of the most isolated and undeveloped regions in Panama.

However, Veraguas is anything but a pristine wilderness. From a height, the Caribbean and Pacific slopes of Veraguas look as different from each other as Canada's Rocky Mountains do from Australia's Great Sandy Desert. While the Caribbean slopes are home to lush virgin forests, the Pacific slope of Veraguas is an environmentalist's nightmare. Since most people living in the province makes their living through farming or ranching, perhaps as little as 5% of the original dry tropical forest remains – the rest was hacked down with ruthless efficiency.

It's fitting that with its history of colonization and environmental devastation, Veraguas Province is now the modern-day battleground for the forces of foreign investment and development versus cultural and environmental conservation. In particular, the region's two all-star highlights, Isla de Coiba and Santa Catalina, are in the midst of redefining themselves. It's hard to predict which side will win out: while the national marine park around Isla de Coiba was recently protected as a Unesco World Heritage site, the beaches around Santa Catalina, famous for their tremendous waves, are primed to boom.

HIGHLIGHTS

- Exploring the astounding natural beauty of **Parque Nacional Coiba** (p185), above or below the water line

- Surfing some seriously sick waves at **Playa Santa Catalina** (p182), Panama's legendary surf spot

- Escaping to the highland retreat of **Santa Fé** (p179), famous for its mountain air, bright flowers and lush forests

- Visiting the **Iglesia San Francisco de Veraguas** (p178), one of the Americas' best examples of baroque religious art and architecture

★ Santa Fé

Iglesia San Francisco de Veraguas ★

Parque Nacional Coiba ★

Playa Santa ★ Catalina

POPULATION: 210,100	AREA: 10,050 SQ KM	ELEVATION: SEA LEVEL TO 3478M

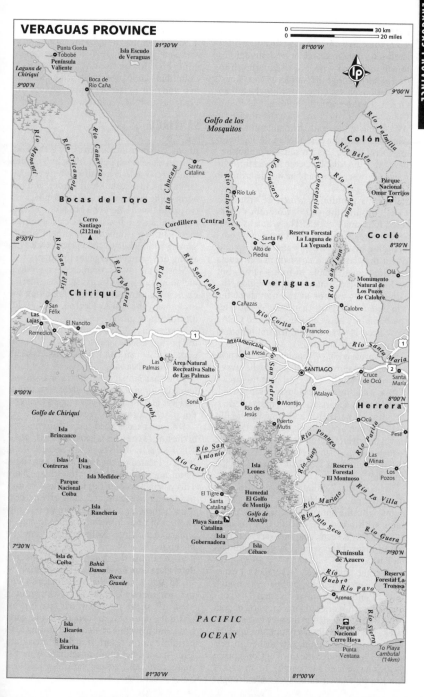

VERAGUAS PROVINCE

0 ___ 30 km
0 ___ 20 miles

Punta Gorda
Tobobé
Península
Valiente
Isla Escudo
de Veraguas
Laguna de
Chiriquí
9°00'N
Boca de
Rio Caña

Golfo de los
Mosquitos

Río Palmilla
Río Belén
Co l ó n

Río Manatí
Río Cricamola
Río Cañaveral

Santa
Catalina
Río Luís

Río Chucará
Río Calovébora
Río Guázaro
Río Concepción
Río Veraguas

B o c a s   d e l   T o r o

Parque
Nacional
Omar Torrijos

Cerro
Santiago
(2121m)

C o r d i l l e r a   C e n t r a l

Santa Fé
Alto de
Piedra

Reserva Forestal
La Laguna de
La Yeguada

C o c l é

8°30'N
8°30'N

Río San Félix
Río Tabasará
Río Cobre
Río San Pablo
V e r a g u a s

Olá

Río San Juan

Monumento
Natural de
Los Pozos
de Calobre

San
Félix
Chiriquí
El Nancito
Tolé
Cañazas
Río Corita
Calobre

Las
Lajas
Remedios

San
Francisco

Río Santa María

1
Interamericana
La Mesa
Las
Palmas
Área Natural
Recreativa Salto
de Las Palmas

Río San Pedro
SANTIAGO

Cruce
de Ocú
Santa
María
2
1

8°00'N
8°00'N

Golfo de Chiriquí
Río Bubí
Sona
Río de
Jesús
Montijo
Atalaya
H e r r e r a

Ocú
Pesé

Isla
Brincanco

Puerto
Mutis

Río Ponuga
Río Parita

Islas
Contreras
Isla
Uvas
Río San
Antonio
Río Cate

Las
Minas

Río Suay

Reserva
Forestal
El Montuoso
Los
Pozos

Parque
Nacional
Coiba
Isla Medidor

Isla
Leones

Isla
Ranchería

El Tigre
Santa Catalina
Humedal
El Golfo
de Montijo
Golfo de
Montijo

Río Marieto
Río La Villa

7°30'N

Playa Santa
Catalina
Isla
Gobernadora
Isla
Cébaco

Río Palo Seco
Río Guera

7°30'N

Isla de
Coiba
Bahía
Damas
Boca
Grande

Península
de Azuero

Río
Quebro
Río Pavo
Reserva
Forestal La
Tronosa

Arenas

P A C I F I C

O C E A N

Parque
Nacional
Cerro Hoya
Río Sierra

To Playa
Cambutal
(14km)

Isla
Jicarón
Isla
Jicarita

Punta
Ventana

81°30'W
81°00'W

History

Columbus' first three voyages westward toward Asia were in search of land, though his fourth and final voyage was undertaken to find a water passage that would, by Columbus' calculation, pass south of Asia into the Indian Ocean. To the north the admiral had found Cuba, which he believed was part of eastern Asia, while to the south, he had found South America, which he described in his log book as a 'New World.' As a result, Columbus believed that the Atlantic Ocean flowed through a strait between them, and he was determined to find it.

For this venture, in which he proposed to sail around the world, Columbus chartered four small vessels. The year was 1502, and the great explorer spent most of it commanding his little worm-eaten fleet up and down the Caribbean coast from Venezuela to Nicaragua. Unable to find a strait, but seeing gold-laden natives in the region, the admiral cast anchor at the mouth of the Río Belén – the river that today constitutes the boundary between Veraguas and Colón Provinces. He was determined not to return to Spain empty-handed.

In February 1503 Columbus gave orders to establish a colony on a hill beside the river's silt-filled mouth. The Quibian, the area's native inhabitants, obviously disapproved. Armed with spears, the tribe massacred an exploratory party that had gone up the Río Belén. When Spanish corpses came floating down the river, Columbus, fearing an attack, loaded the ships and set sail for Hispaniola (island of modern-day Dominican Republic and Haiti).

In his journal, Columbus wrote: 'I departed, in the name of the Holy Trinity, on Easter night, with the ships rotten, worn out, and eaten with holes.' He died three years later believing he'd seen Asia, unaware that he'd found instead the second-largest landmass on Earth.

Over the next 30 years, several other expeditions were attempted by Spanish, though they all ended in similar disaster. The conquistadors, not ones to forget reports of gold in Veraguas, returned to the area two decades later, and eventually overcame the Quiban. They soon found gold, established mines, and in 1560 founded the town of Concepción (which has since disappeared), 10km west of the Río Belén. African slaves were brought in to extract the gold, and to run the smelter in Concepción, though the mines were completely spent by 1590. Soon after, many miners left for newfound gold deposits in Colombia, while others escaped or were set free, and took to farming throughout Pacific Veraguas and the Península de Azuero.

SANTIAGO
pop 36,000

About 250km from Panama City is the town of Santiago, a small but bustling hub of rural commercial activity. Halfway between the capital and the Costa Rican border, and just north of the Península de Azuero, Santiago is a crossroads town where you can easily get a hot meal and a clean bed. For the casual tourist, there's little reason why you should stop in Santiago, though it's a good place to break up a long drive and recharge for the night.

Most of the town's commerce and services, including stores, banks, gas stations, internet cafes, restaurants and hotels, are along the Interamericana and Av Central, which splits off from the highway.

Approximately 25km south of Santiago is the port of Puerto Mutis, which is the most popular disembarkation point for boats heading to Coiba Island (p185).

Note that Santiago also serves as a convenient base for visiting the **Iglesia San Francisco de Veraguas** (San Francisco de Veraguas Church). For more information, see p178.

If all you need is a bed and a bathroom, one of the town's cheapies is **Hotel Gran David** (☎ 998 4510; s/d with fan US$10/15, s/d with air-con US$20/25; P ✖), located on the Interamericana about 500m north of the Av Central intersection. This palatable option has fairly clean rooms, tile floors, adequate beds and private hot-water bathrooms. Although there are certainly cheaper options in town, it's nice to stay in a place that charges by the night and not by the hour.

Also along the Interamericana is the **Hotel Plaza Gran David** (☎ 998 3433; s/d US$25/30; P ✖ ⊠), which is the nicest place to stay in town, mainly because it has a swimming pool. All of the rooms, which face out towards the pool, have air-con, tile floors, good beds and private hot-water bathrooms. It's certainly not a resort, but the Hotel Plaza Gran has a quiet location set back from the main road, and a pool can do a lot for a hotel's character.

THE LEGACY OF COLUMBUS

Despite the fact that Christopher Columbus never made landfall in what was to become the United States, he is nevertheless revered by the majority of Americans as a national hero. Every year, Americans celebrate his discovery of the New World on October 12, 1492, though it's usually observed on a Monday so everyone can spend the day shopping – it's hard to pass up Columbus Day sales.

Recently however, several cities across America have removed the national holiday from their calendars. Claiming that Columbus's life was anything but admirable, critics view the day as a celebration of conquest and genocide. In the US Virgin Islands, Columbus Day has been replaced by Puerto Rico–Virgin Islands Friendship Day, which honors the indigenous peoples of the Caribbean who suffered under the Spanish colonialism. In the state of South Dakota, Columbus Day has been replaced by Native American Day, which is aimed at increasing awareness of the past history and modern plight of this oft-overlooked indigenous group.

The growing dissent in America over the legacy of Columbus brings about a simple question: what did Columbus actually discover? Prior to his arrival in 1492, America had already been 'discovered' by other explorers and immigrants, not to mention the native peoples that were living there. However, Columbus's impact on history is simply to do with the fact that his journeys came at a time when mass media was improving across Europe. By reporting what he saw to Europeans across the social spectrum, Columbus was attributed in the public eye with the discovery of the New World.

In 1828, the great American storyteller Washington Irving published a historical narrative titled *The Life and Voyages of Christopher Columbus*, which was aimed at building a foundation of American folklore. His efforts propelled Columbus into the national spotlight, though adulation of the explorer peaked in 1892 when the country celebrated the 400th anniversary of his arrival in the Americas. All across the country, monuments to Columbus were erected, while cities, towns, and streets changed their names, including the capital cities of Columbus, Ohio and Columbia, South Carolina. The admiration of Columbus was particularly embraced by Italian-American and Catholic communities, who began to view their ancestor as one of the founding fathers of America.

The need to separate myth from reality brings about a second question: what did Christopher Columbus actually achieve? If you ask any American school child, they'll proudly explain to you that Columbus proved the world was round even though everyone in Europe thought the world was flat. By defying the conventions of the time, and sailing west to get to the Far East (Columbus died believing that he had arrived in the East Indies), Columbus is often hailed as a model of the American 'can-do' attitude. Of course, it stands to reason that Columbus didn't actually prove that the world wasn't flat, especially since Portuguese explorer Ferdinand Magellan was the first person to circumnavigate the globe. (Actually, Magellan didn't circumnavigate the globe in one trip since he was killed in 1521 at the Battle of Mactan in the Philippines. Instead, it was the 18 survivors of his expedition that finally returned to Spain after a journey of more than three years.)

Unfortunately, history often has a way of succumbing to popular myth and lore. Since Columbus Day in America is generally thought of as a celebration of the nation's history, there is little room for public discourse on the subject. Today, the majority of Americans remain ignorant about the realities of Columbus, and critics of the holiday argue that disregarding history is an injustice to the surviving indigenous communities of the New World.

Not surprisingly, this theme has been picked up by politicians across Latin America, most notably left-wing Venezuelan President Hugo Chávez, who campaigned in 2003 to wipe out Columbus Day across the Americas. Of course, it's unlikely that Chávez's message will fall on receptive ears in America, especially since both countries have recently enjoyed less than lukewarm relations. In the meantime, school children in America will continue to learn about the Niña, the Pinta and the Santa Maria, though it's unlikely they'll hear the whole story about the New World's first genocide which followed in the wake of his discoveries.

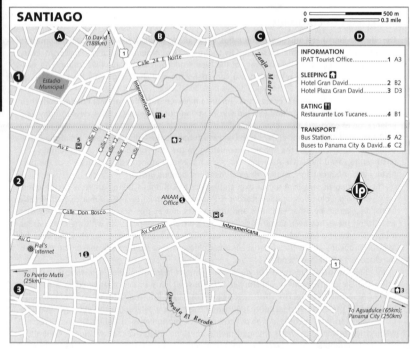

SANTIAGO

```
0        500 m
0        0.3 mile
```

To David (188km)

Calle 24 E Norte

Zanja Madre

Interamericana

Estadio Municipal

Calle 10
Calle 11
Calle 12
Calle 13
Calle 14

Av E

ANAM Office

Calle Don Bosco

Av Central
Interamericana

Av G
Hal's Internet

To Puerto Mutis (25km)

Quebrada El Recodo

To Aguadulce (65km);
Panama City (250km)

INFORMATION
IPAT Tourist Office...................**1** A3

SLEEPING 🛏
Hotel Gran David......................**2** B2
Hotel Plaza Gran David............**3** D3

EATING 🍴
Restaurante Los Tucanes...........**4** B1

TRANSPORT
Bus Station...............................**5** A2
Buses to Panama City & David..**6** C2

If you're looking for a bite to eat, the **Restaurante Los Tucanes** (mains US$4-7) is a favorite for David–Panama City buses passing on the Interamericana. In addition to daily specials such as roast chicken, chicken parmesan and shrimp *criolla* (tomato and onion sauce), you can grab hot sandwiches to go if you're looking to keep on traveling.

From the **bus terminal** (☎ 998 4006), buses depart for David (US$6, three hours) hourly from 9am to 2am, and for Panama City (US$6, four hours) hourly from 3:15am to 9:15pm.

Buses to destinations in Veraguas depart from Santiago's bus station on Calle 10, near Av E. For Santa Fé, buses depart half-hourly from 5am to 6pm (US$2, 1½ hours). You can also hail these on the turnoff from the Interamericana, north of Calle 24. Buses to Soná (from where you can get a bus to Santa Catalina) depart half-hourly from 7am to 6pm (US$1.50, one hour).

If you don't have your own wheels, taxis are the way to travel within Santiago – they are easy to hail and they go anywhere in town for US$2 or less.

IGLESIA SAN FRANCISCO DE VERAGUAS

In the small town of San Francisco, 16km north of the Interamericana on the road from Santiago to Santa Fé, is the historic **San Francisco of Veraguas Church**, which is one of the best and oldest examples of baroque art and architecture in the Americas.

The centerpiece of this church, which was built by local indigenous communities, is the highly ornate altar of ash and bitter cedar. Although most colonial altars in the Americas were brought over from Europe, this altar was carved locally around the same time that the church was constructed. The date of completion is estimated to be 1727, but no one can confirm this, as written records have not survived to the present.

Carved into the altar and elsewhere around the church are the usual images (the crucifixion, the Virgin, the saints), but also throughout the church are finely carved and well-preserved images of the artisans and prominent natives. Their faces are cleverly inserted into the religious scenes – some appear atop the bodies of cherubs. One large carving also includes items that had special meaning for the natives or otherwise impressed them – an eagle piercing its own heart with its beak, three large dice, a Spanish sword, a lantern and a human skull.

The steeple, incidentally, is not original. The original bell tower survived until 1942, when it suddenly collapsed without warning. Unfortunately, the new one doesn't resemble the old one. The original served two purposes, one good, one questionable – it was, of course, used for religious purposes, but the Spaniards also used it as a lookout tower to monitor the movements of the natives and slaves in the community.

To reach the church, head 16km north on the San Francisco turnoff from the Interamericana, until you reach the police substation – you'll see a stop sign there, and the station is conspicuously located on the main road. Veer right, proceed 400m, and then turn right again at the Supermercado Juan XXIII de San Francisco. Another 100m on, you'll see the church on the left.

A bus leaves the Santiago station for San Francisco (US$1, 25 minutes, every 30 minutes from 7am to 6pm).

If you're short on time, an alternative is to hire a taxi in Santiago to take you to the church and, if you wish, on to Santa Fé. Expect to pay US$12 roundtrip to and from San Francisco, and another US$18 if you hire the taxi to take you all the way to Santa Fé.

Near the church in San Francisco is **El Chorro del Spiritu Santo** (Holy Spirit Waterfall), which has a fine swimming hole. To get to here, follow the road as it winds around the church, and then take the road just behind the church. After a few hundred meters, take the first right; after another several hundred meters the road will bring you to the small cascades.

Note that there are no places to stay in San Francisco, though you easily stop by on your way to Santiago or other destinations in Veraguas.

SANTA FÉ
pop 3000

This tiny mountain town lies in the shadow of the Continental Divide about 52km north of Santiago. At an altitude of 1000m, Sante Fé is much cooler than the lowlands, and much of the surroundings forests remain as they did when the Spaniards founded the town in 1557.

Like Boquete (p201), Santa Fé is famous for its fresh clean air and bucolic surroundings. However, while Boquete has become a hot-spot tourist destination, Santa Fé see few foreign visitors, though the town remains incredibly popular with weekending Panamanians from the capital. With lush mountainsides, waterfalls and mountain streams right outside the town, Santa Fé is an ideal destination for hikers, bird-watchers and those simply wanting to soak up the beauty of the highlands.

LOCAL LORE: EL DORADO

The Spanish colonization of the New World may have taken place under the guise of spreading civilization and Christianity, though early explorers were seemingly driven by simple greed. In the months prior to his landing in Panama, Columbus wrote in his journal about the need to acquire more treasures in order to help finance his expedition and to appease the Spanish royalty. Thus, it's not surprising that his attempts to start a colony in Veraguas were fuelled by rumors of the vast cities of gold that lay waiting in the jungles.

Perhaps the most famous legend was of El Dorado, a legendary city of pure gold that was ruled over by *El Indio Dorado* or 'The Golden Indian.' Although the myth originated in the 1530s when conquistador Gonzalo Jiménez de Quesada came across the nation of Muisica in the Colombian Andes, the legend quickly spread throughout Central and South America.

Awed by the quantities of gold that the indigenous population in the Americas used for adornment, the Spanish swept through both continents in search of El Dorado. Eventually, the lore took on epic proportions, and some conquistadores believed they were searching for a lost kingdom or even an empire. However, after claiming most of the Americas, the Spaniards quickly realized that there were no golden cities, just rich mines. Of course, this didn't stop them from mining their empire to the ground, and shipping their riches back to Spain across the Isthmus of Panama.

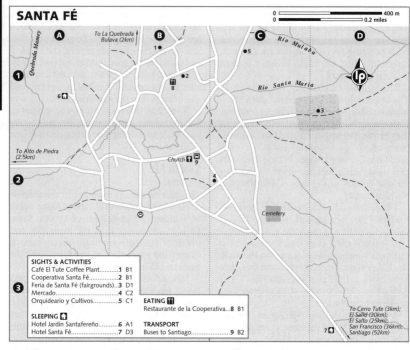

SANTA FÉ

SIGHTS & ACTIVITIES
Café El Tute Coffee Plant...........1 B1
Cooperativa Santa Fé.................2 B1
Feria de Santa Fé (fairgrounds)..3 D1
Mercado...................................4 C2
Orquideario y Cultivos.............5 C1

SLEEPING
Hotel Jardín Santafereño...........6 A1
Hotel Santa Fé.........................7 D3

EATING
Restaurante de la Cooperativa...8 B1

TRANSPORT
Buses to Santiago.....................9 B2

To Cerro Tute (3km);
El Salto (20km);
El Salto (25km);
San Francisco (36km);
Santiago (52km)

Orientation & Information

Town planning is not evident in Santa Fé. The road that heads north to town from Santiago and the Interamericana, winding through lovely valleys along the way, branches out in three directions at the southern edge of town. The middle 'branch' forks yet again after a few more blocks.

None of the streets in town have names, and that's just fine with Santa Fé residents – everybody here seems to know where everybody else lives. And the structures in town that aren't homes (the mayor's office, the cooperative, the church and so on) can be counted on both hands.

Sights & Activities
ORQUIDEARIO Y CULTIVOS

Santa Fé is known throughout Panama for its orchids. Here, the person to see about these flowers is **Bertha de Castrellón** (☎ 954 0910), who has an impressive collection of them (no fewer than 265 species) in her own backyard, and enjoys showing them to enthusiasts. Most of the orchids are handsomely displayed in hanging coconut shells.

Among her orchids are some of the largest and some of the smallest varieties in the world, as well as a lovely lavender orchid found only in the hills around Santa Fé.

Bertha, who speaks a little English, can tell you a great many things about her plants if you can communicate with her in Spanish. Bertha and her brother are also the area's top birding guides, and can organize tours throughout the surrounding area.

To get to Bertha's house, take the right 'branch' at the point where the Santiago–Santa Fé road forks at the southern edge of town. Then take the second right and proceed 100m or so further, until you see a driveway flanked by a sign that reads: 'Orquideario y Cultivos Las Fragacias de Santa Fé.' Her house is located at the intersection of the right fork road and the road leading to the fairgrounds.

Although Bertha does not charge a fee for showing her orchids, feel free to leave a donation. Please remember you are visiting a home, so be considerate: don't show up before 9am or after 5pm, and if you call out to her from her gate and there's no answer, assume she's not home – don't open the gate unless she instructs you to do so.

RIVERS & WATERFALLS

Not far from Santa Fé are a number of lovely waterfalls (including one that's pictured on IPAT's Veraguas glossy publication) and empty mountain streams, and the most accessible swimming spots are all within walking distance from town. Head along the same road as Bertha's, and you'll soon reach several spots that make for a nice dip. Continuing on, you'll reach a bridge – cross it, take the second turnoff on the right and you'll find a place to rent inner tubes (US$1), allowing you to float idly down the river.

Behind the Café El Tute coffee factory, there's a lovely swimming hole, **La Quebrada Bulava**, about 30 minutes' walk away. Ask one of the local kids to show you the way.

El Salto is among the most impressive falls in this area. It lies about 30 minutes south of Santa Fé along a bad road fit only for a 4WD (and only accessible during the dry season). There are also three waterfalls in Alto de Piedra, though you shouldn't enter this area without first hiring a local guide.

ALTO DE PIEDRA & CERRO TUTE

There are two heavily forested mountainous areas near town that offer some fine birding. Many specialties of eastern Chiriquí and Veraguas Provinces can be found here, including the rufous-winged woodpecker and the crimson-collared tanager. Both areas require a 4WD vehicle, a horse or strong legs.

Alto de Piedra, reachable by a road that leaves the western side of town, is an excellent place to explore if you have the time and the will. This vast, mountainous area contains thousands of hectares of pristine wilderness, and extends from the northern edge of Santa Fé to the Caribbean Sea. The entire northern portion of the province – the area where Columbus, Nicuesa and the other Spanish explorers had so much trouble – contains not a single road, and is sparsely inhabited. The edge of the awesome forest is only a couple of kilometers from town, and the forest becomes thick jungle once you clear the ridge and proceed down the Caribbean slope.

Cerro Tute, a few kilometers south of town, on the western side of the Santiago–Santa Fé road, is less rugged and more accessible than Alto de Piedra. In addition to the area's famed birdlife, Cerro Tute is also home to a towering set of waterfalls and a cliff with wind currents that seemingly prevent anyone from falling off. The extensive trail network here that winds through both primary and secondary rainforest.

You'd be wise to access either destination with someone who knows the area well, such as Bertha de Castrellón and her brother or Edgar Toribio from Hotel Santa Fé (p182).

CAFÉ EL TUTE COFFEE PLANT

This famous Sante Fé **coffee plant** (admission free; ☉ 6am-8pm) is the flagship institution in a four decade-old cooperative named Esperanza de Los Campesinos (Hope of the Farmers). Started by Father Héctor Gallego, who was working in Veraguas in the late 1960s, the original aims of the cooperative were to wrest power from local coffee barons and to put the profit from the crop back in the hands of the farmers.

According to the co-op's history, the initial idea came when the priest decided to purchase 50kg sack of salt from the lowlands rather than from the company store in town. By showing the local farmers that he could circumvent the rich and powerful ruling families, he rallied the necessary support to start the co-op. Although the priest was eventually murdered by government forces wary of his teachings, Esperanza de Los Campesinos continues to thrive today.

Café El Tute is only sold for domestic consumption, though every stop of the growing, harvesting and roasting process is 100% organic. Stop by for a free Spanish tour, and start your day off right with a hot, steamy cup of mountain-grown coffee.

COOPERATIVA SANTA FÉ

The **Santa Fé Cooperative** (☉ 6am-8:30pm) and the cooperative's store above the Restaurante de la Cooperativa sell hats made of mountain palm (called *palmilla*) that are much more durable than hats found elsewhere in Panama – and they cost much less (from US$5 to US$15). They are not as refined as the hats available in Ocú and Penonomé, but if you're looking for a rugged hat in classic panama style, you can't do better.

While in the cooperative, you might want to pick up some Café El Tute, the locally grown coffee.

MERCADO

Much larger than the Cooperativa is the open-air **market** just past the entrance to town. In addition to fruits and vegetables, you'll find woven handmade bags, a wide range of hats, leather goods and many other interesting items – it's a fun place to browse.

Festivals & Events

Agricultural Fair This lively event is hosted by the producers of northern Veraguas from 28 January to 2 February – if you're in the area don't miss it. The fair features traditional dancing, horse races, a multitude of food stands and an occasional boxing match or rodeo competition. It's held in the Féria de Santa Fé in the east of town.

Orchid Exposition Collectors from all over Panama display their finest orchids in the Féria de Santa Fé at this popular event each August; the **IPAT office** (☎ 998 3929) in Santiago can provide you with the precise date, as can Bertha, the orchid lady.

Sleeping & Eating

Hotel Jardín Santafereño (☎ 954 0866; cabins US$12; P) On the western edge of town, a good walk from the center, is this bare-bones, budget hotel, which offers the cheapest bed in town. The cabins are, not surprisingly, little more than concrete cells to shield you from the elements, and the mattresses should have been replaced decades ago. But, the cold shower works, and the hotel is attractively perched on the highest point in town overlooking the surrounding forest.

Hotel Santa Fé (☎ 954 0941; d without/with air-con US$15/25; P ✹) This friendly spot just south of the town center is a good place to inquire about hiring a guide. The owner, Eudosia, has a great deal of knowledge to impart about Santa Fé, and he can put you in touch with Fidel and Edgar, two recommended local guides. The rooms at the hotel run the gamut from 'a little wear and tear' to 'has seen better days,' though with private cold-water showers and decent beds, you could definitely do worse.

In addition to the restaurants situated in the two hotels, there are a handful of places to dine at near the center of town. The best of the lot is the **Restaurante de la Cooperativa** (mains US$3), which serves up fish, pork, beef and chicken with locally grown vegetables and heaping portions of rice. Self-caterers can stock up on fresh provisions at the local mercado.

Getting There & Away

Buses from Santa Fé to Santiago (US$2, 1½ hours) depart every 30 minutes from 5am to 6pm.

CERAMICA LA PEÑA

This **artisans' market** (⏰ 9am-4:30pm Mon-Fri) is on the Interamericana, 8km west of Santiago. Here you can find wood carvings and baskets made by the Emberá and Wounaan peoples of the Darién, woven purses and soapstone figurines made by Ngöbe-Buglé people living in the area and masks from the town of Parita in Herrera Province. There's also a workshop on the premises where you can occasionally see ceramics being made, as well as a good selection of pots and sculptures available for purchase.

LAS PALMAS

There's nothing of special interest in sleepy Las Palmas, a town 10km south of the Interamericana and 32km northwest of the town of Soná. But if you love waterfalls and have your own wheels, you'll want to know about the nearby cataract and its enticing swimming hole. The scene is set amid light forest, and you'll likely have the place to yourself.

To get to the **falls** from the Interamericana, take the Las Palmas turnoff and drive 10km. Bypass the first road into town, but turn left at the second road just before the town's cemetery. Follow this dirt road for 200m and then take the fork to the right. This last 1km to the falls, along a much rougher road, requires a 4WD vehicle. If you aren't driving one, it's best to play it safe and walk the last 1km to the falls. Be sure to lock up and take your valuables with you.

SANTA CATALINA

Although lagging behind Costa Rica in terms of tourist development (there is yet to be a beachside Pizza Hut), Santa Catalina has the potential to be the next great Central American beach destination (for better or for worse). Although difficult access and a remote location have so far kept the foreign investors away, the secret about Santa Catalina's incredible surf is out. Regarded as one of the best surf hot spots in Central America, you can choose from any number of beach breaks on Playa Santa Catalina. On a good day, the rights and lefts here are easily comparable to Oahu's Sunset Beach.

SURFING IN VERAGUAS PROVINCE

Although it's not as popular among the international surfing community as Bocas del Toro, Veraguas is home to the country's best surf. Serious surfers should head straight to Playa Santa Catalina, which has some of the biggest breaks in the whole of Central America, though there are plenty of other less-crowded spots to get your surf on.

- **Playa Santa Catalina** As good as it gets. Sharp rock bottom right and left break. Main wave is the right. Incredible tubes, long rides with lots of power. Surfed mostly medium to high tide. For more information, see opposite.
- **Estero Beach Break** A 15-minute walk from Santa Catalina. A long beach break, has lefts and rights over sand bottom. Popular with beginners at low tide.
- **Punta Brava** Just west of Estero. Point breaks at low tide over sharp rock bottom. Has lefts and rights, but the lefts are the best. Very powerful. Has a great tube section. Booties needed.
- **Punta Roca** A 30-minute walk from Santa Catalina. Left point break surfed at low tide over a rock-bottom ledge, with short rides but big hollow tubes.
- **Isla Cébaco** Island near Santa Catalina. Four breaks, with rights and lefts. Area known for sharks.
- **Playa Mariato** Faces Isla Cébaco. Soft rock-bottom break with lefts, rights.

Santa Catalina is home to several hundred people who lead simple lives as fishers, and the town has a laid-back feel to it with one good outdoor pizzeria that forms the nexus of the dining and nightlife scene. However, the real-estate signs are starting to go up, and rumors run the gamut from constructing a mega-resort and an airstrip to establishing a protected area and a marine park. It's hard to know what the future of Santa Catalina holds, but in the meantime, enjoy it while it still is what it is – remote, undeveloped and home to some seriously wicked surf.

Orientation & Information

To get to the ocean-side surf hotels from the bus station, take the dirt road on the left side of the road into Santa Catalina just before the road ends. Each hotel has its own sign marking the turnoff. There is only one public phone, and there are no banks or internet cafes in Santa Catalina. Make sure you arrive with cash – no one takes credit cards.

Activities

Many of the local fishermen make excellent guides, and can easily take you out to some superb snorkeling and spearfishing spots as well as some remote surf breaks. Their lifelong knowledge and love of the area is apparent, and although you will need some basic Spanish to contract them, this

is the best way to support the community. Look for guides on the beach or simply ask around. You can also find locals who will lead horseback riding tours through the nearby forests.

SURFING

For more information on surfing in the Santa Catalina area, see the boxed text, above.

The best waves are generally from December to April, though there is surf here year round. Unlike the Caribbean, the Pacific offers fairly consistent sets, though a good swell will really give a boost to the surfing here.

Most of the accommodations in town rent boards in addition to offering surf lessons. Be advised that many of the breaks in the area are over rocks, and can easily snap your board if you don't know what you're doing.

SCUBA DIVING

Run by an experienced Austrian dive master, **Scuba Coiba** (☎ 263 4366; www.scubacoiba.com) offers divers a chance to experience some of the spectacular marine life around Isla Coiba. Two-tank dives start US$70 per person, though diving in the park costs more since the distance is much greater. Scuba Coiba also offers day trips (US$130) as well as two-day trips (US$320) to Isla de Coiba, which include entry into the national park, lodging at the ANAM station on Coiba and meals;

there's a two-person minimum for these trips. You can also get PADI-certified here for US$225, and snorkeling gear is available for hire (US$6 per day). The dive shop is located on the main road into town, between the restaurant La Fonda and Cabañas Rolo.

FISHING
The area around Santa Catalina is famous for its big fish, including yellow fin tuna, wahoo, dolphin, Spanish mackerel, jacks and rooster fish. Although there isn't a major sportfishing operator in town, there is no shortage of local fishermen willing to rent their boat and services to you for the day. Prices vary depending on the amount of the people in your party and the distance you want to go – remember that petrol is very expensive these days.

If you'd prefer to go after reef fish including snapper and grouper, there are some hidden spots along the coast that are perfect for spearfishing. There are also plenty of rocky ledges in the area that serve as hideouts for lobster, though make sure that you only harvest adults – lobster are in danger of being overfished throughout Panama. Scuba Coiba (see p183) can set you up with the gear you need, and the local fishermen can help you get your feet wet.

Sleeping
IN TOWN
Sol y Mar (☎ 596 1521; www.solymarpanama.com; basic cabins per person US$8.50, deluxe cabins s/d/tr US$40/50/60; P ✖) As you're coming into town, you'll pass a bright blue building on the rightside about 150m before Rolo's – this is the entrance to this cheery Portuguese-Panamanian–owned spot. If you're a surfer on a budget, and in need of a place to lie down and a shower to clean yourself up, the basic cabins here will serve you fine. However, if you're in search of your creature comforts, the recently constructed deluxe cabins feature private terraces, hot-water showers, ocean views, satellite TV and air-con.

Cabañas Rolo (☎ 998 8600; r per person US$10; P) One of Santa Catalina's only locally owned hotels, these eight cabins are a favorite of baby-faced surfers from around the world. Each simple cabin has one to three good beds, a fan, and a shared cold-water bathroom, though it's the great international vibe that makes this place a winner. The owner, Rolo Ortega, speaks Spanish and English, cooks

meals by request (typically US$3), rents surfboards (US$10 per day), and can arrange fishing trips and gear rental.

La Vida Buena (michelle@labuenavida.biz; cabins from US$40; P ✖) This reader-recommended spot is located on the main street in Santa Catalina, and is the newest accommodation in the area. Although the friendly owners, Mike and Michelle, are still putting the finishing touches on the cabins and working on the restaurant, this promises to be a welcome addition to the Santa Catalina scene. Bright and cheerful cabins can comfortably hold two to three people, and the hot-water showers, satellite TV and firm mattresses really pull the place together.

BEACH
You can reach the following places by taking the turnoff on the left after arriving in town – it's the only other road in town.

Casablanca Surf Resort (☎ 226 3786; campsites US$3, d from US$20; P ✖) Although its resort moniker is a bit of a stretch, this surfer's retreat has a number of housing options in a park-like setting bordering the beach. Whether you rent a tent for a night, bed down in simple thatched-roof bungalow or splurge on the tiled-floor duplex with private cold showers, there's a place here for you to crash regardless of your budget. The English-speaking owner spent several years surfing in the States, so he speaks English well, and can give you the low-down on the local surf.

Surfers' Paradise Camp (☎ 595 1010; surfcatalina@hotmail.com; r per person US$10; P) On a breezy bluff overlooking the ocean, you'll find eight rustic and ready wooden rooms on offer here. Owned by a father-son combination of expert surfers, this is cheapest accommodation on the beach, and you can literally roll out of bed in the morning and head down to the water. There are certainly more comfortable spots in Santa Catalina, but if you're a shoestring surfer who is not too fussy about the surroundings, Paradise can't be beat.

Kenny's Surf Camp (☎ 672 0089; www.panamasurftours.com; r from US$10; P ✖) This all-surfers spot is a regular stop on the Panama Surf Tour (see p312) junket, though feel free to stop by even if you're not on an organized tour. This all-wooden surf shack has a college-dorm feel to it, especially since it's chock full of young surfers from around the world. Guests can take advantage of the onsite kitchen and the outdoor deck, which has immaculate views of the huge break right below the surf camp.

Punta Brava Lodge (☎ 614 3868; www.puntabrava .com; s/d from US$15/30; P) This recently renovated beachside lodge is now sporting a fresh coat of paint and some well decorated rooms with air-con and private hot water bathrooms, though the same old dramatic sea views are still there. Although it's perfectly OK to show up and grab yourself a room, this lodge specializes in affordable package tours to Santa Catalina and nearby Isla de Coiba. Tours including transfers from Tocumen Airport, seven night's accommodation, three meals a day, local surf guides and a boat trip to Coiba costs for US$999/799/699 for one/two/three people.

Oasis Surf Camp (per person with breakfast US$20, half/full-board US$25/30; P) Located on Playa Estero near the mouth of the river, this rustic surf camp is owned by a no-nonsense retired Italian policeman. He opened up this remote camp because he takes his surfing seriously, though not as serious as he takes his cooking – authentic Italian meals can be yours for the price of a few bucks. The rooms themselves are located in cabins overlooking the black-sand beach, and have simple but adequate facilities including cold-water showers and ample hammocks.

Eating

There are several places in town and on the beach where you can buy excellent fresh fish to prepare yourself. There are also a number of small shops that sell basic groceries, which is ideal if you're a surfer on a budget. However, although the restaurant scene in Santa Catalina is limited, there are two locally famous places where you can get a hot meal without straining the budget.

Restaurant La Fonda (dishes US$1-3) Just before Rolo's, this long-standing local restaurant offers fresh and healthy Panamanian cuisine at ridiculously low prices. Tuna sandwiches, fresh *batidos,* and fruit with granola are aimed more at the surfers, though there's no shortage of local staples including rice and beans with chicken and plantains.

Pizzeria Jamming (pizzas US$3) Something of a Santa Catalina institution, this pizzeria offers delicious thin-crust pizzas made from fresh ingredients, any of which go nicely with the cold beer on hand. Located on the road to the beach-facing hotels, this stylish, open-air ran-

cho is Santa Catalina's liveliest gathering spot – it gets crowded, so arrive early in the night.

Getting There & Away

To reach Santa Catalina from Panama City, first take a bus to Soná where you can take one of the three daily buses to Santa Catalina, leaving at 5am, noon and 4pm (US$3, 1½ hours). Unless the driver is pushed for time, he will take you to any one of the hotels listed for an additional US$1. If you miss the bus, you can hire a taxi from Soná to Santa Catalina for around US$25.

From Santa Catalina, three buses serve Soná daily, leaving at 7am, 8am and 2pm. In Santa Catalina, the bus stops near the Restaurant La Fonda – a conch-shell's throw from Cabañas Rolo. If you're staying at one of the other hotels, it's a 1km walk to them on mostly flat terrain. Note that there are never taxis in town, unless of course someone is arriving from Soná.

PARQUE NACIONAL COIBA

With the exception of the Galapagos and Isla de Coco, few destinations off the Pacific coast of the Americas are as exotic (and difficult to access) as this national park, which is centered on the 493 sq km Isla de Coiba. Although the island is just 20km offshore in the Golfo de Chiriquí, Coiba is a veritable lost world of pristine ecosystems and unique fauna. Left alone for the past century due to the creation of a notorious penal colony on its shores, Coiba offers intrepid travelers the chance to hike through primary rainforest, snorkel and dive in a marine park and come face to face to increasingly rare wildlife. However, with virtually no tourist infrastructure in place, you're going to have work hard (and empty the pockets) to get here.

Of course, things are going to change eventually on Coiba (see the boxed text, p188), though it's difficult to know what the future holds. Unfortunately, it's increasingly likely that some form of tourist infrastructure will soon manifest itself on the island, though conservationists are hoping that it will be a low-impact lodge and not a mega-resort. In the meantime however, don't miss the chance to explore this little-known ecological jewel.

Orientation & Information

On the northern end of the island is an **ANAM ranger station** (☎ 999 8103; park fee US$10), which

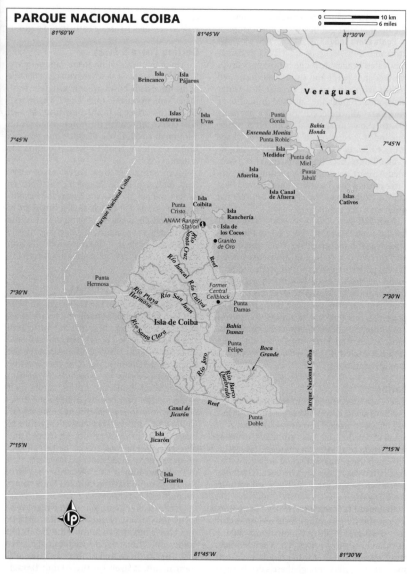

PARQUE NACIONAL COIBA

consists of several basic cabins, a camping pitch, showers and toilets, and is located beside an attractive beach alongside a scenic cover. A few model prisoners work at the ANAM station – preparing meals, washing clothes, and even leading tourists on snorkeling jaunts in the cove – they are allowed to roam freely in the vicinity of the station

and to chat with guests. Although they are a friendly bunch, and no doubt curious about the outside world, please keep in mind that they are prisoners nevertheless.

Since Coiba is still operating as a penal colony, visitors to the island (even day-trippers) must register upon arrival at the ANAM ranger station. This is especially true if you arrive on the island as an independent traveler – it's best to call ahead to confirm that there is space, though the phone lines are not always working (and when they are, there's no guarantee anyone will be around). Also, keep in mind that the majority of the island is a restricted area, though there is a large distance between the ANAM station and the main prison complex. As the future of the Coiba becomes clearer, it's likely that the prison may close down all together. At the time of writing however, it was not known exactly how many prisoners remained on the island, though there are rumored to be less than 100 left.

Coiba is home to the second-largest eastern Pacific coral reef and some of the finest diving and snorkeling to be found along the Pacific coast from Colombia to Mexico. The entire island is covered with a heavy virgin forest, except for the prison camps and along the lower courses of the larger streams where there are swampy woodlands. Rocky headlands project along the coast, and there are sandy beaches broken by mangroves at river mouths.

In addition to Coiba (50,314 hectares), islands within the park include Isla Jicarón (2002 hectares), Isla Brincanco (330 hectares), Isla Uvas (257 hectares), Isla Coibita (242 hectares), Isla Canal de Afuera (240 hectares), Isla Jicarita (125 hectares), Isla Pájaros (45 hectares) and Isla Afuerita (27 hectares).

Watching Wildlife

Although the list is far from complete, to date 147 species of bird have been identified on the island. If you're a serious birder, the prize sighting is the Coiba spinetail, a little brown-and-white bird found only on Coiba. However, the majority of visitors are searching for scarlet macaws, which are limited in Panama to Parque Nacional Coiba. Although they nest in the Barco Quebrado region of the park, they are frequently sighted while flying over clearings in the canopy, and their distinctive calls are easy to recognize, even amongst nonbirders.

It's believed that the national park is home to about 40 different species of mammals, though unfortunately little is known about their range and numbers. Due to the continued presence of the penal colony, few scientists have been granted access to Coiba, and a proper survey of the island's wildlife has yet to be done. Even more pressing is the fact the fact that Coiba has two rare mammals endemic to

the island, namely the Coiba agouti and the Couti howler. Although these two animals are difficult to spot, most visitors to the island are content by simply watching the howlers and white-faced capuchins playing on the beach.

Seventeen species of crocodiles, turtles and lizards, as well as 15 species of snakes (including the very dangerous fer-de-lance, coral snakes and boa constrictors) are found in the park. The crocodiles on the island are enormous, so it's best not to take a dip in any rivers or ponds without first consulting your guide – you're a long way from a hospital if something happens out here. With that said, although snakes tend to be extremely shy, and are easily scared away by ground vibrations, you should always walk slowly and carefully through the jungles. You can also minimize your chances of being bitten by wearing thick leather jungle boots.

The marine life in the park is simply astounding. Over 23 species of dolphins and whales have been identified, and humpback whales and spotted and bottle-nosed dolphins are frequently seen in the park. Killer whales, sperm whales and Cuvier's beaked whales are also present in park waters, but in much fewer numbers.

One of the reasons why Coiba has been such an effective penal colony is that the waters surrounding the island have a notorious reputation for big sharks. Although this is enough to keep prisoners at bay, it's heaven for avid scuba divers looking for a shark encounter. The most commonly sighted species are black- and white-tip reef sharks, though hammerheads school in frighteningly large numbers here as well. Lucky divers will have the chance to see the occasional whale shark. Unlucky divers will have the chance to see the occasional tiger shark, though the danger is highly overestimated. As long as you are confident in the water, sharks tend to view divers as an oddity rather than a potential meal.

The waters around Coiba are also home to large numbers of manta rays, as well as the occasional sea turtle (leatherback, olive ridley and the increasingly rare green). There are also some seriously large fish, and you're almost guaranteed to spot schools of snapper and jacks as well as large grouper and barracuda.

Activities
HIKING
Starting at the ANAM ranger station, the **Sendero del Observatorio** (Observatory Trail)

GREAT ESCAPES: ISLA DE COIBA

Virtually absent of human development let alone tourist infrastructure, Isla de Coiba is an untouched ecological gem. With an approximate area of 500 sq km, Coiba is the largest of a group of islands lying approximately 20km off the Pacific coast of Veraguas. Although historically the island hosted pre-Columbian cultures as well as a colonial-era pearl industry, Coiba was sectioned off as a penal colony in 1912.

Isla de Coiba has a dark and shrouded history as a spirit-crushing prison, and it's impossible to say exactly what has transpired here over the past century. With impenetrable jungles in its interior and vast expanses of shark-infested waters in every direction, Coiba has first and foremost a reputation as a place best avoided. However, it is exactly because of this belief that the island was spared the widespread destruction of the rainforest that swept through Panama this past century.

With the exception of the agricultural and pastoral land surrounding the prison, virtually the entire island is home to primary rainforest that is teeming with wildlife. Isla de Coiba is most well-known for its resident 150 bird species and the island is probably the last place in Panama where you can see the colorful scarlet macaws. Isla de Coiba is also home to about 40 different species of mammal as well as a whole slew of reptiles including the infamous fer-de-lance. There are even unique creatures endemic to the island ranging from Coiba spinetail birds to Coiba agoutis.

Coiba's underwater world is equally spectacular, especially since the island is surrounded by one of the largest coral reefs on the Pacific coast of the Americas. It gets even better – the warm Indo-Pacific current through the Gulf of Chiriquí create a unique underwater ecosystem atypical of this region, and Coiba is part of the same underwater mountain chain that includes Isla de Coco in Costa Rica and the Galapagos in Ecuador. Together, these elements attract large populations of pelagics including sharks, whales, dolphins and manta rays as well as enormous schools of fish.

In 1991, the Panamanian government established Parque Nacional Coiba, which protected both Isla de Coiba and its surrounding waters as a national park. The legislation also allowed for the penal colony to keep operating, especially since its presence was seen as a continued deterrent against mainland squatters moving to the island. In 2004, the Panamanian government passed a second law that doubled the size of the park to include several outlying islands and their surrounding waters. In July of 2005, Unesco followed suit and declared Parque Nacional Coiba a World Heritage site.

However, despite all of the national and international legislation protecting both the terrestrial and marine ecosystems of Coiba, the future of the national park remains uncertain. With the Panamanian tourist industry experiencing its highest ever rate of annual growth, developers view Parque Nacional Coiba as a prime piece of real estate. Specifically, they are arguing that constructing tourist facilities on the island will strengthen the Panamanian economy and generate the revenue needed to maintain the park. And, it seems as if the government is listening with a keen ear, especially since it has already started to scale back the size of the penal colony and has tried on several occasions to lighten the existing park legislation in order to allow for foreign investment.

Over the past few years, the country's largest private conservation organization, ANCON, has been lobbying to prevent the government from awarding hotel concessions in the park. The argument is simply that Coiba is a rare and unique ecosystem that should not be endangered by allowing massive construction projects on the island. ANCON also points to the success of the Galapagos as an example of how tourist revenue could be generated without resorting to traditional models of tourist infrastructure.

Unfortunately, there are powerful investors behind the scenes, and although ANCON has thus far postponed any construction on Coiba, it's difficult to say whether or not it will win out in the end. However, the granting of Unesco World Heritage status means that Panama's actions are being watched, so there is reason to be optimistic that if development does occur on the island, its impact will be minimal.

is a short, 500m long trail that terminates at a secluded bird-watching platform. The entrance to this trail is behind the cabins, through there is also a second part that starts behind the kitchen. After a few hundred meters, you will reach the top of a hill, which has views out to neighboring Isla Coibita.

The entrance to the **Sendero de Los Monos** (Monkey Trail) is near the Granito de Oro islet, and is accessible only by boat. The trail is only a few kilometers long, though it access several beaches and is home to several species of monkey. You're most likely to spot howlers and capuchins, especially in the dry season when the foliage isn't as dense.

SWIMMING & SNORKELING

The cove near the ANAM ranger station is home to a tiny island that you can snorkel around during high tide. If you choose to do this, be warned that the current on the island's far side is sometimes very strong. If you're a poor swimmer, do not venture outside the cove.

Two other popular spots for swimming and snorkeling are the islet of Granito de Oro and the mangrove forest close to Punta Hermosa in the west. Both the mangroves and Granito de Oro can be reached only by boat.

SCUBA DIVING

Currently, there are no dive centers on Coiba, though this will most certainly change if tourist infrastructure is ever allowed on the island. In the meantime, the majority of visitors to Coiba arrange their diving through their tour operators. For more information on tours, see right.

If you're an independent traveler, the easiest option is to arrange your diving through **Scuba Coiba** (p183) in Santa Catalina. Other options include the **Twin Oceans Dive Center** (p250) in Portobelo and **Centro de Buceo Isla Grande** (p254) in the Caribbean as well as the nationwide operator, **Scubapanama** (p312).

SPORTFISHING

The seas around Coiba are home to some seriously large fish, and lucky anglers can hook everything from marlin and sailfish to roosters and tarpon. If you're looking to test your luck, consider a trip with **Coiba Adventure** (www.coibadventure.com; Panama City ☎ 999 8108; USA ☎ 800-800-0907), a recommended sportfishing operation run by Tom Yust, who is widely regarded as Panama's top sportfishing captain.

Tom runs an extremely personalized operation, and he offers a variety of boats and rigs to accommodate your wildest fishing fantasies. Tours can also be custom tailored to meet your needs, and Coiba Adventure's offerings also take the hassle out of planning your transport to the island. Rates vary depending on the time of year, boat used and the size of the party, and include transportation from Panama City, meals, accommodations and fishing charters

Tours

Even if you're normally a fiercely independent traveler, Coiba is one destination where it's probably worth joining up with an organized tour. Although you may be able to save a bit of money organizing your own transport to Coiba, you'll have an easier time getting ANAM to grant you access to the island's interior if you go with an operator. Being part of a chartered expedition also means that you can explore more of the marine park, which is more convenient and ultimately may be cheaper than arranging activities on your own.

The most reputable operator is **Ancon Expeditions** (☎ 269 9415; www.anconexpeditions.com; El Dorado Bldg, Calle 49A Este, Panama City), the for-profit arm of the conservation organization ANCON, which has played a major role in the conservation of Coiba. Prices vary depending on group size, length of stay, activities and other factors. Tours emphasize the ecology and environment of Coiba, and can be catered to your interests. For more information on Ancon Expeditions, see p89.

If you're looking for a little more luxury, the **MV Coral Star** (☎ 800-215-5169 in USA; www.coral star.com) is a 115ft live-aboard ship that offers classy quarters and top-notch service. The MV Coral Star cruises the islands in and around Parque Nacional Coiba, carrying its passengers to some great diving spots. In addition, guests can sea kayak, fish, snorkel or explore the beaches and rainforests on uninhabited islands. Accommodations consist of two master staterooms on the main deck, two deluxe and four standard cabins on the lower deck. Weekly all-inclusive rates start at US$2250 per person.

Sleeping & Eating

The only accommodation on the island is the **ANAM ranger station** (per night US$10), which offers six split-cabins that share common cold showers and toilets. Owing to the isolation of Coiba, you shouldn't expect too much from the cabins. They're furnished with a spartan aesthetic and functional in form, though surprisingly they come equipped with air-conditioning (there's a catch – keep reading). However, the entire station has a certain deserted island charm to it, especially since, well, you're on a deserted island. If you have a tent or a jungle hammock, there is also a space for you to pitch or string up for the night.

There is electricity at the station, though it's produced by a diesel generator that's only turned on from dusk to dawn. Depending on the available gas supply, you might not be allowed to use the air-conditioning, though no one will stop you from turning it on if you bring your own fuel in from the mainland. Of course, if you've made it as far as Coiba, you probably have experience sleeping at night without air-con in tropical climes – plus, it's better for the environment to leave it off.

If you're traveling independently, be advised that there is no food available on the island. So, unless you're planning on fasting for a few days, you will need to purchase supplies in advance on the mainland. At the ANAM ranger station, you can hire one of the prisoners to cook your meals for you in the main kitchen. If you're traveling as part of a tour, you will not have to worry about meals as everything will be arranged for you.

If you're spending the night at the ranger station, bring insect repellent as there will be lots and lots of mosquitoes and the ever-so-pleasant sand fleas.

Getting There & Away

The most common departure point for boats heading to Isla de Coiba is Puerto Mutis, a small port about 25km southwest of Santiago. Typically, this trip takes about two to three hours, though it varies depending on the size and speed of both the boat and the waves. Boats also depart for Coiba from the port of Pedigral near David and Santa Catalina, though these two destinations are less convenient. There is also an airstrip on Coiba Island, though this is reserved for private charter flights.

If you're arriving on Coiba as part of an organized tour, your operator will take care of all the necessary transportation arrangements. However, if you're planning on trying to reach the island independently, the best place to hire a boat and a guide is Puerto Mutis. Prices are negotiable and ultimately dependant on the price of fuel, the size of your party and your intended length of stay on the island (eg whether or not your driver has to return to the mainland).

Although hiring boats is perfectly feasible, please keep in mind that the open sea can get extremely rough, and many fishermen have been lost at sea over the years. Before making the journey, you need to have absolute confidence in the seaworthiness of both your vessel and its captain.

PARQUE NACIONAL CERRO HOYA

On the southwestern side of the Península de Azuero, this 32,577-hectare park protects the headwaters of the Ríos Tonosí, Portobelo and Pavo, as well as 30 endemic plant species, and rare fauna including the elusive carato parakeet. The national park also contains some of the last remaining rainforest on a huge peninsula that is one of the most agriculturally devastated regions of Panama. Although the park was created in 1984, much of the forest had been chopped down prior to that time, and unfortunately it will be a long time before the park really looks like a park.

There are no accommodations for visitors in or near the park, and the trails into it are ill defined. In short, until the park is more accessible and facilities are developed for tourists, visits to the park are reserved for intrepid types truly looking to get away from it all.

The best way to get to the park is by boat from Playa Cambutal in Los Santos Province. There, it's always possible to find a boatman to make the two-hour trip; the cost is generally US$60 to US$80 per party (one way). If you happen to come upon a boat going from Playa Cambutal to the park or to Punta Ventana nearby, the ride could cost as little as US$5 per person.

It's also possible to reach the park by a road that winds along the western edge of the Península de Azuero. However, even with a 4WD vehicle (dry season only), visitors are only able to get as far as Restigue, a hamlet south of Arenas, at the edge of the park.

Chiriquí Province

Chiricanos claim to have it all and there's an element of truth to what they claim: Panama's tallest mountains, longest rivers and most fertile valleys are in Chiriquí. The province is also home to spectacular highland rainforests and the country's most productive agricultural and cattle-ranching regions.

Bordering Costa Rica to the west, Chiriquí is often the first province in Panama encountered by overland travelers and serves as a subtle introduction to the not-so-subtle beauty Panama has to offer. Although the mist-covered mountains near Boquete are slowly being colonized by waves of North American and European retirees, the town is a good base for exploring the flanks of Panama's highest point, Volcán Barú (3478m). The town is also the center of Panama's coffee industry, which means that a potent cup of shade-grown Arabica is never more than a café away.

Chiriquí is home to the Parque Internacional La Amistad, which offers excellent hiking through lush rainforests that are largely unfettered by tourist crowds. If you're a serious whitewater rafter, the region boasts over 20 different runs, yet sees a fraction of the river-runners that descend annually on Costa Rica.

As if this wasn't enough of a tourist draw-card, the province is also home to the pristine Golfo de Chiriquí, which boasts powder-white sand beaches and a rich diversity of marine life. With so much to offer, it's no surprise that some Chiricanos dream of creating an independent República de Chiriquí (Chiriquí Republic).

HIGHLIGHTS

- Fueling yourself with mountain-grown coffee in **Boquete** (p201), the town of eternal spring

- Climbing to the top of **Volcán Baru** (p209) and spotting both coastlines – if the weather is clear!

- Hiking through cloud forests along the **Sendero Los Quetzales** (p209) in search of the elusive quetzal

- Wondering why you're the only one around in the pristine but under-touristed **Parque Internacional La Amistad** (p213)

- Island-hopping in the national marine park in the **Golfo de Chiriquí** (p198), the 'other side' of Chiriquí

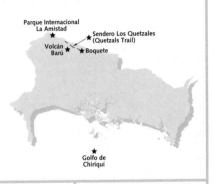

POPULATION: 397,000	AREA: 8653 SQ KM	ELEVATION: SEA LEVEL TO 3478M

CHIRIQUÍ PROVINCE

CHIRIQUÍ PROVINCE

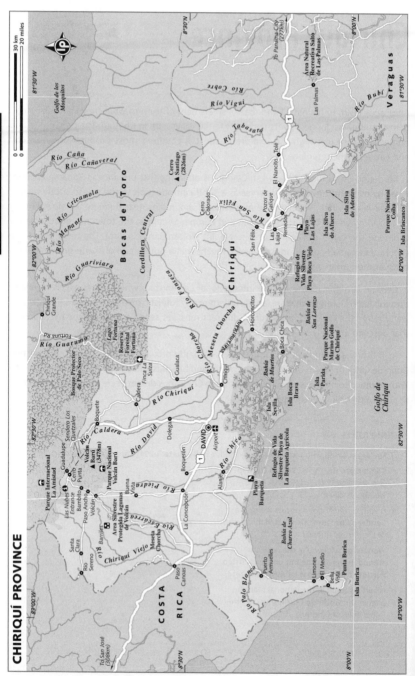

HISTORY

When the Spaniards first visited Chiriquí in the early 15th century, they were astonished by what they found. Instead of discovering one or two main population groups, they encountered a large number of tribes living in relative isolation. Often separated by only a few kilometers, each group maintained a distinct language, culture and religion.

Of course, this didn't stop Spanish missionaries from doing what they did best, namely converting everyone they laid eyes on to Christianity. In the early 17th century, Spanish missionaries led by Padre Cristóbal Cacho Santillana rounded up 626 natives from across the region. Hoping that his work would be easier if he could identify similarities in the languages, Santillana started to record a vocabulary of the most common words, and he was successful in identifying six distinct languages.

Sadly, measles brought by the colonists swept through the towns and killed half the study population. The survivors, having had enough of the Spaniards, their linguistic studies and their religion, took to the hills. Unfortunately, their fate was already sealed – of the Cotho, Borisque, Dorasque, Utelae, Bugabae, Zune, Dolega, Zariba, Dure and others, only the Ngöbe-Buglé survived. Today, the Ngöbe-Buglé are the most populous of Panama's seven indigenous groups, though their numbers are but a fraction of what they once were.

During the 17th century and into the 18th century, Chiriquí Province was the subject of pirate attacks, much like the rest of Panama. It was just outside Remedios in 1680 that English buccaneer Richard Sawkins, attempting to lead an assault against the well-defended city, was fatally wounded. Six years later, English privateers from Honduras sacked the towns of Alanje and San Lorenzo. Even the Miskito tribes from up north behaved like pirates after invading the region in 1732, and plundering and burning the city of David.

In the 19th century, farmers from North America and Europe viewed the climate and slopes of the Chiriquí highlands as prime for coffee, timber and other crops and their descendants still work the fields today. Although the wave of immigration hasn't subsided, recent arrivals are mainly foreign retirees and real-estate speculators, which has led many Chiricanos to question who it is that actually owns the land they love so much.

THE NGÖBE-BUGLÉ

The Ngöbe-Buglé are comprised of two separate ethno-linguistic categories, the Ngöbe and the Buglé, though the distinction is minor, and both are commonly referred to in conjunction with one another. As Panama's largest indigenous population, the Ngöbe-Buglé number close to 200,000, and retain their own *comarca* or autonomous region. Like the Kuna, the Ngöbe-Buglé implement their own system of governance and economy while still maintaining their language, representation in the Panamanian legislature and full voting rights.

The Ngöbe-Buglé are largely confined to the Chiriquí highlands, and predominantly survive on subsistence agriculture, much like their pre-colonial descendants. Their social structure is based on a system of small villages comprised of *chozas* or thatched huts with dirt floors. In the villages, men practice slash and burn agriculture in order to produce staple crops such as plantains, bananas, corn, cassava and rice. During the coffee harvest season, many of the younger men work as migrant laborers in the fields around Boquete, which generates a significant amount of income for the village.

In the villages, women are primarily responsible for raising the children, though many work as skilled artisans, especially since their crafts can fetch a high price. The two most common items produced by Ngöbe-Buglé women are the *chacara*, a woven bag of plant fibers that is meant to mimic the landscapes of the rainforest; and the *naguas*, a traditional dress of hand-sown appliqué that is traditionally worn by both women and girls. Throughout Chiriquí Province, you can find both items for sale in traditional markets and shops.

Like other indigenous groups in Panama, the Ngöbe-Buglé are struggling to maintain their cultural identity, especially as foreign pressures continue to descend on the *comarca* (district). However, although the Ngöbe-Buglé are not as politically organized as the Kuna, they are far greater in number, and they control large tracts of undeveloped land. As a result, the Ngöbe-Buglé have been more successful than other groups such as the Emberá and Wounaan in maintaining their cultural identity and resisting the drive to modernize.

CHIRIQUÍ PROVINCE

CHIRIQUÍ PROVINCE

GETTING TO COSTA RICA

The most heavily trafficked Panama–Costa Rica border crossing is at **Paso Canoas** (☽ 24hr), 53km west of David on the Interamericana. Allow at least one to two hours to get through the formalities on both sides. Buses from David depart frequently for the border (US$1.50, 1½ hours, every half hour) from 4:30am to 9:30pm. On the Costa Rican side of the border, you can catch regular buses to San José or other parts of the country.

The least trafficked crossing into Costa Rica is the border post at **Río Sereno** (☽ 9am-5pm Mon-Sat, 9am-3pm Sun), located 47km west of Volcán. Buses to the border depart from David and travel via La Concepción, Volcán and Santa Clara (US$4, three hours, every 30 minutes). On the Costa Rican side of the border, you can take a 15-minute bus or taxi ride to San Vito, where you can catch buses to regional destinations.

Note that you can be asked for an onward ticket if you are entering Costa Rica. If you do not possess one, it is acceptable to buy a return bus ticket back to Panama. Also note that Costa Rica is one hour behind Panama – opening and closing times in this box are given in Panama time.

LOWLANDS

Chiriquí is much more than its famous highland rainforests – the lowlands are home to Panama's second largest city as well as large stretches of striking Pacific coastline.

DAVID

pop 124,000

Although it feels more like a country town, David is Panama's second-largest city, the capital of Chiriquí Province and a major agricultural center. David is rapidly growing in terms of wealth and importance as a result of the powerful wave of foreign capital flowing into Chiriquí. With tens of thousands of North American and European retirees expected to settle in the region in the years to come, David's economy is expected to boom.

For most travelers, David serves as an important transportation hub for anyone heading to/from Costa Rica, the Chiriquí highlands, Golfo de Chiriquí, Panama City and Bocas del Toro. Although the city has few attractions in its own right, David is a pleasant enough place to stay, and there's no shortage of interesting things to see and do in the surrounding area.

Orientation

David is halfway between San José (Costa Rica) and Panama City – about seven hours by road from either place. The Interamericana does not go through the town, but skirts around its northern and western sides.

The city's heart is its fine central plaza, the Parque de Cervantes, about 1.5km southwest of the highway.

Information

BOOKSTORES

Livraría Regional (Av Bolívar) This modest bookstore stocks a handful of titles in English.

CONSULATE

Costa Rican consulate (☎ /fax 774 1923; cosurica@chiriqui.com; cnr Calle B Norte & Av 1 Este; ☽ 8am-3pm Mon-Fri)

INTERNET ACCESS

Internet Fast Track (Av 2 Este; per hr US$1; ☽ 24hr)
Planet Internet (Calle Central; per hr US$1; ☽ 9am-midnight)

MEDICAL SERVICES

Chiriquí Hospital (☎ 777 8814; Calle Central & Av 3 Oeste) One of the best hospitals in the country.

MONEY

Banistmo With branches on Calle C Norte near the park and on Av Obaldía north of the bus station.
HSBC (Av Central)

POST

Post office (Calle C Norte; ☽ 7am-6pm Mon-Fri, to 4:30pm Sat)

TOURIST INFORMATION

ANAM (Autoridad Nacional de Ambiente; ☎ 775 7840; fax 774 6671; ☽ 8am-4pm Mon-Fri) Provides tourist information and advice, and gives permits to camp in the national parks.

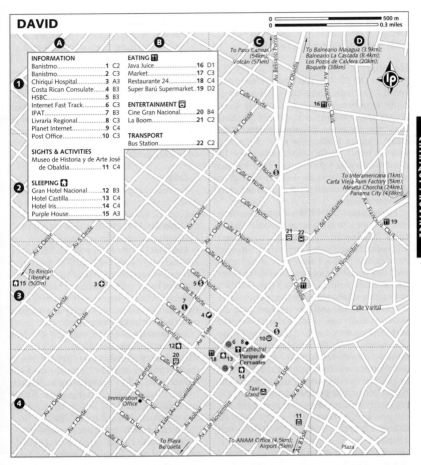

DAVID

0 — 500 m
0 — 0.3 miles

INFORMATION
Banistmo.....................1 C2
Banistmo.....................2 C3
Chiriquí Hospital..........3 A3
Costa Rican Consulate....4 B3
HSBC............................5 B3
Internet Fast Track.........6 C3
IPAT............................7 B3
Livraría Regional...........8 C3
Planet Internet.............9 C4
Post Office..................10 C3

SIGHTS & ACTIVITIES
Museo de Historia y de Arte José
de Obaldía..................11 C4

SLEEPING
Gran Hotel Nacional......12 B3
Hotel Castilla..............13 C4
Hotel Iris...................14 C4
Purple House...............15 A3

EATING
Java Juice...................16 D1
Market.......................17 C3
Restaurante 24.............18 C4
Super Barú Supermarket..19 D2

ENTERTAINMENT
Cine Gran Nacional........20 B4
La Boom.....................21 C2

TRANSPORT
Bus Station..................22 C2

To Paso Canoas (54km); Volcán (57km)

To Balneario Majagua (3.9km); Balneario La Cascada (8.4km); Los Pozos de Caldera (20km); Boquete (38km)

To Interamericana (1km); Carta Vieja Rum Factory (5km); Meseta Chorcha (24km); Panama City (438km)

To Rincón Libenésa (500m)

To Playa Barqueta

To ANAM Office (4.5km); Airport (5km)

CHIRIQUÍ PROVINCE

IPAT (☎ 775 2839; Av Central; ⏰ 8:30am-4:30pm Mon-Fri) Provides information on Chiriquí Province.

Sights & Activities

Despite its size and role as a provincial capital, most of David's attractions lie outside the city. However, David serves as a great base for exploring the Chiriquí lowlands, and it's likely you'll pass through here a few times during your travels in Panama. For tips on how to explore the area, see the boxed text p197.

David's sole attraction is the modest **Museo de Historia y de Arte José de Obaldía** (Av 8 Este btwn Calles Central & A Norte; admission US$1; ⏰ 8:30am-noon & 12:45-4:30pm Mon-Sat), a two-story colonial home that was constructed in 1880, and is furnished with original art and decor. Named after the founder of Chiriquí Province, the museum also houses local archaeological artifacts and old photos of the canal constructions.

If you're looking to get your adrenalin fix, consider spending the day **white-water rafting** on the Río Chiriquí or the Río Chiriquí Viejo. Tour operators in Boquete pass by David on their way to the launch point, and with advanced notice, they'll be happy to pick you up at your accommodation. For more information, see p204.

Festivals & Events

Feria de San José de David This big international fair is held for 10 days each March; contact the IPAT tourist office for exact dates, as they vary from year to year.

Concepción A half-hour drive west of David, Concepción celebrates its patron saint's day on 2 February (or the following Saturday if the 2nd lands on a weekday).

Sleeping

Hotel Iris (☎ 775 2251; Calle A Norte; r from US$12; P 🐕) The faded three-story Iris has definitely seen better days, and its fairly worn rooms are unfortunately starting to show their age. However, it's a good deal, especially if you're looking for a bit of privacy, and you're not too fussy about where you lie down to sleep. It's also conveniently located across from the park, so it's easy enough to flop down here for the night and get out early in the morning.

Purple House (☎ 774 4059; www.purplehousehostel .com; cnr Calle C Sur & Av 6 Oeste; dm US$8.80, r US$18-23; P 🖥 🐕) Owned and managed by a warm and welcoming Peace Corp veteran named Andrea, the Purple House (yes, it's all purple!) is a popular spot to link up with other backpackers. Andrea provides guests with a communal kitchen, an outdoor patio, Cable TV, DVD rentals and free internet, and she is an incredible source of information on the surrounding area. Located in the San Mateo commercial area, the Purple House is also close to lots of restaurants, supermarkets and pharmacies. There is limited availability in October – call or email first. The Purple House also offers private transportation on request for both guests and non-guests to the port for Isla Boca Brava in the Golfo de Chiriquí (p198) – from here, you can catch a water taxi out to this gorgeous island. If you're not staying at Purple House and you'd like to arrange transport, call a day before the desired departure to make a reservation. Prices start at US$30 for one to two people, and decrease depending on the size of the party. Note that there is a US$2 surcharge for non-guests.

Hotel Castilla (☎ 774 5260; Calle A Norte; r from US$30; P 🐕 🖥) Although rooms at the Castilla are more expensive than the Iris, this centrally located hotel is one of the best values in David. Every room at the Castilla is fairly cheap, cheerful and equipped with air-con, private hot-water bathrooms and cable TV. You'll have to dig a little deeper to stay here, but it might be worth it if you're in need of some creature comforts.

Gran Hotel Nacional (☎ 775 2222; Calle Central; d from US$60; P 🐕 🖥 🐾) David's most upscale hotel is a modest affair at best, and its offering of modern yet fairly sterile rooms are more suited to traveling domestic businessmen than to discerning upscale tourists. But the hotel isn't short on amenities, and the on-site bar-restaurant, pizzeria, casino and secure parking sweeten the deal considerably. David also has the somewhat warranted reputation as the hottest city in Panama, which is something you won't have to give much thought to while you're doing laps in the hotel's large swimming pool.

Eating

If you're looking for cheap produce, look out for the bustling market near the junction of Avs Bolívar and Obaldía. Self-caterers can head to the **Super Baru** (Cnr Avs Francisco Clark & 3 de Noviembre), a large American-style supermarket.

Restaurant 24 (Av 2 Este; mains US$2-3; ⏲ 24hr) Popular with locals for its grilled meats and inexpensive lunch specials, this is the perfect spot to get your fill without breaking the budget. But don't come here in a rush as some staff members aren't in a hurry to take your order before the kitchen closes.

Java Juice (Av Francisco Clark; mains US$2.50-4) Iced coffee, fresh-fruit smoothies, healthy salads and juicy grilled burgers are the fare at this charming outdoor café northeast of the bus terminal. Like its sister store in Boquete (p208), Java Juice seems more suited to Northern California than to Chiriquí but the satisfied customers aren't complaining.

Rincón Libenésa (Interamericana; mains US$4-7) Located three blocks past the McDonald's on the Interamericana, this authentic Lebanese restaurant provides welcome relief from a steady diet of rice and beans. Homemade hummus, tabouleh and *baba ghanooj* will make you stop and wonder if you're in the Middle East – 15 seconds later, the sounds of blaring reggaeton will remind you where you are.

Entertainment

La Boom (Av Obaldía, near Av 1 Este) David's largest bar and disco features a sleek dance floor packs in young crowds on Friday and Saturday night. Things can definitely get rowdy here, but a good time can be had assuming you don't pull anyone's date out onto the dance floor.

Cine Gran Nacional (Av 1 Este) This aging movie theater is the perfect spot to catch up on all

---

EXPLORE MORE OF THE DAVID AREA

Tired of the tourist crowds? Looking for a bit of an adventure? Here's a list of Lonely Planet author-tested excursions to spice up your travels:

- **Rest those tired bones in the Los Pozos de Caldera hot springs** Take a bus to the town of Caldera, hike along the dirt road for 45 minutes and soak up the health-giving properties of the spring; see p198.

- **Learn to appreciate rum before you down a tumbler or two** Contact Mr Garcia (☎ 772 7073) to arrange a private tour of the Carta Vieja rum factory, which is located on the outskirts of town.

- **Swim with Chiricanos at Balneario Majagua and Balneario La Cascada** Hop on a Boquete-bound bus and jump off at either of these popular local swimming spots; see below

- **Beat the David heat with a trip to nearby Playa Barqueta** Grab some friends and take a taxi to the lovely dark-sand beach of Playa Barqueta for a day of fun in the sun; see p198.

---

the 'latest' Hollywood films, especially since the majority are spoken English with Spanish subtitles.

Getting There & Away

AIR
David's airport, the Aeropuerto Enrique Malek, is about 5km from town. There are no buses to the airport; take a taxi (US$2).

Air Panama (☎ 721 0841; www.flyairpanama.com /tickets) and **Aeroperlas** (☎ 721 1195; www.aeroperlas .com) fly direct from Panama City to David (US$60, 45 minutes). Air Panama has two daily flights from Monday to Saturday and one flight on Sunday while Aeroperlas has two flights daily. Aeroperlas also has one daily flight from Monday to Friday to Bocas del Toro via Changuinola (US$35, 35 minutes).

BUS
The David **bus station** (Av del Estudiante) is about 600m northeast of the central plaza.

Boquete (US$1.50; 1hr; every 30min, 6am-9:30pm)
Caldera (US$1.50; 45min; hourly, 8:15am-7:30pm)
Cerro Punta (US$3; 2¼hr; every 20min, 5am-8pm)
Changuinola (US$12.50; 4½hr; hourly, 5am-6:30pm)
Guadalupe (US$3; 2½hr; take the Cerro Punta bus, which continues on to Guadalupe)
Horconcitos (US$1.50; 45min; 11am & 5pm)
Las Lajas (US$2; 1½hr; 4 per day, 11:45am-5:20pm; from Las Lajas take a taxi, US$5, to the beach)
Panama City (US$12.60; 7-8hr; every 45min, 6:45am-8pm; Express (US$15; 6hr; 10:45pm & midnight)
Paso Canoas (US$1.50; 1½hr; every 10min, 4:30am-9:30pm)
Puerto Armuelles (US$3; 2½hr; every 15min, 5am-9pm)
Santiago (US$6; 3hr; hourly, 7am-9pm)

Río Sereno (US$4; 2½hr; every 30min, 5am-5pm)
Volcán (US$2.50; 1¾hr; take the Cerro Punta–bound bus)

Tracopa (☎ 775 0585) operates direct buses between David and San José, Costa Rica. Buses depart every day at 8:30am from the David bus station and arrive in San José about eight hours later. From San José, buses depart for the return trip to David at 7:30am. The fare is US$12.50 one way. Bus tickets can be purchased up to two days in advance.

Getting Around
David has a complex network of local buses, though the easiest way to get around is by taxi – fares within the city are generally around US$1, and it's only US$2 to reach the airport. If you're planning on renting a car, all of the major car rental companies have booths at the airport.

THE ROAD TO BOQUETE
If you're heading up to Boquete (p201), there are a number of interesting attractions to check out along the way. If you have your own wheels, you'll be able to go at your own pace and really explore the area, though all of the following places can be accessed via public transportation.

There's no doubt about it – David bakes in the sun virtually year round, which is why the locals have taken to cooling off in the nearby waterfalls. Along the road to Boquete, there are two popular swimming spots: just under 4km north of David is the **Balneario Majagua**, a stretch of waterfall-fed river that's been outfitted with a bar that serves refreshments.

CHIRIQUÍ PROVINCE

Not to be outdone by its neighbor, **Balneario La Cascada**, just over 8km north of David, offers similar waterfall-side swimming, and also features a small bar. Both spots can get very crowded on weekends, though the atmosphere is always 'family fun in the sun.' If you don't have your own wheels, one of the Boquete-bound buses can drop you off at either swimming spot.

If you're in need of a good book, the small town of **Dolega**, about halfway between David and Boquete, boasts a fine second-hand bookshop. The **Book Mark** (9am-5pm Tue-Sun) stocks mostly English-language titles (with a handful of Spanish books as well), including some old and rather obscure works. It's worth stopping in for a browse, especially if you've been re-reading the same Harry Potter book for weeks on end. Once again, any Boquete-bound bus can drop you off in Dolega.

The area's most famous attraction is the **Los Pozos de Caldera** (admission US$1), natural hot springs that are renowned for their health-giving properties. The springs are located on private land near the town of Caldera, 14km east of Boquete.

To get to the springs, take a bus or drive to the town of Caldera (the turnoff to Caldera is 13km south of Boquete). From where the bus drops you off, continue to the end of town, where you'll see a sign indicating the turnoff to the springs. You'll turn right along this rugged dirt road, accessible by 4WD only. If you're walking it's about 45 minutes from here. Continue along the road until you reach a suspension bridge. Cross it, and take the first left leading up the hill. After 100m, you'll see a gate which marks the entrance to the property.

If you're driving, don't leave anything in the car as there have been reports of break-ins here. If you get overheated in the springs, the pleasant Rio Caldera is just a stone's throw away, and is a pleasant spot to cool off. Hourly buses run from both David and Boquete (both US$0.75, 45 minutes) to the town of Caldera.

PLAYA BARQUETA

This long and lovely dark-sand beach southwest of David is a popular weekend escape for city-folk, though you'll have the place all to yourself if you stop by here during the week. As inviting as the ocean seems, the riptides can really pick up here, but this is a great place to break out your surfboard if you've got one. With that said, wading in up to your ankles sure beats sweating through your socks on the David streets.

Capping the eastern end of the beach is the **Las Olas Resort** (772 3000; www.lasolasresort.com; s/d US$134/180, ste s/d US$144/200; P X □ ☎), a low-impact, ecologically-minded resort that was designed to protect the neighboring mangroves and their population of migratory birds. The resort itself is comprised of a number of terraced rooms and suites that are decorated with soft, natural color and feature sweeping ocean views. There is also an extensive facilities list including a number of bars and restaurants, a spa, gym, yoga center, equestrian center and marina. Room rates are cheaper in the low season (April to November), and all-inclusive deals are available if you book via the internet.

Unfortunately, there is no public transportation connecting Playa Barqueta to David, though it's easy to access by private vehicle or taxi (US$20, one hour). If you can fill the cab, you should be able to negotiate a reasonable price, especially if you arrange for a pick-up and a ride back to David.

GOLFO DE CHIRIQUÍ

The undisputed gem of the Chiriquí lowlands is the Golfo de Chiriquí, which is home to the **Parque Nacional Marino Golfo de Chiriquí**, a national marine park with an area of 14,740 hectares protecting 25 islands, 19 coral reefs and abundant wildlife. The marine park also protects the 3000-hectare **Isla Boca Brava**, a lovely little island that is criss-crossed by hiking trails and is home to monkeys, nesting sea turtles and 280 recorded bird species. Whether you want to lie on the beach, snorkel clear waters or go wildlife-watching underneath the rainforest canopy, there's something for everyone in this off-the-beaten-path destination.

A great place (and the only place) to stay on Boca Brava is at the **Restaurante y Cabañas Boca Brava** (676 3244; r US$10, cabins US$18-35, hammock per person US$3), which is comprised of four spacious cabins with private bathrooms and four rustic rooms with shared bathrooms. Owners Frank and Yadira Köhler speak English, German and Spanish. Reservations are not accepted, but they'll always find you a place to stay if you're willing to sleep in a hammock.

The breezy **restaurant-bar** (meals US$4) features a large selection of seafood (such as red snap-

SURFING IN CHIRIQUÍ PROVINCÉ

Owing to difficult access, surfing in Chiriquí is not as popular as in other provinces, though there is still some great surf to be had here. The following list will help you get started, though it's best to hire a local guide or contact a tour operator if you really want to explore the region. The following surf spots are featured on Map pp68–9:

- **Isla Silva de Afuera** Remote island off the coast. Two breaks: one right, one left. Right is a big peak breaking over a shallow rock ledge at medium tide. Occasionally throws a big tube with steep drops and no wall. Other break is a good left that breaks over a rock reef at medium tide. This spot catches almost every swell.
- **Isla Silva de Adentro** Remote island off the coast. A right-hand break over a rock reef that can get really big with strong swell.
- **Morro Negrito** Near Morro Negrito town. About five breaks, variety of lefts and rights with occasional tubes.
- **Playa Las Lajas** East of David. Beach-bottom break with rights and lefts, but in infrequent waves.
- **Playa Barqueta** Near David. Beach-bottom break with rights and lefts. Breaks at all tides, but medium to high tide is best.
- **Punta Burica** On Costa Rican border. Four left points that break along the point for long, tubing rides. Catches any swell. Better waves than Pavones of Costa Rica and less crowded.

per), and Frank and Yadira can arrange any number of excursions around the islands, involving snorkeling, whale-watching or just lounging on a gorgeous uninhabited island (prices range from US$12 to US$70 depending on the tour and the number of participants). From the restaurant, you're a stone's throw from the boundary of the national marine park.

To reach the island, take a bus to the Horconcitos turnoff, which is 39km east of David. You can also take any bus going by the turnoff (any bus heading from David to Panama City), as long as you tell the driver to drop you at the Horconcitos turnoff.

From the turnoff, take a pickup-truck taxi 13km to the fishing village of Boca Chica (US$15; one hour). If you see no taxis at the turnoff, walk into Horconcitos and call either **Jovené** (☎ 653 1549) or **Roberto** (☎ 628 0651); both are taxi drivers in the area. At the Boca Chica dock, hire a water taxi (per person US$1) to take you 200m to the island.

With advance notice, the Purple House (p196) in David are able to arrange all of your transportation.

If you drive your own vehicle, you can safely leave it near the village dock, but the road between Horconcitos and Boca Chica is impassable save for 4WD vehicles.

PUNTA BURICA

This lush peninsula jutting into the Pacific is a lovely spot for absorbing the beauty of both the rainforest and the coastline.

our pick **Mono Feliz** (☎ 595 0388; mono_feliz@hotmail .com; cabin 1st night/every night thereafter per person US$20/15, campsite per person per day US$5; P ☻) offers visitors a chance to enjoy this untouched natural beauty. Wildlife is a key feature here, and the Mono Feliz (happy monkey) certainly has its share of its namesake.

Facilities include three stand-alone cabins – two in the garden and one on the beach. There is also a large pool (fed by cool spring water, and you may be surrounded by monkeys at times), fresh water showers and an outdoor kitchen for guest use. Those who'd rather not cook can pay US$20 per day extra for three home-cooked meals, ranging from fresh seasonal fish to conch or lobster when available (individual meals available for US$6/8/10 breakfast/lunch/dinner). Beds have mosquito nets. Camping on the beach is also available (bring your own gear), and you have access to pool and bathrooms.

The friendly American and Canadian owners (Allegra and John or 'Juancho' as he's known to locals) offer a range of activities including nature walks (an excursion to Isla Burica at low tide is a highlight), fishing, surfing, bird-watching and horseback riding. Remedial massage and yoga is available for guests in need of deeper relaxation. All activities are free, except horseback riding (US$5 an hour). English, French and Spanish are spoken.

Owing to its isolation, Mono Feliz requires a bit of work getting there. You'll first need to go to the small coastal town of Puerto Armuelles. Services from David to Puerto Armuelles leave every 15 minutes (US$2.75, 2½ hours). Be sure to arrive in Puerto Armuelles no later than noon. The bus drops you off in the *mercado municipal,* and from there you'll take a truck to Bella Vista. From here, it is approximately a one-hour walk down the hill to Mono Feliz. You can also get off at El Medio, the last stop before the trucks go inland to Bella Vista. From El Medio it's an hour's walk along the beach. Mono Feliz is directly in front of the island Isla Burica.

If you have a 4WD, you can drive directly to Mono Feliz in the dry season (mid-December to mid-April). From Puerto Armuelles keep heading south along the coast toward Costa Rica. Go through the Petroterminal and then veer directly onto the beach (attempt this only at low tide). About 15km along you will pass though Limones, Puerto Balsa and then, around 20 minutes later, El Medio. Keep going on the beach for another 10 minutes and you will see where the dirt road starts, marked with a 'Mono Feliz' sign. Keep to this road and 30 minutes later, when you cannot go any further, you will reach Mono Feliz.

PLAYA LAS LAJAS

Playa Las Lajas, 51km east of David and 26km south of the Interamericana, is one of several long, palm-lined beaches along this stretch of the Pacific coast. Playa Las Lajas gathers crowds on the weekends, but often lies empty during the week, when you can have some serious stretches of sand all to yourself.

Although several new accommodations are currently in the works, in the meantime you can stay at **Las Lajas Beach Cabins** (☎ 720 2430 & 618 7723; dm/d US$6.50/35, cabin US$25). There are nine small rustic *cabañas* (cabins) right on the beach, a clam's toss from the surf, while the bathrooms are communal in a nearby concrete structure. There is also an additional concrete structure 50m back from the beach with six private rooms and two dormitories.

Back where the road dead-ends at the beach sits **La Estrella del Pacífico** (dishes from US$3), the only restaurant in the area. Simple fish dishes are especially good when the catch is fresh, though you can count on great ocean views anytime.

To reach Las Lajas, take any bus from David (US$2, 90 minutes, hourly) that travels by the Las Lajas turnoff on the Interamericana. At the turnoff, take a taxi (US$5) to where the road reaches the sea. Turn right and proceed 1.5km until you arrive at the cabins.

Ngöbe-Buglé people sell **handicrafts** in a wooden-walled structure 500m west of the turnoff – most of the residents of San Félix, 3km north of here, are Ngöbe-Buglé.

THE ROAD TO VERAGUAS PROVINCE

If you're heading out to Veraguas Province (p174), there are a number of interesting attractions to check out along the way. If you have your own wheels, you'll be able to go at your own pace and really explore the area, though all of the following places can be accessed via public transportation.

Twenty-four kilometers east of David, on the northern side of the Interamericana, is the enormous **Meseta Chorcha** (Chorcha Plateau), which photographers won't want to miss. As you approach the plateau from the west, you'll see a white streak running down its glistening granite face – a closer look reveals that this streak is actually an extremely tall waterfall. Unfortunately, the highway is as close to the falls as you can get without trespassing. The land between the highway and the foot of the falls belongs to a rancher who doesn't like strangers on his property, and it's advisable that you respect his wishes. If you don't have your own wheels, peer at the view from the window while on any eastbound bus.

Nearly opposite the turnoff for Playa Las Lajas is **Cerro Colorado**, one of the world's largest copper mines – mineralogists estimate that there's approximately 1.4 million tons of it in the mine. Although the mine isn't open for tours, it's worth stopping for a moment to size up the mountain, and dream about how many copper pennies could be minted from its stash. Again, if you don't have your own wheels, peer out the window while on any east-bound bus.

If you're looking to soak your travel-worn bones, the **Pozos de Galique** (Springs of Galique) are three no-frills hot springs, each of which can accommodate several people. Bring lots of cold drinks with you, and try to reach them in the early morning before the day heats up and the crowds arrive. The easy-to-miss turnoff for the road to the springs (which requires a 4WD vehicle to access) is 4km east of the turnoff for Playa Las Lajas. The 3.8km-long turnoff leading to the springs is 30m west of a small bridge with 'Galique' written on it.

About 5km west of the town of Tolé is a turnoff for El Nancito, a small community known for its **rock carvings**. Locals say that the carved boulders were made more than 1000 years ago, though no one really knows for sure since the carvings have yet to be studied – few people outside Chiriquí even know about their existence.

From the Interamericana, turn north onto the road to El Nancito. When you reach the 'Cantina Oriente' sign, turn west and drive 75m until you come across some rather large boulders. If you are relying on public transportation, jump off any east-bound bus at El Nancito, and then hike the 1.5km to the boulders. Be careful doing this in the late afternoon as you'll have difficulty catching a return bus after sunset.

HIGHLANDS

The highland rainforests are the heart of Chiriquí Province – from the rugged mountains of Parque Internacional La Amistad to the misty hills of Boquete, the highlands seem to have it all.

BOQUETE
pop 5000

The mountain town of Boquete is known throughout Panama for its cool, fresh climate and pristine natural setting. Flowers, coffee, vegetables and citrus fruits flourish in Boquete's rich soil, and the friendliness of the locals seems to rub off on everyone who passes through.

CHIRIQUÍ PROVINCE

HIGHER GROUNDS

During the 19th century, farmers from North America and Europe discovered that the cool climate and rich volcanic soil of Chiriquí were perfectly suited for the cultivation of coffee. Since dried beans are relatively non-perishable and thus easy to ship, coffee quickly surpassed other cash crops, and became an important source of revenue for the area. Although Panamanian coffee has never attained the popularity of Costa Rican coffees, it is still highly praised for its high caffeine content and acidic, multi-dimensional flavor.

In the past 20 years, however, the Panamanian coffee market, along with other Central American countries, has suffered greatly. Following a collapse in the world quota cartel system, the world coffee price plummeted nearly 40% in just a few years. Although the market eventually stabilized in 1994, this was the same year that Vietnam entered the world market following the lifting of the US trade embargo. Since the market rewarded the efficiency of Vietnamese coffee suppliers, many coffee-exporting nations (Panama included) lost a large percentage of their traditional market share.

Today, Panamanian coffee continues to be grown in Chiriquí Province. Harvesting occurs primarily in the dry season, and is dependent on cheap, seasonal labor that predominantly consists of Ngöbe-Buglé. Once picked, the ripened berries are transported to *beneficos* (processing plants) where they are separated from the fruit and sun-dried. Green coffee beans are then vacuum sealed to retain their characteristic acidity, and shipped to roasters throughout the world.

In recent years, it's ironic that the price of green coffee beans plummeted at the same time that the price of a cup of coffee skyrocketed. While coffee suppliers like Starbucks continue to run lucrative enterprises, coffee farmers (not to mention migrant workers) are receiving an absurdly small percentage of the profits. This phenomenon initiated a push for free trade, which is an economic (and increasingly political) term referring to the unhindered flow of goods and services between countries. When a coffee advertises itself as free trade, it is usually sold at a higher price to ensure that profits are more evenly distributed.

With the consequences of the CAFTA (Central American Free Trade Agreement) already being felt, trade barriers are about to be redefined throughout the Americas. However, since Panama is a comparatively small player in Latin America, it is difficult to say whether this legislation will be enough to secure a market niche in light of the growing production capabilities of countries like Brazil.

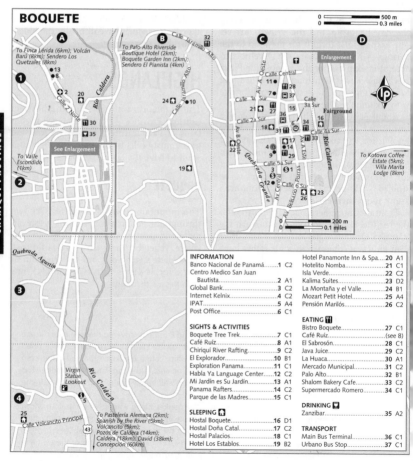

BOQUETE

INFORMATION

Banco Nacional de Panamá	**1** C2
Centro Medico San Juan Bautista	**2** A1
Global Bank	**3** C2
Internet Kelnix	**4** C2
IPAT	**5** A4
Post Office	**6** C1

SIGHTS & ACTIVITIES

Boquete Tree Trek	**7** C1
Café Ruíz	**8** A1
Chiriquí River Rafting	**9** C2
El Explorador	**10** B1
Exploration Panama	**11** C1
Habla Ya Language Center	**12** C2
Mi Jardín es Su Jardín	**13** A1
Panama Rafters	**14** C1
Parque de las Madres	**15** C1

SLEEPING

Hostal Boquete	**16** D1
Hostal Doña Catal	**17** C2
Hostal Palacios	**18** C1
Hotel Los Establos	**19** B2
Hotel Panamonte Inn & Spa	**20** A1
Hotelito Nomba	**21** C1
Isla Verde	**22** C2
Kalima Suites	**23** D2
La Montaña y el Valle	**24** B1
Mozart Petit Hotel	**25** A4
Pensión Marilós	**26** C2

EATING

Bistro Boquete	**27** C1
Café Ruíz	(see 8)
El Sabrosón	**28** C1
Java Juice	**29** C2
La Huaca	**30** A1
Mercado Municipal	**31** C2
Palo Alto	**32** B1
Shalom Bakery Cafe	**33** C2
Supermercado Romero	**34** C1

DRINKING

Zanzibar	**35** A2

TRANSPORT

Main Bus Terminal	**36** C1
Urbano Bus Stop	**37** C1

Boquete was very much intent on remaining on a small town, but was faced with changes beyond anyone's control – Baby Boomers started getting old. When *Modern Maturity* magazine of the American Association for Retired Persons chose Boquete in 2001 as one of the four top places in the world to retire, a flock of foreign retirees started snatching up mountain plots. Today, gated communities dot the hillsides, and the face of Boquete is slowly being transformed.

For travelers, Boquete is one of the country's top destinations for outdoor lovers. From Boquete, you can hike, climb, raft, visit coffee plantations, soak in hot springs, study Spanish or go on a canopy tour. And of course, there's nothing quite like starting your day with a glass of freshly squeezed OJ, or perking up with a cup of locally grown coffee.

Orientation

Boquete's central area is only a few square blocks. The main road, Av Central, comes north from David, passes along the western side of the plaza and continues up the hill past the church.

Information

INTERNET ACCESS
Internet Kelnix (Av Central; per hr US$1)

MEDICAL SERVICES
Centro Medico San Juan Bautista (☎ 720 1881)

CHIRIQUÍ PROVINCE

MONEY
Banco Nacional de Panama (Av Central)
Global (Av Central)

POST
Post office (7am-6pm Mon-Fri, to 5pm Sat)

TOURIST INFORMATION
IPAT (9:30am-6pm) Before arriving in Boquete (about 1.5km south of town), this office sits atop a bluff overlooking town. You can pick up maps here and obtain information on area attractions. On the 2nd floor is an exhibit detailing the history of the region (Spanish only).

Sights
With its flower-lined streets and forested hillsides, Boquete is an ideal spot for taking picturesque strolls. A quick jaunt around town will bring you to the **Parque de las Madres**, which is home to flowers, a fountain and a children's playground. It's also worth exploring the attractive fairgrounds and riverside, where you'll come across an old railway and an exhibition wagon that's left over from the days when a train linked Boquete with the coastal town of Puerto Armuelles.

COFFEE PLANTATIONS
A trip to Boquete just isn't complete without learning the secrets of a perfectly blended cup of joe.

Café Ruíz (720 1392; www.caferuiz.com; 3hr tour US$14), located on the main road about 600m north of the town center, is Panama's most famous coffee-grower. It offers a tour that includes transportation to a nearby coffee plantation, a presentation on the history of coffee in Boquete, a tour of a roasting facility and the obligatory tasting session. Tours depart at 9am daily except Sundays and holidays, but you have to make advance reservations.

Kotowa Coffee Estate (720 1430; 2½hr tour US$19) is a gourmet grower offering the most comprehensive coffee-estate tour in the area. It features a description of the estate's history (beginning with a Canadian's arrival in 1918), a full tour of the production facilities and processing mill, and again, the obligatory tasting session. The estate requests 24 hours' notice prior to your visit.

GARDENS
Just uphill from Café Ruíz, **Mi Jardín es Su Jardín** (admission free; daylight hr) is a magnificent garden surrounding a luxurious private estate. The residence is off-limits to the public, but you are free to stroll about the gardens unhindered.

The private garden of **El Explorador** (775 2643; Calle Jaramillo Alto; admission US$2; 10am-6pm daily mid-Dec–mid-Apr, Sat & Sun only mid-Apr–mid-Dec) is located in a hilly area about 45 minutes' walk from the town center. The gardens are designed to look like something out of *Alice in Wonderland*, and there's no shortage of quirky displays to catch your eye.

HOT SPRINGS
Boquete is a good base for exploring the **Los Pozos de Caldera** (admission US$1; dawn-dusk), an undeveloped hot spring that is rumored to have health-giving properties. A taxi cab from the town center to the hot springs should cost about US$6 roundtrip.

Activities
HIKING
With its breathtaking vistas of mist-covered hills and nearby forests, Boquete is one of the most idyllic regions for hiking and walking. Several good paved roads lead out of town into the surrounding hills, passing coffee plantations, fields and farms, gardens and virgin forest.

Although saunterers will be content with picturesque strolls along the river, the more ambitious can climb **Volcán Barú** (3478m). There are several entrances to the park, but the trail with easiest access to the summit starts near Boquete. For more information, see p209.

You can also access the **Sendero Los Quetzales** (Quetzals Trail) from Boquete, though the trail is uphill from here – you'll have an easier time if you start hiking from Cerro Punta (see p212). For more information on the Sendero Los Quetzales, see p209.

A pleasant day hike is along the **Sendero El Pianista** (Pianist Trail), which winds through dairy land and into humid cloud forest. To access the trailhead, take the first right fork out of Boquete (heading north) and cross over two bridges. Immediately before the third bridge, about 4km out of town, a track leads off to the left between a couple of buildings. You need to wade across a small river after 200m, but then it's a steady, leisurely incline for 2km before you start to climb a steeper, narrow path. The path winds deep into the forest, though you can turn back at any time.

RAFTING

Those who seek a bit of adventure shouldn't miss the excellent white-water rafting within a two-hour drive of Boquete. The Río Chiriquí and the Río Chiriquí Viejo both flow from the fertile hills of Volcán Barú, and are flanked by forest for much of their lengths. At some places, waterfalls can be seen at the edges of the rivers, and both pass through narrow canyons with awesome, sheer rock walls.

The Río Chiriquí is most often run from May to December, while the Chiriquí Viejo is run the rest of the year; the rides tend to last four and five hours, respectively. Depending on the skill level of your party, you can tackle thrilling class 3 and class 4 rapids or some seriously scary class 5 rapids.

The country's two best white-water rafting outfits are **Chiriquí River Rafting** (☎ 720 1505; www .panama-rafting.com; Av Central) and **Panama Rafters** (☎ 720 2712; www.panamarafters.com; Av Central), both of which are located in downtown Boquete. Both companies staff bilingual employees, so you can get all the information you need in either English or Spanish. All-day trips are offered for US$75 to US$100, depending on the run and the size of the party.

CANOPY TOURS

Although canopy tours are about as prevalent as rice and beans in Costa Rica, they're still quite new to the Panama tourist scene. For the uninitiated, a canopy tour consists of a series of platforms anchored into the forest canopy that are connected by zip lines. Although they were originally used by biologists to study the rainforest canopy, today they function primarily as a way for gringos to get their eco-kicks.

If you're game to strap yourself into a harness and zip along the tree line, the **Boquete Tree Trek** (☎ 720 1635; www.aventurist.com; 3hr US$60; Av Central) is located in secondary forest, and consists of 14 platforms, 13 zip lines, a rappel and a Tarzan-swing. Although the company stresses fun instead of ecology, these lines pick up some serious speed, so you might want to consider going a little heavy on the hand-break.

BIRD-WATCHING

Finca Lérida (p207), located about 6km northwest of town, is a coffee farm owned by the Collins family, who are long-time residents of Boquete. Bordering their farm is prime habitat for the quetzal, the national bird of Guatemala that's nearly extinct there, but has found refuge in Chiriquí Province. In total, several hundred bird species have been identified in these woods, which makes Finca Lérida one of the premier birding spots in Panama. The per-person cost of US$150 (party of one), US$75 (party of two) or US$65 (party of four to six people) includes lunch and transportation. The quetzals are most likely to be seen January through August. For more information on accomodations, see p207.

BOAT TOURS

Exploration Panama (☎ 720 2470; www.exploration panama.net; Av Central) offers a wide variety of excursions in and around the Golfo de Chiriquí. Aboard a 50ft vessel, which is a former US Coast Guard Search & Rescue ship, you can take a 'jungle cruise' (per person US$75, four-person minimum), exploring the mangroves, small rivers and coastal forests south of David. Ron Mager, the owner-captain of *Exploration Panama*, also offers sea-kayaking trips (led by personnel from Chiriquí River Rafting), fishing trips and scuba-diving trips. He's a very safe and reliable captain – he has his US Coast Guard license and is a former Green Beret. His ship can accommodate up to six passengers on overnight trips, which allow for excursions into some gorgeous unexplored waters.

TRUCK TOURS

Boquete Mountain Cruisers (☎ 720 4697; boquete cruisers@hotmail.com) is an expat-owned outfit offering two daily tours through some scenic back-country roads in its open-air trucks. The first leaves at 8:30am (per person US$20) and makes a number of stops in and around Boquete – highlights include coffee, basalt formations and waterfalls. The second tour departs at 2pm (per person US$15), and heads straight for the Caldera hot springs. Both tours last four hours. There is no booking office, so call for reservations; trips include pickup at your hotel.

Courses

Spanish by the River (☎ /fax 720 3456; www.span ishbythesea.com) is the sister school to the popular Spanish school in Bocas del Toro (p225). Rates for group/private lessons are US$70/130 for two hours a day, five days a week, although cheaper rates are also available for more comprehensive packages and longer stays. The school also offers a popular traveler's survival Spanish course (US$40) that includes six hours of instruction. Homestays can be arranged (US$12 per night with breakfast) or you can rent one of their simple dorms (US$7.50 per night) or private rooms (US$12 per night). Spanish by the River is located 5km south of Boquete near the turnoff to Palmira.

The reader-recommended **Habla Ya Language Center** (☎ 720 1294; www.hablayapanama.com; Central Av) offers both group and private lessons. Five hours of group/private lessons starts at US$50/75, though significant discounts are given for lengthier programs – 25 hours of group/private lessons is only US$200/300. The language school is also well-connected to local businesses, so students can take advantage of discounts on everything from accommodations to tours.

Festivals & Events

The town's annual festival is the **Feria de las Flores y del Café** (Flower and Coffee Fair), held for 10 days each January. Another popular event is the **Feria de Las Orquídeas** (Orchid Fair), held every April. Contact IPAT (p203) for exact dates of both events as they vary.

Sleeping

Because of the cool climate, all of the places to stay in Boquete have hot-water showers, but don't waste too much time looking for the air-conditioner – you're not going to need it.

BUDGET
Camping

Nights are chilly here, and temperatures can drop to near freezing – pack some warm clothes if you plan to camp. You can also camp in nearby Parque Nacional Volcán Barú (p209).

La Montaña y el Valle (☎ 720 2211; information@cofeeestateinn.com; Calle Jaramillo Alto; campsites 1-/2-people US$7/10, extra person US$3; **P**) This working coffee

---

LOCAL VOICES: CHIRIQUÍ IS FOR KAYAKERS

John Miller has made more first descents of Panama's white-water rivers than anyone else. The instructor trainer for US-based **Nantahala Outdoor Center** (☎ 800-232-7238 in USA; www.noc .com), the world's largest kayaking school, John is an expert kayaker – especially when it comes to Panama's rivers. He prepared the following report:

'There are other rivers in Panama, but nothing compares to Chiriquí. If someone wants to paddle in Panama, this is where they should go.

The Chiriquí Province of Panama has three elements that make it a paddler's paradise: terrain, rainfall and accessibility. During the rainy season (mid-April through mid-December), the area around Boquete has over 20 different runs within a two-hour drive of this small mountain town, varying from easy Class 1 or 2 to scary Class 5. The Cordillera Central ranges from over 10,000ft near the Costa Rican border in the west to around 6000ft at the border with the Veraguas Province in the east. The river gradient is steep and consistent almost to the Pacific Ocean, resulting in long continuous stretches of white water. In addition, Volcán Barú towers over Boquete at 11,500ft on the Pacific side of the Cordillera Central. This dormant volcano tends to attract rainfall and has six runnable rivers draining its flanks.

Most of the watersheds in this area are small, but thanks to the bountiful precipitation in the rainy season, they are usually runnable every day during the rainy season. During the dry season, only the two biggest watersheds, the Río Chiriquí and the Río Chiriquí Viejo, have enough water to be runnable, and most of the paddling in Panama is found in these two watersheds. By far, the best time of year to paddle is from September through November.

Almost all of the rivers in this area follow a very predictable pattern. They are very steep and continuous at the higher elevations, tending to be small, steep streams. As the rivers flow down the mountains, the gradient gradually levels off, and the rivers pick up tributaries and grow in volume and width. As you approach sea level, the rivers are high-volume but also drop or pool. You can generally gauge how difficult the run will be by the elevation. The hardest runs start as high as 5000ft while anything below 1000ft tends to be no harder than Class 3.'

CHIRIQUÍ PROVINCE

estate, 2.5km from town, has camping on a weather-permitting basis (usually January through March). There are three tent sites, and facilities include hot showers, flush toilets, electricity and a covered cooking area. You must call ahead to let the owners know you're coming.

Hotels

Pensión Marilós (☎ 720 1380; marilos66@hotmail .com; cnr Av A Este & Calle 6 Sur; s/d US$7/11, with bathroom US$10/14; **P**) This cozy, family-run spot is a good choice for travelers looking for a little bit of peace and quiet. Rooms are warmly decorated with assorted knick-knacks and doo-dads, and are somewhat reminiscent of the guest bedroom at your grandma's house. The pleasant owner, Frank Glavas, knows Chiriquí like the back of his hand, and can help you make the most of your time in Boquete.

Hotelito Nomba (☎ 720 1076; Av A Oeste; dm/r per person US$6.60/8.80; **P**) The self-proclaimed chillout hostel is bare-bones, fairly sterile and has about as much personality as a fluorescent-lit cubicle. Of course, if you're on a tight budget, it's certainly cheap, and fairly popular among the shoestring crowd. The management is also laid-back, and a good time can be had here if you meet the right people.

Hostal Palacios (☎ 720 1653; Av Central; dm/r per person US$6.60/8.80; **P**) This long-standing budget guesthouse has a friendly and vibrant atmosphere, thanks in part to the energetic owner, Pancho. From check-in until check-out, Pancho will personally ensure that you're having a good time, and that all your questions about what to do are answered. Although the rooms have definitely seen better days, this place is well-suited to backpackers, especially since there is a shared kitchen, room to pitch a tent and a fireplace out back where you can stay warm while chatting up other travelers.

Pensión Topas (☎ 720 1005; schoeb@chiriqui.com; Av Belisario Porras; s/d from US$10/15; **P**) Built around a small organic garden, this German-run pensión features a variety of rooms to suit all budgets. Cheaper rooms share an outdoor solar-heated bathroom, while the more expensive rooms have private bathrooms with steamy showers. In true German fashion, this budget inn is well-run and kept spic-and-span.

Hostal Doña Catal (☎ 720 1260; Av Central; d with shared/private bathrooms US$10/15; **P**) On the central plaza, the faded-blue Hostal Doña Cata is suffering from a bit of wear and tear, though the price is right, especially if you splurge for the upstairs rooms. For a few bucks more, you can enjoy a private bathroom and a balcony overlooking the park. It's not as cozy as some of the other family-run guest houses in town, but it's certainly more private, and you can't beat the park-side location.

Hostal Boquete (☎ 720 2573; Calle 4a Sur; s/d US$15/20; **P**) Overlooking the Río Caldera, this quaint country inn is excellent value, especially if you want a quiet location away from the town center. The interiors of the rooms are utterly basic and none too exciting, though they do have attractive terraces overlooking the river. If you're a light sleeper, this is the place for you – just close your eyes at night and drift off to sleep to the sounds of the flowing water.

Mozart Petit Hotel (☎ 720 3764; coyaldps@hotmail .com; Calle Volcancito Principal; camping US$5, cabins from US$20; **P**) Located near the IPAT office about 1.5km from the town center, this adorable little hotel is a bit far from the action, though it's a great choice if you're looking to slow down a bit and soak up the rural ambience. Consisting of several self-contained cabins with rustic furnishings, terraced patios and sweeping views that reach as far as the Pacific (on a clear day of course!), these cabins epitomize the idea of a mountain retreat. If you really want to get close to nature, you can even pitch a tent here in the well-groomed campsite.

MIDRANGE

Kalima Suites (☎ 720 2884; www.kalimasuites.net; Av A Este; d US$40, each additional person US$5.50; **P** 🖳) This all-suites hotel features 10 modern suites decorated with simple but sturdy furniture and including a bedroom, living room and kitchenette. Although there are definitely more atmospheric midrange options, it's hard to beat the price here, especially if you're planning on self catering. The terrace out back serves as a communal meeting area, and there's an internet café next door that's free for guests.

Isla Verde (☎ 720 2533; islaverde@cwpanama.net; Av B Oeste; small/large cabins US$50/65; **P** 🖳) These centrally located cabins are one of the best deals in Boquete. Set in a beautiful, lushly landscaped garden are a clutch of Alpine-inspired two-story cabins, with vaulted ceilings, professional kitchens and roomy tiled-bathrooms. Although you're only a few blocks from the town center, the gardens here are a veritable oasis, though it can be hard to drag yourself out of bed here – the mattresses are about as plush as you'll find in these parts.

Villa Marita Lodge (☎ 720 2165; www.panamainfo .com/marita; d from US$55; P 🖳) These seven stand-alone cabins on the edge of a plateau overlook a vast expanse of coffee farms, and have striking views of Volcán Barú (when it's not cloudy). Well-maintained by their proud owner, each gorgeous cabin contains a comfortable sitting area, hardwood accents and country-inspired furnishings. There's also an on-site restaurant and gathering room that's perfect for mingling with other guests and swapping stories over a home-cooked meal.

Hotel Panamonte Inn & Spa (☎ 720 1327; www .panamonteinnandspa.com; d from US$65; P 🖳) Located on a quiet road at the northern end of town, this historic inn with dollhouse-like charm lies in perfect harmony with its surroundings. The hotel has handsomely furnished guestrooms, a fine restaurant-bar complete with a stone fireplace and landscaped gardens that make excellent use of the local flora. The hotel also features a highly recommended day-spa that's the perfect complement to your mountain-top getaway.

Boquete Garden Inn (☎ 720 2376; www.boquete gardeninn.com; d US$75-90; P 🖳) Perched on the edge of the Río Palo Alto, this garden inn is overflowing with blossoming tropical flower beds. Airy and romantic rooms are awash in earthy tones, though they're brightened up each morning with the addition of fresh-cut flowers. The biggest perk, however, is the riverside gazebo, which doubles as a lounge-bar, and is the perfect spot for a reflective glass of wine.

Finca Lérida (☎ 720 2285; www.fincalerida.com; Calle 2 Norte; B&B r US$65-120, ecolodge r US$146-162 with 2 meals; P 🖳) Famous throughout Panama for its legendary bird-watching, Finca Lérida is a working coffee plantation that happens to be one of the best spots in the country to see quetzals, though hundreds of unique species have been spotted here. Finca Lérida consists of two premises, a Scandinavian-inspired B&B that's centered on a fireplace-warmed living room, and a recently constructed ecolodge that's nestled in the middle of the coffee plantation. Regardless of which one you choose however, the real reason you're here is to explore the avian hotspot that is Finca Lérida (see also p204).

TOP END

Valle Escondido (☎ 720 2897; www.valleescondido.biz; cabin from US$90; 🔀 P 🖳 🔁) Part of a large, gated expat community on the edge of town, the resort at Valle Escondido is definitely not everyone's cup of coffee. The cabins here are an exercise in hedonistic luxury, though the retiree-atmosphere is about as un-Panamanian as you can get. But, if you're looking for a coffee holiday, the amenities here can't be beat – Valle Escondido is the only place in town with an 18-hole golf course, athletic center, equestrian center and pool complex.

La Montaña y el Valle (☎ 720 2211; www.coffeees tateinn.com; Calle Jaramillo Alto; d US$130; P) Also known as the Coffee Estate Inn, 'The Mountain & the Valley' consists of three luxury bungalows outfitted with a professional kitchen, an enormous living room and dining area, a separate bedroom and a private terrace with breathtaking views of the surrounding mountains and the valley below. The estate is also home to a working coffee farm, and there is an extensive network of trails here that winds into the surrounding forest. According to one reader, the best part of staying here is the fresh coffee and oranges, both of which come from the estate, as well as the incredibly attentive services of the delightful owners, Jane and Barry.

Hotel Los Establos (☎ 720 2685; www.losestablos.net; d/ste US$130/230; P 🖳) One of Boquete's two boutique hotels, Los Establos is an elegant country affair that has the air of a Tuscan villa. Although it was originally built to serve as stables, the lavish quarters here bear no traces of its former purpose, though its history lives on in the equestrian decorations that dot the property. Each of the four guest bedrooms and two suites is immaculately furnished with classically elegant furnishings and private terraces, though the best part of staying here is soaking away those chilly mountain nights in the outdoor glass-enclosed Jacuzzi that seats six.

Palo Alto Riverside Boutique Hotel (☎ 720 1076; www.paloaltoriverside.com; Calle Jaramillo Alto; ste US$165-250; P 🖳) Boquete's most upscale boutique hotel is a casual stunner of white-washed walls, exposed wooden beams, original hanging artwork, elegant picture windows and a hewn-stone fireplace. With six individually decorated guestrooms to choose from, the atmosphere at the Palo Alto Riverside Hotel is

CHIRIQUÍ PROVINCE

relaxed and intimate, and you expect a high level of personal attention here. Guests can also take advantage of the attached gourmet restaurant, which highlights a variety of world cuisines, as well as the holistic wellness center, which is the perfect spot for healing the body and the mind.

Eating & Drinking

Boquete has a numerous well-priced restaurants to choose from, and the produce and coffee here is among the best in Panama. However, you can hear a pin drop at night, so don't expect a wild night out on the town.

The area's fresh produce is sold at the mercado municipal, on the northeastern corner of the plaza. **Supermercado Romero** (Av A Este), a block east of the plaza, has all your basic groceries.

Café Ruiz (Calle 2 Norte; coffee US$1-2) The outdoor patio at Ruiz is a good spot to sip a cappuccino and watch the mist move across the mountains. It's also the epicenter of Panama's most famous coffee industry, so you can be sure that your brew had its origin in the surrounding hillsides.

Pastelería Alemana (pastry US$1-2; ☺ 8am-noon) On the main road 2km south of town, this gorgeous spot serves decadent fresh-baked pies alongside strong cups of coffee. If you're missing the motherland, this is also the best place in Boquete to buy authentic German breads.

Shalom Bakery Cafe (Calle 4a Sur; bagels US$1-2) There's no doubt about it – a bagel is a coveted food here in Latin America, and no matter how much rice and beans you eat, it just doesn't compare. It's hard to go past the poppy seeds with an extra smear of veggie cream cheese, but go ahead and have it any way you want.

El Sabrosón (Av Central; mains US$2-3) This much-loved local institution cooks up cheap and filling Panamanian cuisine served cafeteria style. Although Boquete is rapidly being colonized by gringo-friendly boutique eateries, this is one local institution that stays true to its roots.

Java Juice (Av Central; sandwiches US$3-4; ☺ 9am-10pm) Java Juice is your spot for veggie burgers, fresh salads, juices, iced cappuccinos and tasty milkshakes.

La Huaca (Av Central; pizzas US$5-7) North of the plaza, La Huaca is set in a beautifully restored colonial-style building with river and mountain views. It's locally famous for its tasty stone-baked pizzas, and if you phone ahead, they'll deliver one right to your door.

Bistro Boquete (Av Central; mains US$5-9; ☺ 11am-10pm) This handsome yet casual bistro in the center of town serves a range of eclectic cuisine ranging from grilled mountain trout to chili-rubbed filet mignon. For those with lighter appetites, Bistro Boquete also offers a variety of gourmet sandwiches and salads as well as a rich dessert selection.

Palo Alto (Calle Jaramillo Alto; mains US$6-12) This rustic charmer occupies an open-air spot alongside the rushing Río Palo Alto. The eclectic menu here receives high marks from the local expat community, and emphasizes fresh produce and locally raised meats.

Zanzibar (Av Central; drinks US$1-2) Nightlife in Boquete is about as common as a bad cup of coffee, though this low-key jazz bar has the cure for what ails ya. Your best chance of hearing live music is on weekends, though most of nights of the week you'll find a friendly face sitting at the bar.

Getting There & Around

Buses to Boquete depart from David's main bus terminal regularly (US$1.50, one hour, every 30 minutes) from 6am to 9:30pm. Buses to David depart from the northern side of Boquete's plaza every 30 minutes from 5am to 6:30pm. A taxi between David and Boquete costs around US$12.

Boquete's small size lends itself to easy exploration, and walking is a great way to see the area. The local (urbano) buses winding through the hills cost US$0.50. They depart on the main road one block north of the plaza. Taxis charge US$1 to US$2 to get to most places around town.

PARQUE NACIONAL VOLCÁN BARÚ

This 14,300-hectare national park is home to Volcán Barú, which is Panama's only volcano as well as the dominant geographical feature of Chiriquí. Although Volcán Barú is no longer active (there is in fact no record of its most recent eruption), it has not one but seven craters. Its summit, which tops out at 3478m, is the highest point in Panama, and on a clear day it affords views of both the Pacific and Caribbean coasts.

The national park is also home to the Sendero Los Quetzales, one of the most scenic treks in the entire country. As its name implies, the trail is one of the best places in

---

LOCAL LORE: THE RESPLENDENT QUETZAL

The Central American lore of the resplendent quetzal originated during the era of the Maya and the Aztecs, who worshipped a deity known as Quetzalcoatl (Plumed Serpent). This mythical figure was often depicted as wearing a crown of male quetzal tail feathers, and was believed to be responsible for bestowing corn upon humans.

A popular legend regarding the scarlet-red breast of the quetzal originated during the colonial period. In 1524 in the highlands of Guatemala, the Spanish conquistador Pedro de Alvarado defeated Tecun Uman, the last ruler of the Quiché people. As Uman lay dying, his spiritual guide, the quetzal, stained its breast with Uman's blood and then died of sadness. From that day on, all male quetzals bore a scarlet breast, and their song hasn't been heard since.

Even today, quetzals are regarded in Central America as a symbol of freedom, and it's commonly believed that they cannot survive if held in captivity. In Guatemala, the quetzal is the national bird, and its image is still depicted on the currency. And in Panama, the quetzal is something of a legend as birders from far and wide continue to brave the elements for the chance to see the most famous bird in Central America.

Central America to spot the rare resplendent quetzal, especially during the dry season (November to April). However, even if the Mayan bird of paradise fails to show, the park is home to over 250 bird species as well as pumas, tapirs and the *conejo pintado*, a spotted raccoon-like animal.

Information

Admission to the park (US$3) is paid at either of the trailheads leading to the summit or at the ranger station on the Cerro Punto side of the Sendero Los Quetzales.

The best time to visit is during the dry season, especially early in the morning when wildlife is most active.

Be advised that overnight temperatures can drop below freezing, and it may be windy and cold during the day, particularly in the morning – dress accordingly.

Sights

VOLCÁN BARÚ

There are entrances to the park, with summit access, on the eastern and western sides of the volcano. The eastern access to the summit, from Boquete, is the easiest, but it involves a strenuous uphill hike along a 14km dirt/mud road that goes from the park entrance – about 8km northwest of the center of Boquete – to the summit. If you drive or take a taxi as far up as you can and then walk the rest of the way, it takes about five or six hours to reach the summit from the park gate; walking from town would take another two or three hours each way. It's best to camp on the mountain at least one night; and you should be prepared

for the cold. Camping will also allow you to be at the top during the morning, when the views are best.

The other park entrance is just outside the town of Volcán, on the road to Cerro Punta. The rugged road into the park here – which soon becomes too rough for anything but a 4WD vehicle – goes only a short way off the main road, to the foot of the volcano. The view of the summit and the nearby peaks from this entrance is impressive, and there's a lovely loop trail that winds through secondary and virgin forest. The climb from this side is steep and technical.

SENDERO LOS QUETZALES

The park's most accessible trail is the scenic Sendero Los Quetzales (Quetzals Trail) near Cerro Punta. One of the most beautiful in Panama, this trail runs for 8km between Cerro Punta and Boquete, crossing back and forth over the Río Caldera. The trail can be done in either direction, but is easiest from west to east: the town of Cerro Punta is almost 1000m higher than Boquete, so hiking east is more downhill. A guide is not necessary as the trail is very well maintained and easily visible.

The trail itself takes about four to five hours walking west to east, though getting to and from the trailhead will take another couple of hours of walking on either side. A 4WD taxi can take you to the start of the trail on the Cerro Punta side for about US$12; taxi drivers know the area as Respingo. The trail is 5km uphill from the main road and 2km from the last paved road. When you exit the trail,

---

PAVING THE QUETZALS TRAIL

Ex-President Mireya Moscoso didn't exactly win the hearts and minds of Panamanians during her troubled tenure.

As Panama celebrated its centenary in 2003, nearly 20% of the country was unemployed, the social security system was in shambles and Colombian guerrillas were running amok in the Darién. In fact, about the only thing Moscoso was able to accomplish during her time as president was paying US$10 million to bring the Miss Universe pageant to Panama while parts of the country went without food. Of course, conservationists (and anyone with the slightest bit of regard for the environment) remember Moscoso best for her failed attempts to create a road between Boquete and Cerro Punta, which would have involved paving the Sendero Los Quetzales (Quetzals Trail).

Moscoso celebrated the New Year in 2002 by awarding US$4.6 million dollars in construction contracts to a selection of firms. Although the Quetzals Trail is the main artery of Parque Nacional Volcán Barú, and is home to hundreds of breeding pairs of one of the rarest birds in Central America, Moscoso changed the regulations on the national park in order to circumvent a lawsuit by ANCON, the country's largest private conservation organization. However, ANCON didn't relent, and instead created a broad coalition ranging from concerned citizens to left-wing activists. Although previous environmental issues were not mainstream news stories, the future of the Quetzals Trail became the hottest topic on the streets.

Fortunately, plans to pave the Quetzals Trail were put to rest following tremendous public uproar, though the reasons behind Moscoso's proposal remain unknown. Moscoso acted quickly, especially considering the project received national emergency status at its inception to speed along the ratification process. The end result was a triumph of conservation over development, though the environmentally conscious Panamanians fear that the battle is over, but the war is just beginning.

---

it's another 8km along the road to Boquete, though you may be able to catch a taxi along the road. In total, the hike is about 23km, so plan accordingly if you intend to walk the length of the trail.

After arriving in Boquete, you can stay overnight or take a bus to David and then Cerro Punta; note that the last Cerro Punta bus leaves David at 6pm. You can also leave your luggage at one of the hotels in David (the Purple House will store luggage, as will others) and save yourself the hassle of backtracking. Take only the bare essentials with you on the walk (and a little cash for a good meal and/or lodging in Boquete).

Sleeping

Camping (US$5) is available in the park and on the trail to the summit from the Boquete side, along the Sendero Los Quetzales or at the ranger station at the entrance to the Sendero Los Quetzales on the Cerro Punta side. You can also stay in bunk beds at the **ranger station** (dm US$5); bring your own food and bedding. If you plan to stay in the station, let them know you're coming by calling the **ANAM office** (☎ 775 3163) in David.

Getting There & Away

The trailhead leading to the summit of Volcán Barú is best accessed from the town of Boquete (p201) while the Sendero Los Quetzales is best approached from Cerro Punta (p212).

BUENA VISTA

If you're heading north towards Cerro Punta, Guadelupe or the entrance to the Parque Internacional La Amistad, an excellent place to stop for a few nights is the tiny hamlet of Buena Vista, which is located 16km north of the turnoff from the Interamericana. Here, you'll find the **Buena Vista B&B** (☎ 770 5605; claassendc@email.com; d/ste US$40/45; P ☐), a hidden gem of a country inn. Owned by a friendly Canadian couple named Dorothy and Claus, this mountain inn has two guestrooms and one suite that boast engrossing views of the Pacific Ocean and Volcán Barú – there's even an above-ground swimming pool on the grounds if you want to cool off after a hike through the forests.

The guestrooms are available for rent from 15 November through 15 May, while the whole house can be rented for the rest of the year. The tranquil town is perfect for anyone who's looking for a quiet refuge, or for a temporary home base in the Chiriquí highlands. Note that there is a minimum stay of three nights.

VOLCÁN
pop 8000

Volcán is the first town of major size that you pass along the route to La Amistad, though the town is dwarfed by its namesake. Clinging to the flanks of the towering Volcán Barú, the town of Volcán has a pleasant feel and serves as a good base for excursions, though there isn't a whole lot to do in the town itself. However, if you're feeling nostalgic for the days when Boquete was just another mountain town in Chiriquí, this may be the perfect stop for you.

The road that links Concepción and Volcán forks in the center of town: one arrow points left toward Río Sereno, on the Costa Rican border (47km); the other points right toward Cerro Punta (16km), the entrance to the Sendero Los Quetzales.

There's no tourist information in Volcán, though **Highland Adventures** (☎ 771 4413; ecoaizpurua@hotmail.com; Av Central, Volcán; ⏰ 7am-8pm) is a good source of information on the area (however biased they may be). With that said, Highland Adventures offer a rather good variety of guided tours and activities including rappelling beside a river, bicycle rides through the rainforest, kayaking and water tubing excursions, and guided climbs to the top of Volcán Barú. Most of the tours cost between US$30 and US$50, and are very fairly priced.

On the western side of the Concepción–Volcán road, 3km south of Volcán, you'll see **Arte Cruz Volcán – Artesania en Madera** (☎ 623 0313; ⏰ 8am-noon & 1-5:30pm), where artist José de la Cruz González makes fine-quality signs, sculptures and furniture out of wood as well as impressive etchings on crystal and glass. José was trained in fine arts in Italy and Honduras, and his work has been commissioned by buyers worldwide. Visitors are welcome, and José is happy to demonstrate and explain his art. Items are for sale, and he's more than happy to make you a personal souvenir in just a few minutes.

The ruins of the pre-Columbian culture at **Barriles** are about a five-minute drive from the center of town – the ruins are located on private land, but the family who lives there

accepts visitors. Major artifacts from the archaeological site, including statues, *metates* (flat stone platforms used for grinding corn), pottery and jewelry are currently on display in the Museo Antropológico Reina Torres de Araúz (p87) in Panama City, though there's nothing like getting a sense of the area where they came from.

Four-and-a-half kilometers from Volcán is the **Area Silvestre Protegida Lagunas de Volcán**, the highest lake system (1240m) in Panama. The two lakes here swell in the rainy season, and are extremely picturesque, with lush, virgin forest at their edges and Volcán Barú rising majestically in the background. The lakes and the woodlands around them are excellent sites for bird-watching – of special interest are the masked duck, the northern jacana, the rose-throated becard, the pale-billed woodpecker and mixed flocks of tanagers, flycatchers and antbirds. To get to the lakes from the Concepción–Volcán road, turn west onto Calle El Valle (near central Volcán) and follow the signs. No buses go to the lakes, but you can hire a taxi in Volcán to bring you here. If you take your own vehicle, be advised that there have been reports of thefts of belongings from vehicles here.

About 2.3km from the turnoff for Volcán is **Cabañas Las Huacas** (☎ 771 4363; cabins US$30-90; Ⓟ), which consists of five cutesy two-story cottages, each with a kitchen and a private hot-water bathroom. The cabins are scattered around a peaceful woodland setting, and there's even a small goose pond and a beautiful mountain vista to complete the scene. Cabins can accommodate one to eight people, and are fairly priced according to the size of your party.

Across from the Shell station near the Hotel Las Huacas, **Acropolis** (mains US$4-5) serves superb plates of traditional Greek food (souvlaki, moussaka and pastitsio), with some fantastic baklava for dessert. It's a charming little place and the friendly owners, Elisabet and George Babos, have a wealth of information about Volcán and the rest of Panama.

Buses from Volcán to David depart from the Shell station on Av Central every 15 minutes from 5am to 7:30pm (US$2.50, 1¾ hours). There are also pickup truck taxis available by the Río Sereno–Guadalupe fork in the road.

CHIRIQUÍ PROVINCE

SANTA CLARA

About 30km from Volcán, on the highway to Río Sereno, is the tiny village of Santa Clara, which is little more than a grocery store and a gas station. Although a passing motorist would never think twice about stopping here for the night, Santa Clara is home to the reader-recommended **Finca Hartmann** (☎ 775 5223; www.fincahartmann.com; cabins US$70; **P**)), a working shade-grown coffee farm that is situated in highland rainforest, and is home to a rich variety of wildlife on the grounds.

The owners, Ratibor Hartmann and his sons and daughter, are ardent supporters of conservation, and over the years they have hosted a number of Smithsonian-affiliated scientists. Currently the family rents out basic but handsomely constructed cabins for those wishing to enjoy the fantastic surroundings. Although there's no electricity here, the cabins have clean potable spring water, flush toilets and even hot showers.

The bird-watching here is simply superb, with over 280 unique species spotted on the grounds. Also, since the property is located between elevations of 1300m and 2000m, there are a number of accessible hiking trails that pass through a variety of habitats. Sr Hartmann is also an excellent host with a wealth of information – ask to see his 'museum' (a lifetime's collection of Panamanian insects and pre-Columbian artifacts).

The entrance to Finca Hartmann is located a few hundred meters past the gas station, on the left-hand side – look for the small sign.

PASO ANCHO

Continuing on along the road to the Parque Internacional La Amistad, another great place to stop for a few nights is **Las Plumas** (☎ 771 5541; www.las-plumas.com; guesthouses US$60-130; **P**), a friendly Dutch-owned spot that rests on the edge of Paso Ancho village. Las Plumas occupies a tranquil setting on 2.3 hectares of land, and consists of several roomy guesthouses that can accommodate four people in two bedrooms. Each guesthouse is beautifully furnished with solid wooden furniture, leather couches, tiled-bathrooms and orthopedic mattresses – there's even satellite TV, though this shouldn't distract you too much from the beauty of the surrounding forest. Note that there is a minimum stay of three nights.

Discounted weekly and monthly rates are also available.

BAMBITO

There's no shortage of tiny mountain towns along this route, though Bambito is worth a quick look, even if only to visit the **Truchas de Bambito** (admission US$0.50), a rainbow trout farm where thousands of fish are raised in outdoor ponds. A kilogram of fresh fish costs less than US$5, and the chilly spring-water–fed ponds produce some healthy (and very meaty) trout.

Just over 3km past Bambito in the hamlet of Nueva Suiza is **Hostal Cielito Sur B&B** (☎ 771 2038; www.cielitosur.com; r US$70-80 with breakfast; **P**) which is a great place to stop and recharge your body for the night. Owned by a friendly Panamanian-American couple, this delightful B&B offers four spacious guestrooms that have such incredible amenities as hot-water bathtubs, living rooms with fireplaces and private riverside patios. There's also a *bohío* (rustic hut) that's strung up with hammocks, and a shared bathhouse that's outfitted with a large Jacuzzi.

Before leaving Bambito, look for a small store 1.5km north of the Hotel Bambito named **Alina**, which sells fruit jam, candy and milkshakes using the region's famous wild strawberries. It's a charming spot that any local can point out to you – be sure to stock up on some edible goodies if you're on your way to an expedition in Parque Internacional La Amistad.

CERRO PUNTA

At an altitude of 1800m, this tranquil highland town is reminiscent of an Alpine village. Indeed, you'd be forgiven for thinking you were in Switzerland – as you near Cerro Punta, everything starts to look European, with meticulously tended agricultural plots and European-style houses with steep-pitched tin roofs. Not surprisingly, a Swiss colony was founded here many decades ago, and you can still hear Swiss-German spoken in the area.

Visitors come to Cerro Punta primarily during the dry season (January to April) in order to access the two nearby parks: Volcán Barú and La Amistad. However, the town itself makes a charming stop, especially since the area is known for its succulent strawberries – be sure to pick up a few at either **Fresa de Cerro Punta** or **Fresas Manolo**, both of which are located in the town center.

If you find yourself crashing here for the night, the **Hotel Cerro Punta** (☎ 771 2020; hotelcer@hotmail.com; s/d US$20/30; P) is located on the main road in town, and has your standard-issue concrete rooms, though picture windows and views of the surrounding hillsides definitely brighten up the rooms a bit. Plus, if you're on your way to either national park, enjoy the private hot-water bathroom – it's the last one you'll see for awhile. Whether you stay here or not, drop by the restaurant for a strawberry smoothie, a slice of strawberry pie or pancakes with strawberry compote. You get the idea by now – the local strawberries are delicious.

A bus runs from David to Cerro Punta en route to Guadalupe (US$3, 2¼ hours, every 15 minutes, from 5:30am to 6pm), stopping at Volcán and Bambito along the way. If you're coming from Costa Rica, you could catch this bus at the turnoff from the Interamericana at Concepción. If you're in Volcán, catch one of these buses at the parking lot opposite the Shell station.

If you're driving, the main road continues through Cerro Punta and ends at Guadalupe, 3km further. Another road takes off to the west, heading for the Las Nubes entrance to Parque Internacional La Amistad, 6.8km away – the turnoff is marked by a large wooden sign.

GUADALUPE

Three kilometers past Cerro Punta, Guadalupe is the end of the road, though it's a glorious area where you can walk among meticulously tended farms and gardens. This little community is full of flowers, and the agricultural plots curling up the steep hillsides are out of a picture book. With that said, please do respect the signs that read: 'Esteemed Visitor: we are making all Guadalupe a garden – please don't pick the flowers.'

About 600m beyond the Hotel Los Quetzales at the turnoff to the Cabañas Los Quetzales cabins, lies the **Finca Dracula Orchid Sanctuary** (☎ 771 2070; tour US$7), one of Latin America's finest orchid collections. There are over 2000 species on display here, and the extremely knowledgeable staff takes great pride in showing off this impressive sanctuary to interested guests.

The reader-recommended **Los Quetzales Lodge & Spa** (☎ 771 2182; fax 771 2226; www.losquetzales.com; r from US$120 per person with 3 meals; P ⬚), located in the center of town, is a favorite among hikers heading out to the Sendero Los Quetzales. Each of the rooms and dorms at Quetzales features vaulted ceilings, wood furnishings and private hot-water bathrooms, though most of the guests tend to congregate around the bar-restaurant and lounge. If you're traveling with your significant other, go ahead and splurge on one of the five cedar-walled suites, which feature a romantic hewn-stone fireplace, private bathtub and rainforest-facing balcony. All guests also have access to the on-site full-service spa, as well as access to a private network of trails inside the Parque Nacional Volcán Barú, less than an hour's walk from the hotel – the hotel can also provide transportation. Also on the premises are three riverside whirlpool spas and an equestrian center. WiFi is available.

A bus runs from David to Guadalupe (US$3, 2¼ hours, every 15 minutes from 5:30am to 6pm) via Volcán, Bambito and Cerro Punta. If you're driving, Guadalupe is the end of the road.

PARQUE INTERNACIONAL LA AMISTAD (LAS NUBES)

The 407,000-hectare Parque Internacional La Amistad was established jointly in 1988 by Panama and Costa Rica – hence its name, La Amistad (Friendship). In 1990, La Amistad was declared a Unesco World Heritage Site, and later became part of the greater Mesoamerican Biological corridor. In Panama, the park covers portions of Chiriquí and Bocas del Toro Provinces, contains seven of the 12 classified life zones and serves as a refuge for a great number of endangered flora and fauna.

Although most of the park's area is high up in the Talamanca Mountains and remains inaccessible, there is no shortage of hiking and camping opportunities available for intrepid travelers. Unlike the Wekso entrance in Bocas del Toro Province (see p237), the Las Nubes sector is home to an established trail network, and is more accessible to independent hikers. However, the Naso population has a more established presence in Wekso, so it's better to approach the park from Bocas if you're interested in spending some time with this indigenous group.

CHIRIQUÍ PROVINCE

CHIRIQUÍ PROVINCE

WATCHING WILDLIFE

Panama has long been established as a top destination for watching wildlife – nowhere else in the world are rainforests as easily accessible as they are in this tiny sliver of a country.

In the neotropical rainforests of Central America, over 300 different species of mammals have been tallied by scientists. In fact, this rapidly vanishing ecosystem is one of the few places on Earth where new species are still being uncovered. With the exception of a few versatile colonists from North America such as coyotes and white-tailed deer, the great bulk of mammals in Panama are new world specialists. The Neotropics are also the only place in the world where you can find two early experiments in mammalian evolution, namely sloths and anteaters. The forests of Central America are also home to eight species of primates and 24 species of carnivores, including six species of cat.

Of course, Central America's mammals aren't as diverse or conspicuous as its birds, and it's no secret that the region is firmly entrenched on the world birding circuit. In particular, Panama is home to over 500 species of birds, and is arguably the best destination in Central America for spotting rare endemics. However, as the land-bridge for the continents of North and South America, Panama offers the unique opportunity to spot migrant species in a completely new setting.

To make the most of your wildlife-watching experience, it's recommended that you pick up a good field guide, though the following list will help you get started:

- **Two- & Three-toed Sloths** Found only in Neotropical rainforests, sloths are the ancient remnants of a unique group of mammals that arose when South America was an isolated island. Curled up high above the rainforest floor, sloths can be hard to distinguish, though male three-toed sloths have a distinctive black and yellow patch on their back. True to their name, sloths spend about 16 hours a day asleep or inactive, but most of this time is devoted to digestion.

- **Mantled Howlers** Howler monkeys greet sunrise and sunset with deafening, booming calls that resonate through the forest for kilometers. These unmistakable calls, which become immediately familiar to travelers in the Neotropics, are thought to help space out different family groups. However, howlers are incredibly vocal animals, and will give a hoot and holler if they're disturbed or excited, especially if they see humans traipsing about on the forest floor. They're also good indicators of weather – howlers will cause a ruckus if there are thunder clouds on the horizon.

- **Jaguars** The jaguar is the largest cat in the Americas and the third-largest in the world, though unfortunately size does not convert into visibility. By virtue of their supreme position in the feeding hierarchy, jaguars are incredibly rare and elusive animals, though their evidence is all around, from dried spoors to fresh tracks. Interestingly enough, jaguars are the only big cat that routinely kills its prey by using its massive jaws to bite through the top of the victim's skull – most other cats simply suffocate their prey.

- **Parrots & Macaws** Even non-birders know a parrot or a macaw when they see one, and there's no better place in the world to observe these colorful birds than the Neotropics. Nearly half of the world's 332 species live exclusively in the region, and over 20 species including five macaws can be found in Panama. Although their basic form varies little, parrots range greatly in size, from the 12.5cm long parrotlet to the enormous macaws. Apart from their size, macaws can be identified by their huge bills, bare facial patch and long, tapered tails.

- **Toucans** Toucans are arguably the most recognizable birds in the Neotropics – a toucan's most outstanding feature is of course its spectacular multi-colored bill. Although in some species the bill looks as if it is too heavy for the bird, it is in fact full of air cavities and quite lightweight. Colorful and comical it may be, but the toucan bill is a powerful tool. Serrations on the upper mandible help grip slippery fruits, and help to intimidate the hapless birds whose nests are being raided.

Orientation & Information

Admission to the **park** (admission US$3, parking US$1, camping US$5; ☽ 8am-4pm) is paid at Las Nubes, near Cerro Punta (p212). Permits to camp in the park are payable at the ranger station.

If you plan to spend much time at Las Nubes, be sure to bring a jacket. This side of the park, at 2280m above sea level, has a cool climate – temperatures are usually around 24°C (75°F) in the daytime and drop to about 3°C (38°F) at night.

Activities

HIKING

Three main trails originate at Las Nubes ranger station. The **Sendero La Cascada** (Waterfall Trail) is a 3.4km roundtrip hike that takes in three *miradors* (lookout points) as well as a 45m-high waterfall with a lovely bathing pool. The **Sendero El Retoño** (Rebirth Trail) loops 2.1km through secondary forest, crosses a number of rustic bridges and winds through bamboo groves. The **Vereda La Montaña** (Mountain Lane) is a more strenuous 8km roundtrip hike that ascends Cerro Picacho.

WATCHING WILDLIFE

Although most of Parque Internacional Amistad is inaccessible terrain high up in the Talamanca, the park is home to a recorded 90 mammal species (including all six cat species) and more than 400 bird species (including resplendent quetzals and harpy eagles). For more, see the boxed text on the opposite page.

Sleeping & Eating

A **ranger station** at Las Nubes has a dormitory room with bunk beds where tourists can stay for US$5 per night. Due to the popularity of these beds among school groups from Canada and the USA, reservations are well advisable. To reserve a spot, call the **ANAM** (☎ 775 3163) in David or the co-op **restaurant** (☎ 771 2566) at the park entrance. Guests have access to the kitchen, so you'd be wise to stock up on provisions in Cerro Punta. You'll also need to bring your own bedding, and a mosquito net would also be a good idea.

Near the entrance to the park is a wonderful **restaurant** (dishes US$2-3) that is run by a local women's co-op, and has outdoor seating on a wooden patio where you can watch hummingbirds buzzing nearby. You can get plates of fresh-cooked foods like soup, rice and beans, and grilled cheese. In addition to bottled water, the restaurant also serves hot tea, which hits the spot on a chilly day, as well as homemade strawberry jam. The co-op restaurant is also a good place to inquire about local guides who can lead inexpensive excursions into primary rainforest.

Getting there & Away

The Las Nubes entrance is about 7km from Cerro Punta; a sign on the main road in Cerro Punta marks the turnoff. The road starts out good and paved, but by the time you reach the park, it's a rutted track suitable only for 4WD vehicles. A taxi will bring you from Cerro Punta for US$4 for up to two people, then US$2 per extra person.

FINCA LA SUIZA

If you travel along the paved road that crosses the Cordillera Central from the Interamericana to Chiriquí Grande, providing access to Bocas del Toro, you will pass a wonderful accommodation option that boasts some incredible hiking opportunities.

Located high in the Talamanca range about 41km from the Interamericana is **Finca La Suiza** (☎ 615 3774, 774 4030 in David; afinis@chiriqui .com; s/d with private bathroom US$31/40; ☽ closed Jun, Sep & Oct), a highly recommended place to stay that features 200 hectares of cloud forest and some of the best mountain views in Panama. The lodge has three clean, comfortable rooms with private hot-water bathrooms and large picture windows. On a clear day, you can see the islands in the Golfo de Chiriquí and the bright blue expanse of the Pacific Ocean. The enthusiastic and warm German owners – Herbert Brüllman and Monika Kohler – will also provide a home-cooked breakfast for about US$3.50 and dinner for US$9.

Also on the property are several kilometers of well-marked hiking trails, which pass through primary forest. The scenery features towering trees, hundreds of bird species and views of the Fortuna Park Forest Reserve, the Chiriquí mountains and the Pacific islands. Highlights include waterfalls, dipping ponds and superb vantage points across the forest canopy. Be advised that the owners keep dogs that roam freely at night, and for morning bird-watching, you'll need to ask for them to be tied up. Entrance to the trails costs guests US$8 for the duration of their stay; non-guests pay US$8 per day.

English, Spanish and German are spoken. Be sure to make reservations in advance as it's a long way to the next available lodging in Chiriquí Grande or David. For phone calls, the best time to call is between 7pm and 9pm. Note that the lodge and trails are closed throughout June, September and October – the area's wettest months.

To get to these accommodations, take any Changuinola-bound bus from David (hourly starting at 5am) and ask the driver to drop you off. Coming from the Interamericana, the lodge is to the right just after the Accel gas station (the only gas station on this road). Coming from the north, the lodge is on the left 1.3km after a toll plaza for trucks. You can leave luggage with the caretaker near the entrance gate while hiking.

Bocas del Toro Province

Located 32km from the Costa Rican border, the Archipiélago de Bocas del Toro consists of six densely forested islands, scores of uninhabited islets and Parque Nacional Marino Isla Bastimentos, Panama's oldest marine park. Although Bocas is Panama's principal tourist draw card, a fair measure of authenticity remains. Low-key development has maintained the charm of small-town Caribbean life and the absence of megahotels has preserved the archipelago's idyllic beauty.

The laid-back Caribbean vibe of Bocas is enhanced by the archipelago's spectacular natural setting. The islands are covered in dense jungles of vine tangles and forest palms that open up to pristine beaches fringed by reeds and mangroves. Beneath the water, an extensive coral reef ecosystem supports countless species of tropical fish while simultaneously providing some seriously gnarly surf breaks. In Bocas, hiking through huge swaths of rainforest to arrive at an empty stretch of wave-pounded shore is pretty much the norm. The mainland is home to the Panamanian half of the binational Parque Internacional La Amistad. Here, primary rainforests are home to megafauna including the elusive jaguar, as well as a handful of Ngöbe-Buglé settlements that are still clinging to their traditional ways of life.

Unfortunately, the secret is out, and although local opinion is divided on the merits of increased tourism in Bocas, there's no sign that development is likely to slow. Bulldozers have already started clearing land for condos and resorts, and the influx of foreign investors is an economic force to be reckoned with. It's difficult to predict the future of the province, but one thing is certain – see Bocas now as its unspoiled beauty won't last for much longer.

BOCAS DEL TORO PROVINCE

HIGHLIGHTS

- Soaking up the Caribbean charm of laid-back Bocas del Toro town before venturing out to the beaches and forests of **Isla Colón** (p219)
- Strolling along the pristine beaches of **Isla Bastimentos** (p229) while they're still pristine
- **Surfing** (p224) some of the sickest breaks you'll find in the Caribbean – just watch out for those shallow reefs!
- Exploring the Panamanian side of the **Parque Internacional La Amistad** (p237), home to one of Panama's remaining indigenous groups, the Naso (Teribe)
- Gliding by boat through the wildlife-rich wetlands at **Humedal de San-San Pond Sak** (p236)

Humedal de San-San Pond Sak
Isla Colón
Isla Bastimentos
Parque Internacional La Amistad

■ POPULATION: 95,000	■ AREA: 8,745 SQ KM	■ ELEVATION: SEA LEVEL TO 3300M

BOCAS DEL TORO PROVINCE

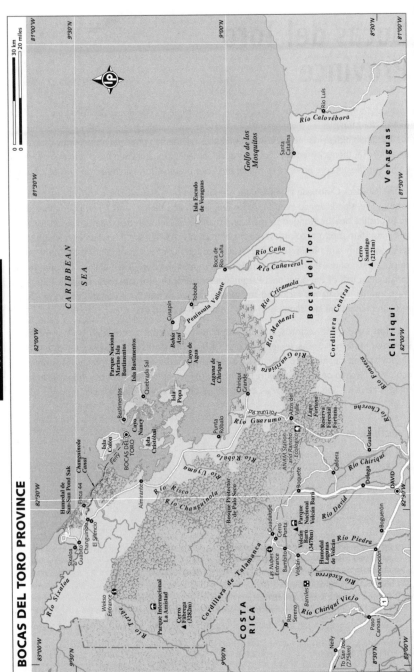

History

When Christopher Columbus visited Bocas del Toro in 1502 during his fourth and final New World voyage, he was so taken by the beauty of the area that he affixed his name to many sites, including Isla Colón (Columbus Island), Isla Cristóbal (Christopher Island) and Bahía de Almirante (Admiral's Bay).

During the 17th century, the archipelago became a haven for pirates. The buccaneers repaired their ships on the islands, built others with wood from their forests and fed upon the many sea turtles that nested on the beaches. The pirates are said to have buried treasure on a number of the islands, but to date none of this loot has been found (or at least reported).

Gold was not plentiful in Bocas del Toro, so the Spaniards did not colonize the region with the same ruthless efficiency that was unleashed on other parts of Panama. However, following the arrival of the French Huguenots on the coast in the 17th and 18th centuries, A Spanish militia was sent to Bocas to dislodge the settlers. As a result, the indigenous populations of Bocas were virtually wiped out by Old World diseases and Spanish swords.

In the early 19th century, wealthy aristocrats looking to establish themselves in the province arrived in Bocas with large numbers of black slaves from the USA and Colombia's San Andrés and Providencia Islands. However, when slavery was abolished in 1850, the blacks stayed put and began to eke out a living as fishers and subsistence farmers. Towards the end of the 19th century, Jamaican blacks joined them as the province's banana industry began to develop.

Bocas del Toro's banana industry dates from 1890, when three American brothers arrived in Bocas del Toro and founded the Snyder Brothers Banana Company. In the years that followed, the brothers planted banana trees all along the shores of the Laguna de Chiriquí. In 1899, however, the United Fruit Company planted itself in Bocas town and took complete control of the Snyders' young company. In the century that followed, United Fruit established vast plantations that stretched across the entire peninsula. They also constructed elaborate networks of roads, bridges and canals as well as entire towns and cities to house their workers.

Today, United Fruit is part of the multinational Chiquita Brands International. Chiquita's workers in Bocas del Toro Province grow and export three-quarters of a million tons of bananas annually. They also comprise the largest workforce in the province and the most diverse workforce in the country; on the payroll are West Indians, Latinos, Chinese and indigenous workers.

ARCHIPIÉLAGO DE BOCAS DEL TORO

For most travelers, the archipelago *is* Bocas – Caribbean clichés aside, there's no shortage of picture-postcard beaches, emerald waters and a healthy dose of swaying palms.

ISLA COLÓN

The archipelago's largest and most developed island is home to the provincial capital of Bocas del Toro, a colorful town of wooden houses built by the United Fruit Company in the early 20th century. Today, Bocas is a relaxed community of West Indians, Latinos and resident gringos, and the town's friendly atmosphere seems to rub off on everyone who visits. In fact, visitors to Bocas have a reputation for cancelling future travel plans – it's an easy place to get stuck and an even easier place to call home.

Owing to its infectious charm (and bargain real estate), Isla Colón is in the middle of a major development boom. Since the mid-1990s, foreign investors have been buying up land like hot cakes and there are constantly new hotels, restaurants and condos springing up around the island. Fortunately, there's still a heavy dose of local flavor left on Isla Colón, and the lack of beachside Burger Kings is a testament to the fact that development is still years behind similar destinations in nearby Costa Rica.

Bocas also serves as a convenient base for exploring the archipelago as *taxis marinos* (water taxis) ply the waters, and can whisk you away to remote beaches and snorkeling sites for a few dollars. However, as most travelers learn after spending their first few days idly wandering the streets, the allure of Bocas is simply slowing down and soaking up the Caribbean vibes.

Orientation & Information

Bocas town is laid out in a grid pattern, with most of the hotels and restaurants on Calle 3.

The only airport in the archipelago is on Av E, four blocks from Calle 3.

Note that the town, the archipelago and the province all share the name Bocas del Toro or simply Bocas. Isla Colón and Bocas del Toro town are also referred to as Bocas Isla.

Bocas gets an incredible amount of rain. Like other regions along the Caribbean coast, rainy and dry seasons don't mean much, especially since it can downpour for days on end in the 'dry' season. The least rainy time of year is mid-August to mid-October, when the seas are calm, and February and March.

For more information on the islands, see the useful English website www.bocas.org. For a rundown on the good, the bad and the ugly, check out the island's monthly bilingual publication, *The Bocas Breeze*.

EMERGENCY
Fire ☎ 103
Police ☎ 104

INTERNET ACCESS
Bocas Internet Café (Map 223; Calle 3; per hr US$2; ☺ 8am-10pm).
Bravo Center (Map 223; Calle 3; per hr US$2; ☺ 10am-7pm)

MEDICAL SERVICES
Hospital (Map 223; ☎ 757 9201; Av G; ☺ 24hr) The island's only hospital has a 24-hour emergency room.

MONEY
Banco Nacional de Panamá (Map 223; cnr Calle 4 & Av E; ☺ 8am-2pm Mon-Fri, to noon Sat) Exchanges traveler's checks and has a 24-hour ATM.

POST
Post office (Map 223; Governmental Bldg, Calle 3)

TELEPHONE
Cable & Wireless (Map 223; Calle 1)

TOURIST INFORMATION
ANAM (Map 223; Autoridad Nacional de Ambiente; ☎ 757 9442; Calle 1) Not really set up as a tourist information office, but they can answer questions about the national park or other protected areas. If you want to camp out in any of the protected areas, you must first get a permit from this or any other ANAM office.
IPAT tourist office (Map 223; Instituto Panameño de Turismo; ☎ 757 9642; ipatbocas@cwp.net .pa; ☺ 8:30am-3:30pm Mon-Fri) In Centro de Facilidades

Turísticas e Interpretación (Cefati) on the eastern waterfront. A color map in English and Spanish is available. The center also houses an interesting display on the natural and anthropological history of the area.

Dangers & Annoyances
The surf can be dangerous on some of the island's beaches, and there are frequently strong riptides – use caution when going out into the waves. For more info on what to do if you're caught in a rip, see the boxed text, p222.

Unlike in most other places in Panama, tap water is not safe to drink in Bocas del Toro. Bocas town has a water treatment plant, but locals say the tap water isn't to be trusted. The water is certainly fine for brushing your teeth, but you're probably best off siding with caution and purchasing bottled water for drinking. Bottled water is readily available and costs about US$1.50 for a 1.5L bottle. Gallon jugs for US$2 are better value if you can find them.

Bocas del Toro is a conservative place and local law prevents men (and obviously women) from walking down the streets topless. Even if you are on your way to the beach, wear a shirt or you will be sent back to your hotel if spotted by police.

Sights
BOCA DEL DRAGO
Located on the western side of Isla Colón, this sleepy beach is famed for its huge numbers of starfish, particularly around the bend. The calm and relaxed atmosphere at Boca del Drago is perfect for beach bums, though the swimming and snorkeling here is good, especially when the sea is calm and the water is clear. Although not as stunning as the wilderness beaches on Isla Bastimentos, the lack of surge means that this is the safest spot for swimming in the archipelago.

The beach is also home to a branch of the **Institute for Tropical Ecology and Conservation** (Map 221; www.itec-edu.org), a nonprofit education, research and conservation organization. Specifically, the field station at Boca del Drago offers field ecology courses to undergraduate and graduate students, provides facilities for tropical researchers, operates marine conservation programs and engages in community development. For more information on research, employment and volunteer opportunities at the station, contact ITEC via email.

ARCHIPIÉLAGO DE BOCAS DEL TORO

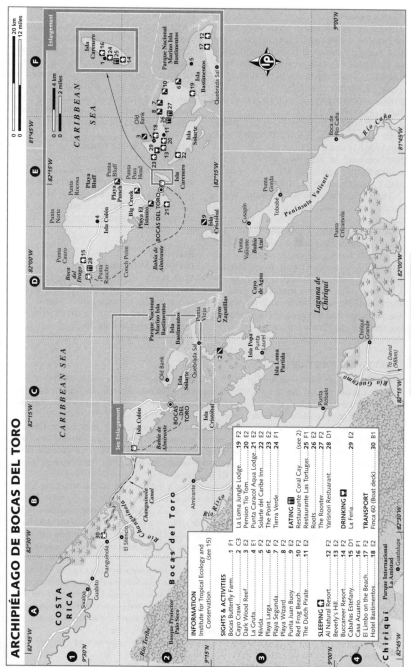

INFORMATION
Institute for Tropical Ecology and
Conservation.......................(see 15)

SIGHTS & ACTIVITIES
Bocas Butterfly Farm.................1 F1
Cayo Crawl..................................2 C3
Dark Wood Reef..........................3 E2
La Gruta.....................................4 E1
Nivida...5 F2
Playa Larga.................................6 F2
Playa Segunda............................7 F2
Playa Wizard...............................8 F2
Punta Juan Buoy.........................9 F2
Red Frog Beach.........................10 F2
The Dutch Pirate........................11 F2

SLEEPING
Al Natural Resort.......................12 E2
Beverly's Hill.............................13 E2
Buccaneer Resort......................14 F2
Cabañas Estéfany......................15 D1
Casa Acuario.............................16 F1
El Limbo on the Beach..............17 F2
Hotel Bastimentos....................18 E2

La Loma Jungle Lodge...............19 F2
Pension Tío Tom........................20 E2
Punta Caracol Aqua Lodge.......21 E2
Solarte del Caribe Inn...............22 E2
The Point...................................23 E2
Tierra Verde...............................24 F1

EATING
Restaurante Coral Cay..............(see 2)
Restaurante Las Tortugas..........25 F1
Roots..26 F2
The Rooster...............................27 F2
Yarisnori Restaurant..................28 D1

DRINKING
La Feria.....................................29 E2

TRANSPORT
Finca 60 (Boat deck).................30 B1

BOCAS DEL TORO PROVINCE

BOCAS DEL TORO PROVINCE

OTHER BEACHES

There is a string of beaches on the eastern side of Isla Colón that can be reached by a road that skirts up the coast from town. There's no public transportation to the beaches, but a 4x4 taxi will take you to any of them and pick you up at an appointed time for a negotiable price – expect to pay US$16 for a round-trip taxi to Playa Bluff.

Playa El Istmito, also called Playa La Cabaña, is the closest beach to town, though it's on Sand Fly Bay and the *chitras* (sand flies) that live here have an itchy bite. This is not the most attractive beach, and unless you're walking, it's worth heading further north.

Further up the coast is **Playa Punch**, which is dangerous for swimming but good for surfing.

After you round Punta Bluff, the road takes you along **Playa Bluff**, a secluded wilderness beach that is pounded by intense waves. Although you wouldn't want to get into the water here without a board, the soft, yellow sand and palm-fringed shores are pristine. Playa Bluff stretches for 5km all the way to Punta Rocosa and serves as a nesting area for sea turtles from May to September.

LA GRUTA

If sun, sand and surf aren't your persuasion, then consider a trip to **La Gruta** (Map 221; The Cavern; admission US$1), where you can wade through waist-high water while trying not to disturb the thousands of sleeping bats overhead. The entrance to the cave, which is marked by a statue of the Virgin Mary, is located 8km from Bocas town along the road to Boca del Drago – a round-trip taxi should cost about US$10.

BOCAS BUTTERFLY FARM

A great afternoon trip from Bocas town is this adorable **butterfly farm** (Map 221; ☎ 648 35741; admission US$5; ☯ 10pm-4am), which houses species from every corner of Panama. Water taxis can whisk you away from Bocas town to the entrance to the farm on nearby Isla Carenero for only US$1.

Activities

DIVING & SNORKELING

With nearly 40 rivers unloading silt into the seas around Bocas del Toro, the archipelago's waters are notorious for their poor visibility. If it has rained a lot in recent days, visibility may be limited to only 3m.

SURVIVING A RIPTIDE

Riptides account for the majority of ocean drownings, though a simple understanding of how these currents behave can save your life. Rip currents are formed when excess water brought to shore by waves returns to the sea in a rapidly moving depression in the ocean floor. They are comprised of three parts: the feeder current, the neck and the head.

The feeder current consists of rapidly moving water that parallels the shore, but isn't always visible from the beach. When this water reaches a channel, it switches direction and flows out to sea, forming the neck of the rip. This is the fastest moving part of the riptide and can carry swimmers out to see with a speed of up to 10km/h. Finally, the head of the riptide current occurs past the breakers where the current quickly dissipates.

If you find yourself caught in a riptide, immediately call for help as you only have a few seconds before being swept out to sea. However, conserve your energy and do not fight the current – this is the principal cause of drownings and it's almost impossible to swim directly back to shore. Instead, try one of two methods for escaping a rip. The first is to tread water and let yourself be swept out past the breakers. Once you're in the head of the rip, you can swim out of the channel and ride the waves back to shore. Or, you can swim parallel or diagonal to shore until you're out of the channel.

Rip currents usually occur on beaches with strong surf, but temporary rips can occur anywhere, especially when there is an off-shore storm or during low tide. Fortunately, there are indicators such as the brownish color on the surface of the water that is caused by swept-up sand and debris. Also, look for surface flattening, which occurs when the water enters a depression in the ocean floor and rushes back out to sea. If you're ever in doubt about the safety of a beach, it's best to inquire locally about swimming conditions.

Remember, rips are fairly survivable as long as you relax, don't panic and conserve your energy.

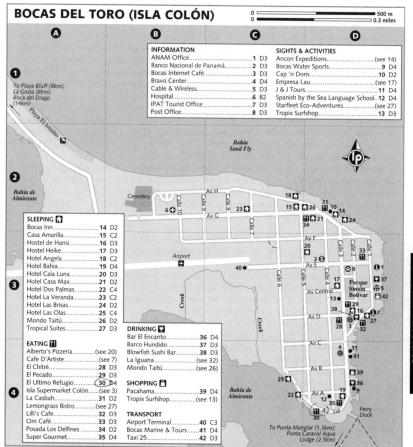

BOCAS DEL TORO (ISLA COLÓN)

INFORMATION
ANAM Office..................................**1** D3
Banco Nacional de Panamá.........**2** D3
Bocas Internet Café......................**3** D3
Bravo Center.................................**4** D4
Cable & Wireless...........................**5** D3
Hospital..**6** B2
IPAT Tourist Office........................**7** D3
Post Office.....................................**8** D3

SIGHTS & ACTIVITIES
Ancon Expeditions..........................(see 14)
Bocas Water Sports.......................**9** D4
Cap 'n Dons................................**10** D2
Empresa Lau................................(see 17)
J & J Tours..................................**11** D4
Spanish by the Sea Language School..**12** D4
Starfleet Eco-Adventures...............(see 27)
Tropix Surfshop...........................**13** D3

SLEEPING
Bocas Inn....................................**14** D2
Casa Amarilla..............................**15** C2
Hostel de Hansi...........................**16** D3
Hostel Heike................................**17** D3
Hotel Angela...............................**18** C2
Hotel Bahía.................................**19** D4
Hotel Cala Luna...........................**20** D3
Hotel Casa Max............................**21** D2
Hotel Dos Palmas.........................**22** C4
Hotel La Veranda.........................**23** C2
Hotel Las Brisas...........................**24** D2
Hotel Las Olas..............................**25** C4
Mondo Taitú................................**26** D3
Tropical Suites..............................**27** D3

EATING
Alberto's Pizzeria.........................(see 20)
Cafe D'Artiste..............................(see 7)
El Chitré......................................**28** D3
El Pecado....................................**29** D3
El Ultimo Refugio.........................**30** D4
Isla Supermarket Colón.................(see 3)
La Casbah....................................**31** D2
Lemongrass Bistro........................(see 27)
Lilli's Cafe....................................**32** D3
Om Café......................................**33** D3
Posada Los Delfines.....................**34** D2
Super Gourmet............................**35** D4

DRINKING
Bar El Encanto............................**36** D4
Barco Hundido............................**37** D3
Blowfish Sushi Bar.......................**38** D3
La Iguana....................................(see 32)
Mondo Taitú................................(see 26)

SHOPPING
Pacahama...................................**39** D4
Tropix Surfshop...........................(see 13)

TRANSPORT
Airport Terminal..........................**40** C3
Bocas Marine & Tours..................**41** D4
Taxi 25..**42** D3

BOCAS DEL TORO PROVINCE

Although experienced divers accustomed to crystal clear Caribbean diving may be disappointed with Bocas, the islands still have much to offer. The emerald green waters of the archipelago are home to the usual assortment of tropical species and with a little luck you might see barracuda, stingrays, dolphins and nurse sharks. Better sites include **Dark Wood Reef**, northwest of Bastimentos; **Hospital Point**, a 50ft wall off Cayo Nancy; and the base of the buoy near **Punta Juan** north of Isla Cristóbal.

Starfleet Eco Adventures (Map 223; ☎ 757 9630; www.explorepanama.com/starfleet.htm; Calle 1) and **Bocas Water Sports** (Map 223; ☎/fax 757 9541; www.bocaswatersports.com; Calle 3) offer diving trips. They cost around US$35 for a one-tank, one-site dive, and US$50 for two tanks and two sites. PADI

open-water and advanced-diver courses are available. Starfleet offers instruction in English and enjoys a sterling reputation amongst locals and travelers.

BOAT

The most popular tours in the area are all-day snorkeling trips, which are perfect for nondivers who want a taste of the area's rich marine life. A typical tour costs US$15 per person, and goes to Dolphin Bay, Cayo Crawl, Red Frog Beach and Hospital Point. A trip to the distant Cayos Zapatillas costs US$20 (plus an additional US$10 for admission to the marine park), and includes lunch, a laze on the beach and a jungle walkabout on Cayo Zapatilla Sur.

SURFING IN BOCAS

Although everyone and their grandmother seems to have picked up surfing in nearby Puerto Viejo, Costa Rica, Bocas del Toro is still emerging as an international surf destination. However, the archipelago offers an excellent mix of beginner beach swells, ripping reef breaks and some seriously suicidal barrels. The following is a rundown of the major surfing spots in the archipelago, though the local fishers assure us that this list is just scratching the surface of what's out there. For a full surfer's map, featuring the following spots, see Map pp68–9.

If you don't have your own board, you can rent fairly thrashed surfboards for US$10 to US$15 per day from **Tropix Surfshop** (Map 223; ☎ 757 9727; ☽ 9am-7pm; Calle 3) in Bocas town. The guys at **Mondo Taitú** (Map 223; ☎ /fax 757 9425; Av H; dm/s/d US$7/8/16) also rent boards for negotiable prices. If you're heading out to Isla Bastimentos or Isla Carenero, you will need to arrange your board in advance as there are no surf shops on either island.

Remember that unlike the Pacific, which has fairly consistent sets of waves most days of the year, the Caribbean can be hit or miss. If the swells are out, the ocean will be calm and glassy, so grab your suntan lotion and work on your tan; if the swells are in, the ocean will be angry and surging, so grab your board and work on your carving. But seriously – watch out for those shallow reefs!

Isla Colón

Beginner surfers looking for a bit of reef experience should check out **Playa Punch**, which offers a good mix of lefts and rights. Although it can get heavy when big, Punch generally offers some of the kindest waves around.

Just past Punch en route to Playa Bluff is a popular reef break known as **Dumpers**. This left break can get up to 3m and should only by ridden by experienced surfers as wiping out on the reef here is a dangerous affair. There is also an inner break known as **Inner Dumps**, which also breaks left but is more forgiving than its outer brother.

Be careful walking out on the reefs as they are sharp and full of urchins – don't go barefoot. If you wipe out and get cut up, be sure to properly disinfect your wounds. Although saltwater heals, seawater doesn't, especially in the Caribbean where the water temperature means that the ocean is full of live bacteria.

The island's most notorious surf spot is **Playa Bluff**, which throws out powerful barreling waves that break in shallow water along the beach, and have a reputation for snapping boards (and occasionally bones). Although the waves close quickly, the tubes here are truly awesome, especially when the swells are strong.

Isla Bastimentos

If you're looking for a solid beach break, both **Wizard Beach** and **Red Frog Beach** offer fairly constant sets of lefts and rights that are perfect for beginner and intermediate surfers. When the swells are in however, Wizard occasionally throws out some huge barrels, though they tend to close up pretty quickly.

Isla Carenero

If you've got some serious surfing experience under your belt, then you're going to want to build up the courage to tackle **Silverbacks**, an enormous barreling right that breaks over a reef and can reach heights of over 5m. On a good day, Silverbacks is a truly world-class break that wouldn't look out of place on Hawaii's North Shore. Silverbacks breaks off the coast, so you're going to need to hire a water taxi (US$3 round-trip) to get out there.

Many 'tours' are really little more than boat transportation to a pretty spot. If you have your own snorkel gear (or if you rent it), you can also get the local boaters to take you around the area in their small, motorized canoes. They know several good snorkeling spots and this option can be cheaper than the dive companies' trips, depending on the size of your group. Agree on a price before you go.

In addition to the dive operators listed above, a recommended tour operator is **J & J Tours** (Map 223; ☎ 757 9915; transparentetour@hotmail.com; Calle 3).

KAYAKING

Although you will need to be wary of boat traffic and the occasional swell, a great way to travel between islands is by sea kayak. **Cap 'n Dons** (Map 223; ☎ 757 9248; Calle 3; ⏰ 9am-7pm) rents kayaks for US$10 per day as well as paddle boats, sailboats and a big water trampoline.

BIKING

Whether you're heading to Boca del Drago on the paved road, or taking the dirt path to Playa Bluff, a bike can seriously increase your mobility. Note that the bike ride to Boca del Drago is taxing, especially when the sun is beaming. If you're unsure of your fitness level, it's advised that you head to Punta Bluff instead, even though the road can flood after heavy rains. You can rent a bike for US$8 per day and support a local Kuna by heading to **Empresa Lau** (Map 223; Calle 3; ⏰ 9am-7pm), located next to Hostel Heike.

HIKING

If you're looking to seriously get off the beaten path, there is a network of undeveloped hiking trails that fan out across the island. One of the more popular hikes starts at the end of the coastal road in Mimbi Timbi and carries on along the coast to Boca del Drago. You will need about six hours of daylight to complete the hike and you must carry in all your fresh water. The trail winds past caves, caverns and plenty of vine-entangled jungle. A bike will help speed things up a bit, though you will be carrying it part of the way, especially if it's been raining recently.

BIRD-WATCHING

While the bird-watching on the islands isn't as good as that on the mainland, it can still be rewarding. Particularly rare birds, or at least those poorly known to Panama, have been recorded on the islands in recent years, and include the semiplumbeous hawk, white-tailed kite, zone-tailed hawk, uniform crake, olive-throated parakeet, red-fronted parrotlet, lesser nighthawk, green-breasted mango, chestnut-colored woodpecker, snowy cotinga, brown-capped tyrannulet, yellow-bellied elaenia, stub-tailed spadebill, purple martin, tree swallow and black-cowled oriole.

FISHING

The best budget option for aspiring anglers is to go surf casting with the local water-taxi drivers. The hand lines are a bit tricky at first, though you'll get the hang of it. It's best to go early in the morning when the fish are biting; prices are negotiable.

Courses

Spanish by the Sea (Map 223; ☎ /fax 757 9518; www.spanish bythesea.com; Calle 4) is a reader-recommended language school that offers affordable Spanish classes in a relaxed setting. Rates for group/private lessons are US$70/US$130 for two hours a day, five days a week, though cheaper rates are available for more comprehensive packages and longer stays. The school also offers a popular traveler's survival Spanish course (US$40) that includes six hours of instruction.

Homestays can be arranged (US$12 per night with breakfast), or you can rent one of their simple dorms (US$7.50 per night) or private rooms (US$12.00 per night). Spanish by the Sea also organizes parties, dance classes and open lectures. English, Spanish, French, German and Dutch are spoken.

Festivals & Events

Bocas celebrates all of Panama's holidays, with a few enjoyable local ones besides. Annual events celebrated on Bocas and Bastimentos include the following:

May Day (May 1) While the rest of Panama is celebrating Labor Day, the Palo de Mayo (Maypole dance) is performed by local girls.

Día de la Virgen del Carmen (third Sunday in July) Bocatoreños make a pilgrimage to La Gruta, the cave in the middle of the Isla Colón, for a mass in honor of the Virgen del Carmen.

Feria del Mar (September 28 to October 2) The 'Fair of the Sea' is held on Playa El Istmito, a few kilometers north of Bocas.

Fundación de la Provincia de Bocas del Toro (November 16) Celebrating the foundation of the province in 1904, this is a day of parades and other events; it's a big affair, attracting people from all over the province, including the Panamanian president.

Día de Bastimentos (November 23) Bastimentos Day is celebrated on the island with a huge parade and drumming demonstrations.

Sleeping

The town of Bocas has become a major tourist draw. Both expats and locals run hotels and a few Bocas residents rent rooms out of their houses. Reservations are a good idea between December and April and during national holidays and local festivals. The following accomodations are featured on Map p221.

IN TOWN
Budget

our pick **Mondo Taitú** (☎ /fax 757 9425; Av H; dm/s/d US$7/8/16) This legendary backpacker joint is reason enough to cancel your travel plans and post up in Bocas for weeks on end. Owned and managed by three fun-loving Americans, Mondo is a wacky treehouselike building that is locally famous for its wild events. On Tuesdays and Fridays, the bar at Mondo hosts a variety of festivities ranging from 'Sake Bomb' parties to '80s Night,' though you can kick back here any time with a beer in one hand and a hookah in the other. All of the usual backpackers amenities are on offer here including a communal kitchen, lounge area, laundry facilities, free bikes and surfboards.

Hostel Heike (☎ 757 9708; Calle 3; dm US$8) The sister hostel to Mondo Taitú, Heike proudly serves as the yin to Mondo's yang. Awash with colorfully painted murals and natural woods, Heike is the perfect spot for chilling out and soaking up the Caribbean ambience. The upstairs balcony overlooks the town's park and is a perfect spot to indulge in a cold beer and a good book. Like Mondo, the amenities at Heike are perfectly suited to backpackers.

Hostal de Hansi (☎ 757 9932; Calle 3; s US$10-16, d $US22) Run by a cheery German woman, this intimate spot features well-designed rooms with colorful wooden planks, set amid a tropical garden. Cheaper singles have shared facilities while the more expensive rooms and doubles have private bathrooms. In the grand German tradition, the hostel is immaculately clean and well run.

Hotel Las Brisas (☎ 757 9248; brisasbocas@cwp.net.pa; Calle 3; d with private bathroom US$17-40; 🟦) On the northern end of Calle 3, Hotel Las Brisas is built over the water and offers a variety of rooms to meet your budget. Cheaper rooms are definitely starting to show their age, but a few extra dollars can get you nicer furnishings, better views and even air-con. Ask to see a few rooms and shop around – variety is the spice of life.

Hotel Casa Max (☎ 757 9120; casa1max@hotmail.com; Av G; s/d/tr with private bathroom US$20/25/30) This Dutch-owned spot offers a handful of brightly painted wooden rooms with high ceilings and private hot-water bathrooms. Some of the rooms come complete with dreamy balconies, which overlook the town and the ocean. The free breakfast of fresh fruits and strong coffee sweetens the deal.

Hotel Dos Palmas (☎ 757 9906; Av Sur; d/tr with private bathroom US$22/28) Proudly touting the hotel as '100% Bocatoreño,' the friendly owners of Dos Palmas offer basic wooden rooms with old-fashioned furnishings. The entire hotel sits above the water and boasts exceptional views of the bay. If you're looking for a locally run spot, the Dos Palmas is your best choice.

Casa Amarilla (☎ 757 9938; Calle 5; d with private bathroom US$35; 🟦 🖥) Run by a lovely retired couple from Denver, this quaint yellow house is one of the best deals on the island. For only a few more dollars more than other budget hotels, you can rack in the amenities, which include cable TV, private hot showers and free wireless internet. The owners are also always on-site to answer any of your questions, or to share a morning cup of coffee with you.

Midrange & Top End

Hotel La Veranda (☎ 757 9211; www.explorepanama.com/veranda.htm; Av G; d US$30-50) This lovely residence-turned-inn was built in 1910 and has been maintained with pride, down to its gleaming hardwood floors and pretty antique windows and doors. None of the six guest rooms are alike, except that all contain early-20th-century antique furnishings. There's a decked-out veranda, which is a great spot for a morning cup of coffee, an afternoon sundowner or a strong nightcap.

Hotel Las Olas (☎ 757 9930; Calle 6; s/d with private bathroom US$37/42; 🟦 🖥) Like a beacon for sailors (or surfers) at sea, the new Hotel Las Olas shines bright yellow from the southern tip of Bocas town. It's a beautiful three-story wooden affair that is built on stilts and acts as a magnet for travelers looking for simple comfort with great seaside atmosphere. The rooms themselves are constructed entirely of polished wood and there's a full range of amenities on offer including private hot-water showers, air-con and wireless internet.

Hotel Angela (☎ /fax 757 9813; www.hotelangela.com; Av H; d US$40-82; 🟦) Hotel Angela is a perennial seaside favorite in a quiet section of Bocas town. The positive vibe, terrific service and perched-over-the-water location has proven a winning combination for this veteran of the Bocas hotel rat race. Choose from units with side-facing balconies or those with ocean views, or splurge on the deluxe suite complete with a Jacuzzi and stunning vistas.

Hotel Bahía (☎ 757 9626; www.panamainfo.com /hotelbahia; Calle 3; d from US$45; ☒) This historic Bocas landmark was built in 1905 by the United Fruit Company to serve as its local headquarters. Today the building serves as a modest hotel, though a series of careful restorations have revived the original splendor of this fine building. The American pine lining the halls is original, as are the oak floors throughout the building, though the modern bathrooms were, needless to say, a later addition.

Hotel Cala Luna (☎ 757 9066; www.calalunabocas .com; Calle 5; s/d/tr/q US$45/55/65/75; ☒ ▣) Built atop legendary Alberto's Pizza, the Italian-owned Cala Luna was built with an impeccable attention to detail. The entire hotel, inside and out, is constructed out of wood and features cathedral windows, brightly lit outdoor spaces and crisp, functional rooms. As an added bonus, guests can watch planes coming in for a landing 30m above their heads from a pair of lookouts on the roof.

Bocas Inn (☎ /fax 757 9226; www.anconexpeditions .com; Av H; d from US$66; ☒) Managed by the highly recommended Ancon Expeditions of Panama (p89), this water's-edge lodge caters primarily to guests on private tours. Spotless rooms with hardwood floors and rustic furnishings are spacious and altogether lovely, and the communal seaside porches are great for lounging around with other guests. It's worth booking a room here through the Ancon office in Panama City, especially since they offer a variety of well-priced packages that include lodging, meals, transfers and tours.

Tropical Suites (☎ 757 9081; www.tropical-ste.com; Calle 1; ste with/without seaview US$140/174; ☒ ▣) If you can't live without your creature comforts, then look no further – Tropical Suites boasts the island's only elevator! Of course, the amenity list doesn't stop there, especially since this bright and cheery hotel consists entirely of shiny new suites. The list goes on, but the most attractive perks include flat-screen TVs, high-tech air-con units, modern bathrooms with Jacuzzis and kitchens with range-tops and refrigerators.

AROUND THE ISLAND

Cabañas Estefany (Map p223; ☎ 618 3155; d US$15; 2-/8-person cabin US$30/55) This cute clutch of cabañas

is one of the only places on Isla Colón to be located on a beach. In addition to basic rooms with shared bathrooms, Cabañas Estefany has small two-person cabins with a bathroom and kitchen, and larger cabins for up to eight people. The cabins are often booked with researchers from the nearby Institute for Tropical Ecology and Conservation, so it's recommended that you call ahead.

our pick Punta Caracol Aqua Lodge (Map p223; ☎ 612 1088; www.puntacaracol.com; s/d with 2 meals & tours in low season US$290/355, high season US$365/440) If you can afford it, do it! Accessible only by boat, this luxury ecolodge is built of wood and *penca* (palm tree leaves) in conformity with traditional Caribbean architecture. Two-story stand-alone cabins feature upstairs bedrooms that are made for romance with a king-size canopy bed, big skylight window with canvas closures, and soft lighting. The living room has fine bamboo furniture and a pair of couches opening onto a private porch-dock with hammock and sun. The small bathroom exudes the same classic, tropical style with bamboo detailing and signature. And the chef is French, so you can expect to eat divinely!

Eating
IN TOWN

Although Bocas town is a small place, there's no shortage of great restaurants serving up an impressive offering of international cuisine. If you're self-catering, the **Isla Supermarket Colon** (Map 223; Calle 3) is the largest supermarket on the island, though the boutique **Super Gourmet** (Map 223; Calle 3) has everything from Japanese *panko* (bread crumbs) to California wines.

A number of food carts ply their wares around town – local favorites include the 'Chicken Lady,' the 'Batido Lady,' the 'Chicken Sandwich Guy' and the infamous 'Meat-on-a-stick Guy.'

Panadería Europeo (Av D; pastries US$0.75-1.50) Sample the island's best baked goods at this tasty bakery, though be warned that the huge, fluffy cinnamon rolls are highly addictive. Wash it all down with a cup of gourmet brew for a fine start to the day.

Cafe D'Artiste (Map 223; Calle 1; coffee US$1.50) This eclectic café is a great place for a freshly brewed cup of Panama's finest grains and you can't beat the views of the harbor and nearby islands. Don't leave without perusing the excellent art and curios that are available for purchase.

BOCAS DEL TORO PROVINCE

Posada Los Delfines (Map 223; Calle 5; breakfast special US$2.50) The cheapest breakfast on the island is yours to be had at this hotel restaurant, which is a popular spot for locals in the know. Order your eggs anyway you want and don't be afraid to get a second helping of rice and beans.

El Chitré (Map 223; Calle 3; plates US$2-3) Adored by locals and travelers alike, this no-frills cafeteria-style hole-in-the wall is the best spot in town for cheap but tasty grub. It will fill the stomach without emptying the wallet and aficionados claim it's the best meal on the island.

Lilli's Cafe (Map 223; Calle 1; plates US$3-6) Whether you feast on an omelet packed with fresh veggies or a club sandwich made with homemade bread, be sure to go heavy on the homemade 'Killin' Me Man' pepper sauce. After all, nothing says the Caribbean like an ocean view and a fire on the palate.

Alberto's Pizzeria (Map 223; Calle 5; pizzas US$4-6) Nothing fills the gut like a big and cheesy pepperoni pizza, especially if you've been on the road for a while and are in need of comfort food. Stop by this Italian-run spot, and long-time resident chef Alberto will make sure you're well taken care of.

Om Café (Map 223; Av H; mains US$6-10) There are only a handful of tables on offer at this handsome outdoor Indian restaurant, which serves up traditional family recipes that are guaranteed to make your brow sweat. Unadventurous eaters can choose from a variety of standards including tandoori chicken or tikka masala, though die-hard Indian fans will enjoy the chili-packed vindaloo.

El Pecado (Map 223; Calle 3; mains US$8-13; 5pm-10pm) This well-established upstairs restaurant near the park is one of Bocas' best-known institutions. El Pecado specializes in unique Thai-Panamanian combinations, such as fillet of fish smothered in coconut milk–based curry and spicy chicken satays, and uses fresh, local produce.

Lemongrass Bistro (Map 223; Calle 1; mains US$8-12) A new contender in the ever-changing Bocas restaurant scene, this Asian-fusion restaurant gets rave reviews from the local gringo community. The breezy, open-air deck is perfect for enjoying the cool, ocean breezes, though you shouldn't let this distract you from the flavors and aromas of what's cooking.

El Ultimo Refugio (Map 223; 640 1878; Av Sur; mains US$8-13; 11:30am-10pm) This rustic, mellow place on the edge of the sea specializes in seafood dishes such as calamari, red snapper

and tiger prawns. It's located in a quiet spot on the southern edge of the town, which makes it a great spot for a quiet, romantic dinner out.

La Casbah (Map 223; Av H; mains US$8-15) Whether you're a shoestringer living on US$20 a day or you're dropping dollars like they were going out of style, everyone needs a good meal sometimes and there's no better place than this Mediterranean-inspired restaurant. One bite of the steak with blue-cheese sauce and you'll already be planning a second trip here.

AROUND THE ISLAND

Yarisnori Restaurant (Map 221; mains US$6-9; 7:30am-7pm) Overlooking the beach at Boca del Drago, this charming, open-air seafood restaurant is a local favorite. Grab an outdoor table on the sand and feast on the catch of the day – just make sure to wait at least a half hour before swimming!

Drinking

A great place to kick off your crazy Bocas night is at **La Iguana** (Map 223; Calle 1), a popular surfer bar that serves up two-for-one cocktails from 6:30pm to 7:30pm. This is a great spot for a frothy piña colada, though you can't go wrong with an ice cold Balboa lager.

Next, head to backpacker central, namely the **Mondo Taitu Bar** (Map 223; Av I), which always guarantees a good time. On Tuesdays and Fridays, the party-loving owners entertain their guests with a variety of themed events, though the creative cocktail list and hookahs (US$5) make Mondo a good choice any night. If you're feeling brave (and cheap), order a tequila suicide – a snort of salt, a squeeze of lime in the eye and a shot of the worst tequila they can find (at least it's free!).

If you're looking for a little local flair, **Bar El Encanto** (Map 223; Calle 3) is all the rage among the island's youth. Although most nights are heavy on the reggaeton, there is the occasional live performance here.

If you're looking for a wild night out, the **Blowfish Sushi Bar** (Map 223; Calle 1) offers the unlikely combination of raw fish, girls dancing on bartops and a fireman's pole.

Most nights in Bocas end at the **Barco Hundido** (Map 223; Calle 1), an open-air bar that's affectionately known as the 'Wreck Deck' – the name comes from the sunken banana boat that rests in the clear Caribbean waters in the front. A short boardwalk extends from the bar to an island seating-area that's perfect for stargazing. The fun-loving American owner also arranges private parties on his *Barco Loco* (Crazy Boat), which is arguably the most unique sea-going vessel you've ever seen.

Shopping

You'll find a large selection of *molas* (textiles) and a range of other handicrafts for sale by local Kunas at stands near the park.

Pacahama (Map 223; Calle 3) Features arts made by most of Panama's indigenous peoples, plus a range of Guatemalan textiles, Nicaraguan hammocks and Emberá baskets,

Tropix Surfshop (Map 223; Calle 3) Sells custom-made surfboards and a few used boards, as well as a large selection of bikinis and other island apparel.

Getting There & Away

AIR

Bocas del Toro has a fine airport that's the pride of the town. **Aeroperlas** (☎ 757 9341) and **Air Panama** (☎ 757 9841) offer daily flights connecting Bocas with Panama City (US$74, one hour, one to two per day). Aeroperlas also has flights from David to Bocas (US$35, 50 minutes, one daily from Monday to Friday). Air Panama also has flights from San José, Costa Rica to Bocas (US$100, 1½ hours, one per day on Monday, Wednesday and Friday).

BOAT

If you don't fly into Bocas you'll have to take a water taxi to Changuinola on mainland Bocas (for more information, see p236). The majority of travelers prefer to use Changuinola as a jumping-off point for the archipelago.

The boat ride to Changuinola goes through the old canal formerly used by the banana plantations – it's a scenic trip that's well worth taking. **Bocas Marine & Tours** (Map 223; Calle 3) has a regular boat service to Changuinola (one-way US$5, 45 minutes, eight daily); the first departs at 7am, the last at 5:20pm.

Boats coming from either direction can let you off in Boca del Drago (one-way US$3), but make sure your captain knows you're going there. If you go for the day, be sure to arrange a pick-up time with the secretary and the driver.

Getting Around

WATER TAXIS

To reach nearby islands, you can hire boaters operating motorized boats and canoes along the waterfront. As a general rule, you should always sort out the rate beforehand, and clarify if it is for one-way or round trip. Although rates vary, you will get a better deal if you speak Spanish, are with a group and arrange for a pick-up. Although most fishers will perceive you as a rich gringo (and comparatively, you are), don't get angry – most boaters are just trying to feed their families.

Round-trip rates are generally as follows: US$4 to the near side of Isla Bastimentos, US$2 to Isla Carenero and US$10 to Red Frog Beach. Although you should always pay on the return leg – this guarantees a pick-up – most boaters will want some money upfront so that they can buy petrol.

BIKES

You can rent bicycles from **Empresa Lau** (Map 223; Calle 3; 🕒 9am-7pm) for US$8 per day as well as mopeds for US$20 per day.

ISLA BASTIMENTOS

pop 1500

Although it's a mere 10-minute boat ride from the town of Bocas del Toro, Isla Bastimentos is a different world. The northern coast of the island is home to palm-fringed wilderness beaches that serve as nesting grounds for sea turtles, while most of the southern coast consists of mangrove islands and coral reefs that fall within the boundaries of the Parque Nacional Marino Isla Bastimentos.

The main settlement on Bastimentos is the historic West Indian town of Old Bank, which has its origins in the banana industry. Here, you'll hear Gali-Gali, the distinct Creole language of Bocas del Toro Province that combines Afro-Antillean English, Spanish and Ngöbe-Buglé. The island is also home to the Ngöbe-Buglé village of Quebrada Sal, which is separated from Old Bank by a huge swath of jungle.

Unfortunately, the face of Bastimentos is changing rapidly as construction has already begun on the controversial Red Frog Beach Club (p232). Although the development project is outside the confines of the Parque Nacional Marino Isla Bastimentos, it will completely transform the face of island and set a precedent for future development projects in Bocas del Toro.

Orientation

The small village of Old Bank has no roads, just a wide, concrete footpath lined on both sides with colorfully painted wooden houses. From the town, there is a path leading across the island to Wizard Beach and Red Frog Beach, though the route can turn into a virtual swamp following the rains.

LOCAL VOICES: THE GUYS FROM MONDO TAITÚ ON SUSTAINABLE TRAVEL

David Harmatz, Daniel Saxe & Daniel Smetana

Travel is intrinsically linked to the timeless search for self-discovery – we all harbor a common hope that we might return from each adventure wiser than when we left. Unfortunately, sometimes we get so caught up in our own personal exploration that we overlook the environment around us. However, we all have the capacity to travel sustainably and it's not too difficult to leave a place better than we found it.

The basic idea of sustainable travel is that a destination is visited in such a way that the community's environmental, cultural and economic needs are met. Here in Bocas del Toro (and throughout the world), there is no shortage of ways that we can lessen the impact of our stay. For example:

▪ Minimize your impact on the local environment. Although humanity carries the responsibility to protect our world, the power to influence sustainability begins with individuals. We as travelers can easily help to conserve a community's natural resources. Reuse plastic bottles and fill up from rain water collection systems or by purifying tap water. When you arrive in a new town, ask around to see if there are any recycling programs – if a system is in place, spread awareness. While walking along a beach or a trail, pick up any garbage you see – your actions might inspire another traveler or local to do the same. And of course, treat our underwater world with respect. Follow the basic snorkel/scuba guidelines, keep garbage out of the ocean and remember not to eat or purchase endangered or undersized seafood.

▪ Respect the local culture. The cultural ruin of a destination is irreversible, though this is one area where travelers can make the biggest difference. While talking to locals, ask about the area's customs and traditions. An eagerness to learn on the part of the traveler may reassure a local that there is something precious about their customs, even if everything is changing around them. In fact, the best window into a local culture might be sitting next to you on the bus, having a quiet drink on the stool next to you in the bar or sharing a park bench with you. And, you never know where a conversation will take you. Ask a few questions. Show interest. Listen.

▪ Be aware of the power of your money. Many local economies in Panama (and the world) have been adversely affected by this rise in tourism. So, if the opportunity arises to spend money at a locally run business or vendor, give a little back. Enjoy the flavors at a local restaurant. If there is a kid selling an empanada out of his shoulder satchel, don't worry about your stomach – just buy one. Enjoy the creativity of a local artisan. If you spot a piece on display that catches your eye, buy it instead of saying you'll come back later. In all cases, you'll be surprised how far your dollar can stretch, though remember that no one likes people who flaunt their money.

Common sense combined with the basic tenets of sustainable travel will ensure that destinations remain desirable for both the traveler and the local. Regardless of whether you're sitting on a beach, roaming the streets, hiking through the jungle or sitting in a bar, never forget how much power you have to effect change in a positive way. And please, don't be afraid to give suggestions to other travelers – the best advice always comes from your peers.

Take only pictures. Leave only footprints. Kill only time.

'The Guys' from Mondo Taitú originally hail from the San Francisco Bay Area. After completing university in 2004, they moved to Panama to try their hands at running a hostel – they've been stuck in Bocas ever since then.

On the southeastern side of the island is the remote Ngöbe-Buglé village of Quebrada Sal. Tropical forest covers the interior of the island; you can explore it, but go only with a guide, as it's very easy to get lost.

Sights

OLD BANK

Located on the western tip of the island, Old Bank (Bastimentos Town) is a small enclave of 1500 residents of West Indian descent. Until the 1990s, most of the adults in Old Bank traveled to Changuinola daily to tend to the banana fields, though today residents have taken to fishing, farming small plots or just hanging out.

Although Old Bank is very poor and devoid of any real sights, it has a much more pronounced Caribbean vibe than Bocas town and it's a relaxing place to stroll around and soak up the atmosphere. It's also the best place in Bocas del Toro to hear Gali-Gali, a fascinating Spanish-English Creole that's native to the island.

BEACHES

Bastimentos has some amazing beaches, though be careful swimming as the surf can really pick up on the north coast of the island.

The most beautiful beach on the island is **Wizard Beach** (also known as Playa Primera), which is awash in powder-yellow sand and backed by thick vine-strewn jungle. Although Wizard Beach is connected to Old Bank via a wilderness path, the mere 30-minute walk can turn into an all-day trek through the muck if it's been raining heavily.

Assuming the weather is cooperating, you can continue walking along the coast to **Playa Segunda** (Second Beach) and **Red Frog Beach**. Like Wizard, both beaches are stunning and virtually abandoned, though it's likely that this will change as development on the island continues (see the boxed text on p232). If the weather isn't cooperating, you can access Red Frog Beach by water taxi via a small marina on the south side of the island; entrance to the beach is US$2. While you are on Red Frog Beach, keep an eye out for the *rana rojo* (strawberry poison-dart frog) as they might not be on the island for too much longer.

The path continues past Red Frog Beach to **Playa Larga** (Long Beach), where sea turtles nest from April to August. Playa Larga and much of the eastern side of the island fall under the protection of Parque Nacional Marino Isla Bastimentos.

PARQUE NACIONAL MARINO ISLA BASTIMENTOS

Established in 1988, this was Panama's first **marine park** (admission US$10). Protecting various areas of the Bocas del Toro archipelago, including parts of Isla Bastimentos and the Cayos Zapatillas, the marine park is an important nature reserve for countless species of Caribbean wildlife.

You can get current park information from the IPAT or ANAM offices in Bocas del Toro (p220). The dive operators and boaters in Bocas are also good sources of information about the park and its attractions. If you want to camp out anywhere in the park, you are required to first obtain a permit from ANAM.

QUEBRADA SAL

On the southeastern edge of Bastimentos at the end of a long canal cut through the mangrove forest is the Ngöbe-Buglé village of Quebrada Sal (Salt Creek). The community is made up of 60-odd houses, an elementary school, a handicrafts store, a general store and a soccer field. For the most part, the community depends on fishing and subsistence farming, travels mostly by canoe, and resides in wooden, thatched-roof huts without electricity or running water.

Although the Quebrada Sal is slowly modernizing along with the rest of the archipelago, the villagers are friendly and open to visitors, especially if you can speak Spanish. If you have the time, it's worth hiring a local guide to walk with you along the cross-island trail that leads to Playa Larga (about one hour each way). Water taxis can also drop you off at the entrance. You will need to pay the US$1 entry fee and sign the visitor's log.

Activities

DIVING & SNORKELING

Diving trips are offered by **The Dutch Pirate** (☎ 6567 1812; www.thedutchpirate.com). There is a small booking office in Old Bank, though it's best to phone ahead to make a reservation. For more information on diving and snorkeling, see p222.

BOCAS DEL TORO PROVINCE

THE RED FROG BEACH CLUB

In October of 2006, Lonely Planet author Scott Doggett published an open letter in the *Bocas Breeze* calling attention to the Red Frog Beach Club (RFBC), a massive residential development project that is well underway on Isla Bastimentos. According to the developers, the RFBC will consist of luxury villas, condos and three marinas, and will provide resort amenities including a clubhouse, swimming pools, restaurants and an 18-hole golf course. Although the development project is outside the confines of the Parque Nacional Marino Isla Bastimentos, it will completely transform the face of Red Frog Beach and set a precedent for future development projects in Bocas del Toro.

The poignancy of Scott Doggett's letter caused uproar in Bocas, especially since it pointed out what locals, resident expats and concerned tourists were already thinking. The RFBC has launched a flashy public relations campaign espousing their involvement in rural development. However, since they are a private residential development, it is unlikely that homeowners will have any impact on the economic livelihood of locals. Furthermore, it is difficult to overlook the effect that the inevitable outcomes of a large residential community, such as air pollution and human wastes, will have a environmental impact on the island.

The principal concern amongst area locals is that future beach access will be restricted once construction of the RFBC is completed. Although beaches in Panama are considered public property, the concentration of wealth at RFBC will necessitate the presence of a private security force. One need only look at case studies of similar residential developments in Mexico, Costa Rica and the Dominican Republic to predict that public access to Red Frog Beach will be tightly controlled if not restricted altogether.

Another concern is that the RFBC will adversely impact sea turtle populations. According to the Smithsonian Tropical Research Institute (STRI), maps provided by the RFBC show encroachment of marine park boundaries and annexation of the land bordering on and including Playa Larga, an important sea-turtle nesting site. As the STRI points out, even if construction does not actually occur on Playa Larga, increased human presence in the area can disturb nesting females and impact habitat suitability. Furthermore, light-pollution from the RFBC will illuminate the coastline and may cause sea turtles to avoid Playa Larga all together.

The final concern is the environmental impact of the proposed 18-hole golf course on Isla Bastimentos. According to the RFBC, the golf course will be built on an existing teak plantation in order to preserve the island's primary forest. Unfortunately, however, access to the construction site is heavily restricted, which makes it near impossible to verify that the primary forest is being preserved. Furthermore, golf courses require huge amounts of agrochemicals and there is little that developers can do to prevent runoff from being absorbed by the outlying reef.

Despite increasing local and foreign opposition to the RFBC, it is unlikely that the project will be halted. Experts ranging from conservationists to marine biologists continue to petition ANAM, Panama's environmental authority, though it is suspected that the RFBC's principal investors are too influential for ANAM to make a difference. However, frequent setbacks have slowed progress and the opposition hopes that this extra time will enable them to influence the RFBC's agenda. It is almost certain that Isla Bastimentos will be the home of an exclusive residential community in the years to come, though there is hope that the developers will take it upon themselves to make their community more ecofriendly.

For more information on the Red Frog Beach Club, visit their website at redfrogbeachclub.com.

SURFING

For information on surfing near Isla Bastimentos, see the boxed text on p224.

SPELUNKING & HIKING

Nivida is the name of a cavern recently discovered by one of the residents of Bastimentos. Although the cave is one of the island's most fascinating natural wonders, half the fun of the place is getting there. To reach Nivida, go to Roots (p234) to arrange a trip (prices negotiable) with Oscar, a very reliable local guide. You'll then travel by small motorboat up a channel through lush vegetation full of wildlife. A short walk through the jungle leads to a massive cavern complete with swarms of nectar bats and a very swimmable subterranean lake.

Oscar can also arrange a challenging hike to Laguna de Bastimentos, a jungle lake completely surrounded by dense vegetation. This swath of rainforest is the terra firma section of the Parque Nacional Marino Isla Bastimentos.

Sleeping

Although the majority of the action is on Isla Colón, accommodations on Bastimentos are perfect for travelers seeking rustic digs and a laid-back atmosphere.

BUDGET

Hotel Bastimentos (Map 221; ☎ 757 9053; dm/d US$5/10) On a hill off the main path, this rough-and-ready budget hotel has bright and airy rooms with balconies overlooking the shoreline. More in-touch with backpacker needs than other hotels on the island, Bastimentos offers a common room with a bar, TV, dartboard and views as well as a well-equipped communal kitchen. Hotel Bastimentos follows the standard recipe for success: offer clean, economic accommodations in a chilled-out setting with shared living space for mingling.

Beverly's Hill (Map 221; ☎ 757 9923; s/d US$10/15) Rooms in clean cabins set amid a lush garden make Beverly's excellent value. Although it's a few dollars more than other budget hotels on the island, the difference here is the personalized service of the friendly hosts, Beverly and Wulf, who will make you feel welcome the moment you arrive. You can also sleep well at night knowing that the on-site composting and water filtration system makes this one of the most environmentally friendly hotels on the island.

Pension Tío Tom (Map 221; ☎ /fax 757 9831; tomina@cwp.net.pa; d without/with private bathroom US$10/20) This plank-and-thatch building has been offering cheap, clean and unfussy rooms for years, which has earned it a reputation as a backpacker palace. Hugely popular and justifiably so, Tío Tom epitomizes the type of rustic backpacker place that blazed the Gringo Trail through Central America. The friendly German owners foster a laid-back environment that's reinforced by the eclectic cast of international characters that are usually found here. It also helps that everyone usually has a full belly – the owners can cook up some seriously gourmet dinners for pennies.

MIDRANGE & TOP END

The Point (Map 221; ☎ 757 9704; cabin US$40) At the northern tip of Bastimentos lie two cabins overlooking the sea, with crashing waves just a few meters from the doorsteps. Each of the cabins boasts handsomely designed rooms with wooden accents, ecologically designed septic systems, and private hot-water bathrooms. Guests also have free use of the kayaks and you can surf right off the tip of the island (bring your own board).

La Loma Jungle Lodge (Map 221; ☎ 592 5162; www.the junglelodge.com; r per person with 3 meals & activities US$80) Integrated into the forest and the community, La Loma is one of those rare places that offers environmentally sustainable and culturally attuned lodging. The handful of bungalows epitomize natural sophistication with locally made furnishings that are adorned with tropical flowers. Each bungalow also has a propane-fuelled, rain-water-fed bathroom, a hand-hewn bed with mosquito net and a solar-powered energy system. The hosts also practice permaculture, which means that your delicious meals incorporate the organic vegetables grown here, plus the fresh-bread baked on the premises.

El Limbo on the Beach (Map 221; ☎ 6205555; www.ellimbo .com; d US$85) Every room is different at El Limbo, with lots of unique touches such as headboards made of driftwood, and seashells arranged in room corners for artistic effect. However, the overall design is understated elegance, which is achieved through a combination of natural building materials, attentive service and a striking location. As the names implies, you're on the beach and there's even a small reef out front that beckons to be explored.

Al Natural Resort (Map 221; ☎ 623 2217; alnatur albocas@cwp.net.pa; r per person with 3 meals & activities from US$100) This desert island hideaway for hippie bourgeoisie beach-lovers lends a bohemian twist to the all-inclusive idea. Based on traditional Ngöbe-Buglé architecture, the round wood-and-palm bungalows here have an open design that delivers full frontal sea views, though you need to have a laid-back travel approach to stay here. Being exposed to the elements is not everyone's cup of organic, young-leaf tea, especially if the rain and the wind picks up.

Eating & Drinking

Although you're just a short boat ride away from Isla Colón, there are a handful of interesting spots on the island worth checking out.

The Rooster (Map 221; mains US$2-4) This inexpensive, low-key spot is run by the friendly and garrulous Pete, who bills himself as the 'antifried guy.' Pete is a talented and creative cook who likes to use the region's fresh fruits and vegetables, and everything that comes out of his kitchen tastes fresh and healthy.

Roots (Map 221; mains US$3-5) This universally loved over-the-water restaurant is a Bocas institution and is famous for its masterfully prepared dishes of local meats and seafood that are perfectly accented with fresh coconut milk. Coowner Oscar Powell has also done much for the community of Isla Bastimentos and he's a personable fellow with a sharp sense of humor.

Restaurante Coral Cay (Map 221; dishes US$6-12; ✆ 8am-5pm) An island unto itself, this place is a cluster of thatched-roof *bohios* on stilts beside a clump of mangrove and a field of coral reef. This is a terrific place to relax, lie in the sun, snorkel and eat, and the boat ride out is an adventure in itself.

Built partially over the water, the large, barnlike La Feria (Map 221) is the seat of Bastimentos' nightlife. After the sun sets it's an easy spot to find – just follow the sound of reggae.

Getting There & Away

To get to Isla Bastimentos from Bocas del Toro, just walk down to the waterfront and ask a boaters to take you over. The ride will cost about US$2 to get to the near side of the island or US$4 to the far side.

ISLA CARENERO

A few hundred meters from Isla Colón is the oft-forgotten island of Isla Carenero. The island takes its name from 'careening,' which in nautical talk means to lean a ship on one side for cleaning or repairing. It was on Careening Cay in October 1502 that ships under the command of Christopher Columbus were careened and cleaned while the admiral recovered from a bellyache.

Today, the wave of development that transformed Isla Colón is also making headway on Isla Carenero. Although the majority of the accommodations on Isla Carenero are borderline resorts, staying on this lovely island is a great alternative to Isla Colón, especially if you're looking for a bit of peace and quiet.

Orientation

Water taxis dock at the small marina on the tip of the island. From here, there is a path that leads to the island's fledgling town and continues across the island.

Activities

SURFING

For information on surfing near Isla Carenero, see the boxed text on p224.

Sleeping & Eating

Although not as popular as Isla Colón or Isla Bastimentos, Isla Carenero is a good option for travelers who want a different view of the islands.

Tierra Verde (Map 221; ✆ 757 9042; www.hoteltierraverde.com; s/d/tr US$45/50/55) Offering excellent value for money, this lovely three-story building sits back from the beach in a shady area full of palm trees. The seven spacious rooms feature beautiful wood details and windows that allow ample light and are designed in a contemporary island style. Tierra Verde is Panaman-run, a rarity for midrange hotels in this expat playground.

Buccaneer Resort (Map 221; ✆ 757 9042; www.bocasbuccaneer.com; d US$65-85, 4-person suite US$200; ✕) Located on a lovely strip of sand, this low-key resort is more of a humble clutch of romantic cabins. Each self-contained unit is elevated and features polished hardwood floors and walls, a thatch roof, a screened porch and a modern tiled bathroom, though the star of the show is the secluded honeymoon-worthy suite. Also located on the grounds is the La Almeja Barbuda, an open-sided restaurant that is a popular expat hangout.

Casa Acuario (Map 221; ✆ 757 9565; d US$75; ✕) Pulling up to the porch-dock that serves as Casa Acuario's welcome mat, you'll see why they named it 'Aquarium House' – the crystal-blue waters here teem with tropical fish. Short of pitching a tent on a wilderness beach, you'll be hard pressed to find accommodations that take such advantage of the archipelago's exquisite beauty. Rooms at this cute, two-story guesthouse are impeccably outfitted with modern amenities and the requisite tropical decor.

Restaurante Las Tortugas (Map 221; mains US$4-6) This low-key restaurant boasts fine views of Bocas town and the local seafood on offer is about as cheap as it gets. If you're staying on Colón or Bastimentos and in need of a change of scene, this Carenero spot is the perfect choice.

Getting There & Away
Isla Carenero is a quick and easy US$1 boat ride from the waterfront in Bocas town.

ISLA SOLARTE
Isla Solarte (Cayo Nancy) is distinguished by Hospital Point, which is named after the United Fruit Company hospital that was built here in 1900. The hospital was established to isolate victims of yellow fever and malaria – at the time, it was not yet known that these diseases were transmitted by mosquitoes. Although the hospital complex eventually included 16 buildings, it was abandoned after two decades of operation following the blight that killed all of United Fruit's banana trees.

Today, most visitors to Solarte are day-trippers on boat tours, who dock just off of Hospital Point to snorkel the 20m underwater wall. Although much of the island is private, an attractive option for anyone looking for a little tropical seclusion is the **Solarte del Caribe Inn** (Map 221; ☎ 757 9032; www.solarteinn.com; d/ste incl breakfast US$65/110), which enjoys the privilege of being the sole hotel on the island. The property has the air of a country inn, complete with a spacious open-sided dining room

---

EXPLORE MORE OF BOCAS DEL TORO

Tired of the tourist crowds? Looking for a bit of an adventure? Hire a boater and try these author-tested excursions to spice up your travels:

- **Cayo Crawl** Clear your schedule and get lost in the mangrove-dotted channels of Cayo Crawl near Isla Bastimentos.
- **Cayos Zapatillas** Apply some sunscreen and set out for the pristine white-sand beaches and virgin forests of the Cayos Zapatillas.
- **Dolphin Bay** Break out your camera and spot dolphins frolicking in your wake at this densely populated breeding ground.
- **Swan Cay** Polish your binoculars and keep your eyes peeled for red-billed tropic birds and white-crowned pigeons in Swan Cay near Isla de Los Pájaros.

---

and cozy guest rooms with lovely hardwood floors and private bathrooms with flushing compost toilets.

Isla Solarte is a quick and easy US$1 boat ride from the waterfront in Bocas town. If you want to snorkel at Hospital Point, you can either organize a private tour or negotiate a price with a water taxi.

MAINLAND

The mainland jungles of Bocas del Toro Province teem with wildlife and are pocketed with remote indigenous villages – the contrast with the archipelago couldn't be greater.

CHANGUINOLA
pop 50,000
Headquarters of the Chiriquí Land Company, the very same people that bring you Chiquita bananas, Changuinola is a hot and rather dusty town surrounded by a sea of banana plantations. Although there is little reason to spend any more time in Changuinola than you have to, overland travelers heading to the archipelago will have to pass through here. Changuinola also serves as the access point for the Humedal de San-San Pond Sak (p236), the Parque Internacional La Amistad (p237) and Las Delicias (p239).

Orientation & Information
The main street, Av 17 de Abril (also called Av Central), runs north to south, and serves as the town's main artery. The bus station is located near the city center, close to a number of restaurants, bars, markets and hotels.

The town has a Banco Nacional de Panamá, an immigration office and an internet café, all located on Av 17 de Abril.

The **ANAM office** (☎ 758 6603, 767 9485; ⏰ 8am-4pm Mon-Fri), near the center of town, should be able to provide information on national parks in the province. Some English is spoken here.

Sights
In 1903 a 15km **canal** connecting the Río Changuinola and Bahía de Almirante was dug parallel to the Caribbean shoreline, running within several hundred meters of it for most of its length. The work was begun in 1897 by the Snyder Brothers to facilitate the barging

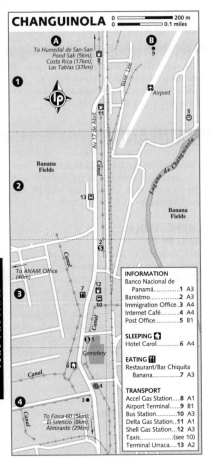

CHANGUINOLA

0 — 200 m
0 — 0.1 miles

INFORMATION
Banco Nacional de
Panamá..............1 A3
Banistmo................2 A3
Immigration Office..3 A4
Internet Café..........4 A3
Post Office.............5 B1

SLEEPING 🏠
Hotel Carol............6 A4

EATING 🍴
Restaurant/Bar Chiquita
Banana................7 A3

TRANSPORT
Accel Gas Station...8 A1
Airport Terminal......9 B1
Bus Station...........10 A3
Delta Gas Station....11 A1
Shell Gas Station...12 A3
Taxis..................(see 10)
Terminal Urraca....13 A2

To Humedal de San-San
Pond Sak (5km);
Costa Rica (17km);
Las Tablas (37km)

Airport

Banana
Fields

Banana
Fields

Laguna de Changuinola

Av 17 de Abril

Base Line

Canal

Canal

Canal

Banana
Fields

To ANAM Office
(40km)

Cemetery

To Finca 60 (5km);
El Silencio (8km);
Almirante (29km)

BOCAS DEL TORO PROVINCE

of bananas from the fields to ships. The 30m-wide channel allowed transfer of the fruit without interference from the open sea.

The canal, which sliced through dense rainforest, was abandoned years ago and until the mid-1990s it was a bird-watcher's dream. Today however, much of the jungle on both sides of the waterway has been cleared for cattle pasture, though there is still wildlife in the area.

Boats running between Changuinola and Isla Colón pass through the canal.

Sleeping & Eating

Hotel Carol (☎ 758 8731; Av 17 de Abril; d with private bathroom US$12-16; 🅿) Although the rooms here could inspire a horror film, it's cer-

tainly the best of the lot. Of course, there is little reason to actually spend the night in Changuinola, but if you end up in a pinch, you could do a lot worse than this spot. The Hotel Carol is conveniently located across from the cemetery – a room with a view.

Restaurant/Bar Chiquita Banana (Av 17 de Abril) On the main road opposite the bus station, this local favorite serves Panamanian fare, but surprisingly no bananas. (Indeed, bananas are hard to find in town as they are marked for export).

Getting There & Away

BOAT

Bocas Marine & Tours operates water taxis between Changuinola and Bocas town (US$4, 45 minutes, eight daily). Departures are from Finca 60, which is located 5km south of town. *Colectivo* buses run regularly from the bus station in town to Finca 60 for US$0.40.

BUSES

Buses depart from the station in the center of town.

El Silencio (Parque Internacional Amistad; US$0.50; 30min; every 20min, 5am-8:30pm)

Guabito-Sixaola (US$0.50; 30min; every half hour; 6am-7pm)

Las Tablas (Las Delicias; US$1.75; 1½hr; hourly)

Panama City (US$24; 10hr; 1 daily; 7am)

David (US$12.50; 4½hr; every half hour; 5am-6pm)

San José (Costa Rica; US$8; 6hr; daily; 10am)

TAXI

You can take a taxi from Changuinola to the Costa Rican border at Guabito (US$3 per person, 15 minutes).

HUMEDAL DE SAN-SAN POND SAK

These relatively undiscovered wetlands are located a mere 5km north of central Changuinola, yet they harbor an incredible variety of tropical fauna. In addition to sloths, river otters, white-faced monkeys, caimans, iguanas, sea turtles and poison-dart frogs, the fresh waters of San-San are also one of the few known Central American habitats for the manatee.

This protected area is administered by a conservation organization called AAMVE-CONA, which works in close conjunction with ANAM. The US$3 park entry fee helps support the conservation organization. To arrange a trip, stop by the Changuinola **ANAM office** (☎ 758 6603) or contact **AAMVECONA** (Association of Friends & Neighbors of the Coast & its Environment, in Spanish; ☎ 758 9461) directly. Trips cost between US$25 and US$35 per day depending on the size of your group, plus an additional US$8 per person for accommodation.

Although it's possible to visit the wetlands in a day trip from Changuinola (or Isla Colón if you get an early start), the best way to appreciate the area is to stay overnight. Located inside the park on a stunning wilderness beach is a rustic house on stilts, which has three simple rooms, cold-water showers, a flush toilet (fed by rainwater) and a cooking area. However, the biggest perk about staying here is that guests are allowed to accompany the rangers at night to observe the turtle nesting sites (see the boxed text, below).

Bring your own food and drink, as well as a sleeping bag or blanket – bedding is not provided. You will also want to bring a mosquito net and bug spray as the sand fleas and mosquitoes here will show no mercy.

PARQUE INTERNACIONAL LA AMISTAD (WEKSO)

The 407,000-hectare Parque Internacional La Amistad was established jointly in 1988 by Panama and Costa Rica – hence its name, La Amistad (Friendship). In 1990 La Amistad was declared a Unesco World Heritage site and later became part of the greater Mesoamerican Biological corridor. In Panama, the park covers portions of Chiriquí and Bocas del Toro Provinces, contains seven of the 12 classified life zones, and serves as a refuge for a great number of endangered flora and fauna.

La Amistad is also home to members of three indigenous groups: the Naso (Teribe), the Bribri and the Ngöbe-Buglé. Although these groups are still clinging to their traditional ways of life, their numbers are dwindling fast, especially as outside influences continue to invade their culture. However, in an effort to preserve their identify while simultaneously providing a means of income, the Naso have created an ecological center at Wekso, the former site of the infamous US-run Pana-Jungla survival school. Today, this ecotourism project is thriving as more and more travelers discover the beauty of both the rugged wilderness of La Amistad and the ancestral culture of the Naso.

The Naso (Teribe)

According to the colonial records of the Spanish empire, the Naso were present in mainland Bocas del Toro when the first explorers arrived in the region in the 16th century. The Spaniards referred to the Naso as the Teribe, or the Tjër Di (Grandmother Water) in Naso, which is the guiding spirit that forms the backbone of their religious beliefs. Nomenclature aside, however, the Spaniards gradually squeezed the Naso off their lands, and drove the population to exile in the highlands near the Costa Rican border.

Although the establishment of the modern Panamanian state has enabled the Naso

---

TURTLES' TRAGIC TROUBLES

Four of the world's eight sea turtle species nest on the beaches of the Archipiélago de Bocas del Toro, particularly the long beaches on the northern side of Isla Bastimentos. The loggerheads appear from April to September, the leatherbacks in May and June, the hawksbills in July and the greens in July and August.

Sea turtles leave the water only to lay their eggs. Two months after the eggs are laid, the hatchlings break loose from their shells, leave their sandy nests and enter the sea – if they are not first eaten by raccoons, birds or dogs. Many hatchlings, which are guided to the sea by moonlight, die because people using flashlights unintentionally steer the tiny turtles into the rainforest, where they are preyed upon or get lost and die from starvation or the heat.

The turtles also have human predators to contend with. Throughout Panama, many communities still eat turtles and their eggs, an unfortunate reality that has contributed greatly to their dwindling populations. Fortunately, AAMVECONA, which is based in the Humedal de San-San Pond Sak, is one community-based organization that is working toward their preservation. If you have time to spare, AAMVECONA accepts volunteers to help with their turtle nesting and hatching projects.

to return to their ancestral home, their survival is threatened by the lack of a *comarca* (autonomous region) of their own. This scenario contrasts greatly with other Panamanian indigenous population groups such as the Kuna, the Emberá, the Wounaan and the neighboring Ngöbe-Buglé. The plight of the Naso is further amplified by the fact that there is tremendous ecotourism potential in Parque Internacional La Amistad, as well as growing national and international interest in building a massive hydroelectric project in the region. Although proposals for establishing a *comarca* are on the table, in true Panamanian form, progress is being held up by bureaucracy.

It is estimated that there are only a few thousand Naso remaining in Panama, the majority of which live in Bocas del Toro Province and survive as subsistence farmers. Although they remained virtually autonomous for generations, the Naso have recently started losing their cultural self-sufficiency due to missionary activity, Latino encroachment and youth migration. Today, most Naso are bilingual (Naso and Spanish), wear Western-style clothing and practice some form of Christianity. However, strong elements of ancestral Naso culture remain, especially considering that they are one of the few remaining indigenous groups in the Americas to retain their traditional monarchy.

Orientation & Information

Admission to the **park** (admission US$3, parking US$1, camping US$5; ⊗ 8am-4pm) is paid at the Wekso entrance near Changuinola. Permits to camp in the park are payable at the ranger station.

Wekso is administered by **ODESEN** (Organization for the Sustainable Development of Naso Ecotourism; ☎ 620 0192), a community-based development organization that promotes ecotourism in the park as well as the cultural preservation of the Naso.

Keep in mind that the guides at Wekso, all of whom are local residents, speak only Spanish and Naso. Although you don't have to be fluent in Spanish to arrive here, a basic understanding of the language is recommended.

Note that the Las Nubes entrance to the park is only accessible from Chiriquí Province. For more information, see p215.

Sights

Before the US invasion of Panama in 1989, Wekso was named Pana-Jungla, and served as a US-run survival school that trained Panamanian and international troops in jungle warfare. Although it was disbanded in 1990 following the ousting of General Noriega, the **dilapidated ruins** of the old structures remain scattered around the Wekso grounds. Highlights include the barracks, mess hall, chapel, armory and the serpentarium.

Activities

Although most of Parque Internacional La Amistad is inaccessible terrain high up in the Talamanca, the park is home to a recorded 90 mammal species (including six cat species) and more than 400 bird species (including resplendent quetzals and harpy eagles).

There's a 3.5km loop trail at Wekso that cuts through secondary and virgin rainforest, which offers good opportunities for wildlife-watching. You can also take a dip in the river

---

LOCAL LORE: INDIOS CONEJOS

The Naso have a rich oral tradition that is rife with lore and mythology, though none of their tales are nearly as evocative as those of the *indios conejos* (rabbit Indians). According to the Naso, these fierce warriors live deep in the jungle, are completely nocturnal, possess super-human attributes and are deadly with a bow and arrow. Physical descriptions vary, but some of the more alluring accounts describe them as being pale white with stripes on their backs and dwarfish in size, like giant rabbits.

Although opinions are divided about whether or not *indios conejos* still exist, most elder Naso are fond of telling stories of battles with these mythical warriors that took place during their youth. According to the Naso elders, *indios conejos* are nearly invincible under cover of night, but they can easily be killed if ambushed while sleeping during the day.

Historians suggest that the lore of the *indios conejos* could stem from real battles that took place with the Miskito tribe. However, when asked where the *indios conejos* are today, most Naso elders will tell you that they're simply too deep in the jungles to be found anymore.

(the current is too fast for crocodiles), though be careful not to wade out very far or you may be carried downstream. There is also a network of trails linking various Naso communities together, though it's best to tackle these with a guide.

From Wekso, it's a five-hour hike into the Parque Internacional La Amistad. If you're planning on entering the park, be advised that the Caribbean side of La Amistad is much less developed than the Pacific side. You will need to hire the services of local boaters and guides, and you must be completely self-sufficient. Also be advised that the terrain is extremely rugged, there are no developed hiking trails and the river can get scary during the rainy season. However, if you're prepared for a serious trek, you're almost certain to have an adventure.

Sleeping & Eating
The heart of Wekso is the Naso-run **guest lodge** (lodgings per person US$12, meals US$3-4), which is staffed by members of the local community and benefits the tribe. Rooms at the lodge are basic and there is a secure water supply, flush toilets and an outdoor shower. Workers can also prepare meals for you, lead you on guided tours through the jungle and answer all your questions about Naso culture and history.

Getting There & Away
To reach Wekso, you first have to catch a bus from Changuinola to the hamlet of El Silencio (US$0.50, 30 minutes, every 20 minutes), and then take a 45-minute boat ride up the Río Teribe. In El Silencio, there's often a *colectivo* boat, which will cost about US$5 per person, though you can always hire a boat yourself for around US$15 to US$25. If you tell the ANAM office in Changuinola (p235) that you want to go to Wekso, they can radio ahead and make sure there is someone at the river's edge.

Once on the river you'll pass hills blanketed with rainforest and intermittent waterfalls. The backdrop is the glorious Talamanca range and the jungle comes all the way down to the river water. After about 45 minutes on the river, you'll see a sign on the right bank that announces your arrival at Wekso.

LAS DELICIAS
Set in a hilly area of lush rainforest, the small indigenous community of Las Delicias lies along the Sixaola River, 20km from the Costa Rican border crossing at Guabito. These local residents have recently shifted their source of income from harvesting and logging to preservation and ecotourism – visiting them is one way you can make a very positive contribution to the environment. Among the attractions here are waterfalls, abundant wildlife and impressive lookout points over the Sixaola River Valley and the Talamanca Mountains.

On a day trip to the area, you'll get the chance to take a boat tour through the Sixaola and Yorkin Rivers, followed by a hike through rainforest or possibly a horseback ride – the possibilities are endless. The villagers will then prepare a lunch – it's usually fresh fish and amazingly good. Prices for an outing are quite reasonable, at around US$20 to US$30 per person. There are also rustic **cabins** (per person US$16) available for overnight visitors, though hardy travelers can string up a hammock or pitch a tent at one of the ranchos. Remember that this is a relatively undeveloped place (there is no electricity), so bring your own supplies, especially a water purifier, a flashlight, a mosquito net and bug repellent.

You can make arrangements to visit Las Delicias through the Changuinola **ANAM office** (☎ 758 6603) or by phoning **Las Delicias** (☎ 600 4042) directly. To reach the community, take a bus from Changuinola to Las Tablas (US$1.75, 1½ hours, hourly), followed by a taxi to Las Delicias (US$1). You can also negotiate a price with one of the 4WD taxis in Changuinola.

BOSQUE PROTECTOR PALO SECO
Located 29km south of Chiriquí Grande on the road to David (also called 'Fortuna Rd' because the road passes by Lago Fortuna reservoir), the **Bosque Protector Palo Seco** (BPPS; Panamanians/foreigners US$1/3) is a lush cloud forest, covering more than 160,000 hectares. It's set high in the Talamanca range and the wildlife here includes monkeys, sloths, armadillos and butterflies. The birdlife includes ashy-throated bush-tanagers, and this is the only place you will find them.

An ANAM station lies at the entrance to the Bosque and here you can pay the park admission fee and obtain information about current hiking conditions. ANAM maintains three trails in the park, each about 45 minutes in duration, allowing visitors the chance to get a taste of the region's natural wonders.

ANAM has rustic facilities for those interested in staying the night inside the center (per

BOCAS DEL TORO PROVINCE

GETTING TO COSTA RICA

The border post at **Guabito-Sixaola** (☷ 8am-noon & 2-6pm), just north of Changuinola, is a straight-forward, less-traveled post and most travelers find it hassle free. Buses from Changuinola depart frequently for the border (US$0.50, 30 minutes, every half-hour) from 6am to 7pm. On the Costa Rican side of the border, you can catch regular buses on to Puerto Limón and San José, as well as regional destinations.

Note that you can be asked for an onward ticket if you are entering Costa Rica. If you do not possess one, it is acceptable to buy a return bus ticket back to Panama. Also note that Costa Rica is one hour behind Panama – opening and closing times in this box are given in Panama time.

BOCAS DEL TORO PROVINCE

person US$5), but be sure to bring your own food and bedding. Guests have access to the kitchen as well as bathrooms. To ensure they have room for you, contact the Changuinola **ANAM office** (☎ 758 660).

Just down from the ANAM station is the home of **Isabel & Onel Guerra-Martinez** (bed with/ without meals US$30/10; **P**), who also provide food and lodging for guests. Accommodations are rustic, but clean and well maintained with flush toilets and showers. The friendly family can cook your meals and they also provide tours of the area in Spanish.

Across the road from them is the sign for **Willie Mazu Rancho Ecologico** (☎ 442 1340 in Panama City; panabird@cwpanama.net; mattress with/without meals US$45/25; **P**), which consists of a large, thatched-roof structure under which four-person tents are pitched. The tents contain mattresses, and guests have access to cooking facilities and a clean bathroom and shower. You can bring your own food or buy your meals here. In the vicinity is a crystal-clear stream that's very refreshing after a long hike. There are several trails on the property, one of which leads to a lovely set of waterfalls and bathing pools. There's also a stand about 100m further up the road that sells fresh fruits and vegetables.

The last place to stay in the area is **Celestine** (☎ 774 4934; hapenagosg@hotmail.com; US$30; **P**), which is a clutch of cabins owned by a local

doctor and his wife. The complex is located up the road from the other spots and is set in the forest with two trails running behind it. The price of lodging includes three meals as well as guided walks along the trails led by an Ngöbe-Buglé villager.

All of these sights lie less than 17km from Lago Fortuna, a picturesque reservoir that also serves a power plant. All around the reservoir is some of the finest forest in Panama, which is strictly protected because it serves as the watershed for the Lago Fortuna. The bird-watching here is superb – keep an eye out for rarities such as the bat falcon, the wedge-billed woodcreeper and the golden-winged warbler.

To reach the Bosque Protector Palo Seco from David, take any bus in the direction of Changuinola (US$4, hourly from 5am to 6:30pm). Tell the driver you want to stop just before Altos del Valle, the community just past the places mentioned above, and then disembark at kilometer 68.5, which is right by the ANAM station. – don't try to reach these areas at night because they're set back from the road and easy to miss. Getting a ride out of the area basically requires catching one of the buses heading in the direction you're going. Buses pass every 45 minutes to an hour heading north to Changuinola (US$5, two hours) and south to David (US$4, two hours).

Colón Province

The mere mention of Colón sends shivers down the spines of travelers and Panamanians, but there is more to the province than its notorious capital. Stretching along the Caribbean coast from Veraguas Province in the west to the Comarca de Kuna Yala in the east, Colón Province is mostly undeveloped and virtually inaccessible, but steeped in a rich, accessible history.

During the colonial era, gold and silver bound for Spain were stored at the Caribbean coastal towns of Nombre de Dios and Portobelo. These were once the world's wealthiest cities, attracting scores of pirates. In 1572 the English privateer Francis Drake sailed into Nombre de Dios and plundered its riches before reducing the city to ashes. In 1739 Portobelo was sacked by Admiral Edward Vernon, forcing Spain to finally abandon the Panama crossing in favor of sailing around Cape Horn. Today, the ruined city of Portobelo and the nearby fortress of Fuerte San Lorenzo stand as testaments to the faded glory of the Spanish empire.

The provincial town of Colón has also long passed its zenith. Although the city itself is an urban jungle racked by violent crime, the surrounding area is home to everything from pristine beaches and lowland rainforests to colonial splendors and modern engineering marvels. Within the span of a few days, you can snorkel in Caribbean waters, spot tropical birds on private reserves, stumble across ruins and admire the massive locks on the lesser-known side of the canal. And of course, it's worth mentioning that the luxury train connecting Panama City to Colón is arguably one of the greatest rail journeys in the Americas.

HIGHLIGHTS

- Traveling in a 1st-class luxury car from Panama City to Colón along the historic **Panama Railroad** (p246)

- Exploring the hallowed ruins of **Portobelo** (p250), once the Caribbean's greatest port

- Living out your *Pirates of the Caribbean* fantasy at the historic fort of **Fuerte San Lorenzo** (p249), a historic Spanish fort that once stood guard over the Caribbean

- Soaking up the natural beauty and laid-back vibe of **Isla Grande** (p254), a picture-perfect gem of a Caribbean island

- Birding in the lowland forests surrounding **Sierra Llorona Panama Lodge** (p247), one of the country's premier birding destinations

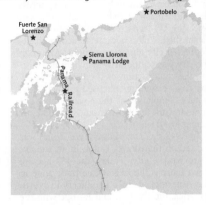

COLÓN PROVINCE

| ■ POPULATION: 205,000 | ■ AREA: 4890 SQ KM | ■ ELEVATION: SEA LEVEL TO 979M |

COLÓN PROVINCE

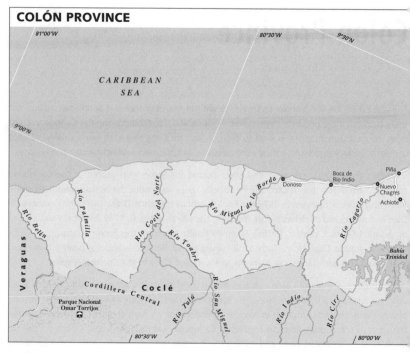

COLÓN

pop 45,000

Simply put, Panama's most notorious city is a sprawling slum of decaying colonial grandeur and desperate human existence. Prior to 1869, the Panama Railroad connecting Panama City and Colón was the only rapid transit across the continental western hemisphere. However, once the US transcontinental railroad was established, Colón became an economically depressed city almost overnight. Although the city was temporarily reinvigorated during the construction of the Panama Canal, the city's economy collapsed following the canal's completion as there was simply not enough work for the thousands of suddenly unemployed laborers.

In 1948 the Zona Libre (Free Zone) was created on the edge of Colón in an attempt to revive the city. Today, the 482-hectare Zona Libre is the largest free-trade zone in the Americas. It links producers in North America, the Far East and Europe with the Latin American market and is home to more than 1600 companies and several dozen banks. Unfortunately, none of the US$10 billion in annual commercial turnover seems to get beyond the compound's walls and the Zona Libre exists as an island of materialism floating in a sea of unemployment, poverty and crime.

History

The discovery of gold in California in 1848 sparked the need for a transcontinental railroad. At the time, most Americans lived on the east coast of the US, and traveling to California via Panama was cheaper and quicker then going across the US. The isthmus route was also less dangerous than traveling through the USA's vast heartland, which was home to hostile indigenous groups. Gold-seekers took steamships from the eastern seaboard to the mouth of the Río Chagres, walked the historic 80km Sendero Las Cruces trade route to the Pacific coast, and then boarded ships bound for California.

In 1850 the city of Colón was established as the Caribbean terminus of the Panama Railroad. It was initially called Aspinwall in honor of William Aspinwall, one of the founders of the Panama Railroad. In 1890, however, the government of Colombia changed the name of

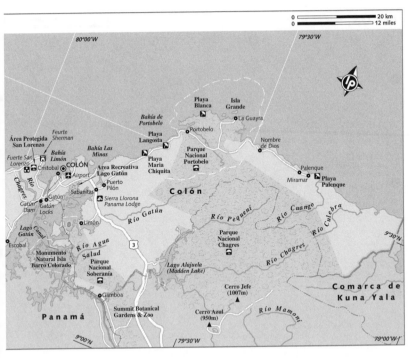

the city to Colón and dubbed the surrounding province Cristóbal.

Following the completion of the Panama Railroad in 1855, Colón became a boom town almost overnight. With scores of Americans passing through the city on a daily basis, Colón attracted entrepreneurs and businesspeople looking to cash in on the gold-rush fever. Unfortunately, the Panama Railroad became insignificant following the completion of the US transcontinental railroad in 1869 and Colón faded into obscurity less than 20 years after its founding.

At the peak of Colón's economic depression in 1881, the French arrived to start construction of an interoceanic canal, but the city was burnt to the ground four years later by a Colombian hoping to spark a revolution. In the years to follow, Colón entered a second golden age as the city was entirely rebuilt in the French colonial architectural style that was popular at the time. Rivaling Panama City in beauty and wealth, life in the Canal Zone was pleasurable and highly profitable.

The French abandoned their efforts eight years later when the monetary costs proved too great, and yellow fever and malaria had killed 22,000 workers, but the US was quick to seize the opportunity. For the next 25 years, the sleepy backwater town of Colón was transformed into a vibrant provincial capital as workers from around the world arrived by the shipload. However, immediately following the completion of the canal in 1914, the sudden lack of employment caused Colón's economy to disintegrate and the city spiraled into the depths of depravity almost overnight. Today, most of the colonial city is still intact, though the buildings are on the verge of collapse, with countless squatters living inside them.

Orientation & Information

Colón sits on a former island that juts into the Bahía Limón (Lemon Bay), though it was linked at its southernmost tip to the mainland via landfill in 1852.

The city is reached via two major roads on the southern side of town. The roads become Av Amador Guerrero and Av Bolívar at the entrance to the town and run straight up the grid-patterned city, ending near Colon's northern waterfront.

COLÓN PROVINCE

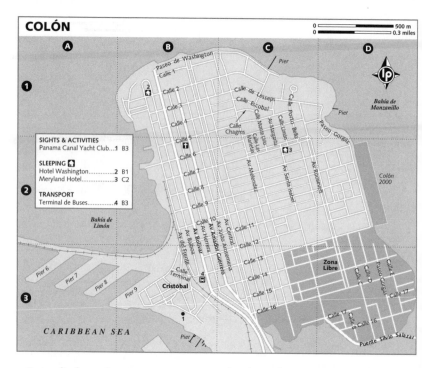

COLÓN

SIGHTS & ACTIVITIES
Panama Canal Yacht Club...1 B3

SLEEPING
Hotel Washington..............2 B1
Meryland Hotel..................3 C2

TRANSPORT
Terminal de Buses.............4 B3

Perpendicular to these avenues are numbered streets; Calle 16 is the first of these you'll cross as you enter the town while Calle 1 is at the northern end of town. The Zone Libre occupies the southeastern corner of the city while the city's cruise-ship port, Colón 2000, is located just north of the free-trade zone. If you turn left on Calle 13, you'll pass the passenger train terminal, which rests 200m before the port of Cristóbal.

Given Colón's high rate of crime, the safest place to withdraw money is the BNP ATM in the Colón 2000 cruise-ship port.

Dangers & Annoyances
Despite Colón's new cruise port on the eastern side of the city, Colón is still a dangerous slum. Violent crime is a serious problem, and you need to exercise caution when walking around, even during the day – always travel by taxi at night.

Sights
ZONA LIBRE
Colón's free-trade zone is a huge fortresslike area of giant international stores selling items

duty free. In fact, it's the world's second-largest duty-free port after Hong Kong. However, most of these stores only deal in bulk merchandise; they aren't set up to sell to individual tourists and the window shopping is not very interesting. If you do buy something, the store usually sends it to the Tocumen International Airport in Panama City, where you can retrieve your purchase before departing the country. You can enter the Zona Libre by presenting your passport at the security office.

PANAMA CANAL YACHT CLUB
This **yacht club** (☎ 441 5882) in Cristóbal is a safe haven for 'yachties' heading through the canal. It has a restaurant, a bar, showers and a bulletin board with notices from people offering or seeking positions as crew. This is the place to inquire about work as a line handler. Don't expect to show up and get work; it can often take several weeks. Still, seeing the canal from the inside is the best way to experience it.

COLÓN 2000
In December of 2000, the self-proclaimed 'Caribbean cruise port of shopping and enter-

tainment' opened on the east side of Colón. It's a rather modest affair, but it does have a good selection of restaurants and souvenir shops.

Sleeping & Eating

There's no shortage of hotels in Colón, but most are in seedy areas and have serious security issues. The hotels listed below are mentioned because they have 24-hour security guards.

There are plenty of places to eat in Colón, but for safety reasons, it's recommended that you eat either in your hotel or at Colón 2000.

Meryland Hotel (☎ 441 7128; cnr Calle 7 & Av Santa Isabel; s/d US$40/45; P ⏹ ❄) This modern business hotel, complete with pseudo-Spanish colonial decor, is located in a comparatively safe part of Colón, especially since it fronts an attractive city park. The fairly standard-issue rooms have air-con, cable TV and private hot-water bathrooms, though you're paying more for security than luxury. There's also an on-site bar-restaurant, which saves you the trouble of having to leave the hotel at night.

Hotel Washington (☎ 441 7133; Calle 2; s/d US$50/60; P ⏹ ❄ ⛱) The Hotel Washington bills itself as the grand dame of Colón's hotels – and indeed it once was grandé – but today its fading colonial elegance is in desperate need of a makeover. Erected in 1870 at the request of US President William Taft, the Washington has hosted dignitaries from around the world, though today it caters more to wholesale shoppers. Still, the hotel's popularity makes it a safe bet, and the amenity-laden rooms are sweetened by the on-site bar, restaurant, casino and swimming pool.

Getting There & Away

AIR

Aeroperlas (☎ 315 7500; www.aeroperlas.com) has five weekly departures to Colón from Albrook airport in Panama City. The 15-minute flight costs US$35 each way.

BUS

From Panama City, a regular bus service to Colón (US$2.50, two hours, every 30 minutes) departs from the Albrook Bus Terminal.

Colón's Terminal de Buses is at the intersection of Calle Terminal and Av Bolívar. It serves towns throughout Colón Province, including:

Escobal (US$1; 1hr; hourly)
La Guayra (US$2.50; 1½hr; hourly) In La Guayra, you can catch the boat to Isla Grande.

Nombre de Dios (US$3; 1½hr; hourly)
Portobelo (US$1.50; 1hr; hourly)

The same buses can be boarded at Sabanitas, the turnoff for Portobelo, thus avoiding a trip into Colón.

TRAIN

For information on the Panama City-Colón railway, see the boxed text on p246.

Getting Around

While in Colón, it's not a good idea to walk around more than you have to. Fortunately, taxis congregate at the bus station, train station and the Zone Libre, and fares across the city are usually around US$1.

AROUND COLÓN
Gatún Locks

The **Gatún Locks** (admission free; ⏰ 8am-4pm), just 10km south of Colón city, raise southbound ships 29.5m from Caribbean waters to the level of Lago Gatún. From there, the ships travel 37km to the Pedro Miguel Locks, which lower southbound ships 9.3m to Lago Miraflores, a small body of water that separates the two sets of Pacific locks. The ships are then lowered to sea level at the Miraflores Locks.

Not only are the Gatún Locks the largest of the three sets, but their size is simply mind-boggling. In his superlative book, *The Path Between the Seas*, David McCullough notes that if stood on its end, a single lock would have been the tallest structure on Earth at the time it was built, taller by several meters than even the Eiffel Tower. Each chamber could have accommodated the Titanic with plenty of room to spare.

The amount of concrete poured to construct the locks at Gatún – 1,820,000 cu meters – was record setting. To put things in perspective, consider that this amount of concrete could be used to build a wall 2.4m thick, 3.6m high and 213km long. The concrete was brought from a giant mixing plant to the construction site by railroad cars that ran on a circular track. Huge buckets that were maneuvered by cranes carried the wet concrete from the railroad cars and poured it into enormous steel forms. The forms themselves were moved into place by locomotives. This protracted process continued virtually uninterrupted

RIDE THE PANAMA RAILROAD

One of the best ways to fully appreciate the extent of the canal is to travel from Panama City to Colón along the historic Panama Railroad. The rails fell into disrepair during the best-forgotten days of the Noriega regime, but in 1998 the Panama government partnered with Kansas City Southern, an American-based railway holding company, to create the **Panama Canal Railway Company** (PCRC; ☎ 317 6070; www.panarail.com). The primary purpose of the joint venture was to reestablish the Atlantic–Pacific rail link and create a profitable alternative to the Panama Canal trade route. Starting in 2001, PCRC also introduced a passenger service that included a fully operational vintage train.

Aimed at foreign travelers and businesspeople looking to relive the golden age of railway travel, the vintage train features exotic wood paneling and blinds, carpeted interiors, glass-domed cars and open-air viewing decks. The hour-long ride runs parallel to the canal and sometimes traverses thick jungles and rainforests. There are daily departures (one-way/round trip US$22/US$38) from Panama City at 7:15am and Colón at 5:15pm. Note that the Panama City terminus is actually located in the town of Corazal, which is a 15-minute cab-ride from the capital.

While you're sipping a hot cup of coffee and admiring Panama's scenic interior, consider for a moment this list of mind-blowing trivia.

- Peaking at US$295 a share, the Panama Railroad was the highest-priced stock on the New York Stock Exchange (NYSE) in the mid-1800s.

- With a total construction bill of US$8 million, the Panama Railroad was, at the time, the most expensive railroad per kilometer ever built.

- Despite being only 76km long, the Panama Railroad required 304 bridges and culverts.

- During the first 12 years of its operations, the Panama Railroad carried over US$750 million in gold and silver, and collected a quarter of one percent on each shipment.

- In 1913 the Panama Railroad hauled 2,916,657 passengers and transported 2,026,852 tons of freight across the isthmus, which was the heaviest per-kilometer traffic of any railroad in the world.

- An estimated 12,000 laborers died during the construction of the Panama Railroad, particularly from malaria and yellow fever.

- Disposing of the dead was such a problem that the Panama Railroad administration started pickling the bodies in barrels and selling them to medical schools...

- ...the proceeds of which were used to build a hospital in the Panama Canal Zone.

until the Gatún locks were completed after four years.

From an intelligently placed viewing stand situated opposite the control tower, you can watch the locks in action. The whole process takes about two hours, though it's probably the most interesting stage of the Canal transit and the English brochure does a good job of clearly describing what you're watching.

Buses to the Gatún Locks leave the Colón bus terminal hourly (US$1.25, 20 minutes). If you arrive by taxi, however, you can stop here before heading on to Gatún Dam – another 2km away. A taxi ride from Colón to the locks and dam and back should cost no more than US$15 per party – agree on a price before leaving.

Gatún Dam

The Gatún Dam, which was constructed in 1908 to shore up the Río Chagres and to create Lago Gatún, was the world's largest earthen dam until the Fuerte Peck Dam was built in Montana (USA) in 1940. And, until Lake Mead was formed by the 1936 completion of the Hoover Dam on the Nevada–Arizona (USA) border, Lago Gatún was the world's largest artificial body of water. In fact, when Lago Gatún was created, it submerged 262 sq km of jungle, entire villages (the people were relocated prior) and large sections of the Panama Railroad. Today, power generated by the dam drives all the electrical equipment involved in the operation of the Panama Canal, including the locomotives that tow ships through the locks.

Although the sight of the dam is impressive enough, it's especially worth coming out here if the spillway is open – millions of gallons of water rushing out is quite the sight. Prior to heading out, ask the guard at the entrance to the Gatún Locks to tell you if the spillway is open.

If you arrive at the Gatún Locks by bus, then it's a leisurely 30-minute walk to the dam. To get there, cross over the bridge spanning the Gatún Locks, turn left and follow the road for approximately 2km. Again, a taxi ride from Colón to the locks and dam and back should cost no more than US$15 per party.

SIERRA LLORONA PANAMA LODGE

our pick Sierra Llorona Panama Lodge (☎ 442 8104; www.sierrallorona.com; s/d/ste with 3 meals & walking tours US$95/138/158, 5-person campsite weekday/weekend US$45/75; P) is located on a 200-hectare rainforest reserve that is home to no less than 213 species of tropical birds. It's something of a legend amongst the international birding community.

The extensive gardens surrounding the lodge are home to numerous varieties of hummingbirds, though the prize sightings are usually spotted along the series of walking paths that crisscross the reserve. Two of the best walking trails, La Poza and El Colibri, are each 4km in length and contain several ground-level observation platforms. More difficult treks, including the network of trails known as Los Nances, cross a variety of mountainous terrain and boast stunning views of the Caribbean Sea, the Canal Zone and the city lights of Colón.

Another advantage to staying at Sierra Llorona is the lodge's proximity to some of the country's top birding hot spots. After you've finished exploring the surrounding reserve, it's easy and affordable to organize private tours to nearby Parque Nacional Soberanía (p110) and the Área Protegida San Lorenzo (p249).

Guests stay in one of a handful of rooms, which are perched around an outdoor swimming pool and offer rustic stylings that are refreshingly absent of modern conveniences. In fact, there are no air-conditioners or TVs on the entire property, though the mountain breezes keep the rooms cool and there's no need for TV when you have the rainforest on your doorstep.

Another accommodation option is the well-equipped and easily accessible campsite, which is located within the reserve. The 5-person pitches surround a thatched-roof rancho complete with composting toilets, showers and washing facilities, and there's no shortage of charcoal stoves and fire pits.

Although it's possible to arrange for a pick-up from the airport in Panama City, Sierra Llorona can be easily accessed if you have your own vehicle. From Panama City, follow the Transisthmian Hwy towards Colón, and take the Santa Rita Arriba turnoff, which is just a few kilometers before the Sabanitas turnoff. Once on this road, just follow signs for the lodge, which is approximately 4.5km from the Transisthmian Hwy. Note that during the rainy season, you will need a 4WD to make it up this road.

FUERTE SAN LORENZO & ÁREA PROTEGIDA SAN LORENZO

Centered on the ruins of the crumbling Spanish colonial fortress of Fuerte San Lorenzo, the 9653-hectare Área Protegida San Lorenzo also includes the former US military base of Fuerte Sherman, as well as 12 different kinds of ecosystems including mangroves, marshlands, semideciduous forests and humid rainforests. Since the departure of the US military in 1999, the area has slowly been recolonized by native fauna, though the future of the San Lorenzo protected area remains uncertain.

As part of the Mesoamerican Biological Corridor, San Lorenzo protects and fosters species migration between the continents, a fact that is being touted by conservation biologists and ecotour operators alike. On the other hand, locals see the area as unoccupied land, and everyone from poachers and loggers to slash-and-burn farmers have already started encroaching on the reserve.

Fortunately, conservation and tourism may win out in the end, due in part to the massive quantities of unexploded ordinance (UXOs) that were left in the area by the US military. For decades, the jungles surrounding Fuerte Sherman were used for target practice and survival training, though America's hasty exit from Panama in 1999 didn't leave much time for cleaning up shop.

COLÓN PROVINCE

Today, most travelers set their sights on the ruins of Fuerte San Lorenzo, but there are plenty of opportunities here for jungle exploration. The secondary forests of the protected area are rich in bird life and there's no shortage of mountainous trails and waterfall-fed ponds to discover.

History

Following the destruction of Nombre de Dios by Sir Francis Drake in 1573, the Spanish hoped to stave off further ransacking and pillaging by fortifying the Caribbean coast. Of principal concern was the Río Chagres, which flowed inland to the town of Venta de Cruces (near the modern town of Gamboa), and then linked up with the trade route leading to the city of Panamá. In 1595, by order of Phillip II of Spain, Fuerte San Lorenzo was built into the side of a steep cliff near the river mouth. Fuerte San Lorenzo, Portobelo and Panamá, the 'three keys' of the Americas, became known as the strategic hearts of the Spanish trade empire.

Once it was established, Fuerte San Lorenzo was under constant pirate attack. In 1596, only one year after its completion, San Lorenzo was seized by the English privateer Sir Francis Drake. Although it was later recovered and rebuilt with greater fortifications, San Lorenzo was again assaulted, this time by Sir Henry Morgan in 1671. Captain Morgan (of the spiced rum fame) succeeded in overpowering its guns and sailing up the Río Chagres. A few months later, Morgan burnt Panamá to the ground, pilfered its riches and sailed back to England with galleons laden with Spanish treasure.

In 1680 a new fortification was built on the highest part of the cliff, but this was no match for British Admiral Vernon, who destroyed San Lorenzo yet again in 1740. In 1761 the Spanish once again rebuilt San Lorenzo, and the decision to abandon the overland trade route in favor of sailing around the Cape Horn meant that the fort didn't suffer further attacks. As a result, Fuerte San Lorenzo was abandoned by Spain in 1821 when Panama became independent. The fort was subsequently used as a Colombian prison, a post office for inbound English mail and a campsite for gold miners en route to California.

In order to defend the Panama Canal Zone, the US military built Fuerte Sherman in 1911 with the purpose of defending the Atlantic side of the canal. Although post-WWII changes in war technology meant that the fortifications were rendered obsolete, the area surrounding the fort became an important jungle warfare training center. In 1963 these operations came under the responsibility of the US-army-run 'School of the Americas' in nearby Fuerte Gullick but five years later the 'Jungle Operations Training Center' became an independent entity. Fuerte Sherman subsequently became the main jungle operations school for the US

SU CASA EN ESCOBAL

Community-based tourism provides travelers with an opportunity that's so grassroots it's almost an adventure. But, hey, that's why you're traveling in the first place, right?

The tiny fishing village of Escobal lies on the banks of Lago Gatún and is inhabited mostly by the descendants of former canal builders and farmers who were displaced with the flooding of the Río Chagres. Escobal also contains one of the most densely diverse populations in Panama – residents are as likely to be the descendants of Haitians, Jamaicans or Colombians as they are Panamanians.

Although Escobal would otherwise be off the tourist radar screen, a community-based tourism program commenced here in 2001 with the help of the US Peace Corps. Today, Escobolanians, who are renowned for their kindness and warm spirits, are literally opening the doors of their houses to foreigners. For a few dollars a night, you can be assured a bed, a fan and a simple breakfast as well as the chance to interact with locals in a relaxed and authentic environment. While in Escobal, it's also easy to hire local guides to take you fishing or boating on Lago Gatún, as well as horseback riding or birding in the nearby rainforest.

If you're interested in arranging a home-stay, contact the program coordinators, **Saturnino Díaz and Aida Gonzalez** (☎ 434 6017, 434 6106). If you show up in Escobal unannounced, you can find Saturnino and Aida at the Restaurante Doña Nelly, which they own. Although you needn't be fluent, it's helpful to have a good command of Spanish before arriving.

army and was used as a training center for Vietnam-bound Special Forces.

On June 30, 1999, under the Torrijos–Carter treaties, Fuerte Sherman, nearby Fuertes Davis and Gullick, and the Área Protegida San Lorenzo were handed back to the Panamanian Government following the abandonment of the Canal Zone by the US military.

Orientation

Fuerte San Lorenzo and the Área Protegida San Lorenzo are located west of the city of Colón and northwest of Lago Gatún. The ruins of San Lorenzo are located 9km southeast of Fuerte Sherman on the Caribbean coastal highway and lie along the northwestern boundary of the protected area. Although there is no official entrance to the reserve, there is a visitors center in the village of Achiote, which is located along the northeastern edge of the reserve between the villages of Piña and Escobal. Fuertes Davis and Gullick, which are home to two of the area's hotels, are located on the Quatro Altos turnoff of the Transisthmian Hwy.

Sights

FUERTE SAN LORENZO

This **fort** (www.wmfpanama.org in Spanish; admission free; ◷ 8am-4pm) is perched at the mouth of the Río Chagres on a promontory west of the canal. Despite its violent history, much of San Lorenzo is well preserved, including the moat, the cannons and the arched rooms. The fort also commands a wide view of the river and bay far below, which was one of the reasons why the Spanish chose to fortify the site. Together with Portobelo, Fuerte San Lorenzo was declared a Unesco World Heritage site in 1980.

Like its contemporary fortresses at Portobelo, San Lorenzo was constructed of blocks of cut coral and armed to the teeth with row upon row of cannons. If you inspect the cannons closely, you'll notice that some of them are actually British-made, which bespeaks the time in the 17th century when Sir Francis Drake and his pirate brethren occupied the fort.

There's no bus service to the fort, but you can take a taxi here from Colón for about US$20. If you're driving, go to the Gatún Locks, continue past the stoplight near the northern entrance to the locks and then follow the signs directing you to the dam, 2km away.

Drive over the dam and follow the 'Fuerte San Lorenzo' signs. These will lead you to the entrance of Fuerte Sherman where you'll be asked to show identification. Once you've done this, you will be allowed to proceed the remaining 9km to Fuerte San Lorenzo.

ÁREA PROTEGIDA SAN LORENZO

The **San Lorenzo protected area** (www.sanlorenzo .org.pa) is renowned for its bird-watching, but hikers and trekkers alike will be more than satisfied with guided romps through its dense secondary forest. You can also take some lovely walks to waterfalls and natural ponds, visit organic shade-grown coffee farms and hike to splendid lookouts with views of the protected area and the Río Chagres.

The protected area is best explored with a guide and this can be easily arranged at the **Centro El Tucán** (☎ 628 9000; ◷ 8am-4pm Mon-Fri), a community learning and visitors center that lies on the edge of the reserve. Guides generally charge US$15 per group for a two-hour hike, though longer and more difficult treks can also be arranged. El Tucán also has an excellent documentation center on the flora and fauna, human ecology and history of the area.

The visitors center is located in the village of Achiote, 13km north of Escobal, on the edge of the reserve. Since there is no public transportation to the town and there are few taxis in the area, Achiote is best accessed by private vehicle.

Sleeping

The helpful staff at the Centro El Tucán can arrange homestays in Achiote for a small, negotiable price. There are also opportunities for unofficial camping within the confines of the reserve, though you will need to be self-sufficient.

You can aslo bed down for a night or two in the former den of dictators, namely Building 400 of the notorious School of the Americas; see the boxed text on p250.

Another unusual option is the **Davis Suites Panama Canal** (☎ 473 0639; www.davis.ste.iwarp.com; d from US$55; P ⬛ ❄), which is housed in a converted US military building smack-dab in the middle of the now-abandoned Fuerte Davis. Needless to say, the entire compound is stark, utilitarian and unsurprisingly militaristic, but there is a certain appeal to bedding down in the former belly of the beast. The friendly

SWEET DREAMS IN THE DEN OF DICTATORS

The borders of the San Lorenzo protected area are home to Fuerte Espinar, which was known as Fuerte Gullick prior to the US handover. Within this compound is the infamous Building 400, which was the former home of the School of the Americas.

Established in 1949, the School of the Americas trained more than 34,000 Latin American soldiers before moving to Fuerte Benning, Georgia, in 1984. The school was created to keep communism out of Latin America, which quickly translated into teaching Latin American soldiers how to thwart armed communist insurgencies.

The school graduated some of the worst human-rights violators of our time, including former Argentine dictator Leopoldo Galtieri, who 'disappeared' thousands during Argentina's Dirty War of the 1970s, and El Salvador's Roberto D'Aubuisson, who led death squads that killed Archbishop Oscar Romero and thousands of other Salvadorans during the 1980s.

In a bizarre twist of capitalism and ill-humor, a Spanish hotel chain has converted Building 400 into a giant resort hotel, namely the **Meliá Panamá Canal** (☎ 470 1100; www.solmelia.com; d from US$80; P ✕ ⚊ ⚟). Not too surprisingly, the Meliá's staff has painted over all evidence that the hotel has ever been anything but an upscale fun center.

The US$30-million hotel features luxurious guest rooms with all the trimmings, a cluster of outdoor and indoor pools complete with swim-up bars, and a formal restaurant overlooking the shores of Lake Gatún. In a bid to keep their clientele busy (and to keep them from snooping around too much), the Meliá offers a wide range of tours including fishing and kayaking expeditions on the adjacent lake, organized tours to the canal and Fuerte San Lorenzo, and day-hikes and night safaris in the Área Protegida San Lorenzo.

In the past, most overnight guests at Building 400 arrived via military convoy or Blackhawk chopper. Of course, today it's recommended that you arrive via private vehicle; take the Quatro Altos turnoff on the Transisthmian Hwy and follow signs for the hotel.

staff can help you arrange tours and guided hikes as well as a hot meal (there aren't too many restaurants in these parts). Fuerte Davis is located on the Quatro Altos turnoff of the Transisthmian Hwy (follow the signs) and is best accessed by private vehicle.

Getting There & Away

As there is no public transportation to either Fuerte San Lorenzo or the Área Protegida San Lorenzo, this area is best explored by private vehicle. It is however possible to take a taxi to Fuerte San Lorenzo from Colón, though taxis are uncommon as you get closer to the reserve.

PORTOBELO

pop 4000

Although today it is little more than a sleepy fishing village on the shores of the Caribbean, Portobelo was once the greatest Spanish port in Central America. Gold from Peru and treasures from the Orient entered Panama City and were carried overland by mule to the fortresses at Portobelo. During the annual trade fair, galleons laden with goods from Spain arrived to trade for gold and other products from the New World. However, much like Nombre de Dio, Panamá and Fuerte San Lorenzo, Portobelo was the target of constant attacks at the hands of English privateers. Considering that the city was destroyed several times throughout its history, it's remarkable that so much of the colonial fortresses still stand.

Today Portobelo is an economically depressed town, and the majority of its inhabitants make their living from either fishing, tending crops or raising livestock. Their homes are situated among the ruins of the colonial fortifications, half of which retain some of their original form, half of which are meager piles of cut stone and coral. However, the city bursts to life every October 21 for the Festival de Cristo Negro (Festival of the Black Christ), one of the country's most vibrant and spiritual celebrations.

Portobelo also attracts dedicated Scuba divers, especially since there are no less than 16 major dive sites in the adjacent waters. Although visibility can't compare to more traditional Caribbean diving destinations, few people leave here unhappy as there is an excellent variety of underwater attractions, including a 110-ft cargo ship and a C-45 twin-engine plane.

History

'Puerto Bello,' the Beautiful Port, was named by Columbus in 1502, when he stopped here on his fourth New World voyage. Since it was common at the time to abbreviate Spanish names, the beautiful port quickly became known as simply 'Portobelo.'

Portobelo consisted of no more than 10 houses when the celebrated Italian engineer Juan Bautista Antonelli arrived in 1586 on a mission to examine the defensibility of the Caribbean. After noting how well Portobelo's bay lent itself to defensive works, King Félipe II ordered that Nombre de Dios be abandoned and Portobelo colonized. However, it wasn't until after Nombre de Dios was completely destroyed by Sir Francis Drake in 1596 that the transfer took place.

The city of San Felipe de Portobelo was founded in 1597 and its 200-year history was riddled with numerous invasions at the hands of English privateers and the Royal Navy. Portobelo was first attacked in 1602 by the English pirate William Parker, but it was the infamous Sir Henry Morgan who sacked the city in 1671.

However, not all of the invasions were the product of superior tactics or numbers. In 1679 the crews of two English ships and one French vessel united in an attack on Portobelo. They landed 200 men at such a distance from the town that it took them three nights of marching to reach it. As they neared Portobelo, they were seen by a farmer, who ran ahead to sound the alarm, but the pirates followed so closely behind that the town had no time to prepare. Unaware of how small the buccaneer force was, all the inhabitants fled.

The pirates spent two days and nights in Portobelo, collecting plunder in constant apprehension that the Spaniards would return in great numbers and attack them. However, the buccaneers got back to their ships unmolested and then distributed 160 pieces of eight to each man. At the time, one piece of eight would pay for a night's stay at the best inn in Seville.

Attacks on Portobelo continued unabated until the city was destroyed in 1739 by an attack led by Admiral Edward Vernon. Although Portobelo was rebuilt in 1751, it never attained its former prominence and in time became a virtual ruin. Later, much of the outermost fortress was dismantled to build the Panama Canal and many of the larger stones were used in the construction of the Gatún Locks. There are, however, still considerable parts of the town and fortresses left and today Portobelo is protected as a national park and as a Unesco World Heritage Site.

Orientation & Information

Portobelo consists of about 15 square blocks of mostly run-down homes and businesses beside a paved, two-lane road. That road intersects with the Panama City–Colón road at the town of Sabanitas, 33km to the west.

COLÓN PROVINCE

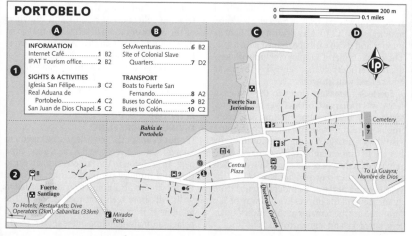

PORTOBELO

0 —————— 200 m
0 —————— 0.1 miles

INFORMATION
Internet Café................1 B2
IPAT Tourism office........2 B2

SIGHTS & ACTIVITIES
Iglesia San Félipe...........3 C2
Real Aduana de
 Portobelo...................4 C2
San Juan de Dios Chapel.5 C2

SelvAventuras................6 B2
Site of Colonial Slave
 Quarters....................7 D2

TRANSPORT
Boats to Fuerte San
 Fernando..................8 A2
Buses to Colón.............9 B2
Buses to Colón............10 C2

Fuerte San Jerónimo

Cemetery

Bahía de Portobelo

Central Plaza

To La Guayra;
Nombre de Dios

Quebrada Gruesa

Fuerte Santiago

To Hotels; Restaurants; Dive Operators (2km); Sabanitas (33km)

Mirador Perú

East of Portobelo, the road forks after 9km. The right branch of the road extends 14km further east to Nombre de Dios; the left branch extends 11km to the hamlet of La Guayra (p254), where you can hire boats to Isla Grande (p254).

The **IPAT tourist office** (☎ 448 2200; ☻ 9am-5pm), just off the main road through town, has a small display of paintings focusing on the Congo in the back room (only Spanish is spoken). Across the street from the tourist office is an **internet café** (per hr US$1.50; ☻ 8:30am-4pm Mon-Fri).

Sights
FORTS
To defend his bullion and galleons from pirates, King Félipe II ordered forts to be constructed at Portobelo based on Antonelli's recommendation. In 1601 Fuerte San Félipe and Fuerte San Diego were built near the mouth of the bay, but were subsequently destroyed by Admiral Vernon in 1739. In the years to follow, **Fuerte San Fernando** was built on top of these ruins, though sadly much of the fort was later taken down by American engineers, who used its walls to create the breakwater protecting the northern end of the Panama Canal. Still, it's a scenic spot worth visiting and boats can be hired from the water's edge (US$2 per person round-trip) to bring you across the bay to the fort.

As you approach the town from the west, the first fort you'll see is **Fuerte Santiago**, which was also built after Vernon's attack. Several of its walls are 3m thick and made entirely of cut coral. Known to the Spaniards as 'reef rock,' coral was extensively used as a building material since it's tough as granite yet light as pumice and it can easily be shaped with a saw. The ruins at Fuerte Santiago include officers' quarters, artillery sheds, a sentry box, barracks and several watchtowers.

Fuerte San Jerónimo, closer to the center of town, was the largest fortress ever built to protect the bay. If you're short on time, San Jerónimo is more complete and makes for a better visit than Santiago. Facing the mouth of the bay are 18 cannon embrasures, some of which remain exactly where the Spanish troops left them when they returned home in 1821 – the year Panama declared its independence from Spain. Beyond the impressive gateway of San Jerónimo are the remains of the officers' quarters, barracks and a guardroom.

On a hill overlooking Santiago and much of the bay is a small but well-preserved watchtower called **Mirador Perú**, which was built at the same time as Fuerte Santiago. There are steps carved into the hillside to reach the lookout and the views of the coastline from here are expansive. Unfortunately for the Spanish, however, the views weren't good enough to save their city from being repeatedly sacked by the English.

REAL ADUANA DE PORTOBELO
The handsome, two-story **Royal Customs House of Portobelo** (admission US$1; ☻ 8am-4pm) was originally built in 1630 to serve as the *contaduría* (counting house) for the king's gold. It was in this building that the treasure brought across the isthmus was recorded and stored until it could be placed on galleons and sailed to Spain. According to early records, no less than 233 soldiers were garrisoned in this building alone.

The customs house consists of two main rooms, which are now used as permanent exhibition halls. One room displays dozens of purple velvet robes, which are placed on the statue of the Black Christ every October when thousands of devotees descend on Portobelo to worship the icon (see opposite). Among the donors are boxer Roberto Duran and salsa star Ismael Rivera. The other room contains replicas of Spanish-colonial rifles, sketches of Portobelo's forts, 20th-century black-and-white photos of the town and a few dozen rusty cannon balls.

Before leaving, don't forget to visit the building's 2nd floor, which features an intriguing collection of photos and drawings of the Spanish-colonial fortresses that exist throughout Latin America. Also, don't overlook the bronze cannon at the entrance – it was recovered from a sunken galleon and bears a Spanish coat of arms as well as the date of manufacture (1617).

Activities
DIVING & SNORKELING
It's not Belize or the Bay Islands, but if you're an avid scuba diver, you'll have a good time here. In addition to the famous sunken cargo ship and military plane, the waters around Portobelo are also home to soft coral-laden walls, off-shore reefs and rock gardens. The good news is that you'll probably see several pelagic animals including nurse sharks, black-

tip reef sharks and eagle rays. The bad news is that you probably won't see them very well, especially if it has been raining. Generally speaking, you can expect about 10m of underwater visibility, but don't be surprised if it gets as low as 3m. Fortunately, scuba diving along this stretch of the Caribbean is fairly cheap and a bad day of diving is always better than a good day of work.

There are two dive operators in Portobelo, both located along Sabanitas–Portobelo road, about 2km west of town. A third operator, Jimmy's Caribbean Dive Resort, is located near the town of Nombre de Dios (p256).

At both of the operators listed below, a one-tank dive will cost about US$60 and a two-tank dive is US$80. An openwater/advanced course will cost US$200/275. If you're planning to dive with either, it's best to phone ahead or make a reservation via the internet.

Scubaportobelo (☎ 448 2147; www.scubapanama .com) The Portobelo branch of Scubapanama (p312) can arrange Scuba diving trips throughout the country.

Twin Oceans Dive Center (☎ 448 2067; www.twin oceans.com) Located inside the Coco Plum Eco Lodge (p254), this professional outfit has over 20 years of diving experience in Panamanian waters.

HIKING

Situated on the town's main road, **SelvAventuras** (☎ 688 6247; www.geocities.com/selvaventuras) is run by a group of charismatic locals eager to show visitors the wilder side of Portobelo. If you're looking to explore the surrounding Parque Nacional Portobelo, these guys can bring you to a number of impressive locales: Catarata de Río Piedras, a towering 45m waterfall; the tranquil waterfall-fed Salto de Tigre; and the rainforest-enshrouded swimming hole of Río Iguanita. Trips start at US$15 per person; you'll need some Spanish.

SWIMMING

If you're looking for a day of fun in the sun, nearby **Playa Blanca** (p254) is a great day trip from Portobelo.

Festivals & Events

For information on the Black Christ Festival, see the boxed text. below.

Los Congos, a festivity in which Blacks assume the role of escaped slaves and run around taking 'captives,' is held in Portobelo during Carnaval, on New Year's Eve and March 20, Portobelo's patron saint day. 'The Congos' is both the name of the festivity and the name of the people who maintain this intriguing tradition, which is based around a satire of colonial Spaniards.

The tradition dates from the days of Panama's slave trade, when Blacks escaped into

---

THE LEGEND OF THE BLACK CHRIST

Every October 21, pilgrims from all over Panama arrive in Portobelo to partake in the **Festival de Cristo Negro** (Black Christ Festival), which honors the 1.5m-high statue of the Black Christ housed in the **Iglesia de San Félipe**. The exact origins of the Black Christ statue are a matter of speculation, especially since all definitive church records were lost in the fire that followed Henry Morgan's sacking of Panamá in 1671. However, there's no shortage of fanciful stories surrounding the origins of the statue.

One story has it that a ship bound for Cartagena, Colombia, tried to leave Portobelo five times, but on each occasion a mighty storm blew the ship back to the town's edge, nearly sinking it in the process. The terrified crew are said to have lightened their vessel by tossing a heavy box overboard. On their sixth attempt to sail out of the bay, the storm did not appear and they were able to go on their way unchallenged. Several days later, local fishers found the discarded box floating off Portobelo and discovered the Black Christ inside.

A second story claims that the box was instead found floating at sea during a cholera epidemic. After being retrieved by local fisherman, the statue was placed inside the Iglesia de San Félipe. Almost immediately, as the story goes, the epidemic passed and the infected were instantaneously cured.

The list of tales goes on, though regardless of the statue's actual origins, the Black Christ Festival is a sight behold. After the sun sets on October 21, the statue is paraded down the streets of Portobelo, while pilgrims bedecked in purple robes and thorned crowns dance and drink until the small hours of the morning.

the jungle and formed communities of exiles. The satire consists of taking someone prisoner and demanding a huge ransom, though the prisoner is freed when he or she pays a token ransom (US$0.50 will suffice). The Congos are generally dressed in outlandish outfits that include tattered clothes, hats that resemble crowns and wooden swords, and usually perform before audiences.

Of course, sometimes a crazy-looking group of men will descend upon a person who's innocently walking down the street and demand thousands of dollars. If you ever find yourself an innocent 'victim' of this tradition, try not to freak out – they'll settle for a few coins.

Sleeping & Eating

Both dive operators in town offer rooms to their customers, though nondivers can stay at either spot without getting their feet wet.

You'll find that many local families also rent out spare rooms for around US$5 to US$10 – ask at the IPAT tourist office (p251).

Scubaportobelo (☎ 448 2147; www.scubapanama .com; 5-person cabin weekday/weekend US$30/50; P 🔀) If you're a nondiver, you might feel a bit out of place here, but avid divers will enjoy the company of other aqua-lovers. Although they are supposed to accomodate five people, the stale and somewhat past their sell-by-date cabins are probably a better fit for two or three.

Coco Plum Eco Lodge (☎ 264 1338; www.cocoplum panama.com; s/d/tr US$35/45/55; P 🔀) Home to the Twin Oceans Dive Center, the Coco Plum is definitely a divers' den, but there are enough landlubbers here to even things out a bit. The maritime theme is definitely a bit kitschy, though the fish prints and beach murals brighten up the otherwise cookie-cutter rooms. Even if you're not staying here, stop by in the evenings for dinner and a drink as the attached bar-restaurant is one of only a handful of spots in town.

Getting There & Away

Buses to Portobelo (US$1.50, one hour, hourly) depart from Colón's Terminal de Buses from 6:30am to 6pm. If you're coming by bus from Panama City, take the bus heading for Colón and get off at Sabanitas, 10km before Colón. Next, catch the bus coming from Colón to Portobelo when it passes through Sabanitas, thus avoiding a trip into Colón.

Getting Around

There are occasional taxis in Portobelo, though they never seem to be around when you need them. Instead, it's best to travel along the Sabanitas–Portobelo road by flagging down any of the buses headed in your direction. After dark, there is no public transportation.

AROUND PORTOBELO
Playa Blanca

A 20-minute boat ride from Portobelo will bring you to this lovely white-sand beach, which fronts a tranquil cove and is surrounded by dense wilderness. Since it is impossible to access the beach by car or bus, you'd be forgiven in thinking that Playa Blanca is an uninhabited island floating in the Caribbean.

Playa Blanca has some of the least disturbed reefs between Colón and the Archipiélago de San Blás and its sheltered waters have better visibility than in nearby Portobelo. There's a colorful reef in the center of the cove that's a mere shell's toss away from the beach as well as a second reef that sits in deeper waters about 100m offshore.

Although it's easy enough to visit Playa Blanca as a day trip from Portobelo, beachlovers can slow things down a bit by spending a night or two at the low-key **Tesoro del Caribe** (☎ 613 5749; www.tesorodelcaribe.com; r per person from US$75). Mellow rooms emphasize comfort and style instead of luxury, and the solar-powered lights, fans and showers help minimize the impact of your stay on the surrounding environment. In keeping with the resort theme, you can take advantage of the available snorkeling gear, canoes, kayaks and sailboats, or just kick-back with a cold beer and some fresh ceviche in the casual bar-restaurant.

Any boat in Portobelo can bring you to the Playa Blanca, though it's possible to arrange for a pick-up if you make a reservation in advance.

ISLA GRANDE
pop 900

Palm trees and white-sand beaches form the backdrop to this lovely little island, just 15km offshore from Portobelo. A popular getaway for Panama City folk fleeing the urban grind, Isla Grande is an ideal setting for snorkeling, scuba diving or simply soaking up the island's relaxed vibe. A few hundred people of African descent live on Grande, most of whom eke out

---

SURFING IN COLÓN PROVINCE

Although it's one of Panama's least surfed provinces, there are a number of great breaks to be had in Colón. And of course, the lack of crowds means that you won't have to share your wave with anyone. The folowing beaches are mapped on pp68–9.

- **Playa Maria Chiquita** In front of Maria Chiquita. Beach break with lefts and rights, but limited to big swell.
- **Isla Grande** In front of La Guayra, best reached by water taxi. Reef bottom break with three peaks, rights and lefts.
- **Isla Mamei** Next to Isla Grande, reached by boat or paddling from Isla Grande. Left-hand point break over shallow reef.
- **Playa Palenque/Cuango** In front of Cuango village. Beach break with rights and lefts. Surfers seldom seen here.
- **Playa Grande Mainland** East of Isla Grande. Beach break with some reef. Waves break left and right.
- **Turtles** Paddling distance from Playa Grande. Waves are great; unreal tubes, if it is glassy with a big swell.
- **V-Land** Near Devils Beach, in Sherman. Unbelievable right-point reef break with great tubes when there's big swell and it's glassy.

---

a living from fishing and coconuts – you'll get a taste of both when you sample the fine island cuisine.

Owing to its location on Panama's northern Caribbean coast, Isla Grande gets an awful lot of rain year-round. Terms like 'rainy' and 'dry' seasons don't apply here, though torrential showers are usually intense and shortlived, much like a traveling fling.

Orientation

Isla Grande is 10-minute boat ride from La Guayra, a tiny coastal hamlet that is connected to Colón via frequent bus connections. Boats arriving at Isla Grande dock in front of the Cabañas Super Jackson, which serves as the island's unofficial landmark.

Activities

Some lovely **beaches** on the northern side of the island can be reached by boat (hire a water taxi at the dock in front of Cabañas Super Jackson) or on foot (there's a water's edge trail that loops around the 5km-long, 1.5km-wide island, as well a slippery cross-island trail).

Some fine snorkeling and dive sites are within a 10-minute boat ride of the island. **Centro de Buceo Isla Grande** (☎ 501 4374; www .buceoenpanama.com; 1-2-tank dive US$60/80), located 50m west of Cabañas Super Jackson, offers a variety of dives around the island and in the Archipiélago de San Blás.

For US$30, one of the boaters in front of Cabañas Super Jackson will take you on a half-day adventure. The possibilities are quite appealing – the **mangroves** east of Isla Grande are fun to explore, or you could go **snorkeling** off the coast of the nearby islets.

Festivals & Events

The **Festival of San Juan Bautista** is celebrated here on June 24 with swimming and canoe races. The **Virgen del Carmen** is honored on July 16 with a land and sea procession, baptisms and masses.

Carnaval is also celebrated here in rare form. Women wear traditional *polleras* (traditional festive dresses) while men wear ragged pants tied at the waist with old sea rope, and everyone dances the conga. There are also satirical songs about current events and a lot of joking in the Caribbean calypso tradition.

Sleeping & Eating

Cabañas Super Jackson (☎ 448 2311; d with fan/air-con US$20/35; ⌘) Closest to the main pier, this Isla Grande landmark offers a handful of budget rooms that have the character and ambience of a hospital waiting room. There are definitely more comfortable spots on the island, but it's hard to beat the price, the convenience factor and the humorous name. If you're looking to fill the gut without breaking the bank, the small on-site restaurant

COLÓN PROVINCE

serves both island cuisine and traditional Panamanian favorites.

Hotel Sister Moon (☎ 226 9861; www.hotelsister moon.com; d from US$70; ❄ ⚑) A 10-minute walk east of the Super Jackson brings you to this lovely clutch of cabins, which are perched on a hillside at the end of the island. Surrounded by swaying palms and crashing waves, each cabin boasts fabulous views from its front porch, though they're best appreciated from the cozy confines of a swinging hammock. The hotel also has an excellent bar-restaurant that's built right over the water and features the island's famous coconut-infused seafood.

Bananas Village Resort (☎ 263 9766; www.bananas resort.com; s/d from US$65/100; ❄ 💻 ⚑) Located on the northern side of the island and only accessible by boat or trail, Grande's most upscale accommodation consists of several two-story A-frame cottages that are backed by jungle and fronted by the sea. Cheerful rooms are highlighted by white-wicker furniture and French doors – ask for the upstairs rooms which are slightly larger and have private balconies. Guests can also take advantage of the full resort amenities on offer including the free use of boats and snorkeling gear, organized tours and live shows.

Getting There & Away

Buses to La Guayra leave from the Colón bus terminal hourly from 6am to 6pm (US$2.50, 1½ hours). These buses can be also be boarded at Sabanitas, the turnoff for Portobelo, La Guayra, and Nombre de Dios.

In La Guayra, there are always skippers hanging about near the water's edge, waiting to take people to the island. The 10-minute boat ride costs US$1 per person; secure parking costs US$1 per day.

NOMBRE DE DIOS
pop 1000

Once regarded as 'treasure house of the world,' Nombre de Dios was destroyed without prejudice by Sir Francis Drake in 1596. Although the Spanish subsequently abandoned the city, Drake's glory was fleeting. With the taste of victory still fresh in his mouth, Drake contracted dysentery and died quietly at sea.

For the past 400 odd years, Nombre de Dios has existed as a backwater hamlet. There are no Spanish ruins to speak of, though local residents, the majority of whom are descended from slaves, occasionally find silver coins on the beach.

Most travelers pass through Nombre de Dios on their way to the popular Jimmy's Caribbean Dive Resort, but you can stop here if you have a burning desire to look for Drake's body (see the boxed text, below).

History

In 1510 Diego de Nicuesa ordered his small fleet to land after they failed to establish a colony at the mouth of the Río Belén in Veraguas. Leading a fleet of sick and starving men, Nicuesa looked upon the seemingly fruitful shore near the northernmost point of the isthmus and exclaimed, '¡Paremos aqui, en el nombre de Dios!' (Let us stop here, in

---

LOCAL LORE: A PIRATE'S GRAVE

Legend has it that Sir Francis Drake's body lies near Nombre de Dios in a leaden coffin at the bottom of the ocean, but it remains undiscovered to this day. The captain was buried at sea within striking distance of the scenes of his earlier exploits, his descent to the ocean floor accompanied by a thunderous salute fired by his fleet.

In Drake's honor, two of his own ships and his share of the Nombre de Dios treasure were sunk near the spot, though these too remain undiscovered to this day. A nearby point and a small island were named after him and a sermon was read aboard Drake's ship, the *Defiance*, with all of the captains of his fleet in attendance. It went like this:

Where Drake first found, there last he lost his name,
And for a tomb left nothing but his fame.
His body's buried beneath some great wave,
The sea that was his glory is his grave.
On whom an epitaph none can truly make,
For who can say, '*Here* lies Sir Francis Drake?'

the name of God!). His followers, sensing something auspicious in his words, decided to call the point Nombre de Dios even before they landed.

Although 800 men had left Hispaniola in November of 1509, only 280 survived long enough to land on shore at Nombre de Dios. Using what little strength they had left, the settlers built a fledgling settlement and survived on rotten provisions and the occasional alligator.

A few months later, a scouting party from the Spanish colony at Antigua in the Darién stumbled upon Nombre de Dios. By this time, only 60 settlers remained, though the majority of the survivors were racked with sickness and hunger. Mortified by the desperate existence of Nombre de Dios, the scouts fled and returned to Antigua with horror stories about Nicuesa and his men.

Hoping to escape their earthly prison, Nicuesa and 17 men sailed to Antigua, but they were forbidden to come ashore by the colony's governor. Racked with desperation, Nicuesa and his men paddled to shore on a lifeboat; they were immediately seized, placed on the worst vessel in the harbor and forced to sail away. The rotting craft left Antigua on March 1, 1511, and the ship and its passengers were never seen again. Back at Nombre Dios, the 43 miserable survivors were rescued and given asylum back in Antigua by its governor, Vasco Núñez de Balboa.

It is rumored that the worm-eaten vessel wrecked on the coast of Veraguas, where these words were found carved into a tree: '*Aqui anduvó perdido el desdichado Diego de Nicuesa*' (Here wandered lost the wretched Diego de Nicuesa). Another rumor has it that while landing on the coast for water, Nicuesa and his men were captured by natives, barbecued and eaten. According to a third rumor, a tree was found in Cuba inscribed with the words '*Aqui feneció el desdichado Nicuesa*' (Here died the wretched Nicuesa) carved into it.

Following the founding of Panamá in 1519, Nombre de Dios was resettled and quickly became the Caribbean terminus of trade across the isthmus. And so it remained until 1598 when it met its fate at the hands of Sir Francis Drake.

Orientation & Information

Nombre de Dios consists of nothing more than a few rows of houses and a small commercial plaza. Jimmy's Caribbean Dive Resort is located on a signed turnoff 5km east of town.

Sleeping

Five kilometers east of Nombre de Dios is the turnoff for **Jimmy's Caribbean Dive Resort** (☎ 682 9322; www.caribbeanjimmysdiveresort.com; divers 4/6/7 nights US$499/799/895, nondivers 4/6/7 nights US$369/519/589; P), a remote retreat of five intimate cabins with private facilities that are perched on the ocean's edge. Jimmy's is a long way from pretty much everything, though the divers staying here don't seem to care, especially since there is an excellent assortment of shore dives, reef dives, wreck dives and cavern dives on offer. If you're the partner of a serious diver and you're not looking to get your feet wet, Jimmy's offers plenty of other distractions including jungle excursions, horseback riding and fishing trips. The heart of the resort is an excellent restaurant-bar, which serves a variety of fresh seafood plates, pastas and grilled meats, and hosts lives bands on weekends. Rates include lodging, three meals a day, two boat dives per day, activities, and transport to and from the airport in Panama City.

Getting There & Away

Buses to Nombre de Dios (labeled 'Costa Arriba') depart from Colón's bus terminal hourly from 6am to 6pm (US$2.50, 1½ hours). These buses can be also be boarded at Sabanitas, the turnoff for Portobelo and La Guayra.

Comarca de Kuna Yala

The Comarca de Kuna Yala is a narrow, 226km-long strip on the Caribbean coast that includes the Archipiélago de San Blás, which stretches from the Golfo de San Blás to the edge of the Colombian border. The islands are home to the Kuna, who run San Blás as a *comarca* (autonomous region) with minimal interference from the national government. Following a violent uprising on February 25, 1925, the Kuna were granted permission to implement their own system of governance and economy while still maintaining their language, representation in the Panamanian legislature and full voting rights. Given that the Kuna have been in contact with Europeans ever since Columbus sailed along here in 1502, this has been no small achievement. Their success is the result of their remarkable tenacity and zealous efforts to preserve a traditional way of life. Today, they have one of the greatest degrees of political autonomy of any indigenous group in Latin America.

The Kuna like to say that their archipelago consists of 'one island for every day of the year.' In fact, there are nearly 400 islands in the chain, all small creations of sand and palms with the turquoise Caribbean lapping at their shores. While the majority of the islands are magazine-cover beauties, the Kuna choose to inhabit no more than a handful of acre-sized cays, which are packed with bamboo huts and people. Although outsiders often wonder why the Kuna choose to live in such crowded conditions, this is a testament to the incredible sense of community and identity that has allowed the Kuna to achieve their remarkable degree of independence.

Difficult access and strict limitations on visitors have invariably stemmed overdevelopment in the region, though San Blás is no longer the off-the-beaten-path tourist destination it once was. However, the archipelago continues to attract intrepid and independent travelers and it's still fairly easy to seek out either vibrant community life or complete and total isolation.

HIGHLIGHTS

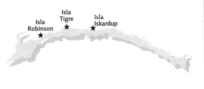

- Interacting responsibly and sustainably with the Kuna (opposite), a fiercely independent people who maintain their traditions in a changing world
- Shopping for *molas* (p263), a traditional Kuna textile that is now the national handicraft of Panama
- Letting your hair down as you party it up with the locals on **Isla Tigre** (p270)
- Living out your wildest desert island fantasy on the backpacker-friendly **Isla Robinson** (p267)
- Escaping to the Kuna Lodge at **Isla Iskardup** (p271), the finest retreat in the archipelago

■ POPULATION: 33,000	■ AREA: 2360 SQ KM	■ ELEVATION: SEA LEVEL TO 748M

THE KUNA
History

Although the Kuna have lived in Eastern Panama for at least two centuries, their origins are fiercely debated by scholars. Language similarities with people who once lived several hundred kilometers to the west would indicate that the Kuna migrated eastward. However, oral tradition has it that the Kuna migrated to San Blás from Colombia after the 16th century, following a series of devastating encounters with other tribes armed with poison-dart blowguns.

Regardless of the Kuna's origins, scholars agree that life on the islands is relatively new for them. Historians at the end of the 18th century wrote that the only people who used the San Blás islands at that time were pirates, Spaniards and the odd explorer. However, the Kuna flourished on the archipelago due to the abundance of fresh fish, lobster, shrimp, crab and octopus. This subsistence diet was also accompanied by food crops, including rice, yams, yucca, bananas and pineapples, which were grown in plots on the mainland, a short distance away.

Today there are an estimated 70,000 Kuna: 32,000 live on the district's islands, 8000 live on tribal land along the coast and 30,000 live outside the district. So communal are the island Kuna that they inhabit only 48 of the nearly 400 keys; the rest are mostly left to coconut trees, sea turtles and iguanas. On the inhabited islands, so many traditional bamboo-sided, thatched-roof houses are clustered together that there's scarcely room to walk between them.

Until the late 1990s, the district's principal currency was the coconut. (In recent years, the sale of *molas* replaced the sale of coconuts as the Kuna's number one revenue source.) The Kuna grow coconuts like crazy: in a good year they'll harvest more than 30 million of them. They barter away most of these to Colombians, who make the rounds of Kuna towns in old wooden schooners, each of which can hold 50,000 to 80,000 coconuts. In return for the fruit, the Colombians give the Kuna clothing, jars of coffee, vinegar, rice, sunglasses, canned milk, batteries, soups and other goods.

In Colombia the coconuts are used in the production of candy, gelatin capsules, cookies, shampoos and other products. Colombia has many processing plants for the fruit, but Panama, oddly, has none. The Colombians also sell Kuna coconuts to other South American countries.

The Kuna are shrewd businesspeople. Since their economy was based on the sale of coconuts until very recently, they protect it by selling the fruit at a predetermined price to prevent their buyers from playing one Kuna off another to bring down the cost. Every year, Kuna chiefs agree on one price for coconuts. If a Kuna is found selling coconuts at another price, they are severely punished by the community. By stabilizing the sale of coconuts and enforcing trade restrictions, the chiefs prevent price wars among the Kuna. Price wars would hurt the community by lowering the standard of living and potentially force some Kuna out of business.

In another protectionist move, the chiefs passed a law a few years ago prohibiting outsiders from owning property in the district. Although they promptly forced out the handful of foreigners living on the islands without compensation, the law ensured limitations on tourism in the region, and prevented foreigners from speculating real estate and driving up living costs. Today, there are fewer than a dozen places to stay on the islands, though each hotel is 100% owned and managed by local Kuna families.

Culture

The traditional Kuna belief structure is based around three principal concepts: god, nature and the cosmos.

According to Kuna religion, the world was created by God, Paba Tummat, and the Great Mother, Nan Tummat, who continue to keep watch over everyone's daily actions. Although Kuna shamans often look into the future and make minor divinations, everything in life is believed to be preordained by God and the Great Mother. In fact, the Kuna make great efforts in their daily lives to ensure that their actions follow the will of Paba and Nan Tummat, even though they do not know their fate.

The Kuna identify strongly with nature and their rich oral traditions are full of songs, hymns and prayers that recount the beauty and majesty of the wind, the land and the sea. To the Kuna, man and nature are considered parts of the same entity and thus the rules of nature follow human life from birth to death. The Kuna also love and admire nature, and believe that true happiness is only experienced within its presence.

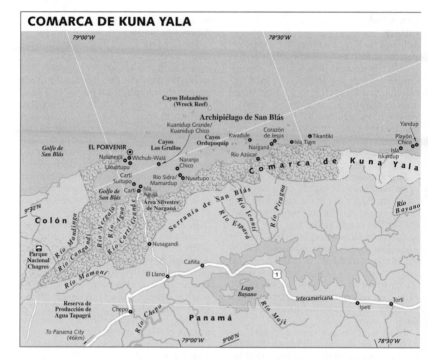

COMARCA DE KUNA YALA

Kuna cosmology is based on the doctrine that the knowledge of a concept allows the knower to manipulate the power of the concept. As a result, Kuna myths and legends have both a literal and a symbolic meaning. For example, the story of the Ibeorkun, who descended to the earth in order to teach the Kuna how to have chiefs, is often associated with most of the moral and ethical teachings of the Kuna.

Not surprisingly, the cornerstone of the Kuna political organization is the Ibeorkun or gathering house. Here, men gather nightly for heated discussions about local events, to make decisions about important problems and to listen to the advice of chiefs. Generally, each island has at least three chiefs and their authority is officially recognized by the Panamanian government. Every year, there are two general assemblies for the representatives from all of the islands in the Comarca where major issues affecting the Kuna are discussed.

Historically, the Kuna were matrilocal, meaning that when a man marries, he moves into the household of his wife's parents and comes under the control of his father-in-law.

Today, this pattern is yielding to neolocality, meaning that newlyweds will establish residence away from both parents. As recent as a generation ago, Kuna households had an average size of seven to 12 people, but today households are often comprised of as few as five people.

The distinctive dress of the Kuna is immediately recognizable no matter where you are in Panama. Most Kuna women continue to dress as their ancestors did. Their faces are adorned with a black line painted from the forehead to the tip of the nose, with a gold ring worn through the septum. Colorful fabric is wrapped around the waist as a skirt, topped by a short-sleeved blouse covered in brilliantly colored molas. The women wrap their legs, from ankle to knee, in long strands of tiny beads, forming colorful geometric patterns. A printed headscarf and many necklaces, rings and bracelets complete the wardrobe. In sharp contrast to the elaborate women's wear, the Kuna men have adopted Western dress, such as shorts and sleeveless shirts.

In recent years, Kuna culture has come under increasing threat of Westernization,

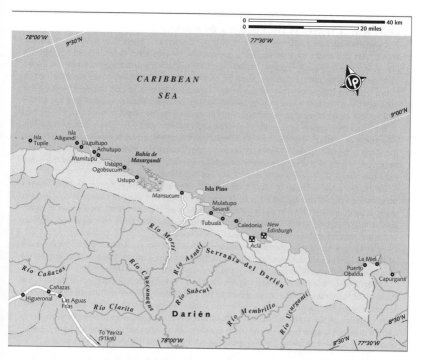

particularly as young Kuna are drawn away from the islands and toward the mainland in search of employment and increased opportunities. However, Kuna culture has survived countless generations of foreign encroachment and communities are just as committed to preserving their identity today as they were when the Spanish first arrived.

ORIENTATION

Few of the islands in the archipelago are more than 10km from the district's mainland. All of the heavily inhabited islands are very close to the coast in order for the Kuna to access agricultural areas and vital natural resources, such as water, firewood and construction materials. Also on the mainland are the giant trees from which the Kuna make their chief mode of transportation – the *cayuco*, a dugout canoe made from a burned and hollowed-out trunk. There are nine towns on the mainland, all within 100m of the sea, though there are no restaurants or hotels in these towns.

The only practical means of visiting the Comarca de Kuna Yala is to fly there, or to depart from Colón on a private sailboat. At the northwest end of the province, El Porvenir is the gateway to the San Blás islands, and one of the most popular destinations for visitors. From here, boat transportation can be arranged to other islands, several of which have basic hotels. If you're planning on staying at any of the far-flung islands, you can also fly into one of several remote landing strips scattered throughout the Comarca.

INFORMATION

Owing to the limited number of flights to the area, you should book as far in advance as possible. It's also recommended that you reserve your hotels in advance, especially since package deals are pretty much the norm in the Comarca. You're also going to want to hit up an ATM before you touch down on the islands.

The best time to visit the Comarca is May through November, when the winds are stronger and the temperatures are generally lower. When there's no breeze and the mercury rises, the humidity sets in and life on the San Blás islands can cease to be a paradise. During January and February, the seas can

RESPONSIBLE TRAVEL IN THE COMARCA DE KUNA YALA

If you're thinking about whether or not to visit the Comarca de Kuna Yala, please consider the impact that you might have on the Kuna community. On one hand, revenue from tourism can play a vital role in the development of the region, particularly if you are buying locally produced crafts or paying for the services of a Kuna guide. However, the Archipiélago de San Blás is not a human zoo and indigenous tourism can be an exploitative force. If you do decide to visit, please remember that Western interests have already caused an irreversible amount of damage to the region – be aware of your surroundings, and be sensitive to the plight of the Kuna.

The Kuna may appear unfriendly to tourists and understandably so, given that most visitors view them as oddities that must be photographed. Cruise ships visit several islands and when the ships arrive, the number of people on an already congested island can triple. Nonetheless, nearly two-thirds of the populace (the tourists) are trying like crazy to photograph the other third (the Kuna). It's a pretty ugly scene that's repeated again and again.

Furthermore, the behavior of many tourists is appalling to the Kuna. For example, Kuna women dress conservatively and always keep their cleavage, bellies and most of their legs covered. Yet many foreign women arrive in Kuna villages in bikini tops and shirt skirts, an act that is nearly always interpreted by the Kuna as a sign of disrespect. Likewise, Kuna men never go shirtless and travelers who do so risk offending local sensibilities.

As a result of repeated violations, the Kuna ask that travelers pay fees for photographs taken of them as well as visitation fees for each island. Travelers who consider these policies intolerable should leave their cameras tucked away and see what a little personal interaction can bring.

Unfortunately, tourism is developing too rapidly in the region and Kuna elders believe the invasion of foreigners poses a major threat to the preservation of their culture. In response, the Kuna Congress has started to debate the extent to which foreigners should be granted access to their Comarca. In the years to follow, it is likely that the Kuna Congress will ban photography in certain areas while prohibiting tourist traffic in others. As an informed and conscientious traveler, please do your best to always inquire locally about proper conduct in the Comarca.

also get extremely rough, which is great for surfers in Bocas, but terrible for boat captains in San Blás.

While in the Comarca, it helps to have a good command of Spanish as few Kuna outside the tourist centers speak English. In fact, not all Kuna speak Spanish and in more remote areas you will have to rely on your guide or boatman to do the talking for you. However, it's fairly easy to pick up a word or two of Kuna, and a little linguistic prowess will win you friends and favors wherever you go. For a quick crash course in the Kuna language, see p268.

As previously mentioned, the Kuna are very particular about what foreigners do on their islands. As a result, the Kuna require tourists to register and pay a visitation fee between US$3 and US$5 on the main islands. The price varies from island to island and you're expected to pay regardless of whether you stay for a week or only half an hour. On smaller, privately owned islands, you must seek out the owner, receive permission to stay on the island and pay a small fee of around US$2.

Visitors are expected to pay for any photographs they take of the Kuna people. If you want to take someone's photo, ask his or her permission first and be prepared to pay US$1 per subject (some Kuna expect to be paid US$1 per photo). You may not be required to pay for a photograph taken of an artisan from whom you buy crafts from, but it depends on the subject. Some islands may charge you US$50 just for possessing a video camera.

If you want to camp on an uninhabited island, US$5 a night per couple will usually do the trick. But camping on such islands isn't wise because you run the risk of encountering drug traffickers in the night. The Kuna do not allow the Panamanian coast guard or US antidrug vessels to operate in the archipelago, so the uninhabited islands are occasionally used by Colombian drug traffickers running cocaine up the coast.

There are only a handful of lodgings on the islands and none on the mainland. Most of these are basic but comfortable. Most densely populated islands in the district have a store selling basic items, as well as coin telephones from which you can place domestic and international calls. The phones are public, but there's usually a Kuna standing nearby charging a telephone tax of up to US$1 per call.

Since there are almost no restaurants on the islands, each hotel provides all the meals for its guests. The meals are usually based on seafood, with lobster and fish the specialities. Quality varies, as some of the fishing stocks have been depleted through overfishing, but there is always a healthy stock of fresh coconuts on hand.

ACTIVITIES

Most hotels offer complete packages, where a fixed price gets you a room, three meals a day and boat rides to neighboring islands for swimming, snorkeling and lounging on the beach. If you seek community life, you can also arrange visits to more populated islands. Before swimming off the shores of a heavily populated island, however, take a look at the number of outhouses built over the ocean – they may change your mind.

Snorkeling is good in places, but many of the coral reefs in the region are badly damaged. You can often rent snorkeling equipment from your hotel, but serious snorkelers should bring their own gear. Hikers can also arrange jaunts to the mainland jungles, but these trips should not be attempted without a guide. Activities aside, most travelers to Kuna Yala are content with simply soaking up the Caribbean sun and perfecting their hammock-swaying.

FESTIVALS & EVENTS

One of the biggest holidays in Kuna Yala is the commemoration of the anniversary of the **Kuna Revolution of 1925**. This is celebrated on February 25, which marks the day when the Kuna rebelled against the Panamanian police who had been occupying the islands, and expelled them from the Comarca. On Isla Tigre (p270) this event is remembered through an emotional re-enactment of the rebellion against the Panamanian police.

Isla Tigre is also the sight of the celebration of the traditional dance, the **Nogagope**, which takes place from October 10 to 12. The event is marked by communities from outlying islands converging on Isla Tigre and dancing for three days straight. This is proceeded by a huge *feria* from October 13 to 16 that includes more dancing as well as art expositions and various games and sports events such as canoe races.

SHOPPING

Molas are the most famous of Panamanian traditional handicrafts. Made of brightly colored squares of cotton fabric sewn together, the finished product reveals landscape scenes, birds, sea turtles, fish and beasts – often surrounded by a mazelike, geometric pattern. Craftsmanship varies considerably between *molas*. The simplest are peddled for a few dollars; more elaborate designs are works of art and can cost several hundred dollars. You can find *molas* on the islands (or rather, the *mola*-sellers will find you).

Mola work originated from the transfer of designs used for body painting to the cloth,

SAILING TO COLOMBIA

Want to be the envy of your jealous friends and a disappointment to your concerned family? One of the best ways to explore the Archipiélago de San Blás is to grab a spot on a chartered sailboat to Colombia. Although there's no shortage of merchant ships plying the waters between Colón and Cartagena, Colombia, sailing with a reputable captain pretty much guarantees that you won't be a stowaway on a ship full of narcotics. Adventure travel is one thing, but getting caught in the crossfire between narcotraffickers and border guards is another.

The best place to enquire about scheduled departures is at any of the youth hostels in Panama City (p90). At these spots, there are usually postings on the noticeboards advertising specific boats and their fearless captains. If you're worried about breaking the bank, don't be – a five-day sailing trip including food, drinks and activities should only cost about US$275; a flight back from Cartagena costs around US$200. And in case your family is worried sick, you can honestly tell them that the walled-city of Cartagena is easily the safest (and most beautiful) city in Colombia. Buen Viaje!

For a brief overview of what awaits in Cartagena, see p264.

COMARCA DE KUNA YALA

particularly on underskirts and blouses. When the Panamanian government tried to modernize the Kuna by prohibiting the wearing of traditional dress, the *mola* emerged as a symbol of independence. Even when Kuna schools were administered by Panamanian officials, girls wore special *molas* that conformed with school colors as a sign of silent protest.

Today there is a wonderful sense of pride among Kuna women regarding *molas*. In addition to being an integral part of the Kuna culture, *molas* are wholly unique to the Comarca.

The Kuna classify *molas* primarily on the basis of differences in the technical process:

Abiniguat One color; refers to a single layer of color sewn onto a base layer.

Obagalet Two colors; refers to two layers sewn onto a base layer.

Mor-Maralet Few colors; refers to two or more layers sewn onto a base layer.

Morgonikat Many colors; refers to two or more layers sewn onto a base layer with additional filler layers, embroidery and/or appliqué.

GETTING THERE & AWAY
Air
Both **Air Panama** (☎ 316 9000; www.flyairpanama.com /tickets) and **Aeroperlas** (☎ 315 7500; www.aeroperlas .com) fly to the Archipiélago de San Blás. Air Panama has one flight per day to Achutupu, Cartí, Corazón de Jesús, El Porvenir, Playón Chico and Río Sidra. Aeroperlas has three flights per day to all of these destinations, except Achutupu.

Book as far in advance as possible as demand far exceeds supply. Note that planes may stop at other islands in the archipelago, loading and unloading passengers or cargo before continuing on.

Flights depart from Albrook Airport in Panama City and arrive at their destinations in about 30 minutes to an hour. A one-way flight ticket to each destination is typically

---

LONELY PLANET GUIDE TO CARTAGENA (ABRIDGED) Michael Kohn

Sailing to Colombia? Wishing you had a bit of info on Cartagena? Here's a brief rundown of what awaits you in South America:

CARTAGENA

A fairytale destination of romance and legends, Cartagena de Indias is arguably the most beautiful city in South America. With its maze of cobbled alleys, historic houses shrouded in bougainvillea and leafy plazas fronted by massive churches, Cartagena invokes images of the long-gone era of the Spanish Empire.

Founded in 1533, Cartagena swiftly blossomed into the main Spanish port on the Caribbean coast and the gateway to the north of the continent. As the city grew in wealth and prominence, the Spaniards decided to make Cartagena an impregnable port and constructed elaborate walls encircling the town as well as a chain of forts.

Today Cartagena has expanded dramatically, and the city is now Colombia's largest port. Nevertheless the old walled town has changed very little and exists as a living museum of 16th- and 17th-century Spanish architecture.

Sights

Cartagena's old town is its principal attraction, particularly the inner walled town consisting of the historical districts of **El Centro** and **San Diego**. Almost every street is worth strolling down. **Getsemań**, the outer walled town, is less impressive and not as well preserved, but it is also worth exploring.

The old town is surrounded by **Las Murallas**, the thick walls built to protect it. Construction was begun toward the end of the 16th century, after the attack by Francis Drake; until that time, Cartagena was almost completely unprotected. The project took two centuries to complete, due to repeated storm damage and pirate attacks.

The main gateway to the inner town was what is now the **Puerta del Reloj** (the clock tower was added in the 19th century). Just behind it is the **Plaza de los Coches**, a square once used as a slave market. A few steps southwest is the **Plaza de la Aduana**, the oldest and largest square in the old town. It was used as a parade ground and all governmental buildings were gathered around it.

US$35 to US$50; prices vary according to season and availability.

Car

The rugged El Llano–Cartí road is the only road that leads into the district. It connects the town of El Llano, on the Carretera Interamericana 70km east of Panama City, to the San Blás coastal hamlet of Cartí. The road begins near El Llano at the turnoff for Nusagandi, though even a German assault tank would have difficulty traversing this rugged terrain. To reach Cartí, you will need a 4WD with a powerful engine, a winch, good tires, lots of patience and a little luck.

GETTING AROUND
Air

Inter-island flights are occasionally available, though it's a good idea to inquire directly at regional air strips since schedules fluctuate wildly.

Boat

Boatmen await the arrival of planes to shuttle people to their island destination (US$2 to US$15). If you want to travel by boat between island groups or explore some of the far-flung islets, you can either hire local guides at the docks or have your hotel make the arrangements.

EL PORVENIR & NEARBY ISLANDS
El Porvenir
pop 2000

Situated at the northwestern end of the Comarca, El Porvenir serves as the gateway to the Archipiélago de San Blás. the majority of visitors to the islands arrive here by plane from Panama City, though the best part of El Porvenir is leaving it behind. Fortunately, the island's small dock isn't too far from the airport, and it's quick and easy to take a boat elsewhere. That 'elsewhere' is usually the island of Nalunega (p266),

---

Nearby, the **Plaza de Bolívar** is in a particularly beautiful area of the old town. One block west of the plaza is **Calle Santo Domingo**, a street that has hardly changed since the 17th century. On it stands the **Iglesia de Santo Domingo**, the city's oldest and grandest church.

Several forts were built at key points outside the walls to protect the city from pirates. By far the greatest is the huge stone fortress **Castillo de San Felipe de Barajas** (☎ 5-656-0590; Av Arévalo; admission US$3; ☼ 8am-6pm), east of the old town, which was begun in 1639, but not completed until some 150 years later.

Sleeping

Casa Viena (☎ 5-664-6242; Calle San Andrés, Getsemaní; dm with air-con US$3; d with/without bathroom US$10/5; ✕ ▢) One of the cheapest backpacker haunts in the city, the always popular Casa Viena has nononsense dormitories and shared facilities. It's the best place to link-up with other travelers and get the low-down on the area. The price is certainly right, especially since there is a range of amenities on offer including free internet, a communal kitchen, a laundry room and a book exchange.

    Casa Relax B&B (☎ 5-664-1117; Calle de Pozo No 20-105, Getsemaní; s/d US$36/45; ✕ ▢ ▣) If you're looking for a bit more privacy, look no further than the French-run Casa Relax B&B, which offers 10 individually decorated rooms complete with private luxurious bathrooms. In the mornings, a French breakfast is served around a communal table, allowing you to get to know the other guests.

Eating

A dozen stalls on the Muelle de los Pegasos operate round the clock, and offer an unbelievable selection of fruit juices and plenty of local snacks. Also try typical local sweets at the confectionery stands at El Portal de los Dulces on the Plaza de los Coches. Plaza Santo Domingo hosts six open-air cafés, serving a varied menu of dishes, snacks, sweets and drinks.

Getting There & Away

Avianca (☎ 8-512-3211; www.avianca.com.co) has three flights per week to Panama City. Prices vary according to season and availability, though you can expect to pay around US$200.

    The airport is located in the suburb of Crespo, 3km northeast of the old city, and is serviced by frequent local buses that depart from various points, including India Catalina and Av Santander.

    For information on getting to Cartagena by boat, see the boxed text on p263.

Wichub-Walá (below), Ukuptupu (right) or Cartí (right).

In addition to a landing strip and a dock, the town also proudly boasts a police station, two (sometimes working) public phones, some ramshackle houses and a few small shops. Although there's little reason to spend the night here unless you miss your flight, the **El Porvenir Hotel** (☎ 229 9000; r from US$25) has a few squalid rooms with private cold-water showers and naked hanging light bulbs, but don't count on reading late as the electricity is turned off at night. On the bright side, the management is friendly and the attached bar-restaurant is a good place to pass the time.

Nalunega

pop 500

With a name like 'Red Snapper Island,' it's no wonder that Nalunega's inhabitants spend most of their days fishing the surrounding seas. However, tourism has played an important role on the island for decades, mainly because Nalunega is home to the Comarca's oldest and most established hotel.

Founded in 1972 by Luis Burgos, the **Hotel San Blás** (☎ 262 9812; r per person with 3 meals & tours US$35) is one of the most popular hotels in the archipelago, partly due to the fact that it's just a short boat ride away from El Porvenir. Luis is also a dedicated owner-manager and his hotel has come a long way since the early '70s when it consisted of three Spartan huts and Luis served triple duty as cook, maid and boatman. The hotel features 29 simple yet rustic rooms, which are built out of bamboo and board, with shared bathrooms.

One of the perks of staying here is that you're just a stone's throw away from the sea and Luis employs several local boys to clean and maintain the beach. Another perk is the exceptional food on offer here, especially when the ocean has been kind to the local fishers.

If you phone ahead and tell Luis you're coming (he speaks English), he'll send a boatman to El Porvenir to pick you up.

Wichub-Walá

pop 100

Just a five-minute boat ride from El Porvenir, the sparsely populated island of Wichub-Walá is often touted by travelers as one of the best places in the Comarca to meet Kuna (and not just be paraded in front of them

as a tourist). It also helps that the island is home to one of the most attractive hotels in the Comarca, namely the **Kuna Niskua Lodge** (☎ 225 5200; r per person incl meals & tours US$35). Although the rooms are lacking the ocean views found at other spots, the Kuna Niskua Lodge is an attractive two-story structure of thatch and bamboo. The grounds are also artfully strung up with ample hammocks and the rural charm of the surrounding area is infectious.

Ukuptupu

Just a few hundred meters from Wichub-Walá lies the tiny artificial island of Ukuptupu, which is roughly the size of a basketball court. From 1974 to 1998, Ukuptupu was occupied by the Smithsonian Tropical Research Institute (STRI), though the scientists were kicked off the island following the passing of stricter legislation by the Kuna chiefs.

Today, the former research facility is now the **Ukuptupu Hotel** (☎ 220 9082; r per person with meals & tours US$35), which consists of over a dozen bamboo-sided, tin-roofed dwellings that are built over the water and connected via a series of boardwalks. For isolation and sea views, you can't beat Ukuptupu, though if you want to mingle with or at least observe the Kuna, you're better off on one of the other islands. Note that all of the bathrooms are shared, and that the toilets 'flush' directly into the sea – you might want to leave the snorkeling gear at home.

Cartí

pop 400

Cartí is the collective name for a group of islands and a small strip of coast that is a 45-minute boat trip south of El Porvenir. If you've arrived in the Comarca by car (see p265) and were successful in navigating the horribly rutted jungle trail affectionately known as the 'only road in Kuna Yala,' the coastal hamlet of **Cartí** will be your first port of call. There is also a small airstrip just outside town that caters primarily to non-roadwarriors.

A mere 100m separates Cartí from **Cartí Suitupo** or 'Crab Island,' which is roughly the size of three football fields. However, since islanders can easily access the mainland from here, Cartí Suitupo is one of the most densely populated islands in the Comarca. It's literally packed from end-to-end with bamboo houses – not surprisingly, it's terribly polluted.

Although there are plenty of other real estate options in the area, islanders have it easy here, especially since Cartí Suitupo is a popular port of call for another kind of traveler, namely cruise shippers. Be warned that if there's a cruise ship docked here, this already overcrowded island can feel like a mosh pit at a Metallica concert.

If you're looking to get a better cultural and historical understanding of the Kuna, there is a small but excellent **museum** (☎ 299 9074; admission $2; ☺ 8am-4pm daily) in the main village of Cartí Suitupo. The museum's founder, José Davis, gives guided tours of the museum in either English or Spanish, and can help elucidate everything from Kuna coming-of-age rituals to funerary rites.

Cartí Suitupo also serves as a good base for exploring nearby **Isla Aguja** (Needle Island), a picture-perfect tropical island of lazy palm trees, golden sands and gentle surf. The beaches on Aguja are perfect for swimming (and refreshingly absent of outhouses), and the few friendly souls who live here will make your visit all the more pleasant.

The only accommodation in the area is the **Dormitory Cartí Sugdup** (☎ 299 9002; r US$8) on Cartí Suitupo, a no-frills hotel with sterile rooms and passable shared facilities. Unless it's getting late, you're better off staying on one of the nearby islands.

RÍO SIDRA & NEARBY ISLANDS
Río Sidra

Located 15km east of Cartí Suitupo, Río Sidra serves as a secondary gateway to the Archipiélago de San Blás. Like El Porvenir, Río Sidra's small dock isn't too far from the airport and it's quick and easy to hop a boat elsewhere. That 'elsewhere' is usually Nusatupo (right), Kuanidup Grande (right), Isla Robinson (right) or the far-flung Cayos Los Grullos, Holandéses and Ordupuquip (p269).

Río Sidra is extremely congested and the effects of Westernization are more prevalent here than on other islands (50 Cent isn't exactly traditional Kuna music). If you do need to spend the night, there are a few rooms for rent above the **Refresquería Petita** (☎ 299 9058; r US$25 with 3 meals & tours) in the community of Mamartupo, though don't expect anything too comfortable. The stripped-down rooms are poorly ventilated and they share some rough-looking bathrooms, but the English-

speaking owner is definitely an interesting character to chat with.

Nusatupo

A few minutes by boat from Río Sidra is the rarely visited Nusatupo, or 'Rat Island,' which sees significantly fewer travelers than other destinations in San Blás. However, if island life is starting to make you feel claustrophobic, Nusatupo also serves as a convenient base for striking off to the mainland and exploring the jungles of the Comarca, though this is best attempted with a local guide, proper provisions and a true sense of adventure. A good place to organize a jungle expedition is the island's sole accommodation, namely the **Hotel Kuna Yala** (☎ 315-7520; r per person with 3 meals & tours US$40). Following a recent overhaul, the hotel now features 11 concrete cinderblock rooms and both over-the-ocean and flush toilets, though you needn't be too choosy as 'it' all ends up in the same place.

Kuanidup Grande

Just 30 minutes by motorized *cayuco* from Río Sidra, the tiny islet of Kuanidup Grande is only large in comparison to its nearby kid brother, Kuandip Chico. In fact, the only residents of Kuanidup Grande, aside from the guests lucky enough to be staying here, are some lazy iguanas and a few flocks of birds. Simply put, Kuanidup Grande is breathtaking – with pristine beaches of powdery white sand, swaying coconut palms and little else, the island is the stuff of travel-magazine covers.

Accommodation on the island is at **Cabañas Kuanidup** (☎ 227 7661; r per person with 3 meals & tours US$45), which is comprised of several bamboo-and-thatch cabins with sandy floors and a small shelf to place a lantern (provided). The cabins front a lovely beach that is perfect for swimming, but most guests pass the time by simply swinging in the hammocks and meditating to the sounds of the lapping waves.

Isla Robinson

A hop, skip and a coconut's throw away, the even tinier islet of Robinson is the most popular backpacker destination in the Comarca. Home to the budget-friendly **Robinson's Cabins** (☎ 299 9058; r per person with 3 meals & tours US$17.50), the island is the perfect destination for shoestringers who want nothing more than a thatch roof over their heads, sand beneath their toes and plenty of time on their hands. Of course, it's

A GUIDE TO THE KUNA LANGUAGE

Feeling a little tongue-tied? The following glossary will help you break the ice with the Kuna. Note – the second entry in all listings is Spanish, the third is Kuna.

Getting Started

Yes.	*Sí.*	*Elle.*
No.	*No.*	*Suli.*
Thanks.	*Gracias.*	*Dot nuet.*
Please.	*Por favor.*	*Uis anga saet.*
OK.	*Esta bien.*	*Nued gudii o.*
Good.	*Bueno.*	*Nabir, nuedi.*
Welcome.	*Bienvenidos.*	*Nuegambi uese be noniki.*

Greetings

Hello.	*Hola.*	*Na.*
How are you?	*¿Como esta usted?*	*Bede nued guddi?*
Fine, thank you. And you?	*Bien, gracias. ¿Y usted?*	*An nuedi. Bedina?*
Fine.	*Bien.*	*Nuedi.*
What is your name?	*¿Cual es su nombre?*	*Igi be nuga?*
My name is...	*Mi nombre es...*	*An nuga...*
Nice to meet you.	*Encantado.*	*An yeel itoe.*
Where are you from?	*¿De dónde es usted?*	*Be bia lidi?*
I am from...	*Soy de...*	*An ... ginedi.*

Feelings

I'm hungry.	*Tengo hambre.*	*An ukur itoe.*
I'm thirsty.	*Tengo sed.*	*An gobie.*
I'm cold.	*Tengo frío.*	*An dambe itoe.*
I'm warm.	*Tengo calor.*	*An uerba itoe.*
I'm sleepy.	*Estoy cansado.*	*An nue gapie.*
I'm happy.	*Estoy contento.*	*An yee ito dii.*

Useful Expressions

Let's go.	*Vamos.*	*Anmar nae.*
How much does this cost?	*¿Cuánto cuesta?*	*Qui mani?*
I want to buy it.	*Quiero comprarlo.*	*An bag-bie.*
Do you speak English?	*¿Habla inglés?*	*Be sumake merki galla?*
Come here.	*Venga aquí.*	*Uesik dage.*
Look at that.	*Miralo.*	*Dake.*
Speak slowly, please.	*Hable despacio por favor.*	*Uis binna sunmake.*
I don't understand.	*No entiendo.*	*Aku ittoe.*
I'm sorry.	*Lo siento.*	*An oakue.*
Foreigner	*Extranjero*	*Uaga*

On the Plate

Rice	*Arroz*	*Oros*
Bread	*Pan*	*Madu*
Fish	*Pescado*	*Ua*
Lobster	*Langosta*	*Dulup*
Coconut	*Coco*	*Koibir*
Coffee	*Café*	*Cabi*

Saying Goodbye

Good bye.	*Adiós.*	*Degi malo.*
Good luck.	*Buena suerte.*	*Nuedgine, nuegan bi.*
I'll see you tomorrow.	*Hasta manãna.*	*An banedse be dakoe.*
I had a good time.	*Me divertí.*	*An yer ittosa.*

easy to pass the days when you're hanging out with an interesting cast of travelers from around the world, and there are worse places to be than a tropical island floating in the middle of the Caribbean.

Naranjo Chico

Three kilometers northwest of Río Sidra is the island of Naranjo Chico, Little Orange or Narascandub Pipi, depending on who you ask. Although it's one of the largest islands in the area, Naranjo Chico is sparsely populated and the unspoilt nature here is ripe for exploration. Unfortunately, the only accommodation on the island is the **Cabañas Narascandub Pipi** (per person US$50 with 3 meals & tours), which is somewhat pricey considering the cabañas are only marginally sturdier than refugee shelters. If it's raining heavily, you will get wet, and you'll have to be able to survive without modern amenities such as electricity or water pressure. However, the families who run the cabañas couldn't be nicer and the nearby beaches and forests are under-touristed and impossibly scenic.

The Cays

The undisputed gems of the Archipiélago de San Blás are the Cayos Los Grullos, Holandéses and Ordupuquip, a triangle of three virtually uninhabited island chains that are separated by calm blue-green waters and surrounded by shallow reefs. At the lower left corner of the triangle are the **Cayos Los Grullos**, which are a mere 10km northwest of Río Sidra. Heading clockwise, the tip of the triangle is formed by the **Cayos Holandéses** (Dutchmen Keys), while the **Cayos Ordupuquip** are located in the south-eastern corner. Despite the lack of tourist facilities in the cays, yachties love to anchor near these islands, though it takes skill behind the wheel to keep your boat afloat here.

Approximately 100m north of Cayos Holandéses is a spot known as **Wreck Reef**, which earned its name by snaring all kinds of vessels over the years. The reef's notoriety stems from the fact that it's fairly offshore from the closest island, though the water south of the reef is barely 1m deep – the ocean floor north of the reef plunges 100m in half that distance. From the captain's perspective, this means that the ocean floor rises 100m to a dangerously shallow depth in half that distance.

Over the years, many experienced sailors have met their end here, though these days it's mostly drug runners and contraband smugglers that meet their doom. In 1995, a smugglers' boat filled with TV sets slammed into the reef at night. Although the smugglers had hoped to skip out on import taxes by sailing from Colón's Zona Libre to Cartagena, Colombia, they instead helped the local Kuna communities catch up with their favourite Venezuelan soap operas without paying a cent.

Needless to say, the snorkeling in the Cayos Holandéses is astounding, though you'll see plenty of tropical fish and colorful reefs anywhere in the cays. Unless you're on an organized tour – or you have your own yacht – you're going to need to hire a boat and guide to come out here. Depending on the distance between your hotel and your destination, you can expect to pay between US$50 and US$75 roundtrip to reach the cays. Be aware that the seas can get very rough out here, so make sure you have confidence in the sea-worthiness of your captain and his vessel. You're also going to want to make sure there are enough life jackets on board for everyone – and don't forget your snorkeling gear!

CORAZÓN DE JESÚS & NEARBY ISLANDS

Corazón de Jesús & Narganá

The densely populated islands of Corazón de Jesús and Narganá, which are linked by an arcing wooden footbridge, are of little interest to travelers, especially since they're the most Westernised Kuna communities in the Comarca. On these islands, Kuna families inhabit concrete cinderblock houses, wear Western clothing, dine on processed foods and hold community meetings in front of the television. However, if you've spent any amount of time on some of the more traditional islands, a quick visit to Corazón de Jesús and Narganá emphasizes why Kuna chiefs are so adamant about protecting their rapidly vanishing culture.

For travelers arriving by plane from Panama City, the coastal airstrip in Corazón de Jesús serves as a gateway to nearby Isla Tigre (p270), one of the most traditional islands in Comarca. Although Tigre is just 7km east of Narganá, the contrast in culture couldn't be greater.

At the southwestern end of the bridge is the island of Narganá. It's home to the district's

---

LOCAL LORE: CHOCOSANOS

Historically, most of the boats claimed by Wreck Reef were the victims of *chocosanos* – 'storms that come from the east' in Kuna. *Chocosanos* are ghastly tempests that whip up monstrous waves that can overrun entire islands. Such waves have swept many Kuna and their homes out to sea, though there are early warning signs, such as a purple-black easterly sky and a lack of breeze and birdsong.

As soon as it's evident that a *chocosano* is approaching, tradition dictates that Kuna elders must combat the storm by blowing into conch shells. The sound alerts their benevolent god, Paba Tummat, who tries to intervene and disperse the *chocosano*. If he fails, as he sometimes does, the eerie stillness is broken by ground-shaking thunderclaps, howling winds, pounding downpours and a vengeful sea.

At the southern end of Wreck Reef is a freighter that lies with its hull fully exposed and its deck flat against the ocean floor – a hulking vessel that was once flipped like a pancake by a mighty *chocosano*.

---

only courthouse and jail, so there are a lot of policemen on the island. If any ask for your passport, politely present it – jotting down tourists' names in little books gives them something to do.

The **Banco Nacional de Panamá** (Narganá; ⏱ 8am-3pm Mon-Fri, 9am-noon Sat) has an ATM, though the chance of actually withdrawing money is somewhat akin to getting three bars on a slot machine. However, it is possible to wire money here (allow at least 24 hours) and you can cash Amex traveler's checks here for a nominal fee.

If you have a pressing need to spend a night on the island, the **Nargana Lodge** (r standard/deluxe US$10/15; ❄) in 'downtown' Nargana is a surprisingly clean and modern hotel, especially if you're looking for some unexpected amenities. For an extra five bucks, you can unwind in an air-conditioned deluxe room, catch up on your favorite *telenovelas* (soap operas) and take a somewhat warmish shower.

Looking for a good meal? The island's best restaurant is Nali's Café, which is scenically perched on the beach near the canal separating both islands. Although a good seafood meal should only set you back a few dollars, it's worth splurging on a lobster feast if they're in season.

Isla Tigre

A short boat ride from the 'big city' of Corazón de Jesús and Narganá will bring you to Isla Tigre, one of the most traditional islands in the Comarca. With wide walkways separating homes, the island is surprisingly clean and un-crowded, which makes it easy to interact with local Kuna in a relaxed and stress-free envi-

ronment. Isla Tigre is also culturally vibrant, perhaps owing to the island's fairgrounds, which are home to some of the biggest festivals and events in the Comarca (see p263).

An extremely pleasant place to spend a night or two is at the beachside **Cabañas Tigre** (☎ 229 9006; r per person US$10), which features a clutch of cutesy bamboo-and-thatch cabañas with cement floors and shared facilities. The grounds around Tigre are amply strung up with colorful hammocks, and the ocean here is crystal clear and fairly placid, which is perfect for kayaking (US$5 per day) or snorkeling (free!). Although there isn't a kitchen at the cabañas, there's a small unnamed restaurant nearby that specializes in the 'catch of the day'. There's also a small *refresquería* (refreshment stand), which is popular with the locals.

PLAYÓN CHICO & NEARBY ISLANDS
Playón Chico

With regular air connections to Panama City, Playón Chico serves as a popular gateway to San Blás, especially since it's located near the archipelago's most expensive hotel on Isla Iskardup. If you're looking for more modestly priced accommodations, Playón Chico also serves as a convenient jumping-off point for nearby Yandup (opposite).

While much of the island is still covered by traditional dwellings, the main drag in Playón Chico is home to everything from missionaries and concrete churches to video shops and liquor stores. Although Playón Chico isn't set up to receive tourists, a quick stroll from the airstrip to the docks reveals the conflicting pressures shaping modern Kuna life.

Yandup

Just five minutes by boat from Playon Chicon, the tiny islet of Yandup is home to the **Yandup Lodge** (☎ 261 7229; cabin per person US$60 with 3 meals & tours), an admirable community-run venture that is administered by the non-profit organization **Dobbo Yala** (www.dobboyala .org.pa). This organization is dedicated to conservation and sustainable development, and works with several indigenous communities across the country. Accommodations are a handful of comfortably fitted thatched-roof cabins with private facilities, and guests are well cared for at this low-key spot. Yandup is also home to an attractive white-sand beach with good snorkeling and there's a variety of hiking trails leading through the island's jungle interior.

Isla Iskardup

Although you have to pay to play here, Isla Iskardup is the center of a cluster of uninhabited islands and is home to the finest retreat in the archipelago.

our pick **Sapibenega 'The Kuna Lodge'** (☎ 226 8824; www.sapibenega.com; s/d/tr/q with 3 meals & tours US$175/250/300/340) is a collection of 13 individually decorated water's-edge cabins with plank floors, bamboo walls and thatched roofs, which emphasize style and modernity. Gorgeous *molas* and other traditional Kuna handicrafts bring the cabins to life, while modern conveniences such as 24-hour solar-powered electricity and composting flush toilets provide creature comforts. The lodge is also centered on a breezy open-air bar and restaurant where you can dine on scrumptious

---

LOCAL VOICES: THE SAILA DUMMA (CHIEF) OF THE COMARCA DE KUNA YALA

Greg Benchwick

Sometimes travel is as much about luck as it is about serendipity and magic.

Prior to boarding a plane in Panama City en-route to El Porvenir, my Kuna guide whispered in my ear, 'See that man behind us? That's the Saila Dumma of the Comarca, the chief.' Although I was too nervous to walk right up to the man right there and shake his hand, I yearned to talk to him about the future of tourism in the region. While other indigenous groups in Central America often showcase their traditions to tourists in ways that wouldn't look out of place in an amusement park or, Las Vegas for that matter, the Kuna have adopted a strong model of cultural conservation. With this in mind, I decided to travel to the Comarca in the hope that I could witness first-hand how the Kuna have created this strong model of heritage tourism.

After arriving in El Porvenir, I mustered up the courage to introduce myself to the Saila Dumma, and to see if he would grant me an interview. Well, sometimes, all you need to do is ask. That very same afternoon, I chatted with Gilberto Arias over some Coca-Colas. Speaking through a translator, I prompted the chief to talk about the future of tourism in the region.

'In recent years tourism has been developing too rapidly. More and more people are coming,' said the aging leader. He looks around 65 years old, with a long, dignified nose, penetrating eyes and wrinkled hands. The Saila Dumma is used to being heard and he elucidates his views with the slow precision and confidence of a world leader. Despite the Kuna's communal practices, Gilberto Arias is the closest thing you find to a king in this region. 'We want to develop tourism, but we will be doing it together, as a community. We are not going to do any large-scale development in the region. This would have too strong an effect on our community – we have a very small, vulnerable culture.'

According to Arias, the invasion of tourists poses a major threat to the Kuna. 'Our children aren't used to this. They will see this new outside culture and suddenly want to change their lifestyle. And we, in turn, will start losing our culture. So, we are going to regulate and control how tourists visit the community.'

At present, most of the Comarca is open to tourists, including major cruise operators. But all that may change in the upcoming years, especially as the Kuna Congress begins to elucidate which places in the Comarca are sacred, and which places tourists shouldn't be allowed to visit.

I am filled with hope and trepidation for the Kuna. By inviting tourists into their communities, they have developed a means of promoting their culture to the world, but they are also exposing themselves to potentially damaging foreign elements. As conscientious travelers, we can help preserve the Kuna's identity by striving to visit their communities with sensitivity and responsibility.

Greg Benchwick is one of the commissioning editors of this guidebook.

EXPLORE MORE OF THE COMARCA DE KUNA YALA

With more islands than days of the year, Kuna Yala is an amazing destination for anyone looking to get off-the-beaten-path. Independent travelers often complain that they feel trapped inside their hotels, but striking off on your own and exploring the Comarca is definitely within the realm of possibility. Of course, arranging activities outside the normal hotel offerings becomes trickier as you will need to negotiate boat rides between islands and find places to stay and eat. However, if you speak a fair bit of Spanish (or better yet, a smattering of Kuna), this is entirely possible. Another option is to grab a spot on a chartered sailboat to Colombia (see p263).

Plenty of adventurous travelers succeed in hiring a boat and a guide to take them to the far-flung reaches of the Comarca, though this takes a bit of time and cash. Costs, however, can be kept to a minimum if you're prepared to camp on small islands or stay with local families. Although it can get tough-going at times, this is perhaps the best way to truly experience the lifestyle and culture of the Kuna. And of course, there's something to be said for spending days or weeks out at sea without laying your eyes on another gringo traveler.

---

seafood spreads or simply indulge in a cocktail or two with the other guests. Owner-manager Paliwitur Sapibe, who speaks English, Spanish and Kuna, also offers a variety of optional excursions to keep his guests busy and entertained. Possibilities include day-hikes to nearby waterfalls on the mainland, boat trips up jungle-flanked rivers and fishing excursions using the Kuna method of nylon, hook and stone.

ACHUTUPU & NEARBY ISLANDS
Achutupu

With regular air connections to Panama City, Achutupu (like Playón Chico to the west) serves as a popular gateway to San Blás, especially since it's located near the archipelago's second most expensive hotel (on Uaguitupo.) West of Uaguitupo, however, tourist infrastructure ceases.

Although the densely populated island of Achutupu isn't set up to receive overnight visitors, it's a popular day-trip for visitors from Uaguitupo who are interested in seeing Kuna village life. Of particular interest is the community gathering house at the center of the island, which often hosts important meetings, rituals and celebrations.

Uaguitupo

Although it's a mere 100m from Achutupu, the grassy isle of Uaguitupo is uninhabited and pristine, though like nearby Isla Iskardup, it's a destination aimed at high-rolling travellers. Taking up virtually all of Uaguitupo, the **Dolphin Island Lodge** (☎ 225 8435; s/d/tr US$110/190/255) is a clutch of concrete-floor stand-alone cabins with wooden walls and traditional thatch-roofing. Although the amenities here pale in comparison to Sapibenega 'The Kuna Lodge,' the unpretentious rooms are all equipped with private cold-water showers and environmentally friendly flush toilets. The atmosphere of the Dolphin Island Lodge is also much more relaxed and traditional than its upmarket brethren, especially at the breezy open-sided restaurant that faces a long set of breakers. The Dolphin Island Lodge receives rave reviews from readers, which is probably why it hosts so many repeat foreign visitors. The English-speaking staff are extremely attentive to their guests, especially if you're looking to hire a boat to explore the surrounding area.

BEYOND ACHUTUPU

If you're sailing to Colombia, be advised that tourist infrastructure is virtually non-existent west of Achutupu and Uaguitupo. Although there are several communities that allow foreigners on their islands, generally speaking the southern stretches of the Comarca are off-limits. However, adventurous souls can expect a healthy smattering of striking scenery and empty seas.

Be advised that the ocean can be treacherous along this part of the archipelago, particularly as you venture further away from the islands and into open water. Here, 3m swells are the norm and the waves can reach frightening heights if there is a storm on the horizon. If you've been frightened by the sea in other parts of the archipelago, you can expect to be terrified here. Again, if you plan to travel these waters and have any doubts about your boatman, consider hiring another one before attempting this trip.

Darién Province

Mention that you're going to the Darién to anyone and you'll no doubt be greeted with everything from fear and panic to horror and disbelief. Bad press and grave misconceptions about safety in the region would have you believe that the Darién is a no-go zone of Colombian guerrillas and narcotraffickers, but while the dangers of the province shouldn't be underestimated, they should at least be contextualized. There are certainly regions that shouldn't be visited unless you're looking to get kidnapped. However, these are few and far between and easily avoided by anyone with the slightest regard for personal welfare.

Home to a 576,000-hectare national park, southern Darién is where the primeval meets the present and the scenery appears much as it did a million years ago. Even today, the local Emberá and Wounaan people maintain many of their traditional practices and retain generations-old knowledge of the rainforest. Parque Nacional Darién is also one of world's richest biomes and is home to the legendary bird-watching destination of Cana. But while the south is home to Panama's most spectacular rainforests, the north is home to its worst scenes of habitat destruction. Although most news items focus on the spilling over of Colombia's civil war into Panama's borders, the real battle lines surround the province's rapidly disappearing forests.

With the right planning, the Darién offers spectacular opportunities for rugged exploration and is best approached by travelers with youthful hearts, intrepid spirits and a yearning for something truly wild.

HIGHLIGHTS

- Spotting macaws by the dozens in the historic gold-mining town of **Cana** (p286)
- Flying in on a chartered puddle jumper to **Reserva Natural Punta Patiño** (p281), a lush jungle reserve on the edge of Golfo de San Miguel
- Interacting with the Emberá in **Mogué** (p282), a traditional village on the banks of the Río Sambú
- Hiking along the spectacular jungle trails surrounding **Rancho Frío** (p285), a ranger station on the edge of the national park
- Going for a world record at the **Tropic Star Lodge** (p289), a remote fishing lodge that's been the site of some of the world's largest catches

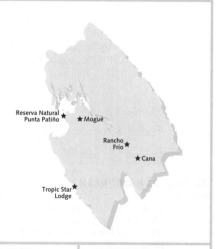

- POPULATION: 397,000
- AREA: 8653 SQ KM
- ELEVATION: SEA LEVEL TO 3478M

DARIÉN PROVINCE

DARIÉN PROVINCE

THE EMBERÁ & WOUNAAN
History
Living within the boundaries of the Darién are the Chocóes, as they are commonly called, who emigrated from the Chocó region of Colombia thousands of years ago. Anthropologists place the Chocóes in two linguistic groups – the Emberá and the Wounaan –

though with the exception of language, the groups' cultural features are virtually identical. However, both groups prefer to be thought of as two separate peoples.

Some historians contend that the Emberá emigrated from northern Ecuador and southern Colombia from 1830 and that the Wounaan emigrated from the Río San Juan

---

LOCAL LORE: NEW EDINBURGH

On November 2, 1698, five Scottish ships known as *Saint Andrew, Caledonia, Unicorn, Dolphin* and *Endeavour* made landfall on the Caribbean coast of the Darién. The settlers christened the colony New Edinburgh and set out to make a life on the edge of an unchartered jungle. However, despite early successes in cutting a canal, constructing fortifications, erecting huts and clearing farmland, the settlement was abandoned by the following July and no more than one ship carrying less than 300 survivors made it back to Scotland.

Although it's unclear exactly what happened during those ill-fated months, the Scots had all of the odds stacked against them. Stifling heat and humidity caused fever to spread throughout the colony, while malaria and yellow fever helped to bump up the mortality rate. It's also believed that they failed to establish a successful trading colony because of their poor choice of goods, namely wigs, shoes, bibles, woolen clothing and clay pipes. It didn't help that the Spanish conquistadores were determined to annihilate the colony, though it wasn't too hard to kill starving and ill men.

Today little remains of New Edinburgh, but the abysmal failure of the Scottish colony is legendary. Of course, had New Edinburgh thrived, then perhaps the Darién would have looked dramatically different today.

---

area of Colombia (where the greatest concentration of them lives today) around 1910. Other historians say the tribes arrived much earlier. Of course, the tribes themselves aren't sure as they do not possess a written history.

Before the introduction of the gun, the Emberá and Wounaan were expert users of the *boroquera* (blowgun) and they envenomed their darts with lethal toxins from poisonous frogs and bullet ants. Many scholars believe that it was these people who forced the Kuna out of the Darién and into the Caribbean coastal area they now inhabit.

The Emberá and Wounaan are famous throughout Panama for their incredibly fine dugout canoes. Known as *piraguas*, these boats have very shallow bottoms, so they can be used during the dry season when the rivers run low. Throughout its history, the Panama Canal Authority has employed Emberá and Wounaan craftsmen to make the *piraguas* which are used by officials to reach the higher parts of the canal's watershed.

Until it left Panama in the late 1990s, the US Air Force turned to the Emberá and Wounaan for help, but for an entirely different reason: jungle survival. Because both groups have the ability to survive and thrive in tropical wilderness, quite a few of them were added to the corps of instructors that trained US astronauts and air force pilots at Fuerte Sherman, near Colón.

Today, the majority of the 8000 Emberá and Wounaan in Panama live deep in the rainforests of the Darién, particularly along the Sambú, Jaqué, Chico, Tuquesa, Membrillo, Tuira, Yapé and Tucutí rivers.

Culture

The Emberá and Wounaan continue to survive on subsistence agriculture that is supplemented by limited fishing and poultry raising. Historically, both population groups were more reliant on slash-and-burn agriculture and hunting, but both practices are now restricted within the confines of the national park. However, the increasing number of commercial rice and maize plantations in the Darién have enabled the Emberá and Wounaan to work as seasonal migrant laborers.

The Emberá and Wounaan are also exceptional woodcarvers and basket weavers. Traditionally the men carved boas, frogs and birds from the dark *cocobolo* hardwood, though recently they have taken to carving tiny animal figurines out of the rock-hard *tagua* nut. The women produce some of the finest baskets in Latin America, which are woven from palm fibers, and require several months of intensive labor to complete. Both carvings and baskets fetch a high market price, and provide a much needed secondary income for most communities.

Emberá and Wounaan homes are extremely well suited to the rainforest environment. Built on stilts that are 3m to 4m off the ground, the floors consist primarily of surprisingly thin, but amazingly strong, strips of palm bark. This vaulted design protects occupants and food from ground pests and swollen rivers, and the palm bark is plentiful in the forest and easy to fashion. A log with stairs carved into it provides easy access to the home.

To permit breezes to enter, more than half of the typical Emberá and Wounaan home is open sided. The roofs are made of thatch, which keeps the rain out and acts as good insulation against the tropical sun. The kitchen typically occupies one corner and has an oven made of mud. Beneath the home, medicinal plants and edible vegetables and roots are grown. Pigs and poultry are often raised in pens.

Over the past few decades, the Emberá and Wounaan have gradually replaced their traditional attire with Western wear. Except for a few older individuals, the men have set aside their loincloths for short pants and now prefer short-sleeved shirts to going around bare chested. The women, who traditionally wore only a skirt, increasingly don bras and some have taken to wearing shirts as well. However, many women still wear traditional jewelry, especially wide silver bracelets and elaborate necklaces made of silver coins. Many Emberá and Wounaan also continue to stain their bodies purplish black with juice from the *jagua* fruit. The dye from this fruit is believed to have health-giving properties and it has the added bonus of warding off insects.

Like the Kuna, the Emberá and Wounaan have a strong measure of political autonomy, though their culture is at danger due to increasing external pressures. In the Darién, the biggest threat is encroachment by Latino settlers and habitat destruction by loggers, which has accelerated in recent years due to the paving of the Interamericana. Missionaries, particularly evangelical Christians, are fiercely active throughout the province and have almost entirely eliminated the core religious values of both groups. The younger generation is also being lured to the cities by increased employment prospects, which has prompted fears that both populations are dwindling fast.

Ultimately, the survival of the Emberá and the Wounaan is dependent on whether or not the Interamericana is brought into Colombia. If the road is finished, then all of the external pressures currently facing the Emberá and the Wounaan will exponentially increase and it's unlikely that such small populations will be able to survive assimilation. Fortunately, there are still a number of hurdles in completing the road, namely a civil war in Colombia, which means that it's likely that both populations will continue to survive for at least another generation.

ORIENTATION & INFORMATION

The Interamericana does not go all the way through Panama. It terminates in the middle of the jungle near a town called Yaviza in the vast wilderness region of the Darién, before starting again 150km further on in Colombia. This transportation break between Central and South America is known as the Darién Gap – it's literally the end of the road.

Despite occasional announcements by international authorities eager to improve transportation and trade between the continents, it is unlikely that the Interamericana will be pushed through the Darién Gap any time soon as Panamanians are concerned that a road could help Colombia's civil war spill over into Panama. A road could also increase illegal immigration and drug traffic and may help spread foot-and-mouth disease in cattle, which is presently limited to South America. A paved road would also make logging easier, perhaps leading to deforestation of the largest forested area in the country.

Any printed information on the Darién can become rapidly outdated. Travelers should always seek up-to-date information on local dangers. The best source of this information is a guide who leads frequent trips to the area.

Local Autoridad Nacional del Ambiente (ANAM; National Environment Authority) offices in towns such as El Real or La Palma can provide some information on the park and help you find guides. Travelers should also check in with the police in these towns before heading out into the jungle.

Panama City's Instituto Geográfico Nacional (p74) usually sells topographical maps for some regions of the Darién.

Keep your baggage to a minimum on any trek through the jungle. You will need insect repellent, sun block, a hat and rain gear. Food can only be found in the few towns and it is not available at the ranger stations. Bring drinking water or a means of purifying water.

Remember to plan your trip to coincide with the dry season (mid-December through mid-April); otherwise, you'll be slogging your way through thick mud and swatting at moth-size mosquitoes.

DANGERS & ANNOYANCES

The greatest hazard in the Darién is the difficult environment. Trails, when they exist at all, are often poorly defined and are never marked. Also, the many large rivers that form the backbone of the Darién transportation network create their own hazards. Any help at all, much less medical help, is very far away – if you get lost out here, you are done for. To minimize these risks, it's recommended that you explore the Darién either as part of an organized tour or with the help of a local guide. Hiring a knowledgeable guide will also provide up-to-date information on the no-go areas and it provides safety through numbers.

Dengue and malaria are serious risks in the province. Take a prophylaxis or chloroquine – and cover up as much as possible, especially at dawn and dusk. Areas of the Parque Nacional Darién are also prime territory for the deadly *fer-de-lance* snake. The chance of getting a snakebite is remote, but you should be careful – always wear boots while walking in the forest. Although they don't carry Lyme disease, ticks are everywhere in the Darién. In reality, they're nothing more than a nuisance, but you'd be wise to bring a good pair of tweezers and a few books of matches.

The US State Department has strongly advised against crossing an imaginary line drawn from Puerto Obaldía in the north to Bahía Piña in the south, with Yaviza in the center. Unfortunately, this ill-conceived advisory includes the entirety of Parque Nacional Darién, which is a shame as the destinations listed in this chapter are completely safe to visit.

Particularly treacherous, however, are the areas between Boca de Cupe and Colombia, the traditional path through the Darién Gap – there is minimal police presence in this area, and it is unlikely that you will be given assistance if (when) trouble arises. Although the forest trails from Boca de Cupe to Cana are generally safe, it's recommended that you avoid the towns of Balsal, El Naranjal, Púcuro, Limón, Paya and Palo de las Letras. The areas north and east of this are also considered dangerous, including the mountains Altos de Limón, the Río Tuquesa and the trail from Puerto Obaldía.

Although the no-go zones in the Darién are well removed from the traditional tourist destinations, the dangers in these spots cannot be underestimated. Narcotraffickers utilize these jungle routes and they don't

---

RESPONSIBLE TRAVEL IN THE DARIÉN

If you're thinking about whether or not to visit the Emberá and Wounaan communities in the Darién, please consider the impact that you might have. On one hand, revenue from tourism can play a vital role in the development of the region, particularly if you are buying locally produced crafts or paying for the services of a local guide. However, a living community is not a human zoo and indigenous tourism can be an exploitative force. If you do decide to visit, please remember that Western interests have already caused an irreversible amount of damage to the region – be aware of your surroundings and be sensitive to the plight of the Emberá and the Wounaan.

Unlike Kuna Yala, the Darién sees few foreign visitors, and it's unlikely that the cruise-ship circuit will swing this far south anytime soon. As a result, the Emberá and Wounaan tend to view tourists with equal parts respect and awe, and at times you will be amazed at the hospitality of your hosts. Although they are tough people that have made lives for themselves in an unforgiving habitat, the Emberá and Wounaan have smiles that could melt gold.

Of course, you should still make an effort to respect the sensibilities of your hosts. Although some men and women still walk around topless in the village, these are still fairly conservative societies and it's recommended that you cover up as a sign of respect. In regards to photography, the Emberá and Wounaan are less shy (and capitalistic) about photos than the Kuna. Although most villagers will be happy to pose for a photo, you should always ask before flashing your camera at a subject. Generally speaking, you will not be asked to pay for a photo, but it's best to ask your guide what is expected from you.

Tourism has a long way to develop in the region, which is one reason why a visit to an Emberá or Wounaan village is so refreshing. However, let's all work together to keep it that way. As an informed and conscientious traveler, please do your best to keep informed about proper conduct in the Darién.

STRIKING A DELICATE BALANCE

As little as 50 years ago, over 70% of Panama's total land mass was covered by forest. This sobering statistic gives a quick indication of the country's gravest environmental problem, namely deforestation. Today, trees continue to be felled at a frightening pace, with the Darién serving as the ecological ground zero.

While travelling in the Darién, you will undoubtedly see huge trucks transporting felled trees to saw mills in either Chepo or 24 de Diciembre, a village near Tocumen Airport. However, an even greater number of trees are moved to the mills by barge. Others are sprayed with a chemical that prevents rot, floated down the rivers and picked up at various mills along the way. This chemical wrecks havoc on the local environment, particularly on the health of agricultural plots and fish stocks.

Unfortunately, most Panamanians seem unconcerned with the rainforest's ongoing destruction. For much of the population, hunting and logging have been a way of life for generations and many communities maintain the belief that their economic welfare is dependent on these practices. Furthermore, Panama's national parks are staffed by only a handful of rangers, though their areas of coverage are colossal. For instance, in the Parque Nacional Darién, there are never more than 20 rangers assigned to protect 576,000 hectares, an area more expansive than some entire countries.

The destruction of the rainforest not only wipes out the animals that inhabit it, but also migratory animals that move with their seasonal food supplies. It also threatens the traditional cultures of the Emberá and the Wounaan, who still rely on the bounty of the rainforest for their survival. Finally, deforestation results in regional water shortages during the dry season, as well as a whole list of other environmental problems ranging from pollution to erosion.

Regardless, Panamanian politicians agreed in 2000 to pave the Interamericana as far as Yaviza, which will permit logging trucks to work the Darién year round and accelerate the region's destruction. In Panama, the loggers have a lot of influence.

For more information on the environmental situation in Panama, visit the home page of ANCON at www.ancon.org (in Spanish).

---

appreciate bumping into travelers trekking through the woods. Parts of the Darién Gap have also become areas of activity for guerrillas from neighboring Colombia, although they usually come to rest and hide, not to attack. However, Colombian paramilitary forces often cross the border to hunt the guerrillas and the last place you want to be is caught in the crossfire. Missionaries and travelers alike have been kidnapped and killed in the southern area of the Darién.

Despite these warnings, there are parts of the Darién that can be visited in complete safety – these areas are covered in more detail later in this chapter.

TOURS

The Darién is the only major part of Panama where a guide is necessary. If you speak Spanish, you can hire guides locally who can show you the way and cook for you. The cost is reasonable, about US$10 to US$20 per day, but transportation costs can be expensive, especially since the price of fuel has

skyrocketed in recent years. However, it's advised that you go with a tour operator, who will take care of all arrangements, provide food and relieve you of the necessity of speaking Spanish.

Ancon Expeditions (p89), in Panama City, is the sole operator in the Darién, though they are highly recommended for the quality and professionalism of their tours. Offerings include:

Coastal Darién Explorer A three-day trip to Ancon's lodge in Punta Patiño on the Pacific coast; the cost is US$575 per person (minimum four people) and the trip is available on request (subject to availability).

Darién Explorer Trek A two-week trip aimed at serious hikers that includes Punta Patiño on the Pacific coast, Mogué village, Rancho Frío and Cana; the cost is US$2450 per person and the trip leaves on fixed departure dates with a minimum of four people.

The Realm of the Harpy Eagle A four-day trip to Ancon's lodge in Punta Patiño and a visit to the Emberá village of Mogué; the cost is US$695 per person (minimum four people) and the trip is available on request (subject to availability).

Ultimate Darién Experience A five-day trip to Ancon's field station in Cana, which is an outstanding spot for bird-watching; the cost is US$1300 per person and the trip leaves on fixed departure dates in the high season (December to April) with a minimum of four people. An eight-day version is also available.

VOLUNTEERING

An excellent organization that sometimes takes volunteers is the **Fundación Pro-Niños de Darién** (☎ 254 4333; www.darién.org.pa). This nonprofit organization started in 1990 and works on a variety of projects throughout the Darién. The foundation aims to improve the lives of *niños* (children) through educational and nutritional programs. The organization also works to help residents develop sustainable agriculture.

GETTING THERE & AWAY

The 266km Interamericana journey from Panama City to Yaviza passes through Chepo, El Llano, Cañita, Ipetí, Tortí, Higueronal and smaller, unmapped communities in Panamá Province before crossing into the Darién. All of these towns are served by buses running between Panama City and Yaviza. There are eight buses daily to Yaviza between 5am and 3:45pm (US$15, seven to 10 hours). Be sure to tell the bus driver your destination.

Travelers can also fly into the region. **Aeroperlas** (☎ 315 7500; www.aeroperlas.com) has three flights per week and **Air Panama** (☎ 316 9000; www.flyairpanama.com/tickets) has one flight per week to La Palma (US$40, one hour). From La Palma, Aeroperlas offers three flights per week to El Real (US$35, 15 minutes).

GETTING AROUND

In the vast jungles of the Darién Province, rivers are sometimes the only means of getting from one point to another, with *piraguas* providing the transport. In La Palma you can hire a motorized boat for US$120 to US$200 per day, which can take you to the Río Mogué or the Río Sambú. From either of these rivers you'll have to negotiate with indigenous villagers (in Mogué or La Chunga) to take you further upriver in *piraguas*. Hiring boats in Río Jaqué is possible but strongly ill-advised owing to the dangers of guerrilla activity. A shorter (and cheaper) boat trip goes from Puerto Quimba to La Palma.

THE ROAD TO YAVIZA

The Interamericana runs along the spine of the Darién Province, edging closer to Colombia with each passing decade – for now however, Yaviza is the end of the road.

PUNULOSA

This community is notable for its border police checkpoint. Get used to it – this is the first of many. Here, motorists traveling in either direction are stopped and asked where they are coming from and where they are going. Sometimes travelers headed southeast are asked to present identification; if you're a foreigner, your ID is your passport. The soldier will return your identification to you in a few minutes. Occasionally, a soldier will give you a lecture about the dangers near the border – that's because these soldiers are the ones who have to go there if something happens.

METETÍ

Punulosa is something of a suburb of Metetí, which is located only 1km southeast of the police checkpoint. You can stop here if you want to break up the trip to Yaviza or if you're planning on hopping a boat to La Palma. Both are good options as it's still a long way to the end of the road and the scenic boat ride to La Palma is a great way to penetrate the heart of the Darién.

If you're spending the night, the **Hotel Felicidad** (☎ 299 6188; r with shared/private bathroom US$8/15) is one of the more decent hotels along this stretch of road. Of course, decent still means concrete cubicles and there are more hourly paying guests than you may be comfortable with, but what do you expect along a trucker route? If you're looking for a hot meal, the downstairs **La Felicidad** (meals US$2-4) serves up heaping plates of rice and beans to truckers who just worked up an appetite.

If you're interested in taking the boat to La Palma, take the turnoff for Puerto Quimba, a port on the Río Iglesias. The road between Metetí and Puerto Quimba is about 20km long, and surprisingly is paved. From Puerto Quimba, boats to La Palma leave hourly from 7:30am to 6:30pm (US$2.50); they depart from La Palma hourly from 5:30am to 12:30pm, and from 2pm to 5pm. There is a pickup-truck shuttle service between Metetí

GETTING TO COLOMBIA

The Interamericana stops at the town of **Yaviza** and reappears 150km further on, far beyond the Colombian border. Although a trickle of travelers have walked through the infamous Darién Gap, the presence of Colombian guerrillas, paramilitaries, smugglers and bandits make this a potentially suicidal trip.

However, the border can also be crossed at a rugged point on the Caribbean coast between **Puerto Obaldía** on the Panamanian side, where you can obtain your exit stamp, and the town of **Capurganá** on the Colombian side, where you can obtain your entry stamp. **Aeroperlas** (☎ 315 7500; www.aeroperlas.com) has one flight per week from Panama City to Puerto Obaldía (US$40, one hour). From Puerto Obaldía, you can either walk or boat to the Colombian village of Sapzurro. On foot, this takes about 2½ hours, but the track is indistinct in places, and the presence of bandits, smugglers, narcotraffickers, guerrillas and paramilitaries (just to name a few) in the area makes boating the better option. From Sapzurro, it's a two-hour walk to Capurganá – be advised that there is a fair amount of risk crossing here and you should get solid information about the security situation before attempting it. Tourists have made it safely to Colombia along this route, though the point worth emphasizing is that not everyone has made it.

For information on sailing to Colombia, which is by far the safest of the available options, see p263.

---

and Puerto Quimba every 30 minutes from 6am until 9pm (US$1.25).

Traveling to La Palma by boat from Puerto Quimba is an excellent alternative to flying straight in from Panama City. The scenery along this 30-minute river trip is virgin jungle and dense mangrove forests – and you're bound to meet an interesting cast of characters onboard the boat.

YAVIZA

Yaviza is the end of the road – literally. Here, the Interamericana stops abruptly without so much as a sign announcing that you've reached the famous Darién Gap. From here, a narrow stretch of dirt road is lined with a few odd buildings and people who appear to have nothing but time on their hands.

If you have a pressing need to spend the night in Yaviza, the **Hotel 3Americas** (r from US$8) has some tired-looking rooms with a mess of a communal bathroom. Unless you have any compelling reason to be in Yaviza, it is recommended that you take the turnoff at Metetí, proceed to Puerto Quimba and take the boat to La Palma. The scenes from the boat to La Palma will give you a good sense of the wild frontier and natural beauty that still remains in the majority of Darién Province, whereas the views from the highway between Metití and Yaviza convey mostly destruction.

There are eight buses daily between Panama City and Yaviza (US$15, seven to

10 hours). From here, foolish travelers can hike along the Darién Gap if they so desire, though you'd best sort out your personal affairs prior. If you do make it to Colombia – and we can't emphasize enough how seriously dangerous and inadvisable this is – send us a postcard.

PARQUE NACIONAL DARIÉN

Although it's overshadowed by the security situation in the province, the Darién is the crown jewel of Panama's national parks – leave your fears behind and explore the jungle out there.

LA PALMA

La Palma is located at the mouth of the Río Tuira, where the wide river meets the Golfo de San Miguel. It is the provincial capital of Darién Province and the most populous town in the region. However, despite its lofty position as capital of the largest province in Panama, La Palma is literally a one-street town.

Most travelers pass through La Palma for one of two reasons: they're here to catch a plane to somewhere else, or they're here to take a boat ride to somewhere else. The two most popular boating destinations are the Ancon nature reserve and lodge at Reserva

Natural Punta Patiño (right) and the Emberá villages that line the banks of the Río Sambú (p283).

Every facility of possible interest to the traveler is located on the main street, which is within 300m of the airstrip. La Palma is home to the only bank in the Darién Province, the Banco Nacional de Panamá. There's also a hospital, a port and a police station (if you intend to go anywhere near the Colombian border and you speak Spanish, you should talk to the police here first), as well as three hotels, three bars and several food stands.

If you have to spend the night in La Palma, the **Hotel Biaquira Bagara** (☎ /fax 299 6224; r with shared/private bathroom US$15/20) is run by the friendly Ramady family, who live in a home beneath the rooms they rent. All of the rooms have private cold-water bathrooms with a tub, which is a godsend after a week or two in the jungle. There's also a lovely sitting area facing the river, which is a nice place to stew on the fact that you're actually in the Darién.

If you're planning a boating excursion, it's probably best to stock up on groceries here as the selection in the minimally stocked local supermarket is about as good as you'll get in these parts.

There's no shortage of cheap and somewhat cheerful eateries in town, though the **Restaurante El Regocijo** (plates US$2-4) is one of the more popular, given that it's also a cantina. As a word of caution, steer clear of *puerco de monte* (mountain pig) – this dish is actually wild peccary, which is illegal to hunt and even more illegal to serve up in a restaurant. Unfortunately, no one in La Palma really seems to be paying attention, though a foreigner washing down a plate of poached meat is bound to attract some unwanted attention.

Air Panama (☎ 316 9000; www.flyairpanama.com /tickets) and **Aeroperlas** (☎ 315 7500; www.aeroperlas .com) fly direct from Panama City to La Palma (US$40, one hour). Air Panama has one flight per week while Aeroperlas has three flights per week.

If you're looking to hire a boat and a guide, you can usually find someone in the vacinity of the dock who owns a vessel and is willing to go on an adventure with you for the right price (US$120 to US$200 per day, gas included).

RESERVA NATURAL PUNTA PATIÑO

On the southern shore of the Golfo de San Miguel, 25km from La Palma, is this 26,315-hectare wildlife preserve, which is owned by the private conservation group ANCON and managed by the organization's for-profit arm, Ancon Expeditions (p89). The only way to reach the preserve, short of hacking your way through endless expanses of jungle, is by plane (or boat). However, landing on the tiny strip of oceanside grass that's called a runway in these parts is definitely part of the Punta Patiño experience.

The preserve contains species-rich primary and secondary forest, and is one of the best places in Panama to spot harpy eagles. However, even if the mother of all eagles doesn't show, Punta Patiño is a great place to rack up the bird count, and there's a good chance of seeing everything from three-toed sloths and howler monkeys to crocodiles and capybaras, the world's largest rodents.

In the waterways around the reserve, you'll almost certainly see brown pelicans, magnificent frigate birds and laughing gulls, though don't forget about the cetaceans – bottlenose dolphins and humpback wheels frequent these waters. Other birds to keep an eye out for include terns (royal, sandwich and gull-billed), American oystercatchers and waders on the beach near the lodge.

In the mangrove patches near the waterways, you'll have a good chance of spotting Amazon kingfishers, white ibises and great and little blue herons as well as waders including willet, whimbrels and spotted sandpipers. A specialty of the area is the black oropendola, which has a higher than normal frequency near Mogué (see p282). Late afternoon and early morning are good times to look for crab-eating raccoons venturing down to the water's edge.

A swampy flat near ANCON's lodge supports large communities of capybaras, though as with all mammalian sightings, a little luck is needed to spot them. Not surprisingly, this community of tasty morsels attracts a few large crocs as well as the elusive jaguar, though you have a much better chance of spotting the former rather than the latter. Other commonly spotted mammals include gray foxes around the lodge (especially at night) and tayras in patches of nearby dry forest.

Visitors to the preserve are treated to guided nature hikes and night tours of the preserve.

THE MOTHER OF ALL EAGLES

The harpy eagle, Central America's most striking raptor, is considered by many to be the most powerful bird of prey in the world. Unfortunately, opportunities to see the bird in the wild are limited as they are rare throughout most of their range and are hard to spot in the canopy even when they are present. Fortunately, you're in the Darién and the area surrounding Reserva Natural Punta Patiño is home to a healthy nesting population. Although the chances of spotting one are still low, your chances are better here than anywhere else in Central America.

Harpy eagles are enormous birds with a wingspan of 2m and a height of 1.5m – they are immediately recognizable. Adults tend to have white breasts with a broad black chest band and faint leg barring as well as grey upperparts. They also have piercing yellow eyes which can be seen from the forest floor, as well as powerful yellow talons and a hooked bill.

Anyone who has had the privilege to watch a harpy eagle hunt will tell you that it is simply awesome. For instance, a harpy seen with a large male howler writhing in her grip will shift her talons with a resounding 'pop' in order to crush the monkey's skull and carry it back to the nest unhindered. With massive claws as big as a grizzly bear's and legs as thick as a man's wrist, the harpy is an undeniable killing machine.

A female harpy can weigh up to 9kg and such a large predator obviously has high energy requirements. As a result, harpies hunt all but the largest forest mammals, as well as other large birds and a whole slew of snakes and lizards. As an apex predator (like the jaguar), the harpy eagle probably never occurred in high densities, though deforestation has removed much of its prey base and its habitat. Furthermore, its habit of perching for long spells, even when people approach, makes it vulnerable to poachers.

Harpies rarely soar above the treetops, and usually hunt by rapidly attacking prey through the canopy. Monkeys are plucked from the foliage, unwary birds are taken from tree limbs and snakes are swept off the forest floor. However, the majority of the harpy's diet consists of sloths, which are extremely vulnerable in the morning when they are basking in the sun. A harpy will sit nearby – sometimes for days – until it is hungry, and then snatch the sloth at its leisure.

There's also the option to explore the mangroves lining the gulf by boat, or to just relax on one of the several wilderness beaches that hug this isolated stretch of coastline.

One of the best parts of visiting Patiño is staying at ANCON's private lodge, which is surprisingly sophisticated considering the remote location. Although you shouldn't expect five-star luxury, it's definitely more sophisticated than a simple rustic retreat. Each of the cabins has air-con, comfortable mattresses (for those sleepless nights) and private cold-water showers – you won't miss having hot water in these humid climes.

The lodge itself is perched atop a ridge overlooking the gulf and has arresting panoramas of the Golfo de San Miguel, particularly at daybreak. The staff is also extremely professional and attentive to the needs of the guest, and it's unlikely that you'll go hungry when they're working their magic in the kitchen.

Ancon Expeditions offers a package tour that includes the roundtrip airfare between Panama City and Punta Patiño, lodging, food and activities. This can also be combined with a trip up the Río Mogué to the Emberá village of Mogué and a guided hike to a harpy eagle's nest. Punta Patiño is also a destination on Ancon's highly recommended two-week Darién Explorer Trek (p278).

If you prefer, you can hire boats in La Palma to reach Punta Patiño on your own without booking a guided tour, but you must notify Ancon Expeditions in advance so that they can reserve a cabin for you. However, it's recommended that you book a package through Ancon, especially since you'll probably save money in the long run.

MOGUÉ

Although there are countless indigenous villages in the Darién, the majority of tourists ultimately end up spending a night or two in Mogué, an Emberá village located on the banks of the Río Mogué, roughly equidistant between Punta Patiño and La Palma. Over the past decade, Ancon Expeditions has helped developed the tourism potential of Mogué, especially since the villagers here are keen to show off their culture and lifestyles, and are extremely adept at finding harpy eagle nests in the surrounding jungle. As a result, a visit to the village allows an up-close and personal encounter with the Emberá and a high chance of spotting one of Central America's rarest birds.

Despite the fact that Mogué is set up for tourism, it is still very much a traditional village. Unlike Emberá villages in Panamá Province and Kuna villages in the Comarca, Mogué may only see a few visitors a month, which means that a complete abandonment of its traditional ways is not possible. Although everything done for the benefit of tourists certainly has a price tag on it, the atmosphere in the village is extremely relaxed and there is no pressure to buy crafts, give gifts or spend money.

While in Mogué, there is the option to watch a performance of traditional dance, purchase crafts including woven baskets and tagua-nut carvings and get a *jagua*-juice 'tattoo,' in the same manner that the Emberá paint themselves. Like henna, the tattoo stains the skin for up to two weeks, so it's wise to consider where you'll be heading after the Darién before you get painted. However, the experience is truly memorable – after being painted, the *jagua* dries on your skin for several hours before you're instructed to wash it off. Although a faint tattoo will appear immediately on your skin, the next morning when you wake up, you'll be about as blue as a Smurf.

Aside from interacting with the Emberá villagers, the majority of whom speak Spanish, the highlight of Mogué is taking a guided walk to a nearby harpy eagle nest. At the time of writing, a young adult female harpy eagle was living in a nest about two hours on foot from Mogué. Although there are no guarantees that you'll spot the bird, the hike itself winds through lush secondary forest that is brimming with tropical birds and the local 'harpy-eagle whistler' will do his best to call this incredible bird back to its nest. And of course, there's nothing quite like the thrill of the hunt, especially if it's rewarded with a clear view of this magnificent bird – bring a camera as harpy eagles are not scared away by human presence and thus easily photographed if you have a strong lens.

While in Mogué, you have the option of sleeping in a tent underneath the communal gathering hall, or stringing up a jungle hammock if you've brought one along with you. Visitors have access to a private outhouse and cold shower, which is only unlocked when tour groups arrive. The villagers will also feed you until your stomach explodes and although the cuisine of rice, beans, meat and plantains is very simple, it's certainly tasty and unbelievably filling. Although the village sounds are part of the whole experience, light sleepers may want to bring earplugs to ensure a good night's rest.

Ancon Expeditions offers a package tour that includes the roundtrip airfare between Panama City and Punta Patiño, lodging, food, activities and an overnight excursion to Mogué. Mogué is also a destination on Ancon's highly recommended two week Darién Explorer Trek (p278).

In theory, it's possible that you could visit Mogué by hiring a boat in La Palma, but it's not recommended. Ancon Expeditions has worked hard to regulate the development of tourism in the village in order to minimize its ill effects, so it's best not to complicate things by going outside the market and visiting independently.

RÍO SAMBÚ

The mouth of the wide, brown Sambú river is 1½ hours by boat south of Punta Patiño. Traveling it is a heart-of-darkness experience: you will pass through spectacular jungle while gliding past traditional Emberá and Wounaan villages.

Be forewarned: a trip far up the Río Sambú is not everyone's cup of tea. Even before you reach the river, you will be on a boat rather a long time under a broiling tropical sun. And if riding in a boat that's loaded down with leaking gasoline cans bothers you, you should probably pass on the Sambú – you'll need to bring several large containers of gasoline along from La Palma to fuel the canoe that you'll hire upriver.

There are also other minor hardships, such as the lack of showers and toilets, and the abundance of creepy crawlies and biting insects. But, a trip up the Río Sambú offers you true adventure, something that may not even be possible anywhere in the tropics 50 years from now. Even if you travel deep into the Amazon, you'd be hard-pressed to find such wilderness these days.

At night, you can make camp where you please if you have a tent or a jungle hammock. However, unless you've brought a second hammock or tent for your boater, he will prefer an alternative – making a deal to sleep on the floor of an Emberá or Wounaan family's home. If you can speak Spanish, finding a family to move in with for the night isn't difficult, and even getting a hot meal is easy. Expect to pay about US$10 per person for shelter and US$5 for food.

If you speak Spanish, boats and guides can be hired in La Palma, but once you reach the Río Sambú, you will need to hire a separate *piragua* and a guide to get further upriver. You need to do this because the *piragua* you'll hire in La Palma to reach the Sambú will sit too low in the water to navigate the upper portions of the river to get any further upriver, you must negotiate the use of a shallow dugout in one of the Emberá villages. During the rainy season, the river is navigable by *piragua* all the way to Pavarandó, the most inland of the eight indigenous communities on the Sambú.

EL REAL

El Real dates from the days of the early conquistadores when they constructed a fort beside the Río Tuira to prevent pirates from sailing upriver and attacking Santa María. Gold sourced from mines in the valley of Cana, to the south, was brought to Santa María and stored until there was a quantity sufficient to warrant assembling an armada and moving the bullion to Panama City. Today, El Real is one of the largest towns in the Darién, though it's still very much a backwater settlement.

For travelers heading to the Rancho Frío (opposite), El Real serves as a transit point since flights arrive here from La Palma. Prior to visiting Rancho Frío however, you must also stop by the ANAM office in town and pay your entry fee of US$3. The best way to locate this office is to ask someone to point

---

LOCAL VOICES: MELIO & THE PLIGHT OF THE EMBERÁ

Melio, the chief of Mogué village, is a widely respected Emberá elder who is renowned in the Darién for his musical prowess, particularly on the local version of the flute. A proponent of both increased tourism in the Darién and the cultural conservation of the Emberá, Melio has travelled as far as Washington DC to promote his aims.

- **What is the history of Mogué?** There is a lot of history in this community. I first came here with my family in 1968 and I was a founding member of Mogué. Now, there are over 600 people in the village and the surrounding area. Before we came here, my family lived in scattered huts along the rivers. It was not in our culture to have a village. But, once we came here and had access to the ocean, we could salt our meat. My distant relatives had never tasted salt before, so they would keep coming here to gather some. They liked it so much they kept moving closer and closer until our community was formed. The same thing happened all throughout Emberá lands.

- **How has tourism affected the community?** Tourism has been good for us because it affects our community directly. The government doesn't do much for us and they only come around during the election times. The government speaks about helping us, but they always abandon and neglect us. They don't help us secure our land, even though we protect it. At least with tourism, people come here to see the forest and our culture and we feel the impact immediately.

- **What is happening now to Emberá culture?** In this community, we've always been concerned about maintaining our culture. But, everywhere else our culture is disappearing rapidly, especially our language. People aren't speaking Emberá as much as they used to because more people are getting access to school and are learning more Spanish.

- **What can you do to help save your culture?** I try to get involved in rescuing our values and instilling our community with pride in our culture, like our *jagua*, our crafts, our dance and our music. This is how it was in the old age. I'm 60 years old and this is what I have left to do. That's my job.

you toward it as none of the wide paths in town have names.

Be advised that before heading up to Rancho Frío, you must either hire a local guide or be part of an Ancon tour – ANAM will not let you proceed if you are unescorted.

If you end up in town too late to start the trek to Rancho Frío, you can spend the night at the **Hotel El Mazareno** (☎ 299 6567; r per person US$8), though it's strongly recommended that you plan accordingly and avoid a night in El Real. If you can't, however, you'll have the privilege of choosing from one of seven mildewy rooms, each of which is equipped with a U-shaped foam mattress and toilets that flush with varying degrees of efficiency.

Before heading up to Rancho Frío, be sure to stock up on groceries in town as food is not available at the ranger's station.

Also before hitting the trail, drop into **Fondo Maná** (plates US$1-2), a friendly spot where there's only one item on the menu and it's whatever the senora is cooking up when you arrive.

From La Palma, **Aeroperlas** (☎ 315 7500; www.aeroperlas.com) offers three flights per week to El Real (US$35, 15 minutes).

RANCHO FRÍO

Thirteen kilometers south of El Real, as the lemon-spectacled tanager flies, is the Rancho Frío sector of Parque Nacional Darién. The sector is home to **Pirre Station**, though this should not be confused with the station at the top of Mount Pirre near Cana (p289). Nomenclature aside, Rancho Frío is, to steal a line from the famous naturalist guide Hernán Araúz, 'Panama's foremost theater of life.'

Although most of the bird species represented here can also be found at Cana, there are a number of rare specialities here including the crimson-bellied woodpecker, the white-fronted nunbird and the striped woodhaunter. However, the real strength of this sector is the network of accessible trails that originate from Pierre Station.

One trail leads to Mount Pirre ridge, which takes most hikers two days to reach, while the other winds through thick jungle to a series of cascades about an hour's hike away. Neither trail should be attempted without a guide as they are not well marked, and if you get lost out here, you're finished.

If you intend to visit Pirre Station, you must first get permission from the ANAM office in El Real and pay US$3; if no one's at the office when you arrive, ask around for Narciso 'Chicho' Bristan, who can take care of business. However, as previously mentioned, in order to hike into Rancho Frío, you must either hire a local guide or be part of an Ancon tour – ANAM will not let you proceed from El Real if you are unescorted. If you're not part of an Ancon tour, the ANAM office is a good place to inquire about hiring a local guide – expect to pay about US$20 per day.

At Pirre Station, there are **barracks** (cots per person US$10) with a front room with fold-out cots for visitors, a small outdoor dining area beside a very basic kitchen, a *palapa* (open-sided shelter) with a few chairs and a number of flush toilets and cold-water showers. There is also a shady **campsite** (per person US$5) where you can either pitch a tent or string up a jungle hammock. There is no electricity at the station.

If you plan on eating (which is always a good idea), you must bring your own food. The rangers will cook your food for you (US$5 a day is most appreciated), but you must provide bottled water. However, if you've got a water-purification system or tablets, the water in the creek is OK to drink, and there are lots of lemon trees in the vicinity of the station. Be sure to try the *zapote* growing at the station – this fruit has a fleshy orange meat with the appearance, taste and texture of mango and it's highly addictive.

Pirre Station can only be reached by hiking or by a combination of hiking and boating. If you prefer to hike, take the 'road' connecting El Real and Rancho Frío – hiking this barely discernible path takes several hours (depending on your pace) and is pretty much impossible without a guide.

The alternative is to hire a boater in El Real to take you up the Río Pirre to Piji Baisal – expect to pay about US$40 plus the cost of gasoline. From Piji Baisal, it's a one-hour hike to the station, and you'll need a guide to lead you to the station as there are no signs to mark the way.

Only 15km separate Pirre Station and Cana, and between the two there's nothing but virgin rainforest. Unfortunately, no trails link the two, but it's possible to backtrack to El Real, take a boat to Boca de Cupe and then follow the old mining trail to Cana. This historic highway is just under 30km long, and can be done in two long days. If you're interested in hiking along this rugged trail, check out the Darién Explorer Trek offered by Ancon Expeditions (p278).

BOCA DE CUPE

The frontier town of Boca de Cupe marks the outer range of the Panamanian Defense Forces. As you edge southeast towards the towns of Balsal, El Naranjal, Púcuro, Limón, Paya and Palo de las Letras near the Colombian border, you're essentially on your own. Of course, there's little reason that any sane person would head in this direction.

At the time of writing, however, the **Boca de Cupe Trail** that heads northwest to the Ancon lodge at Cana was completely safe – and highly recommended. This 30-odd kilometer trail follows the old mining highway that cuts through the Cana Valley and is easily one of the most challenging and rewarding treks in the whole of the Darién if not the whole country. You will walk through a variety of jungled terrain, pass by rusting railway tracks and spot countless tropical birds and the odd mammal or two. There's even a downed US military helicopter along the edge of the trail, though it's anyone's guess as to what happened.

If you're interested in hiking this trail, you will need to join Ancon Expeditions' Darién Explorer Trek (p278) – independent travel along this route is not allowed.

There's not much to Boca de Cupe aside from a few rows of wooden houses and a small military base. Keep in mind that you will need to register at the base before setting out on the trail, and you (or at least your tour leader) will probably be the recipient of a disparaging lecture. The soldiers stationed here are equally shocked and mortified that anyone would have an interest in hiking through the Cana Valley, and they're not afraid to share their displeasure with your group.

Boca de Cupe is accessed via boat from El Real, but you will need to stop at a riverside security checkpoint along the way. However, all of these arrangements will be taken care of by Ancon, so you can just sit back and enjoy how surreal your life has become.

CANA

Nestled in foothills on the eastern slope of Pirre ridge, the historic mining town of Cana has the distinction of being the most isolated

place in the Republic of Panama. It's also one of the world's top birding destinations, with a list of 400-plus species including 60 exclusive to this area. Daily sightings include up to four species of macaws, numerous parrots, jacamars and cotingas, all of which are literally perched at your doorstep. The shoulders of Mount Pirre (1491m) also rise above Cana and are home to a number of rare endemics including the coveted Pirre warbler.

Birding aside, Cana itself is an out-of-this-world destination that sees far few visitors than it should. The area surrounding the old mining camp (now a private Ancon lodge) is home to an impressive network of jungle trails that are dotted with rusting equipment, abandoned shafts and rivers flickering with gold dust. Unfortunately, the Darién's undeserved reputation has kept away the tourist crowds, but the folks at Ancon are working hard to change that.

Orientation & Information

Cana, which is little more than a clearing in the rainforest canopy, simply consists of a grass runway, a few scattered wooden buildings and an extensive network of jungles trails.

Be advised that Cana is a private lodge of Ancon Expeditions, so you will need to make an advance booking before arriving.

History

A geological survey of Cana determined that a lake covered most of the valley's floor during prehistoric times. However, experts speculate that the lake emptied when an earthquake created a divide that allowed the water to drain. As you enter the valley by air, you can still see a marshy area and some ponds, which are believed to be remnants of the prehistoric lake.

During the early 16th century, Spaniards discovered gold in Cana and in the years that followed, they extensively mined the valley using native labor as well as slaves brought from Africa. Las Minas del Espíritu Santo (Mines of the Holy Spirit), as they were once called, attracted over 20,000 people to the Cana Valley. These workers lived in the town of Santa Cruz de Cana, though the entirety of this settlement has long since been consumed by the jungle.

One of the longest rivers in the Darién, the Río Tuira, runs northward past Cana and out to the Pacific Ocean. The Spaniards used to

LOCAL VOICES: RICK MORALES & THE FUTURE OF TOURISM IN THE DARIÉN

Rick Morales works as a guide for Ancon Expeditions, and has lead countless expeditions throughout the Darién and in the rest of Panama. A linguist by training, Rick is completely bilingual and can convey his passion for wildlife and conservation in flawless Spanish and English.

■ **What is your background and how did you become a guide?** I grew up in the western highlands of Panama, surrounded by mountains and by nature, so exploration became a hobby of mine since I was a child. To be honest, I never thought that I could make a living as a guide, so I decided to take a different path and enrolled in university to study linguistics. Later on, by chance, a friend that worked at the same shipping agency as me changed career paths and moved to what was later known as Ancon Expeditions. When we spoke on the phone, she told me that the guides at Ancon had the same interests as I did. The next thing I knew, I was flying to the Darién with Hernán Araúz, one of the most famous guides in the country. That was seven years ago and it was the beginning of my career.

■ **What makes your job unique?** The best part of the job is that you get to travel to all of these amazing places and you're always meeting lots of interesting people. You can learn a lot from the guests who come on our trips, as well as the locals who live in the areas we visit – it's a never-ending learning experience. But, the most exciting part is definitely the hunt. There's a hunter inside every one of us. Even though we may not hunt for survival anymore, there's still that innate instinct. When you're out in the forest, trying to spot something, you have to key into that skill. You hone into a slight sound or movement, and sometimes it's rewarded with a great prize, be it a rare bird, a troop of monkeys or a herd of peccaries. That's the most exciting part – you never know what you'll spot! The only difference between us and the typical hunter is that we carry binoculars instead of firearms.

■ **What makes the Darién special?** The Darién is special because it represents the triumph of nature over human power. The Darién was the first place in the mainland Americas to be colonized by the Europeans, so you would think that with its long history of human intervention, the Darién should be the most developed place in Panama, if not in all the Americas. But, it's not – instead, it's one of the wildest places in the hemisphere, even after hundreds of years. This gives me hope that there are places out there that can resist human colonization, and exist as sanctuaries for nature.

■ **Why has tourism been slow to develop in the Darién?** It is indeed more difficult to travel here without the assistance and support of a reputable outfitter, but that's due to the fact that it's a raw, wild place. Most of the Darién's inhabitants are not bilingual and very few have a service-oriented mentality. But there's a big difference between being 'raw' and being 'dangerous.' The Darién has this negative reputation as a dangerous place and this unfortunately deters a lot of people from coming here. The mainstream belief is that if someone comes to the Darién, they're going to run into trouble. The worst part is that this absurd idea is instilled in tourists by Panamanians themselves. Everywhere you go in the Darién, tourists are warned by police that they're proceeding at their own risk. I really believe that if we could somehow erase this negative reputation, then more people would start discovering the Darién. I'm not implying, however, that the Darién is for everyone. People who are fond of nice hotels with all the creature comforts of civilization should reconsider going to this part of Panama. The Darién is wild and we should keep it that way. That last thing we want to see here is a bunch of foreign retirees living in a gated community called 'The Darién Village.'

■ **What is the future of tourism in the Darién?** If people from all around the world started visiting the Darién, I think that tourism could help stimulate the economy of the region. Right now, people in the Darién depend on farming and fishing for survival. For the most part, farming is an extremely destructive activity because it doesn't yield a lot, yet you need to destroy vast areas of forest for a relatively small plot of corn or rice. Just think about how many locals could get involved in ecotourism if things changed here. People in the Darién could have another means of survival and a new appreciation for their natural wealth. But first, we have to change the Darién's negative image.

send supplies to the Cana Valley via the Tuira and they sent gold from the valley to Santa María, on the western bank of the river. Here, the precious metal was kept for safekeeping until boats arrived to transport it to Panama City. Naturally, the vast quantities of gold at Santa María attracted pirates and the town fell numerous times throughout its history. When the Spaniards left Panama in the 1820s, the mines were abandoned and the jungle quickly reclaimed the valley.

When an English outfit visited Cana in the early 20th century, they discovered that there was still gold to be found in the hills. Hoping to strike it rich, they ran train tracks from the valley to Boca de Cupe and moved men, supplies and gold along them in small locomotives and freight cars. When the Englishmen cleared out 20 years later, they left their trains and heavy machinery behind – today you can still find several rusting locomotives, numerous freight cars and abandoned mine shafts amid Cana's dense jungle.

Wildlife-watching

Everybody's experience is different, but Cana is 'bird central' for the Darién. You'll probably start to identify birds even before you land at the airstrip – king vultures soar overhead along with turkey and black vultures. You'll also be bombarded with flights of mealy, red-lored amazons, brown-hooded and blue-headed parrots as well as flocks of orange-chinned parakeets. Remarkably, Cana is also home to four species of macaws (the chestnut-fronted, blue-and-yellow, great green and red-and-green), which crisscross the valley in their daily search for food. Outstanding amongst the raptors are white hawks and one of Darién's prizes – the crested eagle.

Cana's airstrip is flanked by the forest edge and is the ideal place to scope out dusty-backed jacamars, red-throated caracaras, rainbow-billed and chestnut-mandibled toucans, collared aracaris and crested guans, all seen regularly on tall trees. Flocks of swifts hawk and wheel, particularly at dusk, when they are accompanied by swallows and swallow tanagers.

Flowering bushes attract hummingbirds to Cana all day long. The variety of hummers include rufuos-tailed and blue-chested hummingbirds, white-necked jacobins and green thorntails. Tanagers – golden-hooded, crimson-backed and flame-rumps – flit back and forth. Other visitors include yellow-billed caciques, white-headed wrens and various tyrants. Barred puffbirds perch in trees overlooking the clearing and bat falcons often scan from tall trees.

Great jacamars are often seen near the start of the Sendero Las Minas and you shouldn't have to venture to far to see crimson-crested woodpeckers, slate-colored grosbeaks, dusky-faced tanagers and orange-billed sparrows. Several offshoots from the main trail frequently see army-ant swarms, which prompt obligate ant-followers including bicolored and ocellated antbirds. Cana also boasts numerous scarce and sought after species in this group including immaculate, bare-crowned and dull-mantled antbirds, black-crowned antpittas and rufous-breasted ant-thrushes. And the Darién is one of the best places anywhere to see the elusive rufous-vented ground cuckoo – most sightings have been with large ant swarms on the Mount Pirre and Boca de Cupe trails.

Pauraques are easily spot-lit around the lodge after dark, but keep your eyes (and ears)

THE BIRD THAT SAVED A VALLEY

In the mid-1990s, the mining lease for Cana was up for sale at the same time that the private conservation organization, ANCON, was looking into buying the land. Although the mines still contained unknown amounts of gold, an incredible diversity of wildlife had reclaimed the valley. Unfortunately, under the terms of the lease, the future owners of Cana were obliged to keep mining at Cana.

In a desperate bid to save the valley, ANCON lobbied hard to change the terms of the lease and eventually convinced President Ernesto Pérez Balladares to visit Cana and see for himself what was at stake. Balladares became the first Panamanian president to visit Parque Nacional Darién. While walking along the Las Minas trail, he spotted a great jacamar, a rare iridescent bird. Fortunately, this single sighting was enough to convince the former president that Cana should be a private reserve and not a mine – the bird saved the valley.

open for rufous nighthawks. Both common and great potoos are sometimes seen here. Other nocturnal possibilities include mottled owls and Central American pygmy owls.

Cana isn't just about birds – common primates throughout the area include Geoffroy's tamarins, white-faced capuchins, mantled howlers and brown-headed spider monkeys. White-lipped peccaries and gray foxes are seen regularly, and rare mammals sighted have included bush dogs and Baird's tapirs. The forests around Cana are also home to jaguars, pumas, ocelots and margays, but you'd be extremely fortunate to see one of these cats – they avoid people and generally prowl at night. However, their tracks are all around, especially in patches of mud along well-traversed trails.

Hiking

Three trails begin near the lodge: the Cituro Trail, the Machinery Trail and the Stream Trail.

The **Cituro Trail** begins at the northeastern corner of the lodge and winds a couple of hundred meters through secondary forest, paralleling some old railroad tracks and passing a rusted-out locomotive with the brand name 'Cituro' forged into it.

The **Machinery Trail** is a loop trail that begins at the western edge of the lodge and winds several hundred meters through secondary forest until it reaches the remains of another abandoned Cituro locomotive, a very overgrown smelter and other pieces of mining machinery.

The **Stream Trail** is glorious but short – only 50m – running from behind the field station to a small creek where you can take a refreshing dip.

Beside the valley's grass-and-dirt airstrip, which is about 100m from the field station, the mouths of two more trails disappear into the dense rainforest: the Pirre Mountain Trail and Boca de Cupe Trail.

The **Pirre Mountain Trail**, starting near the western end of the airstrip, offers a six-hour ridgeline hike to a campsite in the cloud forest high above the Cana Valley. The area around Pirre Station (not to be confused with the other Pirre Station in the Rancho Frío sector, p285) is home to some unique endemics including the Pirre hummingbird, greenish puff-leg, green-naped tanager, sooty-headed wren, Pirre warbler and

beautiful treerunner. A visit to Cana usually entails an overnight at Pirre Station.

The **Boca de Cupe Trail** runs north from Cana to the town of Boca de Cupe, which is usually a two- to three-day hike. At the time of writing, this trail was completely safe and one of the highlights of Parque Nacional Darién. If you're interested in hiking along this trail, you must join Ancon's Darién Explorer Trek (p278).

Sleeping & Eating

our pick ANAM/ANCON field station is a wooden structure that was built by gold workers during the 1970s and enlarged in mid-1998 by the wildlife conservation group ANCON. Today it is the star attraction in Ancon Expeditions' portfolio of tour offerings. The building itself offers rustic wood-plank rooms, shared bathrooms and candle-lit evenings. When you consider the awesome hiking and the bird-watching possibilities in the area, the station is simply outstanding. Three meals a day are served in a second wooden structure where you can spot macaws flying overhead and spider monkeys playing in the canopy while you dig into your hot breakfast.

Getting There & Away

Unless you hike into Cana along the Boca de Cupe Trail, the only way into the valley is by chartered aircraft. However, keep in mind that Ancon Expeditions manages the valley's sole lodging, so you must make a reservation with the company prior to your arrival. There have been instances where people have chartered private planes to Cana and were given clearance to land, to be told to turn around and go back to their departure point.

Ancon Expeditions offers an excellent five-day, four-night package that includes an English-speaking guide, all meals, accommodations (including tent camping along the Pirre Mountain Trail) and transportation to and from Panama City. A similar eight-day package is also available. Cana is also the final stop on the two-week Darién Explorer Trek. For more information on tour offerings, see p278.

TROPIC STAR LODGE

Overlooking Bahía Piña, near the southern tip of the Darién, is one of Panama's legendary institutions, namely the **Tropic Star Lodge** (☎ 800-682-3424 in US; www.tropicstar.com; 🔀 🖥 🖳).

THEY DROVE THE DARIÉN GAP

In 1960, back when the Interamericana reached only as far as Chepo, a group of adventurers sought to become the first people to drive between North and South America. Their destination: Bogotá, Colombia, 433km from Chepo by land – 297km of it through the primeval jungle that formed the Darién Gap.

The adventurers consisted of a distinguished crew of six men and two women, as well as nine local woodspeople, who were hired to cut a path through the jungle for their US-built jeep and British Land Rover. Also on board for most of the trip was Kip Ross, a *National Geographic* writer whose fascinating article on the expedition appeared in the society's March 1961 journal.

The entire enterprise took four months and 28 days. The team crossed 180 rivers and streams, and was forced to improvise bridges over 125 of them, built mainly from the trunks of palm trees. At times, progress was slowed to 5km a day and although several major vehicular mishaps occurred, no snakebites or serious injuries were sustained.

Among the group were historian Amado Araúz and his wife, Reina, the finest anthropologist Panama has produced. Reina founded seven museums and wrote the definitive books on Panama's indigenous groups before cancer took her life at the age of 49. Her son, Hernán Araúz, who works for Ancon Expeditions, is now widely regarded as the country's top nature guide.

This is the only lodge that serves Punta Piña, which has produced more International Game Fish Association (IGFA) world records than any other body of water.

The facilities at Tropic Star are 1st-class all the way and no expense has been spared in creating this remote luxury lodge. Stand-alone cabins have modern conveniences such as hot-water bathrooms, air-con and satellite TV, though it's the immaculate grounds that really make Tropic Star shine. Taking advantage of its dramatic hillside location overlooking the bay, guests can lounge in the manicured gardens, wade in the palm-shaded pool and dine on the catch of the day in the sophisticated bar-restaurant. There's even a so-called 'palace' that was built on-site by a Texas oil tycoon as his home away from home in 1961.

Of course, all of this shouldn't distract you from why you're really here – to fish. The lodge's fleet of 31ft Bertrams, the Fer-

raris of sportfishing boats, are all outfitted with top-notch gear and manned by some of the best captains in the world. Everything here is done just right and there's a sense of camaraderie among the guests, many of whom are professional sportfishers, millionaires and celebrities.

Weekly packages include the use of a boat with a captain and mate, all meals, and fishing tackle and leaders. Rates vary according to the number of people on the boat. From April to September, the rates are US$8150/4850 per person for one/two people in a boat and US$4050/3450 per person for three/four people in a boat. The rates go up from January to March.

Tropic Star can arrange a charter flight to transport you from Panama City to their tiny runway in Bahía Piña. From here, a short dirt road links the airstrip to the Tropic Star Lodge.

Directory

CONTENTS

ACCOMMODATIONS

Prices cited in this book for accommodations are 2006 high-season rates, and they include Panama's 10% tax on hotel rooms.

There is usually no shortage of places to stay in Panama, except during holidays or special events outside Panama City, when advance reservations may be necessary.

In this book, accommodations are categorized as budget (where lodgings typically range from US$5 per person to US$30 for a

---

> **BOOK ACCOMMODATION ONLINE**
>
> For more accommodation reviews and recommendations by Lonely Planet authors, check out the online booking service at www.lonelyplanet.com. You'll find the true, insider lowdown on the best places to stay. Reviews are thorough and independent. Best of all, you can book online.

double room), midrange (usually from about US$31 to US$75 for a double room) and top end (anything above US$75).

B&Bs

Almost unknown in Panama until the start of this millennium, the bed-and-breakfast phenomenon is gaining popularity across the country. Rates at B&Bs range from midrange to top end. You'll find them at major tourist destinations throughout the country including Panama City, Boquete and Bocas del Toro.

Camping

Camping facilities are available in many of the national parks; typical fees are US$5 per person per night. Camping isn't available in most towns.

Homestays

Informal homestay opportunities are available throughout the country – the best place to inquire about this is through local tourist information centers. Travelers who are exploring Kuna Yala and the Darién can often find lodging in local villages by asking around. Many villagers would be happy to rent out a spare room (or set aside a hammock space) for US$5 to US$10 a night.

Hostels

As Panama becomes increasingly more popular among backpackers, youth hostels are beginning to pop up across the country. At the time of writing, none of them were connected with international youth hostel federations, though all of them seem to offer excellent facilities for backpackers.

PRACTICALITIES

- Panamanians use the metric system for weights and measures, except that they pump gasoline by the *galón* (gallon) and occasionally use pounds and miles.

- Electrical current is 120 volts in Panama City and 110 volts, 60Hz elsewhere. Plugs are two-pronged, the same as in the US and Canada.

- The most widely circulated daily newspaper in Panama is *La Prensa* (www.prensa.com in Spanish).

- *The Panama News* (www.thepanamanews.com) is published in English every two weeks and distributed free in Panama City.

- There are three commercial TV stations in Panama (channels two, four and 13) and two devoted to public broadcasting (five and 11). Most hotels (midrange and up) have cable TV with Spanish and English channels.

- Popular radio stations in Panama (the signal's best in and near the capital) include 97.1 and 102.1 (salsa), 88.9 (Latin jazz), 88.1 (reggae), 94.5 (traditional Panamanian), 106.7 (Latin rock) and 98.9 (US rock).

Hotels

Usually there is no shortage of places to stay in Panama, although getting a hotel room during Carnaval, Semana Santa (Easter week) and other holiday times can be difficult in some places. Hotel accommodations can also be tight if there is a special event going on in a particular town.

Some travelers prefer to make advance reservations everywhere; this is generally possible and is recommended in the better places and in the increasingly popular Bocas del Toro town on Isla Colón. Booking through the internet is becoming the most common way of booking a room.

Before accepting a room, ask to see several. The same prices are often charged for rooms of widely differing quality. Even in the US$10-a-night cheapies it's worth looking around. If you are shown a horrible airless box with just a bed and a bare light bulb, you can ask to see a better room without giving offense – you'll often be amazed at the results. Naturally, hotels want you to rent their most expensive rooms; if you're on a tight budget, make a habit of asking if economical rooms are available. (Some Panamanian hotels have them but don't post their lowest prices.)

Lodges

A handful of high-end lodges are scattered about the country. Although these places aren't cheap, they provide an excellent opportunity to be surrounded by nature with access to some spectacular hiking and wildlife-watching nearby.

Rental Accommodations

You can arrange short- or long-term rental accommodations through **Haciendas Panama** (☎ 612 5577; www.haciendaspanama.com). This agency has lovely homes for rent in various locations throughout the country. Prices start at around US$200 a night, and guesthouses can sleep from five to 14.

Resorts

Panama also has a growing number of all-inclusive resorts, which often include meals, activities, private beach access and all the amenities. These can be a good option for those with children, as most resorts offer plenty of diversions for kids and adults.

ACTIVITIES

Panama has scores of ways to spend a sun-drenched afternoon, from hiking through lush rainforests to snorkeling among coral reefs. The diving, surfing, bird-watching and fishing are just a few of Panama's star attractions. For a complete list of what the country offers, see p60.

BUSINESS HOURS

Opening hours for travel agents, tour operators and other businesses are normally 8am to noon and 1:30pm to 5pm weekdays, and from 8am to noon Saturday. Government offices, including post offices, are open 8am to 4pm weekdays and don't close for lunch. Most banks are open 8:30am to 1pm or 3pm weekdays; some have Saturday hours as well. Shops and pharmacies are generally open from around 9am or 10am until 6pm or 7pm Monday to Saturday.

Grocery stores keep longer hours, opening around 8am and closing around 8pm or 9pm. A handful of grocery stores in Panama City stay open 24 hours.

Restaurants usually open for lunch from noon to 3pm and dinner from 6pm to 10pm. Those that offer breakfast open from 7am to 10am. On Sundays, many restaurants close. In Panama City and David, restaurants open later on Friday and Saturday nights, until about 11pm or midnight. Most bars are open from around noon to 10pm, later on Friday and Saturday nights (typically 2am). Nightclubs in Panama City open around 10pm or 11pm and close at 3am or 4am.

CHILDREN

Panamanians have a family-oriented culture, and will generally be very accommodating to travelers with children. The same can't be said of many businesses owned by expats, who state very clearly the age requirements of their guests.

High chairs in restaurants are a rarity in Panama, but safety seats in hired cars can be provided upon request. For diapers, creams and other supplies, the best places to stock up are in Panama City and David. Generally speaking, the supermarkets are excellent in Panama, and you can find just about any product you'd find in the US. However, fresh milk is rare and may not be pasteurized – packet UHT milk and powdered milk are more common.

Most of Panama is quite safe to travel with children, through places that present greater health risks include Bocas del Toro, where dengue fever is present, and the Darién Province, where malaria and yellow fever, though rare, still exist.

Among its rainforests, beaches and waterways, Panama has some fantastic sights for children. The Panama Canal is a favorite, and kids are likely to enjoy the interactive new museum at the Miraflores Visitors Center (p107). A cruise up the canal is another option, though the full-transit tour is not recommended, owing to its length. Many Panamanian families enjoy outings to Isla Taboga (p115), where there is both beach and fine walking opportunities, along with plenty of snacking spots – the boat ride out there is quite nice as well.

PREVENTING CHILD SEX TOURISM IN PANAMA

Tragically, the exploitation of local children by tourists is becoming more prevalent throughout Latin America, including Panama. Various socio-economic factors make children susceptible to sexual exploitation, and some tourists choose to take advantage of their vulnerable position.

Sexual exploitation has serious, lifelong effects on children. It is a crime and a violation of human rights.

Panama has laws against sexual exploitation of children. Many countries have enacted extra-territorial legislation that allows travelers to be charged as though the exploitation happened in their home country.

Responsible travelers can help stop child sex tourism by reporting it. It is important not to ignore suspicious behavior. Cybertipline is a website where sexual exploitation of children can be reported. The website can be found at www.cybertipline.com. You can also report the incident to local authorities and if you know the nationality of the perpetrator, report it to their embassy.

Travelers interested in learning more about how to fight against sexual exploitation of children can find more information on the ECPAT International website at www.ecpat.org.

Beyond Borders is the Canadian affiliate of ECPAT. It aims to advance the rights of children to be free from abuse and exploitation without regard to race, religion, gender or sexual orientation. Their website can be found at www.beyondborders.org.

ECPAT – USA (End Child Prostitution & Trafficking; in USA ☎ 1-718-935-9192; www.ecpatusa.org), based in New York, is part of a global network working on these issues with over 70 affiliate organizations around the world.

DIRECTORY

A number of tours, some low-intensity, can be an enjoyable way for you and your children to see Panama's lush environment. Tour outfits such as Ancon Expeditions (p89) will help make arrangements.

For more ideas about making the most of your family travels, get a hold of Lonely Planet's *Travel with Children*.

CLIMATE CHARTS

Panama's tourist season is during the dry season from mid-December to mid-April. This is true for the Pacific slope, but the Caribbean side can get rain throughout the year.

The weather can be hot and steamy in the lowlands during the rainy season, when the humidity makes the heat oppressive. But it won't rain nonstop – rain in Panama, as elsewhere in the tropics, tends to come in sudden short downpours that freshen the air, and are followed by sunshine. If you'll be doing any long, strenuous hiking, the dry season is the most comfortable time.

For more information, see p16.

COURSES

One of the best ways to appreciate a foreign country is to speak the local language – if you're feeling a little tongue-tied, consider enrolling in Spanish classes in either Panama City (p88), Boquete (p204) or Bocas del Toro (p225).

Those who want to go out dancing in some of the capital's nightclubs should learn the right moves: take a few salsa or merengue classes while in Panama City (see p88) for details.

CUSTOMS

You may bring up to 200 cigarettes and three bottles of liquor into Panama tax free. If you try to leave Panama with products made from endangered species – such as jaguar teeth, ocelot skins and turtle shell – you'll face a steep fine and jail time.

DANGERS & ANNOYANCES

Crime is a problem in certain parts of Panama City. The city's better districts, however, are safer than in many other capitals: witness the all-night restaurants and activity on the streets at night. On the other hand, it is not safe to walk around at night on the outskirts of Casco Viejo – be careful in the side streets of this district even in the daytime. In general,

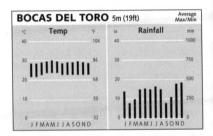

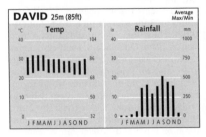

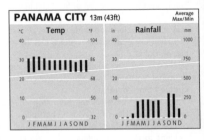

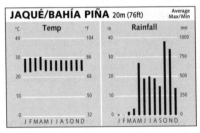

stay where it's well lit and there are plenty of people around.

Colón has some upscale residential areas, but most of the city is a sad slum widely known for street crime. If you walk around, even in the middle of the day, well-meaning residents will inform you that you are in danger.

Parts of the Darién Province, which borders Colombia, are extremely dangerous. Not only is it easy to get hopelessly lost, but parts of the province are used by guerillas from Colombia, the paramilitary chasing the guerillas, and narcotraffickers. Particularly treacherous is the area between Boca de Cupe and Colombia, which is the traditional path through the Darién Gap.

Plying the waters of the Archipiélago de San Blás are numerous Colombian boats that run back and forth between the Zona Libre in Colón and Cartagena, Colombia. It has been well documented that some of these boats carry cocaine on their northbound voyages. If you decide to ride on one of these slow cargo boats, be forewarned that your crew may be trafficking drugs.

Hiking Safety

You should be adequately prepared for hiking trips. Always carry plenty of water, even on short journeys, and always bring adequate clothing – jungles *do* get quite a bit colder at night, particularly at higher elevations.

Hikers have been known to get lost in rainforests, even seemingly user-friendly ones such as Parque Nacional Volcán Barú. A Panamanian hiker who entered that park in 1995 was never seen again, and it's assumed that he got lost, died of hypothermia and was fed upon by various creatures.

Never walk in unmarked rainforest; if there's no trail going in, you can assume that there won't be one when you decide to turn around and come back out. Always let someone know where you are going, in order to narrow the search area in the event of an emergency.

Police

Police corruption is not as big a problem in Panama as it is in some other Latin American countries. However, it's not unheard of for a Panamanian police officer to stop a motorist for no obvious reason, accuse him or her of violating a law, and levy a fine to be paid on the spot. If there are people around, making a big scene will sometimes fluster the officer into letting you go. Most of the time, however, you become an unwilling participant in a waiting game.

Your best option, unless you want to try to wait out the officer, is to negotiate the fine down. Failure to pay anything can result in your being led to jail with the officer insisting you really did break some law.

Swimming Safety

Sadly, in recent years there have been several deaths in Bocas del Toro Province and on other beaches around the country owing to strong currents. Tourist brochures do not mention the drownings that occur every year in Panamanian waters. Of these, about 80% are caused by rip currents. A rip current is a strong current that pulls the swimmer out to sea. It occurs when two currents that move parallel to the shore meet, causing the opposing waters to choose the path of least resistance, which is a path out to sea. It is most important to remember that rip currents will pull you *out* but not *under*.

If you find yourself caught in a rip current, stay calm and swim parallel to the shore to get out of it – rip currents dissipate quickly. When the current dissipates, swim back in at a 45° angle to the shore to avoid being caught by the current again. Do not try to swim directly back in, as you would be swimming against the rip current and would only exhaust yourself.

If you feel a rip current while you are wading, try to come back in sideways, thus offering less body surface to the current. If you cannot make headway, walk parallel to the beach so that you can get out of the rip current.

Thefts & Muggings

Tourist-oriented crime is uncommon in Panama, but it does happen. Be smart – avoid carrying all your money in one place and avoid entering areas that appear unsafe.

If you go out at night, leave your watch, jewelry and expensive clothing at the hotel. Take only the amount of money you think you'll need, and then a little extra tucked away in a shoe. If you look like you don't have anything of value on you, you're less likely to interest a mugger.

It is a good idea to carry an emergency packet somewhere separate from all your other valuables. It should contain a photocopy of the essential pages of your passport. On the back of the photocopy you should list important numbers, such as your traveler's checks' serial numbers, airline ticket numbers, and credit card and bank account numbers. Also, keep one high-denomination bill with this emergency stash.

If you are robbed, you should get a police report as soon as possible. This is a requirement for any insurance claims, although it is unlikely that the police will be able to recover the property. If you don't speak Spanish and are having a hard time making a police report, your embassy can often advise and help.

Panama has a long history of business-related crimes, particularly with regard to real estate. If you want to sink money into any kind of Panamanian business, make sure you check it out *thoroughly*. As a general rule 'if a deal seems too good to be true, it probably is.'

EMBASSIES & CONSULATES
Panamanian Embassies & Consulates
Panama has embassies and consulates in the following countries:

Canada (☎ 613-236-7177; fax 613-236-5775; 130 Albert St, Suite 300, Ottawa, Ontario K1P 5G4)

Colombia (☎ 257-5067, fax 257-5068; Calle 92, No 7-70, Bogotá)

France (☎ 1-47-83-23-32, 1-45-66-42-44; fax 1-45-67-99-43; 145 Av de Suffren, 75015 Paris)

Germany (☎ 228-36-1036; fax 228-36-3558; Lutzow-strasse 1, 53173 Bonn)

Mexico (☎ 5-250-4229; fax 5-250-4045; Schiller 326, 8th fl, Colonia Chapultepec-Morales, CP 11570, Mexico DF)

UK (☎ 171-493-4646; fax 171-493-4499; 48 Park St, London W1Y 3PD)

USA (☎ 202-483-1407; fax 202-483-8413; 2862 McGill Tce NW, Washington, DC 20008)

Embassies & Consulates in Panama
More than 50 countries have embassies or consulates in Panama City. Their contact details can be found in the Panama white pages, listed under 'Embajada de' followed by the country name in Spanish. Many embassies appear in the yellow pages under 'Embajadas' or 'Consulados.' With the exception of the United States and France, most embassies are in the Marbella district of Panama City.

Ireland, Australia and New Zealand have no consulates or embassies in Panama.

Canada (Map p79; ☎ 264 9731; fax 263 8083; World Trade Center, Calle 53 Este, Marbella)

France (Map p80; ☎ 211 6200; Plaza de Francia, Las Bóvedas, Casco Viejo)

Germany (Map p79; ☎ 263 7733; World Trade Center, Calle 53 Este, Marbella)

The Netherlands (Map p79; ☎ 264 7257; Calle 50, Marbella)

UK (Map p79; ☎ 269 0866; Swiss Tower Calle 53 Este, Marbella)

USA (Map pp76-7; ☎ 207 7000; Avs Balboa & Calle 37 Este, La Exposición)

FESTIVALS & EVENTS
Panama has a range of colorful festivals that encompass everything from traditional folkloric fests to indigenous celebrations. For the lion's share of the country's revelry, head to the Peninsula de Azuero (see p151 and p163), where some of Panama's most famous events take place.

The following events are the country's better known celebrations:

February/March
Carnaval On the four days preceding Ash Wednesday, costumes, music, dancing and general merriment prevail in Panama City and on the Peninsula de Azuero.

March/April
Semana Santa On Holy Week (the week before Easter), the country hosts many special events, including a re-enactment of the crucifixion and resurrection of Christ. On Good Friday, religious processions are held across the country.

May/June
Corpus Christi Forty days after Easter, this religious holiday features colorful celebrations in Villa de Los Santos (p162). Masked and costumed dancers representing angels, devils, imps and other mythological figures enact dances, acrobatics and dramas.

October
Festival of the Black Christ On October 21, thousands of visitors come to honor the black Christ in Portobelo (p250).

FOOD
See the Food & Drink chapter (p43) to get an in-depth look at Panama's cuisine. For price listings in the Panama City Eating section, we signify budget restaurants as having main dishes costing US$5 and under, midrange as costing US$6 to US$10 and top end as costing more than US$10.

GAY & LESBIAN TRAVELERS
Other than the gay float during Carnaval in the capital, there are few open expressions of homosexuality in Panama. As in other Latin American countries, gay men and lesbians remain closeted or else suffer a great deal of discrimination.

Panama City has a few gay and lesbian clubs (not openly advertised, however). Outside Panama City, gay bars are hard to come by. In most instances, gays and lesbians just blend in with the straight crowd at the hipper places and avoid cantinas and other conventional lairs of homophobia. There are several Panamanian websites for gays and lesbians that focus on Panama City, upcoming events and parties, new club openings and political issues about town. You'll need at least a little Spanish to maneuver through these sites:

- www.farraurbana.com
- www.rumbanight.com

HOLIDAYS

National holidays (*días feriados*) are taken seriously in Panama, and banks, public offices and many stores close. Public transportation tends to be tight on all holidays and the days immediately preceding or following them – book tickets ahead.

There is no bus service at all on the Thursday afternoon and Friday before Easter, and many businesses are closed for the entire Semana Santa (Holy Week, the week before Easter). From Thursday to Easter Sunday, all bars are closed and alcohol sales are prohibited. Beach hotels are usually booked several weeks in advance for the Semana Santa, though a limited choice of rooms is often available.

The week between Christmas and New Year's, along with the first week of the year, tend to be unofficial holidays. In addition, various towns have celebrations for their own particular days throughout the year. These other holidays and special events are not official holidays, and businesses remain open.

All the official national holidays are listed below, and most are celebrated on Monday to create long weekends. When holidays fall on a Thursday or Friday, they are celebrated on the following Monday; holidays that happen to fall on Tuesday or Wednesday are usually celebrated the prior Monday.

New Year's Day January 1
Martyrs' Day January 9
Good Friday, Easter March/April
Workers' Day May 1
Founding of Old Panama (Panama City only) August 15
Hispanic Day October 12
National Anthem Day November 1
All Souls' Day November 2
Independence Day November 3
First Call for Independence November 10
Independence from Spain November 28
Mothers' Day December 8
Christmas Day December 25

INSURANCE

Prior to your trip, signing up for a travel insurance policy to cover theft, loss and medical problems is a good idea. Be advised however that some policies specifically exclude dangerous activities, which can include scuba diving, motorcycling, even trekking.

You may prefer a policy that pays doctors or hospitals directly, rather than you having to pay on the spot and claim later. If you have to claim later, ensure you keep all documentation.

Check that the policy covers ambulances or an emergency flight home. For information on medical insurance, see p313.

INTERNET ACCESS

Most travelers make constant use of internet cafés and free Web-based email such as **Yahoo** (www.yahoo.com), **Hotmail** (www.hotmail.com) or **Gmail** (www.gmail.com).

Internet cafés are plentiful in Panama, and with the exception of remote villages, most cities and towns have at least one access point – most charge around US$1 to US$2 per hour.

INTERNET RESOURCES

IPAT (www.ipat.gob.pa) Panama's tourist website in Spanish. Also has a sister site in English (www.visitpanama.com).
Lanic (http://lanic.utexas.edu/la/ca/panama) Outstanding collection of links from the University of Texas Latin American Information Center.
Panama info (www.panamainfo.com) Also in English.

LEGAL MATTERS

The legal drinking age in Panama is 18, which is strictly enforced in Panama City and generally ignored elsewhere. In Panama you are presumed guilty until found innocent. If you are accused of a serious crime, you will be taken to jail, where you will likely spend several months before your case goes before a judge. Some simple but valuable advice: stay away from people who commit crimes. For example, you can expect to go to jail if the car you are in is stopped and found to contain illegal drugs, even if they aren't yours.

In Panama penalties for possession of even small amounts of illegal drugs are much stricter than in the USA, Europe, Australia and most everywhere else. Defendants often spend years in prison before they are brought to trial and, if convicted (as is usually the case), can expect sentences of several more years in prison. Most lawyers won't even accept drug cases because the outcome is certain: conviction.

If you are jailed, your embassy will offer only limited assistance. This may include a visit from an embassy staff member to make sure that your human rights have not been violated, letting your family know where you are and putting you in contact with a lawyer (whom you must pay yourself). Embassy officials will not bail you out.

Remember that you are legally required to carry identification at all times. This should be a photographic ID, preferably a passport. Although this may seem like an inconvenience, police officers reserve the right to request documentation from tourists at all times, and several readers have been forced to spend the night in prison for failure to produce proper ID.

Please bear in mind that Panama is a conservative society. Generally speaking, displays of gratuitous flesh are not looked kindly upon, though this is waived once a year when the country hits the Carnaval season.

With that said, it is illegal for men (and women) to walk around topless, even if you are on your way to the beach. This rule is strictly enforced in Bocas del Toro town on Isla Colón (p219), and you can expect to be stopped on the streets by police officers if you don't cover up.

MAPS

International Travel Maps (in Canada ☎ 604-879-3621; www.itmb.com) publishes an excellent 1:800,000 color map showing the geographical features, cities, towns, national parks, airports and roads of Panama.

At the **Instituto Geográfico Nacional** (Tommy Guardia; p74) in Panama City, you can buy topographical maps of selected cities and regions. Various free tourist publications distributed in Panama also have maps, though hiking maps are rarely available at national park ranger stations.

MEDIA
Newspapers & Magazines
La Prensa (www.prensa.com in Spanish) is the most widely circulated daily newspaper in Panama. Other major Spanish-language dailies include *La Estrella de Panamá*, *El Panamá América*, *El Universal* and *Crítica*.

The **Panama News** (www.thepanamanews.com) is published in English every two weeks. It is distributed free in Panama City. *The Visitor*, written in English and Spanish and targeting tourists, is another free publication. The *Miami Herald International Edition* is available in some upscale hotels.

Radio & TV
There are three commercial TV stations in Panama (channels two, four and 13) and two devoted to public broadcasting (five and 11). Many hotels have cable TV with Spanish and English channels.

Panama has over 90 radio stations that are mostly commercial based. The more popular play the following styles:
Classical 105.7
Latin jazz 88.9
Latin rock 106.7
Reggae 88.1
Salsa 97.1 and 102.1
Traditional Panamanian 94.5
US rock 93.9 and 98.9

MONEY
Panama uses the US dollar as its currency. The official name for it is the *balboa,* but it's exactly the same bill, and in practice people use the terms *'dólar'* and *'balboa'* interchangeably. Panamanian coins are of the same value, size and metal as US coins, though both are frequently used. Coins include one, five, 10, 25 and 50 *centavos* (or *centésimos*) – 100 *centavos* equal one *balboa*. Most businesses won't break US$50 and US$100 bills, and those that do may require you to present your passport.

For exchange rates, see inside the front cover.

For information on the cost of travel, see p17.

ATMs
Throughout Panama, ATMs are readily available except in the most isolated places – look for the red *'sistema clave'* sign. Generally speaking, ATMs accept cards on most networks (Plus, Cirrus, MasterCard, Visa, Amex), though a charge is usually levied depending on your issuing bank. The amount that can be withdrawn at one time varies from bank to bank, though it is usually around US$500.

Credit Cards

Although they are widely accepted at travel agencies, upscale hotels and many restaurants, credit cards can be problematic almost everywhere else. In short, carry enough cash to get you to the next bank or ATM.

There are several places where it's essential to show up with cash. Among tourist destinations, the following places have no banks, and it's a long way to the nearest ATM: Santa Catalina, Santa Fé, Boca Brava, Isla Contadora, Isla Grande, Portobelo, Isla de Coiba and the Darién.

At the time of research, very few businesses on Bocas del Toro accepted credit cards. Find out if your hotel does *before* you go to avoid any unpleasant surprises.

Moneychangers

The only bank that exchanges foreign currency is the Banco Nacional de Panamá counter at Tocumen International Airport. Once you have departed from the airport, the only place that can change foreign currency for dollars is a *casa de cambio* (exchange house), which can be difficult to find outside Panama City.

Taxes

A tax of 10% is added to the price of hotel rooms. When you inquire about a hotel, ask whether the quoted price includes the tax. Note that hotel prices given in this book include the 10% tax.

A 5% sales tax is levied on all nonfood products.

Tipping

The standard tipping rate in Panama is around 10% of the bill, though in small cafés and more casual places, tipping is not necessary. Taxi drivers do not expect tips.

Traveler's Checks

Although they can be cashed at a few banks. traveler's checks are rarely accepted by businesses, and traveler's checks in currencies other than US dollars are not accepted anywhere in Panama. In addition, some banks will only accept American Express traveler's checks. The banks that do accept traveler's checks typically charge an exchange fee equal to 1% of the amount of the check.

PHOTOGRAPHY

Panamanians make wonderful subjects for photographs. However, most people resent having cameras thrust in their faces, and some attach price tags to their mugs. In the Comarca de Kuna Yala, subjects typically expect US$1 per photo. As a rule, you should ask for permission if you have an inkling your subject would not approve.

Tropical shadows are extremely strong and come out almost black on photographs. Often a bright but hazy day makes for better photographs than a very sunny one. Photography in open shade or using a flash will help. As a general rule, the best time for shooting is when the sun is low – the first and last two hours of the day. Remember, too, that flash equipment is forbidden in Panama's churches and museums.

Since digital cameras are well on their way to replacing traditional cameras completely, it can be difficult to purchase high quality film in Panama. On the other hand, most internet cafés in the country can burn your digital pictures on CD, and cheap media is available for purchase in most large towns and cities.

POST

Airmail to the USA takes five to 10 days and costs US$0.35 (postcards US$0.25); to Europe and Australia it takes 10 days and costs US$0.45 (postcards US$0.40). Panama has neither vending machines for stamps nor drop-off boxes for mail. You may be able to buy stamps and send mail from an upscale hotel to avoid going to the post office and standing in line.

Most post offices are open from 7am to 6pm weekdays and from 7am to 4:30pm Saturday. General delivery mail can be addressed to '(name), Entrega General, (town and province), República de Panamá.' Be sure the sender calls the country 'República de Panamá' rather than simply 'Panamá,' or the mail may be sent back.

RESPONSIBLE TRAVEL

Traveling sensitively in Panama means being mindful of the environment around you. Try to patronize local businesses and industries, and spend your money where it will go directly to the people working for it.

DIRECTORY

Don't support businesses that keep caged animals around. It's an offense to keep a parrot, toucan or macaw in a cage; if it bothers you report the crime to **Ancon** (☎ 314 0060). And – hopefully this goes without saying – don't eat endangered species. If you see *tortuga* (sea turtle), *huevos de tortuga* (turtle eggs), *cazón* (shark), *conejo pintado* (paca), *ñeque* (agouti) or *enado* (deer) on the menu, take your business elsewhere.

For information on responsible tourism in the Comarca de Kuna Yala, see the boxed text (p262).

For information on responsible tourism in the Darién, see the boxed text (p277).

SHOPPING

A remarkable variety of imported goods, including cameras, electronic equipment and clothing, is sold in Panama, both in Colón's tax-free Zona Libre and in Panama City. The giant stores in the Zona Libre cater mostly to mass buyers, and most of them will not sell individual items. However, Panama City gives tourists and foreigners better shopping opportunities, offering a wide selection of high-quality handicrafts and traditional artwork.

The favorite handicraft souvenir from Panama is the *mola*, a colorful, intricate, multi-layered appliqué textile sewn by Kuna women of the Archipiélago de San Blás. Small, simple souvenir *molas* can be bought for as little as US$5, but the best ones are sold on the islands and can fetch several hundred dollars.

It's possible to purchase high-quality replicas of *huacas* – golden objects made on the isthmus centuries before the Spanish conquest and placed with Indians at the time of burial. These range in price from US$5 to more than US$1000.

Other handicrafts that can be purchased include wood carvings (from the *cocobolo* tree), *tagua* carvings (from the egg-sized *tagua* nut) and baskets. These are all made by the Wounaan and Emberá tribes.

SOLO TRAVELERS

Traveling alone isn't uncommon in Panama, and there are plenty of places to meet other travelers. In particular, Bocas del Toro (p217) has emerged in recent years as a major backpacker destination, and the good network of hostels and budget hotels here means that it's hard to be alone for long.

Language schools, in either Bocas, Boquete and in Panama City, are also good spots to meet other travelers while in Panama.

TELEPHONE

Panama's country code is ☎ 507. To call Panama from abroad, use the country code before the seven-digit Panamanian telephone number. There are no local area codes in Panama.

Telephone calls to anywhere within Panama can be made from pay phones. Local calls cost US$0.10 for the first three minutes, then US$0.05 per minute. You can buy Telechip phonecards at pharmacies, corner shops and

---

TRAVEL WIDELY, TREAD LIGHTLY, GIVE SUSTAINABLY – THE LONELY PLANET FOUNDATION

The Lonely Planet Foundation proudly supports nimble nonprofit organizations working for change in the world. Each year the foundation donates 5% of Lonely Planet company profits to projects selected by staff and authors. Our partners range from Kabissa, which provides small nonprofits across Africa with access to technology, to the Foundation for Developing Cambodian Orphans, which supports girls at risk of falling victim to sex traffickers.

Our nonprofit partners are linked by a grass-roots approach to the areas of health, education or sustainable tourism. Many – such as Louis Sarno who works with BaAka (pygmy) children in the forested areas of Central African Republic – choose to focus on women and children as one of the most effective ways to support the whole community. Louis is determined to give options to children who are discriminated against by the majority Bantu population.

Sometimes foundation assistance is as simple as restoring a local ruin like the Minaret of Jam in Afghanistan; this incredible monument now draws intrepid tourists to the area and its restoration has greatly improved options for local people.

Just as travel is often about learning to see the world with new eyes, so many of the groups we work with aim to change the way people see themselves and the future for their children and communities.

Cable & Wireless offices (the national phone company) in denominations of US$3, US$5, US$10 and US$20. You then plug this into the phone and dial the local number. Some public phones accept both cards and coins, but many accept only cards. Note that calling cell phones (which typically begin with a '6') is much pricier (US$0.35 for the first minute, then US$0.10 per minute thereafter).

International Calls

Travelers wishing to make international calls can do so with a phonecard or via an internet café. A Telechip Total card has a scratch-off code and can be used from any phone. They come in denominations of US$1, US$3, US$5, US$10 and US$20. Buy at least US$5 for an international call.

Connecting to an international operator from a residential, business or pay phone is easy. To connect with a local international operator, simply dial ☎ 106. For an international operator in the USA, dial ☎ 108 (MCI), ☎ 109 (AT&T), ☎ 115 (Sprint) or ☎ 117 (TRT). To reach a Costa Rican operator, dial ☎ 107; for a Colombian operator, dial ☎ 116.

Due to the increasing popularity of voice-over IP services like Skype, it's sometimes possible to skip the middle man and just bring a head-set along with you to an internet café. The increasing frequency of ethernet connections and wireless signals in accommodations also means that if you're travelling with a laptop, you can just connect and call for pennies.

TIME

From the last Sunday in October through to the first Sunday in April, Panama time is in line with New York and Miami. Because Panama does not observe daylight saving time, during the rest of the year (April through October), Panama is one hour behind New York. Panama is five hours behind Greenwich Mean Time (GMT) and one hour ahead of the rest of Central America. If you're coming from Costa Rica, be sure to reset your watch.

TOILETS

Panamanian plumbing generally is of high quality, although most places will ask you to place your used paper in the trash bins provided instead of flushing it away. That's because narrow piping was used during construction and the owners fear clogging.

Putting used toilet paper into a trash bin may not seem sanitary, but it is much better than clogged bowls and overflowing toilet water.

Be advised that in Kuna Yala and in some parts of Bocas del Toro, whatever you flush goes straight out to sea. While you certainly can't stop nature from calling, be sure not to flush anything else down the toilet that doesn't belong in the sea.

Public toilets can be found mainly in bus terminals, airports and restaurants. In Spanish, restrooms are called *baños* and are often marked *caballeros* (gentlemen) and *damas* (ladies). Outside the cities, toilet paper is not always provided, so you may want to consider carrying a personal supply.

TOURIST INFORMATION

The **Instituto Panameño de Turismo** (Map pp74–5; IPAT, Panamanian Institute of Tourism; ☎ 226 7000; www.ipat .gob.pa; Centro Atlapa, Vía Israel, San Francisco, Panama City) is the national tourism agency. In addition to this head office, IPAT runs offices in Bocas del Toro, Boquete, Colón, David, Paso Canoas, Penonomé, Portobelo, Santiago, Villa de Los Santos, Las Tablas, El Valle and Pedasí. There are smaller information counters at the ruins of Panamá Viejo, in Casco Viejo, and in both the Tocumen International Airport and the Albrook domestic airport.

IPAT has a few useful maps and brochures, but often has a problem keeping enough in stock for distribution to tourists. Most offices are staffed with people who speak only Spanish, and the helpfulness of any particular office depends on the person at the counter. Some employees really try to help, but others are just passing the time. As a general rule, you will get more useful information if you have specific questions.

TRAVELERS WITH DISABILITIES

The **Instituto Panameño de Habilitación Especial** (IPHE; Panamanian Institute for Special Rehabilitation; ☎ 261 0500; Camino Real, Betania, Panama City; ☑ 7am-4pm) was created by the government to assist all disabled people in Panama, including foreign tourists. However, the law does not require – and Panamanian businesses do not provide – discounts to foreign tourists with disabilities.

Panama is not wheelchair friendly; with the exception of wheelchair ramps outside a few upscale hotels, parking spaces for the disabled and perhaps a few dozen oversize bathroom stalls, accommodations for people with physical

DIRECTORY

disabilities do not exist in Panama. Even at the best hotels, you won't find railings in showers or beside toilets.

If you have a disability and want to communicate with person with disabilities who might have been to Panama recently, consider becoming a member of **Travelin' Talk Network** (TTN; in USA ☎ 303-232-2979; www.travelintalk.net; membership per year US$20). This organization offers a worldwide directory of members with various disabilities who communicate among themselves about travel.

Other organizations include:

Access-Able Travel Source (☎ 303-232-2979; www .access-able.com; PO Box 1796, Wheat Ridge, CO 80034) An excellent website with many links.

Gimp on the Go (www.gimponthego.com) Reported to be the most informative of the free internet-based newsletters written for persons with disabilities who love to travel.

Mobility International USA (☎ 541-343-1284; fax 541-343-6812; www.miusa.org; PO Box 10767, Eugene, OR 97440) Advises disabled travelers on mobility issues and runs an educational exchange program.

Society for Accessible Travel & Hospitality (SATH; ☎ 212-447-7284; www.sath.org; 347 Fifth Ave, Suite 610, New York, NY 10016) Lobbies for better facilities and publishes *Open World* magazine.

VISAS & DOCUMENTS
Onward Tickets

Travelers officially need onward tickets before they are allowed to enter Panama. This requirement is not often checked at Tocumen International Airport, but travelers arriving by land should anticipate a need to show an onward ticket.

If you're heading to Colombia, Venezuela or another South American country from Panama, you may need an onward or roundtrip ticket before you will be allowed entry into that country or even allowed to board the plane if you're flying. A quick check with the appropriate embassy – easy to do via the internet – will tell you whether the country that you're heading to has an onward-ticket requirement.

Passports, Tourist Cards & Visas

Every visitor needs a valid passport and an onward ticket to enter Panama, but further requirements vary by nationality and change occasionally. Anyone planning a trip to Panama would be advised to check the internet to obtain the latest information on entry requirements. Ticketing agents of airlines that fly to

Panama and tour operators that send groups there often can provide this information.

A valid passport is required to enter Panama, though additional requirements vary by country. Note that as of January 2007, US citizens can no longer enter Panama with just a driver's license and a birth certificate.

A tourist card costs US$5, and it's available at the airport or at border posts upon arrival. Most airlines serving Panama issue the tourist cards before you arrive, as do most buses arriving from Costa Rica.

No matter where you are coming from, you will generally be given a 90-day stamp in your passport when you enter Panama. This means you are allowed to remain in Panama for 90 days without having to obtain further permission from the authorities. After 90 days, visas and tourist cards can be extended at *migración* (immigration) offices.

Travelers entering Panama overland will probably be asked to show an onward ticket and a show of sufficient cash (US$500) or a credit card.

At the time of publication, people holding passports from the following countries needed to show only their passports to enter Panama: Argentina, Austria, Belgium, Chile, Costa Rica, Denmark, Egypt, El Salvador, Finland, France, Germany, Greece, Guatemala, Holland, Honduras, Hungary, Israel, Italy, Luxembourg, Paraguay, Poland, Portugal, Northern Ireland, Scotland, Singapore, Spain, Switzerland, the UK, Uruguay and Wales.

People from the following countries need a passport and a tourist card: Antigua, Australia, Bahamas, Barbados, Belize, Bermuda, Bolivia, Brazil, Canada, Colombia, Granada, Guyana, Iceland, Ireland, Jamaica, Japan, Malta, Mexico, Monaco, New Zealand, Norway, Paraguay, San Marino, South Korea, Suriname, Sweden, Taiwan, Tobago, Trinidad, the USA and Venezuela.

Citizens from countries that do not appear on this list will need to obtain a visa, available at Panamanian embassies or consulates. Contact the one nearest you or call the **immigration office** (☎ 227 1448, 225 8925; fax 227 1227, 225 1641) in Panama City.

In the event that you lose your passport while in Panama, you'll need proof of when you entered the country to be able to leave it. That proof, strangely enough, does not come from an immigration office but from the airline you flew in on. You need to go to the airline's main office in Panama City and request a certification of your entry date *(certificación de vuelo)*. There's no charge, but you'll likely be asked to come back the next day to pick it up. When you leave the country, along with your new passport (obtained from your embassy in Panama City), you'll present your *certificación de vuelo* to an immigration agent.

Visa Extensions

Visas and tourist cards are both good for 90 days. To extend your stay, you'll have to go to an office of Migración y Naturalización in Panama City, David or Chitré. You must bring your passport and photocopies of the page with your personal information and of the stamp of your most recent entry to Panama. You must also bring two passport-size photos, an onward air or bus ticket and a letter to the director stating your reasons for wishing to extend your visit. You will have to fill out a *prórroga de turista* (tourist extension) and pay US$10. You will then be issued a plastic photo ID card. Go early in the day as the whole process takes about two hours.

If you have extended your time, you will also need to obtain a *permiso de salida* (permit) to leave the country. For this, bring your passport and a *paz y salvo* (a certificate stating you don't owe any back taxes) to the immigration office. *Paz y salvos* are issued at Ministerios de Economia y Finanzas, found in towns with immigration offices, which simply require that you bring in your passport, fill out a form and pay US$1.

These documents can be obtained in Panama City or in David at the following locations:

Migración y Naturalización office (Immigration Office; Map pp76-7; ☎ 225 1373; Av Cuba & Calle 29 Este, La Exposición, Panama City; ⏰ 8am-3pm Mon-Fri)

Ministerio de Economia y Finanzas, Dirección de Ingresos (Map p79; ☎ 207 7748; cnr Via Españ & Calle 52 Este, Panama City) For a *paz y salvo*.

WOMEN TRAVELERS

Female travelers find Panama safe and pleasant to visit. Some Panamanian men make flirtatious comments or stare at single women, both local and foreign, but comments are rarely blatantly rude; the usual thing is a smiling *'mi amor'* (my love), an appreciative hiss or a honk of the horn. The best way to deal with this is to do what Panamanian women do – ignore the comments and don't look at the man making them.

Panamanians are generally fairly conservative in dress. Women travelers are advised to avoid skimpy or see-through clothing. And although Emberá women in the Darién go topless, it would be insulting for travelers to follow suit.

Women traveling solo will get more attention than those traveling in pairs or groups. Although assault and rape of foreign travelers is rare, avoid placing yourself in risky scenarios. Don't walk alone in isolated places, don't hitchhike and always pay particular attention to your surroundings.

WORK

It's difficult for foreigners to find work in Panama. The government doesn't like anyone taking jobs away from Panamanians, and the labor laws reflect this sentiment. Basically, the only foreigners legally employed in Panama work for their own businesses, possess skills not found in Panama or work for companies that have special agreements with the Panamanian government.

Small boats transiting the Panama Canal sometimes take on backpackers as deckhands (line handlers) in exchange for free passage, room and food. Inquiries can be made at the Panama Canal Yacht Club in Colón. Alternatively, boat owners sometimes post notices in pensions.

Volunteer Work

The **Asociación Nacional para la Conservación de la Naturaleza** (National Association for the Conservation of Nature, ANCON; ☎ 314 0061; www.ancon.org) offers opportunities for volunteering on projects in national parks and other beautiful natural areas. Volunteers might protect nesting turtles near Bocas del Toro, do environmental-education work in the Darién or assist park rangers. You can volunteer for any length of time from a week to several months; you won't get paid, but Ancon will supply basic necessities such as food and shelter. Contact Ancon for details.

Another excellent organization that takes volunteers from time to time is the **Fundación Pro-Niños de Darién** (☎ 254 4333; www.darien.org.pa). This nonprofit organization started in 1990 and works on a variety of projects throughout the Darién. It's targeted at the improvement of the lives of *niños* (children), including educational and nutritional programs. The organization also works to help residents develop sustainable agriculture.

Transportation

CONTENTS

GETTING THERE & AWAY

ENTERING THE COUNTRY

The proceedings for entering Panama by air are much less scrutinized than crossing by land. When you arrive at Tocúmen in Panama City or in David, depending on your nationality (see Visas, p302) you may have to fill out a tourist card (US$5). These are available either from an airline attendant during the flight or from a small desk near the passport checkpoint. It's a straightforward and painless procedure.

The same cannot be said for the most popular overland crossing from Costa Rica at Paso Canoas. Many travelers have complained about this border crossing, and the Panamanian officials – who act as if their instructions were to keep people out – receive low marks for their officious attitude. At this crossing, you will sometimes be asked to show an onward ticket – a

---

THINGS CHANGE

The information in this chapter is particularly vulnerable to change. Check directly with the airline or a travel agent to make sure you understand how a fare (and ticket you may buy) works and be aware of the security requirements for international travel. Shop carefully. The details given in this chapter should be regarded as pointers and are not a substitute for your own careful, up-to-date research.

CLIMATE CHANGE & TRAVEL

Climate change is a serious threat to the ecosystems that humans rely upon, and air travel is the fastest-growing contributor to the problem. Lonely Planet regards travel, overall, as a global benefit, but believes we all have a responsibility to limit our personal impact on global warming.

Flying & Climate Change

Pretty much every form of motorized travel generates CO_2 (the main cause of human-induced climate change) but planes are far and away the worst offenders, not just because of the sheer distances they allow us to travel, but because they release greenhouse gases high into the atmosphere. The statistics are frightening: two people taking a return flight between Europe and the US will contribute as much to climate change as an average household's gas and electricity consumption over a whole year.

Carbon Offset Schemes

Climatecare.org and other websites use 'carbon calculators' that allow travelers to offset the level of greenhouse gases they are responsible for with financial contributions to sustainable travel schemes that reduce global warming – including projects in India, Honduras, Kazakhstan and Uganda.

Lonely Planet, together with Rough Guides and other concerned partners in the travel industry, support the carbon offset scheme run by climatecare.org. Lonely Planet offsets all of its staff and author travel. For more information check out our website: www.lonelyplanet.com.

return bus ticket to Costa Rica will suffice – and a credit card or US$500. The border post at Sixaola/Guabito is much more low-key. There's a third crossing at Río Sereno that's little used by travelers despite being a good option.

AIR
Airports & Airlines
Panama has two international airports. Panama City's **Tocumen International Airport** (☎ 238 4322; airport code PTY) lies 35km from downtown, and it's where most international flights to Panama arrive. **Aeropuerto Enrique Malek** (☎ 721 1072; airport code DAV), in David, which is 75km southeast of the Costa Rican border, frequently handles flights to and from San José.

COPA is Panama's national airline, offering flights to and from the USA, numerous Latin and South American countries, and the Caribbean. The US Federal Aviation Administration recently assessed COPA Airlines as Category 1, which means they are in full compliance with international aviation standards.

The following listed airlines fly in and out of Panama:

Aires (☎ 265 6044; www.aires.aero; airline code 4C; hub Cartagena, Colombia)
Aerolíneas Argentinas (☎ 269 3815; www.aerolineas.com.ar; airline code AR; hub Buenos Aires)
AeroMexico (☎ 263 3033; www.aeromexico.com; airline code AM; hub Mexico City)
Air France (☎ 223 0204; www.airfrance.com; airline code AF; hub Paris)
Alitalia (☎ 269 2161; www.alitalia.com; airline code AZ; hub Rome)
American Airlines (☎ 269 6022; www.aa.com; airline code AA; hub Dallas & Miami)
Avianca (☎ 223 5225; www.avianca.com; airline code AV; hub Bogotá)
Cathay Pacific (☎ 263 3033; www.cathaypacific.com; airline code CX; hub Hong Kong)
Continental Airlines (☎ 263 9177; www.continental.com; airline code CO; hub Houston & Newark)
COPA (☎ 227 2672; www.copaair.com; airline code CM; hub Panama City)
Cubana (☎ 227 2291; www.cubana.cu; airline code CU; hub Havana)
Delta Air Lines (☎ 214 8118; www.delta.com; airline code DL; hub Atlanta)
Grupo TACA (☎ 360 2093; www.taca.com; airline code TA; hub San Salvador)
Iberia (☎ 227 3966; www.iberia.com; airline code IB; hub Madrid)
Japan Airlines (☎ 223 1266; www.jal.com; airline code JL; hub Tokyo)

> **DEPARTURE TAX**
>
> Panama levies a US$20 departure tax for outbound passengers on international flights.

KLM (☎ 264 6395; www.klm.com; airline code KL; hub Amsterdam)
Korean Air (☎ 315 0356; www.koreanair.com; airline code KE; hub Seoul)
Lan Chile (☎ 226 7119; www.lanchile.com; airline code LA; hub Santiago)
Mexicana (☎ 264 9855; www.mexicana.com; airline code MX; hub Mexico City)
Singapore Airlines (☎ 264 2533; www.singaporeair.com; airline code SQ; hub Singapore)
United Airlines (☎ 225 6519; www.united.com; airline code UA; hub Los Angeles)
US Airways (☎ 263 3033; www.usairways.com; airline code US; hub Philadelphia)

Tickets
In addition to websites such as **Travelocity** (www.travelocity.com), **Orbitz** (www.orbitz.com) and **Expedia** (www.expedia.com), all of the major carriers have their own website with online ticket sales, and tickets are sometimes discounted for online customers. You can find a comprehensive list of all international airlines with links to their websites at http://airlinecontact.info/index.html.

From Panama
The best place to buy tickets out of Panama is Panama City. Throughout the city, there are travel agencies scattered around that can arrange onward travel. However, the easiest way is to simply book your tickets online through any of the airlines listed.

From Asia
In Asia, there's a proliferation of **STA Travel** (Bangkok ☎ 02-236 0262; www.statravel.co.th; Singapore ☎ 6737 7188; www.statravel.com.sg; Hong Kong ☎ 2736 1618; www.statravel.com.hk; Japan ☎ 03-5391 2922; www.statravel.co.jp). Another resource in Japan is **No 1 Travel** (☎ 03-3205-6073; www.no1-travel.com); in Hong Kong try **Four Seas Tours** (☎ 2200 7777; www.fourseastravel.com/fs/en/index.jsp).

From Australia & New Zealand
The cheapest routes usually go via the USA (often Los Angeles). If you're planning a

TRANSPORT

longer trip through Latin America, an open-jaw (into one city, out of another) or even an around-the-world ticket will be your best bet. For online bookings try www.travel.com .au. The following are well-known agents for cheap fares with branches throughout Australia and New Zealand:

Flight Centre Australia (☎ 133-133; www.flightcentre .com.au); New Zealand (☎ 0800-243-544; www.flight centre.co.nz)

STA Travel Australia (☎ 1300 733 035; www.statravel .com.au); New Zealand (☎ 0508-782-872; www.statravel .co.nz)

From Canada

There were no direct flights from Canada to Panama at the time of writing. As a result, travelers need to connect through one of the gateway cities in the USA. United Airlines, Continental Airlines and American Airlines all have good connections from major Canadian cities.

A recommended Canadian travel agency is **Travel Cuts** (☎ 800-667-243-544; www.travelcuts .com), Canada's national student travel agency. Websites such as www.expedia.ca and www .travelocity.ca are also good bets.

From Central America, Cuba & the Caribbean

Grupo TACA provides services between all the Central American capitals and Panama City. In addition, COPA (the Panamanian airline) offers flights between Panama City and Costa Rica, Cuba, the Dominican Republic, El Salvador, Guatemala, Haiti, Jamaica and Mexico. Cubana has the cheapest flights in the region between Panama City and Havana.

From Europe

At the time of publication, Iberia was the only airline flying direct from Europe to Panama; the cheapest fares are usually via Madrid. Air France and Lufthansa also fly from Europe, connecting in the USA. Recommended UK ticket agencies include the following:

Journey Latin America (☎ 020-8747 3108; www.jour neylatinamerica.co.uk)

STA Travel (☎ 0870-2300 040; www.statravel.co.uk) For travelers under the age of 26.

Trailfinders (☎ 0845-058 5858; www.trailfinders.co.uk)

For online booking, try www.dialaflight.com or www.lastminute.com.

From South America

In South America you'll discover that services to and from Panama are offered by Avianca and Aires in Colombia, LAB in Bolivia, Lan Chile in Chile and Aerolineas Argentinas in Argentina. American Airlines, Continental Airlines, Delta Air Lines and United Airlines all have connections from Panama City to several different South American countries.

From the USA

The principal US gateways to and from Panama are Miami, Houston, Newark, New York, Washington DC, Dallas and Los Angeles. At the time of writing, sample roundtrip economy fares for direct flights from Miami to Panama City ranged between US$400 and US$600. Fares from Los Angeles ranged between US$500 and US$700.

The following websites are recommended for online booking:

- www.cheaptickets.com
- www.expedia.com
- www.lowestfare.com
- www.orbitz.com
- www.sta.com
- www.ticotravel.com

LAND

Many travelers arrive in Panama by bus from Costa Rica. It's recommended that you get to the border early in order to ensure that you don't miss onward transportation on the other side. There are no roads into Colombia, and travelers are strongly discouraged from crossing overland due to the instability of the border region.

Border Crossings

There are three road border crossings between Costa Rica and Panama. The most frequently used (and least pleasant) crossing between the two countries is on the Interamericana. Border-crossers should note that Panama is always one hour ahead of Costa Rica.

To enter Panama from Costa Rica, you'll need a passport, an onward ticket and proof of solvency – US$500 or a credit card. At the border you'll fill out a US$5 tourist card (some nationalities are exempt, while others need a visa to enter; see p302).

PASO CANOAS

This chaotic and heavily used border is on the Interamericana, not quite halfway between Panama City and San José. If you've been traveling overland through other countries, you're liable to find this one of the least pleasant crossings in Central America. The border hours here change frequently; at last check the border was open 7am to 11pm daily. Note that there are hotels on the Costa Rican side of Paso Canoas but none on the Panamanian side.

Make sure you get all of your stamps – proof of exiting from Costa Rica, proof of entry in Panama. A few travelers in the past have gone through without the proper entry/exit stamps only to encounter problems later on.

If you don't have an onward ticket and are asked to show one, you'll have to buy a bus ticket from either Panaline or Tica Bus at the border. This will be a Panama City–San José ticket and will cost US$25.

Among the services here is a **Banco Nacional de Panamá** (8am-3pm Mon-Fri, 9am-noon Sat) just beyond the immigration window. At the bank you can use their ATM, cash traveler's checks and get cash advances against credit cards. However, it's not possible to change Costa Rican *colones* to US dollars. Men on the street will offer to change money if they see you standing in front of the bank looking perplexed. To lower the risk of being cheated, ask for their exchange rate and calculate how many US dollars you should receive for the amount of *colones* you intend to unload *before* reaching for your cash.

Once you have entered Panama, you will see taxis and buses stationed just past the border, on your left and ahead 50m. The nearest Panamanian city with a hotel is David. Buses depart Paso Canoas from this station (immediately to the left) for David (US$1.50, 1½ hours, every 10 minutes, 5am to 9:45pm); look for a bus with 'Frontera – David' on its windshield. Three buses depart daily for Panama City (adult/child US$12/US$6, 10 hours, 8:30am, 11am and 4pm) making numerous stops along the way; a fourth bus departs at 10pm (adult/child US$17/$8.50, 8 hours) making only a couple of brief food stops.

Fifty meters east of that bus station is an unmarked, often-overlooked bus station that features bus rides to Panama City (US$12, about 9 hours; 5:45am, 7am, 8:30am, 10am, 11:30am, 2pm, 4pm and 6:45pm), including two express services (US$17, about 7½hours; 9:45am and 10:45pm). These buses make stops at David and all the other major cities along the way (they'll even stop at a hamlet along the Interamericana or at a turnoff *if* you ask the driver to stop ahead of time).

There is a taxi stand near the first bus station. Taxis are available 24 hours a day. A taxi ride from the border to David will cost from US$25 to US$30 per party, depending on the driver and the hour.

If you are entering Costa Rica, you may be required to show a ticket out of the country, although this is rarely requested.

SIXAOLA/GUABITO

This crossing is on the Caribbean coast. Sixaola is the last town on the Costa Rican side; Guabito is its Panamanian counterpart. There are no hotels or banks in Guabito, but stores there will accept your Costa Rican *colones,* Panamanian balboas or US dollars. *Colones* are not accepted south of Guabito.

The border is officially open from 7am to 11pm daily. However, immigration and customs officers often don't work past 7pm, which is when bus service on both sides also grinds to a halt. During the day, there are frequent minibuses from Guabito to Changuinola ($US1), 17km away. The minibuses can be found on the southern side of the elevated entrance road, just past the immigration office. Taxis are found on the northern side of the road; the fare to Changuinola is US$5.

In Changuinola there are numerous hotels, several banks, some decent restaurants and an airstrip with daily services to David and Panama City. You can catch a water taxi from here to Bocas del Toro (see p217 for details).

RÍO SERENO

This little town at the eastern terminus of the scenic Concepción–Volcán road sees so few tourists that locals often stare at those who pass through. If you arrive here from Costa Rica by small bus (as most people do), you'll be hard pressed to figure out where one country ends and the other begins. The Río Sereno crossing is open from 7:30am to 5pm daily.

The little immigration office is near the base of a huge police communications tower – look for the orange-and-black 'Migracion' sign.

The **Banco Nacional de Panamá** has an ATM and provides services such as offering cash advances against major credit cards and cashing traveler's checks. However, foreign currency cannot be exchanged here.

There's a bus terminal two blocks northeast of the bank (ie along the same street and away from the border). Buses depart from Río Sereno to Volcán (US$2.65, 40km, hourly) and continue on to David (US$4), with the first bus departing at 5am and the last at 5pm.

Bus

At all three border crossings, you can take a local bus up to the border on either side, cross over, board another local bus and con-

TRANSPORT

DRIVING TO PANAMA FROM NORTH AMERICA

Every year, readers send us letters detailing their long-haul road trip across the continent. If you think you're game for a little overland adventure, here is a selection of reader-tested tips for making the most of the big drive:

- **Think it through.** Driving yourself through Central America is *not* a cheap option. Having your own car will afford you greater comfort and flexibility, though you *will* spend more than you expect on petrol, insurance and import fees. Unless you are planning to spend a lot of time off the beaten track or detest the idea of slumming it on local buses, public transport will probably be a cheaper and easier way to go.

- **Buy a Japanese car.** Toyotas, Hondas and Nissans are extremely popular in Central America, which makes them substantially easier to service if problems arise. Their popularity also makes them easier to sell in Panama, though you should not expect to recoup your initial expenditure.

- **Get insurance in the USA or Canada.** Since most Central American countries will not offer fully comprehensive insurance for vehicles with foreign license plates, this may be your last opportunity to ensure that you're covered.

- **Learn to service your car.** A degree of mechanical know-how will allow you to make minor repairs yourself, and help you avoid being ripped off by unscrupulous mechanics. If you do need to repair your vehicle, be advised that mechanics charge much more in Panama than in other Central American countries.

- **Be prepared.** It's a good idea to plan for the worst, so make sure you bring along a good tool kit, an emergency jerry can of petrol, plenty of emergency food and water, and the always handy roll of industrial-strength duct tape. A spare tire or two is also a good idea, especially if you're planning on going off-road or traveling over rough terrain.

- **Know the law.** Panamanian law requires that all vehicles be fitted with a catalytic converter. Bear this in mind if you remove your catalytic converter elsewhere in Central America due to the poorer grades of fuel, which can cause clogging of the catalytic converter.

- **Nationalize your car**. If you plan on selling your car in Panama, you will probably have to nationalize it before selling it – this should cost you approximately 20% to 25% of the vehicle's value in taxation. Note that any damage to the vehicle will reduce its value – do not have any mechanical or aesthetic work carried out until after you nationalize it. Technically, the buyer can also nationalize the vehicle, though most don't want the hassle of dealing with customs.

- **Advertise your wares**. The easiest way to sell your car in Panama is to take out a classified in the *La Prensa* newspaper. The best day to do this is Sunday when the majority of car buyers are looking. If you place your advertisement on a Thursday morning, you should be able to get inclusion for both Saturday and Sunday editions, only paying for one of those days.

And most importantly:

- **Drive defensively**. As one reader puts it, 'Understand that many drivers are clinically insane.' Driving in Panama and the rest of Central America is not for the faint of heart – be smart, be safe and arrive alive.

tinue on your way. Be aware that the last buses leave the border crossings at Guabito and Río Sereno at 7pm and 5pm, respectively; the last bus leaves Paso Canoas for Panama City at 10pm.

Two companies, **Panaline** (☎ 227 8648; fax 227 8647) and **Tica Bus** (☎ 262 2084; fax 262 6275), operate daily *directo* (direct) buses between San José, Costa Rica and Panama City, departing from the Albrook bus terminal. Both recommend that you make reservations a few days in advance.

Car & Motorcycle

You can drive your own car or motorcycle from North America to Panama, but the costs of insurance, fuel, border permits, food and accommodations will be much higher than the cost of an airline ticket. As a result, many people opt for flying down and renting cars when they arrive in Panama City. However, if you can sell your car when the journey is complete, it is possible to recoup some of the travel costs.

If you consider driving, factor in the following: driving Central American roads at night is not recommended – they are narrow, rarely painted with a center stripe, often potholed and subject to hazards such as cattle and pedestrians in rural areas. Also bear in ming that traveling by day from the USA or Canada takes about a week, considerably more if you want to visit some of the fantastic sights en route.

If you decide to drive to Panama, get insurance in advance, have your papers in order and never leave your car unattended (fortunately, guarded lots are common in Latin America). US license plates are attractive to some thieves, so you should display these from inside the car.

If you are bringing a car into Panama, you must pay US$5 for a vehicle control certificate *(tarjeta de circulación)* and another US$1 to have the car fumigated. You will also need to show a driver's license, proof of ownership and insurance papers. Your passport will be stamped to show that you paid US$6 and followed procedures when you brought the vehicle into the country.

For tips on driving to Panama from North America, importing your car and selling it afterwards, see the boxed text, opposite.

SEA

For information on crossing to Colombia by sea, see the boxed text on p263.

GETTING AROUND

AIR

Panama has two major domestic carriers: **Air Panama** (☎ 316 9000; www.flyairpanama.com/tickets) and **Aeroperlas** (☎ 315 7500; www.aeroperlas.com). Domestic flights depart Panama City from **Aeropuerto Albrook** (Albrook Airport; ☎ 315 0403) and arrive in destinations throughout the country. For most flights it's wise to book as far in advance as possible – this is particularly true of flights to the Comarca de Kuna Yala. At the time this was written, most islands had only one flight leaving per day, with flights booked weeks in advance. Fares run from US$35 to US$70 one way.

BICYCLE

You can bicycle through the country easily enough, but using a bicycle to travel within larger Panamanian cities – particularly Panama City – is not a wise idea. The roads tend to be narrow, there are no bike lanes, bus drivers and motorists drive aggressively and it rains a lot, reducing motorists' visibility and your tires' ability to grip the road.

Outside the cities, the Panamanian stretch of the Interamericana is the best quality in Central America, although parts are extremely narrow, leaving little room to move aside should a car pass by. Of course, once you leave the well-paved Interamericana, roads in many of the provinces (especially in Veraguas and Colón) are in bad shape – plan accordingly and bring lots of spare parts.

There's one professional outfitter in Panama City if you need gear, maintenance or to purchase a quality bicycle – see Bicicletas Rali on p86.

Lodging in Panama is rarely more than a day's bike ride away.

BOAT

Boats are the chief means of transportation in several areas of Panama, particularly in Darién Province, the Archipiélago de las Perlas, and the San Blás and Bocas del Toro island chains. And while at least one eccentric soul has swum the entire length of the

TRANSPORT

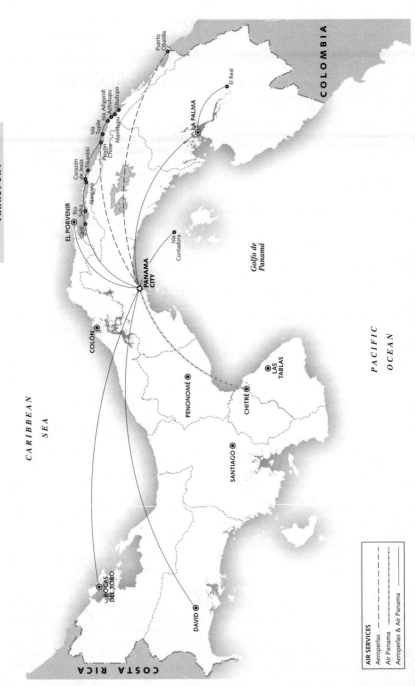

Panama Canal, most people find that a boat simplifies the transit enormously.

From Panama City, frequent boats depart from the Causeway (p86) and head to the nearby island of Isla Taboga (p115). Panama City is also the jumping-off point for partial and full Panama Canal transits (see p109).

If you're planning an excursion to Isla de Coiba and the national marine park, the best way to reach the island is through an organized boat tour – for more information, see p189. Local fisherman also ply the waters off the coast of Veraguas (p190), though this is a much riskier proposition as the seas can really get rough in these parts.

The tourist mecca of Bocas del Toro on Isla Colón is accessible from Changuinola by speedy and inexpensive water taxis – see p235 for details.

Colombian and Kuna merchant boats carry cargo and passengers along the San Blás coast between Colón and Puerto Obaldía, stopping at up to 48 of the islands to load and unload passengers and cargo. However, these boats are occasionally used to traffic narcotics, and they're often dangerously overloaded. Hiring a local boatman is a wiser option – see the Comarca de Kuna Yala section (p265) for more details.

Since there aren't many roads in the eastern Darién Province, boat travel is often the most feasible way to get from one town to another, especially during the rainy season. The boat of choice here is a long canoe, or *piragua*, carved from the trunk of a giant ceba tree. *Piraguas'* shallow hulls allow them to ride the many rivers that comprise the traditional transport network of eastern Panama. Many such boats – including the ones travelers usually hire – are motorized. See the Darién Province section (p279) for more details.

BUS

You can take a bus to just about any community in Panama that is reachable by road. Some of the buses are huge, new Mercedes Benzes equipped with air-con, movie screens and reclining seats. These top-of-the-line buses generally cruise long stretches of highway.

More frequently used – and often seen on the Carretera Interamericana – are Toyota Coaster buses that can seat 28 people. These are affectionately called *chivas*, and are not as comfortable as the Mercedes Benzes, but they aren't bad and they're less expensive. They are

an excellent way to visit towns on the Península de Azuero and along the Interamericana.

Also seen on Panamanian roads – particularly within cities – are converted school buses. They are neither comfortable for most adults (they were designed for children) nor convenient (they stop every 10m, or so it seems), and they are usually crowded. Still, they are an extremely cheap way to get around and they beat hoofing it.

CAR & MOTORCYCLE

Few tourists drive to Panama in their own vehicles, though it is certainly possible to do so. Renting a car is also a possibility. Because of difficult driving conditions, there are speed limits of 80km per hour on all primary roads and 60km per hour or less on secondary roads. Drivers should carry their passports as well as driver's licenses.

If you are involved in an accident, you should not move the vehicles (even if they're blocking traffic) until after the police have arrived and made a report. This is essential for all insurance claims. If you see oncoming cars with headlights flashing, it often means that there is some kind of road problem or a police speed trap ahead. Slow down immediately. Also be on the lookout for a pile of branches placed on the road near an edge; this often means that a vehicle is broken down just ahead.

Rental

Due to the low cost and ready availability of buses and taxis, it isn't necessary to rent a vehicle in Panama unless you intend to go to places far off the beaten track. Should you choose to rent, however, you'll find car-rental agencies in major cities such as Panama City and David. Several agencies also have offices at Tocumen International Airport in the capital. To rent a vehicle in Panama, you must be 25 years of age or older and present a passport and driver's license – if you are over 21 and can present a valid credit card, some rental agencies will waive the age requirement.

Prices for rentals in Panama run from US$45 per day for a tiny car to US$100 per day for a 4WD vehicle (or a *'cuatro por cuatro'*). When you rent, carefully inspect the car for minor dents and scratches, missing radio antennae, hubcaps and the spare tire. These damages *must* be noted on your rental agreement; otherwise you may be charged for them when you return the car.

There have been many reports of theft from rental cars. You should never leave valuables in an unattended car, and you should remove all luggage from the trunk when you're checking into a hotel overnight – most hotels provide parking areas for cars.

HITCHHIKING

Hitchhiking is not as widespread in Panama as elsewhere in Central America; most people travel by bus, and visitors would do best to follow suit. The exception is holiday weekends, when buses are full to overflowing and hitchhiking may be the only way out of a place. If you get a ride, offer to pay for it when you arrive; *'¿Cuánto le debo?'* (How much do I owe you?) is the standard way of doing this.

Hitchhiking is never entirely safe in any country, but it's not uncommon as you arrive in rural areas.

LOCAL TRANSPORTATION

Local buses serve the urban and suburban areas, but services can be difficult to figure out and there are few roadside signs indicating destinations. Panamanians are usually friendly, and this includes bus drivers; they'll often be able to tell you where to wait for a particular busy, if you ask in Spanish (few bus drivers speak English). But in general, unless you've come to Panama specifically for its urban-bus experience, leave that for another lifetime and take taxis – they're cheap and will save you a lot of time and hassle.

Taxis

Panamanian taxis don't have meters, but there are some set fares. Taxis are cheap and, most of the time, they are plentiful. However, they can be difficult to hail late at night and just before and during holidays. At times like these, it's best to call for a radio taxi. Listings for reliable radio taxis can be found in the yellow pages of phone directories throughout Panama, under the heading Taxis.

There is one group of taxis that do charge more than others. These 'sedan' taxis operate from particular upscale hotels, including the Hotel Caesar Park (p93) and the El Ejecutivo Hotel in Panama City. Taxi drivers generally mill about the front doors of the hotels and ask every exiting individual if he or she would like a cab. These drivers charge at least twice what you'd pay a hailed cab.

TOURS

Although Panama has much to offer the tourist, the country's tourism industry is still young and the number of local tour operators quite small. With that said, the quality of available operators is extremely high, and many of Panama's top attractions including the Darién (p273) and Coiba (p188) are relatively inaccessible without a guide. So, even if you're a staunch independent traveller, Panama is one destination where you might want to consider joining an organized tour. And remember: good guides are like flying first class – they make the trip so much more enjoyable.

Prices vary depending on the services you require. Two people wishing to travel with a private English-speaking guide and a private vehicle will obviously pay more than two people who are prepared to join a group.

Each of the agencies listed below is highly recommended for anyone in search of a guided tour of Panama.

Ancon Expeditions of Panama (Map p79; ☎ 269 9415; www.anconexpeditions.com; El Dorado Bldg, Calle Elvira Mendez) Created by Panama's top private conservation organization, Ancon Expeditions employs the country's best nature guides and offers a superlative level of service. For more information on offerings, see the boxed text on p89.

Scubapanama (☎ 261 3841; www.scubapanama.com) This is the country's oldest and most respected dive operator, and offers a variety of dive trips throughout the country. It's recommended that you book a tour prior to your arrival.

Panama Surf Tours (☎ 6671 7777; www.panamasurf tours.com) The only tour operator in Panama that offers customized surf tours throughout the country – guides are local surfers who have lived and surfed Panama all their lives. It's recommended that you book a tour prior to your arrival.

TRAIN

The country's only rail line is the historic Panama Railroad, which runs from Panama City to Colón. In 2001, the **Panama Canal Railway Company** (PCRC; ☎ 317 6070; www.panarail.com) introduced a passenger service that included a fully operational vintage train. Aimed at tourists looking to relive the heyday of luxury rail travel, the hour-long ride runs parallel to the canal, and at times traverses thick jungles and rainforests.

There are daily departures (one-way/roundtrip US$22/38) from Panama City at 7:15am and Colón at 5:15pm. Note that the Panama City terminus is located in Corazal, which is a 15-minute cab ride from the capital.

For more information on train services, see the boxed text on p246.

Health Dr David Goldberg

CONTENTS

Panama has a high standard of hygiene and very few travelers get seriously sick during their stay. However, food-borne as well as mosquito-borne infections do exist and though many of these illnesses are not life-threatening, they can certainly ruin your trip. Besides getting the proper vaccinations, it's important that you take insect repellent and exercise care in what you eat and drink.

BEFORE YOU GO

Since most vaccines don't produce immunity until at least two weeks after they're given, visit a physician four to eight weeks before departure. Ask your doctor for an International Certificate of Vaccination (otherwise known as the 'yellow booklet'), which will list all the vaccinations you've received. This is mandatory for countries that require proof of yellow-fever vaccination upon entry, but it's a good idea to carry it wherever you travel.

Bring medications in their original containers, clearly labeled. A signed, dated letter from your physician describing all medical conditions and medications, including generic names, is also a good idea. If carrying syringes or needles, be sure to

HEALTH

RECOMMENDED VACCINATIONS

There are no required vaccines for Panama, but a number are recommended:

Vaccine	Recommended for	Dosage	Side effects
hepatitis A	all travelers	1 dose before trip; booster 6-12 months later	soreness at injection site; headaches; body aches
typhoid	all travelers	4 capsules by mouth, 1 taken every other day	abdominal pain; nausea; rash
yellow fever	all travelers	1 dose lasts 10 years	headaches; body aches; severe reactions are rare
hepatitis B	long-term travelers in close contact with the local population	3 doses over 6-month period	soreness at injection site; low-grade fever
rabies	travelers who may have contact with animals and may not have access to medical care	3 doses over 3-4 week period	soreness at injection site; headaches; body aches
tetanus-diphtheria	all travelers who haven't had a booster within 10 years	1 dose lasts 10 years	soreness at injection site
measles	travelers born after 1956 who have had only one measles vaccination	1 dose	fever; rash; joint pains; allergic reactions
chickenpox	travelers who've never had chickenpox	2 doses one month apart	fever; mild case of chickenpox

MEDICAL CHECKLIST

- Acetaminophen (Tylenol) or aspirin
- Adhesive or paper tape
- Antibacterial ointment (eg Bactroban) for cuts and abrasions
- Antibiotics
- Antidiarrheal drugs (eg loperamide)
- Antihistamines (for hay fever and allergic reactions)
- Anti-inflammatory drugs (eg ibuprofen)
- Bandages, gauze, gauze rolls
- DEET-containing insect repellent for the skin
- Iodine tablets (for water purification)
- Malaria pills – recommended if going to the Darién (see p273)
- Oral rehydration salts
- Permethrin-containing insect spray for clothing, tents and bed nets
- Pocket knife
- Scissors, safety pins, tweezers
- Steroid cream or cortisone (for poison ivy and other allergic rashes)
- Sun block
- Syringes and sterile needles
- Thermometer

have a physician's letter documenting their medical necessity.

Most doctors and hospitals expect payment in cash, regardless of whether you have travel health insurance. If you develop a life-threatening medical problem, you'll probably want to be evacuated to a country with state-of-the-art medical care. Since this may cost tens of thousands of dollars, be sure you have the insurance to cover this before you depart. You can find a list of medical-evacuation and travel-insurance companies on the **US State Department** (www.travel.state.gov/travel/abroad_health.html) website. If your health insurance does not cover you for medical expenses abroad, consider supplemental insurance. Find out in advance if your insurance plan will make payments directly to providers or reimburse you later for overseas health expenditures.

INTERNET RESOURCES

There is a wealth of travel-health advice on the internet. For further information, the **Lonely Planet** (www.lonelyplanet.com) website is a good place to start. A superb book called *International Travel and Health*, revised annually and available online at no cost, is published by the **World Health Organization** (www.who.int/ith/). Another website of general interest is **MD Travel Health** (www.mdtravelhealth .com), which provides complete travel-health recommendations for every country, updated daily, also at no cost.

It's usually a good idea to consult your government's travel-health website before departure, if one is available:
Australia (www.dfat.gov.au/travel/)
Canada (www.hc-sc.gc.ca/pphb-dgspsp/tmp-pmv /pub_e.html)
United Kingdom (www.doh.gov.uk/traveladvice/index .htm)
United States (www.cdc.gov/travel/)

FURTHER READING

For further information, see *Healthy Travel Central & South America*, also from Lonely Planet. If you're traveling with children, Lonely Planet's *Travel with Children* may be useful. The *ABC of Healthy Travel*, by E Walker et al, is another valuable resource.

IN TRANSIT

DEEP VEIN THROMBOSIS (DVT)

Blood clots (deep vein thrombosis) may form in the legs during long-haul plane flights, chiefly because of prolonged immobility; the longer the flight, the greater the risk. Though most blood clots are reabsorbed uneventfully, some may break off and travel through the blood vessels to the lungs, where they could cause life-threatening complications.

The chief symptom of deep vein thrombosis is swelling or pain of the foot, ankle, or calf, usually but not always on just one side. When a blood clot travels to the lungs, it may cause chest pain and difficulty breathing. Travelers with any of these symptoms should immediately seek medical attention.

To prevent the development of deep vein thrombosis on long flights you should walk about the cabin, perform isometric compressions of the leg muscles (ie contract the leg muscles while sitting), drink plenty of fluids and avoid alcohol and tobacco.

JET LAG & MOTION SICKNESS

Jet lag is common when crossing more than five time zones, resulting in insomnia, fatigue, malaise or nausea. To avoid jet lag, try drinking plenty of fluids (nonalcoholic) and eating light meals. Upon arrival, get exposure to natural sunlight and readjust your schedule (for meals, sleep etc) as soon as possible.

Antihistamines such as dimenhydrinate (Dramamine) and meclizine (Antivert, Bonine) are usually the first choice for treating motion sickness. Their main side effect is drowsiness. A herbal alternative is ginger, which can work like a charm for some people.

IN PANAMA

AVAILABILITY OF HEALTH CARE

Good medical care is widely available in Panama City. The following hospitals and clinics are generally reliable:

Centro Medico Paitilla (☎ 265 8800; cnr Av Balboa & Calle 53, Paitilla)

Clinica Hospital San Fernando (☎ 278 6300, emergency ☎ 278 6305; www.hospitalsanfernando.com; Vía España, Las Sabanas Apartado 363)

Clinica Hospital San Fernando Hospital Pediatrico (☎ 229 2299/229 2477; www.hospitalsanfernando.com; Vía España, Las Sabanas 363)

Hospital Nacional (switchboard ☎ 207 8100, emergency room 207 8110; Av Cuba btwn Calle 38 & 39)

Medical facilities outside Panama City are limited. David has the best hospitals outside the capital:

Hospital Centro Medico Mae Lewis (☎ 775 4616; Vía Panamericana, Apartado 333)

INFECTIOUS DISEASES
Chagas' Disease

Chagas' disease is a parasitic infection that is transmitted by triatomine insects (reduviid bugs), which inhabit crevices in the walls and roofs of substandard housing in South and Central America. In Panama, Chagas' disease occurs in rural areas. The triatom-

ine insect lays its feces on human skin as it bites, usually at night. A person becomes infected when he or she unknowingly rubs the feces into the bite wound or any other open sore. Chagas' disease is extremely rare in travelers. However, if you sleep in a poorly constructed house, especially one made of mud, adobe or thatch, you should be sure to protect yourself with a bed net and a good insecticide.

Cholera

Cholera has not been reported in Panama in recent years. Cholera vaccine is not recommended.

Dengue Fever (Breakbone Fever)

Dengue fever is a viral infection found throughout Central America. In Panama, most cases occur in San Miguelito and in the Panama City metropolitan area. Dengue is transmitted by aedes mosquitoes, which bite preferentially during the daytime and are usually found close to human habitations, often indoors. They breed primarily in artificial water containers, such as jars, barrels, cans, cisterns, metal drums, plastic containers and discarded tires. As a result, dengue is especially common in densely populated, urban environments.

Dengue usually causes flu-like symptoms, including fever, muscle aches, joint pains, headaches, nausea and vomiting, often followed by a rash. The body aches may be quite uncomfortable, but most cases resolve uneventfully in a few days. There is no treatment for dengue fever except to take analgesics such as acetaminophen/paracetamol (Tylenol) and drink plenty of fluids. Severe cases may require hospitalization for intravenous fluids and supportive care. There is no vaccine. The cornerstone of prevention is to avoid being bitten.

Hantavirus Pulmonary Syndrome

This is a rapidly progressive viral infection that typically leads to respiratory failure and is frequently fatal. The disease is acquired by exposure to the excretions of wild rodents. Most cases occur in those who live in rodent-infested dwellings in rural areas. An outbreak of hantavirus pulmonary syndrome was recently reported from Los Santos Province.

Hepatitis A

Hepatitis A is the second most common travel-related infection (after traveler's diarrhea). It's a viral infection of the liver that is usually acquired by ingestion of contaminated water, food or ice, though it may also be acquired by direct contact with infected persons. The illness occurs throughout the world, but the incidence is higher in developing nations. Symptoms may include fever, malaise, jaundice, nausea, vomiting and abdominal pain. Most cases resolve without complications, though hepatitis A occasionally causes severe liver damage. There is no treatment.

The vaccine for hepatitis A is extremely safe and highly effective. If you get a booster six to twelve months later, it lasts for at least 10 years. You really should get it before you go to Panama or any other developing nation. Because the safety of hepatitis A vaccine has not been established for pregnant women or children under age two, they should instead be given a gammaglobulin injection.

Hepatitis B

Like hepatitis A, hepatitis B is a liver infection that occurs worldwide but is more common in developing nations. Unlike hepatitis A, the disease is usually acquired by sexual contact or by exposure to infected blood, generally through blood transfusions or contaminated needles. The vaccine is recommended only for long-term travelers (on the road more than six months) who expect to live in rural areas or have close physical contact with the local population. Additionally, the vaccine is recommended for anyone who anticipates sexual contact with the local inhabitants or a possible need for medical, dental or other treatments while abroad, especially if a need for transfusions or injections is expected.

Hepatitis B vaccine is safe and highly effective. However, a total of three injections is necessary to establish full immunity. Several countries added hepatitis B vaccine to the list of routine childhood immunizations in the 1980s, so many young adults are already protected.

HIV/AIDS

This has been reported from all Central American countries. Be sure to use condoms for all sexual encounters. Reliable, American-made brands are available at most pharmacies.

Leishmaniasis

Leishmaniasis occurs in rural and forested areas throughout Panama, especially the eastern and south-central regions. The disease is generally limited to the skin, causing slow-growing ulcers over exposed parts of the body, but the infection may become generalized, especially in those with HIV. Leishmaniasis is transmitted by sandflies, which are about one-third the size of mosquitoes. There is no vaccine. To protect yourself from sandflies, follow the same precautions as for mosquitoes, except that netting must be finer-size mesh (at least 18 holes to the linear inch).

Leptospirosis

Leptospirosis is acquired by exposure to water contaminated by the urine of infected animals. In Panama, leptospirosis is reported throughout the country. The greatest risk occurs at times of flooding, when sewage overflow may contaminate water sources. Outbreaks have been reported among military personnel performing jungle training exercises. The initial symptoms, which resemble a mild flu, usually subside uneventfully in a few days, with or without treatment, but a minority of cases are complicated by jaundice or meningitis. There is no vaccine. You can minimize your risk by staying out of bodies of fresh water that may be contaminated by animal urine. If you're engaging in high-risk activities in an area where an outbreak is in progress, you can take 200mg of doxycycline once weekly as a preventative measure. If you actually develop leptospirosis, the treatment is 100mg of doxycycline twice daily.

Malaria

Malaria is transmitted by mosquito bites, usually between dusk and dawn. The main symptom is high-spiking fevers, which may be accompanied by chills, sweats, headache, body aches, weakness, vomiting, or diarrhea. Severe cases may involve the central nervous system and lead to seizures, confusion, coma and death.

In Panama, malaria pills are recommended for rural areas in the provinces of Bocas del Toro, Darién and Kuna Yala. For Bocas del Toro, the first-choice malaria pill is chloroquine, taken once weekly in a dosage of 500mg, starting one to two weeks before arrival and continuing through the trip, and for four weeks after departure. Chloroquine is safe, inexpensive and highly effective. Side effects are typically mild and may include nausea, abdominal discomfort, headache, dizziness, blurred vision or itching. Severe reactions are uncommon.

Protecting yourself against mosquito bites is just as important as taking malaria pills, since no pills are 100% effective.

If you may not have access to medical care while traveling, you should bring along additional pills for emergency self-treatment, which you should take if you can't reach a doctor and you develop symptoms that suggest malaria, such as high-spiking fevers. One option is to take four tablets of Malarone once daily for three days. If you start self-medication, you should try to see a doctor at the earliest possible opportunity.

In areas east of the Canal Zone, including the Darién and Kuna Yala, there are chloroquine-resistant mosquitoes. Your options there are mefloquine (which has severe side effects for some travelers), doxycycline (which is milder on the system, but makes you more susceptible to sunburn) or Malarone.

If you develop a fever after returning home, see a physician, as malaria symptoms may not occur for months.

Rabies

Rabies is a viral infection of the brain and spinal cord that is almost always fatal. The rabies virus is carried in the saliva of infected animals and is typically transmitted through an animal bite, though contamination of any break in the skin with infected saliva may result in rabies.

In Panama, rabies is transmitted mainly by vampire bats. All animal bites and scratches must be promptly and thoroughly cleansed with large amounts of soap and water, and local health authorities contacted to determine whether or not further treatment is necessary (see p74).

Tick-Borne Relapsing Fever

This fever, which may be transmitted by either ticks or lice, is caused by bacteria that are closely related to those which cause Lyme disease and syphilis. The illness is characterized by periods of fever, chills, headaches, body aches, muscle aches and cough, alternating with periods when the fever subsides and the person feels relatively well. To minimize the risk of relapsing fever, follow tick precautions as outlined below and practice good personal hygiene at all times.

Typhoid

Typhoid fever is caused by ingestion of food or water contaminated by a species of salmonella known as *Salmonella typhi*. Fever occurs in virtually all cases. Other symptoms may include headache, malaise, muscle aches, dizziness, loss of appetite, nausea and abdominal pain. Either diarrhea or constipation may occur. Possible complications include intestinal perforation, intestinal bleeding, confusion, delirium or (rarely) coma.

Unless you expect to take all your meals in major hotels and restaurants, typhoid vaccine is a good idea. It's usually given orally, but is also available as an injection. Neither vaccine is approved for use in children under the age of two.

The drug of choice for typhoid fever is usually a quinolone antibiotic such as ciprofloxacin (Cipro) or levofloxacin (Levaquin), which many travelers carry for treatment of traveler's diarrhea. However, if you self-treat for typhoid fever, you may also need to self-treat for malaria, since the symptoms of the two diseases may be indistinguishable.

Yellow Fever

Yellow fever is a life-threatening viral infection transmitted by mosquitoes in forested areas. The illness begins with flu-like symptoms, which may include fever, chills, headache, muscle aches, backache, loss of appetite, nausea and vomiting. These symptoms usually subside in a few days, but one person in six enters a second, toxic phase characterized by recurrent fever, vomiting, listlessness, jaundice, kidney failure and hemorrhage, leading to death in up to half of the cases. There is no treatment.

HEALTH

Yellow-fever vaccine is not required for travel to Panama, but is strongly recommended for all travelers greater than nine months of age, especially those visiting Chepo, Darién and Kuna Yala.

The vaccine is given only in approved yellow-fever vaccination centers, which provide validated International Certificates of Vaccination (yellow booklets). The vaccine should be given at least 10 days before any potential exposure to yellow fever and remains effective for approximately 10 years. Reactions to the vaccine are generally mild and may include headaches, muscle aches, low-grade fevers or discomfort at the injection site. Severe, life-threatening reactions have been described but are extremely rare. In general, the risk of becoming ill from the vaccine is far less than the risk of becoming ill from yellow fever and you're strongly encouraged to get the vaccine.

Taking measures to protect yourself from mosquito bites (see right) is an essential part of preventing yellow fever.

TRAVELER'S DIARRHEA

To prevent diarrhea, avoid tap water unless it has been boiled, filtered or chemically disinfected (iodine tablets); only eat fresh fruits or vegetables if cooked or peeled; be wary of dairy products that might contain unpasteurized milk; and be highly selective when eating food from street vendors.

If you develop diarrhea, be sure to drink plenty of fluids, preferably an oral rehydration solution containing lots of salt and sugar. A few loose stools don't require treatment but, if you start having more than four or five stools a day, you should start taking an antibiotic (usually a quinolone drug) and an antidiarrheal agent (such as loperamide). If diarrhea is bloody or persists for more than 72 hours, or is accompanied by fever, shaking chills or severe abdominal pain, you should seek medical attention.

ENVIRONMENTAL HAZARDS
Animal Bites

Do not attempt to pet, handle or feed any animal, with the exception of domestic animals known to be free of any infectious disease. Most animal injuries are directly related to a person's attempt to touch or feed the animal.

Any bite or scratch by a mammal, including bats, should be promptly and thoroughly cleansed with large amounts of soap and water, followed by the application of an antiseptic such as iodine or alcohol. The local health authorities should be contacted immediately for possible post-exposure rabies treatment, whether or not you've been immunized against rabies. It may also be advisable to start an antibiotic, since wounds caused by animal bites and scratches frequently become infected. One of the newer quinolones, such as levofloxacin (Levaquin), which many travelers carry in case of diarrhea, would be an appropriate choice.

Insect Bites

To prevent mosquito bites, wear long sleeves, long pants, hats and shoes (rather than sandals). Bring along a good insect repellent, preferably one containing DEET, which should be applied to exposed skin and clothing, but not to eyes, mouth, cuts, wounds or irritated skin. Products containing lower concentrations of DEET are as effective, but for shorter periods of time. In general, adults and children over 12 years of age should use preparations containing 25% to 35% DEET, which usually last about six hours. Children between two and 12 years of age should use preparations containing no more than 10% DEET, applied sparingly, which will usually last about three hours. Neurologic toxicity has been reported from DEET, especially in children, but appears to be extremely uncommon and generally related to overuse. DEET-containing compounds should not be used on children under the age of two.

Insect repellents containing certain botanical products, including oil of eucalyptus and soybean oil, are effective but last only 1½ to two hours. DEET-containing repellents are preferable for areas where there is a high risk of malaria or yellow fever. Products based on citronella are not effective.

For additional protection, you can apply permethrin to clothing, shoes, tents and bed nets. Permethrin treatments are safe and remain effective for at least two weeks, even when items are laundered. Permethrin should not be applied directly to skin.

Don't sleep with the window open unless there is a screen. If sleeping outdoors or in accommodations that allow entry of mosquitoes, use a bed net, preferably treated with permethrin, with edges tucked in under the mattress. The mesh size should be less than 1.5mm. If the sleeping area is not otherwise protected, use a mosquito coil, which will fill the room with insecticide through the night. Repellent-impregnated wristbands are not effective.

Snake Bites

Panama is home to several venomous snakes and any foray into forested areas will put you at (a very slight) risk of snake bite. The best prevention is to wear closed, heavy shoes or boots and to keep a watchful eye on the trail. Snakes like to come out to cleared paths for a nap, so watch where you step.

In the event of a venomous snake bite, place the victim in an restful position, keep the bitten area immobilized and move the victim immediately to the nearest medical facility. Avoid using tourniquets, which are no longer recommended.

Sun

To protect yourself from excessive sun exposure, you should stay out of the midday sun, wear sunglasses and a wide-brimmed sun hat and apply sunscreen with SPF 15 or higher, with both UVA and UVB protection. Sunscreen should be generously applied to all exposed parts of the body approximately 30 minutes before sun exposure and should be reapplied after swimming or vigorous activity. Travelers should also drink plenty of fluids and avoid strenuous exercise when the temperature is high.

Water

Tap water in Panama City *is* safe to drink, as is the water in most other parts of the country. However, you're better off buying bottled water or purifying your own water in the provinces of Bocas del Toro and Kuna Yala.

If you have the means, vigorous boiling for one minute is the most effective way of water purification. Another option is to disinfect water with iodine pills; add 2% tincture of iodine to one quart or liter of water (five drops to clear water, 10 drops to cloudy water) and let stand for 30 minutes. If the water is cold, longer times may be required.

TRAVELING WITH CHILDREN

In general, pregnant women and children less than nine months of age should avoid going to Panama, since yellow-fever vaccine, which is strongly recommended for all parts of the country, may not be safe during pregnancy or the first few months of life.

Older children may be brought to Panama. However, you should be particularly careful not to let them consume any questionable food or beverage. Also, when traveling with children, make sure they're up-to-date on all routine immunizations. It's sometimes appropriate to give children some of their vaccines a little early before visiting a developing nation. You should discuss this with your pediatrician.

HEALTH

Language

CONTENTS

THE LANGUAGES OF PANAMA

Although Spanish is the official language of Panama, there are several indigenous languages spoken throughout the country. In general, Spanish is widely spoken among minority groups, though this is not always the case amongst older people and in extremely isolated areas.

The country's largest indigenous group, the Ngöbe-Buglé, are actually subdivided into two separate ethno-linguistic categories, the Ngöbe and the Buglé. However, since the distinction is minor, both are commonly referred to in conjunction with one another.

Living within the boundaries of the Darién are the Emberá and the Wounaan. Although the groups' cultural features are virtually identical, they prefer to be thought of as two separate peoples, a fact that is reinforced by their divergent languages.

The Kuna, Panama's most independent indigenous group, implement their own system of governance and economy while still maintaining their unique language. As a result, Spanish is not widely spoken in their *comarca* (autonomous region), though this is now changing rapidly due to rapid Westernization.

On the island of Bastimentos in Bocas del Toro, the town of Old Bank is home to a West Indian population that originally emigrated to Panama to work in the banana industry. Here, you'll hear Gali-Gali, the distinct Creole language of Bocas del Toro Province that combines Afro-Antillean English, Spanish and Ngöbe-Buglé.

LEARN SOME LINGO!

Just as most Panamanian immigrants have learned to speak Spanish as a second language, any traveler to Panama would be wise to learn at least a little Spanish as a matter of courtesy and convenience. Basic Spanish is easily acquired (perhaps more so for speakers of English and Romance languages), and a month-long language course taken before departure can go a long way toward facilitating communication and comfort on the road. Language courses are available in Panama City (see p88) for those interested in the added benefits of learning Spanish while in the country. Even if classes are impractical, you should make the effort to learn a few basic phrases and pleasantries. At the very least your Spanish should cover 'good morning,' 'good afternoon,' 'good evening,' 'goodbye,' 'thank you' and 'glad to meet you.' Don't hesitate to practice your language skills – in general, Latin Americans meet attempts to communicate in the vernacular, however halting, with enthusiasm and appreciation. If you try speaking Spanish in Panama and the person you are talking to speaks English, that person will usually respond in English.

PHRASEBOOKS & DICTIONARIES

Lonely Planet's *Latin American Spanish Phrasebook* will be extremely helpful during your trip. Another very useful resource is the University of Chicago *Spanish-English, English-Spanish Dictionary*. It's small, light and has thorough entries, making it ideal for travel. It also makes a great gift for any newfound friends upon your departure.

SPANISH IN PANAMA

Think you know enough Spanish? Here's a quick rundown on some of the local expressions and colorful colloquialisms you may hear while traveling in Panama.

salve – street slang for propina, or tip
tongo – street slang for cop
hota – street slang for police car
diablo rojo – 'red devil'; refers to public buses
mangajo/a (m/f) – someone who is filthy
buena leche – 'good milk'; means good luck
salado/a (m/f) – 'salty'; refers to someone who is having bad luck
Eso está bien pretty. – refers to something nice
¡Eso está pretty pretty! – refers to something supernice
¡Entonces laopé! – Hey, dude!
¡Hey, gringo! – Hey, white person! (friendly)
¡Juega vivo! – Be alert, look out for your best interests!
Voy por fuera. – I'm leaving right now.
¡Ayala bestia! – Holy cow!
¡Chuleta! – common expression similar to 'Holy cow!'
pelao or pelaito – common expression for a child
Pa' lante. – Let's go now.
enantes – just now
Eres un comemierda. – refers to someone pretentious
¡Pifioso! – a showoff, or something that looks cool
Tas buena, mami. – You're looking good, mama.
Nos pillamos. – We'll see each other later.
una pinta or **una fría** – literally, 'one pint' or 'a cold one'; means a beer
Dame una fría. – Give me a cold one (a beer).

guaro – hard liquor
chupata – an all-out drinking party
¡Bien cuidado! – 'Well taken care of!'; often used by a street person when asking for a tip for taking care of your car, normally in parking lots at restaurants, cinemas, bars, etc
Me estoy comiendo un cable. – 'I'm eating a cable'; I'm down on my luck.
rabiblanco/a (m/f) – 'white tipped'; pejorative reference to a member of the socioeconomic elite; the term comes from *paloma rabiblano/a* (white-tipped dove), a bird that walks with its head held out high and its chest thrust out in a seemingly pretentious way
racataca – also *meña*; both terms refer to women who wear lots of gold jewelry and are perceived as low class
chombo/a (m/f) – an acceptable reference to a black person of Antillean descent
ladilla – 'crab louse'; refers to an annoying person
nueve letras – 'nine letters'; refers to Seco Herrerano (the word 'Herrerano' has nine letters)
vuelve loco con vaca – 'makes crazy with cow'; refers to drinking *seco* and milk
vaina – common word that substitutes for 'thing,' as in *Pasame esa vaina.* (Pass me that thing.)
yeye – refers to kids and adults who wear fancy clothes and maybe drive a fancy car and who pretend to be rich but who in reality are living well beyond their means for as long as they can

LATIN AMERICAN SPANISH

The Spanish of the Americas comes in a bewildering array of varieties. Depending on the areas in which you travel, consonants may be glossed over, vowels squashed into each other, and syllables and even words dropped entirely. Slang and regional vocabulary, much of it derived from indigenous languages, can further add to your bewilderment.

Throughout Latin America, the Spanish language is referred to as *castellano* more often than *español*. Unlike in Spain, the plural of the familiar *tú* form is *ustedes* rather than *vosotros*; the latter term will sound quaint and archaic in the Americas. Another notable difference is that the letters **c** and **z** are never lisped in Latin America; attempts to do so could well provoke amusement.

PRONUNCIATION

Spanish spelling is phonetically consistent, meaning that there's a clear and consistent relationship between what you see in writing and how it's pronounced. In addition, most Spanish sounds have English equivalents, so English speakers shouldn't have too much trouble being understood.

Vowels

a   as in 'father'
e   as in 'met'
i   as in 'marine'
o   as in 'or' (without the 'r' sound)
u   as in 'rule'. Note that the 'u' is not pronounced after **q**, or in the letter combinations **gue** and **gui**, unless it's marked with a diaeresis (eg *argüir*), in which case it's pronounced as English 'w'

y at the end of a word or when it stands alone, it's pronounced as the Spanish **i** (eg *ley*); between vowels within a word it's as the 'y' in 'yonder'

Consonants

As a rule, Spanish consonants resemble their English counterparts. The exceptions are listed below.

While the consonants **ch**, **ll** and **ñ** are generally considered distinct letters, **ch** and **ll** are now often listed alphabetically under **c** and **l** respectively. The letter **ñ** is still treated as a separate letter and comes after **n** in dictionaries.

b similar to English 'b,' but softer; referred to as 'b larga'
c as in 'celery' before **e** and **i**; otherwise as English 'k'
ch as in 'church'
d as in 'dog,' but between vowels and after **l** or **n**, the sound is closer to the 'th' in 'this'
g as the 'ch' in the Scottish *loch* before **e** and **i** ('kh' in our guides to pronunciation); elsewhere, as in 'go'
h invariably silent. If your name begins with this letter, listen carefully if you're waiting for public officials to call you.
j as the 'ch' in the Scottish *loch* (written as 'kh' in our guides to pronunciation)
ll as the 'y' in 'yellow'
ñ as the 'ni' in 'onion'
r a short **r** except at the beginning of a word, and after **l**, **n** or **s**, when it's often rolled
rr very strongly rolled
v similar to English 'b,' but softer; referred to as 'b corta'
x usually pronounced as **j** above; in some indigenous place names **x** is pronounced as the 's' in 'sit'; in other instances, it's as in 'taxi'
z as the 's' in 'sun'

Word Stress

In general, words ending in vowels or the letters **n** or **s** have stress on the next-to-last syllable, while those with other endings have stress on the last syllable. Thus *vaca* (cow) and *caballos* (horses) both carry stress on the next-to-last syllable, while *ciudad* (city) and *infeliz* (unhappy) are both stressed on the last syllable.

Written accents will almost always appear in words that don't follow the rules above, eg *sótano* (basement), *América* and *porción* (portion).

GENDER & PLURALS

In Spanish, nouns are either masculine or feminine, and there are rules to help determine gender (there are of course some exceptions). Feminine nouns generally end with -**a** or with the groups -**ción**, -**sión** or -**dad**. Other endings typically signify a masculine noun. Endings for adjectives also change to agree with the gender of the noun they modify (masculine/feminine -**o**/-**a**). Where both masculine and feminine forms are included in this language guide, they are separated by a slash, with the masculine form first, eg *perdido/a*.

If a noun or adjective ends in a vowel, the plural is formed by adding **s** to the end. If it ends in a consonant, the plural is formed by adding **es** to the end.

ACCOMMODATIONS

I'm looking for ...	Estoy buscando ...	e·stoy boos·kan·do ...
Where is ...?	¿Dónde hay ...?	don·de ai ...
a cabin	una cabina	oo·na ca·bee·na
a camping ground	un camping/ campamento	oon kam·ping/ kam·pa·men·to
a guesthouse	una casa de huéspedes	oo·na ka·sa de wes·pe·des
a hostel	un hospedaje/ una residencia	oon os·pe·da·khe/ oon·a re·see·den·sya
a hotel	un hotel	oon o·tel
a youth hostel	un albergue juvenil	oon al·ber·ge khoo·ve·neel

Are there any rooms available?

¿Hay habitaciones libres?	ay a·bee·ta·syon·es lee·bres

I'd like a ... room.	Quisiera una habitación ...	kee·sye·ra oo·na a·bee·ta·syon ...
double	doble	do·ble
single	individual	een·dee·vee·dwal
twin	con dos camas	kon dos ka·mas

How much is it per ...?	¿Cuánto cuesta por ...?	kwan·to kwes·ta por ...
night	noche	no·che
person	persona	per·so·na
week	semana	se·ma·na

MAKING A RESERVATION

(for phone or written requests)

To ...	A ...
From ...	De ...
Date	Fecha
I'd like to book ...	Quisiera reservar ... (see the list under 'Accommodations' for bed and room options)
in the name of ...	en nombre de ...
for the nights of ...	para las noches del ...
credit card ...	tarjeta de crédito ...
number	número
expiry date	fecha de vencimiento
Please confirm ...	Puede confirmar ...
availability	la disponibilidad
price	el precio

---

full board	pensión completa	pen·syon kom·ple·ta
private/shared bathroom	baño privado/ compartido	ba·nyo pree·va·do/ kom·par·tee·do
too expensive	demasiado caro	de·ma·sya·do ka·ro
cheaper	más económico	mas e·ko·no·mee·ko
discount	descuento	des·kwen·to

Does it include breakfast?
  ¿Incluye el desayuno?   een·kloo·ye el de·sa·yoo·no
May I see the room?
  ¿Puedo ver la   pwe·do ver la
  habitación?   a·bee·ta·syon
I don't like it.
  No me gusta.   no me goos·ta
It's fine. I'll take it.
  Está bien. La tomo.   es·ta byen la to·mo
I'm leaving now.
  Me voy ahora.   me voy a·o·ra

CONVERSATION & ESSENTIALS

In their public behavior, Latin Americans are very conscious of civilities. You should never approach a stranger for information without extending a greeting, such as *buenos días* or *buenas tardes*.

Central America is generally more formal than many of the South American countries, and the usage of the informal second-person singular *tú* and *vos* differs from country to country. When in doubt, use the more formal *usted*, which is used in all cases in this guide; where options are given, the form is indicated by the abbreviations 'pol' and 'inf.'

You should use only the polite form with the police and public officials.

Hi.	Hola.	o·la (inf)
Good morning.	Buenos días.	bwe·nos dee·as
Good afternoon.	Buenas tardes.	bwe·nas tar·des
Good evening/ night.	Buenas noches.	bwe·nas no·ches

The three most common greetings are often abbreviated to simply *buenos* (for *buenos días*) and *buenas* (for *buenas tardes* and *buenas noches*).

Bye/See you soon.	Hasta luego.	as·ta lwe·go
Goodbye.	Adiós.	a·dyos
Yes.	Sí.	see
No.	No.	no
Please.	Por favor.	por fa·vor
Thank you.	Gracias.	gra·syas
Many thanks.	Muchas gracias.	moo·chas gra·syas
You're welcome.	De nada.	de na·da
Apologies.	Perdón.	per·don
May I?	Permiso.	per·mee·so
(when asking permission)		
Excuse me.	Disculpe.	dees·kool·pe
(used before a request or when apologizing)		

How are things?
  ¿Qué tal?   ke tal
What's your name?
  ¿Cómo se llama usted?   ko·mo se ya·ma oo·sted (pol)
  ¿Cómo te llamas?   ko·mo te ya·mas (inf)
My name is ...
  Me llamo ...   me ya·mo ...
It's a pleasure to meet you.
  Mucho gusto.   moo·cho goos·to
The pleasure is mine.
  El gusto es mío.   el goos·to es mee·o
Where are you from?
  ¿De dónde es/eres?   de don·de es/er·es (pol/inf)
I'm from ...
  Soy de ...   soy de ...
Where are you staying?
  ¿Dónde está alojado?   don·de es·ta a·lo·kha·do (pol)
  ¿Dónde estás alojado?   don·de es·tas a·lo·kha·do (inf)
May I take a photo?
  ¿Puedo sacar una foto?   pwe·do sa·kar oo·na fo·to

DIRECTIONS

How do I get to ...?
  ¿Cómo llego a ...?   ko·mo ye·go a ...
Is it far?
  ¿Está lejos?   es·ta le·khos
Go straight ahead.
  Siga/Vaya derecho.   see·ga/va·ya de·re·cho

LANGUAGE

Turn left.
Voltée a la izquierda.   vol·*te*·e a la ees·*kyer*·da
Turn right.
Voltée a la derecha.   vol·*te*·e a la de·*re*·cha
Can you show me (on the map)?
¿Me lo podría señalar   me lo po·*dree*·a se·nya·*lar*
(en el mapa)?   (en el *ma*·pa)

SIGNS

Entrada	Entrance
Salida	Exit
Información	Information
Abierto	Open
Cerrado	Closed
Prohibido	Prohibited
Comisaria	Police Station
Servicios/Baños	Toilets
Hombres/Varones	Men
Mujeres/Damas	Women

---

north	*norte*	*nor*·te
south	*sur*	soor
east	*este*	*es*·te
west	*oeste*	o·*es*·te
here	*aquí*	a·*kee*
there	*ahí*	a·*ee*
avenue	*avenida*	a·ve·*nee*·da
block	*cuadra*	*kwa*·dra
street	*calle/paseo*	*ka*·lye/pa·*se*·o

HEALTH

I'm sick.
Estoy enfermo/a.   es·*toy* en·*fer*·mo/a
I need a doctor.
Necesito un médico.   ne·se·*see*·to oon *me*·dee·ko
Where's the hospital?
¿Dónde está el hospital?   don·de es·*ta* el os·pee·*tal*
I'm pregnant.
Estoy embarazada.   es·*toy* em·ba·ra·*sa*·da
I've been vaccinated.
Estoy vacunado/a.   es·*toy* va·koo·*na*·do/a

I'm allergic to ...	*Soy alérgico/a a ...*	soy a·*ler*·khee·ko/a a ...
antibiotics	*los antibióticos*	los an·tee·*byo*·tee·kos
peanuts	*los maníes/ cacahuates*	los ma·*nee*·es/ ka·ka·*wa*·tes
penicillin	*la penicilina*	la pe·nee·see·*lee*·na

I'm ...	*Soy ...*	soy ...
asthmatic	*asmático/a*	as·*ma*·tee·ko/a
diabetic	*diabético/a*	dya·*be*·tee·ko/a
epileptic	*epiléptico/a*	e·pee·*lep*·tee·ko/a

EMERGENCIES

Help!	*¡Socorro!*	so·*ko*·ro
Fire!	*¡Fuego!*	*fwe*·go
Go away!	*¡Déjeme!*	de·*khe*·me
Get lost!	*¡Váyase!*	*va*·ya·se

Call ...!	*¡Llame a ...!*	*ya*·me a
the police	*la policía*	la po·lee·*see*·a
a doctor	*un médico*	oon *me*·dee·ko
an ambulance	*una ambulancia*	oo·na am·boo·*lan*·sya

It's an emergency.
Es una emergencia.   es oo·na e·mer·*khen*·sya
Could you help me, please?
¿Me puede ayudar,   me *pwe*·de a·yoo·*dar*
por favor?   por fa·*vor*
I'm lost.
Estoy perdido/a.   es·*toy* per·*dee*·do/a
Where are the toilets?
¿Dónde están los baños?   don·de es·*tan* los *ba*·nyos

I have ...	*Tengo ...*	*ten*·go ...
a cough	*tos*	tos
diarrhea	*diarrea*	dya·*re*·a
a headache	*un dolor de cabeza*	oon do·*lor* de ka·*be*·sa
nausea	*náusea*	*now*·se·a

LANGUAGE DIFFICULTIES

Do you speak English?
¿Habla/Hablas inglés?   a·bla/a·blas een·*gles* (pol/inf)
Does anyone here speak English?
¿Hay alguien que hable   ai al·*gyen* ke a·ble
inglés?   een·*gles*
I (don't) understand.
(No) Entiendo.   (no) en·*tyen*·do
How do you say ...?
¿Cómo se dice ...?   *ko*·mo se *dee*·se ...
What does ... mean?
¿Qué significa ...?   ke seeg·*nee*·fee·ka ...

Could you please ...?	*¿Puede ..., por favor?*	*pwe*·de ... por fa·vor
repeat that	*repetirlo*	re·pe·*teer*·lo
speak more slowly	*hablar más despacio*	a·*blar* mas des·*pa*·syo
write it down	*escribirlo*	es·kree·*beer*·lo

NUMBERS

1	*uno*	*oo*·no
2	*dos*	dos
3	*tres*	tres

4	cuatro	kwa·tro
5	cinco	seen·ko
6	seis	says
7	siete	sye·te
8	ocho	o·cho
9	nueve	nwe·ve
10	diez	dyes
11	once	on·se
12	doce	do·se
13	trece	tre·se
14	catorce	ka·tor·se
15	quince	keen·se
16	dieciséis	dye·see·says
17	diecisiete	dye·see·sye·te
18	dieciocho	dye·see·o·cho
19	diecinueve	dye·see·nwe·ve
20	veinte	vayn·te
21	veintiuno	vayn·tee·oo·no
30	treinta	trayn·ta
31	treinta y uno	trayn·ta ee oo·no
40	cuarenta	kwa·ren·ta
50	cincuenta	seen·kwen·ta
60	sesenta	se·sen·ta
70	setenta	se·ten·ta
80	ochenta	o·chen·ta
90	noventa	no·ven·ta
100	cien	syen
101	ciento uno	syen·to oo·no
200	doscientos	do·syen·tos
1000	mil	meel
5000	cinco mil	seen·ko meel

PAPERWORK

birth certificate	certificado de nacimiento
border (frontier)	la frontera
car-owner's title	título de propiedad
car registration	registración
customs	aduana
driver's license	licencia de manejar
identification	identificación
immigration	migración
insurance	seguro
passport	pasaporte
temporary vehicle import permit	permiso de importación temporal de vehículo
tourist card	tarjeta de turista
visa	visado

SHOPPING & SERVICES

I'd like to buy ...
Quisiera comprar ...   kee·sye·ra kom·prar ...
I'm just looking.
Sólo estoy mirando.   so·lo es·toy mee·ran·do
May I look at it?
¿Puedo verlo/a?   pwe·do ver·lo/a

How much is it?
¿Cuánto cuesta?   kwan·to kwes·ta
That's too expensive for me.
Es demasiado caro   es de·ma·sya·do ka·ro
para mí.   pa·ra mee
Could you lower the price?
¿Podría bajar un poco   po·dree·a ba·khar oon po·ko
el precio?   el pre·syo
I don't like it.
No me gusta.   no me goos·ta
I'll take it.
Lo llevo.   lo ye·vo

Do you accept ...?	*¿Aceptan ...?*	a·sep·tan ...
American dollars	*dólares americanos*	do·la·res a·me·ree·ka·nos
credit cards	*tarjetas de crédito*	tar·khe·tas de kre·dee·to
traveler's checks	*cheques de viajero*	che·kes de vya·khe·ro

more	*más*	mas
less	*menos*	me·nos
small	*pequeño/a*	pe·ke·nyo/a
large	*grande*	gran·de

I'm looking for the ...	*Estoy buscando ...*	es·toy boos·kan·do
ATM	*el cajero automático*	el ka·khe·ro ow·to·ma·tee·ko
bank	*el banco*	el ban·ko
bookstore	*la librería*	la lee·bre·ree·a
exchange house	*la casa de cambio*	la ka·sa de kam·byo
general store	*la tienda*	la tyen·da
laundry	*la lavandería*	la la·van·de·ree·a
market	*el mercado*	el mer·ka·do
pharmacy/ chemist	*la farmacia*	la far·ma·sya
post office	*la oficina de correos*	la o·fee·see·na de ko·re·os
supermarket	*el supermercado*	el soo·per·mer·ka·do
tourist office	*la oficina de turismo*	la o·fee·see·na de too·rees·mo

What time does it open/close?
¿A qué hora abre/cierra?
a ke o·ra a·bre/sye·ra
I want to change some money/traveler's checks.
Quisiera cambiar dinero/cheques de viajero.
kee·sye·ra kam·byar dee·ne·ro/che·kes de vya·khe·ro
What is the exchange rate?
¿Cuál es el tipo de cambio?
kwal es el tee·po de kam·byo

I want to call ...
Quisiera llamar a ...
kee-*sye*-ra lya-*mar* a ...

airmail	*correo aéreo*	ko-*re*-o a-*e*-re-o
letter	*carta*	*kar*-ta
registered (mail)	*certificado*	ser-tee-fee-*ka*-do
stamps	*timbres*	*teem*-bres

TIME & DATES

What time is it?	*¿Qué hora es?*	ke *o*-ra es
It's one o'clock.	*Es la una.*	es la *oo*-na
It's seven o'clock.	*Son las siete.*	son las *sye*-te
Half past two.	*Dos y media.*	dos ee *me*-dya
midnight	*medianoche*	me-dya-*no*-che
noon	*mediodía*	me-dyo-*dee*-a

now	*ahora*	a-*o*-ra
today	*hoy*	oy
tonight	*esta noche*	es-ta *no*-che
tomorrow	*mañana*	ma-*nya*-na
yesterday	*ayer*	a-*yer*

Monday	*lunes*	*loo*-nes
Tuesday	*martes*	*mar*-tes
Wednesday	*miércoles*	*myer*-ko-les
Thursday	*jueves*	*khwe*-ves
Friday	*viernes*	*vyer*-nes
Saturday	*sábado*	*sa*-ba-do
Sunday	*domingo*	do-*meen*-go

January	*enero*	e-*ne*-ro
February	*febrero*	fe-*bre*-ro
March	*marzo*	*mar*-so
April	*abril*	a-*breel*
May	*mayo*	*ma*-yo
June	*junio*	*khoo*-nyo
July	*julio*	*khoo*-lyo
August	*agosto*	a-*gos*-to
September	*septiembre*	sep-*tyem*-bre
October	*octubre*	ok-*too*-bre
November	*noviembre*	no-*vyem*-bre
December	*diciembre*	dee-*syem*-bre

TRANSPORT
Public Transport

What time does	*¿A qué hora ...*	a ke *o*-ra ...
... leave/arrive?	*sale/llega?*	*sa*-le/*ye*-ga
the bus	*el bus/autobús*	el bus/ow-to-*boos*
the ferry	*el barco*	el *bar*-ko
the minibus	*el colectivo/*	el ko-lek-*tee*-vo/
	la buseta/	la boo-*se*-ta/
	el microbus	el *mee*-kro-boos
the plane	*el avión*	el a-*vyon*
the train	*el tren*	el tren

the airport	*el aeropuerto*	el a-e-ro-*pwer*-to
the bus station	*la estación de*	la es-ta-*syon* de
	autobuses	ow-to-*boo*-ses
the bus stop	*la parada de*	la pa-*ra*-da de
	autobuses	ow-to-*boo*-ses
the train station	*la estación de*	la es-ta-*syon* de
	ferrocarril	fe-ro-ka-*reel*
the luggage locker	*la consigna para*	la kon-*see*-nya para
	el equipaje	el e-*kee*-pa-khe
the ticket office	*la boletería/*	la bo-le-te-*ree*-ya/
	ticketería	tee-ke-te-*ree*-ya

A ticket to ..., please.
Un boleto a ..., por favor.
oon bo-*le*-to a ... por fa-*vor*
What's the fare to ...?
¿Cuánto cuesta hasta ...?
kwan-to *kwes*-ta a-sta ...

student's	*de estudiante*	de es-too-*dyan*-te
1st class	*primera clase*	pree-*me*-ra *kla*-se
2nd class	*segunda clase*	se-*goon*-da *kla*-se
single/one-way	*de ida*	de *ee*-da
return/round trip	*de ida y vuelta*	de *ee*-da e *vwel*-ta
taxi	*taxi*	*tak*-see

Private Transport

I'd like to	*Quisiera*	kee-*sye*-ra
hire a ...	*alquilar ...*	al-kee-*lar* ...
4WD	*un todo terreno*	oon *to*-do te-*re*-no
car	*un auto/carro*	oon *ow*-to/*ka*-ro
motorcycle	*una motocicleta*	oo-na mo-to-see-*kle*-ta
bicycle	*una bicicleta*	oo-na bee-see-*kle*-ta

pickup (truck)	*camioneta*	ka-myo-*ne*-ta
truck	*camión*	ka-*myon*
hitchhike	*hacer dedo*	a-ser *de*-do

Where's a gas (petrol) station?
¿Dónde hay una gasolinera/bomba?
don-de ai oo-na ga-so-lee-*ne*-ra/*bom*-ba
How much is a liter of gasoline?
¿Cuánto cuesta el litro de gasolina?
kwan-to *kwes*-ta el *lee*-tro de ga-so-*lee*-na
Please fill it up.
Lleno, por favor.
ye-no por fa-*vor*
I'd like ... worth of gas (petrol).
Quiero ... en gasolina.
kye-ro ... en ga-so-*lee*-na

diesel	*diesel*	*dee*-sel
leaded (regular)	*gasolina con*	ga-so-*lee*-na kon
	plomo	*plo*-mo

ROAD SIGNS

Acceso	Entrance
Acceso Permanente	24-Hour Access
Acceso Prohibido	No Entry
Ceda el Paso	Give Way
Construcción de Carreteras	Roadworks
Curva Peligrosa	Dangerous Curve
Despacio	Slow
Desvío/Desviación	Detour
Mantenga Su Derecha	Keep to the Right
No Adelantar	No Passing
No Hay Paso	Road Closed
No Pase	No Overtaking
Pare/Stop	Stop
Peligro	Danger
Prohibido el Paso	No Entry
Prohibido Estacionar	No Parking
Salida (de Autopista)	Exit (Freeway)

petrol (gas)	*gasolina*	ga·so·*lee*·na
unleaded	*gasolina sin plomo*	ga·so·*lee*·na seen *plo*·mo
oil	*aceite*	a·*say*·te
tire	*llanta*	*yan*·ta
puncture	*agujero*	a·goo·*khe*·ro

Is this the road to ...?
¿Por acquí se va a ...?
por a·*kee* se va a ...

(How long) Can I park here?
¿(Por cuánto tiempo) Puedo estacionar aquí?
(por *kwan*·to *tyem*·po) *pwe*·do ess·ta·syo·*nar* a·*kee*

Where do I pay?
¿Dónde se paga?
don·de se *pa*·ga

I need a mechanic/tow truck.
Necesito un mecánico/remolque.
ne·se·*see*·to oon me·*ka*·nee·ko/re·*mol*·ke

Is there a garage near here?
¿Hay un garaje cerca de aquí?
ai oon ga·*ra*·khe ser·ka de a·*kee*

The car has broken down in ...
El carro se ha averiado en ...
el *ka*·ro se a a·ve·*rya*·do en ...

The motorbike won't start.
La moto no arranca.
la *mo*·to no a·*ran*·ka

I have a flat tire.
Tengo una llanta desinflada.
ten·go *oo*·na *yan*·ta des·een·*fla*·da

I've run out of petrol.
Me quedé sin gasolina.
me ke·*de* seen ga·so·*lee*·na

I've had an accident.
Tuve un accidente.
too·ve oon ak·see·*den*·te

TRAVEL WITH CHILDREN

I need .../Do you have ...?
Necesito .../¿Hay ...?
ne·se·*see*·to .../ai ...

a car baby seat
un asiento de seguridad para bebés
oon a·*syen*·to de se·goo·ree·*da* pa·ra be·*bes*

a child-minding service
un club para niños
oon kloob pa·*ra* nee·nyos

a créche
una guardería
oo·na gwar·de·*ree*·a

(disposable) diapers/nappies
pañales (de usar y tirar)
pa·*nya*·les (de oo·*sar* ee tee·*rar*)

an (English-speaking) babysitter
una niñera (que habla inglesa)
oo·na nee·*nye*·ra (ke a·bla een·*gle*·sa)

formula (milk)
leche en polvo
le·che en *pol*·vo

a highchair
una silla para bebé
oo·na *see*·ya *pa*·ra be·*be*

a potty
una bacinica
oo·na ba·see·*nee*·ka

a stroller
una carreola
oona ka·re·o·la

Are children allowed?
¿Se admiten niños?
se ad·*mee*·ten *nee*·nyos

Also available from Lonely Planet:
Latin American Spanish Phrasebook

Glossary

For terms for food, drinks and other culinary vocabulary, see p47. For additional terms and information about the Spanish language, see the Language chapter on p320. This glossary contains some words in Kuna (K) - for more on their language, see the boxed text on p268.

ANAM – Autoridad Nacional de Ambiente; Panama's national environmental agency
ANCON – Asociación Nacional para la Conservación de la Naturaleza; National Association for the Conservation of Nature, Panama's leading private environmental organization
apartado – post office box
árbol – tree
artesanía – handicrafts

bahía – bay
balboa – the basic unit of Panamanian currency
baño(s) – restroom(s)
biblioteca – library
bohío – a thatched-roof hut
boleto – ticket; for bus, museum etc
boroquera – blowgun once used by the *Emberá* and *Wounaan* Indians
bote – motorized canoe
buceo – diving

caballero(s) – gentleman (gentlemen)
cabaña – cabin
cacique – *Kuna* tribal leader
calle – street
campesino/a – rural resident; peasant
carretera – highway
casa de cambio – money-exchange house
cascada – waterfall
catedral – cathedral
cayuco – dugout canoe
centavos – cent(s); 100 *centavos* equal one US dollar (or one Panamanian *balboa*)
cerro – hill
certificación de vuelo – certification of entry date into Panama
cerveza – beer
chévere – cool (slang)
chitra – sand fly
chiva – a rural bus, often a 28-seat Toyota Coaster bus
chocosano (K) – storm that comes from the east
chorro – waterfall
cielo – the sky; the heavens
cigarro – cigarette
cine – cinema

ciudad – city
cocina – kitchen
cocobolo – a handsome tropical hardwood; used for carving life-size images of snakes, parrots, toucans and other jungle wildlife
comarca – district
conejo pintado – raccoonlike animal abundant in Parque Nacional Volcán Barú
cordillera – mountain range
corredor de aduana – customs broker
cuatro por cuatro – 4WD vehicle
cuidado – caution
Cuna – see *Kuna*

dama(s) – lady (ladies)
directo – direct bus
día feriado (días feriados) – national holiday(s)

edificio – building
Emberá – indigenous group living in Darién Province

feria – festival
finca – farm
floresta – forest
frontera – border
fuerte – fort

Gali-Gali – the distinct Creole language of Bocas del Toro Province; it combines English, Spanish and Guaymí
galón (galones) – gallon(s); fluid measure of 3.79L
gruta – cave
guacamayo – macaw

habano – Havana cigar
haras – stable (for horses)
herida – injury
hombre – man
hormiga – ant
hospedaje – guest house
huaca(s) – golden object(s); made on the Panamanian isthmus in the pre-Columbian era and buried with Indians

iglesia – church
INAC – Instituto Nacional de Cultura; Panama's National Institute of Culture
Interamericana – the Pan-American Hwy; the nearly continuous highway running from Alaska to Chile (it breaks at the Darién Gap)
invierno – winter
IPAT – Instituto Panameño de Turismo; the national tourism agency
isla – island

kilometraje – mileage
Kuna – the 70,000-strong indigenous tribe living in the Comarca de Kuna Yala

ladrón – thief
lago – lake
lancha – motorboat
lavamático/lavandería – laundromat
librería – bookstore
llanta – tire
llantería – tire repair shop
lleno – full
lluvia – rain
loro – parrot

manglar – mangrove
mariposa – butterfly
mercado – market
Merki (K) – North American
mestizo/a – person of mixed indigenous and Spanish ancestry
metate – flat stone platform; used by Panama's pre-Columbian Indians to grind corn
migración – immigration
Migración y Naturalización – Immigration and Naturalization office
mirador – lookout point
molas (K) – colorful hand-stitched appliqué textiles made by Kuna women
mono – monkey
montaña – mountain
montuno – fine embroidered shirt; typically worn during festivals on the Península de Azuero
muelle – pier
mujer(es) – woman (women)
museo – museum

nadar – to swim
Naso – an indigenous group scattered throughout the Bocas del Toro Province; also called the Teribe
Ngöbe Buglé – an indigenous tribe located largely in Chiriquí Province

ola(s) – wave(s)

pájaro – bird
palapa – thatched, palm leaf–roofed shelter with open sides
panadería – bakery
parada (de autobús) – bus stop
Patois – a local dialect on the islands of Boca del Toro; a blend of English, Spanish and Gali-Gali
PDF – the Panama Defense Forces; the national army under Manuel Noriega
penca – palm tree leaves
permiso de salida – exit permit
pescador – fishers

pescar – to fish
piragua – canoe carved from a tree trunk
playa – beach
polleras – the intricate, lacy, Spanish-influenced dresses of the Península de Azuero; the national dress of Panama for festive occasions
pozo(s) – spring(s)
preservativo(s) – condom(s)
prohibido – prohibited; forbidden
propina – tip; gratuity
prórroga de turista – a permit that resembles a driver's license, complete with photo; it allows you to stay in Panama for longer than the 90 days permitted for tourists
protector solar – sunscreen lotion
puente – bridge
puerto – port
punta – point
puro – cigar

quebrada – stream

rana – frog
rana dorada – golden frog
rancho – a thatched-roof hut
regalo – gift; present
río – river

selva – jungle
Semana Santa – Holy Week; preceding Easter
sendero – trail
serpiente – snake
serranía – mountain range
sol – sun
supermercado – supermarket

tabla – surfboard
tagua – an ivory-colored nut that is carved into tiny figurines
taller – workshop
tarjeta(s) – plastic phonecard(s)
tarjeta de circulación – vehicle control certificate
taxi marino – water taxi
tigre – jaguar
típico – typical; traditional Panamanian folk music
tortuga – sea turtle
traje de baño – swimsuit
trucha – trout
urbano – local (as in buses)

valle – valley
verano – summer
viajero – traveler
viento – wind
volcán – volcano

waga (K) – tourist
Wounaan – indigenous group living in Darién Province

The Authors

MATTHEW D FIRESTONE   Coordinating Author

Matt is a trained biological anthropologist and epidemiologist, though he prefers moonlighting as a freelance travel writer. His first visit to Panama was in 2001 during an alternative spring break from college. While his classmates were partying on the beach in Panama City, Florida, Matt was dining on tapas and dancing salsa in Panama City, Panama. Although he may have missed his big chance to appear on *MTV Spring Break*, Matt now knows how to prepare a mean ceviche and his three-step ain't half bad. The secret to both is simple – spice things up with either diced habaneros or a few rounds of rum and coke with lime.

CONTRIBUTING AUTHOR

Dr David Goldberg MD wrote the Health chapter. David completed his training in internal medicine and infectious diseases at Columbia-Presbyterian Medical Center in New York City, where he has also served as voluntary faculty. At present he is an infectious-diseases specialist in Scarsdale, New York state, and the editor-in-chief of the website MDTravelHealth.com.

Behind the Scenes

THIS BOOK

This 4th edition of *Panama* was researched and written by Matthew D Firestone. The 1st and 2nd editions were written by Scott Doggett, and Regis St Louis wrote the 3rd edition. The boxed text on travel to Colombia was adapted from material written by Michael Kohn. This guidebook was commissioned in Lonely Planet's Oakland office and produced by the following:

Commissioning Editors Greg Benchwick, Catherine Craddock-Carrillo, David Zingarelli

Coordinating Editor Chris Girdler

Coordinating Cartographer Herman So

Coordinating Layout Designer Jacqueline McLeod

Managing Editors Imogen Bannister, Barbara Delissen

Managing Cartographers Alison Lyall

Managing Layout Designer Adam McCrow

Assisting Editors Susie Ashworth, Justin Flynn, Phillip Tang, Fionnuala Twomey, Jeanette Wall

Assisting Cartographers Joshua Geoghegan, Jolyon Philcox

Cover Designer Marika Kozak

Project Manager Fabrice Rocher

Language Content Coordinator Quentin Frayne

Thanks to Owen Eszeki, Emma Gilmour, Chris LeeAck, Malcolm O'Brien, Andrew Smith, Celia Wood

THANKS
MATTHEW D FIRESTONE

First of all, my warmest thanks goes to my family. To my always supportive mother and father, thank you for teaching me how to live life to its fullest, even though I have a hard time keeping up with your Vegas lifestyle! To my incredibly successful sister, thank you for abandoning your New York stylings for a taste of life on the road with your wanderlust-ridden brother. I'd like to give a big shout out to the main man behind the Lonely Planet scenes, namely my editor-extraordinaire Greg; it's been a pleasure working with you on *Costa Rica* and *Panama* over the past two years, and I wish you the best luck in your newfound career on the other side of the desk. Finally, I'd like to thank my friends, both old and new, that made my time on the road so special. To my best friend Ronnie, thanks for following me to the edges of Panama and for continuing to remind me of who I am and where I came from. To the members of the Darien Explorer Trek, especially our fearless leader Rick, let's never forget what will surely be one of the greatest adventures of our lives! And, to my fellow *gaijin* at Sakura House Uguisudani B, thanks for keeping me well-hydrated with bottle after bottle of *shochu*.

OUR READERS

Many thanks to the travelers who used the last edition and wrote to us with helpful hints, useful advice and interesting anecdotes:

A Christina (Tina) Alefounder, **B** Norm Bader, Loreto Barcelo, Beryl Benderly, Peter Bergsten, **D** Oya Berk Demirel, Ruben Bijker, Saskia Boesjes, Philip Boley, Wanda Bolt, Herveline Bordier, Monique Born, Aaron Brown, **C** Tracey Cobb, Luigi Calvo, Alison Cawood, Vicky Chacón, Debra Chalhoub, Connie Cochrane, **D** Jennifer Dacosta, Gary Dandy, Timothy Davis, Joe Depeau, Duane Dickinson, Jane Dominey, Simon Dunne, Chris Dyke, Chris Dyke, **E** Omar Enciso,

THE LONELY PLANET STORY

The story begins with a classic travel adventure: Tony and Maureen Wheeler's 1972 journey across Europe and Asia to Australia. There was no useful information about the overland trail then, so Tony and Maureen published the first Lonely Planet guidebook to meet a growing need.

From a kitchen table, Lonely Planet has grown to become the largest independent travel publisher in the world, with offices in Melbourne (Australia), Oakland (USA) and London (UK). Today Lonely Planet guidebooks cover the globe. There is an ever-growing list of books and information in a variety of media. Some things haven't changed. The main aim is still to make it possible for adventurous individuals to get out there – to explore and better understand the world.

At Lonely Planet we believe travelers can make a positive contribution to the countries they visit – if they respect their host communities and spend their money wisely. Every year 5% of company profit is donated to charities around the world.

Leila Fonseca, **F** Stephen Fox, Miriam French, **G** Lina Galleguillos, Glyn Garratt, Hayley Gee, Max Gefter, Lonnie Glazer, David Graham, Fela Grunwald, Alfredo Guicciardi, **H** Dave Hall, Melanie Hanlon, Stuart Harkness, Emilio Ho, Amy Hoke, Andrea Hudson, Andrea Hudson, **J** Goeran Jaeger, Jack Joyce, **K** Walter Kassoway, Sean Kelly, Beth King, Bob Kippola, Wendy Kirkby, Kit Kirkpatrick, Tsuyuki Kita, Danielle Koning, Mark Kowalsky, **L** Francis Lagace, Stéphan Lam, Barbara Landi, Stefan Laube, Michiel Lenstra, Kate Lewis, Diane Longhouse, Alexei Lougovtsov, Lorraine Luciano-Singer, **M** James N Maas, Brian Macharg, Yossi Margoninsky, Rita Medak, M Mercer, Stefan Mettler, Noelle Morris, Monica Mulcahy, Jean Murialdo, BJ Murphy-Bridge, Arlyn Musselman, **N** Linda Natho, Becky Nemec, Linda Nijlunsing, **O** Aleida Ormel, Catherina Ostick, Anna O'Reilly, **P** Janie Pageau, Jason Paiement, Robert Parker, Peter Pasyk, Sandra Patel, Ellen Paul, Gustavo & Stina Pena, David Phillips, Alex Porras, Alana Prashad, **R** Nyoka Rajah, Judith Ravin, Jessica Reilly, Renee Cossitt, Bert Richmond, Daniel Riggan, Alfonso Rivera, Roxanna Robbins, Ana Isabel Rojas Aragones, Javier Romero, Louis Rossi, Jocelyn Roy, **S** Jesus Sanchez, Therese Sandgren, Flavia Schepmans, Tobias Schmetzer, Muriel Schmid, Michael Schwebel, Laura Sciolla, Kate Skinner, Angelina Skowronski, Nicole Smith, Paul Smith, Nona Snell, Gabriela Sosa, Peter Sultan, Herbie Sunk, Michelle Swanson, **T** Thomas Taxer, Jennifer Teerlink, Philippe Theys, Carlo Trulli, **U** Kathy Utigard, **V** Tata Valencia, Arnoud Van Houten, **W** Anne Walker, Micheal White, Justin White, Christoph Wieser, Dan Wiseman, Brad Wolfe, **Y** Umut Yasar, John Yates, Jayson Young, **Z** Manuele Zunelli

ACKNOWLEDGMENTS

Many thanks to the following for the use of their content:

Globe on title page ©Mountain High Maps 1993 Digital Wisdom, Inc.

Internal photographs p10 Danny Lehman/Corbis; p8 Robert Harding Picture Library Ltd / Alamy.

All other photographs by Lonely Planet Images, and by Paul Kennedy p7 (#5); Alfredo Maiquez p5, p6, p7 (#2), p9, p12; Eric Wheater p11.

All images are the copyright of the photographers unless otherwise indicated. Many of the images in this guide are available for licensing from Lonely Planet Images: www.lonelyplanetimages.com.

BEHIND THE SCENES

Index

INDEX

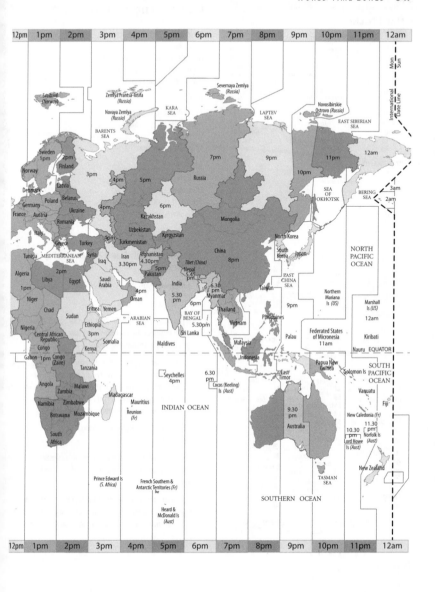

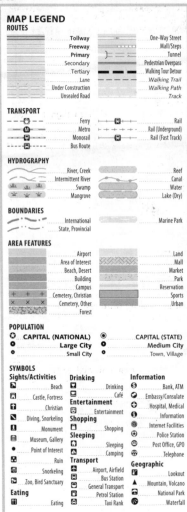

MAP LEGEND

ROUTES
Tollway · Freeway · Primary · Secondary · Tertiary · Lane · Under Construction · Unsealed Road · One-Way Street · Mall/Steps · Tunnel · Pedestrian Overpass · Walking Tour Detour · Walking Trail · Walking Path · Track

TRANSPORT
Ferry · Metro · Monorail · Bus Route · Rail · Rail (Underground) · Rail (Fast Track)

HYDROGRAPHY
River, Creek · Intermittent River · Swamp · Mangrove · Reef · Canal · Water · Lake (Dry)

BOUNDARIES
International · State, Provincial · Marine Park

AREA FEATURES
Airport · Area of Interest · Beach, Desert · Building · Campus · Cemetery, Christian · Cemetery, Other · Forest · Land · Mall · Market · Park · Reservation · Sports · Urban

POPULATION
CAPITAL (NATIONAL) · CAPITAL (STATE) · Large City · Medium City · Small City · Town, Village

SYMBOLS

Sights/Activities: Beach · Castle, Fortress · Christian · Diving, Snorkeling · Monument · Museum, Gallery · Point of Interest · Ruin · Snorkeling · Zoo, Bird Sanctuary

Eating: Eating

Drinking: Drinking · Café

Entertainment: Entertainment

Shopping: Shopping

Sleeping: Sleeping · Camping

Transport: Airport, Airfield · Bus Station · General Transport · Petrol Station · Taxi Rank

Information: Bank, ATM · Embassy/Consulate · Hospital, Medical · Information · Internet Facilities · Police Station · Post Office, GPO · Telephone

Geographic: Lookout · Mountain, Volcano · National Park · Waterfall

LONELY PLANET OFFICES

Australia
Head Office
Locked Bag 1, Footscray, Victoria 3011
☎ 03 8379 8000, fax 03 8379 8111
talk2us@lonelyplanet.com.au

USA
150 Linden St, Oakland, CA 94607
☎ 510 893 8555, toll free 800 275 8555
fax 510 893 8572
info@lonelyplanet.com

UK
72–82 Rosebery Ave,
Clerkenwell, London EC1R 4RW
☎ 020 7841 9000, fax 020 7841 9001
go@lonelyplanet.co.uk

Published by Lonely Planet Publications Pty Ltd
ABN 36 005 607 983

© Lonely Planet Publications Pty Ltd 2007

© photographers as indicated 2007

Cover photograph: Uninhabited island, Greg Benchwick. Many of the images in this guide are available for licensing from Lonely Planet Images: www.lonelyplanetimages.com.

Printed through Colorcraft Ltd, Hong Kong
Printed in China